Sir William Jones is best known for his famous Third Discourse of 1786 in which he proposed that Sanskrit's affinity to Greek and Latin could be explained by positing a common, earlier source, one known today as Indo-European. This brilliant thesis of language families laid the groundwork for modern comparative linguistics. Jones's interests and achievements, however, ranged far beyond language. He studied and made contributions to anthropology and archaeology, to astronomy, botany, history, law, literature, music, physiology, politics, and religion. He served as a Supreme Court justice in India and founded the Asiatic Society, which stimulated worldwide interest in India and the Orient. He was friends with many of the leading intellectuals of his day and corresponded with Benjamin Franklin in America and with Burke, Gibbon, Johnson, Percy, and Reynolds in Britain. In his short life he mastered so many languages that even in his own time he was regarded as a phenomenon, and so he was. Garland Cannon, editor of *The Letters of Sir William Jones*, has written a new and definitive biography of this fascinating man, who in his life and works teaches us that the path to understanding and appreciating the art and literature of a great culture very different from our own is through devoted study, a tolerant spirit, and an unquenchably curious mind.

The Life and Mind of Oriental Jones

Jones at the age of forty-seven, by A. W. Devis. Reproduced by permission of the British Library (India Office Library and Records).

The Life and Mind of Oriental Jones

Sir William Jones, the Father of Modern Linguistics

GARLAND CANNON
Department of English, Texas A&M University

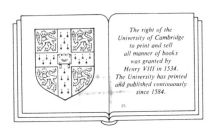

The right of the University of Cambridge to print and sell all manner of books was granted by Henry VIII in 1534. The University has printed and published continuously since 1584.

CAMBRIDGE UNIVERSITY PRESS

Cambridge
New York   Port Chester   Melbourne   Sydney

Published by the Press Syndicate of the University of Cambridge
The Pitt Building, Trumpington Street, Cambridge CB2 1RP
40 West 20th Street, New York, NY 10011, USA
10 Stamford Road, Oakleigh, Melbourne 3166, Australia

First published 1990

Printed in Canada

Library of Congress Cataloging-in-Publication Data
Cannon, Garland Hampton, 1924–
The life and mind of Oriental Jones : Sir William Jones, the
father of modern linguistics / Garland Cannon.
p.   cm.
Includes bibliographical references.
ISBN 0-521-39149-0
1. Jones, William, Sir, 1746–1794.   2. Orientalists – Great
Britain – Biography.   I. Title.
PJ64.J6C36   1990
950'.07202 – dc20
[B]   90-1580
                                                              CIP

British Library Cataloguing in Publication Data
Cannon, Garland
The life and mind of Oriental Jones : Sir William Jones,
the father of modern linguistics.
1. Asian studies. Jones, Sir William, 1746–1794
I. Title
950.07202

ISBN 0-521-39149-0 hardback

Contents

v

Preface

In 1964 my earlier biography of Jones, *Oriental Jones,* was published. Intended to replace the previous, unsatisfactory biographies, it was a somewhat sketchy narrative. It lacked the necessary historiography at that time on the intercivilizational encounter between Britain and India, as well as the experience from extensive travel and residence in India needed to appreciate the cultural situation in which Jones found himself. Although I did use Jones's manuscript letters at Althorp, the lack of annotations precluded my using them fully. My later *Letters of Sir William Jones* (1970) made available all of his letters known at that time, but many of them were unknown in 1964 and more letters have turned up since 1970. Indeed, six previously unpublished letters are included in this new biography.

His correspondence overall reveals such a confiding, articulate man that it is now possible to trace his life in minute detail and to know his ideas, motives, and aspirations. Moreover, the Manuscript Proceedings of the Asiatic Society detail his association with that innovational group that he founded in Calcutta, and the contemporary London and Calcutta newspapers provide additional information. Also, new, scholarly insights have appeared in numbers of specialized studies since 1964, including studies from the bicentenary celebrations of 1984 and 1986. Many of these are listed and annotated in my *Sir William Jones: A Bibliography of Primary and Secondary Sources* (1979). Thus this new biography contains at least 30 percent new material, which has been integrated so as to present a more rounded picture of Jones's life and particularly his intellectual development within the historical setting. The scholarly documentation and elaboration are provided as endnotes, so that the general reader who is interested in history, biography, and Oriental studies can more easily pursue the story of a fascinating man and his times. The scholar can pursue specialized interests by utilizing the endnotes and particularly the references in *Letters,* for which this biography is in some ways a complementary volume, even as the scholar can find in *Letters* additional details about people and events mentioned in the biography.

Though the broad outlines of Jones's life as detailed in *Oriental Jones* have not substantially changed, the picture that emerges is of a more profound, humanitarian, and varied man, with continuing influences on posterity and a world that has integrated and advanced Oriental influences in most areas of human endeavor. This fuller description and evaluation of his writings and ideas required a new book, not a second edition of *Oriental Jones,* which is indicated by the title *The Life and Mind of Oriental Jones.*

Because he knew so many people and knew about or participated in so many important events, it was difficult to keep his biography within reasonable bounds. At some points it could have been more of a chronicle showing interrelations with hundreds of people and events, rather than primarily a straightforward biography and intellectual history intended to meet historiographic standards. The subject matter dictates that the book be thus primarily addressed to South Asianists and Indologists (including anyone interested in the history of India), linguists and language historians particularly of Middle Eastern and Indic languages, as well as persons interested in literature and law, and in eighteenth-century studies in almost any discipline, not to mention readers who like their history and ideas to be presented through biographies.

The necessary excisions may sometimes disappoint scholars of a given discipline, though my notes specify the particular sources, and a bibliography lists the principal sources used. As Jones attained his greatest achievements in India, I condensed the literary and political material on his activities in England that had no particular bearing on his career. For example, his unsuccessful efforts in 1780 for a seat in the House of Commons from the University of Oxford illuminate eighteenth-century politics; but because the details and annotated catalogue of names can be found in *Letters,* the material is condensed here so as to focus on Jones. Similarly, his activities were often so intellectual, and he was involved in so many disciplines of his day, that the story might have become principally a history of eighteenth-century ideas and their relationship to posterity. A detailed narrative account might well have provided much information about social and military history. Because of the extraordinary breadth of Jones's learning, it was not easy to keep the general reader always in mind, and the provision of additional background would have lengthened the already long story without contributing new scholarly information.

Completion of the long project required the assistance of numerous institutions and individuals, who stopped their own work to answer pressing questions and provide needed information. My notes and bibliography express my principal indebtedness, but some institutions merit particular thanks. Texas A&M University provided generous assistance, as did the University of Michigan, the Indian Council for Cultural Relations and the Indian government (which funded two trips to India), and the American Philosophical Society (which funded three trips to England). Among the libraries where I did most of my research, special assistance was provided by the Bodleian Library, especially its Indian Institute; the British Library, including the Western and the Oriental Departments of Manuscripts, as well as the India Office Library and Records; the University of Calcutta Library; the Asiatic Society Library in Calcutta; the Beinecke Library and other collections at Yale University; and the New York Public Library. All of them also assisted with some of my earlier books.

Numerous individual scholars provided selfless help, among whom are Hans Aarsleff, Princeton University; H. B. Carter, Yeo Bank, Somerset; Llewelyn Gwyn Chambers, University College of North Wales; Hertha Kirketerp-Møller, Kongelige Bibliotek, Copenhagen; David Kopf, University of Minnesota; Sidney I. Landau, Cambridge University Press; Peter Marshall, King's College, London; Leslie Mitchell and Roy Hyde, University College, Oxford; Robert J. Morris, Jr., Oregon State University; James M. Osborn, Yale University; N. H. Robinson, Royal Society; Rosane Rocher, University of Pennsylvania; J. C. Sainty, London; Dame Lucy Sutherland and Valerie Jobling, History of the University of Oxford; Derek T. Whiteside, Cambridge University; William B. Willcox, Papers of Benjamin Franklin, Yale University; and Edwin Wolf II, Library Company of Philadelphia.

Finally, for permission to reproduce plates and texts, I am grateful to the director of the Indian Office Library and Records (the British Library) for A. W. Devis's portrait of Jones, and to the Asiatic Society for the logo used for the Asiatic Society Bicentenary. For permitting the first publication of six letters, thanks are due to the Gloucestershire County Council for Jones's four letters to Dr. William Adams in 1780 (housed in the Gloucestershire Record Office, #D6/F141), to the Princeton University Library for Jones's letter to Richard Johnson of 1787 (Elizabeth Montague Collection, Box 1, Folder 27), and to the British Library's India Office Library and Records for Thomas Law's undated letter to Jones (MSS Eur. D. 491).

Introduction

Three previous biographies of Jones are unsatisfactory. Teignmouth's *Memoirs of the Life, Writings and Correspondence of Sir William Jones* (1804) includes numbers of valuable letters, the holographs of many of which have been lost. Teignmouth records important personal information about his close friend Jones that only a contemporary could have known. But a check of his omissions and other changes in his publication of some of the Spencer letters at Althorp reveals his efforts to fit Jones into a near-model of Clapham evangelicalism, as is easily seen if one compares Teignmouth's version with the whole text as reproduced in *Letters*. Jones's free-thinking politics and religion are simply excised. Henry Morris's short *Sir William Jones, the Learned Oriental Scholar* (1901) goes even further toward reshaping Jones into a kind of Christian missionary. This view is quickly disproved when one scans through Jones's praises of Hinduism in letters that Morris probably could not have seen and might not have used anyway, in view of Morris's bias. Nor is Durgaprasanna Raychaudhuri's *Sir William Jones and His Translation of Kālidāsa's "Śakuntalā"* (1928) suitable as a biography, as this valuable study is restricted to one major aspect of Jones's Sanskrit work.

The first scholar to use the Spencer letters constructively was A. J. Arberry, whose incisive *Asiatic Jones: The Life and Influence of Sir William Jones* (1946) is, lamentably, only forty pages long. The 1946 bicentenary celebrations provided additional critical materials, which are unfortunately not integrated into a comprehensive biography. Volume 11 (1946) of the *Bulletin of the School of Oriental and African Studies* contains several excellent research articles, as does *Sir William Jones: Bicentenary of His Birth Commemoration Volume* (1948). There are two short proceedings (1946): *150th Jubilee of the Royal Asiatic Society of Bengal (1784–1934)* and the *Bicentenary of Sir William Jones (1746–1946)* and the Oxford *Proceedings of the Sir William Jones Bicentenary Conference*.

Of the several doctoral dissertations on Jones, two published ones are notable. Fatma Moussa-Mahmoud's *Sir William Jones and the Romantics*

(1962) is a study of Jones's literary influences. S. N. Mukherjee's *Sir William Jones: A Study in Eighteenth-Century Attitudes to India* (1968) is generally intellectual rather than literary or linguistic, but is undependable because of Mukherjee's mistakes in transcribing and annotating parts of the Spencer letters and because of his dubious literary and linguistic conclusions in a book not designed primarily as a biography. My *Oriental Jones* (1964) is badly out of date, as various reviewers of *Letters* noted in calling for a new biography. Two excellent, short chapters on Jones in 1967 indicated what might be done in such an extended story – linguistically in Hans Aarsleff's *The Study of Language in England, 1780–1860* (pp. 115–61) and politically in Peter Brown's *The Chathamites* (pp. 339–420).

The worldwide observances of the Asiatic Society Bicentenary in 1984 and 1986 (Calcutta, New Delhi, Bombay, London, Oxford, Brussels, New York, Princeton, Cornell, Syracuse, and Washington, D.C.) gave unprecedented scholarly attention to Jones, in some ways bringing his name more into public consciousness than even during the halcyon days of his own life. Numerous specialized studies in varied disciplines appeared in various journals and proceedings. This scholarly and popular treatment, disseminated widely in newspapers and on television, and in special programs on All-India Radio and BBC World Service and the Voice of America, has reelevated Jones to the lofty place that he held until the mid-nineteenth century and has provided new insights into his goals and achievements. At the Calcutta celebrations, Mrs. Indira Gandhi grandly praised Jones and declared the Asiatic Society to be "an institution of national importance." At that celebration I called the Society "a hope for world peace, where *scholars* can resolve problems rather than leaving the problems to politicians with Cruise missiles and SS–20s." At the end of my Indian lecture tour of 1984, I had planned to meet with Mrs. Gandhi again to see whether the Society might become a vehicle for peace through her leadership of the Third World nations, but the meeting was prevented by her tragic death. In any case, the information in this new biography will shed new light on the history and substance of various disciplines, when placed in the context of posterity's use of Jones's many contributions in anthropology and archaeology, astronomy, botany, history, language and linguistics, law and judicature, literature, music, physiology, politics, religion and mythology, general scholarship, and the history of ideas. Jones was a significant figure in several of these disciplines, not to mention his fascinating personal activities amid great events like the American Revolution and the governing of British India.

Much of my new biography is necessarily drawn from Jones's letters, the veracity of which can hardly be doubted because of the independent confirmation in other sources. Nor is there reason to doubt his truthfulness in his letters. In most cases, as when he was still in England or was writing to a colleague in India or England, his correspondent was in a position to know about the situation that Jones was describing, so that Jones neither could nor would have altered facts. Nonetheless, I have used caution in regard to a few passages in his letters that cannot be verified in such ways.

A second caveat should be mentioned here. I shall directly address the Orientalism question, which is of concern to many Indologists, only in the following paragraphs, rather than systematically in the body of the book, which is, again, a biography rather than a historical survey of the Orientalism question. Similarly, the historiography of the intercultural contacts between India and Britain – materials that are needed to set the broad historical scene – is likewise best handled compactly in this brief introduction rather than by interrupting the flow of the narrative. By having such topical materials here, the reader will recognize the roles of historical figures like Lord Macaulay and James Mill when they are mentioned in the narrative, but will not be distracted by interpolated history. The contributions of Jones and his colleagues to Orientalism in India may then be appreciated without interfering with the unfolding sequence of events in his biography.

Jones was always the humanitarian. His Indian law digest was designed to improve justice in the English courts in India, where the people deserved constitutional rights and respect for their culture and laws. He had a double strategy in proposing his digest. Despite his own occasional ethnocentrism, he recognized that Europeans must discard their biased opinions about colonial people before they could appreciate India's intellectual, artistic, and spiritual achievements and recognize the Asians' place in the family of human beings. His second strategy was humanitarian, as illustrated by his efforts to find a cure for Asian elephantiasis and to introduce a fruit tree into Bengal to combat famine. He contributed generously to charity, just as he gave his book royalties to imprisoned debtors. These are distinct personal achievements that time should not diminish.

But historians and changing attitudes in the nineteenth century did change at least the British view of Jones and the other early Orientalists. Basically, his scholarship and translations drastically altered the West's view of India, stimulating the general interest in Asia that is still seen in the West, and introducing the vast Oriental knowledge that has been interpolated into the body of total Western thought. By the mid-nineteenth century "works encyclopedic in form were multiplying: composite anthologies of texts, textbooks, and catalogs of world history. Asia seemed on the verge of entering decisively into the sphere of classical humanism."[1]

There were at least three major nineteenth-century blows to Orientalism. First was the philosopher James Mill's immensely popular, strongly anti-Asian *History of British India* (London, 1818). David Kopf cogently synthesizes Mill's devastating argument:

Fundamentally, Mill argued, beneath the shining veneer of Brahman achievements lay a primitive and barbaric state of society held together from earliest times by despotism and priestcraft. Being a rationalist and a Benthamite, Mill viewed tyranny – not religion – as the root evil of Hindu culture. The absence of political liberty, natural in a society that condoned extreme caste rigidity and complete license of religious superstition, resulted from the twin tyranny of the despot and Brahman. Mill went so far as to suggest that "despotism and priestcraft taken together, the Hindus, in mind and body, were the most enslaved portion of the human race." (p. 240)

Mill's Utilitarian concept of despotism was used to justify European overseas empires and eventuated in the Victorian "master race" days.

Despite strong rebuttals by Bengali intellectuals, who defended the concept of a Sanskrit golden age in arguments borrowed from Jones and his colleagues, such Utilitarian attacks prevailed. Next came Macaulay's Minute on Education of 1835, which was even more definitive in ending the British Orientalist movement. Third, hoping to develop an Indian intelligentsia trained in Western literature and sciences, Governor-General Lord Bentinck instituted a system of English education and essentially stopped the translating of English books into Sanskrit and Arabic. The College of Fort William was closed, the Asiatic Society experienced major financial problems, and the Calcutta Madrasah and the Calcutta Sanskrit College almost perished. Of course, Macaulay thought that he was right in attempting to bury ancient Indian civilization, which he viewed as decadent. The subsequent, catastrophic drop in the reputation of Jones and his colleagues was hardly affected by Horace H. Wilson's widely read, comprehensive refutation of Mill in *Two Lectures on the Religious Practice and Opinions of the Hindus* (Oxford, 1840).[2] Bentinck had constituted the Indian system of education so as to develop an essentially English culture.

Some twentieth-century developments somewhat ameliorated the situation. Scholars were beginning to realize that Indian society was not static, but had experienced creative changes over the earlier centuries that disproved the deterministic idea underpinning the Utilitarian and Victorian views of Orientalism. Among the major positive scholarly works that might be mentioned, Raymond Schwab's *La Renaissance orientale* (Paris, 1950) should be singled out. In 1984 this landmark work in the history of ideas was translated, and the notes and bibliography were updated. As Schwab reminds scholars in his prefatory remarks, Anquetil-Duperron and Jones informed Europe that there were other Europes, that is, areas that had had admirable intellectual pasts. Schwab minutely catalogues the whole new dimension in Western literature eventuating from Orientalism, ranging from the British and German Romantics, and the American transcendentalists, to modern poets like T. S. Eliot. He perceives "the birth of an integral humanism, a crucial, unprecedented chapter in the history of civilization."[3]

A second major positive work came in 1969, when Kopf investigated the subject of Orientalism from the Indian point of view, providing vital historiography and intercivilizational background. In tracing the dynamics of Indian modernization in the critical period of 1773 to 1835, his *British Orientalism and the Bengal Renaissance* uses Indian sources, including many Bengali ones, to place the Orientalists in a modern perspective:

The Orientalists served as avenues linking the regional elite with the dynamic civilization of contemporary Europe. They contributed to the formation of a new Indian middle class and assisted in the professionalization of the Bengali intelligentsia. They started schools, systematized languages, brought printing and publishing to India, and encouraged the proliferation of books, journals, newspapers, and other media of communication. Their impact was urban and secular. They built the first modern scientific laboratories in India, and taught European medicine. They were neither static classicists nor averse to the idea of progress; and they both historicized the Indian past and stimulated a consciousness of history in the Indian intellectual. It was they who transmitted a new sense of identity to Bengalis. (p. 275)

The major modern negative note was struck in 1978, when Edward Said's *Orientalism* challenged the virtues of Orientalism for Arabs. Citing some negative political aspects of Orientalism, apart from the salutary intellectual and artistic aspects, Said ends by rejecting Orientalism primarily because of a political image of the Arab as developed by some Western Orientalists (pp. 284–328). He warns against too close a relationship between the scholar and the state, and he urges the scholar to hold allegiance to a discipline defined intellectually rather than to a "field" like Orientalism that can be defined canonically, imperially, or geographically (p. 326). Unfortunately, Said pays comparatively little attention to India and Jones, particularly the vast influence that Jones's 1786 Calcutta lecture had on comparative linguistics in Europe as a whole.

My book is not a defense of Orientalism but an account of Jones's actions and ideas, which stand for themselves and show that he always resisted any political aspects of scholarship. He perceived any relationship between a scholar and the state to be objective and often a matter of needed financing, with the ideal to be a Governor-General like John Shore, who held the rich intercultural views of Jones and other Orientalists. Indeed, the scholar should be a citizen of the world, who can use knowledge to resolve controversies. If Mrs. Gandhi had survived and had championed a scholars' conference of geographers and historians finally to resolve the problem of Kashmir, as a model for other such political disputes, the world would have had the benefit of implementing one of Jones's ultimate visions.

In Jones's view, if the governing of other people falls to the lot of the scholar, their well-being should be the administrator's first concern. The people should be governed by their own laws and customs, without a Westernization of Indian values and attitudes. The only way the scholar can properly do this is to master the *field* (Orientalism) rather than to try to master isolated intellectual disciplines like law or religion, as Jones first tried – disturbingly incompletely – to do. For example, ancient Sanskrit astronomy contained valuable information about history and religion, and it is the integration of such information that particularly distinguishes Jones's work. But as Said perceptively observes, it is regrettable that there is no major journal of Arab studies in the Arab world, and no Arab university comparable to the great institutions of Europe, America, and India. Yet Jones's name does not belong in such a contemporary condition and context, despite his love for Arabic and Persian cultures. The Orientalists' influence was on India, not on the Arab world, where there was no Jones to ameliorate the dreary European conquest of helpless peoples and to help provide an intellectual edifice on which to build the future. One has only to consider the numerous fine universities that are thriving in India today, particularly the Sanskrit institutions that are advancing that knowledge. Jones's life in Calcutta was not really a reflection of the European impact on India, and the colonial situation was such that his life could not have been an illustration of the *Indian* response to European ideas and values. Rather, he was setting the stage for a cultural encounter that partly synthesized both European and Indian forces, but with a necessarily heavy proportion of classical Indian culture.[4]

In Jones's view, if the governed people's culture has waned, it is the administrator's responsibility to master the local languages and to apprehend and appreciate the local religions, culture, and history, with the eventual goal of disseminating that knowledge so as to reestablish the integrity of that heritage among the local peoples. If their civilization has waned, it may need modernization, but only through changes effected by cooperative actions of the native intelligentsia and the Western administrators, not through unilateral actions of Europeans who may consider a given local condition as being an aberration of Western customs and meriting elimination. This change may be stimulated in part by exposing a people to neglected periods of their past, as their knowledge of history is a sure path toward gaining an appreciation of their culture. Jones's achievements aided Indians eventually to take their place among the modern peoples of the world and to participate fully in creative evolutionary changes. He would have welcomed the modern updating of this view by Rabindranath Tagore, one of the major products of the Bengal renaissance particularly inspired by the British Orientalists:

Before Asia is in a position to co-operate with the culture of Europe, she must base her own structure on a synthesis of all the different cultures which she has. When, taking her stand on such a culture, she turns toward the West, she will take, with a confident sense of mental freedom, her own view of truth, from her own vantage ground, and open a new vista of thought to the world. Otherwise, she will allow her priceless inheritance to crumble into dust, and trying to replace it clumsily with feeble imitations of the West, make herself superfluous, cheap and ludicrous.[5]

Time and again in his writings, Jones underlined the necessity that European rule must be temporary, until such time as the people were ready to govern themselves; he was never an exponent of the British Empire tradition. All such views and examples emphasize the value for India of the Orientalism that Jones communicated from Bengal and that continues to hold valuable hints for the the future.

Chronology of Jones's Life

1746   Birth in London.
1753–64   Student at Harrow.
1764   Matriculation at University College, Oxford; election to Bennet Fellowship at Oxford.
1765–70   Tutor to Viscount Althorp (second Earl Spencer).
1766   First meeting with the Jonathan Shipleys and daughter Anna Maria.
1770   *Histoire de Nader Chah* from the Persian (including "Un Traité sur la poësie orientale"); outlining of the unfinished epic "Britain Discovered"; writing of the unpublished "An Essay on Education."
1770–3   Law studies in the Middle Temple (and Oriental publications). Work on an unpublished, revised edition of Meninski's *Thesaurus*.
1771   *Dissertation sur la littérature orientale*; *A Grammar of the Persian Language* ("A Persian Song of Hafiz"); *Lettre à Monsieur A—— du P——*.
1771–2   Work on the unpublished "Essay on the History of the Turks."
1772   *Poems, Consisting Chiefly of Translations from the Asiatick Languages*; second edition in 1777; election F.R.S.
1773   Election to Dr. Johnson's Literary Club; awarding of M.A. from Oxford; *An Oration Intended to Have Been Spoken in the Theatre at Oxford*; *The History of the Life of Nader Shah, King of Persia* (English translation of *Histoire*).
1774–83   London barrister and circuiteer (and Oriental publications).
1774   *Poeseos Asiaticæ Commentariorum*; admission to the bar; first appearance in Westminster Hall.
1775–83   Circuiteer on the Oxford and South Wales circuits.
1775   Appointment as a commissioner of bankruptcy.
1777   Assistance to the city of London on the Millachip impressment case.
1778–83   Efforts for a judgeship on the Bengal Supreme Court.
1779   Translation of *The Speeches of Isæus* from Greek; first of three trips to Paris to see Franklin; "A Fragment of Polybius" given to Franklin as an unsuccessful compromise plan.
1780   *Julii Melesigoni ad Libertatem*; experiences during the Gordon Riots; unsuccessful candidacy for an Oxford University seat in Parliament; *An Inquiry into the Legal Mode of Suppressing Riots*; *A Speech on the Nomination of Candidates to Represent the County of Middlesex*; second trip to Paris to see Franklin.
1781   *The Muse Recalled*; *An Ode in Imitation of Alcæus*; light poems; *An Essay on the Law of Bailments*.

1781–2	Assistance to Burke and others on Indian legislation.
1782	Translation of *The Mahomedan Law of Succession to the Property of Intestates* from Arabic; joining of Cartwright's Society for Constitutional Information; "Plan of National Defence"; *An Ode in Imitation of Callistratus*; *Speech to the Assembled Inhabitants of the Counties of Middlesex and Surrey*; last trip to Paris to see Franklin; quarrel with John Paradise; *The Principles of Government*; Shipley libel trial in 1784; translation of *The Moallakát; or Seven Arabian Poems* from Arabic, with second edition in 1783.
1783	*A Letter to a Patriot Senator*; appointment to a judgeship on the Bengal Supreme Court; knighthood and marriage to Anna Maria Shipley.
1783–94	Indian residence, scholarship, and translations.
1783–92	Delivery of six charges to Calcutta grand jury.
1784	Founding of the Asiatic Society of Bengal; quarrel with Burke; Burke's failure to use Jones's "Best Practicable System of Judicature for India."
1784–5	Serious illness in Bihar; "The Enchanted Fruit" and "On Parent Knees" quatrain.
1784–8	Nine poetic hymns to Hindu deities.
1784–94	Legal assistance to Bengal Governors-General; delivery of eleven Anniversary Discourses; systematic study of botany; Indian botanical writings; essays on Indian anthropology and archaeology, astronomy, chronology and ethnology, geography, music, literature, mythology and religion, languages and inscriptions, physiology, and other subjects; scholarly correspondence.
1785	*Asiatick Miscellany* (including Jones's first Indian poetry).
1785–94	Systematic study of Sanskrit, Jones's "best" language.
1786	Philological passage in the Third Anniversary Discourse; founding of comparative linguistics; "A Dissertation on the Orthography of Asiatick Words in Roman Letters" (the Jonesian System); Chittagong sojourn and Persian studies; planning of translation of "Sohrab and Rustum" from the *Sháhnáma*; *Hitopadesa of Vishnusarman*.
1786–94	Work on unfinished Indian digest of contract–succession laws.
1788	Persian printing of Hátifí's *Lailí Majnún*.
1788–94	Editing of first four volumes of *Asiatick Researches*.
1789	Translation of Jayadeva's *Gīta Govinda* and Kālidāsa's *Śakuntalā* from Sanskrit.
1792	Sanskrit printing of Kālidāsa's *Ṛitusaṃhāra*; translation of *Al Sirájiyyah* from Arabic.
1793	Illness and further weakening of health from overwork; departure of Lady Jones for Europe.
1794	Appearance of tumor; translation of *Institutes of Hindu Law; or, the Ordinances of Menu* from Sanskrit; request to resign from judgeship on completion of the Indian law digest in 1795 or 1796; death from inflammation of the liver; burial in Calcutta.

1   A Barbaric Oriental Conqueror (to 1770)

Jones's parents were remarkable people. Jones's father William is remembered for his personality, entrepreneur's role in promoting contemporary British science, and association with the Royal Society. William's own mother, Elizabeth Rowland, was related to the antiquarian Lewis Morris in a line back to Hwfa ap Cynddelw, one of the fifteen tribes of North Wales.[1] John George, his father, was a small farmer in Llanfihangel, Anglesey, where William was born in 1674 or 1675.[2] When his family moved to Tyddyn Bach, Llanbabo, he did so well in a charity school that the landlord Viscount Bulkeley arranged for him to go to London. William worked in the counting house of a merchant, for whom he visited the West Indies. Next he was a mathematics teacher aboard a warship. Present at the conquest of Vigo in 1702, he plundered only some scissors from a bookshop. Upon his return to London he set out his shingle as a mathematics teacher.

William Jones's first book, *A New Compendium of the Whole Art of Practical Navigation* (London, 1702), was dedicated to the mathematician John Harris, F.R.S., in whose house he had composed this application of plane trigonometry to Mercator's and middle-latitude sailing. The 102 pages of examples and problems supply practical rules for the sailing of ships. *Synopsis Palmariorum Matheseos: Or, a New Introduction to the Mathematics* (London, 1706) brought William to prominence. This beginner's syllabus explains the principles of arithmetic and geometry, and also discusses conic sections, the laws of motion, and gunnery theory. It was the first to employ the symbol π to denote the ratio of the circumference of a circle to its diameter, a use that was later adopted by Leonhard Euler for general use.

If forgettable today for its insights and memorable for its trivia, *Synopsis* was praised by Halley and Newton, with whom William became friends. Newton esteemed him, permitting him to print "De analisi per æquationes numero terminorum infinitas," "Methodus differentialis," and reproductions of some tracts. These appeared, with an elegant preface, as

1

Analysis per quantitatum series, fluxiones, ac differentias (London, 1711), probably William's intellectual pinnacle and a contribution to notation through use of the dot as a sign for differentiation in calculus, but showing little basic understanding. Pleasing Newton but evoking an attack by Leibnitz, the book had a new edition in 1723 and an English translation in 1736.

When an article in *Philosophical Transactions* of 1710 claimed that Leibnitz had published Newton's *Fluxiones* under another name and with a different notation, Leibnitz asked the Royal Society to decide whether he or Newton had developed the infinitesimal calculus. The society then appointed a committee of Halley, William, and others, who decided for Newton, using Newton's own work as their report, *Commercium epistolicum* (London, 1712). Actually, the two scholars had independently arrived at differential calculus as a practical mode of mathematical reasoning. William became a fellow of the society (F.R.S.) on 30 November 1712.[3] The physician Richard Mead was his close associate, and Dr. Samuel Johnson was a later friend.

William was interested in the government prize of up to £20,000 to devise a practical means of determining longitude at sea, but he had no success. One of his letters was even signed "Longitude Jones." A leading mathematician and man of science, William corresponded with the mathematicians Roger Cotes, Nicholas Saunderson, and Brook Taylor, and scientists like James Logan and John Machin. Letters came from Pierre Rémond de Montmort about *Essay d'analyse sur le jeux de hazard* (Paris, 1708), the astronomer Pierre-Louis Moreau Maupertuis, and the mathematician Le P. Charles-René Reyneau. These letters reflect the history of science of the day.[4] William assembled what was considered to be the most valuable mathematical library in England, some fifteen thousand scientific works and fifty thousand to sixty thousand manuscript pages, while also collecting rare shells and fossils. He began a large book modeled on his *Synopsis* to introduce Newtonian and natural philosophy, as he was one of the few to be shown and be permitted to copy many of Newton's mathematical papers. Indeed, some of his errors in copying were long perpetuated, although only the first pages of the book ever went to press.

One of William Jones's notable pupils was Philip Yorke, later first earl of Hardwicke and chief justice from 1732 to 1736, who often took him on the circuit as a companion. After Yorke became lord chancellor in 1736, he made William the secretary for the peace. Another pupil was Thomas Parker, the first earl of Macclesfield. As lord chancellor he made William the secretary of commissions of the peace in 1721, to help with administrative duties in the appointment of justices of the peace. William held the post until 1725, when according to custom, he left office when Macclesfield was found guilty of malversation of funds.

Macclesfield invited William to live as a member of the family at Shirburn Castle, Oxfordshire, where for several years William instructed Thomas Parker in the sciences and Thomas's son George in mathematics. As he seems to have been relatively well off, he was able to continue his scientific work. He had married the widow of his London merchant-employer, whose property he inherited at her death. The Welsh scholar Richard Morris mentions a scandal, which gave rise to the saying "Macclesfield was the making of Jones and Jones the making of Macclesfield."[5] This may imply that William sired Thomas, the third earl, by George's new bride in 1723, as possibly hinted at in Pope's *The Dunciad*, "The Sire is made a Peer, the Son a Fool" (IV. 548), and in the Macclesfield papers. In any case, in about 1729, after William's banker failed, George (a teller of the Exchequer and later president of the Royal Society) arranged the sinecure office of second clerk, which he apparently held until his death. Back in London, William became a justice of the peace for Middlesex and Westminster.

At Shirburn he had met Mary, George Nix's youngest daughter. (Nix had so excelled in cabinet making that he was Chippendale's chief competitor and was invited to the estates of the great.) At twenty-two, Mary became William's second wife on 17 April 1731. Their son George died in infancy in 1732; their daughter Mary was born in 1736.

William's work in the Royal Society continued, and in 1743 the society appointed a committee to compare their standard yard with that used in the Exchequer and elsewhere.[6] While serving as a mathematician in the Shirburn observatory, William was put on the committee, with three of his papers appearing in *Philosophical Transactions:* "A Commodious Disposition of Equations for Exhibiting the Relations of Goniometrical Lines" (1747) and the posthumous "Of Logarithms" and "Properties of the Conic Sections" (1771, 1773).

William's son, the subject of this biography, was born at Beaufort Buildings, Westminster, on 23 September 1746. Jones hardly got to know his father, whose doctor, Mead, discovered that William had an incurable polyp in his heart. When Mead reported this fact to Mary, she resolved not to tell her husband; but then a well-meaning friend wrote him a philosophical condolence, which, she realized, revealed the secret. Cheerfully obeying his request that she read it aloud, Mary spontaneously created such a convincing substitute letter that he never realized the deception. He died on 1 July 1749, leaving a fine reputation but modest assets. Macclesfield never implemented William's request to take charge of the large mathematical project. The proved will of 8 November 1748, preserved in the Public Record Office, gave his gold watch and library to Macclesfield. It reserved £1,000 each for his son and daughter when they became twenty-one, under the executorship of Macclesfield and his "most beloved wife." His diamond ring went to Nix.

William described Mary as "virtuous without blemish, generous without extravagance, frugal but not niggard, cheerful but not giddy, close but not sullen, ingenious but not conceited, of spirit but not passionate, of her company cautious, in her friendship trusty, to her parents dutiful, and to her husband ever faithful, loving and obedient."[7] Naturally studious, she became proficient in algebra and trigonometry. Upon William's death the naturalist-poet Henry Baker helped arrange the fossil collection so that she could sell it profitably. The countess of Macclesfield urged her and her children to live at Shirburn, but fearing that such residence might hamper her plan of education for her son, she declined. That is, Mary intended to develop his mind and character to the fullest, rejecting severe discipline while leading him to knowledge

by exciting his curiosity, and directing it to useful objects. To his incessant importunities for information on casual topics of conversation, which she watchfully stimulated, she constantly replied, *read, and you will know;* a maxim, to the observance of which he always acknowledged himself indebted for his future attainments. By this method, his desire to learn became as eager as her wish to teach. ... in his fourth year he was able to read, distinctly and rapidly, any English book.[8]

Mary cultivated her son's memory by making him learn speeches from Shakespeare and the best of Gay's fables. She and his sister, who was now fifteen, were devoting themselves to providing him with the best education that a commoner could get with her modest resources.

In his fourth year, while trying to scrape soot from the chimney, Jones fell into the flames, and his clothes caught fire. His screams brought the servants, who had difficulty in saving him. His neck, arms, and face were badly burned. A second accident, soon afterward, had more severe consequences. While he was struggling with the servants who were dressing him, a clothes hook was thrust into his right eye. Mead treated it, but it was permanently weakened.

By his fifth year Jones could read again, developing the habit of reading any book available. The angel described in the tenth chapter of Revelation so impressed him that he never forgot his rapture at reading what he later considered to be a divinely inspired passage. A friend helped him with Latin in his sixth year, but the grammatical lists did not inspire him to learn much about Latin. His mother was not concerned, for she was planning for him to start his classical studies at Harrow, where he was enrolled at Michaelmas in 1753.

Just becoming a leading public school under Thomas Thackeray, Harrow served gentlemen and also provided a classical education for thirty poor boys of the parish. Jones thus would be associating with boys likely to have distinguished careers. The village setting was appealing, with the boys living in boarding houses. Jones stayed at Mrs. King's, where Peter, the Hanover "wild boy," lodged. Said to have been found by George I in a German woods climbing a tree like an orangutan, Peter cut the firewood and carried the water.[9]

Jones did not display any real talents during his first two years at Harrow. Half his time was devoted to his books; the rest, to a small garden. His mother sewed his clothes when funds were short; and as he noted to his sister: "They fit, in my opinion, very well; though Biddy says they are too little in the arms."[10] During his vacations in London, his mother continued his instruction in the English language and began teaching him drawing.

The second year ended with another accident. Jones was sitting under a tree when some pears fell off. In the scramble for the fruit, he broke his thigh, which kept him away from school for a year. Once his pain was gone, his mother, as his constant companion, resumed his education. He so enjoyed reading Pope's juvenile poems and Dryden's *Aeneid* that he composed imitations. Because he considered Latin to have little utility, his mother let him forgo it in favor of literature.

Upon returning to school, he was placed in his former class, now advanced a year. For months the situation was almost intolerable. When he failed in tasks for which he had had no instruction, his classmates thought him lazy or stupid. The master, who was a detestable tyrant, strengthened both impressions by beating him. Jones felt an intense sense of injustice at being punished for his "inability to soar, before he had been taught to fly," as he later said.[11]

The punishment initiated Jones's lifelong distrust of magisterial authority, adding stubbornness to his precocity. Nonetheless, he sought out and studied basic works to derive needed principles, soon earning a respectable standing in his class. The success prompted greater industry: "His compositions were correct, his analysis accurate, and he uniformly gained every prize offered for the best exercise."[12] But being at the head of his class was inadequate, and so he learned prosodic rules in order to compose imitations of Ovid, an assignment never required of lower-school students.

Jones was beginning to construct a kind of educational model to supplement Harrow's apparent inadequacies. Games could be useful in this respect: As they were designed for amusement on the playing fields, he devised one to provide exercise while strengthening the boys' knowledge of ancient Greece. Samuel Parr and William Bennet, his best friends, acted as Leander and Nisus; and Jones was Euryalus, king of Arcadia. They mapped the fields into Greece, persuading other boys to be the barbarian invaders of the trio's hillock kingdoms, which they defended. During the simulated wars they held councils and composed memorials.

Jones also wrote plays and classical imitations. The trio wrote and performed a play in a parlor thronged with school fellows, who exuberantly applauded the actors clad in flowing robes and turbans. Sometimes they acted the roles of great people, haranguing and debating. They studied logic, syllogistically debating on natural history or metaphysical questions suggested in Plato's dialogues. Jones and Parr liked to imitate English writers: "While they excelled in the ordinary exercises of the school in the learned languages, they improved their English style by a diligent perusal of Addison, Johnson and other elegant authors, whose comparative merits they discussed in conversation, and whose peculiar forms of writing they selected as models for imitation."[13] Though the three boys did not participate in the usual school games, they did join in the "Pugna Maxima" of December 1757, when the boys from Thackeray's house attacked those at another's house in order to seize some fireworks.[14]

In his twelfth year Jones was promoted to the upper school. His memory was so well developed that when his school fellows decided to stage a play and accepted his suggestion of *The Tempest,* he wrote out the text from memory upon discovering that copies were not available. His own role was that of Prospero. Having learned the Greek alphabet for amusement, he set out to master Greek. True to form, his teachers praised his imitations of Sophocles as having the qualities of the original; Thackeray predicted that Jones's active mind would gain Jones fame and riches even if he were naked and friendless on Salisbury Plain. Stimulated by Robert Sumner, who became headmaster in 1760, Jones then mastered Latin. At the principal assistant's suggestion he drew up for the new headmaster a plan of the lectures and exercises in the upper school. For two years he wrote the exercises for many of the boys in the two superior classes, while his own classmates became his pupils. Not surprisingly, the holidays declared as the result of his excellent compositions helped make him more popular.

Jones also gave Sumner a collection of his compositions, including a translation of Virgil's pastorals. Composing a tragedy about Meleager, in which his school fellows performed, Jones played Meleager.[15] His metrical knowledge enabled him to scan Terence; Jones's "Limon," classical poetic imitations, would lie unpublished among his papers for a decade.

For his holidays he planned further studies – French, Italian, and arithmetic. Books were plentiful, because his mother allowed unlimited funds for them. Henry Baker, a family friend, invited him to the informal meetings of scientific and literary men at Baker's house. On one occasion Jones's mother recommended that he read Antoine Pluche's *Le Spectacle de la nature* (Paris, 1732–51) as preparation, but the nine volumes proved less entertaining than did the *Arabian Nights Entertainments* and Shakespeare, which he often read. He was proud of his friendship with Baker, whose *Medulla poetarum Romanorum* (London, 1737) was one of his favorites.

Headmaster Sumner declared that Jones, who was an open favorite, knew more Greek than his master did. Yet the very comprehensiveness of the classical instruction revealed the school's overemphasis on these two languages – such a school obviously did not prepare children for mercantile careers.[16] In any case, Jones began an independent study of some writings in modern languages, primarily to gain the ideas and cultural values contained in them. He added Hebrew to underpin his religious studies, reading some of the Psalms, as his mother had taught him only the Lord's Prayer and the Apostles' Creed. Later, when a private tutor at Harrow recommended Beveridge's popular *Private Thoughts upon Religion* (London, 1709), Jones was struck by the idea that one should profess Christianity out of a candid inquiry and conviction, not because others profess it. The linguistic relationship of Hebrew to Arabic led him to study the Arabic writing system. In this way he filled gaps in Harrow's traditional, Western-oriented curriculum, building toward a world perspective of the Renaissance man. He even utilized nature in his education, as in the botanical study developed from his garden.

Jones's father had made a distinguished name without the fine education that the boy was receiving from his father's modest estate, and much was expected of him. Sometimes he studied all night, kept awake by coffee or green tea. Toward the end of his Harrow days his reputation had so spread that strangers often inquired about the Great Scholar, the first of several epithets given him.

Jones was distilling his reading into usable form. Thus a consoling letter to his sister (*Letters*, 1:1–3), written when he was fourteen, reveals an amazing maturity. Jones gently wrote that her friend's death could be a cause not for grief but for rejoicing at his having peacefully left "a state so perilous and uncertain" at a time when his reputation was wholly virtuous: "We should therefore compare our afflictions with those who are more miserable, and not with those who are more happy."

Eyestrain was a problem in Jones's final months at Harrow, as he wrote Sumner:

Sir, my mother has brought a medical gentleman from London to examine my eyes. He says, I must be taken home, because I must not be allowed to look into a book. If I go home, there will be nobody to read to me; but if I am suffered to remain here, I give you my word, that I will not read myself, but can come into the school to hear the lessons done, and Parr, Bennet, &. &. can read to me in the evenings.[17]

Sumner let him miss classes, and he dictated his compositions to younger students. During this period he learned chess by practicing the games in Philidor.[18] The result was Jones's first important poem, "Caissa," which was not published for a decade.

When his seventeenth birthday passed, it was time for the next stage in his education. Such a fine record by a commoner might have dictated a legal career. Accordingly, his father's friend Samuel Prime (a king's serjeant in the Common Pleas) and others urged placement under an eminent barrister, as his talents and industry would ensure wealth and fame. Intrigued, Jones read Sir Edward Coke,[19] frequently amusing legal friends by discussing old cases normally studied only by legal scholars. But because a career in law would require his giving up Cicero and Demosthenes so as to plead cases in Westminster Hall, such study was not appealing, and it would strain his limited inheritance.

Jones's mentors, particularly Sumner, urged him to complete his formal studies at a university, where the costs would be more moderate. Sumner recommended Cambridge, but a tutor suggested Oxford. Jones and his mother, who wanted to live near him, preferred Oxford, and he was admitted as a commoner at University College on 15 March 1764.

At Harrow, whose term had just begun, Jones completed a course of lectures before taking up residence at Oxford. There he became a founder's exhibitioner, a position that paid a tiny sum to two Harrovians at Oxford and that he retained for three years. Jones left a glorious name at Harrow, with Sumner often citing him as the ornament of Harrow and a model of classical learning.

Jones's friendship with nine boys was to continue for many years. That with Parr and John Parnell (later chancellor of the Irish Exchequer) was to influence both their careers. As William Bennet, later the bishop of Cloyne, reflected: "I loved him and revered him, and, though one or two years older than he was, was always instructed by him from my earliest age. In a word, I can only say of this amiable and wonderful man, that he had more virtue, and less faults, than I ever yet saw in any human being." Parnell had a similar opinion: "He gave very early proofs of his possessing very extraordinary abilities. His industry was very great."[20] When Parnell left school, Jones gave him a collection of English poems containing the later-published "Arcadia." Another, addressed to Parnell, was a translation of a moody ode by Horace.[21] Six other close friends were Joseph Banks, Charles Combe, Sir Fletcher Norton's son Fletcher, William Dean Poyntz, Richard Brinsley Sheridan, and Richard Warburton.

Because Jones was anticipating a literary career, upon returning to Oxford on about 13 May he followed Sumner's advice and began to edit his Greek and Latin compositions, including "Mormo," a comedy imitating Aristophanes. But the juvenile book was postponed, though not because of an enhanced appreciation of classical literature derived from the public lectures:

They were much below the standard of his attainments, and, in fact, were considered as merely formal; and, instead of pure principles on subjects of taste, on rhetoric, poetry, and practical morals, *he complained* that he was required to attend dull comments on artificial ethics, and logic detailed in such barbarous Latin, that he professed to know as little of it as he then knew of Arabic.[22]

Jones so objected to the school Latin that in an oration in University College, "he declaimed violently against Burgersdiscius, Cracanthorpius, and the whole body of logicians" in Queen's College.[23]

Oxford's dons did not have the literary zeal and dedication to advancing their best student to his maximum ability that Sumner had had. Initially Jones found no Parr among his fellow students, whose bell ringing, horseback riding, walking tours, and frequenting of taverns were not his idea of recreation, although he strenuously exercised to counter the effects of prolonged study.

As Jones's mother and sister were still in London, he spent his vacation from 20 July to 6 October there, daily attending Angelo's schools of riding and fencing, to learn these gentleman's graces while getting exercise. But he devoted most of his spare time to his family, by, for instance, helping his sister Mary with Greek. Like their mother, she also was dedicating herself to his interests.[24]

In October 1764 Jones was elected to one of the four scholarships offered by Sir Simon Bennet's foundation. His name first appears among the Common Room charges in the Buttery Account of 9 November, when he presumably began dining there. Because three seniors were ahead of him for a fellowship, that more lucrative award seemed remote.

Jones brought to Oxford an Arabic informant, Mirza, who was from Aleppo. Jones already knew the Arabic writing system, and a friend was lending him basic books. He was anticipating that his colleagues might also study Arabic, while helping pay the informant's expenses. But he was disappointed: Few used Pococke's superb manuscripts at the Bodleian Library, which showed the Arabs' literary and intellectual greatness, or to communicate discoveries about past Asian civilizations. Without the hoped-for support, paying Mirza's expenses for several months almost bankrupted Jones.

He nonetheless spent part of every morning on Galland's twelve-volume *Les Mille et une nuits* (Paris, 1704–17), transcribing Mirza's Arabic version and later refining it.[25] His other method was innovational within the matrix of prescientific linguistics: Attic Greek and Latin obviously offered no possibility of working with a native contemporary of Aristotle or Cicero, whereas Jones was imitating a native pronunciation so as to help him learn Arabic. Yet he viewed writing as language and stressed written literature. Using a prescriptive approach, he tried to correct Mirza's speech, with the goal of reading classical Arabic literature. On this slender base "he raised the edifice of a sound knowledge of the language."[26]

Persian opened another door. Written in Arabic characters, it contains numerous Arabic loanwords and grammatical features, as well as a rich literature to be translated. As Persian was the "official" language of India, the East India Company's natural interest raised the possibility of patronage or place. Jones used the only grammar available, Greaves's *Elementa linguæ Persicæ* (London, 1649). His text was Saʻdí's *Gulistán,* which he checked against Gentius's version (Amsterdam, 1651); and his lexicon was Meninski's *Thesaurus linguarum orientalium Turcicæ, Arabicæ, Persicæ* (Vienna, 1680–7). He made rapid progress.

Such industry led Jones's tutors to excuse him from their lectures, which were directed to the less ambitious. Using the time more advantageously, he did not abuse this freedom: "He perused with great assiduity all the Greek poets and historians of note, and the entire works of Plato and Lucian, with a vast apparatus of commentaries on them; constantly reading with a pen in his hand, making remarks, and composing in imitation of his favourite authors."[27] He stressed Aristotle because of Oxford's placement of that philosopher at the heart of its curriculum. Milton's "Of Education" (1673) also so impressed Jones that he memorized it, following Milton's plan by reading the best Italian, Spanish, and Portuguese authors and doing physical exercises. In short, as he observed, he was giving himself a prince's education with a peasant's means. His systematic supplementing of Oxford's offerings began to assume the form of an educational theory modeled on Milton, whereas the Oxford curriculum was devoted more to style than content, and virtually ignored the major philosophical and linguistic developments in Germany. Jones added the needed content, in individualized learning that implemented his ambitious self-study plan at his own rate.

Although Oxford was now eminently satisfactory, in the spring of 1765 he became concerned: Even after careful economy, he was draining the limited income of his mother, who never complained. His sister and his "virtuous and affectionate parent" had now moved to Oxford "in hopes of passing the remainder of her life" in his company (1:72). Despite Jones's record, a first-year student had little chance for a fellowship. But just when he began to think about leaving college, his record at Harrow provided the means for him to make a place for himself at eighteen years. This success helped him decide on a life that would permit scholarship.

Jonathan Shipley, dean of Winchester, had liked Jones's Harrow compositions and had recommended him to Baron Spencer as the tutor of George John, Viscount Althorp and Spencer's only son. Although neither man had met Jones, Spencer offered him the post. The generous terms were conveyed by William Arden, Spencer's former tutor. Meeting the seven-year-old Althorp in London, Jones was so charmed that he forgot about a possible profession in order to devote himself to a post where he might employ his educational theory. Baron Spencer would let Jones remain at Oxford during the terms, with time for writing and with opportunities to travel and improve his knowledge of languages. The financial drain on his mother would cease. After Althorp's preliminary instruction Jones could rejoin Sumner when the boy enrolled at Harrow. Jones returned to Oxford until 19 July, when he moved to Wimbledon House.

He entered the Spencer household much as his father had joined the Macclesfields'. It was a way in which someone of recognized talents who had pretensions to gentility could move into a front rank of society, in an intimate but tense social arrangement with his betters by fortune and birth.[28] The new world of Wimbledon was quite agreeable to Jones. The splendor of the estate and the aristocrats who visited there, Althorp's keen intelligence, the charm of his eight-year-old sister Georgiana (the future duchess of Devonshire) and his four-year-old sister Henrietta Frances, and the elegant life-style of Lady Spencer (Georgiana, a daughter of the diplomat Stephen Poyntz) were impressive. Because Althorp was eager to learn, the tutoring was pleasant.

At Oxford for most of the period of 14 October to 13 May 1766, Jones continued his studies, composing several poems. His recent work with Arabic led him back to Hebrew, and he read most of the Old Testament in the original. His chief interest was the Book of Job and the Prophets.

The summer of 1766 brought three important developments. First, when two of the four Bennet fellowships unexpectedly became available, he and Samuel Swire were summoned to University College. George Horne (later bishop of Norwich), John Coulson, and the master (Nathan Wetherel) elected Jones on 7 August, and then Swire. Jones was immediately given two terms of absence, not being formally admitted until 7 February 1767. The Buttery Account of 6 February first lists him with 0–0–0 charge among the fellows; his usual daily charge of 7s 4d is listed in the Common Room group for that date. His first payment under the fellowship was for £19 14s 0d, which was paid annually on 25 February through 1783, and his share of dividends and fines for 1767 was £43.

Jones had thus achieved independence. His room and a manservant would always be waiting, and sometimes only one other fellow shared the Senior Common Room with him. The Bodleian manuscripts and books were but steps away, with a constant company of scholars. Because he was not married and lived prudently, the stipend more than ensured a life of learning at any time that he might return to Oxford. Now he had enviable security if he ever chose to leave the Spencers. Rarely has a fellowship been so richly justified or better used.[29]

Soon after Jones's election, his scholarship was rewarded in a second way: The duke of Grafton, secretary of state for the Northern Department, offered him the post of interpreter for Eastern languages. Although it would not have interfered with his tutorship or studies, Jones declined the offer, instead strongly recommending Mirza. When someone else was appointed, he regretted his naïveté, as he could easily have performed the few duties and given the pay to Mirza.

The third development was personally important. The Shipleys visited Wimbledon, enabling Jones to thank the dean for the recommendation. Soon to be bishop of St. Asaph, Shipley moved in high circles and was a friend of Benjamin Franklin. Anna Maria (b. 1748), the oldest of Shipley's five daughters, captivated Jones. But he believed in honorable independence: He would never owe his fortune to a wife or her parents, although opportunities were likely in his situation in the Spencer household. Without a profession or substantial income, he rejected all notions of an alliance with the well-to-do Shipleys, despite Anna's friendliness. Under different circumstances, he might have proposed to her that summer.

Life with the Spencers was revealing deficiencies in Jones's view of a gentleman's graces. Dancing was a necessary refinement. Thus when the Spencers moved to London in the autumn of 1766, he secretly took lessons from the famed master Giovanni Gallini, who was teaching Henrietta. Besides studying, he further cultivated his skills of riding and fencing. When a scarred pensioner offered to teach him to use the broadsword, Jones acquired this skill. Consequently, when he attended the balls at the manor at Althorp, Northamptonshire, that winter, not only could he dance with Anna and the other girls, but he also showed that he could excel at dancing.

Spencer's excellent library compensated for the disadvantages of country life, miles from the Bodleian and London. It contained rare books, which Jones studied. Indeed, he inspected virtually every book, weighing its utility in his continuing education. Robert Lowth's *De sacra poesi Hebræorum prælectiones* (Oxford, 1753) inspired him to begin his Latin *Commentariorum* on Asiatic poetry in imitation of the Hebrew study, and he drafted a Persian grammar for a friend who was planning to go to India.

From 4 February to 8 March 1767 he was at Oxford. Because Spencer was ailing, the family went to Spa in the summer, but Jones's three weeks on the Continent permitted only dancing lessons and German study. The dancing master Janson was his teacher for the former. For the latter, because at Oxford he had gained some command of German sounds from a friend – just as he had studied Arabic under Mirza – he preferred a native master. But as none was available in Spa and as his pay was inadequate to bring one from Aix-la-Chapelle, Jones concentrated on the grammar and dictionary that he had brought with him. His delightful text was Gessner's epic *Der Tod Abels* (Zurich, 1758).

The month of 11 October to 12 November found Jones at Oxford; the winter, at Althorp. Spencer was involved in the three-man contest for the two Northampton Town seats, in a violent general election. It proved enormously expensive, for he opened Althorp to the "jolly Voters" and others who wandered in for free food and drink. Jones was initially detached but then became concerned, his feelings influenced by his reading. Nonetheless, the election furor permitted him to confine himself to the library and extend his literary knowledge. One year after he had started his *Commentariorum,* it was nearly complete, although its publication would be long delayed. He also practiced his Arabic by transcribing a manuscript on Egypt, and he practiced writing out Chinese characters.

Out of curiosity Jones opened and then studied Fortescue's *De laudibus legum Angliæ* (London, 1616). This praise of English laws led him to compare them with Greek and Roman laws, whereupon he delightedly concluded that the English ones were superior, a generalization that he had not previously considered and that would help determine his career. He had strongly favored classical orators and poets, and now he had evaluated classical jurisprudence. The 1768 election, however, was showing English jurisprudence to be less perfect than its theoretical perfection might suggest.

The political situation was deteriorating. Amid the spectacle of Sir George Brydges Rodney's spending £30,000 to narrowly win a Northampton seat in the election, Jones was hearing "the uproar of seditious people," whose renowned liberty had been "changed into unbridled license" upon John Wilkes's return from flight after expulsion from the Commons. The London riots were in the name of "Wilkes and Liberty" following his election for Middlesex. Jones disapproved of "that villain Wilkes – a man, it is true, of energy and intelligence, but a trouble-maker and a sort of firebrand to light the flames of sedition," but he regretted some of the aristocratic supporters' betrayal of Wilkes. Jones was placing trust in the English constitution, which was received "almost by divine intervention, so that no Greek or Roman state seems to have had a more perfect one" (trans., 1:9–11). He felt that no legislator could have conceived a better constitution, even in the abstract. The flexibility built into the English mixture of the classical types of states could overcome the present problems: royal authority undiminished by the aristocracy's influence, the people's freedom undiminished by prominent citizens' power, and the quality of the laws undiminished by popular freedom.

Jones expressed his growing trust in the constitution – together with his opposition to mob action as a way to redress acknowledged grievances – to Count Charles Reviczky, the first of several scholars with whom he would carry on a lifelong correspondence in Latin and French. When the Hungarian-born diplomat had sold his classical library to Spencer while in London in early 1768, the pair had had time for only a half hour's conversation about Persian poetry, but even that stimulus was enough to influence Jones's career. Jones enthusiastically recalled their talk:

We are ardent devotees of the same things; but there is one difference between us: you assuredly have the deepest knowledge of Asiatic literature, whereas I struggle, strive, and toil in order to obtain *some* knowledge of it. But I will not allow that your enthusiasm is greater than mine; my delight in such literature is so incredible that nothing could surpass it. (trans., 1:5)

He had once felt that nothing could surpass Greek poetry; now his introduction to Arabic and Persian had diminished that enthusiasm.

Reviczky sent translations of two Háfiz odes, together with classical parallels. Jones responded with additional parallels and queries about Oriental prosody. He made suggestions about his friend's Latin versions of other odes, which appeared as *Specimen poeseos Persicæ* (Vienna, 1771). The sensuous images appealed to him; and he thought sadly about English poetry, burdened by stereotyped phraseology, the constricting heroic couplet, and the rejection of emotion. The ode "Shírazí Turk" especially impressed him. After Reviczky explained the probable meaning of the first couplet, Jones began a translation that was to become "A Persian Song of Hafiz."

He spent the month of 15 April to 14 May 1768 at Oxford. Then, back at Wimbledon he revised his *Commentariorum* and began making a copy for Reviczky. In the summer there was new fruit of his scholarship. The geographer Carsten Niebuhr had given the Danish Royal Library a copy of Mahdi Khan's rare official biography of Nadir Shah, *Ta'rikh-i-Nadiri*. When Christian VII visited England, he requested its translation into French. The Danish ambassador talked to the duke of Grafton, who promptly recommended Jones, perhaps the only Englishman capable of translating the complicated manuscript. But the eighteenth-century style was difficult, different from the classical Persian that Jones knew, and the subject was dry. In his refusal of the offer, he stressed that he lacked the leisure and ability for such a fruitless, laborious task. Though honored, he recommended Alexander Dow on the basis of *Tales Translated from the Persian of Inatulla of Delhi* (London, 1768) and a translated history. He did not mention a major objection: Such biographies should be translated only in order to reveal the tyrants' wickedness.

Because Dow was busy with his career, the application was renewed. There were hints that Jones's acceptance would assist his career, that the translation would provide a pleasing distinction, and that the king's otherwise having to seek a translator in France would reflect badly on England. Jones later reflected:

> Incited by these motives, and principally by the last of them, unwilling to be thought churlish or morose, and eager for the bubble Reputation, I undertook the work, and sent a specimen of it to his Danish Majesty; who returned his approbation of the style and method, but desired, *that the whole translation might be perfectly literal, and the Oriental images preserved.*[30]

The task would have been much easier had the king wished a Latin version, because Jones's mastering of a French style was tedious. As his French lacked "certain peculiarities of idiom, and nice shades of meaning, which a foreigner can never learn to perfection," every chapter had to be checked by a native French speaker. The task was made unpleasant by repeated hints that Christian VII was impatient for its completion. By neglecting his own work, Jones was able to finish it in a year. He asked permission to present a beautiful copy to Oxford and to print the book with a dedication to the king. The reply was that such a presentation was a royal prerogative, which could hardly favor Oxford over Cambridge. The second request was granted, and Jones was asked whether this favor was sufficient reward, as the Danes clearly wished to settle with as little money as possible.

By August 1769 the book was in press. Printed by Peter Elmsly, *Histoire de Nader Chah* appeared in April 1770 in two quartos at Jones's expense and is introduced by his public, dedicatory letter to the king. Despite his conventional praise like "véritable appréciatrice du génie," Jones notes that he will leave Oriental flattery to Mahdi, for posterity will differentiate between the baseness of adulation and the pure praise of truth (1:62). Forty copies on large paper were sent to Copenhagen. The king's was elegantly bound; the others were presents for the courtiers. Jones told Reviczky that the king was very pleased: "[He] is thinking of giving me some sort of decoration. One of my friends, a most noble man, told him, when the King was thinking of the appropriate way to reward me, that I was not desirous of money and did not think much of it, but, in his opinion, was most eager for Honour" (trans., 1:61). What Christian VII did do was to send a Latin testimonial to Britain's George III on 15 February 1771, which the London newspapers promptly printed. Jones received a copy and a diploma for membership in the Royal Danish Academy of Sciences and Letters. In a private letter to Adolph Siegfried van der Osten, Denmark's minister of foreign affairs, Jones praised the king (trans., 1:92–93).

Although Jones may have thought the king was niggardly, the rewards did not upset him. Advertisements in London newspapers for censure led him to explain the whole matter and briefly defend the "amiable monarch" in the preface to his English abridgment. Friends like Richard Warburton thought that "a very different reward would have crowned his labours" if Jones's letters to Denmark had included "that *eastern adulation* in which Asiatic productions generally abound."[31] Jones later told Edmund Burke that if given the opportunity, he would reward the translators of any Oriental works done for him, but "not as government has rewarded" him for *Histoire* (2:522).

He was hardly sanguine about his translation's success. He had not chosen the subject, and he had done the work before his scholarship was mature. Though he would not accept responsibility for Mahdi's extravagant style or faults, he was uncomfortably aware of his likely numerous errors caused by his rush to complete the work, which also had offered no opportunity for creativity. But Jones's French is good, his translation demonstrates an understanding of Modern Persian, and his notes are factual and helpful. His most serious flaws are the mutilation of many proper names and the incorrect conversion of Moslem dates, but, then, he had no modern conversion table.[32] Lacking personal information about Persia, he had to rely on poor maps and references – he used no commentary – and even today, some of Mahdi's names cannot be identified.

The task made Jones extend his mastery of French, which he used to advantage in one pleasurable aspect of the work. This was the treatise that the king had requested, which Jones hoped to publish separately but never did. "Un Traité sur la poësie orientale," completed in 1769, was begun as an introduction for his *Commentariorum*. In it he argues that there is excellent poetry in Persia and Arabia. By contrast, stale European poetry is chained to classical images, subjects, plots, and themes. It needs Arabic and Persian influences to rejuvenate it. These languages are not difficult and useless, but actually are easy, instructive, and entertaining. Throughout the "Traité," his poetic examples in French illustrate the possible European revitalization.

Few of Jones's readers would know anything about this literature. Yet he uncritically attributes some of the Arabic and Persian literary genius to the people's happy lives, a warm climate, and a beautiful, fertile homeland. He assumes the dubious value judgment that the two languages are suited to poetry, permitting strong expressions, bold metaphors, animated pictures, and fiery sentiments. The poetry contains heroic, amorous, elegiac, didactic, satirical, and panegyric types, which Jones broadly compares with European types. For example, he introduces Firdausi's *Sháhnáma,* enthusiastically comparing that epic with the *Iliad.* Samples from the Sohrab and Rustum story, in an Oriental richness of coloring, illustrate his argument. He also praises the Arabic collections *Mu'allaqát* and *Hamása,* together with Abu 'l- 'Alá's eulogies and other works. Jones takes every opportunity to paint brooding forests, racing camels, desert raids, ruby wine, and lovely damsels. He includes separate French versions in prose and in poetry of ten odes by Háfiz, including two translated into Latin by Reviczky.

The reaction to *Histoire* and the appended "Traité" dispelled any doubts that Jones may have had. Scholars on the Continent praised both the French and the content. At home his reputation spread throughout England in a way that his unpublished efforts at Harrow and Oxford could never have done. Examples of this praise include "This ingenious gentleman, who had procured a very deserved reputation for his knowledge in languages, has executed his task with success"; and his notes reveal "great sagacity, and an extensive knowledge of oriental literature."[33] In February 1771 Elmsly was still advertising the book.

Perceiving a need for an English abridgment, over the next two years Jones collected materials for an Asian history, to include geography, philosophy, and literature. When he did not have time to shape these materials into a book, he used them in a long introduction to the abridgment, consisting of a preface, "A Description of Asia," "A Short History of Persia," and "The History of the Persian Language." The last section extensively employs the illustrations designed for the Persian grammar that Jones had long been composing but had decided to exclude so as to avoid ostentation. No longer inhibited from criticizing Nadir Shah, he asserts that Mahdi's manuscript would have been the last one in the world that he would have translated if Christian VII had not requested it. The works of Háfiz or Sa'dí are better and worthier, and they might have been printed faster and for half the expense. Moreover, Mahdi had probably been induced to paint Nadir Shah in "more pleasing colours than he deserved; to cast a veil over the deformities of his character, and to present us only with the beauties ... which border upon the meanest flattery."[34] To answer the charge that the king was parsimonious, Jones includes in his English abridgment the king's public testimonial and his own letter of thanks to Osten.

Having completed the account of Jones's first book, we shall return to the summer of 1768. He was with Althorp at Wimbledon, beginning a long correspondence with Georgiana, Lady Spencer, whose husband John was now an earl. Jones's first letter to her reveals a keen sensitivity. While devoted to study and believing that it was the way to achieve his ambitions, he also wanted the aristocracy's social approval. It seems that a mutual friend had first praised Jones to someone, but then described him as "the most silent and unsocial of all beings, as a nonconformist in society, as a mere hermit, as one who locked himself up all day, and took no part in the amusements that usually employ young men" (1:14). In fact, this report was partly right. At that time Jones seems not to have been very likable. He needed to learn that he must not appear bookish. Defending himself with affected classical examples, he said that his supposed reservedness, proceeding from hidden discontent, might have upset Lady Spencer. If so,

I would have bid farewell to all studies that were not absolutely necessary, and would have endeavoured to lay myself out for the more social qualities, and to convince your Ladyship that my most romantic wishes could not have formed even an idea of a situation so entirely agreeable to me as that which I have enjoyed for more than two years, and which I shall always consider as the glory of my life.

Actually, Jones had no intention of abandoning his studies, even though he wanted to acquire the nobility's social graces. Lady Spencer answered that she had never disapproved of his conduct, which had been exceedingly pleasing to her and Spencer.

This incident in his social education came just as his scholarship was again displaying fair prospects. Joseph Spence, Oxford's Regius Professor of Modern History, had died. Friends repeatedly informed Jones of the post, which "requires no sort of residence and may be held with a fellowship." Because the king had pointed out that the successor must be recommended by Oxford, "my Oxford friends are partial enough to me to think I am fit for such an employment, and as my book on the Oriental poetry will come out soon, I fancy the university would readily grant me their recommendation." Would Lady Spencer ask Spencer to talk to Grafton, the principal elector (1:17)? After four days Jones wrote her again, nonchalantly noting that he was not really interested in the "full four hundred a year," but that friends might think him indolent if he slighted their advice.

In reality his qualifications were not impressive. He was only twenty-one years old and had no publications; he had barely started on his *Histoire*. In addition, three major candidates were competing. The vice-chancellor and heads of houses had asked the king to require a term's residence and fifty lectures annually so as to change the post from a sinecure. John Vivian submitted a proposal upon being invited, and *Gentleman's Magazine* of August 1768 (p. 399) erroneously reported that Thomas Gray had been appointed (actually at Cambridge). Jones may have heard these reports, but in any case he learned the truth during his Oxford residence from 29 September to 8 October. Apparently he never submitted a proposal, not even when Vivian's early death reopened the post.

Jones returned to Oxford on 26 October, receiving his B.A. degree on 10 November. The ceremony was ridiculous:

> It was absolutely necessary for me (as it is for every one that takes a degree) to get nine batchelors to recommend me to the convocation, in these words Scio Jones esse habilem et idoneum ad hunc gradum, I *know,* that Jones is fit for this degree. ... I was a long time before I could get any nine Scio's but at last they came and every thing went on well.

As he would not have to reside often at Oxford to complete his M.A. degree, he told Althorp that they would be together for years: "We will apply ourselves diligently to parsing Greek & Latin, to verse, and to Latin Composition, and then, away we go to the land of play, I mean, school" (1:21).

Jones's enthusiasm about education permeates these years. In London from 14 November, he continued refining his ideal plan for preparing a pupil for Harrow and then Oxford, as developed from his own experiences. The Spencers had little voice in the plan, although he carefully described the subjects, procedures, and goals to Lady Spencer and Althorp. It provided one of the most systematic experiences that even a modern educator might construct for a young eighteenth-century nobleman. Overall, it presented humankind fully, treating the ten-year-old as an adult. At that time, children were a more natural part of the adult world than they are today, and Jones did not dilute the subject matter. He told Lady Spencer that Althorp was showing the dawning of great genius: "I shall make my commendation of him pretty comprehensive in saying, He is just as I should desire him to be" (1:14). From the outset he had dominated Althorp's education. Now his pupil's progress seemed to validate his plan, which was curiously traditional except for his egotistical conviction that he had discovered the Truth about education.

Their amusements were chess and Shakespeare. They used grammars and dictionaries to study Latin and Greek, in order to acquire the knowledge contained in classical writings. Althorp constantly wrote translations, followed by imitations. There was composition of Latin poetry, which supposedly would help Althorp read the classics with more pleasure and appreciation. Comenius's *Orbis sensualium pictus* (London, 1700) was basic to much of the study. Such work extended Jones's classical knowledge.

Althorp seemed bright enough to become a major scholar: "The vulgar notion that a little learning is sufficient for a gentleman, is extremely absurd" (1:16). What the Spencers thought about his being trained for scholarship – as first lord of the Admiralty he would assign the British admiral Horatio Nelson to the Mediterranean command that would eliminate Napoleon's threat to the East – is unknown. Now Althorp was concentrating on languages. In Italian he ranged back to Dante, and forward to Galland's French version of Bidpai's fables and the *Arabian Nights Entertainments*. His only reservation was in leaping into the cold pond in his physical training, which Lady Spencer approved to counteract his asthmatic tendency. One September morning he hesitated until Jones swam across and warned that the boys at Harrow would laugh at him if he hesitated; but "he will grow perfectly reconciled to the bath, which I am convinced will confirm his health, and strengthen him against the colds he is apt to have" (1:19). His assignments were grueling, but Jones inspired him to persevere. The plan of education was superhuman if not divine. Being so tutored must have been like being hitched to the tail of a comet.

Jones did not neglect the social aspects of his own study. While periodically freeing himself from his labors on *Histoire* that winter, he filled the musical gap in his background. His father's nationality led him to the Welsh harp, on which he took lessons. But as he had not yet studied musical principles, acquiring instrumental skill gave him little pleasure. In addition, because he wanted every activity to have an intellectual end or relationship, he never seriously practiced on any instrument.

Jones was extending and deepening his friendships. Besides his father's friends, the first great man whom he came to know well was Joshua Reynolds, who painted him. The oil, now at Althorp, cost his mother £37, according to Reynolds's receipt of 5 June 1769. Reynolds also painted "Sir William Jones as a Boy," depicting a reading student with dark eyes and short brown hair.[35] In preparing his first discourse as president of the Royal Academy, Reynolds probably submitted his drafts to the criticism of friends like Burke, Johnson, and Jones.[36] To celebrate his knighthood, he invited intimates to dinner on 29 April 1769. Thomas Percy catalogued them: "Sam Johnson, Esq.; Edm. Burke, Esq.; Mr. Chambers, Vinerian Prof.; Dr. Nugent; Mr. Langton; Mr. Jones, the great Linguist; Dr. Leland of Dublin, Author of the Life of Philip of Macedon; Dr. Hawkesworth; Dr. Percy."[37]

Percy's esteem for Jones, as well as the number of those present who belonged to Johnson's Literary Club, is noteworthy. Apparently the only members whom Jones did not yet know were Topham Beauclerk and Anthony Chamier. Like his father, he was constructing a reputation based on scholarship, unassisted by fortune or family. He did not fawn on great men so as to be able to eat at their tables and hear their conversations. They were starting to welcome him, for they appreciated his mind.

When Jones was at Oxford, he sometimes ate with Johnson. This was not so often that he could be blasé:

I dined and supped yesterday with four extraordinary men; Dictionary Johnson, Dr. Goldsmith, author of the Good-Natur'd Man, Mr. Chambers, the Professour of Law, and Mr. Percy, who published the famous collection of old songs. They were in high spirits, and I was very much entertained and improved with their conversation. (1:24)

The host was Robert Chambers, whom Jones did not know well. As Jones would complete his five-hundred-verse draft of "The Palace of Fortune" the next morning, Oriental literature may have been discussed.

During the term at Oxford, he became closer to William Scott, a college fellow and friend of Johnson. He increasingly participated in those memorable evenings when Johnson would comfortably consume three bottles of port.[38] This decade between 1765 and 1775 was the golden age of University College under Wetherel.[39] By 1769 Jones's reputation in languages was rivaling that of Chambers in law, and Scott was a fine tutor.

Thirteen of Jones's best Oxford friends were University College men. Between 1764 and 1774, when he was most often there, these were Jacob Pleydell-Bouverie, Viscount Folkestone and later earl of Radnor, who took his B.A. in 1770 and his M.A. in 1773; and fellows Robert Chambers, John Coulson, and George Horne, who was vice-chancellor from 1768 to 1780. Fletcher Norton, Jones's Harrow friend, was MP for Appleby in 1773–4 and then for Carlisle before becoming baron of the Scottish Exchequer. William Dean Poyntz, another Harrow colleague, matriculated in 1767, was created M.A. in 1773, and was later a clerk of the Treasury. Seventh, Thomas Plumer took his B.A. in 1775 and was master of the Rolls between 1818 and 1824. Besides Scott, there was George Strahan, who took his M.A. in 1771 and was a friend of Johnson. Jones's Harrow friend Richard Warburton had arrived in 1765. Thomas Francis Wenman, a fellow of All Souls from 1775, was MP for Westbury, Wiltshire, from 1774 to 1780. John Eardley-Wilmot took his B.A. in 1769 and was a master in chancery from 1781 to 1804 and MP for Tiverton and then for Coventry from 1776 to 1796. William Windham, matriculating in 1767, became a major in the Norfolk Militia, and was a close friend of Johnson.

Jones had seven close friends in other colleges. There were Thomas Caldecott, a fellow of New College from 1770; and Thomas Day, who enrolled at Corpus Christi in 1765. Charles James Fox, matriculating at Hertford in 1764, began his career as MP for Midhurst between 1768 and 1774. Nathaniel Brassey Halhed, entering Christ Church in 1768, was inspired by Jones to study Arabic and then become a fine Orientalist. Richard Paul Jodrell, matriculating at Hertford in 1764, became a classical scholar. Thomas Milles, who took his B.A. at Queen's in 1773, was a fellow of All Souls between 1777 and 1803. And the polyglot John Paradise, created M.A. in 1769 and D.C.L. in 1776, also was a friend of Johnson.

Of these twenty men with whom Jones most frequently associated, nine became longtime friends. Chambers, Scott, Warburton, and Wilmot often spent "a very merry Evening" with him at his mother's, playing "at dumb crambo, at Bouts Rimès, and all our old games" (1:21–22). The others were Caldecott, Day, Halhed, Milles, and Paradise. Warburton was the principal founder of the Oxford Grecian Club, which included Chambers, Day, Jodrell, Jones, Paradise, and others. They met in one another's rooms, serving an unostentatious dinner and discussing topics befitting "their rank and character in the literary world."[40]

Jones was at Oxford from 3 February to about 9 March 1769. One day in the public schools he had to stay in the cold from one till five doing nothing. Then "I was forced to the great trial of my patience to sit an hour listening to a sermon that was called Latin, but might have been Dutch for any thing I could understand of it. But my trouble is not yet at an end. I shall be obliged to dispute four times, and to stay in the schools three hours each time" (1:22–23). Such requirements for the M.A. contributed nothing to his own study schedule.

Back at Wimbledon, Jones finished translating his *Histoire,* with the preface and notes still to be composed. He immersed himself in Italian, reading Petrarch a second time and assembling the loveliest lamentations for Laura into an elegy, which went into his stack of unpublished poems. It was a romantic spring, and he attended the "donzelle vezzose e tenerolle, by whose beauties I confess myself easily overcome" (1:26). Like the donzellas, he wrote many letters. There was time for Robertson's *History of the Reign of the Emperor Charles V* (London, 1769), which he judged inferior to the classical historians' works.

When Althorp enrolled at Harrow on 8 June, the pair took rooms in a nearby house. Jones had an assistant introduce him to some diligent boys, who then studied together. Althorp was placed in the lower part of the third form. Once the boy's classes began, Jones resumed his association with Summer: "Their enthusiasm for literature was equal: the master contemplated, with delight unmixed with envy, a rival of his own erudition in his scholar, who acknowledged with gratitude his obligations to his preceptor."[41]

When the brother of Jones's friend Wilmot asked for help in learning Persian, Jones may have lent the draft of his Persian *Grammar.* He recommended interleaving a translation of the Latin rules in Greaves. He had not polished the draft, partly because of the East India Company's apparent lack of interest in his proposed revision of Meninski's *Thesaurus*, which contained many Persian words. Jones had begun to construct a Persian dictionary from his reading, illustrated by quotations from famous authors, but then decided to abandon it unless the company purchased it for a considerable price.

Besides asking Sumner, Jones turned to two clerics at Harrow to help him resolve doubts about his Christian beliefs. When they could not help, he read the Bible in the original Hebrew, so as to compare the age and authenticity of the Old and New Testaments. This study produced a series of propositions that demonstrated divine authority to him. These concluded: "Jesus was the subject of their writings, which are consequently inspired, and he a person of an extraordinary nature, that is, the Messiah. If this be just reasoning, we may believe his miracles, and *must* obey his law."[42] Thus Jones fitted religion intellectually into his overall education, an attitude that later enabled him to view other religions objectively.

With the approach of the holidays, he secured reports from Althorp's teachers, who praised the boy. Several classmates confirmed that Althorp was well liked. As Althorp seemed in better health than ever, Jones went to Oxford on 31 July, remaining until 11 September. During the vacation Coulson was the only other man at University College and almost the only one with whom he talked. He quickly developed a routine: "I rise, I read in the Bodleian till twelve, I dress, I dine, I walk, I sup, I sleep, I rise again &c. &c." (1:33). With his *Histoire* now in press, he could breathe more easily, although his proofreading the first sheets showed that its publication was still a long way off.

While working with Persian writing, Jones recalled his transcript of the Chinese writing system. He read the *Ta Hsüeh* (Great learning), *Chung Yung* (Doctrine of the mean), and *Lun Yü* (Analects), aided by Couplet's Latin translation in *Confucius, Sinarum philosophus sive scientia Sinensis Latine exposita* (Paris, 1687). Several pretty verses, surprisingly, were older than all known poetry except that by Homer and the Hebrew prophets.

Because Althorp was suffering from shortness of breath, the Spencers delayed his return to Harrow, thereby permitting Jones to work in the Bodleian a bit longer. His Oxford residence was inexpensive. For example, his charges for 1769 were £12 15s 2d, which, when deducted from his fellowship payment of £62 9s 3d, left him £50 for the year.

Much of the Oxford talk was about the forthcoming Jubilee. Having composed *An Ode upon Dedicating a Building and Erecting a Statue to Shakespeare at Stratford-upon-Avon* (London, 1769), David Garrick was expected to deliver the recitative part dramatically. After Jones's unsuccessful hint to Althorp that the Spencers reserve apartments for him too, he decided to go alone, despite the expense of a costume for the masquerade. But heavy rains prevented his going and assisted the wits who attacked Shakespeare, making this first Stratford festival a failure in spite of Garrick's rapturous delivery.

Instead, Jones and a friend walked to nearby Forest Hill, where Milton had resided. He took his much-used copy of "the most perfect scholar, as well as the sublimest" English poet. Recounting his almost-mystical experience to Lady Spencer, he described their approach by means of images from "L'Allegro" (I.37–9): Ascending the hill, he felt great pleasure at the stillness and natural simplicity until they reached the spot "whence Milton undoubtedly took most of his images." Evidently Milton had not used a single useless word in his "exact and lively representation of nature." Thus Jones's adulation led him to find realism rather than the actual idealization. The pair were told of the discovery of papers in Milton's handwriting. They examined a wall that had formed part of his chamber, and an old man recollected "The Poet." In youthful enthusiasm, Jones contemplated the renting and repair of the ruined mansion for a festival if he ever spent six weeks at Oxford in the summer: "Such an honour will be less splendid, but more sincere and respectful, than all the pomp and ceremony" at Stratford (1:39).

Jones was also moved by Milton's essays, especially by some ideas in "Of Education." First, language is only an instrument conveying useful things. Second, one should intensively study Latin and Greek – composing themes, verses, and orations in them – in order to master the subjects written in them, such as mathematics, politics, logic, rhetoric, and poetry. Reflecting on his own plan, developed from his experience and tested on his receptive pupil, Jones composed "Plan of an Essay on Education," which he expanded into an analytical treatise in Aristotelian style on educating young people. Perhaps seeing himself as an educational philosopher and ideal teacher, he read Milton's essay and his now-lost treatise to Lady Spencer, who liked them both.[43]

Jones's purpose is to trace education "from its beginning with the elementary parts of language, to the great end proposed by it, that is, the ability to benefit mankind and ourselves, either in war or in peace, by action or by speculation." The primary end of liberal education is "the good of ourselves and our fellow-creatures"; the secondary ends, cultivating understanding and acquiring knowledge. Knowledge, which helps one differentiate good actions from apparently good actions, must be acquired and conveyed to others. It must be supplemented by "the accumulated experience and wisdom of all ages and all nations." Thus the languages of peoples of superior knowledge must be understood by scholars, who should convey their findings "to *other nations*, either in their respective dialects, or in some language, which, from its peculiar excellence and utility, may be in a manner universal." An immediate object, therefore, is to learn the languages of nations such as China. Jones's "Plan" indicates that this part of the treatise had sections on language, understanding, knowledge, and the good of mankind.

The last part concerns one's own happiness. Besides the grander acquisitions, one should pursue "those which refresh and enliven the mind, and those which improve and adorn the body." After the day's study, one should relax and prepare for new study by enjoying literature, painting, and music. Dancing, swimming, riding, and fencing will keep one's body healthy and accustom it to graceful motions. These exercises should be supplemented by oratorical declaiming.

Revealing Jones's early capacity to universalize from particulars, his "Plan" reflects the successful end of his social education. He had had no appropriate model up to 1765. The dress and behavior of Anna and the other sophisticated young ladies he now encountered were different from those of the few young women whom he had previously known. At Oxford he had been reserved, seldom participating in the usual recreation. However, he was extremely adaptable, determined to master the graces to complement his intellectual attainments. After observing the urbanity of Lady Spencer and her friends, in his lost treatise he recommended music and dancing. But in early 1769 he was still mildly defensive: "We are to have another ball the beginning of next week; so you see we are not so dull and philosophical at Oxford as some people imagine" (1:24). When he moved to London in 1770, he was soon accepted into social and literary circles, an acceptance perhaps due as much to his amiable personality as to intellectual accomplishments.

Stimulating endeavors like the treatise were interrupted by Henrietta Spencer's being stricken with tuberculosis, at which time her father decided to send her and Althorp to southern France. Although this was almost a Grand Tour, Jones was not pleased, as Althorp was well and his Harrow education would be interrupted. And Jones's own study would be hampered. He could carry along few books, with separation from friends and Oxford coming at an unpropitious time.

The travel group included the two children, Henrietta's girl friend, Mrs. Anna Maria Poyntz (Lady Spencer's mother), a doctor, and a nurse, who died shortly thereafter. After a long stay in Paris, the group sailed down the Rhone, past Avignon. Jones could not miss visiting Vaucluse, and in a rapturous moment at Petrarch's Helicon he added a description of the fountain to his elegy "Laura." They then went to Marseilles and Nice, arriving in October 1769 for what turned out to be a seven-month stay.

Jones concentrated on literature, temporarily enjoying his stay. He planned a trip to Florence, which was canceled because of the doctor's failing health. Proudly he wrote Reviczky: "All my thought and feeling are concentrated on anything sensitive and delicate in the fine arts, anything that is difficult or obscure in the sciences, anything that is sublime or charming in painting or poetry" (trans., 1:45). By January 1770 he finished his verse translation "A Persian Song of Hafiz" and "De epigrammate Græcorum," which joined his growing stack of compositions. He also wrote "Suleiman," a tragedy on the Ottoman sultan's murder of his son. Using Shakespeare as a model, Jones attempted to portray Turkish manners, which he had extensively studied. His dramatic principles were explained in a prefatory discourse discussing such discourses by Dryden and Corneille.[44]

In May he wrote Reviczky of his devotion to civilized arts and letters. His goal was "Excellence, the most divine of all things, and Fame, the most precious of all things for mortal men" (1:53). The poor mail service hampered his correspondence, which he preferred to conduct in Latin, French, or Greek. When Halhed requested help in the collaboration with Sheridan, by which the pair hoped to gain £200 by producing the farce *Jupiter,* Jones obligingly wrote his friends. He asked Halhed to correspond in Latin.

By now the novelty of tropical fruits and flowers in winter was no longer pleasing, and he impatiently awaited the Spencers' departure. He had tried to dissuade Lady Spencer from the decision not to send Althorp to Harrow in the summer, but not even his praise of Althorp's unfolding disposition convinced her that the pair should return to Harrow.

Unable to meet any great Continental literary men, Jones was disappointed even on the return trip. He journeyed to Lake Geneva with the hope of meeting Voltaire, who had been out walking and was just entering the house. Jones penned a conventional "note with a few verses, implying that the muse of tragedy had left her ancient seat in Greece and Italy, and had fixed her abode on the borders of a lake, &c." A servant brought the answer: "The worst of French poets and philosophers is almost dying; age and sickness have brought him to his last day; he can converse with nobody, and entreats Mr. Jones to excuse and pity him. He presents him with his humble respects" (1:55).[45] The servants pointed to a window, where they said Voltaire was standing. Jones scarcely glimpsed the semiretired man, who was not as ill as he imagined or he would not have been walking: "I am inclined to think that Voltaire begins to be rather serious, when he finds himself upon the brink of eternity; and that he refuses to see company, because he cannot display his former wit and sprightliness." But his not criticizing Voltaire to Lady Spencer shows Jones's urbanity, whether or not the philosopher felt that the twenty-three-year-old should have brought an introduction or was presumptuous in claiming to be a fellow poet.[46]

After Jones's group reached Paris on 2 June, he wrote Lady Spencer of his wish to visit Oxford on their return, or else to wait until August if Althorp went back to Harrow, as he preferred. The Paris stay was again longer than he wished. He did locate Ode 55, an encomium that he had earlier read in Couplet's Latin version. He found it in the fine *Shih Ching* in the Royal Library by means of *Sapientia Sinica* (Kiam Province, 1662), in which the first line is in Chinese and Latin (p. 4). Finally able to decode the ideograms, he wrote a Latin translation ("Ode Sinica"), "The Verbal Translation," and "The Paraphrase."[47] He sent his three versions to Reviczky to introduce that scholar to Chinese, praising Confucius as the Chinese Plato some six centuries before Christ. He also arranged for Reviczky's *Traité de la tactique* (Vienna, 1769), translated from Efendi Ibrahim, to be sent to George III, an action partly excused by Christian VII's recent testimonial to the king.

Accompanying Jones's fame from his *Histoire* were stories about his language exploits. For example, he had mastered the various dialects of France during his residence, impressing Louis XVI at court with his dialectal brilliance. Because the king never exchanged a word with the foreigners introduced at Versailles, the story is probably untrue.[48]

Jones's group moved on to Spa, where he shaped materials once intended for his *Commentariorum* into introductory essays for his *History of Nader Shah*. He thought seriously about "Britain Discovered," an epic "on the excellence of our Constitution, and the character of a perfect king of England" that he had been contemplating for a year. The idea came from Spenser's letter to Raleigh about a possible epic depicting Arthur's political virtues as king. Jones sketched the plot, composing the twelve prose arguments and a few stanzas.[49]

He rejected the medium of prose, because poetry better instills "moral precepts in a manner more lively and entertaining." Pope's *Iliad* and Dryden's *Aeneid* were his models for heroic couplets: "It has been found by experience, that the verses of those poets not only make a deeper impression on the mind, but are more easily retained in the memory, than blank verse, which must necessarily be too diffuse." As other activities were to interfere, it was another year before he could think about this "verse epic of tremendous scope, called the *Britanneis,* though I shall have to postpone that task until I am somehow granted some spare time in remarkable circumstances" (trans., 1:85). He was not able to consider the epic seriously for another twelve years.

At Spa, as the summer crawled by, Jones contemplated his future. He had been a tutor for five years, and soon the twelve-year-old Althorp would not need him. The boy's health continued to be good, but the Spencers had not let Jones go directly from Paris to Harrow, thus again delaying his educational plan. His prospects as private tutor – even living essentially as one of the family – were limited. The year on the Continent had severely delayed his studies, making him entrust the proofreading of *Histoire* to someone else. Such interruptions upset his spirited independence and could block what should eventually be a successful career, which ideally would serve England and humanity. His mother had sacrificed for an education that he was hardly utilizing as preparation for a high place. Therefore, he would have to change to a part-time tutorship or perhaps resign, in order to concentrate on a career.

Oriental scholarship and languages were appealing. But as Jones's interest in the Oxford professorship had been unrewarded and as his first book had appeared at his own expense, a career in Orientalism for a fortuneless scholar was impractical. Rather, his career should provide fame and financial comfort, as well as support for his mother. After objectively weighing the alternatives, he talked with his mother and close friends, stressing his high ambition. They recommended law, his own preference.

Some of Jones's friends in the legal profession praised it. Day had been admitted to the Middle Temple in 1765, and Wenman was just being called to the bar from the Inner Temple. The bibliophile Caldecott would shortly enter the Middle Temple. Fletcher Norton, whose father was speaker of the Commons, was a barrister. Wilmot, Jones's best Oxford friend, had chosen the Inner Temple. Wilmot's father, who was chief justice of the Common Pleas, wrote his son: "Mr. Jones has been with me this morning – he seems a genius – and you may rely on my shewing him all the civility in my power."[50] Jones also consulted with John Parnell, who had been admitted to Lincoln's Inn in 1766.

He explained his final decision to Reviczky:

As soon as I arrived back in England, I was caught in a web, consisting of a huge variety of worries. I was surrounded by friends, acquaintances, and relatives, who encouraged me to expel from my way of life, for a short time, poetry and Asian literature. They said I should devote my life to public speaking and legal studies, that I should frequent the law-courts and, in a word, become a barrister and be devoted to ambition. As it happens, I followed their advice without much regret, since a legal career is the only way open for those who seek my country's highest honours. (trans., 1:85)

Imbued with the ideal of a democratic society, which he construed to be based on law, he was intellectually inclined toward law. On 19 September 1770 he was admitted to the Middle Temple as "William Jones, only son of William J., of Beaufort Buildings, in the parish of St. Martin in the Fields, Middx, esq., decd."

Jones apparently never considered taking Holy Orders and entering the church, the normal route to a scholarly career. Even if he found no patron, as a fellow of a college he would have ultimately qualified for a living, with its ease, leisure for study, and right to marry. With the patrons that he had, it would have been far easier for them to help him to preferment in the church than in any other field. A man of his talents and reputation would have made a comfortable if not distinguished career there. Perhaps it was a matter of principle that made him reject the advantages that others in his position might have exploited, as well as his intense desire to stress his standing as a gentleman. Nor could the church offer the opportunity to serve his country and mankind the way that law could.

The "web" that Jones had mentioned had begun with the Spencers' decision to keep Althorp at home because of the boy's cough. This new delay helped motivate Jones to enter the Middle Temple but not to inform the family, as his entrance would seriously affect his tutoring. Responding to Lady Spencer's request for "a line or two," he showed his independence:

Lord Althorp seems to himself, and to me to be very well. It were much to be wished that his Education were as settled as his health seems to be. At present he is as much to be pitied, as he is amiable; which is, surely, saying a great deal. As for me, I am going immediately to Oxford, whither I am called by my interest, my inclination, and my duty. (1:64)

Then he left Althorp to the servants and went to Oxford.

Ironically, Lady Spencer was pleased with Althorp's health upon her return: "I could not help regretting your having left London before we got there, as I think we should certainly have been tempted to have sent him immediately to Harrow; be so good as to let me know how soon it will be convenient to return as (if he continues well) the sooner he goes to school now the better" (1:64). But why was Althorp to be pitied? The Spencers wanted him to "pass a few years in a publick education if his health & strength will permit him to continue it, but if there should be the least doubt of its disagreeing with him we cannot think it so very material." If so, Jones could give Althorp every necessary improvement. She delicately inquired about the dissatisfaction that she detected in Jones's letter: "If it is so I wish you would be more explicit; if not it will give me pleasure to hear it."

His answer on 10 October (1:66–68) lectured her on the kinds of education and on the changes in his "very enlarged system" necessitated by the Spencers' moving Althorp around and by switching him from public to private education. Althorp was ready for essential learning: "I do not want his hours only, but his months and years; I wish to be with him at meals, at our amusements, in our hours of rest as well as of study that I may give his thoughts a right turn upon every subject, and strengthen his mind while I seem to relax it." He should spend three to four years either at Harrow without interruption or else at a "private house" formed for that purpose and protected from the Spencers' avocations if his health prevented an extended residence at Harrow. Jones's plan would direct the education. At sixteen Althorp should go to Oxford, losing not a single hour until then. Jones's nature would not let him take orders, and only his regard for Althorp had made him quit "vast prospects" at Oxford so as to accept the tutorship. Overall, he asserted his independence and dictatorial intention of controlling the boy's life in a rigorous education. He was probably contemplating a part-time role, which would permit law studies, if the Spencers would agree once he asked them.

Meanwhile, Mrs. Poyntz told various people that Jones's abrupt departure had distressed the Spencers because it had given them no time to find a new tutor. Parnell reported this disturbing fact, as well as the news that Sumner had offered "attendance" for three months until a tutor could be found. After protesting to Sumner about "the mean and servile offer," Jones confided to Parnell: "Lord & Lady Spencer neither do complain of my conduct, nor have a right to complain; they do not even suspect that I intend to leave them" (1:68). Then he wrote Lady Spencer. Had she or Spencer made the highly injurious statement quoted by her mother? If neither had, she should correct Mrs. Poyntz and stop its circulation. He would not apologize for the tone of his brief letter, as he had always written freely to her and had been more pointed to Christian VII.

Spencer answered decisively. He had flattered himself that Jones was the proper tutor, whose sentiments on education did not essentially differ from his own: "I am sorry now to find they do almost in every particular" (1:70). Jones's letter about going to Oxford was "an abrupt method of conveying your intention of quitting my son." Jones lengthily protested, expressing surprise at the disagreement about education. Lady Spencer had approved Milton's "Of Education" and his own treatise, and William Arden had told Jones that Althorp would go to Harrow after a year of a "fixed and permanent" tutorship. Jones would have been honor bound to acquiesce in any other plan, except that (1) the difficulty had been divulged immediately to Mrs. Poyntz, (2) Lady Spencer had written him insincerely, and (3) his letter had not been benevolently answered before steps were taken regarding the tutorship. His resentment burst through: "I take it so ill that Lord Althorp should be *sent to school and put under another tutour before I was consulted or my letter answered, that I am now detached from your Lordship's family beyond all possibility of a reunion*" (1:72). Finally, he wanted assurance that the parting was caused solely by their differing views about education, which they had not previously known.

While expressing gratitude and underlining the amicability of the parting, Spencer answered by reiterating that Jones had apparently intended to quit immediately unless he surrendered his son's education in every particular and under a plan quite different from his own ideas. Spencer would give no tutor, however talented, such freedom.

As it was vital to Jones's career that the parting be absolutely amicable, he now expressed complete satisfaction. He had never wished the entire management of Althorp's education; parents had a natural right to govern their son. Admittedly he had spoken strongly, but his papers left in his room at Wimbledon should have proved that he intended to return. He was willing to help as a friend if Althorp's health prevented study at Harrow or if a domestic tutor could not be found. As Jones would be living at University College, with convenient vacations and free summers, the boy could use his two apartments. But when Spencer responded that Althorp would never again have a regular private tutor, Jones agreed that his connection should cease: "In my last letter from Oxford (which is now rendered useless) I took the liberty to tell your Lordship that I should enter at the Temple, and practise the Laws of my country. If I retain my strength of memory and habit of application, I shall certainly, have the success which I flatter myself your Lordship wishes me" (1:76).

He remained friends with the Spencers. The sudden parting was surprising only in that he had been able to implement his rigorous plan as well as he had for five years, that his dogmatic though idealistic views had not precipitated an earlier rupture. Jones's general education was completed. Before him beckoned a barrister's career, which friends, talents, and ambition assured him could lead to a high place. Twenty-four-years old, he naively thought that a man of principles – through great industry if not genius – could so rise without compromising them. When he went to Oxford in late September, he could visualize himself in a distinguished political post.

2 Delicate Arab Maidens and Liquid Ruby (1770–1772)

Once Jones was certain of the Spencers' willingness for him to be friends with Althorp, he answered the boy's letter:

I have entirely dropped my connexion with your papa as your tutor, for many reasons which at your age you will not be able to comprehend, but which I will fully explain to you five or six years hence. I am now a member of the Middle Temple, and am studying the Laws of my country: I shall be called to the bar this time three years, where I hope you will come and hear me plead. Till that time I shall live chiefly at Oxford; but after that I shall enter into publick life. (1:77)

The ending of the tutorship did not end Jones's practice of composing instructional letters. Now they were openly modeled on Cicero's letters to Atticus, in informal adult tutoring that was to continue throughout his life. The relationship was sensitively qualified: "You will be a man as far superior to Atticus, as I shall be inferior to Cicero." He urged Althorp to read "Middleton's short account of Cicero's studies from the time of his wearing the *toga virilis* to his first publick magistracy, or rather Cicero's own account of them at the end of his *Famous Orators*. What on earth can hinder you from pursuing the same course?" Later, on the law circuits, he wrote letters "in the old Ciceronian method upon the road or even at table" (1:152, 191–2; 2:486). Once he resumed writing to Lady Spencer, he repeated his recommendation of Euclid, Locke, and Blackstone: "The first will open to him the principles of all natural knowledge, the second will show him the nature and extent of human reason, and the third will offer to him a specimen of that reason reduced to practice in the admirable Laws of our country" (1:121).

Jones was permanently attached to Althorp, a closeness that each expressed. His affection had been continually increasing: "I concentrated all my hopes of perfect satisfaction in this life in the prospect of your becoming a virtuous and able man, a lover of your country, and a benefactor of mankind" (1:210). Althorp was Jones's strongest personal tie except for his relatives and perhaps Anna, and so his affection helped make these letters his best. He was one of the fine "English letter-writers of the golden

32

age of letter-writing. The early letters Jones wrote to Lord Althorp are what Chesterfield's to his son should have been; the later English letters at times suggest Walpole's, although Jones gives the impression of being more involved in what he is writing about. His letters, often pleasantly witty, reveal great passion, great compassion."[1] Those to Althorp "show a unique relationship, made of mutual trust, respect, and affection, that would be the dream of any teacher – or student."[2] In view of the rigorous tutoring, one wonders how Jones would have fared with Chesterfield's son or even whether the two would have remained friends.

Surrounded by his books, not to mention the Bodleian collections, Jones returned to his Oriental studies for several months. He reveled in Persian history, philosophy, and poetry, especially Jámí's *Yúsuf va Zulaykhá;* and he fondly thought about publishing his own text of Jámí if he could find the time. He did have the original of "A Persian Song of Hafiz" engraved on a copper plate, hoping to engrave Jámí's works when he had the money. An edition on silken India paper might please the Governors-General of India. Jones also had complex book-length projects, as we will see. From his translations and Oriental imitations he was selecting the best poems for publication. Longingly he reread his outline for "Britain Discovered."

Jones's career concern was law. On 3 January 1771 he characterized Wilmot's father's resignation from the chief justiceship as permitting "the greatest happiness of human life, ease with dignity, after having passed through the most honourable labour without danger" (1:78). If he could similarly proceed in his small sphere, gaining a competency at the bar before retiring to the bowers of learning, he would think himself blessed. Law was not dull: "It seems so to those only, who would think any study unpleasant, which required a great application of the mind, and exertion of the memory." Garrick was sent a copy of these sentences to Wilmot about law, perhaps one of Jones's several brief letters to literary acquaintances announcing his career.

Jones studied the first two volumes of Blackstone's *Commentaries on the Laws of England* (Oxford, 1765–9). The citation of authorities in the margin gratified his scholarly expectation, and he began commonplace books on oratory and law that drew on favorite sources like Demosthenes and Cicero. To him the acquisition of legal information was especially justified when it was transmitted at the bar with a style and elegant method that at once pleased and persuaded. He distinguished oratory from popular eloquence, which he disliked. His early goal was to locate and translate the important works of Henry de Bracton, John Breton, Fortescue, Ranulf de Clanville, Ralph de Hengham, and Sir Thomas Littleton.

Yet Jones did not forgo youthful pleasures, because he enjoyed singing, dancing, moderate wine-drinking, and pretty women. His classical idealism made him subordinate such pleasures to glory: "Glory I shall pursue through fire and water, by night and by day" (trans., 1:86–87).

On New Year's Day 1771 Jones dined with Scott, Wetherel, and others, having missed all the holiday dinners in 1770. With the end of his tutorship he attended more of these memorable dinners, missing only the Candlemas one in 1771, because he had to be at the Middle Temple. Although he wanted to buy chambers there, they were so scarce that he remained at University College until 3 January. Meanwhile, in London he could live at Westminster or accept apartments on Duke Street, Westminster, from one of his father's friends, who had nephews in school. He chose these apartments, where he could relax from his studies by helping the boys with their exercises. His sister sent his books and clothes, and he was quite comfortable.

Paradoxically, while telling Wilmot of his immersion in law, Jones noted that he would have to neglect it for six weeks. He had to see through the press his long-finished Persian *Grammar,* from which much was expected and which should be made as perfect as possible before he began attendance at the Court of King's Bench. While reading law at his own speed, a procedure best accommodating his talents, he had supposedly given up Orientalism; in reality, he had not. Europeans were interested in the Orient, which offered literary treasures. His scholarship had earned him a reputation that he could easily enhance by publishing his completed drafts, which might also provide a humanistic enrichment of European literature. So he published four Oriental books and had a fifth almost ready for the press by the time he was admitted to the bar.

All five of these books utilize prescientific linguistic views of the day. Educated in the classical tradition, Jones first thought Greek and Latin to be the most beautiful and perfect languages of all time. But finding aesthetic and intellectual values preserved in several Oriental languages, he decided that these were valuable for the knowledge buried in manuscripts written in these tongues. He never viewed language as worthy of study per se, but only as a tool and a means to an end, a view that helps explain impressive projects throughout his career. Thus one who prepared a dictionary and a grammar, without properly applying one's knowledge, was little more useful to society than one who sought to learn the language only by studying such materials. By contrast,

it is impossible that he who reads the admirable words of the ancients, should not at the same time that he studies the language, become master of the valuable things they contain: for instance a man might live many years in all the hurry and bustle of publick life, without gaining half the knowledge of human nature, which may be learned from the satires and epistles of Horace. (1:16–17)

Once Jones had discovered that there was literature in Arabic and Persian, he rejected the idea of their supposed inferiority, but he could not communicate the values to Europe until the bias was eliminated. Because Europeans thought the two languages to be less beautiful, poetic, and lexically adequate than Greek and Latin, his initial goal was to rebut ideas; for example, Persian is not difficult and baroque. In rejecting such value judgments, he did not anticipate the modern view that one language is not abstractly superior or inferior to another, but is adequate for its communicational purposes. He employed other value judgments; for example, Arabic is expressive, strong, and sonorous, and perhaps has the largest vocabulary. Also, the Arabs' natural poetic genius, delicacy, and sentiments had helped change their language into one of the softest and richest. He presented similar arguments for Persian and Turkish.

Elmsly published Jones's second book, *Dissertation sur la littérature orientale,* on 2 March 1771. Only fifty pages long, with no front or end matter, it sold for one shilling. Using much of his remaining material not included in the Persian *Grammar* or reserved for his *Commentariorum,* this companion piece to "Traité" demonstrates Jones's further drift from classical languages and attacks several prejudices. That is, Europeans should not assert that Middle Eastern poetry has no taste or spirit, as it has all the vivacity of those peoples. They also err in thinking that Middle Easterners are illiterate and uncivilized, and that the poetry consists of passion and intemperance and lacks delicacy and elegance. Rather, all people have the germ of the same passions. The chief differences between European and Middle Eastern poetry derive from language. Jones argues that Arabic and Persian are elegant, rich, uncomplicated, and musical, and are used to produce fine poetry. If a poem in each of Persian, Arabic, Greek, and Latin were translated literally into a "useful" language, the classical poems would not be superior if idiom, setting, and customs were disregarded. To illustrate, he offers French prose versions of Háfiz's tenth ode and Horace's thirty-second ode.

Jones's *Dissertation* utilizes his recent studies in Arabic history and philosophy, although he doubts that Europe, with men like Newton and Leibnitz, needs translations of Arabic philosophy. He favorably compares the historian Abu 'l-Fída with Xenophon, and al-Iṣfahání with Thucydides: Europeans should profit from any Middle Eastern poetic irregularities by correcting their own; they cannot competently judge this poetry until they know the languages. Jones lauds the love poetry of Imru'u 'l-Qays, Mesíhí, Háfiz, and Nizámí; the moral poetry of Saʿdí and ʿAṭṭár; and the heroic poetry of 'Antara and Firdausi. Finally, he urges European rulers to encourage the study of Asiatic languages.

John Langhorne reviewed *Dissertation* in the June 1771 issue of the *Monthly Review* (pp. 425–32). As the claims about the comparative excellence of Oriental works were a bit startling, he makes no judgments. Still, his detailed, journalistic review recommends "this ingenious pamphlet to the attention of our learned Readers." But Jones did not expect particular enhancement of his reputation from this book.

His long-awaited *Grammar of the Persian Language* had been advertised in London newspapers since February. The book had originated in 1766 as descriptive formulations from his reading. It was popularly thought that, because many Indian princes corresponded in Persian, they used it in daily activities, so that people concerned with India should welcome the book. Jones continued his revision, partly because much was expected from it. As much of what became the 153-page book would have to be printed in Persian, costs would be high. He vainly attempted to secure advance help from the East India Company, which customarily bought numerous copies of linguistic-cultural works about Asian peoples. Finally it was published by the nephews of Samuel Richardson, William and John, on 3 April. The Bodleian still has the inscription copy that Jones presented.

His corpus was collected from Persian literature. When Jones observed a certain grammatical form in Háfiz, he searched for it elsewhere, slowly building a tentative description. He refined his classifications, combining or subdividing them as additional data came to light, rather than systematically analyzing representative corpora as later linguists would have done. Yet his corpus gradually became more dependable for his purposes. His love for literature, together with his lack of access to native Persian speakers, made him rely on writing rather than speech. He chiefly chose writing in what might be called the Shiraz literary dialect of 1000 to 1500. His corpus was not "Indian Persian," despite his statement in the preface that his major purpose was to help East India Company employees learn the language. It was not even representative of eighteenth-century nonliterary Persian writing, but he could defend his data on the basis of an unsound premise of the day: Historical change, particularly that which comes about through everyday speech, can eventually debase a language. Therefore, what could surpass his Háfiz, Nizámí, and Firdausi? Jones found examples in Mahdi's biography of Nadir Shah to illustrate the supposed deterioration.

In his preface Jones assigns professional students of language to a lower rank in his ideal world because they compose only grammars and dictionaries, which, though essential, do not sufficiently advance learning. As his book was not designed as a linguistic grammar, there is no inquiry into

كتاب

شكرستان

در نحوي زبان پارسي

تصنيف

يونس اوكسفردي

A

G R A M M A R

OF THE

PERSIAN LANGUAGE.

BY W I L L I A M J O N E S, ESQUIRE,

FELLOW OF UNIVERSITY COLLEGE, OXFORD.

چو عندليب فصاحت فروشد اي حافظ

تو قدر او بسخن كفتن دري بشكن

L O N D O N:

PRINTED BY W. AND J. RICHARDSON, SALISBURY COURT,

FLEET STREET.

M DCC LXXI.

Title page of Jones's famous *Grammar*.

general grammar or other subjects, such as are discussed in Robert Lowth's *Short Introduction to English Grammar* (London, 1762) and the English grammar prefixed to Johnson's *Dictionary* (1775). Jones's pedagogical grammar sketches a reading method that he optimistically predicts will prepare a student in less than a year to translate and answer any Indian prince's letter. If the student also practices with a native informant, in a year he will supposedly be able to talk fluently with the Indian people, who actually did not know Persian. Although Jones disavows any real intention of describing the language, he first studied similar grammars so as to compose a better one, perhaps pointing toward an ideal form that succeeding linguists were to follow. That is, grammarians should use Jones's Persian rules in their own research, as their task is to open the literary mine. Those who want the gems must find them independently.

The book was a remarkable achievement. Working without modern linguistic knowledge or an informant, Jones nonetheless makes a generally accurate phonemic and morphological analysis, giving some attention to syntax. Like the German philologists who built on his advances in the next century, he speaks of letters, not sounds, cautioning that pronunciation must be learned from a native speaker. He spells Persian in the Roman alphabet according to English pronunciation, a dubious method in view of the unphonetic spelling of English vowels, not to mention the differences between the two phonologies. His descriptions are auditory, such as "soft *g* in *gem,* extremely harsh, another harsh Arabick letter, answers generally to our broad *a,* a very strong aspirate, exactly like our *ch* in the words *cherry, cheek.*" Yet he understands matters like aspiration, liquids, and initial-medial-terminal positions. He could hardly have used physiological transcription at a time when the concept of the phoneme had not yet been developed. Moreover, the twin difficulties of printers' resistance and an audience unable to read such transcription still obtain today. He was later to resolve the major phonetic problems with his pioneering Jonesian System, which contributed to his success with Sanskrit.

The book can still be profitably read for its innovations, description of Persian, and insights into analysis. Jones hints at the reconstruction of earlier forms, which is essential to modern linguistics: "This remark on the formation of the Persian imperatives from an obsolete verb, may be useful to those who are curious in ancient dialects; as it will enable them to trace out a considerable part of the old Persian language."[3] Thus Pahlavi is to Modern Persian, as Old Norse is to Danish, and Old English is to Modern English.

Jones's preface was "a veritable turning point in the history of humane studies, for it comprises the most informed and eloquent *apologia pro litteris orientalibus* which had yet been penned, perhaps that has ever been penned."[4] Its complementary purposes are to convince (1) readers that Persian poetry could provide the needed enrichment for neoclassical staleness, and (2) scholars that they should translate Persian manuscripts. European rulers share the blame for the neglect of this rich literature. Jones interlaces the book with vibrant examples from Háfiz, appending a moral fable as an exercise, presented in both Persian prose and poetry and English.

Inclusion of "A Persian Song of Hafiz" helped ensure the book's success. Among Jones's contributions to the development of Persian studies in Europe, none was more consequential than his paraphrasing of several of Háfiz's lyrics. None bore sweeter fruit than his version of "Shírazí Turk." He really had no choice except to expand it: He wished to transmit the whole, and coherence required elaboration of the foreign tropes, even as contemporary taste "preferred elegant prolixity to epigrammatic succinctness."[5] Each of the nine rubaiyats became a stanza of *abcabc*, expanding the lyric by about 50 percent and somewhat changing the rhyme. Octosyllabics permitted close imitation of the cadence and accent, while allowing inclusion of four exotic place-names. This was Jones's early versification at its best.

Jones communicates the mosaic of sounds and symbols, even if his line "Like orient pearls at random strung" mistakenly suggests that Háfiz was a careless jeweler of words.[6] He was not interested in literal translation; rather, his poem was a labor of love to see whether he could convert an Oriental original into good English poetry, which might stimulate European translators and rejuvenate jaded conventions. His sense of morality dictated his altering the sex of the male, so that the male is charmed by a maid instead of by another male, a change that his contemporaries never suspected.

The poem has a "very pleasing and unusual movement, conveying a sense of exotic charm and mystery" largely by means of magical place-names.[7] This precursor of Romanticism contains emotion, music, exotic allusions, and simple diction, as in the opening stanza:

> Sweet maid, if thou wouldst charm my sight,
> And bid these arms thy neck infold;
> That rosy cheek, that lily hand
> Would give thy poet more delight
> Than all Bokhára's vaunted gold,
> Than all the gems of Samarcand.

Radiating a refreshing hedonism, it is one of Jones's best poems.

His *Grammar* brilliantly satisfied the needs of the time. The influential

Monthly Review now took a stand on Jones's claims about Middle Eastern literary richness, in James Robertson's two-part review (January and February 1772, pp. 36–43, 81–92). Jones "is more full and copious than any grammarian whom we have had an opportunity of consulting; and he merits due praise for his industry and taste." Every learner of Persian must be eagerly awaiting Jones's history of that language and the copious praxis of literature extracted from fine writers, promised as a separate work (it became the introduction to his *History of Nader Shah*). Declaring the book to be the most linguistically useful one on Persian yet, Robertson complains only that Jones did not suggest the preliminary learning of Arabic.

He was now one of the most famous Orientalists in Europe, having been given the epithets of Persian Jones and Oriental Jones. Johnson presented a copy of the book to John Hussey, who was going to Asia. Another went to Warren Hastings: "That literature is not totally forsaking us, and that your favorite language is not neglected will appear from the book which I should have pleased myself more with sending if I could have procured it bound: but time was wanting."[8] In 1775 a second edition principally added an index. As Jones's friends were cautioning him against exuberance for Orientalism at a time when he had committed himself to law, he added a note to the preface:

My professional studies having wholly engaged my attention, and induced me not only to abandon oriental literature, but even to efface, as far as possible, the very traces of it from my memory, I committed the conduct and revisal of this edition of my grammar, and the composition of the index to Mr. [John] Richardson, in whose skill I have a perfect confidence.

Public enthusiasm was still high by the sixth edition: "The public is indebted for one of the most early, and most pleasing means, of access to treasures which are not likely to be exhausted. Never was there a more successful attempt, to render the elements of any language easy and delightful."[9] Not until long after the ninth edition of 1828 was the book superseded. There also was a French edition in 1772, followed by a second French edition in 1845. Although it did enhance Jones's reputation, the book did not persuade people to study and translate Persian.[10] Later, however, Edward FitzGerald was the major convert, and the book had an indirect influence on Matthew Arnold's *Sohrab and Rustum*. The scholar A. J. Valpy credited the book's style and admirable poetic samples with inducing him to begin Oriental studies.[11]

Persian Jones deserved his name. His *Grammar* contained an advertisement for his revised edition of Meninski, which also often appeared in the *London Chronicle* and *Gazette* from 1 October 1770. In March 1771 he sent Reviczky a sample of the new characters, urging criticism of any inelegance, so that he might correct it. His edition was proceeding satisfactorily once he had secured the patronage of Oxford and Cambridge, which he exploited in his advertisement: "The protection of the most celebrated Universities in the world, sufficiently proves its high importance to the progress of learning; and the encouragement which the Hon. East India and Turkey Companies have given it, shows, that they consider it as extremely serviceable to them in their transactions and correspondence with the powers of Asia." Jones's advertisement announced that his edition would go to press in April 1770 and would be completed in 1773.

Jones was checking all the Turkish, Arabic, and Persian items in Meninski's *Thesaurus*. After the East India Company lent its name, he expanded the project by planning an English translation and a Portuguese one to capitalize on Portugal's Indian possessions. John Uri, who had started his twenty-year compilation *Bibliothecæ Bodleianæ codicum manuscriptorum orientalium* (Oxford, 1787), was supplying many additional items discovered by combing manuscript dictionaries like the Bodleian's "Farhang Jehanguiri, which comprises the Substance of Forty Persian Lexicons."

To keep the price of the book moderate – the *Thesaurus* was selling for sixty guineas – the printers John and William Richardson would deliver the work in sheets. The cost was six guineas at the time of subscription, with six more payable on delivery. Nonsubscribers would pay twenty guineas. Subscriptions were collected from a number of distinguished people; but the project did not attract enough subscribers, despite the *Monthly Review*'s public encouragement (February 1772, p. 92), scholars' anticipation, and advertisements. The East India Company did not even answer Jones's direct request for financial assistance to the extremely expensive project, perhaps feeling that its servants would have little use for the four impractical folio volumes. And as governmental and publishing groups also advanced no money, Jones had no intention of emulating Meninski, who had sacrificed health and fortune, borrowing money for an Oriental press and dying unnoticed: "A prudent man should not launch out into unknown waters, with the dangers, even, of his fortunes being wrecked" (trans., 1:168).

The project was not advertised in the 1775 edition of the *Grammar,* as Jones had given the project to John Richardson in gratitude for having prepared the index. Jones also helped with the books that established Richardson's reputation, *A Grammar of the Arabic Language* (London, 1776) and *A Dictionary, Persian, Arabic, and English* (Oxford, 1777), by lending sources and reviewing the plan for the latter, which was modeled on the Persian *Grammar*. This abridged Meninski edition omitted the

Turkish words and added words chiefly from Golius.[12] It almost involved Jones in Richardson's quarrel with Jacob Bryant, who felt that Jones had contributed to the prefatory dissertation and its attack on *A New System, or, an Analysis of Ancient Mythology* (London, 1774–6), although Richardson nowhere indicated such aid.[13]

Lettre à Monsieur A—— du P——, Jones's third publication in 1771, was his only answer to a book that had provoked him. It caused not the usual literary quarrel, but an erroneous view that misled Avestan scholars for half a century. The sequence began with the texts in unknown script given to the Bodleian Library in 1718. Supposedly Zoroaster's *Zend-Avesta*, the texts defied the efforts of Thomas Hunt and others to decipher them. When Abraham-Hyacinthe Anquetil-Duperron saw them in 1754, he became a private soldier with the French East India Company so as to get to India and learn how to read them. After eight difficult years, he returned to Oxford and quickly disagreed with Hunt and John Swinton about the texts. After years of toil, his *Zend-Avesta, ouvrage de Zorastre* (Paris, 1771) appeared.

Volume 1 irritated Jones. The prefatory discourse egotistically narrated the Indian search, with praise of Anquetil's handsomeness and pink-and-white complexion. His nationalistic derogation of England, Oxford, and Hunt likewise did not belong in scholarship. The seventy-five-year-old Hunt, Regius Professor of Hebrew at Oxford, had preceded Jones's father as a tutor in the Macclesfield household. Anquetil claimed that his pointing out some errors to Hunt had led to an exchange of sharp words disguised as pleasantries.[14] He said that he had presented a Sanskrit alphabet to Hunt (who then boasted of knowing Old Persian), and had promised another Oriental alphabet to Swinton. The bulk of his three volumes was devoted to his French translation.

In view of the unwarranted criticism, Jones asked Hunt a series of questions to determine Anquetil's veracity. Hunt replied that he had never claimed to know Old Persian and that Anquetil had not given him or his friends any alphabets. Anquetil seemed to have been lying. Actually, he was poorly trained in philology, making mistakes in the translation and not improving on the priests' understanding of the Zend texts. Jones found only "a farrago of puerile fables, tedious formulæ, wearisome repetitions, and grotesque prescriptions."[15] Instead of the elegant, profound philosophy that one might expect from the founder of Zoroastrianism, Jones found only dreary ideas. Had Anquetil been duped?

For perhaps the only time in his life, Jones approached a scholarly problem with real bias. There was no counterevidence, as scholars did not yet know the kinds or extent of linguistic change since Old Persian, and he had no conception of the change's magnitude. The manuscripts used by Anquetil had suffered orthographic alterations that would long delay reconstruction of Zoroaster's spelling. So everything pointed to an unreliable translation of modern forgeries. Jones thought he had found Arabic items (really Aramaic), although Arabic loanwords had not entered Avestan before the seventh century. Some ideas in the manuscripts were suspiciously similar to the French traveler Sir John Chardin's. Anquetil's promise to translate the Brahmans' sacred texts – an incredible task even today – suggested a poor knowledge of Oriental languages.

The book required an answer that simultaneously should inform Europeans that Oriental philosophy was spirited, rich, and profound, an idea that Jones had already advanced. He was the logical defender of scholarship and Oxford: His *Grammar* had just shown him to be the best Persian scholar in the country, and his *Histoire* had demonstrated his fluency in Anquetil's language. The stage was set for a typical literary pattern – a satire on a new, well-known book. Forgeries were in the public eye: Jones agreed with those charging Thomas Chatterton with forging the Rowley manuscripts, and James Macpherson's hoax with the Ossian materials was being exposed. Jones modeled his answer on Voltaire, making personal attacks quite untypical of him; yet he chose to write anonymously. After Elmsly published Jones's *Lettre* on 23 November, Daniel Prince sold the fifty-two-page pamphlet at Oxford.

Jones's thesis is that Zoroaster could not have composed such materials, which must be a modern patchwork. He then defends the Oxford Orientalists: "The holy fathers of your dear country never braved such perils, to further the true faith, as you have endured to discover the false." He polemically assails Anquetil's conceit, errors, and style. The style is termed harsh, low, inelegant, and sometimes bombastic.[16] The page numbers of examples are not supplied for the quoted passages, inasmuch as no one would read such a book. Yet Jones, who surely knew that his identity would be recognized, was apparently not seeking to destroy Anquetil's reputation, but only to display his own literary invective and mastery of French.[17] On the Continent, however, his authorship was not identified for a time; French critics thought that some *bel esprit* of Paris was the writer.

Jones's view easily prevailed in England. The *Monthly Review* took its usual laudatory stance:

[Anquetil's] absurd pretentions to eastern literature are treated with the utmost pleasantry: and we have a full exposition of the total insignificance of those writings which he has impudently ascribed to Zoroaster. The public in general, and the learned professors at Oxford in particular, whom M. Du Perron has mentioned in his work with the highest disrespect, are indebted for this publication to the ingenious Mr. Jones.

Gentleman's Magazine paraphrased this review.[18]

Hunt sent thanks from Swinton and himself: "I have read it over and over again, and think the whole nation, as well as the University and its members, are much obliged to you for this able and spirited defence."[19] Although Swinton doubted that there had been as much general destruction of ancient Persian writings as Jones imagined, the pair urged him to translate his *Lettre* into English. Thus Jones, refusing to see the importance and reality of Anquetil's work, strongly reflected scholars' disappointment with the *Zend-Avesta*. Chardin, Richardson in England, Christoph Meiners in Germany, and others concluded it to be spurious.[20] The damage was done.

Perhaps because of the tide against him, Anquetil did not defend himself, though his silence may have strengthened Jones's convictions. In 1772 Jones observed: "Many productions, invented in *France,* have been offered to the publick as genuine translations from the languages of *Asia.*" Then in 1773: "It is sufficient for us to have exposed his follies, detected his imposture, and retorted his invectives, without insulting a fallen adversary." And as late as 1780: "A foul-mouthed and arrogant Frenchman . . . attacked Oxford in three large volumes of misrepresentation and scurrility."[21] When Jones visited Paris in 1780, Anquetil studiously avoided him. A friend later said: "Those who have heard Sir William Jones speak of Perron, well know that he held the talents of that vain and malignant author in very low estimation."[22]

The *Zend-Avesta* soon received in France the linguistic recognition that is now universal.[23] In 1826 Ramsus Rask's "Über das Alter und die Echtheit der Zend-Sprache und des Zend-Avesta" finally demonstrated that Avestan was not corrupted Sanskrit, but was related to Modern Persian and written at least before 334 B.C. Indeed, Rask called Jones's *Lettre* "a libel full of venom and gall and quite unworthy of its author's name."[24] Thereupon scholars redirected Avestan studies, but the correction in literary circles was even slower. Alexander Chalmers maintained that Jones had corrected "the French writer with more asperity than perhaps his mature judgment would have approved, but yet without injustice, for Perron stood convicted not only of loose invective, but of absolute falsehood." Across the Atlantic, Emerson proposed that a committee investigate the "extraordinary fragments" and report "their true history."[25]

Even before writing *Lettre,* Jones had made considerable progress on a work potentially as important as his *Grammar.* Displeased with Elmsly and the Richardson cousins as printers, Jones turned to Thomas Cadell, who did perhaps the best books of the day and treated the authors generously. The work was "An Essay on the History of the Turks," modeled on Montesquieu's *Considérations sur les causes de la grandeur des Romains et de leur décadence* (Amsterdam, 1734) and begun during an August holiday at Weymouth. Jones told William Bennet on 10 November: "I give up my leisure hours to a Political Treatise *on the Turks*, from which I expect some reputation; and I have several objects of ambition, which I cannot trust to a letter" (1:103). The "Essay" was designed to supply his previous omissions about Turkish literature and to demonstrate his knowledge of Turkish affairs.

Sir James Porter, the ex-ambassador who was writing books about Turkey, had introduced him to Lord Chancellor Henry Bathurst. As John Murray had held the ambassadorship since 1765 and would be relieved some day, Jones resolved to seek it openly once he could learn the outcome of the confusing Russian–Turkish war: "For the moment it must be done with secrecy and whispers. The King is very well disposed toward me, the nobility is sympathetic, and the commercial group is quite favourable. The only thing I fear is that some more powerful rival may appear on the scene and overtake me" (trans., 1:108). Shortly afterward Jones gave up his naive assumption that ambassadorships were awarded for relevant scholarship and language competence, and he pursued the post primarily to keep potential patrons aware of his aspirations. But long before Murray's death in 1775, he abandoned his diplomatic aspirations. The abandonment also meant the end of his languishing revision of Meninski, for now the Turkish portion could not directly assist his career.

Jones worked on the "Essay" for three years, advising Cadell that the prefatory discourse would soon be ready for printing. The earl of Radnor, the father of Jones's Oxford friend Jacob Bouverie, granted permission to inscribe the "Essay" to him. It was scheduled for the press on 20 January 1772, but Jones became involved in publishing his early poems and then his *Commentariorum*. Otherwise, "the only *original* work, except upon law, that I mean to publish for the next twenty years, is a short *History of the Turks* . . . in about 300 pages in 8 vo. You see it will be the Iliad in a nutshell" (1:136). By 1775 he considered his career in law to be much more important, and he paid for the five sheets already printed. With the loss of these sheets in a 1776 fire that burned Cadell's warehouses, fate seemed to intervene to end the project.

It had started with Jones's discovery that there was little dependable information about Turkey. Not knowing Turkish and Arabic, Europeans could not study relevant sources and, more importantly, could not live among the Turks and converse with persons of various social levels. One major source described in Jones's prefatory discourse is Meninski's "great repository of Eastern learning," which contains phrases and proverbs that illuminate customs and attitudes.[26] Thus language study is necessary for cultural research. Jones rejects the European view that Orientals are rude, ignorant, and savage; Muhammad advised Moslems to apply themselves to learning. Jones also seeks to raise the Turks' stature in poetry, rhetoric, moral philosophy, and history, which he illustrates. In addition, he was planning to map out the outline of a complete history, interwoven with English commercial history, leaving until later the filling in of details.

The "Essay" was not his only major, unfulfilled project pursued while he was a law student. In 1771 he considered producing "Suleiman." After all, Alexander Dow had begun as an Oriental scholar and had achieved some reputation at Drury Lane with *Zingis*. But Jones was unable to arrange for the proper actors. He later lent the manuscript to Lady Cork, which he attempted to retrieve when she died in 1788. Nor did he find the time to publish Jámí's *Yúsuf va Zulaykhá* from a copper-plate engraving.

Oriental treasures were tempting. The religious scholar James Bate owned an edition of Nizámí's *Khamsa* containing thirty miniatures. Gratefully accepting the invitation to inspect it, Jones sent a glowing report in Latin, which Bate preserved with the comment: "In times to come, a piece of your handwriting will be looked upon as a curiosity by virtuosi yet unborn."[27] But Bate did not respond to the suggestion that he or some other Cantabrigian might edit Nizámí's works, even though Jones had no time for the vast project.

Only Jones's habit of strenuous study could sustain his pace during the winter of 1771. He attended the public speeches of the best barristers and MPs and studied English laws, "the most noble example of human wisdom that the mind of man can contemplate" (1:103). Drawing on Demosthenes and others, he visualized law and oratory as an ideal union. Then he measured speakers like Burke and Pitt against this ideal so as to gain insight into the optimum and yet practicalities of his future career. His Westminster attendance was intended to complete his professional training at the Inns of Court.

Such application kept him from Oxford in 1771 except for the holiday dinners, two weeks in May, and the vacation of 24 December to 9 January 1772. Jones let one of Scott's pupils use his apartment, stipulating that he be able to have it at vacation. He would not give it up entirely, though he seldom used it, as it was the only place that he could properly call his home.

During the Christmas vacation he burned most of his childhood compositions. As he fed more than two thousand pages to the fire, he reflected on his golden dreams at Harrow and on Sumner's urging him to publish these immature works. Now he intended to publish the poems that deserved to see the light. The selecting had been going on for years, as when "Laura" and another poem were read by Wilmot, whose father praised them highly.

Going about the publication in neoclassical fashion, Jones circulated the surviving nine English poems and some classical imitations among close friends like William Hawkins (Oxford professor of poetry, 1751–6), Parr, Shipley, and Reynolds. He hoped to compare their reactions and add his own emendations, on the model of "Variations" in Pope's posthumous *Works* (London, 1751). He would print the variations, or first readings, in the margin. Joseph Warton was added to his critics after a party at Reynolds's house: "He paid me a compliment before the whole company, which I cannot write without blushing: he said, my Greek poems which he had seen in manuscript, were worthy of ancient Greece." Hawkins thought that the dates of composition were inconsequential, but Jones chose to specify them in the book. People must not think that he was still applying himself to poetry: "I mean to insinuate that I have given it up for several years, which I must explain more fully in the preface. For a man who wishes to rise in the law, must be supposed to have no other object" (1:109, 102). As the favorable winter season for publication approached, he discarded the idea of a critical apparatus. He had prepared as well as he could for what would be his most famous literary book.

Poems, Consisting Chiefly of Translations from the Asiatick Languages is misleadingly imprinted "At the Clarendon-Press," which was not reserved by the delegates for their publications until 1780. As the warehouse keeper's 1772 accounts show a surcharge of £3 5s 6d on the printer's bill to cover the overhead, the delegates did not publish the book at their expense. The facts are not clear: One review carries the name of Elmsly, although the title page specifies Elmsly and Prince as the booksellers.

Poems contains nine poems and two essays. Jones is almost apologetic in his short preface: "I should not have suffered even the following trifles to see the light, if I were not very desirous of recommending to the learned world a species of literature, which abounds with so many new expressions, new images, and new inventions." However, the reader's enjoyment was not the only purpose:

It has been my endeavour for several years to inculcate this truth, that, if the principal writings of the *Asiaticks,* which are reposited in our publick libraries, were printed with the usual advantage of notes and illustrations, and if the languages of the *Eastern* nations were studied in our great seminaries of learning, where every other branch of useful knowledge is taught to perfection, a new and ample field would be opened for speculation; we should have a more extensive insight into the history of the human mind; we should be furnished with a new set of images and similitudes; and a number of excellent compositions would be brought to light, which future scholars might explain, and future poets might imitate.[28]

Though Jones does not have the remotest intention of doing the needed translations, a writer acquainted with the original can effectively imitate it in English or other Western language. Firdausi's *Shâhnâma* "might be versified as easily as the *Iliad,* and I see no reason why *the delivery of Persia by Cyrus* should not be a subject as interesting to us, as *the anger of Achilles,* or *the wandering of Ulysses.*" Even so, Jones does not place Asiatic literature in competition with Greek and Roman works, which he specifies as the standard of true taste. Thus he exalts Asiatic literature while stressing classical perfection. He draws his meter from Dryden and Gray and mainly employs the heroic couplet. Four poems have classical sources – with pastoral subjects from Spenser, Addison, and Petrarch – so that Jones's title is somewhat misleading. Yet by presenting tantalizing short translations, he was exploiting the market that he had created.

Jones makes an innovational intercultural suggestion: Scholars should translate the greatest Arabic and Persian works for Europeans who cannot read the originals. These translations would provide elements for the re-shaping and enlivening of unoriginal European poetry, in a grand plan to improve cultures by means of language. Thereby he pointed toward the modern concepts of comparative and world literature, in a vein of inter-national education.

Jones's "Solima, an Arabian Eclogue" originated in 1768 from verses on benevolence, in which he shapes figures, sentiments, and descriptions into fifty-two couplets praising a princess's caravanserai. Albeit indirectly, he may have been thinking of Lady Spencer and her Society for Charitable Purposes, as he told her that he would never have composed "Solima" if he had not known her. The poem is full of sensuous Oriental coloring like "Where every breeze sheds incense o'er the vales, / And every shrub the scent of musk exhales!"

Until now, Jones had meant Arabic and Persian or occasionally Turkish when speaking of Oriental literature, for he had seen almost no Indian poetry. Indeed, his only "Indian" work in *Poems* is "The Palace of Fortune, an Indian Tale," based on Dow's tale of Roshanara. To Dow's Persian plot, questionably Indian, Jones adds Eastern descriptions and episodes; and by changing the moral, he asserts his right to change any work that he translates. Thus his ambitious maiden sees a series of visions in which Pleasure, Glory, Riches, and Knowledge are granted their wishes, only to be destroyed by the fruits of these wishes. In Oriental fable tradition the maiden learns the vanity of human wishes. The narrative is interesting, with Jones's revision halving it to 253 closed couplets.

"The Seven Fountains, an Eastern Eclogue," composed in 1767, is based on Ibn 'Arabsháh's allegorical *Fatihatu'l-Khulafá*. Jones's engrafting of the Agib episode, from Night 57 of the *Arabian Nights Entertainments*, produces a parable of man and his worldly friends similar to *Everyman*. A prince experiences the various pleasures of the senses until rescued by an old man representing religion. The rich coloring in the 271 couplets echoes Shakespeare:

> High on the burnish'd deck, a gilded throne
> With orient pearls and beaming diamonds shone.

Amid such morality is "A Persian Song of Hafiz," whose reprinting in *Poems* ensured wide circulation and acceleration toward acceptance as a standard British poem. A Roman translation is included for "those who may have any doubt of its being genuine." Its appeal led to its inclusion, along with "Solima" and two other poems, in the *Annual Register* of 1772 (pp. 196–205), the first complete reprinting of any of Jones's works in a periodical. A headnote credits "the very ingenious and learned Mr. Jones, so well known for his extraordinary knowledge in the Oriental Languages." *Gentleman's Magazine* of January 1786 (p. 86) and the *Annual Register* of 1797 (pp. 178–9) also reprinted it. Among many other collections, it went into Southey's *Specimens of the Later English Poets*, helping create the dreamworld of pleasure, soon echoed by Beckford's *Vathek* that itself was so influenced, which haunted many Romantics.[29] Today it remains one of the most famous English renderings from Persian, surpassed only by the *Rubáiyát* and *Sohrab and Rustum*.

Jones's fifth and sixth poems are Petrarchan. "Laura, an Elegy from Petrarch," completed in seventy-five couplets in 1769, is juxtaposed with Oriental translations to suggest the similarities in culturally different literature. It exemplifies a comparative spirit. Because Italians "have written in the true spirit of the *Easterners*," he includes "An Ode of Petrarch, to the Fountain of Valchiusa" and Canzone 27 (his source for the "Ode") to show his knowledge of Italian. In a playful contest with Voltaire, who paraphrased the first stanza, Jones also includes a French paraphrase.

"A Turkish Ode of Mesihi," the only literal translation of an Asiatic poem in the book, celebrates the return of spring in thirty-three closed couplets. Suggesting refreshing colors and perfumes, each stanza ends in the refrain "Be gay: too soon the flowers of Spring will fade." The last stanza introduces Europeans to the Persian fable of the nightingale's attachment to the rose, a fable that was one of Jones's favorites. He provides a Roman transliteration and a prose paraphrase of the fifteenth-century work. Because the original is similar to "Pervigilium Veneris" in measure and refrain, he also appends a Latin imitation.

The last two poems are classical types. "Arcadia, a Pastoral Poem," composed in 330 lines in 1762, was extensively polished as an imaginative critique on pastoral styles. Number 32 of the *Guardian* is included so that one may see where Jones copied Addison's "hint" and where he changed the allegory. In the narrative, various shepherds sing as suitors for the daughters of Theocritus, who chooses Virgil for Daphne, and Spenser for Hyla. The suitors represent the pastoral types: elegant/polished and simple/unadorned. Virgil's offspring is Pope; Spenser's is Gay. Since then, "No shepherd rules th' Arcadian mead."

"Caissa: or, the Game at Chess," composed while Jones was mastering chess in 1763, was stimulated by the game in Vida's "Ludus scacchiæ." Jones provided most of the descriptions, the story of Caissa, and the explanation of the origin of chess, in imitation of Ovid. The game is vigorously narrated in 179 graceful couplets, as in

> The dark-brow'd hero, with one vengeful blow
> Of life and place deprives his ivory foe.
> Now rush both armies o'er the burnish'd field,
> Hurl the swift dart, and rend the bursting shield.

"Caissa" drew critics' plaudits and went through many editions in chess books.[30] The Scottish historian Gilbert Stuart praised its "singular art and delicacy, with a command of language, and a power of harmony, which few poets have displayed" (*Monthly Review,* May 1772, p. 516). But never did the poorer "Caissa" equal the popularity of Pope's *The Rape of the Lock,* also derived from Vida, which Jones must have had in mind as a classical contest.

These nine poems are a successful fusion of classical conventions with Middle Eastern themes and images, producing poetry as innovative in its limited way as is Wordsworth and Coleridge's *Lyrical Ballads.* The two essays concluding Jones's *Poems* continue the neoclassical and exotic amalgamation characterizing pre-Romanticism. The first philosophizes on the value of Oriental literature; the second develops an aesthetic theory for his argument. However, poems like "Caissa" were composed long before this venture into poetic theorizing and could not have been forced into a form exemplifying his theory.

The essays should be considered in the history of British criticism. "An Essay on the Poetry of the Eastern Nations," designed as the introduction to Jones's still-unpublished *Commentariorum,* laments the staleness of European poetry. He urges people to learn Oriental languages so as to study the principal works written in them. Up until then, Persia has produced more writers, chiefly poets, than has all of Europe. Significantly, in his succeeding essays on this theme he introduces additional authors and treats subjects besides literature, his comparative approach thus becoming more universal. That is, pastoral tradition is more alive in Arabic poetry than in European, suggesting that the pastoral is a simple, living form that appeals to everyone. Jones's effort to revive the pastoral is the most important essay on that subject in the late eighteenth century and brings the pastoral again into a vital relationship with literature.[31]

"On the Arts, Commonly Called Imitative" theorizes from Jones's experiences in transmitting literature from one culture into another. Presumably "*poetry* was originally no more than a strong and animated expression of the human passions of *joy* and *grief, love* and *hate, admiration* and *anger,* sometimes pure and unmixed, sometimes variously modified and combined." Primitive people spontaneously praised God by "bursting into an extasy of *joy,* and pouring his praises to the creator." Although poetry and music can imitate a human's manners and several objects in nature, they produce their greatest effect by assuming the power of Nature, not by imitating. Thus Jones rejects Aristotle's supposed doctrine that all poetry consists of imitation. The artist achieves great effects by capturing the spirit of the piece in a beautiful simplicity, not by painting minute details in a gaudy composition. When "vehement passion is expressed in strong words, exactly measured, and pronounced, *in a common voice,* in just cadence, and with proper accents," the result is genuine poetry. Because the passions and, consequently, sympathy are generally the same for all people until weakened by age or other causes, Jones is philosophically able to justify Oriental literary sublimity.

His essay, fresh and original in aesthetics, boldly challenges the doctrine that art should imitate Nature. It anticipates and probably influenced the views of Wordsworth, Coleridge, and Shelley.[32] Jones seeks to revise neoclassical foundations by harmoniously blending ideas from "Longinus, the old doctrine of poetic inspiration, recent theories of the emotion and imaginative origin of poetry, and a major emphasis on the lyric form," together with his own emphasis on supposedly primitive, spontaneous poetry. It was the first English essay to weave such disparate threads into "an explicit and orderly reformulation of the nature and criteria of poetry and of the poetic genres."[33] The threads were to be developed by much better critics; Jones never again delved into poetic theory.

Like any new poet, he anxiously awaited the reaction to *Poems.* He wrote Hawkins, who had provided extensive suggestions:

It has not yet been in my power to learn what reception my publication has met with in the great world, but all my friends, and even my slightest acquaintance, are perpetually saying fine things concerning it. . . . I hear, he is very well received by the Ladies.– If you are willing to compliment your friends at Oxford, or elsewhere, with presents of the Poems, let me beg you take of Prince as many copies as you please. (1:110–11)

The book added the name of *poet* to Jones's expanding fame in Orientalism and translation. The review in *Universal Magazine* is typical: "It discovers the true spirit of poetry, and does honour to the genius of the Asiatics. It is to be hoped, that the novelty and the merit of the pieces, which comprise it, will encourage men of letters to pay an attention to the languages of Asia" (May 1772, p. 265). Having garbed Oriental thoughts and feelings in attractive English dress, in one slim book Jones had temporarily become a major poet of the day.

The book was the talk of London. Mrs. Montagu, a Blue Stocking who may not have known him yet, observed:

There is a gayety & splendor in the poems which is naturally derived from the happy soil & climate, of the Poets & they breathe Asiatick luxury, or else Mr. Jones is himself of a most splendid imagination. The descriptions are so fine, & all the objects so brilliant, *that the sense aches at them.* . . . Every object in these pieces is blooming & beautiful; every plant is odouriferous; the passions too are of the sort which belong to Paradise. (1:111)

Only Walpole, holding his own view of exoticism, was grumpy: "There is a Mr. Jones too, who has published imitations of Asiatic poets: but as Chambers's book was advertised by the title of *ornamental gardening,* instead of *oriental,* I think Mr. Jones's is a blunder of *oriental* for *ornamental,* for it is very flowery, and not at all Eastern."[34]

Though *Poems* achieved less than it intended, it started "lines of advance in English poetry which were to continue for at least half a century."[35] As the *Times Literary Supplement* remarked at Jones's 1946 bicentenary, his diction is often stilted, the imagery worn, and the allegories the same old clothes with new buttons; but *Poems* retains a pleasant freshness in the effort to reintroduce the lost lyrical evocation into British poetry.[36] After a second edition in 1777, it went through seven more editions by 1822, besides being included in numerous anthologies. Since then, only "A Persian Song of Hafiz" has not faded from memory and still helps guard Jones's small niche in British poetry.

3   Persian Jones and Constitutional Law
         (1772–1777)

Jones's origin placed him outside the social categories in an age of sharp distinctions, although men of letters occasionally moved between classes. He employed a small inheritance, a good education, "precocious intellectual gifts, intense and unusual intellectual interests and a pleasant personality" to earn an initial place befitting his talents and ambition.[1] As the tutorship had not really provided an independent livelihood, he had chosen the route that others like him sometimes took, and law gratified both his higher ambition and his love of scholarship, especially comparative study.

Once *Poems* appeared, he sent all his books unrelated to law or science to Oxford, "where they shall be till I resume my former pursuits in my old age. You will see my shelves filled with reports and abridgements. Tully and Demosthenes alone have preserved their places, and I read no other books in the ancient languages. These I devour – these I get by heart" (1:124). Thus he sought to implement his promise to abandon Orientalism, even as he thought tantalizingly of his long-finished *Commentariorum*. He read Cicero's works annually "to pervade and fathom the soul of a man, like himself: accomplished in every great attainment of the human genius, and applying them to the interests of active life. The close study of the Greek orators was to him a part of a course of the philosophy of law and legislation."[2]

Jones's classical bent kept him in close association with Samuel Parr, whom he frequently visited after Parr became head assistant at Harrow. Shocked one morning to hear of Sumner's death, he dashed off a note to Parr. Parr sent a Latin epitaph, to be inscribed in Harrow Church. Jones was good-natured in offering corrections: "How can a man who reads every day such words as maritagium, marriage, and warrantizo, to warrant, be expected to criticise one who lives perpetually with Terence and Cicero? However, since you desire it, and the thing itself is of no small consequence, I must try to rub up my old Latin" (1:96).[3] Jones liked the epitaph; Sumner could not have composed a better one, and his own delicate suggestions were adopted in the much-revised final version. He considered composing

53

an epitaph in couplets modeled on Pope, but rejected the idea because of the labor required. Too, perhaps in the back of his mind was disillusionment with Sumner, who, he felt, had violated principle by volunteering to be Althorp's temporary tutor.

During the revising, Parr heatedly contested for the headship, which he lost, he said, because of his vote for John Wilkes. His politics was having no real effect on Jones, who professed no interest in Wilkes's campaign for the lord mayoralty of London in late 1772. Jones probably did support Parr, who persuaded numbers of pupils to accompany him to the competing school that he established at Stanmore. Jones often visited there, where he met two bright pupils. Walter Pollard was the son of a Barbados physician. Thomas Maurice, like everyone else, was charmed with Jones's instructive conversation and engaging manners.[4] They became his longtime friends.

Among Maurice's recollections is the suicide of the seventeen-year-old Thomas Chatterton. The future Orientalist and others hurried to the obscure London lodging, but Jones had been so intrigued that he and Thomas Day had already been there. His friend William Hayley's seven couplets about the "poisonous phial" in the chill room by the vile bed so impressed Jones that he copied them in his commonplace book and read them with great animation to Pollard and Maurice,[5] confiding that internal evidence in the Rowley poems had convinced him of Chatterton's fabrication, even before Walpole's revelations. In this, Jones demonstrated his linguistic knowledge of Middle English, just as he had done in regard to Persian and Arabic. His evidence was sound, as the poems employed the measure and often the phraseology of Dryden's and Pope's classical translations. Chatterton had borrowed from Collins and Gray, whom a medieval poet could not have known; and he had used spellings from Chaucer and Spenser to attempt an antique appearance, intermingling obsolete words and even his own coinages. He had overused the prefix y- and had unlinguistically "antiqued" some words. In short, Chatterton had created "a jargon of every species of dialect, ancient and modern, of every age and date," though capable of producing an *Iliad*. Jones never entered the tempting controversy, in which he would have been as certain of success as he died thinking his attack on Anquetil had been.

Jones's law studies did not interfere with closer friendships. When Althorp visited "of his own accord with all his former openness and gayety," Jones asked Lady Spencer whether the family might welcome him as warmly as when he had been a tutor (1:100–1). Heedless of the influence that they might have wielded on his career, he had not attempted a reconciliation. Now Althorp's visit made Jones realize his negligence, for Lady Spencer had always treated him as an equal. He remembered her retort:

I should want sincerity as much as you say I do if I did not tell you I think you have accused me very unjustly; I am not conscious of any insincerity in my letter from Southampton; I never dictated any letters to you, nor can I think your *supposing I did* a sufficient answer for you to rob me of the most valuable quality I boast of. (1:100)

He eloquently apologized. After people had characterized her letter as insincere, he had inconsiderately adopted their opinion, which proved to be groundless. Others' insinuations had provoked his earlier, peevish lines about going immediately to Oxford. So he asked her to accept his "full apology – and as to the unfortunate word that I let fall, it must be considered, that my very daring to call in question any single quality of your Ladyship was a proof of my being no flatterer in the just encomium that I gave at the same time of all your other excellences."

Having left the tutorship, Jones took delight in law. Though intending to be a learned lawyer, "I am not covetous and am only ambitious of an honest Fame, not that I shall decline either fortune or honour, if I can gain them consistently with my principles, but I shall not make myself unhappy, if I miss them" (1:130). What was in reality a higher ambition required comprehensive study. At Oxford in the summer of 1772, he studied law and history seven to eight hours a day, beginning at seven and ending at midnight.

Jones's association with acquaintances was not always professional: He discussed literature with Pitt, whose creativity had been provoked by Garrick's "An Invitation to Ld. Chatham Passing into Devonshire." London was titillated by Pitt's rejecting Garrick's "landscape proudly gay" in favor of his "primæval seat." When the old statesman would not give a copy to Jones or other acquaintances, Jones heard it from Pitt's sister. It was not good verse, but Pitt's character inspired Jones to memorize the eight couplets.[6]

Of the students at the Middle Temple, Day and Arthur Lee were Jones's closest friends. The future author of *A History of Sandford and Merton* (London, 1783), Day had attended Blackstone's Oxford lectures with Jones, sharing a love of classical studies. Jones reproved his deism, the fashionable doctrine that Day followed because he believed an action was truly virtuous only if performed without hope of mortal or spiritual reward.[7] This difference was sometimes amusing:

One day, upon removing some books at the chambers of Sir William Jones, a large spider dropped upon the floor, upon which Sir William, with some warmth, said, "Kill that spider, Day, kill that spider!" "No," said Mr. Day, with that coolness for which he was so conspicuous, "I will not kill that spider, Jones; I do not know that I have a right to kill that spider! Suppose when you are going in your coach to Westminster Hall, a superior being, who, perhaps, may have as much power over you as you have over this insect, should say to his companion, 'kill that lawyer! kill that lawyer!' how should you like that, Jones? and I am sure, to most people, a lawyer is a more noxious animal than a spider.'"[8]

Lee, a Virginian who was a fellow of the Royal Society, was not admitted to the bar until 1775. His "Junius Americanus" letters had impressed American leaders, and his nationalism was influencing Jones's increasingly liberal politics. Injustice, exemplified by rotten boroughs and other corruption, was blatant. The best hope for correction lay in barristers with principles, the two men felt. Such people did not necessarily include Charles James Fox, who "is studying the law; a powerful rival! He offers twenty guineas to receive five hundred when he is Attorney-general. I cannot answer for the truth of this report; but I am not much afraid of him; though I see many wolves in one Fox" (1:124).

Jones often spent his evenings with members of Johnson's Literary Club, especially Percy. On 21 February 1772 Percy dined with Reynolds, Jones, Burke, Johnson, and others; then Jones and Percy conversed for the rest of the evening. He joined Beilby Porteus (later bishop of Chester) and others at Percy's on the night of 10 December, and he and Anthony Chamier were there on the next night. On 17 April 1773 Jones accompanied Percy and Oliver Goldsmith – who was thinking about suicide at least in the abstract – to Chatterton's fatal lodging.[9] He gave Percy an inscription copy of his *History of Nader Shah*.

Another good friend was John Paradise, who knew Turkish and six more languages, thus being one of the few European polyglots able to talk with Jones on equal terms. On 25 January 1772 they and the botanist Daniel Solander were guests at the Royal Society Club,[10] probably the only time that Jones attended one of the weekly dinners, as he was never elected.

Two days before, Jones had made the traditional statement at the Royal Society: "William Jones of the Middle Temple Esqr. Fellow of University College Oxford and of the Royal Society of Copenhagen, a Gentleman well known for his learning in polite literature and the Oriental Languages being desirous of becoming a Member of this illustrious Society. . . . " The elections book recorded this statement weekly until his election on 30 April, with his admission as a fellow on 14 May. Paradise was the first to sign the ballot, and then the physician Anthony Askew, Reynolds, Charles Morton and Matthew Maty of the British Museum, Richard Jodrell, and the explorer Reinhold Forster signed. The natural philosopher Henry Cavendish had first invited Jones as a visitor in May 1771.

Association with the society stimulated a massive study in addition to what Jones called his "unremitted application" to law. He started mastering mathematics so as to edit his father's papers. This scientific work did not violate his resolution to abandon literature, and he felt obliged to complete the work as he associated with his father's aging friends. In a year he was able to advertise the big book for subscription, retaining the general management but letting Cadell receive the money. After Jones's admission to the bar, his expanding responsibilities indicated that he could not print the book for years, and so he had Cadell return the fifty subscriptions that he had received, as well as those paid directly to Cadell. As this work was the most distant from his interests and probably no great loss to mathematics, it never appeared. Possibly he had a hand in the printing of two of his father's papers in *Philosophical Transactions* in 1771 and 1773.

Jones's Oriental reputation was continuing to attract scholars, to whom he felt an obligation. Robert Orme, historiographer of the East India Company, presented a copy of his *History of the Military Transactions of the British Nation in Indostan from the Year 1745* (London, 1763), which helped establish him as a historian. Jones praised it in polished Latin, encouraging composition of the second part (finished in 1778). Jones's exalted standard was Xenophon: "The strategy, action, and outcome are so clearly delineated by you that I thought, while reading the book, that I was actually a participant in the events, and not merely reading and imagining them" (trans., 1:113). Orme's style was exceptional, with careful, appropriate diction in an attractive arrangement: "In literary criticism this is virtually the highest praise." Macaulay later confirmed the high judgment.

Jones's praise initiated a long friendship, opening the possibility of his using the rich East India Company records. After receiving help with Persian, Orme attached a note to a letter from the Bengal Governor-General: "Mr. Jones has been so kind to explain the Persic terms in the margin, which renders the copy very curious and valuable."[11] Orme sent a copy of the second edition of the *History* (1773), which Jones termed an elegant, enjoyable treasure. He later made a loan to Orme, who paid him £200 due on 11 November 1778.

In October 1772 Jones received Hendrik Albert Schultens's just-published *Anthologia sententarium Arabicarum*. He complimented the young Leiden scholar's translation and notes, offering to help during Schultens's stay at Wadham to study Pococke's manuscript of Al-Maidání's Arabic proverbs, and urging translation of the *Hamása*. Thereupon began a scholarly correspondence rivaling that with Reviczky.

Jones went to Oxford on 19 November and remained until 11 January 1773, joining the earl of Radnor, Robert Chambers, and others at the Christmas and New Year's dinners at University College. On his return he attended the Commons debates. On 15 February he stayed till midnight, entertained by the debate about the unjust expedition against the Caribs on St.Vincent.

He spent the next Sunday at Harrow, talking with the masters to confirm Althorp's progress. Now engaged in an urbane correspondence with Lady Spencer, Jones reported that Althorp "is modest, attentive, and sweet-tempered, has fine parts and uncommon industry, which cannot fail to make him a truly valuable man" (1:121). Jones noted that although he had enjoyed the music of Sacchini's *El Cid,* he considered the dancing superior. Clearly, he wanted her to know that he had filled the musical gap in his education, for the London appearance of major composers and performers had given him a gentleman's competence in music. Lady Spencer usually agreed with him, in motherly fashion.

Soon Jones received a new honor, election to the Club. Reynolds had proposed the group in 1764, and Johnson had agreed. Other original members were Burke, Goldsmith, Topham Beauclerk, Anthony Chamier, Bennet Langton, and Christopher Nugent. Meeting weekly at the Turk's Head, they ate, drank, and talked until a late hour.[12] Membership permitted conversation and conviviality with outstanding men of the time, but the mandatory unanimous vote made election extremely difficult. Garrick and Gibbon were blackballed. Only Percy, Chambers, and George Colman were added until the election of five new members in 1773.

James Caulfeild, earl of Charlemont, was added, followed by a successful ballot for Garrick this time. Agmondesham Vesey and Jones were admitted on 2 April. Chambers proposed his Oxford colleague, with Percy recording the election of "the great Orientalist,"[13] the youngest member.

James Boswell's turn came four weeks later. Beauclerk, the earl of Charlemont, Johnson, and Reynolds accompanied Boswell to the Beauclerks' house, where they dined with Lady Diana. Burke, Garrick, Goldsmith, Jones, and Nugent ate at the Turk's Head. Boswell remained anxiously behind while the Club voted. Soon he was summoned to meet a society, as he said, such as was seldom seen. In high spirits, Goldsmith spoke of equality. Burke observed, "Here's our monarchy man growing Republican. Oliver Cromwell, not Oliver Goldsmith." Goldsmith retorted, "I'm for Monarchy to keep us equal." "Ay," said Boswell, "a King like a great rolling stone to make all smooth," Jones completed the image: "To grind to powder." Boswell concluded the entry in his journal by remarking, "Pleased to see Jones so young and jolly."[14]

Jones was already a well-liked participant in the repartee. He was never boastful; in fact, the others considered him quite modest. On one occasion Johnson and Thomas Barnard were discussing whether a man might improve himself after the age of forty-five. After Johnson expressed his opinion uncivilly, Barnard composed verses on the different perfections that one might learn from the members. One couplet was

> Jones teach me modesty – and Greek;
> Smith how to think; *Burke* how to speak.

Mrs. Hester Thrale reported: "[Johnson] pronounced one day at my house a most lofty panegyric upon Jones the Orientalist, who seemed little pleased with the praise, for what cause I know not."[15]

During the few years that Jones had been on sufficiently close terms to call on the lexicographer, they had often talked about linguistics. But in 1773 he told Parr: "We must call upon Johnson at the beginning of the week; you will win the old man's heart. As for me, my ideas of philology are so faded, and other habits of study begin so strongly to prevail, that I have no great pleasure in his conversation" (1:124). He then quoted a line from Cicero meaning "intercourse with political opponents is an unpleasant thing." Despite Johnson's keen interest in law, Jones never mentions their discussing it, perhaps because law underpinned his increasingly advanced Whig views.

Johnson admired Jones's Oriental learning. Once Boswell suggested to Johnson that the Club might set up a college in St. Andrews, which would draw a wonderful concourse of students. Entering into the spirit of the idea, Johnson made several assignments: Jones had Oriental learning; Chambers, law; and Goldsmith, poetry.[16]

One reason that Jones was invited into such groups was his incisive mind, which complemented a winsome personality. Once Wilmot sent a Chinese text, which Jones could not decipher until the weather was warm enough for him to read in the Bodleian. He recommended a Cantonese: "I cannot recollect where he lodges, but shall know when I come to town" (1:79). This was Whang Atong, whom Reynolds had befriended. Sometimes Jones joined the pair in fascinating dinners.

A more exotic acquaintance was Omiah, the chieftain whom Joseph Banks had brought from Tahiti. Jones liked Omiah: "He is a tolerable chess player, as Banks tells me; which gives me a high idea of his capacity" (1:176).[17] Banks was not yet a member of the Club; Jones met his Harrow friend mainly in the Royal Society. Sir Charles Bunbury, George Fordyce, Fox, Gibbon, and George Steevens were admitted to the Club in 1774. After Jones was called to the bar, he was often too busy to attend. The circuits took him away for months, and intricate cases in London required extensive study. On 5 April 1775, he, Burke, and Garrick were fined for absence; Jones then attended the other five meetings in 1775. The languishing state of the twenty-man group is indicated by Adam Smith's election in December by five members – Beauclerk, Gibbon, Jones, Percy, and Reynolds. In 1776 Jones attended four of the fifteen meetings; in 1777, three of the fifteen.

Probably Parr aspired to membership in the Club, even if there is no record of his asking Jones to propose him. He did request help in borrowing costumes for a play at Stanmore. Jones could not predict Garrick's reaction: "I am by no means intimate with him, and never visited him, nor paid him any other attention than common civility. I will, however, most certainly write to him (for our club will not meet till the meeting of Parliament)" (1:173).[18] This letter led to a closer association. When the two dined together in June 1776, Garrick confided that, having just retired with great éclat, he was alarmed by the queen's having told him of her hopes of seeing him act again (1:219). But once Jones had abandoned the staging of "Suleiman," he had little interest in the stage.

His new friend was Gibbon, who published volume 1 of *The History of the Decline and Fall of the Roman Empire* in 1776. Jones considered it pleasurable reading, with an elegant and easy style, but with very little verve. As Gibbon continued his vast work, he delved more deeply into Oriental matter. Jones's publications were useful, and he asked detailed questions that could not be answered in his many Eastern sources. Gibbon thanked Jones in lavish footnotes, expressing his appreciation of Jones's love of Orientalism.

This sketch of Jones's association with the Club members to the mid-1770s (excepting Johnson for now) ends with his dinner with Fox, Gibbon, and others. Gibbon had just received Richard Watson's *Apology for Christianity,* a popular antidote to Gibbon's fifteenth chapter. Jones wrote Althorp: "The company told him it was written with great civility: I hear it is a very masterly work; but, to speak sincerely, I would advise you to read it, indeed, but not to busy yourself too much with controversies of that nature" (1:224). For Jones, the truth of Christianity was highly probable, if incapable of demonstration, and a part of English law. Althorp should not be concerned with such objections as Gibbon's, though "if some men are mad enough to make objections, it is the duty of others to answer them, for the sake of the populace, who are apt to be staggered by objections of any kind, without comprehending them."

Jones had a strong integrity, which, when he publicly advocated unpopular minority positions, was to impede his career. In 1773 he was involved in an incident with political implications, which further liberalized his views. He went to Oxford in May, preparatory to receiving his M.A. degree on 18 June. As an official had asked him to speak at the Encaenia, he expected to spend a month in preparing an oration, as well as in writing the required compositions.

Jones was naive about the ramifications of Prime Minister Frederick Lord North's forthcoming installation. Its militant independence defeated in North's uncontested election, Oxford was reverting to the Restoration situation, when the chancellor was the king's favorite minister. Nathan Wetherel (Jones's master), supported by "most of the academic political connexions which had been influential in the past," played a major role.[19] The question was whether the situation could be overcome at the next vacancy for a burgess, as Jones was personally to discover. Meanwhile, there were preparations for "a greater appearance of Nobility and Persons of Fashion than has been known on any former occasion.– Great numbers of the Nobility will be accommodated with apartments in the different Colleges."[20] Reynolds, Henry James Pye (future poet laureate), and Elijah Impey (soon to be chief justice of the Bengal Supreme Court) were to receive honorary degrees.

Jones carefully composed what might be his most important oration to date. It treats scholarship and freedom of inquiry, with the avowed purpose of rebutting prejudices against men of letters. Learning does not destroy manly spirit or anticipate obsequiousness to the rich and powerful. Cambridge and Oxford surpass the classical bowers, and at Oxford one can master all disciplines under an English mentor. Jones exalts the Oxonians Lowth and Blackstone, showing that England surpasses even France in poetry, music, and mathematics. And Jones relates scholarship to liberty: Knowledge lets scholars serve "our friends, our country, and all mankind. . . . arts, literature, science, cease to be laudable, as soon as they cease to be beneficial." His abstract eulogy of liberty praises John Selden, Milton, and Locke as three of England's greatest men.

With the exception of a few pointed statements, Jones's oration is almost conventional, if one overlooks its political matrix. But after Oxford's famous scholar had been pressed to close the Encaenia with a formal oration on which he had lavished much time in articulating the scholarly spirit, those who had pressed him indicated that he was not flattering enough, though he had included nothing that could offend the most obsequious courtier. Then he realized that they wanted a slavish compliment to the ministers, which was a violation of his principles. When key Oxonians exhorted him not to read his paper without a lot of softening, he decided not to speak at all. Nor was he sorry: "Most of the compositions, that were repeated, were so full of flattery, that my bold strain would hardly have met with a favourable reception" (1:133).

As Jones was not even given a ticket, he and William Poyntz (Lady Spencer's older brother, with a Christ Church M.A.) followed the procession of North and the doctors in their scarlet robes, through the High Street and into the crowded Sheldonian. Thus they secured fairly good seats among the nearly four thousand people for the degree conferring, the English and Latin verse reading, and the concerts. The whole business amused him.

Having labored to compose, revise, memorize, and rehearse his oration in the classical manner, Jones had a few copies anonymously printed for friends. The eighteen-page *Oration Intended to Have Been Spoken in the Theatre at Oxford, on the 9th of July 1773, by a Member of the University* was not reviewed for years, until *Gentleman's Magazine* summarized it and named Jones as the author. Even then, the attempted coercion was not publicly known: "Why it was not spoken, we are not told, but have reason to rejoice, if to that we owe the pleasure of perusing it" (July 1776, pp. 317–18).

This was Jones's first political encounter. His study of common law had based his principles on the settlements of the Glorious Revolution; he acted according to his belief in personal liberties, regardless of the consequences. If subservient to royal control, the scholar could not make objective conclusions. At a time of parliamentary corruption, the insertion of harmless compliments in the *Oration* would have been conventional, but Jones's principles had rejected compromise. He could have offended powerful Oxford Tories in this initial contact with attempted restriction on freedom of the press, such as it was. The experience confirmed his course in a later confrontation with executive restrictions against political publication.

In London, as he neared the end of his studies in the Middle Temple, Jones tried to concentrate on law so as to be truly learned at his forensic debut. He ceased all mathematical studies except geometry, which had a just manner of reasoning. But the proofreading of new books again intervened, keeping him in his quarters except for exercise.

Cadell was the publisher. First, Jones ordered Oriental bindings for his *Grammaire Persanne* (1772), *Dissertation, Lettre,* and *Histoire* as French books. Second, though *The History of the Life of Nader Shah* had gone to press in March, it did not appear until 25 November. Even then, several pages did not include the running title, which he tried to insert. Vainly he urged Cadell to advertise this English abridgment in the newspapers and to have Cambridge and Oxford booksellers sell it: "I am strongly inclined to think, from the peculiar circumstances of it, and the variety, as well as novelty, of its subjects, that it will go off extremely well" (1:135–6).

Jones inserted in his *History* a new statement of his quitting Oriental studies because of his career. Reviewers like Ralph Griffiths, the influential editor of the *Monthly Review,* lamented the cessation (October 1773, p. 285); and *London Magazine* praised "the learned and ingenious writer" (December 1773, pp. 610–11). T. H. Gadebusch made German translations of Jones's *Grammaire Persanne* and *Histoire* (Greifswald, 1773).

Jones did extensive proofreading on his *Commentariorum,* which was nearing publication after seven years. In view of his comparative method and desired polish, he submitted successive revisions to various scholars. Parr thought the book was studiously designed and happily executed:

The observations are just and curious, and equally free from indiscriminate approbation, licentious censure, and excessive refinement. Through the hurry of the first composition, the same expression frequently occurs, and sentences begin in the same manner, and now and then two words are improperly combined.

These inaccuracies are very rare, and very trifling. On the whole, there is a purity, an ease, an elegance in the style, which shew an accurate and most perfect knowledge of the Latin tongue. . . . I have received infinite entertainment from this curious and learned performance.[21]

Jones had expected to publish the book in 1772, at a cost of £200, but when the plan fell through, he arranged for Cadell to have a half-share. He retained the other half, according to the Stationers' Company records (3:4). The 542-page book was advertised in the *London Chronicle* of 8 February 1774, but Richardson's slowness delayed the publication of *Poeseos Asiaticæ commentariorum libri sex, cum appendice; subjicitur Limon, seu miscellaneorum liber* until 1 March.

The book contains a dedication to Oxford ("the most illustrious of all universities, as long as she remains the most free"), a preface, a summary of the six parts, the text, and an appendix. An eloquent eight-line epilogue, "Ad musam," bids a new farewell to poetry. The preface eulogizes Sumner, who is described in Ciceronian terms as the only master qualified to educate youth, and rededicates the book to England and Oxford, for which Jones's labors are intended to be useful. Necessity, he says, now compels him to abandon literature, so as to relieve the oppressed, assist the miserable, and restrain the tyrannical. But when his career is over, he will retire to Oxford for an uninterrupted cultivation of literature.

The first part of Jones's *Commentariorum* develops his favorite thesis: Asians have an aptitude for and a devotion to poetry. Though stressing Arabs and Persians, he now adds Chinese and Turks. The second part describes poetic form, in which he reviews Asiatic metrics, described in classical terms and compared with Hebrew metrics. After introducing Arabic idyls, especially the *qasida,* he presents an Arabic elegy in Latin verse.

Persian songs receive somewhat more attention, and he compares Háfiz's ghazals with classical works.

The third part, the longest, studies Oriental imagery, which contains some fanciful figures, although some Arabic metaphors were too graphic for Jones's strong morality for him to translate. He favorably compares Asiatic poets with Apollonius, Callimachus, and Homer. There is a chapter on "relic" imagery and on the meaning of Asiatic mystical poetry, with comparisons from Anacreon. Jones's mystical examples come from Háfiz. "Exultant" poetry is compared with biblical and Greek poetry. Included in his description of amatory poetry is a Mesíhí ode presented in Latin quatrains.

The fourth part, probably the most important, discusses subject matter. As in Europe, the poetry is chiefly heroic, funereal, didactic, amatory, eulogistic, satirical, or descriptive, with a chapter devoted to each type. Firdausi, Jones believes, is the best Asian epic poet, and Jones illustrates his story of Rustum with pages in Persian and then Latin verse, which is compared with Virgil. The funereal poems are dirges or sorrowful eulogies. Didactic passages are short and modulated, expressed by contempt, taciturnity, or other means. After comparing the amatory poetry with Pindar's, Jones gives samples of laudation alongside reproduced classical passages. Perhaps the greatest Asiatic satire is Firdausi's masterpiece against Sultan Mahmud. The fourth part ends with translated descriptions of gardens, pleasant situations, and human beauty, always accompanied by the original passages.

The next part is a short chapter about Arabic, Persian, and Turkish poets. The last part, on diction, presents rhetorical, philosophical, and historical examples.

Jones's compressing the vast subject of Asiatic poetry into 473 pages, despite contemporary European ignorance, necessitated superficiality and unevenness. He omits writers and does not systematically analyze any type or poet, often describing the literature in superlatives and reducing Arabic metrical units to classical feet.[22] His desire to incorporate fresh style and matter into European poetry constantly shows through. For example, Firdausi is called the Persian Homer; Háfiz, the Persian Anacreon because of his superb drinking songs and panegyrics.

The overwhelming impression of the book is scholarship, which demands that the reader have a knowledge of classical literature. Jones wrote in Latin and illustrated copiously from Greek; yet classicists, who became his chief audience, could not read the many Persian and Arabic quotations. He avoids contemporary sources, though he does use Burke's definition of beauty from *A Philosophical Enquiry into the Origin of Our Ideas of the Sublime and Beautiful* (London, 1757). Despite such limitations, he was determined to transmit key portions of an Asiatic literary knowledge probably unrivaled in his day. This unique book deserves to be translated into English.[23] It presents information and criticism derived from his own perceptions, with little use of the commentaries. Some of its semiformulations were later to be articulated in the development of comparative literature.

The book's long appendix includes Jones's best childhood Greek and Latin compositions. Besides two prose pieces, it contains eleven Greek and six Latin poems in "Limon," a title borrowed from Cicero. Four polished Latin songs and a Latin verse translation from the Greek complete this classical, curiously discordant appendix.

Jones was wise to have revised his *Commentariorum* so painstakingly. Waiting for it even longer than they had waited for his Persian *Grammar,* the literary world expected a major achievement. Beauclerk wrote Charlemont: "Mr. Jones, of our club, is going to publish an account, in Latin, of the eastern poetry, with extracts translated verbatim in verse. I will order Elmsly to send it to you when it comes out; I fancy it will be a very pretty book."[24] The book was enthusiastically received by both Continental and English Orientalists. Thomas Hunt, who had criticized the manuscript for Jones, lauded its striking observations and judicious criticism, and expressed the hope that the book would become "what you intended it to be, an happy instrument in the hands of learned and inquisitive men, for unlocking the rich treasures of wisdom and knowledge" preserved in Oriental languages.[25] English periodicals also praised Jones's extensive learning, pure taste, and elegant style. *Gentleman's Magazine* termed him "this truly classical writer" (Suppl., 1774, p. 624). John Langhorne, in the *Monthly Review,* liked "the happy imitative powers and command of language which Mr. Jones possesses, in so eminent a degree" (July 1774, p. 22).

In the book, Jones was one of the first to work with two charming poems by Anacreon. Their modern state is at least partly due to the attentions of this unusual scholar of understanding and grasp of the manuscript tradition,[26] who had now achieved international fame. In 1777 Gottfried Eichhorn produced a second edition of the book, wisely omitting "Limon." Gibbon later recalled: "I have perused with much pleasure Sir William Jones's Latin Commentary on Asiatic Poetry (London, 1774, in octavo), which was composed in the youth of that wonderful linguist."[27]

During much of Jones's publishing experience in England, he was seeking an arrangement for the best printing, distributing, and profits. For a time he considered Richardson's printing for Cadell to be the best solution. But

Cadell's large business made him dilatory, and sometimes reports to his authors omitted important information. As Jones now bought books only out of profits from his publications, he asked: "I am desirous of seeing *how many* copies of my two works have been sold here and abroad, since they were published, and *for what,* and like wise, on the other side, what the expenses &c. amounted to, and consequently how many copies of the impression remain unsold" (1:259). Also, he had heard that few copies of the *Commentariorum* were available in Amsterdam. When Cadell's reply raised further questions, Jones chided him as to whether he did not have insurance covering the 1776 fire.[28] This third-person letter, Jones's most formal communication to him, shows impatience. Jones would now change publishers.

Having traced the story of Jones's *Commentariorum,* we can return to 1773. He went to Oxford about 10 December before going to Cambridge. It was a pleasant vacation: "I shall become a member of this University, as well as of Oxford; for the convenience of having access to many rare Manuscripts in our Laws and History, which are not any where else; besides, I receive all imaginable civility from this Academical body, and they vie with each other in obliging and entertaining me" (1:139). On 6 January he was admitted as a pensioner at Emmanuel. Perhaps, like Percy, he was considering taking a Cambridge doctorate. Bennet, now a fellow and chief tutor at Emmanuel, welcomed him. He was urged to enjoy a week of music by leading artists at Hinchinbrook, where the earl of Sandwich was entertaining the whole county and University. Jones reluctantly turned down his Royal Society colleague so as to study law and go through his Elzevir's ten-volume edition of Cicero (Leiden, 1642). Pollard's apartment at Emmanuel was next to Jones's, and having earlier fenced together, now they became close.

Back in London, Jones anticipated admission to the bar on 28 January. His principles were firm, drawn primarily from reading. He believed in

the justice of the highest court in this kingdom, which always regulates its decrees by the soundest principles of equity, and which claims it as its distinguishing prerogative to protect the weak and friendless; and I may truly say, and I hope not arrogantly, that, while I wear the gown, no helpless or injured person of any nation shall want an advocate, without a fee, in any of our courts. (1:142)

Jones wanted to make an impressive debut, showing extensive legal knowledge and masterly oratory. Yet even his immersion in classical principles and methods did not give him total confidence, for he had never heard his own voice in court. He solved this problem in the Court of King's Bench:

When I first spoke, I cured myself in some measure, of my terrors, by considering, that out of an hundred hearers, not above five, perhaps, were judges of my speaking; and I thought it inconsistent, to speak with confidence before those *few* in private, yet to be alarmed at speaking before them, when there were ninety-five more in company, who did not know whether I spoke well or ill. (1:145–6)

The case involved the separation of a husband and a wife, with the court to decide custody of the daughter:

A perfect silence prevailed – the attention of all present being attracted to hear what "Linguist Jones," as he was even then called, would say. . . . I believe this was his forensic debut; he, nevertheless, spoke with the utmost distinctness and clearness, not at all disconcerted by the novelty of his situation. His tone was highly declamatory, accompanied with what Pope has called "balancing his hands," and he seemed to consider himself as much a public orator as Cicero or Hortensius could have done. His oration, for such it must be called, lasted, I recollect, near an hour.[29]

Ironically, Jones was trying to be an orator, perhaps seeking to set a standard, and so the comparison with Cicero would have pleased him. Yet his mannerism made a less favorable impression than did the conventional approach employed by Thomas Erskine, who also made his debut about this time. And another problem troubled Jones's debut when he mentioned a previous case:

He stated in the same high declamatory tone in which he had delivered the whole of his speech, that he found "that it had been argued *by one Mr. Baldwin.*" Not being very conversant with the state of the bar, he did not know that this *one Mr. Baldwin* was, at the time of which I am speaking, a barrister in great business, and was then sitting not half a yard from the orator's elbow. It occasioned a smile, or perhaps more than a smile, on every countenance in Court; but the orator proceeded as steadily as before.

Shortly thereafter Jones referred to the daughter's governess in terms indicating that she was too improper to remain with the child. The next morning he resumed in his declamatory tone, begging to inform the court that he had learned with the deepest regret that, in what he had had the honor to say, he had been misinterpreted as calling the governess a harlot. "The gravity of every countenance in Court yielded to the attack thus made upon it, and a general laugh was produced."[30] After the judges stopped laughing, they assured him that he had conveyed no unfavorable idea of her morals. Thus some practical joker apparently misled Jones and nicely punctured his artificial manner.

A friend, probably Chamier (now deputy secretary of war), reported intriguing news: John Robinson, the secretary of the treasury, was likely to retire or die from a serious illness. If so, the acting secretary would succeed him, thus vacating the post of undersecretary to the secretary of state for the Northern Department. Would Jones accept if offered it? He replied that he would accept any post of equal confidence in which he could serve his king and country, if he could still occasionally plead as a barrister. The friend promised to pursue the matter. As Jones was planning to leave on his first circuit, where he would be isolated, he tried to see Lady Spencer. When he was unsuccessful, he wrote her a long letter asking to be notified if she heard of the undersecretary's resignation. Such a post would not remain vacant long, and the profession of law bore real fruit only in twenty years: "I should not be at all eager to raise myself so early, if I were not desirous that my mother should partake of my prosperity while she lives" (1:143).

Jones planned to join his new colleagues as a counsel at the semiannual assizes, in the Lent season and in the summer. The Oxford circuit began with Berkshire (rotating between Reading and Abingdon) and proceeded to Oxfordshire, where he would stay in college. Next came Worcestershire and Worcester City, Gloucestershire and Gloucester City, Monmouthshire, Herefordshire, Staffordshire, and Shropshire. At the sessions the judges of the high court of justice, who chose their respective circuits, chiefly tried prisoners and causes at *nisi prius*.

Most of the counsel on the Welsh circuits first followed the Oxford one, apparently being entitled to practice because they were barristers of the Inns of Court. The South Wales sessions were held semiannually in each county town for six days, operating like the Court of King's Bench in England and holding Pleas of Assizes like the Common Pleas.[31] One justice served three counties for an annual fee of £50. Another served the circuit that Jones chose – Carmarthen, Cardigan, Pembroke, and Carmarthen borough and Pembroke town.

He never joined the 1774 circuits. Planning for six weeks of travel was so complicated that he decided not to join the spring circuit until Stafford. Then heavy rains, together with his scholarly application, made him decide to study more and usefully observe his profession. As he must be absolutely ready when he began practicing, so as to meet his own high standards, he elected to miss the summer circuit, too. His career would begin with the new parliament.

In September Jones vacationed at Margate. Permitting himself more leisure than he had had in months, in the mornings he swam and rode horseback, and he explored Thanet to visualize Roman history. His afternoons were devoted to law, with two readings of Isaac Watts's famous *Logick* (London, 1725). To do more reading, he avoided the social rooms and aristocratic friends who were vacationing there.

Back in London, Jones threw himself into his profession: "The Term

. . . allows me no leisure from seven in the morning till midnight, when I am generally overpowered with sleep" (1:173). As the statement in his *Commentariorum* that he had concluded his last major Oriental work had surprised scholars, he declined the friendly expostulations of Schultens, whom he met during the Arabist's study at Oxford. In London he kept materials only on law and oratory: "I have decided to work hard for at least twenty years at only legal or political studies" (trans., 1:166).

Scholars' questions, coupled with their praise of the *Commentariorum,* made Jones's complete abandonment of Orientalism impossible. He wrote Johann David Michaelis, a biblical expert, that he would not write or even think about Asiatic poetry; yet his answer to Michaelis's question had required him to read the German's *Recueil de questions, proposées a une société de savants* (Amsterdam, 1774). Carl Godfrey Woide, a Polish Orientalist, had asked him about a problem raised by Michaelis and presumably presented *Recueil,* but Jones had been unable to go to Oxford to check sources and confer with Lowth.[32]

In 1774 Jones's significant scholarly correspondence expanded. Hunt, delighted by an inscription copy of the *Commentariorum,* urged him to explore Hebrew. Next, John Alleyne, whom he knew at the Middle Temple, asked linguistic questions about the Bible, necessitating work with Arabic and Hebrew. The answers helped Alleyne complete *The Legal Degrees of Marriage Stated and Considered* (London, 1774), and appropriately the advertisement to Alleyne's second edition (1775) praised Jones's "able and critical exposition" of Leviticus.

The Spanish scholar Francisco Pérez Bayer sent his *La Conjuracion de Catilina y la Guerra de Jugurta . . . del Alfabeto y Lengua de los Fenices y de Sus Colonias* (Madrid, 1772). In return, Jones sent a copy of the *Commentariorum* by the antiquarian Robert Darley Waddilove (embassy chaplain at Madrid), who requested criticism of *La Conjuracion* for a Latin edition. Waddilove included news about deciphered Moorish inscriptions, along with a translation of Sallust by Don Gabriel, Charles III's son. This was not being formally published; a few magnificent copies were being given to kings and universities. Jones responded with a learned letter about Spanish and Spanish literature, generalizing about ruling families:

In Spain the brilliance of the fine arts and the sciences will greatly increase, since the young Spanish prince is endowed with such intelligence and learning that he can brilliantly interpret the prince of Roman historians and can illuminate Sallust's work with erudite notes. . . . For an ordinary scholar to do all this would be praiseworthy; for a young man, it would merit outstanding honour, whereas for a young man who is also prince of young men (heir-apparent), the highest honours should be announced by public proclamation. (trans., 1:161)

Jones recommended that Gabriel carefully read Cicero, particularly the letter warning rulers to shun tempting art, beautiful women, and money.

A valuable manuscript of the Islamic poet Al-Mutanabbí was relayed from the traveler Edward Wortley Montagu, who paid Jones many compliments introduced by an Arabic verse letter. Jones stored the manuscript at University College, modestly answering: "How little I have deserved the many honours I have lately received from the learned in Europe and Asia; I can ascribe their politeness to nothing but their candour and benevolence" (1:158).[33]

To Schultens he recounted meeting James Bruce, who had recently returned from an attempt to discover the source of the Nile. Bruce had been peevish and resentful:

[Bruce] may be trying to be like my pet "French" monkey Perron! The Enoch book, which he had deposited in the Royal Library in Paris, was copied, with no deception intended, by a worthy man whom you know, Woide or Voide, who is Polish or Hungarian. But then Bruce became angry and refused to give Woide a chance to see him, although Woide had suffered all the indignity and inconvenience of travelling to see this arrogant man. Banks the Englishman and Solander behave ever so much better than this, and they have travelled much further afield and endured much graver perils. (trans., 1:169)

Commending Schultens's long study resulting in *Specimen proverbiorum Meidanii* (London, 1773), Jones encouraged Schultens's friend Everardus Scheidius to complete his *Abu Nasri Ismaëlis ebn Hammad Al-Gieuharii* (Harderwijk, 1776).

Lytton (Richard Warburton), who had inherited Knebworth Park in Hertfordshire, invited Jones and Parr for dinner. An eccentric, he had married Jodrell's sixteen-year-old daughter. The pair were her guardians. Parr ranked Lytton second only to Jones in Oriental languages.[34] At the dinner was Thomas Maurice, who wanted to impress Jones, "this superior genius, by translating into English some of the very elegant Latin poems which occasionally flowed from his pen, and were circulated in manuscript among his more select acquaintances." These translations received Jones's applause and "proved the prelude to a long series of obliging attentions." Maurice often called on Jones, arriving one morning and finding Percy there.[35]

Jones went to Oxford for the Christmas vacation in 1774. His rooms there seemed particularly agreeable, partly because he could relax. The weeks were not wholly leisurely, for he had a rule that he should become wiser or better every day. For amusement he composed an elaborate self-testing list crystallizing his conclusions about education. Naming it an *an-*

drometer (*andro-* 'man' + *meter* 'measure'), he explained it to Althorp:
One's mind should develop in step with one's strength and physical activity:

It will enable you to *measure* every *man's* merit by looking for his *age* in the scale,
and then comparing it with the other side, and seeing to what *degree* he has risen
in arts, sciences and ornamental qualifications. Thus, if at age 16 he has composed
and translated in prose and verse, chiefly in his own language, if he has learned
the Greek, Latin and French tongues grammatically, and so on to the bottom of
the scale, we may be sure that he has kept his station in the road to Glory; and if
he has acquired still higher accomplishments, as oratory and publick speaking, we
may then pronounce, that he has risen a *degree* above his age. (1:175)[36]

Jones had been behind schedule at eighteen, knowing "little of history,
less of law, and nothing of mathematicks." Despite years lost on Oriental
rambles, he had almost reached the degree specified for his twenty-eight
years, but not quite the degree when Cicero began to take part in public
affairs.

Though Jones called the andrometer a joke, it was also a stern schedule.
The achievements of Cicero and Demosthenes were mirrored in the pro-
gression, and they were realistic models for few people; however, Jones
always pushed himself. Such testing lists, though not as finely calibrated,
were not uncommon in his day. Franklin used one; Boswell did not, but
there is constant self-examination in his journal.

After his happy, four-year residence on Duke Street, Jones was finally
able to move into the Temple, an area between Fleet Street and the
Thames. His quarters were in Lamb Building, the principal edifice within
the Middle Temple.[37] His days were busy. For example, on 7 February
1775 he called on Lady Spencer at St. James's Place, then went to the
Court of Chancery, where an important point of law was argued. That
afternoon he met Spencer by appointment, so as to secure admission to
the Lords–Commons conference in the painted chamber. After Pitt's overwhelming defeat in proposing American reconciliation by removing the
British troops from Boston, the Commons requested the Lords' concurrence in a loyal address declaring the colonies to be in a state of rebellion.
In the Lords' debate Jones silently identified himself with the Opposition
and stood for more than four hours as Rockingham and others attempted
to block the resolution, perceiving the debate as an *Iliad*-like battle. Finally
it passed by eighty-seven to twenty-seven votes, with eighteen Lords' "Dis-
sentient" that it amounted to a declaration of war.[38] After dinner Jones
studied for two hours, having passed a day modeled on Cicero.

Satisfied that his preparation was adequate, he made plans to begin the
spring circuit: "I promise myself great pleasure in travelling through eight
or nine counties in England and part of Wales; I shall see, as the poet says,

many men and many cities, and expect to return in April with a variety of new ideas" (1:185). Romantically recalling Ulysses, Jones set out on the first of eight years of circuits, with the twin goals of helping people and learning more about human nature and legal conduct. His colleagues, he discovered, had "easy and agreeable manners with the utmost liberality of sentiments" (1:185–92). Few cases were tried at Reading, because parliamentary business prevented the famous lawyer John Dunning and others from attending.

Jones took up residence at Oxford, where several unpleasant cases ended the way others did on the circuit. For instance, a journeyman shoemaker was ordered executed and dissected for murdering his master. A capital conviction for theft of a mare was reprieved at the last minute. Four people were ordered transported for seven years for separate thefts of wheat, spoons, silver, and food. Another thief was to be "burnt in the hand" and to serve a year at hard labor. There were similar harsh judgments for other crimes.

Because his little gray horse could not make the long journey, Jones engaged hacks for himself and a servant. In a select party he reached Woodstock and then took a miserable road under incessant showers to Worcester on 12 March. After those assizes were finished, the lawyers rode to Enville, where Serjeant James Adair, a serjeant at law, treated them to claret to celebrate his election to the Commons. At Stafford they were joined by Dunning, who had been summoned to lead an important case. When it had to be deferred, the Whig who was to figure significantly in Jones's career left "with 300 guineas for not opening his lips: He means however, like a man of honour, to attend the trial next circuit without a fee." At Ludlow, Jones romantically toured the ruined castle where Milton had written *Comus.*

The weather was delightful except for snow at Hereford, where there was little business. The lawyers were entertained at a ball, where Jones danced with a very pretty woman. They invited the junior canons of the cathedral to supper. In the summer an elite group of ten lawyers always sailed down the Wye to Monmouth. Their acceptance of Jones is reflected in the fact that they promised to add him at the next vacancy in the group. He and two friends then left the circuit, skipping Monmouth and Gloucester, to enter Wales. At Llandovery they dined with the judges, with whom they lived "in perfect familiarity." At Carmarthen he secured excellent lodgings, which he decided to keep.

As a new lawyer on the Oxford circuit, Jones had been involved in only three or four cases. But as the son of a Welshman, in Wales he immediately participated in a variety: "We have a court of chancery as well as of common law, we make motions, we draw bills and answers, and special pleadings, and we try causes both civil and criminal." He did not get to make a set speech, which was always made by the senior: "If Cicero himself or Hortensius had been Englishmen, they would have had no opportunity of showing their oratory for some years." He would have to be an apprentice for four or five years. Five days of continual hurry brought him much larger gains than anticipated. At Haverfordwest he was advocate for four men accused of murder, but his success troubled him because he suspected one to be guilty. The circuit ended at Cardigan. Jones had received infinite pleasure from the two circuits, discovering that his profession could provide adequate worldly honors and advantages. Leaving on 19 April, he stayed at Oxford until 24 April.

Here he heard discouraging news: Robinson's return to the Treasury ended any hope of Jones's gaining the undersecretaryship; and so a few weeks later, hearing of another promising place, he wrote Lady Spencer. Personally esteeming Robinson, he was as grateful as if he had become the undersecretary: "It has left me impressed with an equal sense of gratitude to my lord and your Ladyship for the kind zeal with which you listened to me" (1:57).

The new place was the duke of Devonshire's auditorship. Jones had been at a ball until quite late, when he learned of Beaumont Hotham's promotion that day to the seat of a baron in the Exchequer. At 2:00 A.M. he penned a request that Lady Spencer recommend him before a successor was named, that is, if she thought him worthy. The auditorship was in his "very line." He did not specify her obvious influence: Her daughter Georgiana was the duke's wife. When Lady Spencer immediately asked how she should forward Jones's application without actually requesting the post, he hurried an answer to her. She might say that he had offered his services and that his studies had qualified him, while disclaiming any intention of bypassing Devonshire's choice. But he would not apply unless she thought a direct application proper: "If there be the least chance of success, every hour is precious, where there are so many competitors." She tried, but the lucrative surveying of the lands and an annual voyage went to Devonshire's longtime steward, of whose interest Jones had known. Jones thanked her for her efforts, rendered despite her indisposition during one tremulous day: "Had your letter contained an account of my success, I should not have felt a warmer sense of gratitude for your kind act of friendship" (1:196).

On 25 May he received an impressive honor, admission as a fellow of the Society of Antiquaries, for which he had been recommended by his Lincoln's Inn friend Edmund Calamy, James (Athenian) Stuart, and William Norris (the secretary). Another bright spot of 1775 was Jones's summer circuit. He stayed at Oxford while attending the Abingdon and Oxford sessions, becoming friends with the judges – Hotham and Sir James Eyre. One great pleasure was his joining the ten-man group on the boat trip down the Wye. It was a luxurious day, with panoramas of castles, concluded by a feast even grander than the lawyers' usual meals.

When the Oxford circuit ended on 19 August, Jones and two other lawyers spent the eight days before the Carmarthen circuit in touring North Wales. Again he described his travels in a report to Althorp enriched by allusions ranging from Cicero to Lyttelton (1:196–205). A day's ride took them to Chester, where, following the Dee, they visited tin mines and then St. Winifred's Well. That evening they went to St. Asaph; Bishop Shipley was away, but his son William (the dean) urged them to stay the night. Lacking the time, however, they visited a baronet and sampled his tasty fruits. After their horses were ferried across to Conway, they went to Bangor and hired a boat. At Viscount Bulkeley's manor they had a light meal and discussed an actor's paper war with a duchess. Jones did not challenge Bulkeley's remark that "persons of rank were already treated with too little respect," but to Althorp he stressed that mere rank does not entitle one to great respect unless one is virtuous and meritorious. The trio next visited the nearby druidic ruins. Once they left the Irish Road, the roads and inns were terrible. At Caernarvon they joined the judge and North Wales circuiteers at dinner. After viewing the castle ruin they traveled beside Snowdon and large lakes to "the most romantick scenes in the world." Overtaking Daines Barrington (the other judge), they all enjoyed a gallop along the coastal road before traversing Festiniog to Harlech. After taking the sea ferry, they crossed the mountains, and from Aberdovey they crossed a rather dangerous arm of the sea, reaching Aberystwyth by dinner. On the last day Jones's little gray horse tired, but unable to hire another horse or a chaise, he rode it the forty miles to Cardigan.

The Welsh circuit began on 28 August, and he finished this second experience of travel-cum-business with a goodly share of cases. Reaching Oxford on 19 September, he stayed there three weeks. His gray was still fresh after the seven hundred miles, but he retired it to a meadow along the Cherwell. He was tired but pleased, for his profession seemed likely to support him in a manner that he would never have had the conscience to expect the Spencers to do had he remained with them.

Jones resumed his studies until the term began on 6 November, whereupon he was continually at Westminster Hall. The last bright spot of 1775 – the first official recognition of his legal distinction – came in December. The lord chancellor appointed him as one of the sixty commissioners of bankruptcy. Later he publicly thanked Bathurst: "Without any solicitation, or even request on my part, You gave me a substantial and permanent token of regard, which You rendered still more valuable by Your obliging manner of giving it."[39] This office, which Jones viewed as his first step in public advancement, served a valuable function, but the hours consequently subtracted from his law practice made it less lucrative than the £100 it paid per annum.

Pollard had been admitted to the Middle Temple, where he enjoyed "the advice and soothing friendship of Mr. Jones, with whom he daily associated, either at dinner, or in the enjoyment of a literary evening." Their friendship was lifelong. Pollard thought Jones had an ideal relationship with his mother, to whom he owed so much: "He was all-sufficient, tender, attentive, and affectionate, invariably reserving one day in each week to a domestic party; of which, in due time, he invited me to partake, at her private lodging with his sister."[40]

Recalling his earlier Christmas at Cambridge, Jones hoped to have a leisurely stay at Emmanuel. However, his commissionership and a full schedule made him restrict his visit to Christmas week. Although he had hoped that Althorp would have matriculated at Trinity by now, at least he enjoyed seeing Bennet before returning home for a hurried two days and then to Oxford for the quarter sessions, where he pleaded several causes until 10 January 1776.

Just before Jones departed for the circuit, Althorp presented an elegant, twenty-volume edition of Cicero, which showed his former pupil's advancement in learning. Indeed, Jones was tempted to reread all of Cicero, although his profession temporarily precluded that pleasure. To him, Cicero was almost the only person who was truly a "great man." His letters to Althorp were now more political, reflecting his associations with Americans like Lee and a hatred for injustice derived partly from the classics. Shipley and Parr were also influencing Jones. Day had just published *The Devoted Legions,* an anonymous classical satire: "I like it extremely, not only because I know and esteem the author, but because I begin to be as warm as your friend the bishop of St. Asaph in condemning the American War" (1:213).

Starting the 1776 spring circuit, Jones stayed at Oxford until 10 March, a long residence that caused him to miss the Worcester assizes. After successfully completing the Carmarthen circuit, he prolonged a pleasant stay at University College to 24 April.

Lady Spencer, accepting his offer to help the poor, requested legal aid to personal charities and her Society for Charitable Purposes. She had befriended a penniless Syrian, and Jones had gotten Robinson to prevail upon North to discharge the man's debts and send him home: "If I had not continually pleaded with important men in England, who have greatest influence with the King, he would either have lived on in London in great misery or else have died" (trans., 1:169).[41] Through such cases Jones met Lady Spencer's charitable society, including John Burrows (rector of Hadley, St. Clement Dane's) and Burrows's sisters, who were Blue Stockings. Her newest case involved an old will, a dishonest executrix, and an unsuccessful effort for a year and a half to assist a poor woman.

In the spring Jones spent a week at Cambridge, staying at Emmanuel, where he was delighted by Althorp's learning and friends. He was especially impressed by Philip Yorke, the future earl of Hardwicke; Frederick Ponsonby, Viscount Duncannon; and William Pitt.

From time to time Jones visited Johnson, who was bearing his gout with good humor. He insisted on composing Goldsmith's epitaph for Westminster Abbey in Latin; Jones first teased him by suggesting Greek or Arabic as equal alternatives. Then Jones and five others expostulated with him, recommending English: "Some body said that Dr. Warton and most of Goldsmith's friends were of our opinion – 'What! said Johnson, is Warton too such a fool?' An elegant compliment to the company!" (1:219). But Johnson triumphed, disregarding the round robin sent by Burke and others that urged English. Jones did not sign it, for he was not at Reynolds's dinner when the group decided to compose it.

Soon Jones was off on the summer circuit, beginning with a sojourn at Oxford until 18 July and then following the entire circuit. There were "fine weather, excellent roads, cheerful company, perfect health, amusement, business, causes, speeches, gold, fame" (1:221). On the way home he visited the Chepstow estate of Valentine Morris, whom he had met some years before Morris became governor of St. Vincent. Jones then went briefly to Oxford.

In London he was at once busy at Guildhall: "I sate the other day as judge, and had a point learnedly argued before me by two advocates: we delivered our opinions solemnly; my assessors were of a different opinion from me, and they, being a majority, prevailed" (1:221). His commissionership, studies, and a heavy schedule of advising clients on legal points prevented the visit to Amsterdam that he had promised Schultens. After an intermittent fever confined him for weeks, he was at Oxford from 4 to 10 October for air and exercise, taking quantities of cinchona for malaria.

Fully recovered, he resumed his duties, attending the important debates in the Commons, as he did until 1783. His evaluations were often oratorical:

[Fox] spoke extremely well on Thursday; but I cannot prevail with him to compose his speech, in the manner of the Ancients, for the publick eye. He is a man of very quick and lively parts; but I think he wishes rather to display them than to convince his audience. Were I in parliament (which I sincerely do not wish to be, though I suppose it will be my fate some time or other) I would speak with more effect, or not at all, and I would, certainly, write my speeches afterwards for the inspection of my countrymen. (1:223)

Sometimes Jones was severe:

Lord Chatham spoke with a notable vigour for a veteran orator, and your bishop [Shipley] pronounced an elegant harangue. . . . Charles Fox poured forth with amazing rapidity a continued invective against lord G. Germaine; and Burke was so pathetick, that many declare they saw him shed tears. The ministers in both houses were sullen and reserved; but lord Sandwich boldly contradicted the duke of Richmond on the state of the navy. I grieve, that our senate is dwindled into a school of rhetorick, where men rise to display their abilities rather than to deliberate, and wish to be admired without hoping to convince. (1:247-8)

Recently Jones had been reviewing classical oratory. His exploration led to less noted orators like Isaeus, who may have been Demosthenes' guide in speaking because of his effective style. Jones enjoyed having "the same instructor in the laws of Athens and forensic eloquence" (1:226). Delighted with Isaeus' reasoning and manly sense, he translated into English the original Greek and the Latin version of the extant speeches, and by December he was writing a commentary.

Because his books were now producing profits, Jones was able to expand his law library. Though the income from his law practice was modest, he had his quarters in the Temple redecorated. He decided to take a month's vacation at Bath with a few friends, where he conversed with them and enjoyed the countryside rather than dancing and going to parties. Bath was crowded but he mixed little; and so when he reached Oxford on 7 January 1777, he was unable to answer questions about the new assembly rooms, concerts, gambling, and other "nonsense," as he termed such activities. But he had enjoyed the leisure and self-denial, despite one unhappy moment. With the arrival of news about General Washington's forced evacuation of New York City, he felt insulted when strangers exulted. Instead, "I sigh and pant for a reconciliation; but tremble at the idea of seeing our colonies extirpated . . . or, before the end of the eighteenth century, we shall see an end of law and liberty in England" (1:229). This was his strongest known statement about the war to date; he was becoming an advanced Whig.

At Oxford a letter from St. Vincent awaited him. There was some Arabic writing from a recently purchased black slave, whom Morris was using as a shepherd. Jones could only rationalize that such indulgence, as long as the detestable traffic in human beings continued, might be acceptable, as the black might be seized again and resold to a bad master. There was a new request from Parr, who had enlisted Jones's aid in a hopeless case of an insane Englishman imprisoned in Calais. Stanmore had declined so much that Parr now wanted the vacant headmastership at the Colchester grammar school. Johnson (by way of Bennet Langton), Jones, and others were being asked for recommendations. Accordingly, Jones devoted 19 January to writing the letters. He finished by the evening post, but it was too late for his servant to make copies for the successful candidate.

After the long ride home the next day, Jones pursued his usual relentless schedule until he went back to Oxford from 4 to 7 March to begin the 1777 spring circuit. The pattern continued – moderate success on the Oxford circuit, and real profits on the Carmarthen one. There was hardly a day in Wales when he did not make a speech, either as accuser or defender. He had earlier adjudged English laws preferable to Roman laws. Now he preferred the Roman procedure, in which one chose one's side, rather than having to be retained as an advocate by one side before knowing its merits.

Returning home by way of Oxford, Jones learned of a development that might let him use his talents nationally. John Millachip, freeman and liveryman of London, had been impressed. After the Admiralty denied the city's request for discharge on the grounds that Millachip's position did not exempt him from service if he were liable, on 27 March a court affirmed the city's right to claim his discharge. When he was still not released, the city's marshal went to Portsmouth with a writ of habeas corpus. Perhaps at Lord Mayor Wilkes's suggestion, Jones was taken into the city's confidence. If the government could not prevent the case from being argued, Jones would have the great pleasure of speaking against impressment "and of being able to say hereafter 'prima cause *publica* pro Libertate dicta' " (1:232). Then startling news arrived: After Millachip was freed, a press gang seized him. The city decided to apply for a new writ of habeas corpus and to prosecute the officers involved. Back in London, Jones found himself potentially opposing Edward Thurlow (attorney general) and Alexander Wedderburn (solicitor general), who were preparing the defense. Despite a taxing schedule, he studied old cases for the city. In the preliminary hearing on 17 June, Dunning urged Millachip's release because of his office. Although Jones had prepared materials for a three-hour speech, the important case was postponed.

The delay was disconcerting. He had been planning a trip to Rome, part business and part pleasure. If the case were argued while he was away, he would never forgive himself, as he was now an expert on impressment. Even if the case never came up, he intended to publish his intended speech: "This opposition to *prerogative* is not, you will say, the road to preferment. I know it, my dear friend, and am wholly unconcerned about it" (1:241).[42]

Canceling the trip to Rome, Jones planned a week with Althorp at Whitsuntide. He bought a tall chestnut to carry him to Cambridge, but "unseasonable abominable provoking business" kept him in town and made him return the horse (1:236). He had been looking forward to seeing the young Pitt, who had recently stopped by his quarters when he was out.

That spring he declined tempting invitations for him to indulge in Orientalism. Ralph Griffiths, whose *Monthly Review* always treated Jones's books kindly, asked him to review Nathaniel Halhed's *Code of Gentoo Laws* (London, 1776), which would later influence his career. Despite his esteem for Halhed, Jones's dedication to his profession left him no time to read the book. Then, proposing a critical miscellany intended as a periodical, Schultens asked Jones to search his shelves for any completed writing. The Arabist would willingly translate it into Latin, and Latin scholars would check the version before it appeared, with or without Jones's name. But his *Commentariorum* was intended to be his last major nonlegal work. His continual study, judicial obligations, legal advising, thinking about speeches, and conducting cases barely left him time for meals. He discreetly overlooked Schultens's suggestion that he ask Elmsly to accept twenty copies on assignment.

Jones now had a satisfactory arrangement with William Bowyer's Press, which had just done the second edition of his *Poems,* and this connection continued when John Nichols took over after Bowyer's death. Nichols did nine books for Jones by 1783, frequently doing the printing for the brothers Charles and Edward Dilly, who were then the publisher.

The main change in Jones's *Poems* was the addition of twelve Latin works entitled "Carminum Liber," including five reprinted from "Limon." These impressed the reviewer in the *Monthly Review:* "We attend to this second edition of Mr. Jones's elegant poems, and on account of some additional Latin poems, which are, in every respect, worthy of their learned and ingenious Author" (October 1777, p. 326).

To Jones, the dedication to Lady Spencer was an important addition, as the need for a new edition of *Poems* gave him the opportunity to express his gratitude publicly for her earlier assistance. As the first edition had had no dedication, he suggested that her "name would, doubtless, give great splendour to the list of its encouragers, and it could not fail of success with such a patroness" (1:130). Securing her permission, he first attempted a metrical dedication, but he had not composed poetry for so long that he had to be content with an inscription: "To the Right Honorable *The Countess Spencer,* these Eastern pieces, and, particularly, the poem of *Solima,* are most respectfully inscribed by her ladyship's most obliged and faithful servant, *The Author.*" She was pleased: "I shall always look upon that poem, as a model you have set up for my imitation, and shall only be sorry I do not approach nearer to it."[43]

Parr proudly wrote in his inscription copy of the second edition: "The gift of the writer, my schoolfellow and friend." He also received *Opera et fragmenta veterum poetarum Latinorum profanorum et ecclesiasticorum* (London, 1713). He told Jones how he had been allured by the title *Joannis Meursii elegantiæ Latini sermonis, seu Aloisia Sigaea Toletana, de arcana amoris & veneris* (Leiden, 1774). Thinking the notorious book to be philological, he had read only a few pages before discovering his mistake. Hearing the story, Jones laughed at him as an ignoramus. But fearing that his pupils might find the book, he gave it to Jones.[44] Jones later strongly recommended him to Lowth, bishop of Oxford, who was quite impressed.[45]

Jones had long known Lowth. In his *Commentariorum* he acknowledged the inspiration of *Prælectiones,* and in his Persian *Grammar* he praised Lowth's book on English grammar. Now he anticipated Lowth's translation of Isaiah. The two were good friends. Indeed, when Jones offered condolences at the death of Lowth's son, he was overwhelmed with anguish for the suffering father. Pollard called soon after, and Jones still showed his grief: "Alas! Pollard, who would be a father!"[46]

Jones went to Oxford from 6 to 14 July and traveled on the 1777 summer circuit. By now he was friends with most of the circuiteers. Eyre was again a judge on the Oxford circuit. Another friend was George Hardinge, who often rode with Jones. Walpole's correspondent, Hardinge had taken an expensive trip to the Continent, prompting Jones's sonnet urging him to forget low desire and emulate Lord Chancellor Earl Camden and Demosthenes.[47]

The Welsh labors fatigued Jones. But after he returned to Oxford for a fortnight, he completely relaxed, finally reading Jacob Bryant's *New System,* which he considered entertainment rather than scholarship because of the uncertain system and fanciful etymologies. It was one of the few long works unrelated to law that he had read in years. On his way to London he spent two delightful days with Bryant, whom he wanted Althorp to meet: "I love the man and am wonderfully diverted with his book. I am sure you would like him" (1:242). This warmth continued until Jones had to react publicly to Bryant's expansive speculative theorizing.

Because one invitation arrived late, he missed a pleasurable visit at Midgham Hall on his way home. After the difficulty with Mrs. Poyntz as the tutorship was ending, he had now been accepted into the large family like a brother. Her son William had inherited her estate and was enjoying life as a sportsman.

Jones resumed his work in Guildhall, spending many nights in tracing complicated points through many volumes. The 1777 edition of Philidor's chess book was serving as an excellent work on logic because of its science and exact reasoning. Jones also was correcting his translation of Isaeus in his leisure and studying cases with a view to composing a vast legal work in a few years. The quarter sessions took him to Oxford until 12 October, when, as usual, he made himself hoarse by striving to communicate law and reason to the justices. He was beginning to perceive law as a science that had its own internal logic.

During these years Jones frequently attended the Royal Society, bringing nine different visitors, including Schultens, Charles Combe, Thomas Plumer, and Thomas Francis Wenman. The last three became fellows.

Jones had a severe stomach disorder in November. Sir George Baker, the royal physician, prescribed relaxation and forbade all but light reading. Accordingly, Jones decided to take the Bath waters rather than visit Schultens. Amusing himself just before departure, he was reading Demosthenes when news arrived that the impressment case was likely to come up soon. Public tranquility demanded that the issue be decided:

I have seen their *plea,* as we call it in writing; it states that, when the press-warrants issued, there was *an open & unnatural rebellion* in America; whence they mean to insist on the *necessity* of the measure; but, as there was full time for parliament to have authorized such warrants, there could be no *necessity* for the King alone to issue them *without parliament;* and that is the single question to be discussed. (1:250)

Coincidentally, Arthur Lee, now an American commissioner to France, had written him on the subject, in a letter that initiated their lifelong correspondence:

Put forth your utmost strength upon the great question of the legality of impressment. It is of the last importance to the security of the subject, and to the honour of the police of the kingdom, that this question should be decided. For what can more abase the dignity of the constitution, or endanger the security of the subject, than that the least enlightened and most abandoned of the community, for of such press-gangs are usually composed, should be supposed to have a legal power of judging and executing in what concerns the dearest object of legal protection, personal liberty?[48]

Lee requested Jones's arguments and opinions for use if anyone ever tried to introduce impressment in America. Thus an American official urged him to defeat a method used to supply the men fighting America. But when Jones realized that the case was being indefinitely delayed, he thanked Lee belatedly and observed how their opinions coincided. He discreetly did not mention impressment and referred only to "the case of

John" followed by an illegible word that Lee would interpret as *Millachip* (1:273).

When Jones left for Bath on 1 December, he was hopeful that he would soon be arguing against impressment. There he wholly recovered from his exhausted spirits and nervous stomach. Drinking the warm waters for a month was pleasurable, although his regular exercising was more beneficial. Reluctantly he abstained from dancing, which would have made him hotter, for the idler diversions of Bath lacked even the attraction of novelty. He did join some hunters and was in at the death of the hare, an activity that seemed dull if not cowardly. Lacking his law books, he enjoyed reading Captain James Cook's new *Voyage towards the South Pole, and round the World*. In addition, he attended a concert, but was more struck by the violinist's adultery than by the music.

The uninhibited activites disturbed Jones. Worse than the adultery was a prominent physician's stealing from the charity plate that he was holding in the church. Still worse was communicated by Wilkes, with whom Jones was now political friends. Wilkes's diary records their dining together with the writer William Dodd, the Dilly brothers, and others on 4 December 1776.[49] Dodd then had the same company for dinner.

In Bath the dissipated Wilkes displayed a letter from Denis Diderot, who chastised him for appearing ridiculous in his efforts to reform the English government. Jones concurred in Diderot's praising Wilkes for condemning the American war, but not Diderot's profligate advice: "Be cheerful, drink the best wines, keep the gayest company; and should you be inclined to a tender passion, address yourself to such women as make the least resistance: they are as amusing and as interesting as others; one lives with them without anxiety, and quits them without regrets" (1:253). It is unlikely that Jones expressed his disgust to Wilkes. He was as fond as any Frenchman was of cheerful company and virtuous pleasures, but he belonged to a different sect than did the French academicians. His personal life was as spotless as his professional life.

Though he felt sorry for the needy people amid the expensive activities in Bath, he recognized the impossibility of one individual's aiding them all. Yet the misery of an unemployed musician and eight children prompted Jones to help a clergyman collect a fund. He himself contributed and added a guinea for Lady Spencer, perhaps hoping that she would involve her Society for Charitable Purposes.

So it was that Jones was again in perfect health at the end of 1777. His profession let him help the oppressed and secure redress. The first stage of his career was over, with prospects more promising than he had anticipated. He was accepted in literary and professional circles. His law abilities were becoming known, and his circuit business in Wales was expanding. After halfhearted efforts for a place, he could visualize a loftier future, even a seat in Parliament. As he had not yet focused on a career goal, he would pursue his general goals – improving his faculties and extending his knowledge, so as to be useful to England and humankind. These goals, he felt, should provide as much happiness as he could enjoy on earth.

4 The Athenian and Eleutherion (1778–1780)

Before Jones finished the quarter sessions and left Oxford on 19 January 1778, he was engaged in his first direct political activity. Although he had known Burke for nine years, the two were not close, but Jones's observations in Parliament had shown him the oratorical power of the MP for Bristol. The event triggering their association was General John Burgoyne's surrender at Saratoga, New York, which marked the turning point of the American Revolution. The national income plummeted because of the lost colonial markets, but the king needed many recruits and large sums to continue the war. Subscriptions were opened at Birmingham, Coventry, and Halifax. The London Court of Common Council defeated a motion on 16 January to open a bounty subscription in London, because assistance in "the present ruinous and destructive war, whilst offers of just and honourable terms are withheld from America" would reflect dishonor on the City. Yet a successful subscription began.

Probably Burke initiated the correspondence, which may have assisted him in the Opposition's attack on raising troops by means of private subscription. Unable to meet Burke in London at the time suggested, Jones dispatched "cursory considerations" (1:257–60). First, the Declaration of Rights bars the Crown from receiving supplies from a subject to support the army through any medium except Parliament. However, long usage permits paying a bounty to volunteer sailors; ancient statutes permit the raising of compulsory forces in a time of "extreme Necessity, sudden Invasion or formidable Insurrection." Jones believed that none of these conditions existed, but his trust in the legal process made him generalize that "whether the distinction be well or ill-founded it is generally received." Second, the London Court's debate about City subscriptions did not decide the issue constitutionally. Jones enclosed a "fugitive sheet" attacking the whole concept, which permitted arbitrary exactions that created a trend toward absolutism. Perhaps his communications to Burke had a role in the attacks partially leading to North's promise on 11 February to bring forth conciliatory propositions.

84

For a few weeks Jones was extremely busy. Then came the Reading assizes, followed by residence at Oxford for those sessions, before he proceeded to Worcester. If the circuit was his most successful yet, his effort to add a major activity to his schedule was disappointing. A letter arrived from Parr, who made valuable suggestions about Jones's translation of Isaeus. Deciphering Parr's handwriting and Greek, however, entailed more fatigue and eyestrain than had the entire translation. Jones was trying to correct and return the proofs to John Nichols from the circuit towns: "Every page occasions some little doubt or other, which cannot be cleared without consulting a number of books; and my reputation, both as a Scholar and a Lawyer, depends on my making this little Work as accurate as possible" (1:261). He requested a new proof of sheet L, and he mailed sheet M from Monmouth, thereupon stopping the proofreading until his return to London. He was finding that combining his law profession with scholarly avocations was very difficult.

After the circuit ended at Cardigan, Jones went to the Poyntzes' house for a crowded but enjoyable week with aristocratic people. There were three other house guests: Lady Cork, who borrowed his only copy of "Suleiman"; Charles Moore, earl of Drogheda; and Lady Drogheda. Jones adopted their leisurely style, for example, rising after eleven o'clock on 24 April. Shortly thereafter a French agricultural writer and Lady Granard arrived. Jones thought her extremely clever: "She reasoned with great vivacity in praise of unlimited *sincerity,* courage in women, and ardour in friendship" (1:264). The following day, General Richard Smith, the Bengal commander in chief before becoming active in East India Company politics, came for lunch, on his way to Baron Craven's to rehearse a play that he, Ladies Craven and Granard, Isabella Poyntz (William's wife), and others were performing for charity. Smith brought Lady Craven's special invitation to Jones, who was charmed, if terrified that she might command him to take a role and thus commit his next week to rehearsals. He and Poyntz did not get back to Midgham until 2:00 A.M.

Jones's schedule, requiring several speeches at Oxford, would have been best served by his speaking the next morning. But Mrs. Elizabeth Montagu had asked Lady Cork to call on 27 April, and Lady Cork requested him to be her knight on the ride. Returning her and her sister Isabella at midnight, he reached Oxford at dawn. Shortly his chamber was full of clients, his floor spread with plans, and his table covered with briefs. When the court sat that afternoon, he exerted himself to finish his business. That night he received an invitation from Poyntz to see the king review the fleet at Portsmouth. Despite leaving at 4:00 A.M., Jones reached Midgham too late, and Poyntz was not at Portsmouth when he arrived.

Amid cheering thousands, the king arrived on 2 May. After the king was conducted to the governor's house, Jones watched the firing of the forty-two pounders. Baron Mulgrave, whom he knew in the Royal Society, invited him aboard the *Courageux,* where he spent twelve hours watching the magnificent review. Then Poyntz suddenly turned up, suggesting tea on the eighty-gun *Foudroyant,* but rain and obstinate boatmen prevented Jones's keeping the engagement. As no horses were available, he hired a boat to Southampton. He was sorry to have missed Sandwich, first lord of the Admiralty, who had been so busy with the king that Jones thought it improper to call. He had hoped to discuss the vacant advocate generalship of the Bengal Supreme Court of Judicature, whose annual pay of £3,000 would give him independence:

I wish to have it before I am old, that I may be enabled to exert myself, while my mind and body are in full vigour. My professional gains are continually encreasing, but my expences encrease with them; and, with all possible frugality, I could not hope to amass in thirty years *here* the same sum that I might save in a fifth part of the time at Calcutta. (1:269)

Jones intended to spend three months in strengthening his interest in the ministry, the East India Company, and his profession. His appointment, which should depend on North and Sandwich, would let him return home with £30,000 at the age of thirty-eight, and then he would have the necessary independence to defend the constitution and amend laws. Were the post vacant, he might be appointed immediately.

Actually, news of a more important Indian vacancy had arrived. Stephen Lemaistre, a puisne judge of the Supreme Court, had died. The Court had been established by North's Regulating Act of 1773, which imposed general governmental supervision on the East India Company while granting funds to stave off its bankruptcy. The events producing this statute were complex. The Tea Act had supposedly enabled the company to sell tea directly to America, except that the Americans again objected to taxation without parliamentary representation, preferring to buy smuggled tea even at a higher price. When pressure was applied, the first Boston Tea Party took place, and the retaliatory Coercion Acts made war almost inevitable.

The East India Company should not have been in need. India's riches permitted factories that provided work for laborers and generated funds from rents and land sales, while also producing jute and other things. But the company became a giant colonial parasite, capitalizing on the princes' greed and feuds to expand its empire. In reality, the company was its officers, who endured a kind of unhealthful, expensive exile. Resented if not feared by the Indians, they chiefly wanted to make money, which was abundant as a result of bribery and corruption. Robert Clive's efforts to restore honesty caused him to face severe criticism before he committed suicide. Conditions reached a new low, with officers concentrating on amassing personal fortunes. Without police or court protection for the people, lawlessness was rampant. With virtual anarchy in its empire, the company asked London for loans.

The grant was accompanied by the Regulating Act, which declared the company's territory to be Crown property. The Bengal Presidency was made superior to the Bombay and Madras Presidencies, and the Calcutta Council was replaced by a four-man Supreme Council led by Governor-General Hastings. This would be supervised in England by an elective Court of Directors, which would be governmentally supervised. To ensure dual responsibility, a Supreme Court would protect the Indians, with jurisdiction of important cases delegated to its chief justice and three puisne judges. Of the judges, only Sir Robert Chambers enjoyed any reputation. Jones had witnessed the conferring of an Oxford degree on Sir Elijah Impey (the chief justice), and John Hyde was the other judge. The court and the council members were forbidden to trade with Indians or accept gifts.

When Jones learned of the vacant judgeship, he immediately preferred it to the advocate generalship. His reputation in Orientalism surpassed that of Hastings and Chambers; he could employ his legal knowledge more productively than he now could in England. He loved Eastern subject matter, and he could unite Persian and law in the post. The £6,000 salary would let him save £4,000 annually after deducting for living expenses, so that he could later proceed at the bar or in Parliament, insulated from all need of patronage.

Key people encouraged him; his appointment seemed almost automatic. The chancellor said that he would recommend Jones to the king as Lemaistre's successor. The earl of Mansfield, lord chief justice of the King's Bench, had been so kind to Jones that his support was certain. North, whom Jones had never known to raise false hopes, talked to Jones both at his house and at his levee in a manner indicating favorable intentions. Such support made Jones fairly confident: "But many things may intervene; and, as no ships will sail to Bengal till late in the autumn, they may keep me in suspense for the whole summer, unless my friends exert their interest to have the matter decided as soon as possible" (1:271–2).

Lady Spencer obediently arranged a meeting with Sir Grey Cooper, the joint secretary of the treasury, who might expedite Jones's appointment: "Lord Bathurst would have appointed me directly, if I had been of full standing at the bar, which I shall not be till November, before which time I could not embark for India. My object therefore is to procure a present nomination and a patent, which need not be sealed till the winter" (1:272).[1]

As the statute stipulated five years' standing, Jones could not be legally named until January 1779. His optimism seems to have been well founded. Laurence Sulivan, a company director, mentioned in a letter that there was a thought of sending Jones out as Lemaistre's replacement.[2] Bathurst was prepared to name him as soon as he was eligible.

The weakness of North's cabinet led to a call for Earl Bathurst to resign in June. With public opinion not supporting the war, a stronger chancellor was named. He was Edward Thurlow, who often relied on Lloyd Kenyon and Francis Hargrave to prepare his judgments. As a reward, he favored Hargrave, a King's Counsel who had gained fame in a habeas corpus case but who made quite an unimpressive appearance.[3] Jones heard about this disturbing possibility and wrote Hargrave about his desire for the judgeship. Would Hargrave accept a mastership in chancery, assuming that there was an option?

Hargrave's high regard for Jones had originally caused him to hesitate, but the urging of Thurlow and others had persuaded him to aspire to the post while acknowledging Jones's superiority. Then Jones's letter almost made him retract his application, an action that would have contradicted his own and others' judgment. All this he explained in a delayed answer, hoping that Jones would understand and thus relieve him of much pain.[4] This answer was hardly comforting: None of the reluctance and praise could overturn the fact that he was a competitor.

Jones had little time to pursue the matter, as he left for Oxford on 16 July for the summer circuit. After the prosperous Welsh circuit, he stayed at Oxford until 15 October. Returning to London, he found the situation unchanged. Many people doubted that Hargrave would be nominated: "I think he will *not,* unless the Chancellor should press it strongly. It is still the opinion and wish of the bar, that I shall be the man. I believe the Minister hardly knows his own mind" (1:276). Many people told Jones that the post was being kept open until he was eligible. If he were appointed and could save £20,000, he would never need to sell his liberty to a patron, as many lawyers did unashamedly. He might be speaker of the Commons in his full vigor, whereas a slow career in Westminster Hall could not provide independence until the age at which Cicero was killed. But "if the minister be offended at the style in which I have spoken, do speak, and will speak, of publick affairs, and on that account should refuse to give me the judgeship, I shall not be at all mortified, having already a very decent competence" (1:277).

The instability of Bengal, however, was contributing to North's doubts about a candidate of outspoken convictions. As Thurlow advocated full use of English power against the rebellious colonies, he would hardly want a judge who opposed the war. Even after he perceived Hargrave's limitations, he tenaciously blocked the appointment chiefly because of Jones's advanced Whiggism. Yet Jones was not really disturbed that nothing had been done about the nomination.

Jones was busily correcting proof of his translation of Isaeus, the first master of strict forensic argument, who merited an English version. He dedicated his first legal book to Bathurst, who praised it. As he said in the epistle dedicatory, his commissionership was the sole fruit "gathered from an incessant course of very painful toil." Bathurst, his only benefactor, had intended to reward him in the manner most agreeable to his inclinations and studies, except for one event. Naturally he did not specify the changing of chancellors, which ended the immediate prospects of his judgeship. The epistle also praised Sir James Porter, who had encouraged a translation showing that "ancient literature, properly directed, may be applied to many useful purposes beyond those intended" in education.

In 1776 Jones had started a Latin translation of Isaeus' ten speeches and some fragments.[5] He asked Parr for all available information on Isaeus, as he was planning an English version and an elaborate prefatory discourse: "My work will be more creditable to me if no one has yet translated the speeches; for they are not easy, and are full of obscure allusions" (1:226). As Jones discovered, the Latin version of the ten speeches was full of errors.[6] Parr examined Jones's English translation and was still making suggestions while the book was going into proof.

The Stationers' Company records (3:129) show that *The Speeches of Isæus in Causes Concerning the Law of Succession to Property at Athens* was published on 24 February 1779 by the Dilly brothers, who owned the whole share. Nichols was the printer. Besides the prefatory matter and the translation, the book contains a summary of relevant Attic laws, notes, and an elegant commentary.

This book is important for several reasons. It permanently corrects assumptions from Dionysius: (1) Isaeus is actually at least as significant in his own right as for his having been Demosthenes' teacher, and (2) he copied Lysias' style only in his early works. This first English translation of Isaeus' speeches makes a major evaluation of his place in Attic oratory. Jones liberally utilizes Roman, Hebrew, Koranic, and English law to describe and compare ancient Athenian inheritance law. He suggests reform in the complex English land laws on the basis of Isaeus, with little expectation of practical reform.[7] He encourages the study of law – ancient and modern, Asiatic and European – which, he points out, is more pleasing than even fine arts. Finally, while seeking to raise law to the status of a science, he makes one of the earliest pleas for the development of comparative law. The opening of his prefatory discourse sets the tone:

There is no branch of learning, from which a student of the law may receive a more rational pleasure, or which seems more likely to prevent his being disgusted with the dry elements of a very complicated science, than the history of the rules and ordinances by which nations, eminent for wisdom and illustrious in arts, have regulated their civil polity: nor is this the only fruit that he may expect to reap from a general knowledge of foreign laws both ancient and modern; for, whilst he indulges the liberal curiosity of a scholar in examining the customs and institutions of men, whose works have yielded him the highest delight, and whose actions have raised his admiration, he will feel the satisfaction of a patriot in observing the preference due in most instances to the laws of his own country above those of all other states; or, if his just prospects in life give him hopes of becoming a legislator, he may collect many useful hints, for the improvement even of that fabrick which his ancestors have erected with infinite exertions of virtue and genius.

The barrister John Touchet praised the book (*Monthly Review,* June 1779, pp. 452–9): Jones has perfectly combined the abilities of lawyer and "critic of considerable reputation and talents," while presenting solid, ingenious reflections on the value of ancient literature. Alexander Chalmers later stated: "The elegant style, profound research, and acute criticism displayed in this translation attracted the applause of every judge of classical learning."[8]

The book established Jones as a legal scholar, with a capacity to discover penetrating, relevant comparisons in other systems and to apply them to English law. Despite this fine reaction, his stream of small clients did not become a torrent, nor were clients with cases involving large fees attracted. There was no serious consideration of another edition, unlike most of his previous works. Rather, this was a labor of love, a refined translation for scholars primarily concerned with law.

One of the first lawyers to whom Jones sent a copy was Burke. In a modest letter accompanying the book, Jones observed that Athenian eloquence could not change current English politics. His preface and commentary were only a sketch; nor was he satisfied with the translation, which was not highly polished because of the possible consequent loss of the Attic flavor. Still, he hoped that Burke would be entertained: "The approbation of such a reader is the highest reward that a writer can desire; and will give [me] the greatest pleasure" (1:287). Burke answered elegantly:

I give you many thanks for your most obliging and valuable present, and feel myself extremely honoured by this mark of your friendship. . . . orators have hitherto fared worse in the hands of the translators, than even the poets; I never could bear to read a translation of Cicero. Demosthenes suffers I think somewhat less; – but he suffers greatly; so much, that I must say, that no English reader could well conceive from whence he had acquired the reputation of the first of orators. I am satisfied that there is now an eminent exception to this rule, and I sincerely congratulate the public on that acquisition. (1:287)

Praise also came from John Symonds, who had succeeded to the Cambridge professorship of modern history. Jones was gratified: "Writers would be incited to exert themselves, if they could expect to find such readers as yourself."[9] Gibbon praised the book, too. Pleased with Parr's help, Jones asked his old friend to read Demosthenes' five speeches on Athenian maritime contracts, which he was considering translating if they had been rendered only into French and Latin.[10] Although he worked on the project, he never completed it, despite his love of Demosthenes. Burke had been involved with Bristol shipping when he first requested Jones's help, and now there was much maritime interest because of the war.

While headmaster at Colchester in 1777–8, Parr often saw Jones. Parr was just starting to write seriously. First came a work occasioned by a quarrel with the trustees, a privately printed diatribe about which he asked legal advice. Jones returned it with many passages marked "Too strong" or "Too violent!" Because Parr was now interested in the headmastership of the grammar school at Norwich, he never published it because Jones and others explained that it would hardly commend him to those with appointive power.[11] He also requested editorial help, submitting several questions about the draft of "A Sermon on the 27th of February, 1778." Jones advised: "If your Sermon be not likely to hurt you and your family by giving fruitless offence to men in power, I will answer for your reputation, and exhort you to print it *with your name;* without it, you must not expect to have the charges of publication defrayed, as few men read a book with so unpromising a title" (1:260). Jones promised to give attentive criticism if the handwriting were legible.

When Parr became the Norwich headmaster, the distance prevented their seeing each other as often. But he reported his various quarrels, and Jones urged him to desist so as not to part with his peace of mind for a shadow. Jones was quite negative about one question: The Cambridge M.A. degree conferred on Parr by mandamus gave him no title to such privileges at Oxford; it was valid only at Cambridge. Before informing Parr that he could not be admitted to an Oxford M.A., Jones verified this opinion, as, when Jones started to describe the case in classical pseudonyms, other Oxonians anticipated the opinion.

Besides such correspondence and activities concerning the judgeship, there was a new political theme in Jones's multifaceted life. It started with the fervent opposition to the war of men like Shipley and Franklin. Franklin, who was perhaps the major cause of Shipley's adopting the American position, spent three weeks with the Shipleys in 1771. There he composed half of his *Autobiography* and explained the American view, confirming a natural sympathy that had attracted him to the bishop. When Shipley's sermon to the Society for the Propagation of the Gospel in Foreign Parts criticized the government's policy, Franklin sent copies to America for republishing in a number of editions. If the sermon helped the American cause, it also cost Shipley the archbishopric of Canterbury. Helping later in the House of Lords, he voted against the Coercion Acts.[12]

Franklin was an agent of several American Colonies, serving as a kind of ambassador extraordinary and attempting to aid Pitt's fruitless efforts toward conciliation. Jones had met him through the Royal Society and Shipley. Both men influenced Jones's deepening American sympathy, which was the logical outcome of principles derived from the constitution and the settlements of the Glorious Revolution, and of experiences like the undelivered Oxford *Oration*. After Franklin left England, he was appointed to a commission to negotiate a treaty with France. The seventy-year-old arrived in Paris in late 1776 with Silas Deane and Arthur Lee for what became nine years of diplomacy.

Jones's correspondence with Lee about impressment had brought the two into political association. When he became an advocate in a case involving some Parisian witnesses, he planned a visit for September 1778. He had much to tell Lee about old acquaintances: "I should like to be in a little private lodging, where I may spend a week or fortnight, unknown to all, except a few friends" like Franklin (1:274).

Jones had another purpose. He had become John Paradise's legal adviser and the guardian of Paradise's two daughters by marriage with a Virginia heiress. The Virginia House of Delegates' Act for Sequestering British Property had given the commonwealth temporary retention of the rents and threatened eventual confiscation of Mrs. Paradise's property.[13] Paradise was dejected at the suspension of the rents, and Jones reported to Lee that their mutual friend seemed incapable of action. Jones's principles would not let him suggest that Lee, of a famous Virginia family, might exercise influence. But his Parisian trip was hardly urgent, and it was important that he be in London if an unsealed patent for the Indian judgeship became obtainable.

Jones's correspondence was requiring considerable time. Like his father earlier, he always responded when scholars requested assistance, as there were few journals in which to present one's discoveries. Continual correspondence and long visits were the way to gain clarification on some point of difficulty or to build a rebuttal of criticism of one's own views.[14] In this way scholars could share and test their findings before the modern development of formal conferences and sufficient journals.

Until recently, Jones's scholarly correspondence had been mainly confined to Reviczky and Schultens and to others' solicitations about Oriental subjects. In current fashion this was often in Latin; Jones carefully used the writer's language in replying. Even partly personal letters from Orme and Halhed were often in Latin. A sketch of four sets of their letters in 1778 and 1779 will indicate the nature of this correspondence as well as the state of contemporary research.

The classicist Sidney Swinney wrote from his British embassy chaplaincy. Enclosing two Persian and Greek manuscripts, he noted that the public museum at Constantinople contained two thousand Arabic, Persian, and Turkish manuscripts: "People assure me, but I dare not say whether with good authority or no, that the entire Decades of Livy, and the complete history of Curtius, are contained in that very precious repository."[15] He promised to send the catalogue and then copy any manuscripts that Jones wanted. Perhaps George III might want a copy of the putative Livy.

Second, the economist Josiah Tucker, the dean of Gloucester, availed himself of Jones's offer to help, made during a recent conversation. He had sent copies to Oxford of his tract attacking Locke's theory of government; now he wondered whether Oxonians agreed with him. If they did not, he would proceed no further, for his own system could have no chance if they upheld Locke's. But if they agreed, he would present his own theory after consulting with Jones, in what became *A Treatise Concerning Civil Government* (London, 1781). Jones expressed wide disagreement and sent a packet of sources. As Tucker had always expected to compose the second part, he reacted graciously to Jones's constructive evaluation:

I cannot say that your remarks have wrought much conviction in me, (in some places they have,) but they have had what I esteem a better effect, that is, they will make me more cautious and circumspect in some of my expressions; and they will oblige me to bring more proofs and illustrations of some points than I thought were needful. In all these respects, your friendly remarks have done me much greater service than unmeaning compliments; and as to your differing so widely in opinion from me, your frank declaration of this difference proves you the honester man, and the more to be esteemed.[16]

Gilbert Stuart wrote Jones about "the studies of law and government on the great scale of history," perhaps presenting his most important work, *A View of Society in Europe, in Its Progress from Rudeness to Refinement* (Edinburgh, 1778).[17] Though Jones lacked the time to compose the deserved laudation, Stuart was not disappointed: Jones's time was better spent in serving as a model lawyer who was also an orator, philosopher, and historian. As soon as Stuart's *Observations Concerning the Public Law and the Constitutional History of Scotland* appeared, he sent Jones a copy. Having attacked the historiographer William Robertson, he felt that impartial judgment about Scottish freedom could best be rendered in England. He also presented *An Historical Dissertation Concerning the Antiquity of the English Constitution* (Edinburgh, 1768), designed to introduce an extensive work on which he wished Jones's opinion before he began shaping his materials.

Last, Prince Adam Czartoryski, a Polish general, used a typical beginning for addressing a famous scholar:

It is the fate of those who, like you, are an ornament to the literary world, to be known to those who are perfectly unknown to them; each is entitled to call to them for light, and this I hope will be a sufficient apology for my intruding upon you, and interrupting those studious hours which you consecrate with so much success to the instruction of your readers.[18]

Jones's Persian *Grammar* was a main guide along thorny Eastern paths; but it did not explain why Persian contains many words very similar to words in European languages like English, German, and Old Church Slavonic. The prince and Reviczky, now an ambassador in Warsaw, invited Jones to visit and talk about philology for as long as Jones could spare.

Jones's answer in February 1779 expressed the great honor paid him. He was not certain as to why "European" words had come into Persian. Procopius' mention of European intercourse with Persia might suggest borrowing. Then Jones came close to the truth: "Many learned investigators of antiquity are fully persuaded, that a very old and almost primæval language was in use among these northern nations, from which not only the Celtic dialects, but even the Greek and Latin, are derived" (1:285). Illustrating with Greek, Latin, and Persian pairs of words, he concluded that one root could be the source of a given pair, though this approach was uncertain. Jones made no effort to instruct the scholarly prince in the ways of kingship, as he had earlier attempted to instruct Christian VII and Gabriel.

Amid such correspondence, Jones continued writing long letters to Althorp. Now a captain in the Northamptonshire Militia, Althorp invited him to visit the camp at Warley Common, but Jones preferred to stay in nearby Brentwood so as not to inconvenience anyone. Anyway, he wanted to see Althorp, and he wanted to perform a great service for Althorp. The occasion was the expansion of the Club, which Jones attended when he could, for example, half of the sixteen meetings that year. Goldsmith had once told Johnson that he wanted additional members so as to provide an agreeable variety: "There can now be nothing new among us: we have travelled over one another's minds." Johnson was a bit angry: "Sir, you have not travelled over *my* mind, I promise you." Reynolds agreed with Goldsmith: "When people have lived a great deal together, they know what each of them will say on every subject. A new understanding, therefore, is desirable."[19] But Johnson did not oppose the resolution expanding the membership from twenty to thirty, as he wanted a more miscellaneous company of conspicuous men.

There were four nominations on 27 November 1778. First were Banks and William Windham. After Johnson proposed William Scott, there was a pause, and Jones thought of Althorp. With no time for deliberation, he said, "Lord Althorp." Everyone applauded, but Langton called him into another room. Langton, a captain in the Lincolnshire Militia also at Warley, reported talking with Althorp, who had expressed doubts about the propriety of such a young man's admission. Because it was too late to retract, Jones proposed to ask Althorp and shortly sought to convince him in a long letter containing the only known firsthand characterization of all the members (1:278–81).

Though partly motivated by the hope of seeing Althorp more often, Jones would not have nominated him without believing that the meetings would delight Althorp: "Many of our members are sinking into the vale of years, and you will never have such an opportunity of knowing men, of whom all England talks and will talk for centuries to come." Johnson had said that "Europe cannot produce such another club, and that there is no branch of human knowledge, concerning which we could not collectively give the world good information." Jones's roll call is fascinatingly organized:

Our members are, first, three Deans, *Barnard,* dean of Derry, soon to be a bishop, an elegant and lively scholar; *Marley,* dean of Fernes, a man of wit and vivacity; *Percy,* dean of Carlisle, the only agreeable professed Antiquary I know; next, six members of the house of commons; *Burke,* the pleasantest companion in the world; his eloquence all the kingdom knows; *Chamier,* Under Secretary of state, a man of the world with a strong sterling understanding, and my great friend; Sir Charles *Bunbury,* whom you know, of no contemptible natural talents; *Fox,* of great talents both natural and acquired; *Gibbon,* an elegant writer, not without wit in conversation; *Dunning,* the best lawyer, the ablest advocate, and one of the honestest men of the age; next come men connected with the theatre; *Colman* well known by his dramatick pieces; *Garrick,* whom all Europe knows; *Steevens,* a learned critick, and editor of Shakespear; *Sheridan,* a sprightly young fellow with a fine comick genius; very little older than yourself; then appear other writers, *Johnson,* the best scholar of his age; *Warton,* of Winchester, a man of learning and taste; *Smith,* author of a great work on the wealth of nations; – then follows a miscellaneous company; *Reynolds,* a great artist and fine writer on his art; *Boswell* of

Corsica, a good-natured odd fellow; *Fordyce,* a physician, one of the best chymists in the world; *Beauclerk,* of strong parts and fine genius; *Langton* you know; and Lord *Ossory;* Lord *Charlemont,* a man of taste in arts and literature; *Vezey,* good-natured and agreeable; two lawyers close the rear, Sir R. *Chambers* an India judge; and W. *Jones,* likely to be his colleague.

Althorp's youth was no barrier; his having been nominated without his participation eliminated any question of forwardness.

Althorp encountered Garrick, but they did not discuss the nomination. As Jones did not receive a refusal, Althorp was one of the four men elected on 11 December. As Johnson stated, "there is no society in Europe that would not be glad to admit four such men as our present candidates" (1:282). Jones notified Althorp, who could listen or talk as he pleased, as there was no restraint. Regardless of what the world thought, conversation at the Club was seldom erudite: "You will fancy that you are dining with men of the world, as most of them indeed are." If modesty made Althorp wish to delay Jones's introduction, this could be done, although Jones had been only four years older at his own election.

As Althorp was concerned about not being a man of letters, Jones was reassuring:

It was never the spirit of our society to admit only men of letters: Mr. Chamier, Captain Langton, Major Wyndham, Sir C. Bunbury, Lord Ossory, &c. are accomplished men and polite scholars, but none of them set up for wits; nor would I indeed, though I have dabbled in literature, wish to be thought [so] to professed men of letters. On the whole, you will hear only such conversation as you would hear at the best tables, except from Johnson, who is a phenomenon of knowledge, sagacity, and singularity. He declines very fast, and I should be sorry, if you were to lose an opportunity of seeing so extraordinary a man. (1:283)

The Club had no rules; the presidency revolved, changing from meeting to meeting and involving only presiding.

Jones may have introduced Althorp on 18 December. Then Garrick died, one of the sad moments of Jones's tenure. On 1 February the Club somberly rode to Westminster Abbey in Coaches 18 through 22 of the procession – Jones, Reynolds, Fox, and Scott were in Coach 21. That day Johnson summarized the actor's life to Jones: Garrick made acting respectable, and acting made him rich.[20] Four days later the goodly number of thirteen members met. Besides Jones and Banks, who served as president, there were Beauclerk, Bunbury, Colman, Dunning, Gibbon, Johnson, Langton, Marlay, Percy, Reynolds, and Scott. On 24 April, Jones was at Beauclerk's house, along with Johnson, Reynolds, Langton, and Paradise. Soon Boswell came. They talked about Wilkes's attack on Johnson's eulogy of Garrick, and Boswell recorded in his journal: "Paradise did not say a word; Jones little more than to ascertain exactly what Johnson said of *Wilkes's* having a cheerful countenance and a gay voice."[21]

Let us now turn to Jones's associations with five members and his social standing. The Beauclerks' house was a social center, where he often dined. For example, he was there on 21 November 1779 but did not enjoy the evening once Beauclerk reported the fluxes in Althorp's camp.

Chamier, now an MP from Tamworth, was hoping to advance Jones's judicial endeavors. Hearing that Lady Spencer had given away many of her birds and intended to dispose of the rest, he asked Jones to request a bullfinch and curassows. Jones did so in the very words of the "excellent man and zealous friend," like Homer's ambassadors, as he said jocularly (1:288). Eight months later Chamier belatedly acknowledged her offer, but noted that the birds had been intended for a friend, who could no longer accommodate them. Now Jones should transmit his thanks. Unembarrassed by the fact that Jones had thought the birds were for Chamier and had praised his bird tending, Jones did so.

The increasingly divisive war was affecting the Club. Members conversed wholly about politics, without any pretension to the literary character that their meetings supposedly had: "We are sadly divided in sentiment: our friend Langton is very vehement against the lovers of freedom in all countries: it is a pity he was not a French officer: his veneration for Kings is really too high for an Englishman" (1:299). Nevertheless, Langton's conversational skills made him Jones's good friend. They frequently dined and had quiet literary talks. Jones always found him instructive and felt great affection for him, but would have dispensed with his royalist views: "I believe, if all men in this country professed his sentiments upon government, I should not stay three months longer in England, but should hasten to America, where men of liberal principles, instead of being persecuted and proscribed, will be honoured and advanced" (1:301).

Jones sometimes visited the chambers of Johnson, whose propensities he knew well. As he wrote Althrop: "You will be able, when you come to London, to examine with the minutest *scrupulosity,* as Johnson would call it, the properties" of the American eel. Jones was unimpressed by the elaboration of the often inaccurate notes of parliamentary proceedings into "Reports of the Debates of the Senate of Lilliput" for *Gentleman's Magazine:* "Johnson wrote a whole volume of them with few, or no, materials" (1:246, 333).

Jones's bias partly stemmed from Johnson's abusing Milton in a preface to *Works of the English Poets* (London, 1779–81):

Johnson and I are very cool to one another. Can I be *cordial* with the libeller of Milton, whom of all men I most admire? He is displeased with me for not praising his lives. Believe me, I cannot praise him; nor do I wish to have the good word of a man, who abuses all the friends of Liberty, because they are so: his abuse on that ground is true praise, and his praise is defamation. What care I for the friendship of a thousand such men? (1:335)

Jones never forgot the abuse, and even after Johnson's death he recalled the deriding of Milton "for talking of driving sheep a-field, when he had no sheep to drive" (2:793). He could not forgive Johnson's criticism of "Lycidas," one of the best works by the poet who most influenced him.

Too urbane to continue personal coolness, Jones sometimes muted his voice if his principles were not compromised: Langton "and his Socrates, Dr. Johnson, have such prejudices in *politicks,* that one must be upon one's guard in their company if one wishes to preserve their good opinion" (1:275). At the Club, where political discussion was supposedly forbidden, Jones's integrity compelled a response to remarks that he thought unjustified, for, despite his amicability, he was not passive. Yet his harmonious spirit and warm personality let him remain friends with Johnson, even though Johnson's politics so profoundly differed from his that a close friendship was impossible.[22]

The fifth member whom Jones often saw was Banks, in an association that was to lead to the major scholarly cooperation of his career. Essentially a dictator, Banks directed the Royal Society's Club from 1775 to 1784, a separate dining club that met on the Thursday evenings of the Royal Society meetings. John Lloyd, Jones's acquaintance in the Temple, introduced him as a guest three times in 1778, and he and Althorp were Banks's guest on 20 April 1780.

Jones's wide range of friends essentially embraced "the whole literary world; so exalted was his character, and so anxiously sought after was his company."[23] He had cultivated his conversational abilities to complement his great learning. The Blue Stockings accepted him. Mrs. Montagu invited him to Mayfair for her famous conversation parties, having regarded him with affection for years. Jones's modesty also distinguished him, as Fanny Burney reveals in writing about one of Mrs. Montagu's parties: "The star of the evening was Lord Bristol, who shone, indeed, with much resplendency. . . . Mr. Langton, Mr. Stanhope, Mrs. Boscawen, Lord Falmouth, Oriental Jones, and some others were of the party, but Lord Bristol was the only spouter, the rest, Mrs. Mon: excepted, were mere audience."[24] When Mrs. Montagu was at Bath, and Jones was nearby on the circuit, he often called to transmit late news.

The duchess of Devonshire invited Jones to her distinguished parties. In 1780 he was presented to Walpole by Mrs. Vesey, Agmondesham's wife, who entertained every other Tuesday. Walpole described a party at Lady

Lucan's in imitation of Mrs. Vesey's: "Mrs. Montagu kept aloof from Johnson, like the West from the East. There were Soame Jenyns, Persian Jones, Mr. Sherlocke, the new Court wit Mr. Courtney, besides the out-pensioners of Parnassus."[25] Jones was popular socially:

Do you dine to-morrow with Mr. Walsh, (I know he meant to ask you) or on Sunday with the best of Bishops [Shipley], or on Tuesday with the club? At all or any of those places I should be happy to meet you. I could not attend the Royal Society last night, and am prevented this evening from paying my respects to Lady Spencer. (2:515)

Jones attended eleven of the eighteen Club meetings in 1779, and thirteen of the nineteen in 1780.

He was planning to visit Poyntz on the way to the 1779 spring circuit, but troublesome avocations delayed him until the day the Oxford sessions began. Finishing the prosperous Welsh circuit at Cardigan, he spent five days at Oxford in mid-April en route back to London. Although he had fulfilled the five years' requirement, the pending parliamentary discussion of India meant that action on the judgeship was still blocked.

He made plans for what became the first of three trips to Paris. The problem was Paradise's estate. If Jones composed legal papers to restore the income, presumably Franklin would endorse and transmit them to America. Jones also had personal reasons for seeing the American com-missioner: He wished to discuss the military–political situation for a con-templated history of the war. The official British view was distorted, and Gibbon and Orme had increased his interest in writing history. Jones hoped to learn what peace terms the Americans might accept. The Shipleys wanted him to transport gifts and letters.

Two of the Honest Whigs, a "club of friends of Liberty," sent along publications and probably letters for Franklin, who had had a major role in the members' becoming stout champions of America.[26] Some were Jones's friends in the Royal Society, including two radicals – the Noncon-formist minister Richard Price and Joseph Priestley, who probably provided Franklin with the latest news about the club's efforts to help America. Price's publication was likely *Two Tracts on Civil Liberty, the War with America, and the Debts and Finances of the Kingdom* (London, 1778), as Franklin already knew the vastly popular *Observations on the Nature of Civil Liberty* (London, 1776). Priestley, the earl of Shelburne's librarian, might have sent his pamphlet attacking North's attitude; he would have accepted almost any conditions that would end the war. Price had only recently declined an offer to migrate and manage the American finances.

Despite France's increasing aid to America, Jones had little difficulty in arranging passage. He did seek an introduction to the duc de Nivernois or anyone else of high rank who, "in these times, an Englishman at Paris might find useful if not necessary" (1:288–9). Paradise, Jones, and his servant took a four-hour passage to Calais on 16 May. Detained by formalities for two hours, they could not set out for St. Omer, because the gates would be shut before they could arrive. They thought of going on to Boulogne, but accepted their fate when they discovered the customhouse shut and the officials at a play. So they saw the play and then rose at dawn so as to reach Lille that day.

They arrived at Passy on 20 May 1779. Not finding Franklin at home, they left the books and letters, with a note requesting "the honor of waiting upon the most respectable of patriots and philosophers, on any morning when they hear that he is likely to be at leisure" (1:290). During the next fortnight they dined with him twice and talked with him frequently: "He was cheerful and open, in high health and vigour both of mind and body, at the age of seventy five, and much-respected by men of all ranks" (1:298). Jones enjoyed the conversation of the man who had assisted in framing the American Colonies' constitutions and who had derived maximum advantage from his literary and philosophical reputation. Franklin was highly respected in France: "He gives a publick dinner once a week with the plainness and frugality of a Spartan ambassador; and one cannot help admiring the great propriety of his conduct in so difficult a station" (1:305).

Jones quickly discovered the American resoluteness: The colonies must be united, possessing natural rights independent of Britain. Franklin's "no taxation without representation," echoing the Irish call of the 1730s, did not mean the impracticable sending of MPs to Westminster, but, rather, the maintaining of a separate congress.[27] Yet George III, detesting rebellion and sharing the general British feeling that America should contribute to the national debt because much of it had been caused by wars to protect the colonists, would not willingly grant independence.

Jones was envisioning a commercial compact requiring England to make considerable compromise, but his conveying the terms to Franklin required delicacy. Neither country had asked him to draft a treaty. Jones's literary background recalled the semiallegorical accounts of the Lilliputian senate, which circumvented the ban on printing parliamentary debates. He thus composed a transparent allegory for Franklin, supposedly his translation of a "curious fragment" by Polybius, who wrote the great history of Rome from the First Punic War to Carthage's end. Based on the Social War of 357–355 B.C., it contains four principals: Athens (England), the Islands (America), Caria (France), and Eleutherion (Franklin). Jones has a fifth, independent role:

An Athenian, who had been a pupil of Isæus together with Demosthenes, and begun to be known in his country as a pleader of causes, was led by some affairs of his clients to the capital of Caria. He was a man unauthorized, unemployed, unconnected; independent in his circumstances as much as in his principles; admitting no governor under providence, but the laws, and no laws but those which justice and virtue had dictated, which wisdom approved, which his country had freely enacted. He had been known at Athens to the sage Eleutherion; and, their acquaintance being renewed, he sometimes took occasion in their conversations to lament the increasing calamities of war, and to express his eager desire of making a general peace on such terms as *would produce greatest good from the greatest evil.*[28]

Jones's "Fragment of Polybius" ends with a nine-point treaty designed to save English pride. If America would not require formal acknowledgment of independence, England would not have to recognize it like a defeated nation. Yet America would achieve independence through the natural working of this commercial treaty, "connected by a common tie" while enjoying a different form of government and constitution. America would consider England an elder sister with "pre-eminence of honour and coequality of power." An assembly of deputies, perhaps fifty from each of Parliament and Congress, would decide on acts for the general good, but leave national matters to the respective legislature. The assembly would decide "the ratio of the contributions on both sides," which, while evidently requiring American contribution to the British debt, would neatly postpone the critical issue of taxation in order to stop the bloodshed.

Jones was implementing ideas of friends like Adam Smith, such as the precedent of France's taxing the states of certain provinces by requisition, while maintaining a strong mercantile marine. Thus America would not be treated like an unfranchised dependency of England. Jones did not perceive the incredibility of his idea, when Parliament was so unrepresentative that large boroughs like Leeds and Manchester had no representation; North's Parliament would never accept voluntary separation of the colonies. At least Jones avoided the extreme of giving America some representatives at Westminster.

His conclusion underlines the gravity of the situation:

While Athens is Athens, her proud but brave citizens will never *expressly* recognize the independence of the islands: their resources are no doubt exhaustible, but will not be exhausted in the lives of us and of our children: In this resolution all parties agree: I, who am of no party, dissent from them; but what is a single voice in so vast a multitude? Yet the independence of the united states was *tacitly* acknowledged by the very offer of terms.

In his cover letter to Franklin (1:290–1), Jones explained that he had amused himself since their last conversation by doing the appended translation, which might amuse a classicist. His naive solution was unacceptable. Although Franklin professed great pleasure at what he must have recognized as a serious proposal, he thought it too late. Actually, this proposal of a joint American–British congress was quite superficial as a substantive proposition for reconciliation, in light of the Carlisle Commission's far more advanced proposals offered officially by the North government, when America rejected all terms short of independence. As Franklin expressed distrust of the present Parliament, he probably told Jones of his insistence to David Hartley that there be an honest ministry before a realistic possibility of peace could develop. Conditions had so deteriorated that a weak compromise was not possible.

American scholars have concluded that on this trip Jones was not an English agent. Some feel that he was representing the few Englishmen who had championed America since the repeal of the Stamp Act.[29] Jones also might have discussed possible terms with Shipley and Price, who went much further, believing in the express acknowledgment of independence. The interpretation that his visit had a political object may be partly true,[30] particularly after he became more enmeshed with the rebel emissaries. Certainly his allegory did not affect events. A self-appointed meddler and idealist, he was representing only himself. Moved by love for both countries and intrigued by the American democratic experiment even as personal liberties at home seemed to be threatened, he had presented a philosophical compromise. Had it come before Saratoga, it might have had a chance. Now not even his proposal of a meeting of peace commissioners from each side was acceptable. As he had stated the pessimistic alternative, "tens of thousands will perish." But at least he had attempted to put into practice his view that scholars have a pacific responsibility to the world; thus as a legal scholar he should use his knowledge to try to end the war.

Jones's principal purpose was accomplished: Franklin endorsed the papers mailed on behalf of the estate, and soon the courts of inquisition that were continued over others' property were discontinued on Paradise's. An amendment to a new Virginia law allowed two years of grace. If the war were over by then, Paradise could go to Virginia with far less risk.[31]

Jones had a pleasant stay in Paris. Nivernois received him politely, and he requested the discharge of an English merchant imprisoned at Toulon. In return, he procured orders for releasing a Frenchman, later learning that the British had already freed the man. While conversing with Nivernois and other French nobles, he speculated that Admiral Richard Howe would be recalled from retirement to command the British fleet. He intended thereby to vex them because of the tenor of the discussion, but Nivernois knew enough about the distracted English politics to assert that such was impossible. However, the joke was on both, when Howe later relieved Gibraltar. Such sources provided valuable information for Jones's proposed history of the war.

He dined with Turgot, "an unsuccessful minister, and, as I think, rather a romantick politician, but, as even his enemies allow, a man of approved virtue and inflexible integrity. I saw much of Marmontel and other wits, who seem far more deeply engaged in the contest between Gluck and Picini for the prize of musical composition, than concerned for the event of the present war" (1:305–6). Jones attended Gluck's competing masterpiece *Iphigéni en Tauride,* which settled the Parisian argument about the superiority of national operatic traditions. He thought it admirable entertainment with artful accompaniment.

Informed that they needed the French king's passport in order to depart, Jones and Paradise applied to Versailles. After comte de Vergennes responded with a series of questions to Franklin on 1 June, the pair asked Franklin to insert in his passport the facts that Paradise was an American gentleman born in Greece and that Jones was an Englishman with a *valet de chambre.* Franklin procured a pass with dispatch, besides supplying his own, which, if not of immediate use, attested to his friendship. He also gave them two letters to deliver. The one to Price was apparently short, and Price's answer indicates that it probably contained nothing strongly political.[32] The other recipient is unknown.

From Calais the travelers sent hearty thanks for Franklin's attentions and hours of conversation, promising to delight his friends with an account of his health. After a pleasant trip, Jones reached the Temple. He was immediately discouraged: "The affairs of India, and with them my particular business, are at rest till next session: what may happen in the tremendous interval, God only knows" (1:299).

Besides this continuing delay, there was the war, in which Parliament was greatly absorbed. Jones attended the Commons on 17 June to hear the Spanish manifesto, along with the ambassador's notification of his immediate departure. Hearing the hundred supposed insults and Spain's clear intention to join the war, Jones wished for thundering eloquence, but the tame debate culminated in both the Commons' and the Lords' supporting war against Spain. There was an unsuccessful motion for an address asking the king to collect all armies and the fleet against Spain, so that England might explore whether ancient measures might not heal the American wound. Jones preferred stronger wording, which would have been defeated more speedily: "to unite all the force of the kingdom against the house of Bourbon, and at the same time to seek a reconciliation with America on terms of liberty and reciprocal advantages."

On the way to the summer circuit, Jones visited the Poyntzes. Sandwich had recently told his nieces Isabella and Lady Cork that he had heard Jones was a "violent patriot." The sisters loyally denied the charge, but Jones wished that it had been made to his face so that he could rebut it. He was not a warm party man or unreasoning; rather, he was openly a "zealous lover of our genuine uncorrupted constitution and one ready to part with his life for the liberty of his country" (1:301). Though he would always disregard ministers' opinions of him, the charge showed that some did question his politics. Evidently no one would be appointed to the judgeship until Parliament examined the East Indian affairs and decided whether to restrain the Supreme Court. If the vacancy were filled, the question would be "who is to be the man. If they do not mean to send me, they hold out false colours" (1:301).

Reaching Oxford on 11 July, Jones left the sessions to spend two days with Lytton in Buckinghamshire. His Harrow friend had become a farmer. Together they lamented Pollard's indiscretion in Paris, which had caused deep distress; but the sum needed to relieve him and permit him to join his father in Barbados was more than Jones could spare.

Another development was more disturbing. As the French–Spanish fleet potentially threatened invasion, Oxfordshire was probably going to raise a new battalion. Jones was already distressed. Althorp might be killed in the war or at least suffer a delay in the parliamentary career that Jones was depending on to assist America. Now Jones's direct military involvement might be required, though he viewed scholars as essentially citizens of the world and was increasingly concerned about the dangers of nationalism. He would never have participated militarily against America, but the manifest injustice of a French invasion of England would cause him, if required, to defend his country against probable attack. For the time being, he would not stop his career, because he perceived little danger of attack. And still beckoning was the judgeship, which might be endangered if he stopped his law work. The war was a tangled affair. Though Jones's fighting France would ultimately assist the effort against America, his sense of justice and patriotism was so strong that he would nonetheless join the Oxford militia in case of impending attack.

His circuit was hardly serene. The royal proclamation of 9 July had scared the people by ordering "all officers civil and military, in case of an invasion, to cause all horses, oxen, and cattle and provisions, to be driven from the sea coast to places of security, that the same may not fall in the hands of the enemy." He thought sarcastically that, as British subjects were not yet treated like cattle, he could swim in the sea without disturbance. Nor was he pleased by Worcestershire's decision to postpone considering new levies until after the harvest. Tension was heightened when Sir Charles Hardy's English Channel fleet passed Falmouth in search of the combined enemy fleet of about ninety ships. Hardy had thirty-eight sail of the line, besides frigates, fireships, and cutters.

On the circuit Jones became better friends with Lloyd Kenyon, a circuit leader who was building a distinguished career. They dined together on 21 July. The Oxford circuit offered more leisure than he had in London, and so Jones was able to catch up on his correspondence, which permitted his usual comprehensive reports to Althorp during the sometimes tiresome march through nine English and five Welsh counties. Excursions, together with the healthful effect of journeying in the open air, partly obviated his confinement in packed courtrooms, and the constantly differing trials always entertained:

Some are grave, others gay; some requiring the most intense exertion of the reasoning faculty; some naturally calling for humorous observations; in all, the characters, language and deportment of the different witnesses, the conduct of the judges and counsel, and the effects of cool argument or rapid eloquence on the minds of the juries, are no less amusing than improving to all such as think, with you and me, that "The proper study of mankind is Man." . . . I can hardly conceive a higher pleasure of the mind, than the business of conducting a nice cause well-understood, and of speaking to twelve intelligent men. (1:308–9)

Jones liked his sensible, well-informed colleagues. At meals the conversation was not elegant, but the smart raillery and reply suited their profession. Many were temperate and moderately convivial. As the number of circuiteers expanded and as individuals visited local friends, the company at meals varied. There was also local entertainment, so that Jones was seldom idle.

He won almost all his cases, having to make speeches that he had no time to rehearse. His goal was justice. When the Cardigan assizes ended, the military news was still not so threatening as to block his vacation. Rumors had swept the countryside when the enemy fleet stood off Plymouth in mid-August, but it did not attack. Jones wanted to sail to north Devonshire; however, "there was real danger in the passage from some rascally pirates, who take advantage of these perilous times and have done some mischief in the channel: this deterred me; not that I had any serious fear; but, if I must be killed or taken at sea, I should wish to have a nobler enemy" (1:310).

Instead, Jones went to Weymouth for six studious, adventurous weeks. He read Demosthenes and books by good lawyers and outlined a long legal work. His journal-like letters poured out his dismay at what he considered a depraved Parliament. Althorp must serve "manly, rational, intelligible Liberty" to set an example for other qualified men to build a virtuous, patriotic union, which could preserve the constitution if founded on "good sense, liberty, law, and general happiness" (1:318). William Pitt was another such young patriot.

Jones sometimes spent the day on the Isle of Portland, swimming and collecting shells. As he had always been fond of physiology, he was fascinated by some actiniae (sea anemones) adhering to a shell that he pulled out of the water. He put several in a glass, giving them food and water. When they sickened, he released them in the humanitarian spirit that always governed his investigations: "The British fleet, vast as it is, and ingeniously as it is conducted, raises only my *admiration*, whilst a little Actinia, or a sea-weed, or piece of coral, excites my wonder" (1:323). Once he returned from Portland in a storm:

It rained, as if a waterspout had burst; the sea was very rough for a small open boat; and the thunder-clouds just over my head; the clap followed the flash without a moment's interval; the lightning seemed to snap at the head of my boat and the thunder was tremendously loud: in the midst of this hurly one of my sea men was exclaiming, "You will have it presently, sir, I see it coming." To me, who thought I had it already, and that it was then fully come, this prophesy of the man was exceedingly diverting, and, I believe, if I had been preparing to swim for my life, I could not have forborn laughing. (1:313)

After Jones's friends arrived, he indulged more in conversation, particularly philosophy with Bennet. Philip Yorke became a close friend, befitting the descendant of the man whom Jones's father had tutored. Yorke brought news that Pollard was waiting in Amsterdam for passage to Barbados.

During his vacation Jones observed a naval drama. Noticing a fleet approaching Spithead on 2 September, he counted thirty-six sail besides small vessels in Hardy's fleet, and earlier observers had counted fifty ships. He was thrilled at the prospect of witnessing a victory. When the enemy did not pursue Hardy, Jones concluded that they had never intended to invade Plymouth, for whose defense he had been ready to grab a musket. Toward the end of his stay, adverse winds drove Sir John Lockhart Ross's little fleet into the bay, before Jones watched it leave on an unsuccessful hunt for John Paul Jones.

On 3 October he left his independence enjoyed in tranquillity for the Oxford sessions, during which, at University College, he added physiology to his study of law. His fascination with actiniae led him to the description in Pliny's *Natural History,* Drayton's description of the Portland "hair of Isis," and other sources.

An invitation from Lytton took Jones to Chesham, where he had a productive respite. He had brought Lowth's *Isaiah. A New Translation: with a Preliminary Dissertation, and Notes* (London, 1778), which filled him with great ideas. Isaiah had composed "Odes, Elegies, Satires, Panegyricks, and Prophecies, on various occasions in every kind of style; some, extraordinarily grand and sublime; some, exquisitely beautiful and elegant, and all abounding with the noblest figures, and the richest imagery" (1:328–9). Comparing Lowth's version with the Hebrew, Jones perceived a revealed religion, which reconfirmed his Christian beliefs, the system of moral philosophy that he preferred anyway. He thought it highly probable that Christ had come to earth, the events of which the prophets had minutely long foretold. Logically, empirical demonstration was impossible, as all the right evidence and its different degrees could not be gathered. Yet Jones's view provided high probability, which had chiefly made him a Christian and underpinned his lifelong belief, while intellectually strengthening his later objectivity in viewing Oriental religions without the usual Western bias.

Jones did not resume work at the Temple until 5 November 1779, after an absence of four months. Refusing to be so bound to his profession as to forget physiology, he attended John Hunter's anatomical lectures that winter, one of three such courses helping complete what he called his encyclopedia. Of special interest was the inductive method that Hunter relentlessly employed, which would lead toward more scientific research. Jones had probably heard the Cronian Lectures on Muscular Motion presented to the Royal Society. Now he urged Althorp to accompany him to the descriptions of the muscles, which he related to one's pleasure in music: "Playing on the harpsichord and singing are performed by rapid vibrations of muscles belonging to the fingers and the larynx" (1:332). More eye-opening was Hunter's repetition of his introductory course on the whole animal economy. This pioneering evolutionary view pointed toward the modern truth that higher animals experience a series of change from the embryo to adult form, generally repeating the corresponding embryonic states of their ancestor.

During this period Jones was organizing information. His 1780 memorandum "*Resolved* to learn no more rudiments of any kind, but to *perfect* myself in, First 12 languages, and the *means* of acquiring accurate knowledge" of history, arts, and sciences. He defined history as a knowledge of mankind and nature; the arts, a knowledge of rhetoric, poetry, painting, and music. The sciences include law, mathematics, and dialectic. The twelve languages that Jones had mastered were Greek, Latin and its derivations (French, Italian, Portuguese, Spanish), English, German, Persian, Turkish, Arabic, and Hebrew.

Jones's memorandum relatively subordinates law in a more mature organization than did his earlier representation of knowledge by a circle, with law as the hub. The radiating spokes are logic, music, painting, anatomy, chemistry, politics, gymnastics, criticism, ethics, antiquities, poetry, grammar, rhetoric, mathematics, history, and metaphysics. A second circle contains most of these and also declamation, exercises, languages, and natural history. The spokes are not of equal value: "Every classical book should be read *three* times, *once* for the *Imagination* that an *idea* may be formed of the *whole* work and its parts, a *second* time, for the *Reason* that the work may be perfectly understood, and . . . a third time for the *Memory*."[33]

Jones sometimes donated his services, providing free legal help to the poor, as he had promised. Thus he dropped other matters to hear a destitute old woman whom he had aided for several years. Her son, illegally impressed and having a wife and baby to support, was gravely ill. The old woman had heard that a petition for the king's bounty, if endorsed by a person of distinction, would entitle her to a share when it was distributed at Christmas. Lady Spencer obligingly endorsed the petition, but her endorsement of an earlier one meant that a new one had to be prepared at Easter; and by then Jones, who may have made a practice of having her sign such petitions, had secured the son's release.

Jones was close friends with the Spencers. In the winter of 1779 he often saw Althorp, sometimes at the encampment, where he also had literary conversations with Langton. His influence was bearing fruit, as Althorp was attending parliamentary debates and reading constitutional law. Jones now had less interest in the debates, feeling that ninety-nine MPs in every hundred had predetermined votes and thought such conduct necessary. Deploring the king's direct efforts to control Parliament, Jones still hoped for a time when both houses could agree with Demosthenes that "the best counsels may prevail." Althorp could not learn about free parliaments from observing the present one, but observation was essential to a future legislator.

Jones and Yorke were brought closer that winter by the plight of Pollard, who had almost died. They hoped that he would sail, but he declined Yorke's offers of loans and came to London. For a few weeks he was reintroduced to Jones's practice of inviting select friends to dinner and conversation at the lodging of Jones's mother. Then he secured passage for a disillusioning decade in America.

Jones's mornings were sometimes requested by Mrs. Poyntz and Lady Cork. He was with them on 21 November and then again with Mrs. Poyntz, who ordered him to spend a long weekend at Midgham. Because Althorp would be there, Jones finished at Guildhall at 1:00 P.M on 9 December and hastened out.

He dined at Sandwich's house with a large company in early January, exulting in Captain Cook's successes only days before hearing of Cook's horrible death. Sandwich was wonderfully pleasant, with a genius for putting people at ease. His conversation and music were good, but his politics did not harmonize with Jones's, whose principles would not be altered by conversations with ministers. Though not obtruding his opinion at such times, he always gave it openly when asked.

On 9 January he went to the Oxford sessions. Over the years his fellowship had appreciated to £88 3s 5d in 1779. After paying his expenses of £17, Jones signed for the balance.

At Oxford he had a provocative discussion with Blackstone, who complained of gout in the stomach but seemed to have suffered "a violent concussion of the whole nervous system. So limited are our abilities, while our views are so large" (1:338–9). Jones considered the fifty-seven-year-old scholar, who was soon to die, an excellent judge and one of the best English writers. Blackstone's *Commentaries* was constructed on learning, taste, and judgment. Yet Jones had a philosophical objection: Blackstone defined law as "a rule prescribed by a superior power," whereas Jones's definition was "the Will of the whole community as far as it can be collected with convenience" (1:334).

Returning to London, Jones expected the present session of Parliament to end his suspense about the judgeship. He had started a good business, with expanding clientele and hopes of larger income, and the Welsh circuit was profitable. Yet the intense application cost his freedom and comfort. Even if his fairest prospects materialized, he could hardly gain sufficient financial independence to embark on a parliamentary career while at the height of his powers. Because North and others had held out promising hopes for two years, Jones had been unable to give the kind of dedication to his practice that would be necessary if it – rather than the judgeship – had to provide his livelihood.

The confusion surrounding the Supreme Court kept Jones from blaming North for the lack of action. Conditions in India were bad. The French incitement of native wars had provoked military retaliation. Philip Francis's violent opposition to Hastings had split the Supreme Council, which was battling for jurisdiction with the ineffective Supreme Court. Some MPs, having failed to control the judges, were even agitating to abolish the Court. The charter of the East India Company, again in financial straits, would soon expire. Moreover, North's plan for the governmental arrangement with the company, which the secretary of state had just received, did not mention the internal police.

In informally seeking the judgeship, Jones had not compromised his principles. But his determination to think for himself would hardly recommend him even to a political party trying to bring down North. An example was Burke. Despite Jones's and Burke's accord on subscriptions, they differed on other points. An early minor matter was William Dodd's hanging for forgery: "I think *justly;* Burke thinks otherwise; let us both enjoy our own opinion" (1:237). Jones had also differed with Johnson, whose efforts for a pardon resulted in a large petition. Burke's views on three other matters troubled Jones. First, Burke viewed the county petitions, now more widespread and influential after Wilkes's 1768 petition, as lacking constitutional authority. Jones was initially suspicious about the real purpose of the several associations in 1780, for there seemed to be few unselfish English patriots. Burke's opposition began to worry Jones once he decided that the associated counties were seeking redress constitutionally. Still, he did not join the movement. Instead of petitioning to save millions of guineas and many lives by speedy union with America, the associations sought petty reforms and ignored the war, the basic problem.

Second, Burke presented a plan containing "A bill for the more perfectly uniting to the crown the principality of Wales, and the county palatine of Chester, and for the more commodious administration of justice within the same; as also, for abolishing certain offices now appertaining thereto." Intended to strengthen parliamentary independence and reduce spending, the bill would abolish the Welsh judicature. With trials held in London, the judges' travel and other circuit costs would be saved. Jones would have called on him to protest, except that Burke was busy:

He neither does nor can foresee the inconvenience of his alteration. As a circuiteer, I should be interested in the promotion of his plan, because I should have the same business in a more conspicuous scene; but I know so well the expense of instituting suits in Westminster Hall for the principality, and the convenience of watering the borders of my countrymen with the fountain of justice brought to their own doors, that I hope the Welch men will petition against the bill, and, if they please, they may employ me to support their petition at the bar of the House. (1:346)

Nor did Burke espouse Jones's concept of a mixed republic, which had a tripartite balance underpinned by law, the community's aggregate will. Although the constitution had a royal part, Jones would suspect even a mild monarchy, which entailed government by one man. Comparable vigilance was needed to prevent an oligarchy. The people's lack of virtue would preclude pure democracy; yet the people should provide the "real force, the obligation of its laws, its welfare, its security, its permanence" (1:344), in a limited democracy as an ideal form of responsible self-government. The kingship should be an accountable magistracy, hereditary only to avoid inconvenient elections. Jones was to conclude that the monarchy should be restricted to fit his concept even if local militias had to use force. Each component of his tripartite government would have separate powers. Of course, such a view, being unacceptable to North and Thurlow, would hardly advance his ambitious career under a Tory administration.

Still, Jones's personality and learning were so engaging that monarchists welcomed him. He dined at Sandwich's house on 15 January. He was in a social whirl at the time. At Mrs. Montagu's he discussed the Abbé de L'Épée's pioneering work with deaf mutes. Jones was learning sign language. On 20 January he was at the Royal Society to deliberate on memorializing Cook; he preferred a medal to a marble monument because it was easy to circulate on a worldwide basis. The society resolved to "order a Medal to be struck expressive of his deserts."[34] Jones also was often with the Spencers. At dinner in February, he and Spencer discussed politics after the ladies retired, their opinions coinciding perfectly. On 13 February, Beauclerk asked Langton to invite Jones, Gibbon, and Percy to spend the evening with him after the Club, and to invite Jones, Percy, and Reynolds to dinner on 15 February.[35]

Three days later Jones and Yorke went to "the strangest of all places, the new spouting society in Soho Square" (1:345). Six hundred "men and women of fashion, lawyers, parsons, officers, tradesmen, people of all sorts" debated "whether [political] parties were beneficial in a free state." Young men, some ridiculous in masks and dominoes, harangued the crowd. One or two had prepared their speeches, but a former Harrow classmate of Jones disturbed the meeting by drunkenly attempting eloquence. After a curious two-hour debate, a majority decided that parties were beneficial. Though the experience amused Jones, such societies might hold potential for political improvement in England.

On 26 February he visited Mrs. Poyntz and her numerous children. When Lady Cork brought the news of Admiral Rodney's destruction of a Spanish squadron, Jones rejoiced patriotically with the others but concealed his stronger despair: Even brilliant victory was not true cause for joy if it protracted the war. Had Rodney been defeated, Jones would not have rejoiced; yet he would not have sorrowed much if the defeat helped produce a family compact with America.

He attended the four-day Oxford assizes before going to Worcester. As usual, he had brought books to occupy his leisure on the Oxford circuit. Still stimulated by Blackstone, he sketched the nature of laws and government. He also studied bailments and would have devoted more time to that branch of commercial law, except that he received Burke's recent speech, *A Plan for the Better Security of the Independence of Parliament, and the Economical Reformation of the Civil and Other Establishments,* which had four quick printings. Jones read it twice: "It is a noble composition, and the most extraordinary example I ever knew of retentive memory, strong reason, and gay imagination: some passages are no less just and solid than others are brilliant and sparkling" (1:353). Though the metaphors were too profuse and the comic epigrams inappropriate to a speech about a nation facing ruin, the public should be obligated to such a patriot. Friends like Daines Barrington were keeping Jones apprised of progress on the individual clauses of the bill. One was rejected by seven votes, and the one eliminating the Board of Trade carried by seven.

But if the Welsh judicature were abolished, "the saving will be a trifle, the inconvenience great; the increase of expense to the suitors, very considerable. If I find the Welch, in my approaching intercourse with them, averse to the alteration, I will speak to Burke" (1:351). Traveling through "his Welsh counties," as Jones fondly called them, he found that a few gentlemen did not object. As many more were warmly opposed, he probably asked Burke to delete the clause; but Burke, convinced of the need for the total package of bills, pressed on in a slowly losing battle with North.

Jones's circuit was profitable, though the extensive traveling was tiresome. Only once was he indignant, when a girl was hanged for strangling her illegitimate baby. As her seducer had promised to marry her, he deserved execution more than she. Yet the severe law required her death.

Upon returning to London, Jones found that North was still unable to make the judicial appointment. North had heard the East India Company's propositions politely, but replied that Parliament would compose the legislation so as to end the conflict between the Supreme Court and the Supreme Council. Because the Rockingham Whigs were ready to support the company if India became a major issue, North could hardly fill the vacancy. Battle lines were being drawn for a general election.

Besides this political impasse, Jones learned of a personal impasse:

The Chancellor will either have the *sole* appointment or none: he will have no concurrent patronage: Lord North is fearful of offending him and waits for his recommendation, which he will never give in favour of me or any one else. Thus I am kept between *hawk and buzzard,* approved by both and advanced by neither. I hope to have an interview with Lord North. (1:357)

Actually, Thurlow's advocating single patronage was less important than his dislike of Jones's politics, as Jones, if appointed, might apply his principles to judicial questions in Bengal. Notwithstanding the double impasse and the general condemnation of Hastings's harshness in India, Jones wanted the post. But would he ever be appointed?

On the circuit he had made a decision. If the situation were not near resolution and particularly if North did not give him strong encouragement, he would ask key friends whether he should forget India. The election was approaching, and lawyers should join the scene of action. His training was complete; he had a right to address fellow citizens on their important interests. After a few weeks of deliberation and consultation, he might embark on his political career. As he had not been rejected for the judgeship, he could not be angry at North, whose singular disposition often inconvenienced even North's best friends. If Jones so decided, he would take a determined role as a legal scholar and a supporter of the constitution.

5   An Ass Laden with Gold (1780)

Moved by his feelings about the war, Jones had questioned the British policy from the outset, and he had become more sympathetic toward the American cause as the conflict lengthened and the British situation became more hopeless. America required *de facto* independence – at least a family compact. Jones's classical background now persuaded him to use his literary talents to influence others toward his view.

He became a poet and pamphleteer within the heroic milieu of the American Revolution. Contributing to the rising stream of radical publications amid his efforts for the judgeship and a burgess's seat from Oxford, Jones wrote three poems and six prose works between 1780 and 1783 that associated him with the radical Whigs. The first was *Ad Libertatem,* composed about December 1779. Some stanzas are little more than a liberal translation of William Collins's "Ode to Liberty." This animated Alcaic expresses Jones's views about the war, with poetic amplification and coloring. Not really seeking to conceal his authorship, he signed the 172-line ode as *Julius Melesigonus,* an anagram of *Gulielmus Jonesius,* and had John Nichols print copies for friends. When surprising news arrived, he had a limited reprinting on 27 April, with copies going to acquaintances sharing his views.

One copy went to William Adams, Johnson's friend and the master of Pembroke. Jones had thought of sending the poem as a courtesy, but now he used it as a way to inquire about the surprising, impending retirement of Sir Roger Newdigate, a longtime MP for the university and a University College man. Jones knew little of the complicated background, or he might have proceeded more circumspectly. Because Newdigate had often threatened to resign, his major supporter Wetherel did not take him seriously. But this time he was determined because of governmental ambivalence, the unsuccessful American policy, and his colleagues' lack of principles. Arguments by Wetherel and others went unheeded. Then Sir William Dolben was recommended as someone able to continue Newdigate's semi-independence while supporting North.

114

Wetherel turned to Dolben, who sat in seven Parliaments between 1768 and 1806. He had been selected as a stopgap in the old Tory interest for a few weeks in 1768, and represented Northamptonshire between 1768 and 1774, voting regularly with the ministry although essentially an independent. Now he agreed to be powerful Christ Church's candidate, disturbing numerous Oxonians. Scott had opposed North's selection as chancellor, advancing the earl of Radnor until the seventy-three-vote constituency led Radnor to withdraw to prevent humiliation. After Radnor died, Scott had come to consider himself "heir to the tradition of die-hard opposition to whom independence still meant opposition to the Court."[1] Not satisfied with his University College senior tutorship, Scott had been looking for a seat that could be inexpensively secured. After friends encouraged him to stand for Newdigate's seat, he solicited Jones's support and advice. When Jones promised support if his own friends did not declare him a candidate, Scott insisted that their discussion be kept secret. Then, without releasing Jones from the promise of secrecy, Scott immediately began to solicit Jones's friends. Soon there was pressure on some members of Convocation to name him a candidate if his college did not. In justice to his merit, the members had to propose this "mere academical man," who was different from the country-gentleman tradition of burgesses and probably had little chance. After a printed paper was circulated on 29 April for a meeting, the attendance of University College men essentially made Scott their college candidate despite their master's selection of Dolben.

When friends at Oxford first asked Jones about his inclinations, he felt bound by his promise, until he learned that Scott was intensively soliciting his closest friends. Burke was already wholly engaged, and Reynolds had been urged to solicit Dunning's influence, so that Jones's best potential supporters were being lost. Now Jones decided that he would like the seat. Many respectable friends would advance his candidacy, and he could work for liberty and American reconciliation if elected. The time seemed propitious for the first step of his lofty ambition. As Scott and Dolben, whom he had long known, might split the Tory vote, Jones might benefit from the unhealed wounds caused by the arrangement making North the chancellor in return for protection against Dissenters' efforts to overthrow Oxford's Anglicanism. Friends would keep him apprised of informal actions to help him in these early hours. Thus he asked Adams forthrightly:

Now, the great attention and kindness, which you have shown me, Sir tempt me to ask you, who are well able to inform me, whether the writer of the enclosed poem, if his friends were to declare him a candidate, would have *any chance* of respectable support from such members of the University, as would trust the defense of their rights, as scholars and as Englishmen, to a man who loves learning as zealously as he does rational constitutional Liberty. (1:358)

If Jones's small interest at Oxford and his avowed affection for the constitution could not command such support, he would not make a fruitless attempt. Yet even the prospect of an honorable nomination "would be an honour, which no other man or society of men could confer."

Jones wrote Althorp, who had announced candidacy for Northamptonshire, that he was as able as most Oxfordshire squires were "to answer the purpose of the franchise granted to the Academical body, namely, *to protect,* as Blackstone says, *in the legislature the rights of the republick of letters*" (1:360). The Tories were so strong that the author of *Ad Libertatem* would have no real support, nor would he stoop to represent men who disapproved of his politics. Still, he would become a candidate if friends were to reply that, among the hundreds of voters, fifty Whigs would entrust their rights to someone of his principles. He would stand even if he "must finally yield to the forcible impressions of Toryism and the soft but sure influence of the Treasury."

The replies were favorable. Adams was ready to help, and Thomas Milles (All Souls) and Thomas Plumer (University College) approached some members of Convocation. A friend told Newdigate that the members "were forced also to acquiesce in his Nomination. But his friends are chiefly young Men and have shewn more Zeal than conduct in the Affair."[2]

On 2 May the University College bursar visited Jones. He explained that when the decision to fix on Scott had been made, they had thought Jones's Indian appointment would soon be announced. Having attended Scott's announced meeting, they could not withdraw their support, even though they now knew of Jones's doubts about the appointment and of his wish to be nominated by University College. Jones did not tell the bursar of his promise to Scott that had effectively kept him from starting his candidacy at the same time as Scott had. Moreover, he had spent only one day at Oxford after the circuit, leaving friends there uninformed about the judgeship. His candidacy thus became a hurried attempt to exploit a dramatic change in the political situation. He could not have challenged Newdigate, who had American sympathies, or Francis Page, a University MP since 1768. Jones was unprepared.

At the Club a few hours after the bursar's visit, Jones expressed his excitement to Banks, Colman, Langton, Percy, Reynolds, Sheridan, Steevens, and Vesey. Because the president designate was absent, Jones, as the vice-president, took the chair. All eight promised to serve him, although none had an Oxford M.A. degree. When they apparently urged him to solicit other friends, he penned a note to Althorp while they ate. Only the warmest exertions by every Whig and patriot, he wrote, could ensure even respectable support. All his friends must use every way to communicate with Oxford M.A.s, even if their influence seemed remote. What would have happened if Scott or Johnson had attended that unique meeting, when a member announced parliamentary candidacy and sought active help? Events would surely have been different.

Jones's decision to stress his literary and professional character, contrasting with the conventional country gentleman who was not an academic, perhaps derived from that meeting. However, the example of Burke – Sheridan lost his first race – was different in ways that Jones did not perceive for weeks. He naively assumed that such nonpolitical support could influence Oxford voters, who had little connection with literary men at the Club or anywhere else. University elections, unlike others, were normally not contested. His strategy, remarkable in its very failure, demonstrated the political weakness of exalted figures who tried to help. Literary and social support could not withstand the tide for Dolben, especially after Oxford voters were told of Jones's advanced politics.

The next morning Jones began dispatching a one-paragraph solicitation modeled on that to Althorp. One went to Hargrave, whose judicial pretensions were so weak that he was not a serious challenger for the judgeship. The solicitation urged friends' effort, good word, and influence. As a candidate should not canvass at Oxford, their effort would be critical. Another went to Schultens in Leiden, along with *Ad Libertatem*. Prohibited from voting by mail, Schultens offered to solicit language scholars like Joseph White. A third was received by John Burrows, who had no vote: "I have an additional reason for wishing you seated in the British parliament, as I shall take great satisfaction in seeing the dull of all denominations convinced, that men of wit and learning are as capable of excelling in public business, as they call it, as the most illiterate of them all."[3]

The morning after Jones met Walpole at a party, he made the mistake of writing Walpole, who reported:

He sent me an absurd and pedantic letter, desiring I would make interest for him. I answered it directly, and told him I had no more connection with Oxford than with the antipodes, nor desired to have. I doubt I went a little farther, and laughed at Dr Blackstone, whom he quoted as an advocate for the rights of learning, and at some other passages in his letter. However, before I sent it, I inquired a little more about Mr Jones, and on finding it was a circular letter sent to several, I did not think it necessary to answer it at all; and now I am glad I did not, for the man it seems is a staunch Whig, but very wrong-headed. He was tutor to Lord Althorpe, and quarreled with Lord Spencer, who he insisted should not interfere at all in the education of his own son.[4]

Though Walpole soon changed this opinion, Jones probably never learned of the negative reaction to his sometimes careless circularization.

On 4 May the *London Chronicle* summarized the situation: "Three Candidates have begun to canvas for the vacancy, viz. Professor Scott, and Mr. Jones, both of University College, and Sir William Dolben; but it is thought the contest will lie between Dr. Scott and Sir William Dolben." Johnson was similarly doubtful in his reply to Mrs. Thrale: "Scott and Jones both offer themselves to represent the University in the place of Sir Roger Newdigate. They are struggling hard for what, others think neither of them will obtain." Soon he was dogmatic: "Jones and Scott oppose each other for what neither will have."[5] His political principles would not have let him support Jones, but the previous coolness had now vanished. He counseled Jones like a father: "*Persist:* for, if you lose the election you will gain considerable honour by *having stood*" (1:406). Although disliking Johnson's principles, Jones venerated the old man's intellect and was buoyed up. When Jones told him of Scott's forgetfulness in not releasing Jones from the promise of secrecy, he responded: "I hope it *was forgetfulness*" that had permitted Scott to gain unfairly the support of many of Jones's friends at Oxford.

Naively, Jones did not perceive his handicap in not being a college candidate, until friends reported from Oxford that voters were repeatedly and forcibly asking a disturbing question: Why had University College endorsed Scott, when Jones was an older member if a somewhat younger fellow? Had his college rejected him? Some voters said that it was unfair for one college to have two candidates. Because he was not available to reply – and Scott carefully did nothing to defend him – the situation became alarming after only three days. After friends convinced Jones that a public explanation was necessary, Paradise anonymously penned and circulated "To the University of Oxford." Jones cooperated but unfortunately did not moderate the more exuberant passages.

Paradise's four-page paper concludes with quotations from four of Jones's books to emphasize his Oxford loyalty, honesty, and modest aspirations.[6] It defensively apologizes for the fact that his candidacy would split the University College vote, while building sympathy for his awkward situation. It attempts to justify the paper and to explain why Scott was the college candidate: The college would not have selected a candidate if there had been any doubts about Jones's receiving the Indian judgeship. Indeed, Jones has often said that "he would resign the absolute certainty of the most lucrative post to which he could now aspire, either in India or in

England, for the moral certainty of so high an honour" as burgess. His nomination by many friends from different colleges has removed the just objection of one college's having two candidates. Necessary residence in the Temple has prevented his gaining many acquaintances in the university, in contrast with Scott's extensive connections developed during years of residence there. There is no mention of Jones's unfortunate promise to Scott.

Jones's friends pledge not to canvass at Oxford, as he will never disturb "the calm seat of the Muses, by consenting to any such solicitation." He himself will apply only to those who have expressed regard and have no votes: "The Master of Arts in a great University, whose prerogative is cool reason and impartial judgment, must never be placed on a level with the voters of a borough, or the freeholders of a county." The last paragraph pleads: "No exertions must be spared by those who, either personally or by reputation, approve the character of Mr. JONES; into which, both literary and political, as well as moral, his friends desire and demand the strictest scrutiny." He has incurred powerful men's displeasure, as he has in answering the foul-mouthed Anquetil's scurrilous attack on Oxford. He suspended his favorite studies for a year to save Oxford the discredit of not having a son translate *Histoire*. His occupation unfortunately requires his absence from the university, until the election either rejects his toil as a man of letters or provides "the greatest reward to which he can aspire. The unavoidable disadvantage of being so late proposed, and the respectable support with which he is now honoured, will secure him in all events from the least disgrace."

A tactical error, the paper acknowledged Jones's tardy, even minority situation and revealed his willingness to assume a defensive posture, instead of exposing the whisperers' motives and displaying his qualifications. He sent the paper to particular friends, defending it as sensible and necessary and denying that he was actually dispersing it himself. One copy went to Adams, indicating his optimism about significant support at Pembroke. There was some reaction: "This being circulated by his consent if not desire, sounds so like being ones own Trumpeter, & approving yourself before you are approved of others, that I think it will do him much more harm than good."[7] Such typically conservative reaction reached Jones. Although he gave the duchess of Devonshire a copy, he acknowledged that it should have consisted of only two paragraphs explaining why his college had not endorsed him.

With this problem supposedly resolved, Jones took the usual step. Friends received an advertisement for a meeting of his Oxford supporters, whether voters or not, at the Turk's Head on 25 May. He asked the

Spencers to help him secure the needed numbers and splendor for the meeting to appoint canvassing committees and duly declare him a candidate:

Means will be devised of filling up my list as accurately and completely as possible with the names of *patrons* and friends of great weight. Dr. Milman, whom Lord Craven (unless I am misinformed) has fixed in my interest, tells me of an absurd report "that my friends are to *deliberate* to-morrow whether I am to stand a poll or decline." A very uncandid and injurious report! (1:384)

Thomas Milles chaired the meeting, and the voters declared Jones a candidate. Langton attended, despite his monarchism. Jones's gift for friendship permitted him to hold advanced views and yet not alienate Tories like Johnson and Langton. Such standing with major intellectuals partly explains the West's rapid acceptance of his later Oriental discoveries. His affection for the Club, heightened by the recent meeting at which everyone had agreed to serve him, prompted an action that helped preserve the group at a time of lagging attendance.

The 1778 resolution, which increased its membership to thirty, had not rejuvenated the Club. Beauclerk's death in March 1780, while causing a second vacancy, eliminated one of their social centers. Chambers was in India, Charlemont often had to be in Ireland, and the aging Johnson came only two or three times a year. Attendance was averaging about eight members. As the next president designate and wishing to rekindle the spark that the Club had once known, Jones called a "meeting extraordinary" on 9 May to vote on two candidates and his resolution:

Resolved, 1st. That the number of the club be augmented.
2dly. That it be now augmented to thirty-five.
3dly. That it be not hereafter augmented to more than forty, and that the members whose names are underwritten will vote against any other candidate whenever the club shall consist of *forty* members.[8]

Jones was the first of eleven signers – Althorp, Banks, Bunbury, Colman, Fordyce, Langton, Reynolds, Sheridan, Steevens, and Vesey. Among the thirty-four who signed later, one in 1810, were Boswell, Burke, Gibbon, Percy, and Scott. Johnson, who apparently disliked further expansion, never signed. Although he did not attend that Tuesday meeting, he evidently dined out on Monday and then on Thursday and so was not ill. Though four candidates were blackballed that night, the resolution did freeze the maximum membership. Paradoxically, election work kept Jones from attending on 23 May, when only four members came.

Jones was seeking to enlist patronage through the Spencers. Jauntily he notified Althorp that a zealous friend, probably Paradise, would secure the lists of members of Convocation from the college butlers: "One of these you shall immediately have: I will fish out the connexions of the voters. Patronage, I fear, will carry votes against me: it must therefore be exerted for me" (1:365). Jones approached Lady Spencer. As ecclesiastical patronage would decide the race and as his competitors had strongly applied to all the wealthy patrons, he must weaken them by soliciting the same support: "May I hope for your Ladyship's assistance and that of my Lord, as far as his health will permit? It will be a considerable point gained, if we can carry a Whig member for Oxford. . . . if I succeed, it will be a triumph; if not, it will be honourable to have stood" (1:369–70). Naming several nobles who had "infinite weight" with the voters, he enclosed the voting lists, complete but for the elusive Jesus College one.

The duchess of Devonshire, who was mightily assisting Fox, volunteered her aid and began to seek out voters. Immediately thanking her, Jones noted that no more than 200 of the roughly 860 voters were engaged. As the Whigs owned two-thirds of the English property, their influence would be almost irresistible if they united behind him, despite his formidable competition:

Mr. Page's seat is, and ought to be, firm by the rule of the University *once a member always a member:* Sir W. Dolben is supported by Christ Church and by the Tories: Dr. Scott professes *moderation,* but is himself *no Whig* to my certain knowledge: He therefore, if his friends would take off his veil, would weaken and disunite the Tories, by whom he has been already supported; and I should hope that Lord Radnor, his *college-pupil,* would cease to support him so strongly, and would give him a compensation some other way. I am determined, in all events, to stand a poll. (1:371)

Enclosing the lists, Jones requested help with a University College fellow. Misled by his misspelling, the duchess promised to approach the Cambridge MP Richard Croftes. Jones thereupon transmitted the fourth letter between them on 15 May, correcting the mistake but noting Croftes's "great weight with the members of both Universities on account of his literary character" (1:372).

Indeed, Jones's lists, copied from "Members of Convocation 1760–87," had numerous misspellings.[9] It lists 834 college voters and another 27 from the five halls in 1780. Eight colleges had 514 votes:

Christ Church	117	Merton	49
Magdalen	88	St. John's	44
Queen's	79	All Souls	40
Brasenose	57	Jesus	40

University College's 33 votes made it the twelfth largest. But despite Jones's propensity for friendship, he was severely handicapped by virtue of having few really influential supporters resident at Oxford.

Soon he sent the duchess the list from Jesus College, an extremely important page because most of the forty voters lived in Wales. The pursuit of one voter had uncovered a problem: "He must not divide his votes between Dr. Scott and me, lest Mr. Page (whose seat I am trying to secure for the sake of the Foleys) should be injured" (1:378). The reasoning was pragmatic. If a voter supported Jones and Page, the vote for Jones could be the margin defeating Page, as Dolben seemed certain to win the other seat. But one might ensure Page's victory by voting for Page and Dolben, regardless of sympathy for Jones.

There was also a problem with the Welshmen of Jesus College. As the vice-principal was backing Scott, Jones asked the duchess to enlist Viscount Bulkeley and another Welsh noble who might influence nearly the whole college and convert the vice-principal or at least cool his efforts for Scott. Aware of the interconnections of the medical men, Jones pointed out the influence of his physician on another physician, and he listed the other physician-voters for the duchess. Francis Milman was already enthusiastic, having attended Jones's committee of canvassers.

Jones sent Lady Spencer a list of powerful potential patrons, chiefly the nobility. Though he shared the political views of Jacob Bouverie, now the second earl of Radnor, Radnor had advanced Scott as a lesser evil than Dolben and had gone almost too far to assist Jones. Really a Tory in principles, Scott lacked only family prejudice to render him as contemptuous of popular government and as favorable to high prerogative as Dolben was. Jones was proud of the powerful people who were working for him: "Though I find the opposition diffident of their strength, yet I can assure them that it is greater than they imagine" (1:377). He was receiving encouragement hourly; men whom he had never met were volunteering their help. Some who had unwarily engaged their vote by half-promises honorably expressed regrets. As Thomas Wenman (MP for Westbury, 1774–80) had decided not to be a university candidate, Jones was authorized to communicate that important fact. Baron Craven and the earl of Abingdon were also backing Jones.

Only extreme self-control let Jones articulate this catalogue to Lady Spencer, for he could hardly restrain his tears: "*I have now no parent left but my Country.*" After his sister had married a retired merchant in Bristol, he had often dined with his mother. On recent nights they conversed about many subjects, and he amused her by drinking patriotic healths. Despite complaining of pain, she discussed his Oxford chances with high spirits, feeling that a victory would provide him a station for opposing oppressors; if he lost, he would still have demonstrated zeal for a noble cause and would have advanced in his profession. Despite more pain on 16 May, she was so cheerful that he did not suspect any danger. The next morning she started to summon him, but decided not to worry him. She died "without a sigh or a pang with the most placid countenance and a mind completely at rest; the very end for which she had always devoutly prayed" (1:375). When he reached her, her lips were barely cold. He wept convulsively for hours, and his doctors said that only his weeping prevented perhaps the worst consequences.

The shock was doubly severe because of its unexpectedness. She was

one of the most intelligent and accomplished, as well as wisest and most amiable, of women. . . . I have lost the highest pleasure that I could enjoy, that of spending an hour or two with her from time to time, and conversing upon all the variety of subjects on which we perfectly agreed; especially on politicks, of which no Spartan mother ever thought more divinely. (1:380–1)

He controlled his grief by throwing himself wholeheartedly into his campaign.

Jones was enjoying his closest association yet with the Spencers, who always did everything possible to help. In essence, Lady Spencer replaced his mother as confidante. His letters to her reflect the weak, idealistic opposition that some intellectuals offered North's ministry. She tried to assist, but the tasks he gave her were formidable. Thus an earl's little interest had long been engaged to Scott, a duke and his friends were of Christ Church and thus bound to Dolben, and the Spencers did not know Bulkeley well enough to approach him. Overall, she was much discouraged: "If you are not pretty sure you shall make a tolerable figure you had better give it up – which your finding Doctor Scott had been so much before hand with you, would be a sufficient occasion for daring" (1:385).

Her doubts had substance. His competitors were circulating a harmful story that he did not intend to stand a poll. However, many votes were promised, and many men who declined to promise would vote for him. Withdrawing would be imprudent except under two circumstances. First, as there were fewer than 200 resident votes, not all of which were engaged to his competitors, the roughly 660 nonresident votes, of which Jones anticipated a majority, could decide the election. But if this nonresident strategy failed to offer real promise, his supporters should not have to journey to Oxford to cast a useless vote. Second, he must never strengthen the Tories by dividing Dolben's opposition.

Jones did not consider Scott, who had much greater strength amassed through long preparation, a friend of liberty. When Fletcher Norton, calling to express regret at having promised to vote for Scott, proposed a union of interest with Scott, Jones coldly refused. If Scott would unmask his Tory features, Jones might well win because of the ensuing division among the already disunited Tories. But Janus did not, talking like a Tory at Oxford but like a Whig in London. Jones also had difficulty in consolidating the Whigs behind him, for supporters of Whigs who were currently not candidates feared to engage their votes to Jones lest the given Whig might suddenly decide to oppose Dolben.

Jones's strategy was counter to tradition. The usually uncontested election had few nonresident votes cast. Some residents considered his strategy improper, perhaps a step toward reducing the election to just another political contest, with the corruption often entailed. When they murmured that nonresidents should not vote, he privately and indignantly rejected the disfranchising of three-quarters of the electorate: "Would the residents think so, if they could get good livings, for which they all pant? Surely not. – This is a most agreeable canvass, except that it gives much trouble to my excellent friends and patrons. It is attended with no expense" (1:400). Even if he were too optimistic, his supporters would persist in canvassing every voter outside the university, almost with abandon, although no Oxford election had ever been decided mainly by nonresidents.[10]

Except for the unfortunate "To the University of Oxford," Jones's strategy was based on five generalizations:

Proposition 1. It would be a great object to literature and to the nation, if a Whig could be returned for Oxford.

Prop. 2. The Tory party is so strong there, that such an event can *hardly* happen, unless a candidate arise, who, by the circumstances of his character, may disunite them.

Prop. 3. It is not arrogance to say, *what* is already proved, that such circumstances occur in me, from my literary and professional character.

Prop. 4. We shall succeed in this contest, if we can *disunite* the Tories and *unite* the Whigs.

Prop. 5. The instrument of *disunion* must be my professional and literary support: the instrument of *union,* must be my avowed zeal for our excellent constitution; and the united efforts of opposition. (1:363)

Jones had pursued this strategy despite the artifice of Scott's followers in portraying Scott as a moderate. As a result, David Hartley, the influential Whig MP on whom Jones had been counting, had perhaps been lost to Scott. Happily, after Rockingham was assured that Craven and Abingdon supported Scott, a check of the story led Craven to attend Jones's meeting and led Abingdon to promise his support, too.

After just three weeks, considerable influence was being exerted for Jones. Fox was helping at Brooks's gambling club, and General Richard

Smith was canvassing Berkshire and India connections. Sir George Savile, Jones's great friend and a longtime MP for Yorkshire, was seeking to recover Hartley. The three Foley brothers would help if they could convince Page that his seat was secure. The Whig opposition, especially Dunning, favored Jones, as did the Club. Even after reading *Ad Libertatem,* Langton was canvassing, as was Banks, despite his closeness to Sandwich. Milman and another physician had promised their votes. Most judges, serjeants, and King's Counsel were Jones's friends, including the advocate general and the judge of the High Court of Admiralty.

In view of his open Whiggism, few ministerial men could be expected to help Jones. Yet the lord lieutenant of Cardigan had procured two votes, and the admiral of the fleet was soliciting. Jones felt that three-fourths of the electors would vote as their patrons wished: "I know several, who will give no answers, and only wait for some powerful application" (1:390–1). There were disappointments. When friends approached Henry Harington, the author apologetically told Jones that his name was out of the books. When application, perhaps at Parr's instigation, was made to the King's Champion, he was favorable but doubted whether he could change after having voted for Dolben earlier.

Jones's literary friends were working hard, if with little result. Mrs. Montagu volunteered to write her Oxford acquaintances in the strongest manner. She told Weller Pepys: "If the Muses were the Electors he would carry the election from every candidate that could offer. He possesses the keys of all their treasures and can deal them forth for the world."[11] Pepys lamented that he had no university vote.

Jones's most outspoken workers were the radical Whigs, particularly three. First, Edmund Cartwright volunteered his support because of Jones's literary stature, superior talents, and integrity. Jones had received many flattering testimonies, but Cartwright's was "the fairest and most pleasing fruit of the competition" (1:373).[12] Jones was aspiring toward the kind of honor given John Selden, whose political prominence had led to his being offered the mastership of Trinity Hall, Cambridge, by direction of the Commons. If successful, Jones would devote his life to serving his constituents and country, practicing law, and studying. He sent *Ad Libertatem* to Cartwright, whose *Prince of Peace; and Other Poems* (London, 1779) deplores the American war.

Cartwright pledged his vote and sought others. When a friend wrote on behalf of Dolben, Cartwright praised Jones:

A society, principally instituted for the cultivation of letters, and which is supposed at least to consist of literary men, cannot, it is presumed, be so respectably, or indeed so properly represented, as by men who are most conspicuous for literary attainments; and it seems but just that those whose superior abilities and learning reflect honour upon the University, should have in return such honours conferred upon them as the University may have in their power to bestow.[13]

When John Coulson, their old tutor, solicited for Scott, Cartwright offered support only insofar as it would not hamper Jones. The two had considerable correspondence.

Second, Richard Price sought to engage Hartley's vote: Jones "is well known to be one of the first Scholars in the world; but his principal recommendation on the present occasion is the excellence of his public principles which are those of a zealous and decided Whig. I may safely say that in this respect he is far from having an equal among his competitors."[14] Wilkes was also helping. Such aid was innovational, for an Oxford election was normally remote from London politics. Jones told these radicals to stress his Whig principles to anyone who doubted them.

By late May three factors were badly harming his chances, which had never been good. First, there were exaggeration and dishonesty. Lines from "To the University of Oxford" were quoted out of context. With Scott's approval, remarks from Jones's more uninhibited conversations were distributed in a paper seeming to come from him that could greatly damage him. Hearing a description of the paper, Jones urged Parr to explain it whenever it was mentioned.

Second, he should not have distributed *Ad Libertatem* to show his integrity and independence. At Oxford it earned him the names of *American* and *Republican:* "Those, who call me so, do me great injustice, if they mean to insinuate that I prefer the interests of independent America to those of England, and that I should be glad to see a republican form of government in this country: most certainly those charges are groundless" (1:388). His circulating the ode nicely confirmed the charge of republicanism that Scott's friends printed in a pamphlet and placed in college Common Rooms.

Finally, Jones was having to trust some of his more serious expectations to radical Whigs. He was almost compelled to appear as the popular candidate, hardly an appealing image to conservative Oxonians.[15] A friend warned him: "Have you however no apprehension that your enthusiasm for liberty, which is so generally known, may, in these unpropitious times, injure the success of your cause? Will those upon whose votes your election depends, allow the University to be represented in parliament by Julius Melesigonus?"[16] But Jones's integrity would not let him moderate his public opinions.

Law work had principally kept him away from Oxford. Now Jones visited Chesham, accompanying Lytton to the Buckinghamshire meeting at Aylesbury on 27 May. Grieved to witness divisions among patriots, he feared that their zeal might injure England. This time he heard a debate on Pitt's views on short parliaments and expanded county representation, rather than on the critical question raised by the York petition. Jones feared that the people's suspicion about forming associations, coupled with the excess ardor and monarchists' efforts to discourage such meetings, could doom the whole movement, which might otherwise lead to a fine union if the meetings would concentrate on the real object of the petitions and would guide the associations toward that goal. If the movement were dropped or Parliament rejected the petitions, and if the petitioners submitted to this further indignity, Jones would despair of seeing his ideal constitution operate in England. If the same or nearly the same Parliament were elected, he might even migrate to America.

Jones talked with a fellow of All Souls, whose influential family were opposed to a firm commitment to Jones, which could weaken Wenman in case of an unexpected vacancy. More importantly, his conversation about Oxford with another man at the Aylesbury meeting was to have repercussions.

On the whole, he was optimistic if Scott would drop the Whig disguise. When he found two of Oxford's warmest Jacobites canvassing for Scott in London, he considered the conduct honest. But when others argued for Scott's Whiggism, the unexpected strategy siphoned off needed Whig votes. The curious delusion did not make Jones despair; there might be another vacancy before the election. On all sides he was hearing that any failure would be explained by his late start, which would protect him from disgrace if he received few votes. Certainly he had no inclination to withdraw, though North had told Lowth: "I persuade myself that, when the two Literary candidates's are apprized of Sir William's strength, they will decline" (1:407). Jones's later reaction was that he would not let people think he was complying with the minister's wishes so as to favor the court candidate. He would withdraw only to spare his friends much trouble.

Then the domestic unrest that had helped precipitate Jones's candidacy erupted and doomed his remaining chances. Lord George Gordon, president of the Protestant Association organized to seek repeal of the Popish Act, instigated a rally of some 100,000 Protestants on 2 June. The demagogue harangued the mob and then led them to Parliament. MPs, forced to wear blue cockades and cry "No Popery," were beaten. After presenting his petition, Gordon lost control of the mob, which burned two Catholic ambassadors' chapels and began to fan out through London.

In the comparative quiet of 3 June, Jones was saddened by the destruction. Wild enthusiasts, he thought, were injuring the cause of liberty. He continued writing letters for his campaign, not employing a secretary to copy even the less personal ones. The Gordon Riots erupted with fury the next day. As the mobs raged through the city, he uncomplainingly observed the assignment of armed soldiers to street corners, though he philosophically opposed martial law. Unaware that Savile's house had been gutted, amid mounting threats that all Catholics would be killed, Jones sent a messenger to offer his services. However, Savile and many others were in the House of Commons, besieged by a mob quieted only by the reading of the Riot Act.

By the climax on 7 June, Jones was convinced of the need for military force. From the Temple he could hear looters shouting and the wounded screaming, as troops shot down scores of pillagers. Drunken men and women filled the streets, vowing to burn the property of anyone who had even expressed a desire to ease the restrictions against Catholicism. The city was in danger of a second fire and at the mercy of a licentious rabble. Jones had been advocating liberty, but here was liberty unrestrained – anarchy motivated by medieval intolerance, incited by a fanatic. Avoiding the mobs, he went to the Westminster courts, which were supposed to be in session and which might be an answer to the terror. The doors were barred, as were those at Parliament House, after the MPs' savage treatment. Indignant, he picked his way back through the dangerous streets.

What followed was his most harrowing night. At 8:00 P.M. the barristers and the students met to plan a defense of the Inns of Court, following a report that the rioters would attack. As the inmates of the King's Bench, Fleet Prison, and two other prisons were freed and those buildings burned, devastation threatened. In the lurid light from fires burning out of control, and the pandemonium from fleeing thousands, some two hundred members of the Temple, armed with new muskets from the government, took up stations at the gates under the command of a bencher of the Middle Temple, who requested soldiers.

Just before going on duty at 8:30, Jones sent everything of value to a friend's house. He, Wenman, an MP for Derby, and an earl's son were ordered to hold their gate at all costs. At 2:00 A.M. a nearby gate was broken down. When the mob saw the soldiers, they fled. Had they persisted, there would have been much bloodshed, as preparations had been so hasty that the barristers might have shot one another. Jones's post was not the safest, but when no attack had materialized by dawn, the four went to their rooms for sleep interrupted by a summons to a general meeting. They formed one Irish and two English associations, as the societies had earlier done under the regicide Edmund Ludlow.

When Jones joined his division at their station that afternoon, he no longer expected an attack. The troops' shooting into the mobs had ended the riots; the War Office unofficially reported two hundred killed. The order for the troops to fire had made the Temple safe, and peaceable Londoners could now dig up or bring back valuables that had not been lost. The Commons' adjournment had left London protected by army muskets, but Jones began to worry when the soldiers were still at their posts after a week. Though he had approved their protecting the Temple – ironically reacting like the monarchists – he had not changed his principles, which were now almost impossible to defend. When a great magistrate told him, "This is the voice of the people," he was shocked that the man could mistake the wild rabble for the voice of the community and nation (1:404).[17] The precedent would let the king use the army to disperse legitimate gatherings.

The Temple had formed its own militia. Some five hundred gentlemen were divided into companies, armed with muskets that could fire only once. Jones was on duty, without rest, from 8:00 P.M. until 4:00 A.M. on 9 June. Then after making a long argument in a case that morning, he heard that London was now under martial law, thus legally requiring the Commons to adjourn. However, the continued sitting of the courts of common law and equity disproved this disturbing report. He also heard that rioters would be tried by courts martial and, if found guilty, would be hanged instantly. The constitution, however, should bar such action unless all other law was suspended. Parliament, legally in session, could grant the king constitutional powers and even proclaim martial law.

Althorp's Northamptonshire Militia was stationed nearby, as was an army encampment. But Jones did not think the bloody business finished: "The vile rabble that burned the prisons and demanded money in private houses, is crushed effectually; but the spirit of religious enthusiasm only sleeps or rather closes his eyes in meditation of repeated attacks" (1:407–8). He feared the rising reaction that he was hearing from people who should know better: There should be greater royal prerogative, which he considered already too strong.

As he thought this to be the time for putting a flintlock in every gentleman's hands, Jones raised a volunteer company of barristers and students on 10 June. Officers recommended an excellent sergeant, and Jones procured carbines. He encouraged other men, hoping that companies would associate themselves for their defense all over the kingdom. When his company of twenty-four men began training under the sergeant, Jones prevailed on them to act as officers and privates in alphabetical rotation. On 13 June his group, now thirty-six men, laudably performed platoon drill twice; and he also took his turn in the Temple garrison in guarding a gate all night. His company practiced firing in the garden, but shortly the ending of the emergency terminated his noble experiment.

Meanwhile, Althorp had secured Jones a vote, although it raised the delicate question of Jones's accepting a plumper after having promised no hostility to Page. The Foleys' friends would act similarly for Page unless Page's seat was absolutely safe. Althorp persuaded Augustus Keppel, later first lord of the Admiralty, to procure Jones two votes. The Shipleys were soliciting Welsh voters. Other gains were partly offset by a false rumor that Scott was withdrawing, which would end all hope of dividing the Tories and would make Dolben irresistible. When Jones's friends expressed that view to him, he replied that he did not know the truth and would not accept speculation.

His committee had helped little, as men like Milman were busy with their professional concerns. Though intending to learn the voters' connections, they had discovered little that was useful. Their failure was yet more disappointing when Jones learned what his competitors were saying. That is, they accused him of trying to overturn the very constitution that he was laboring to preserve, and of attending the Buckinghamshire meeting in order to be introduced as a university candidate, a ridiculous thought that presumed Aylesbury freeholders might interfere with the Oxford election. Actually, there had been no introduction, and Jones had talked to only two people about Oxford. The only truthful charge was that he had hoped to build a majority of nonresidents, who had the same suffrage rights as did residents.

Weighing the situation amid the ashes of the Gordon Riots, Jones realized that his current chances were hopeless and his future unpromising. The delusions and artifices dividing the Whig interest were preventing his securing sufficient nonresident votes. Yet this was not the time to strike his colors to a court candidate, as there might be some unforeseen event before Parliament was dissolved, and it would be imprudent to decline when all his real friends were canvassing. In fact, on 12 June he learned of the possible gaining of the warden of Wadham's vote, along with three or four other votes.

As has been said, Jones had reacted to the riots by forming a company. After all, had trained militias been available, the army would not have been needed to quell the bloody disturbances. As a legal scholar he now urgently asked "whether the still-subsisting laws and genuine constitution of England had not armed the *civil state* with a power sufficient, if it had been previously understood and prepared, to have suppressed ever so formidable a riot without the intervention of the *military*." He soon discovered common and statute laws supposedly in force, which gave every county enough power, if understood and utilized, to quell any riot or insurrection. This fact needed dissemination, for well-intentioned men kept remarking that the constitution's mixed nature was at fault or that a government like France's would have protected London. Others argued that the danger was over, despite the riots at Bath, Leeds, and Windsor.

Jones recorded his findings anonymously in his first political pamphlet, printed by Nichols for Charles Dilly in July. *An Inquiry into the Legal Mode of Suppressing Riots, with a Constitutional Plan of Future Defence* describes his experiences in the riots, his search for the needed laws, and the provisions of those laws. His thirty-five-page plan is based on the *posse comitatus,* as the law requires the county force to equal a well-disciplined army. Jones cites Blackstone's explanation for the neglect of this law – the vast force of the Riot Act, the expedience of a standing army, general indolence, and executive voluptuousness. The English are accustomed to being protected by the executive power and the army, although they should refuse such reliance and seek to reinstitute the relevant laws.

Jones intends to submit his carefully restricted plan in person to his fellow citizens as the answer to "such riots as savour of rebellion":

1. Any man in the power of the county, with money to buy arms and learn their use, should have a musket.
2. Every county should have several companies of at least sixty such men, voluntarily associated solely to help when summoned.
3. Each company should be privately taught every morning until the men are skilled, avoiding military show and considering themselves part of the civil state.
4. Each member should keep his weapon ready to defend his house and person and should be ready to help his company keep the peace.
5. Severe restrictions must prevent misuse of the company.

Jones presents a general answer to any criticism: People do not have to apply to the king or Parliament for permission to obey the laws, every citizen can act as a soldier to preserve public peace and thereby guarantee liberty, and one's security depends on the assurance that the executive power will not invade one's rights.

The August issue of the *Monthly Review* suggests the educated reader's reaction to this one-shilling pamphlet:

It is impossible to say too much in praise of this concise Inquiry. It bespeaks the hand of a master, deep in legal knowledge, and the heart of a citizen truly virtuous. Within the compass of a few pages, it makes every reader a lawyer upon the question under discussion; and it points out the means of preserving public peace and freedom with so much clearness, that it is not possible, as we conceive, for any reader to doubt of their efficiency, or to see any difficulty in carrying them into practice. (pp. 142–3)

In 1782 there was a second edition of Jones's *Inquiry*.

The city of London attempted to implement his plan. James Townsend, a former MP for West Looe, moved its adoption in the Court of Aldermen, where it lost by two votes. The earl of Mansfield vainly urged the House of Lords to strengthen the civil power at once. Unfortunately, the summer circuit would prevent Jones's speaking at the meeting of Middlesex County, at which, if he received support, he would have made a motion supporting the civil power so as to eliminate the need for soldiers and perhaps eventually to eliminate the standing army.

Jones urged Parr to prod friends in Norfolk to make an effort to preserve the constitution: "They would take pains enough I dare say, to preserve the game. A month's exercise with the firelock would make them useful men" (1:424). He supplied Althorp with answers to expected objections. Preparing armed citizens would not plunge the nation into discord; rather, civil war or anarchy caused by the people's unrestrained power or monarchistic encroachment would be prevented. Ultimately, the implementation of long-neglected laws providing for local militias would preserve the constitution. Jones was proved right by the end of the century, for armed associations were formed under varying names in the British counties.

He intended to recommend his plan on the circuit, revealing his authorship of *Inquiry* and declaring that martial law threatened constitutional government more than did the riots that had led to the imposition of martial law. This view disregarded conservative voters' fear that, because an unarmed citizenry had devastated London, armed militias would be more frightening. Though he had heard little from Oxford, Jones presumed that the riots had made "resident Oxonians more adverse than ever to the advocates for Liberty, which they absurdly confound with Licentiousness, whereas the first is the basis of all human happiness" (1:417). He spent three days at Oxford in early July, encountering a sullen silence when he mentioned the election. With the pressing political issues and riots, "the Tory was overshadowing the Radical in Dolben as in so many of his constituents."[18]

Before his circuit Jones visited Lytton and then went to the Abingdon sessions, spending only one day at Oxford. The month-long circuit provided both business and recreation. Although many worthy men praised his plan as constitutional, they declared that this was not the time for it.

In Pembrokeshire he won a curious case. A man was charged with alarming a village by reporting the approach of an enemy warship. John Holwell (former governor of Bengal) and the other prosecutor were angry at having been made fools, a point that they could not prove, Jones felt, as they were already fools. His subsequent speech included bitter reflections on the state of the country and on Holwell's attempt to import British Indian laws by indicting an honest man who had only done his duty.

Finishing at Cardigan, Jones went to Oxford for four days. Leading men told him that he would have had a majority if only Scott and he had stood. As Dolben's phalanx at the large colleges was irresistible, if Parliament were dissolved in the autumn, Jones would withdraw. He and Paradise would soon leave for Paris to try to save the Virginia estate. But Althorp sent word of the surprise dissolution of Parliament of 1 September, observing that Jones might receive election business that could help the Whigs. Also, it would seem unprofessional to be absent at such a time.

Delaying his trip, Jones reviewed his decision. He had secured ten to twelve more nonresidents' votes on the circuit, but he had no chance against Dolben, and any effort to contest Page would rashly violate his repeated declarations. Jones had always feared failure, but had not expressed his fear lest he dampen his friends' zeal for this race or a future vacancy. As he had not gained much nonresident support, his strategy had not made him a serious contender. He had literary character, which Dolben lacked, but college loyalty overrode that asset.[19] Dolben's supporters could vote without inconvenience, whereas Jones's were faced with long rides. Nor was Scott faring well. His literary character won many Tories in the first week, until the news of Radnor's support prompted a greater number to join Dolben to prevent election of a burgess with the "madness of Radnor politics." The needed dividing of the Tory vote, much less the uniting of all the Whigs behind Jones, never occurred.

Now Jones's concern was withdrawing properly. A friend advised him to notify Wetherel and George Horne, the Oxford vice-chancellor. Because it seemed more appropriate for his committee to make the declaration, Jones sent letters to their houses. He also asked Benjamin Wheeler (Regius Professor of Divinity), who had not been very helpful because of his canonry in Dolben's college but who was one of Jones's truest Oxford friends, to inform the university that Jones would give no further trouble and was heartily sorry for that already given. He had hoped to become an Indian judge and perhaps a burgess. But if success at Oxford required a change of principles, his cause was hopeless, as they would always guide him. Ambiguously, he was not hostile to the ministers, who had been kind to him; but he could not support their measures. When his committee did not answer his letters, he realized that they might be out of town.

Jones himself had to write Wetherel. After stating his withdrawal, he voiced a willingness to keep his promise to give Scott his vote, which would hardly please Dolben's supporters. He could not keep from criticizing events. Friends who had said that he had not proved his attachment to University College had never requested his services, and he had once zealously helped Wetherel when asked. When he wrote these friends sincere, affectionate, absolutely unexceptionable letters, they quoted detached sentences on various occasions, perhaps altering his meaning. Worse, Jones was charged with misrepresenting facts (he was ready to make a deposition on the points in question) and with writing an objectionable paper, which contained an erroneous number that disproved his authorship. Worst of all, he told Wetherel, he was charged with wishing to overturn the very constitution for which he would die. Ever the gentleman, he did not directly accuse Wetherel of having made that charge, though he knew that the master was a culprit. He privately informed Adams of Wetherel's unpleasant role in the unsuccessful candidacy.

Jones's withdrawal was not known publicly for a time. The *London Chronicle* reported on 5 September: "We hear from Oxford, that beside Mr. Page, who (it is supposed) will be re-chosen unanimously, there will be three Candidates to represent that University, in the place of Sir Roger Newdigate, Bart. who voluntarily retires" (p. 224). Then came Jackson's *Oxford Journal* of 9 September: "We have Authority to assure the Publick, that the Election of Representatives for the University of Oxford, comes on in Convocation on Monday next, when Sir William Dolben and Francis Page, Esq. will be chosen without Opposition; Mr. Scott and Mr. Jones having both declined all future Contest." Thus ended Jones's only effort for elective office; Scott would finally succeed Page in 1801, serving until he was elevated to a barony. Dolben was agreeably received when the victors toured the Common Rooms. He verified Jones's pessimism in a letter to his son: "I must be at the meeting, as it is said there will be a Contest for the Chair, and I am sure it is necessary that Government should have a friend and the House a Gentleman placed in it."[20] Even before his first vote, he intended to support North.

Jones had not mentioned his principles to Wetherel. In the abstract they were not radical, but when applied to specific situations like the American war, they would have helped ensure his crushing defeat. Informed at Oxford that *Ad Libertatem* had lost him almost twenty votes, Jones stubbornly denied the report. The rumor that he was a confirmed republican also helped block his being nominated as a formal Whig candidate.[21] This rumor was circulated in a damaging pamphlet and contributed to the delay in his Indian judgeship. "Nothing could have been more calculated to anger North and Thurlow, who controlled all judicial appointments, than his decision to stand as the popular Whig candidate."[22] Yet Jones was not disturbed that his advocacy of popular principles was slowing his career.

Althorp, elected from Northamptonshire, was the one person to whom Jones confided his despair. All he had now was his studies and his law profession. In England a lover of the true constitution was outnumbered twenty to one; now people who coldly applauded his honesty also questioned his wisdom. If the love of pure monarchy continued, Jones might accept improvable property along the James River in Virginia as compensation for saving Paradise's estate. In America his profession could provide as much success as civil society should permit.

Jones sent Edmund Cartwright an eloquent notice of his withdrawal. Despite his respectable support, it would have been unpardonable to let friends make the journey to vote without higher expectations. As victory would not have advanced his law practice but would only have upset him when he vainly tried to promote the public good, he professed no depression. Jones was not really dissembling. Cartwright did not need this admission of defeat, for he had cast into a sonnet the sentiments of his earlier letter to Jones:

> In Learning's field, diversify'd and wide,
>   The narrow beaten track is all we trace!
> How few, like thee, of that unmeasur'd space
> Can boast, and justly boast, no part untry'd?
> Yet rests not here alone thy honest pride.
>   The pride that prompts thy literary chace;
>   With unremitting strength and rapid pace
> 'Tis time to run, and scorn to be deny'd!
> Thy early genius, spurning Time's controul,
> Had reach'd ere others start, the distant goal,
> Marking the bright career that thou has run,
>   With due regard thy toils may Oxford see;
> And, justly proud of her superior son,
>   Repay the honour that she boasts in thee.

Gentleman's Magazine added a footnote to the sonnet: "It was the earnest wish of many of Mr. Jones's friends that he should offer himself as candidate to represent the University of Oxford, that celebrated seminary and patroness of learning, at the late election."[23]

An important supporter whom Jones must not discourage was Wilkes: "I beg my friends (in the number of whom I am happy to rank Mr. Wilkes) will believe, that I think myself no less obliged to them for their kind exertions than if that kindness had been attended with complete success" (1:435). Although he was confident that no one would dare oppose Wilkes's nomination at the next Middlesex meeting, Jones would attend to show his support. Lacking connections, he had only been able to urge friends to apply to voters on behalf of Fox, who professed good principles and had the ability to advance them. Jones would have continued his own candidacy had Parliament not been dissolved, as so much depended on next year's regency, although a Whig had no chance unless the Oxford Tories were equally divided and the national Whig interests were united behind a third competitor like Jones. He had depended on these two conditions, he told Wilkes, but had been defeated without real disservice. A literary reputation had proved to be moonshine, not an asset; but as friends would probably set him up in any new vacancy, he needed Wilkes's printed voting list so as to add the new names and their connections.

This experience would be useful if there were a change in public measures. Besides discovering that the nation preferred a pure monarchy to a mixed republic, Jones had gained valuable insights and numerous friends. He had seriously challenged the longtime assumption that the university was intractably Tory, and had provoked some Oxford Whigs to speak up, while generally worrying Tory leaders.[24]

At the Middlesex meeting at the Mermaid on 9 September, he hoped to speak on the state of the nation. There was no opposition to the nomination of Wilkes and George Byng, whereupon Wilkes made a long speech that was received with great clapping. As only routine business was transacted without debate, Jones felt that he could not speak with propriety.

At home he amused himself by contemplating what he would have said had he been invited to speak. Deciding that he should have spoken anyway, he composed a speech no stronger than what was often said in the Commons or in the associated counties' petitions. In it he savagely congratulates Parliament for six sessions that have deprived England of greater advantages than can be regained in six centuries. The policy toward India and Turkey, colonial commerce, and the slave trade destroyed British commerce and alienated America, while giving the lucrative Turkish trade to the French. He proposes that India's riches and territory be held in trust for the whole community, and condemns the "abominable traffic in the human species" as a violation of natural law. It would be better to lack sugar than to rob one person of the eternal right of freedom. Jones has been informed that the American South will abolish slavery as soon as circumstances permit. His main theme is the war, which "began with injustice, was pursued with malignity, and must end, if it be long protracted, in destruction." If America somehow loses, there will have to be a military occupation, during which the English will lose their constitutional system at home. Only a conciliating parliament can restore trust. Without naming Franklin, Jones presents Franklin's argument against reunion: (1) English constitutional liberty is extinguished, and (2) the many attempts at trickery have made America distrust any ministry. Jones had Nichols print *A Speech on the Nomination of Candidates to Represent the County of Middlesex* for select friends, but this second political pamphlet had a limited audience until it appeared in the second edition of his *Inquiry*.

He made plans for his Paris trip. Although Paradise's estate was legally protected for another year, the steward had pointed out the danger of confiscation unless Jones acted to preserve this annual source of £1,000. As Paradise could not go to Virginia right away, he was contemplating the almost unprecedented step of naturalization. Jones was excited if not a bit awed by this primarily professional trip.[25] He was anticipating seeing Franklin, who might now recall his "Fragment of Polybius," rejected last year as having been proposed too late. As he had offered to carry out commissions for Wilkes and often met with Shipley, who was playing a part in trying to end the war, he presumably wanted to obtain late news from America for Whig friends. Probably Shipley's intermediary, he was carrying letters for Franklin.

Langton had sent a determined invitation to dinner, and so Jones spent a few hours at Chatham. While waiting for Paradise, he began to worry. The weather was usually bad in September, and raiders like John Paul Jones might appear anywhere. He penned an overly dramatic note to Parr that did not specify his straightforward reason for the trip. If he died, Parr and Bennet, his two oldest friends, should use his papers to compose an account of his life and ideas; but they must not print unfinished work, much less any idle thing, thereby perhaps distantly but falsely implying the presence of treasonous communications among the papers. Perhaps Jones saw himself as a modern Roman knight, momentarily turned from the goal of saving his country in a depraved time, to the goal of helping a friend threatened by a consequence of that depravity.

After the arrival of Paradise, "the best natured man in the world with no contemptible stock of various knowledge" (1:440), the pair sailed before daybreak on 20 September. The wind was good, with bright starlight. Just after dawn they were becalmed, but the wind resumed and gave them hopes of soon seeing Flanders. They were deceived, for a southeast breeze blocked them all day. After midnight an abrupt equinoctial squall endangered them until the sails could be struck, and they tossed about until the gates were opened at Ostend. They had had no food for thirty-two hours.

They remained in Paris for two weeks and accomplished their principal objective: Paradise was naturalized preliminary to his anticipated eventual migration. Jones delivered some letters to Franklin, who enjoyed the pair's company and inquired in detail about Price. Franklin's answer to Price noted: "I thank you much for the second edition of your excellent pamphlet. I forwarded that you sent to Mr. Dana, he being in Holland. I wish also to see the piece you have written (as Mr. Jones tells me) on Toleration."[26]

When Jones recounted his Oxford experience and the election results, Franklin was convinced that the new Parliament would not be honest, a quality attainable only by revolution. The conversations deepened Jones's apprehensions: "The result of all I have heard and thought is, that the war, which I have invariably and deliberately condemned as no less unjust than impolitick, will continue very long to desolate the country of our brethren and exhaust our own" (1:442). The naive compromise in his "Fragment of Polybius" had had no chance; he was moving toward embracing independence. One reason for his wish to know many American leaders was his intended history, and he steered conversations to military affairs so as to gain direct information. Later he told Shelburne of his planned "authentick History of the unhappy War" (2:602).

Jones attended some cases at the *palais* and purchased the eight-volume *Œuvres posthumes de M. Pothier* (Orléans, 1776–8). Impressed, he hoped to introduce the legal scholar to English lawyers. In the royal library he found an Arabic manuscript that he hoped to use in a cultural essay to accompany his possible translation of the poetic *Mu'allaqát*.

Jones and Paradise left with letters from Franklin. In one to Georgiana, Shipley's fourth daughter, Franklin stated: "Mr. Jones tells me, he shall have a pleasure in being the bearer of my letter, of which I make no doubt" (1:443). Presumably there was also one for Shipley. James Searle, whom Pennsylvania had sent to Europe to seek a huge loan for military supplies, accompanied the pair to Brussels. Jones had hoped to visit Amsterdam to deliver the letters that he was carrying for John Adams, the American Peace Commissioner, but finally had to forward them, as business called him to London.

There his political gloom was somewhat relieved by a surprising report:

Lord Shelburne, having seated all his particular friends, actually canvassed a borough in my name, and would have succeeded if an unexpected event (the arrival perhaps of *an ass laden with gold,* with which Philip of Macedon used to say that he could *take* any *town* in the world) had not given an adverse turn to the affair. This his Lordship told a friend of mine fully and explicitly. He presumed, I suppose, that, as I was candidate for Oxford, I wished to be in parliament for any other place. I am certainly much obliged to him for his very kind and flattering intentions; nor will I depreciate the value of a seat. (2:457–8)

Certainly he would have liked to have the seat, though the Opposition was pouring forth empty invective and attempting unavailing censures.

The vehement sparring between Dunning and Burke convinced Jones that the Opposition was crumbling. Only Arabic literature helped relieve his anguish: "I reflect on the melancholy times in which we live – times when many of the best men I know have actually resigned their seats in parliament, from a full conviction that no exertions whatever can preserve our free constitution" (1:444). Jones's exaggerated jeremiads reflected the Opposition's dismay at failing to bring down the ministry and rouse the nation against the war. So did Walpole's letters to William Mason on the declining British greatness and the ruin of the constitution, and the correspondence of Burke, Rockingham, and Shelburne. Only Viscount Barrington had idealistically resigned between 1775 and 1780, principally because of the American policy, although Newdigate had had similar motives in not standing.

Jones's dismay was reflected in the mannered, stilted vein of some of his early letters, until his professional career was secure and he was politically mature. Contrasting with his developed warmth in person, his early correspondence often presented a cold pose of Roman republican virtue. For years he compared himself with Cicero, denounced the wicked times, and saw himself as a future savior of his country. Jones's deep classical learning and intense idealism prompted such writing, which is hardly in modern taste. This sensitive, highly intelligent man filled his letters with classical phrases and thoughts. Walpole, who was also scrupulously honest and candid, mocked such affected passages, but he was intent on memorializing himself through thousands of letters. His severe artistic standards demanded fine "gazettes," which Jones's haste and classical elegance usually precluded except in warm letters to Althorp. Chesterfield, who had earlier adopted the stoic pose and would probably have liked Jones's early letters, might have thought Walpole garrulous and lacking in generalizations.

Jones's friends in the Club had fared well in the election. Facing defeat at Bristol, Burke won a seat for Rockingham's borough of Malton. Fox crushed the ministerial candidate for Westminster, and Dunning was reelected for Calne. Sheridan and Althorp were new MPs. Chamier was reelected, but Gibbon lost his seat.

Jones's own experience was greatly discouraging. The Whigs had not acted according to the principles that he considered to be the foundation of their party and that might provide the mixed republic that the real English constitution should sustain. The Whigs had not united behind him, and the principles impelling his candidacy had been distorted into charges that he wished to overturn the constitution. Military defeats, the soaring national debt, and bloody riots had been insufficient to overcome the enormous patronage and corruption when the executive directly interfered with Parliament. A conciliating parliament had not been elected, but North's majority had been reduced from about sixty votes to twenty.

As Jones's candidacy had not endeared him to the ministers, the judgeship seemed distant. He was not beginning the role of an independent MP, but continuing that of a lawyer who could do little for liberty. Campaign activities and a month's absence had retarded his practice, which was unlikely to provide real financial independence for years; yet he was a good lawyer, with much energy. This one defeat need not be a harbinger.

6   Politics: Writings and Activism (1780–1782)

Jones faithfully attended the Club in late 1780: on 31 October; 14, 21, 28 November; and 12 December. He only attended seven of the sixteen meetings of 1781, and six of the sixteen in 1782.[1] As his resolution had authorized expansion to thirty-five members, the meeting of 21 November 1780 was important. However, Bishop Beilby Porteus and Earl Camden were blackballed: "When Bishops and Chancellors honour us with offering to dine with us at a tavern, it seems very extraordinary that we should ever reject such an offer; but there is no reasoning on the caprice of men" (1:451). Camden's hopes may have been compromised years before, when Goldsmith had complained that Camden had paid him no notice at a gathering, and Johnson had answered that Camden should not have neglected Goldsmith.

No bishop had ever been elected directly; Barnard had been consecrated when a member. Now Jones nominated Shipley, the second friend whom he added to the Club. The nomination of a Whig extremist naturally raised the question of Johnson, though the two were social acquaintances. Jones still recalled a night at Shipley's, when Johnson remained silent at dinner and then poured forth invective against music: "Montboddo could hardly get in a word, and was indignant, nor has his indignation yet ceased" (1:359). But Shipley was elected with approbation, Jones happily informed him: "There is no branch of human knowledge, on which some of our members are not capable of giving information, and I trust that as the honour will be ours, so your lordship will receive some pleasure from the company once a fortnight, of some of our first writers and critics, as well as our most virtuous senators and accomplished men" (1:451–2).

This was the only club that Shipley had ever wished to join: "I believe Mr. Fox will allow me to say, that the honour of being elected into the Turk's-Head Club is not inferior to that of being the representative of Westminster or Surrey. The electors are certainly more disinterested."[2] But Jones's future father-in-law did not enjoy a smooth membership; soon Johnson censured him for meeting at a tippling house.

141

One club to which Jones was elected but did not attend, perhaps because he was not interested in their focus on chemistry, was the London Philosophical Society, sometimes known as the Chapter Coffee House Society. Of the several fellows of the Royal Society who were "original members," James Horsfall, treasurer of the Middle Temple, may have suggested Jones as a prospective "original member" prior to the first meeting in December 1780. Many members were nonconformers with advanced political views, including the chemist Thomas Cooper and the honorary members Price and Joseph Priestley. Cooper had known Jones at the Nicotean Society at Oxford, where he often saw Jones, Joseph White, and John Uri enveloped in the smoke of Virginia tobacco.

Jones was devoting himself to his law practice as if his parliamentary race and the rejection of his plan for militias had never occurred. On 22 November he spoke for two and a half hours in Westminster Hall on a knotty point, the following morning on a public question, and the next day on a great cause.

As the holidays neared, Jones made plans to study Arabic at Cambridge. White, the holder of the Laudian Chair of Arabic, had asked some linguistic theological questions in connection with a proposed volume of annotations for his Ḥarklean *Sacrorum evangeliorum versio Syriaca philoxeniana* (Oxford, 1778). But Jones could provide few answers, as he did not know Syriac, and White's questions about certain biblical passages were baffling. Certain Hebrew astronomical words were general, not the names of constellations. Jones preferred not to be thanked in the volume, for he had more linguistic fame than he wished, and a lawyer would be burdened by a scholar's reputation. Nonetheless, White's preface to William Davy's translation *Institutes Political and Military, Written Originally in the Mogul Language, by the Great Timour* (Oxford, 1783) praised Jones's Persian *Grammar* as having a "propriety of arrangement which is peculiar to an elegant mind" (p. xiii).

Jones spent a harried "vacation" at Emmanuel College. For six years he had submerged his old love of Arabic under the dedication to his new career. Now an occasional indulgence should not harm that career, though he was careful not to use time needed to expand his small London practice. As his own copy of the seven-poem *Muʿallaqát*, made from an Aleppo version, was beautiful but not very correct, he devoted every day to translating Trinity College's fine manuscript, which he was unable to finish. Trinity obligingly permitted him to borrow it, and he relaxed during his last week and visited with Bennet. At Oxford from 7 January 1781, he finished translating the manuscript in a few weeks. Because of the approaching circuit, he decided to delay until the summer the publishing of his version, which would need notes and his projected essay on ancient Arabic literature.

He completed a proposal for printing John Uri's intended translation of Saʿdí's *Bústán* by subscription. The Bodleian had let Uri spend work time in combing Persian manuscript dictionaries for words not in Meninski; now Jones repaid the favor by formally proposing Uri's translation and promising to correct it.[3] The poem, he said, conveys

the most striking lessons of Morality . . . illustrated by a variety of tales and fables, written, by the concurrent testimony of all Asia, in the purest and most elegant style; so that the proposed translation will, it is hoped, be acceptable to all lovers of polite learning, and especially to those, who, from their residence in INDIA, have acquired a taste for Eastern literature, and a knowledge of the *Persian language.*

Jones appended a five-couplet fable in Persian and his own English prose version, observing that Addison once used the fable in a *Spectator* essay.

Amid his labors on the *Muʿallaqát,* he met his obligations in the quarter sessions. Somewhat earlier, Robert Raikes, a printer who promoted Sunday schools, had sketched a political system harmonious with Jones's. Missing Raikes at Oxford, Jones penned an elegant letter lamenting his countrymen's willingness to lose the free constitution. He included regards for their mutual friend Josiah Tucker, who had written him about the now-completed attack on Locke. While anticipating seeing Tucker on the circuit, he considered the political situation so bad that such attacks seemed scarcely worthwhile.

Jones sent congratulations upon Althorp's engagement to Lavinia Bingham, the earl of Lucan's daughter. He was convinced that no man could enjoy happiness unless "united by marriage to a lovely and accomplished woman" (2:454). Then why was Jones still a bachelor at thirty-four? The answer was independence: A husband had large responsibilities unless his wife was wealthy (Lucan had gained £20,000 through marriage). Jones's view was the same as it had been when he had met Anna Shipley. He would not marry to make his fortune, refusing to wed someone he did not love, even "if she had all the mines of Peru and all the diamonds of Golconda."

As it was vacation time at Oxford, Jones saw few people who could assess his political standing after his depiction as the popular candidate. Scott had been called to the bar and hoped to practice in the Admiralty and Ecclesiastical courts. Jones was willing to help Scott; however, the two had never had a real friendship, which, he felt had to be constructed on philosophically similar opinions. Scott's notions of power seemed too high for general freedom, whereas Jones's notions were not too republican for public order: "I never dreamt of liberty unrestrained by well-enacted and well-executed laws; and, without *such* liberty, I am very sure, that men cannot enjoy the happiness of *men;* that of *cattle* they may enjoy in any government" (2:456).

Back in London on 23 January, Jones found many papers requiring immediate action. He and Wenman had grown closer during their guard duty in the Temple. Now Wenman wanted help in the contest for Keeper of the Oxford Archives. Although he disagreed politically with Wenman, the two were *gemelli* in other respects. Next, Jones asked Althorp to solicit the vote of a man whom he barely knew: "This is the only way of canvassing friends" (2:457).

He remained in London for the Club meeting of 13 February before going to Oxford to vote, when Wenman narrowly won. Passing the time pleasantly with friends whom he considered the flower of the university, Jones was much sought after: "I have neither obtruded *nor suppressed* any of my political opinions; but, as they know me to have no selfish views, they give me credit for consistency and integrity. Seriously I think that my conduct among them may in time soften a little of their old Tory spirit" (2:465).

His friends' dislike of Radnor, who had "inflexible virtue and solid worth," puzzled him. In case of a new vacancy, they would probably choose Wenman, though hundreds told him that he would have certain success in a race solely against Scott. Curiously, his industry had aroused some envy, while serving as a reproof to loafers.

Jones had to miss the beginning of the circuit because of Althorp's wedding, at which the ladies made much of him. These included Lady Spencer, the duchess of Devonshire, and Henrietta Spencer, who had recently wed Frederick Ponsonby. They and the unmarried Louisa Bingham and Frances Molesworth insisted on an epithalamium. When Jones laughingly protested, "My voice is tuneless, and my harp unstrung," they pointed for inspiration to the beribboned basket prepared for the wedding presents.

Accordingly, he composed *The Muse Recalled, an Ode on the Nuptials of Lord Viscount Althorp and Miss Lavinia Bingham, Eldest Daughter of Charles Lord Lucan, March VI, MDCCLXXXI* almost extempore. But aspiring to the kind of larger horizon that Milton had created in "Lycidas," Jones revised his most distinguished occasional poem so carefully that he missed the Oxford assizes. The 152-line Pindaric begins with rather conventional octosyllabics reminiscent of "L'Allegro," invoking the Muses to return to the lyre that he has fondly hung up and now reclaims. The second stanza imaginatively describes the nuptial basket. Needing to please the ladies, in the next stanza he interweaves jarring names like *Bingham,*

Molesworth, and *Devonshire.* Then his warbled strain announces the bride, whose approach lends ethereal fire to his poetic power. Three stanzas praise her beauty and talent, perhaps less expansively than he might have done if she had been less coarse and her father had not been North's supporter.

Jones's climactic turning to Althorp raises the ode far above a rhetorical performance. Just as Milton had found a universal dimension in an acquaintance's drowning, so Jones finds in the bridegroom the potential of classical patriots. Althorp will charm the applauding senate, while exulting Liberty brings peace and domestic joy. But Truth, Justice, Reason, and Valor have fled to America, which, Jones prophesies, will defeat tyranny and then build magnificent commercial fleets and become the Muses' new abode. This bold vision reaches his imaginative peak, surpassing his early imitations and translations in sentiments worthy of the radical Whigs. Imitating Milton's far-superior close, Jones returns his harp to the sacred well. No longer lightning, it is only glittering wire, for his circuit beckons.

The Lucans asked Walpole to print the ode, and he did 250 copies: "There are many beautiful and poetic expressions in it. A wedding to be sure is neither a new nor a promising subject, nor will outlast the favours: still I think Mr Jones's ode is uncommonly good for the occasion." When a critic questioned Jones's expression "curled smiles," Walpole defended it as intelligible to anyone who had seen Correggio's angels. Though Jones might have dwelled more on the bride's transcendent qualities, Walpole knew that "Mr Jones is not so zealous an idolater at that shrine. However, if the ode is not perfect, still the eighth, ninth and tenth stanzas have merit enough to shock Dr Johnson and such sycophant old nurses, and that is enough for me."[4] Gibbon liked the poem so much that he asked Lady Lucan to give William Hayley a copy. It was reprinted in Paris in 1782 for private distribution, and in *European Magazine* (January 1785, pp. 62–63). The poem later had a role in the radical movement, assisting the cause of rebellion.[5]

Completing the revision, Jones hurried to the advancing circuit. At Hereford he won two cases, but a great one, of which he had the command, was postponed. After the Oxford circuit, he stayed at Abergavenny to meet with Tucker, who had finally published *A Treatise Concerning Civil Government.* Tucker bluntly recalled Jones's criticism: "Accept a work which you will not like." Jones replied: "Why not? frankness and plain dealing are what I most like, and I esteem no man the less, because I dissent from him" (2:463). Skimming through the book, Jones agreed that Locke was too insistent that one cannot be made a member of a state without one's express consent. Though accepting Tucker's argument for an implied contract or consent, Jones upheld one's right to migrate if one's original state ever no longer deserved the name of *country.* He thus anticipated the United Nations' Universal Declaration of Human Rights: "Everyone has the right to leave any country, including his own, and to return to his country." Jones conceded that a person has "an instinctive propensity to social life, subordination, and government"; yet people are more sociable than bees, ants, or other animals. If natural propensity goes any further, Jones argued, it should lead to equality and a pure republic, the only rational form of government when circumstances permit.

Still imbued by his vision in *The Muse Recalled,* Jones completed his greatest political poem as he rode in his chaise on 1 April. Joining "A Persian Song of Hafiz" as his two best poems, it had been drafted by December 1779. The organist Charles Burney had set the draft to Attic notes, and it had been sung after dinner. The literary image of a free city had first tantalized Jones in 1773, when he found Alcaeus' Fragment 29 in Aristides. Returning to Greek poetry for comparable political expression, he began revising his 1779 draft. He borrowed from James Thomson's Preface to *Areopagitica: A Speech of Mr. John Milton* (London, 1738): "What makes a city? Not walls and buildings; no – but men, who know themselves to be men, and as sensible that liberty alone exalts them above brutes" (p. iv).

An Ode in Imitation of Alcæus expresses Jones's system of government and morality in eight famous quatrains beginning with

> *Althorp,* what forms a state?
> Not high-rais'd battlement or labour'd mound,
>   Thick wall, and moated gate;
> Not cities proud with spires and turrets crown'd.

High-minded men who know their rights and crush the tyrant constitute a state, over which Law is sovereign. "This heav'n-lov'd isle" once enjoyed such freedom. Jones ends by answering his rhetorical question:

> Shall *Britons* languish, and be *Men* no more?
>   Since all must life resign,
> Those sweet rewards, which decorate the brave,
>   'Tis folly to decline,
> And steal inglorious to the silent grave.

Jones made Parr a copy as the last sign of his *"departed hope* for a renovation of our free Constitution" (2:466). Shipley thought it was truly Grecian; Jones's genius had quickened Alcæus' seed "into a noble production. I cannot help observing that Alcæus, like other good poets and patriots, was condemned for life to be in the minority."[6] But Jones did not esteem the ode: "It is very *true,* and consequently wants the essence of poetry" (2:498).

He had several copies printed without bibliographical markings for Priestley and others. Sometimes the copy was accompanied by a statement about "this absolutely criminal war, my deep hatred of tyrants, and my enthusiasm and support for true liberty" (trans., 2:471). Franklin received a copy along with other poetic enclosures that were "the fruit of a few idle hours: they contain sentiments, which, I trust, you will approve" (2:492). Franklin's fourteen-year-old grandson printed the ode on Franklin's press in 1783.

The ode soon gained the wider audience that it deserved. The *Annual Register* of 1781 reprinted it without the poet's name (p. 183), as did *European Magazine* (February 1782, p. 146). The radical Society for Constitutional Information published it as a broadside without bibliographical markings in 1783. Perhaps the moving expression of liberty accounts for its fame, for patriotic Common Councilmen and MPs often dramatically quoted inciting lines. The ode further reduced Jones's acceptability for the judgeship in the eyes of the ministry. He later altered only the opening line, deleting Althorp's name to produce the more universal "What constitutes a State?" Soon a standard poem, it helps maintain Jones's place as a minor eighteenth-century poet.

Not all his poems were serious, for he celebrated his love of gaiety in occasional poems of "happy wit and fine imagination, tempered by the chastity of his mind and the elegance of his language."[7] Often written for friends' amusement, they provided aesthetic respite after courtroom strain. The best were composed in the beautiful Welsh countryside that he loved. Thus the elegant "Damsels of Cardigan," probably written in the summer of 1780, was composed at the circuiteers' *fête champêtre* beside the Teifi. Set to the time of "Carrickfergus," the flowing rhythm suggests a link between Matthew Prior and Gray on the one hand, and Thomas Moore on the other.[8] Each of the seven octets ends with a refrain, as in

> Yet weak is our vaunt, while something we want.
> More sweet than the pleasure which *prospects* can give;
>   Come, smile, damsels of Cardigan,
> Love can alone make it blissful to live.

Even if the barristers gain ermine robes or coronets, the damsels are sweeter. Fair women, not yearbooks and parchments, are the proper books. *Gentlemen's Magazine* gave the poem the lead position in its poetry section (September 1782, p. 446); and the Philadelphia *Port Folio* reprinted it: "The very amusements of Sir William Jones were of a literary character, and in his festal hour, he seems always disposed to associate Minerva and the Muses with Bacchus and the Nymphs. From such a post, the following Song, adorned with all the classical graces, will be read more than once, by all, who have an ear for the sweetest notes of the Muse" (4 May 1805, p. 133).

The poem was composed for the Druids, a circuiteers' society who dined by a romantic spring. Jones wrote the eighty-one-line fragment "Kneel to the Goddess" in one hour for them in 1780.[9] Under a majestic oak he dedicates the occasion to passionate lovers, decreeing exile for men of steely hearts. Mock-heroically he describes Parsees, Hindus, Moslems, and pagan Greeks, all of whom kneel to Fair Maiden.

"The Fountain Nymph" was apparently composed in 1781. The three octets of this *chanson à boire* celebrate the Druids' beautiful spring "in a wild grotesque style to the tune of a very lively country-dance, and it was admirably sung by one of our party" (2:498).[10] Inferior to "Damsels of Cardigan," it too conveys paganism, sensually contrasting the Teifi's azure couch with the "sweet paps lilied and roseal" of the spring's arched grotto.

Fearing that Althorp might think Jones to be one of the "licentiously profligate" circuiteers, he explained how he maintained his popularity. On an early circuit he had deliberately overimbibed so as not to appear critical. By means of that excess he had demonstrated that his future temperance would not be dictated by sullenness or reserve, as "they now let me drink as little as I please, and very little I please to drink. Even on the day when my song was produced, I confined myself to three or four glasses, with a copious mixture from the fountain."[11]

At least three other light poems that he wrote in this period have survived. When a beautiful maiden galloped past, he composed the undistinguished fifteen-quatrain "On Seeing Miss——— Ride by Him, Without Knowing Her," at a time when he was just beginning to accept his looming Oxford defeat. Jones was probably the author of the six-sestet doggerel "A New Song, on the Alteration of the Times." Written before Rockingham's succession in 1782, it portrays a peasant woman appealing to George III to dissolve Parliament and restore the days when five quarts of beer cost a shilling, before it is too late to save England. The poem is a kind of common people's counterpart to the electors' petitions.[12]

Jones did a sixteen-line unrhymed translation of Horace's ode to Pyrrha (I.5), in "a whimsical contest with Milton, who professes to have rendered it 'as near the Latin measure *as may be*' " (2:505–6).[13] Feeling that his English was closer to the original measure, Jones sent the two versions to Parr, who presumably recognized Milton's artistry, which Jones's competent version lacks.

Jones had a scanty harvest at Carmarthen, though he conducted every case and continued to be delighted with his profession: "There is none in which all the passions, interests, and good or bad qualities of mankind are so clearly seen and so decisively proved. . . . I believe many men to be wise, benevolent, upright, virtuous; but the *generality* are the reverse, as I hear proved *upon oath* every term and every circuit" (2:465). His talents were being employed to protect the oppressed. For example, the previous autumn he had successfully defended a poor farmer attacked by a powerful landowner, who had begun a new action, which he dared not bring on this circuit because he knew that Jones would lash him with redoubled asperity. Jones had gained a foe but had saved a better human being.

At Haverfordwest he resumed his usual fatiguing exertions in Wales, winning two cases on 12 April. Jones defended a man indicted for poisoning a woman, whom he had made pregnant and then had given a potion that was intended to cause an abortion but that killed her. Jones's evidence suggested that she had voluntarily and knowingly taken the medicine to cause an abortion. As her act was self-murder, the law required that the man be acquitted as *principal;* he could only be an accessory before the fact. The jury found him not guilty. This was an interesting case, as Jones always rigorously argued according to the law. The fact that the man was morally guilty and that the poisoned woman was the oppressed was irrelevant in this case, because Jones perceived the man's prosecution to be illegal according to the perhaps ultimately unfair law. His feelings were nonetheless strong, as he reported his indignation to Althorp about another case, when the law required a girl to be hanged for strangling her illegitimate baby, after having been seduced with a solemn promise of marriage: "How much more deserving of death was her seducer!" (1:350).

In the second case Jones won a verdict for a client impressed by a military man. The matter was supposedly finished; however, the loser waited outside with a press gang. Had the client been unable to secure a messenger to carry his frantic appeal to Jones, he would shortly have been at sea. Jones procured his release, with an attachment against the culprits. Impressment, Jones felt, kept English peasants as effectively in bondage as did Turkey's enslavement of the Turks, and it made the legislative branch as bad as the executive. Jones wondered how much longer he could withhold his argument proving warrants to be illegal, regardless of his friendship with Sandwich. As matters were to develop, this was his last serious thought about attacking impressment.

After the circuit he went to Oxford to consult commentaries on the *Muʿallaqát* for notes for his projected translation. Then his London practice kept him busy until he returned on 29 May, offering to perform Oriental commissions for Orme at the Bodleian. Enclosing a letter to Davy, probably about Jones's view that the supposedly nonliterate Tamerlane could not have written the original of Davy's forthcoming *Institutes,* he asked

Orme to notify him of any developments in the Indian judicature. There was no reason for optimism, because North had opposed the General Court of Proprietors' proposals; and a warmly debated resolution declared that three-fourths of the East India Company's net profits belonged to the public, and that the Exchequer should receive £600,000 in installments.

Jones's life was complex. Besides his practice, actions taken on behalf of the judgeship, work on the materials for his *Mu'allaqát,* proofreading of his first original legal book (as opposed to his translation of Isaeus), and time spent with friends, he was contemplating a trip to Paris. Paradise's estate was not really in jeopardy, as Franklin had just written Jefferson to explain the Paradises' inability to leave: "As they have ever been firm in the Sentiments of good Americans, I hope their absence will not be prejudicial to them."[14] Jones could talk politics with Franklin, if not learn about opportunities in America for a lawyer. Memories of the English Channel storm the previous year, besides wartime dangers, did not deter him. But he decided against the trip anyway and composed an answer to Franklin's recent letter, which he tried to send along with the letter that Georgiana Shipley had given him to deliver. His answer was lost, however, possibly when an informal courier plying the channel to the "American agents Adams and Franklin" destroyed the packet upon seeing a British warship.[15]

Jones did the final work on his new book, sending the last of the proofs to Nichols on 11 June. Long enthralled by English laws, he had recommended them in his *Speeches of Isæus.* Law in the abstract was also appealing. He considered law a science founded on principles and holding high rank in the empire of reason, with subordinate systems connected by nice links and beautiful dependencies reducible to a few elements. It employs reason and memory for the ultimate purpose of serving humankind, with English civil law supreme in regulating affairs at home and in the growing empire. Jones had recognized the relationship of history to literature and law at University College, where Robert Eden's *Jurisprudentia philologica* (Oxford, 1744) had started the tradition of linking law with literature. But Jones limited his new book to bailments, a branch of commercial law that he intended to explain by means of a new method.

His original plan was to begin with an encomium of Blackstone. But disappointed by the inadequate treatment in Blackstone's *Commentaries,* Jones only briefly praised it as "the most correct and beautiful outline, that ever was exhibited of any human science." Blackstone's indeterminate, three-paragraph description was the least satisfactory part, although bailments was the most generally interesting while the least precisely determined branch, actually a foundation of civil society. As virtually all persons often contracted lending or hiring obligations, liability ought to be determinable for any loss in which someone had another's property through agreement; yet bailments had caused more confusion in England than perhaps had any other aspect of commercial law.

The purpose of *An Essay on the Law of Bailments* is stated in Jones's opening lines – "a short and perspicuous discussion of this title, an exposition of all our ancient and modern decisions concerning it, an attempt to reconcile judgments apparently discordant, and to illustrate our laws by a comparison of them with other nations, together with an investigation of their true spirit and reason." This practical use of his legal knowledge was an effort to produce as essential a work on the specialized branch as *Commentaries* (which had earned Blackstone enormous fame and profits) was on general law. Expecting his book to sell well, Jones retained the whole share, according to Charles Dilly's declaration to the Stationers' Company on 29 June.

Jones's comparative sources are chiefly Roman laws, along with Greek, Hindu, Mosaic, Moslem, and Visigoth laws. He innovationally uses three approaches: (1) analytical, describing the bailee's obligation to restore the item bailed and the degrees of care that must be exercised in different situations, and relating every part to the principles of reason; (2) historical, comparing Roman and English laws in terms of the harmony in which nations have established those principles; and (3) synthetic, stating precisely the rules governing bailments.[16] Jones praises "the extraordinary merit of the treatises of Pothier upon the principal branches of commercial law. Nor is his eulogy upon this great man, warm and vigorous as it is, too strongly colored."[17]

The book first generalizes that one should be as careful of another's property as one would be of one's own, assuming ordinary prudence and the capacity to govern a family. Any lesser care constitutes negligence. A review of bailments decisions traces the principles back to Roman law; here Jones condemns Augustus for having subverted an excellent constitution with the tyrannous *lex regia*. Among important English decisions, he revises Sir John Holt's famous system, combining the third and fifth divisions and expanding another. Then, explaining his own five divisions, he corrects Holt's mistranslation of *diligentissimus*. Last comes a bailments dictionary constructed from various legal codes.

In extensively discussing Coggs *v.* Barnard, which contains Holt's system, Jones's perspicuity lags. By hoping to show perfect harmony on bailments "in the codes of nations most eminent for legal wisdom," he occasionally and unintentionally changes the facts. Yet his legal knowledge, in view of the poor foreign sources, was remarkable. Many contemporaries could have handled the yearbooks and later English materials, but perhaps none could have distilled into one specialized book so many relevant laws from so many languages.[18] His accomplishment was, furthermore, immediately recognized. John Touchet praised him in the *Monthly Review* for treating a dry subject with a master's skill, perspicuity, and grace; his luminous method "is the justest model of a Law-tract that we recollect any where to have met with" (April 1782, p. 299). The book gave Jones a juridical reputation.

Jones asked Hargrave to check the unbound sheets: "You will oblige me infinitely if you will point out such inaccuracies in it, as may occur to you. I could cancel a sheet or two without much delay. One or two slips I have myself detected; but they were of no great moment. New materials or cases, of which I am not now apprized, I must reserve for a second edition" (2:475–6). He never had time for this revision. After the Dublin edition of 1790, it had more editions and reprintings than even his Persian *Grammar* had, particularly in America, where the third London edition was reprinted in Philadelphia in 1836. It was the standard source on bailments for British and American lawyers for fifty years and remains a classic among English law-treatises. *Black's Law Dictionary* still cites Jones's five divisions. The book guaranteed his place in legal scholarship.[19] Justice Joseph Story, whose *Commentaries* superseded it in 1832, stated:

What remained to give perfect symmetry and connexion to all the parts of that system, and to refer it to its principles, has been accomplished in our times by the incomparable essay of Sir William Jones. ... Had he never written any thing but his Essay on Bailments, he would have left a name unrivalled in the common law, for philosophical accuracy, elegant learning, and finished analysis.[20]

Even today its formulations, varied research, and abundant learning are impressive.

Lack of time eventually caused Jones to abandon the vast legal work that he had been writing since 1777. This was a treatment of "*every* branch of *English* law, *civil* and *criminal, private* and *publick,*" organized into analytical, historical, and synthetic parts. It would fill out Blackstone's outline in *Commentaries* and remedy the defects, while adding a treatise on maritime contracts as illustrated by Demosthenes' speeches.

Jones had been revising his translation of Littleton's *Anciennes loix des François* (Rouen, 1766), completed in 1773. Containing notes, it was to be introduced by a discourse on English laws. His model was Gabriel's rendering of Sallust, and the discourse was to be extracted chiefly from Coke. His title page names the Clarendon Press as the publisher of the two quarto volumes in 1776; but professional obligations made him abandon such projects, preventing his doing for other branches of law what he did for bailments. His scope is revealed in a memorandum listing the laws that he had studied: Arab, Athenian, Britonic, Chinese, English, French, German, Gothic, Indian, Italian, Jewish, Lombardian, Norman, Persian, Roman, Russian, Saxon, Spanish, Spartan, and Turkish.[21]

Not having had an opportunity to thank Gibbon for the compliment paid him in the *History,* Jones sent a copy of *An Essay on Bailments* as a token of appreciation: "The subject is so generally important, that I make no apology for sending you a professional work" (2:480). Gibbon was again complimentary: "The public must lament that Mr. Jones has suspended the pursuit of oriental learning," as declared in the *History of Nader Shah.* Besides praising Jones's *Commentariorum,* Gibbon made four other graceful salutes. *An Essay on Bailments* is ingenious and rational: "He is perhaps the only lawyer equally conversant with the year-books of Westminster, the commentaries of Ulpian, the Attic pleadings of Isæus, and the sentences of Arabian and Persian cadhis." The *Speeches of Isæus* was done by "a scholar, a lawyer, and a man of genius."[22] The gift book and Gibbon's greater use of Jones's scholarship in the remainder of the *History* brought the two closer.

In his letter Jones told Gibbon that he would have to abandon Oriental studies so as to concentrate on his law practice, unless North were to think him worthy of the vacant judgeship. If he heard nothing by the autumn, he would construe the silence as a polite refusal and forget India. If his political system offended the ministers, they should tell him so. It was purely speculative: "I should hardly think of instructing the Gentoos in the maxims of the Athenians." Thus he discreetly sought Gibbon's help. He was not compromising his principles, because he strongly believed that lawyers and judges must not question or vary from the law, however they might disagree with it. Unfortunately, Gibbon's influence was slight.

A communication from Burke had further deepened Jones's interest in India:

I do not know how I can justify myself in the liberty I take with you, but confiding in your humanity and condescension, I beg, if you have leisure for it, that you would be so kind as to breakfast with me, and assist me with your opinion and advice on the conduct of the Bengal Bill. The natives of the East, to whose literature you have done so much justice, are particularly under your protection for their rights. (2:479)

Frustrated by his unsuccessful Oxford candidacy, Jones felt that Parliament could not stop the country from sinking into despotism; his attempted assistance had been rejected. Yet he supported Burke's wish to reduce the king's use of faction and sinecures as a chief cause of parliamentary corruption, and he loved Oriental studies. As his assistance would serve both the Indians and his judicial aspiration, he began searching relevant Arabic and Persian books, supplying the start of Burke's massive knowledge about India.

Burke wanted more than the foreign-language information that Jones was best qualified to gather. Because some would go into legislation, Jones's legal ability would also be helpful. General Smith's Select Committee had brought in the East India Judicature Bill, which would bar the Supreme Court from revenue administration and indemnify the Governor-General and Supreme Council and their resistance to the Court's decrees. North had posed alternatives: (1) Was it proper for the Crown to take over the Indian lands and revenues, or to leave them for the East India Company? (2) Was it proper to open trade to India, or to give another country the monopoly? and (3) If the company were given a new charter, should it be for a short term? On 1 June, North brought in the East India Agreement Bill, which would let the company temporarily (1) control the Indian lands, (2) continue exclusive trade, and (3) receive the revenues. The Opposition retorted: "Public robbery!"

Jones faced a delicate situation. Dunning's politics was more congenial with his own than Burke's was, but Dunning opposed the Judicature Bill. As Jones was regularly but separately consulted by its promoters and its opponents, he steered a middle course: "I really think parts of the bill wise and salutary, though I have strong objections to other parts: many amendments have been made, and one whole clause struck out, on my remonstrance. I have been much with Burke on this business, and have heard many animated speeches from him in the House" (2:478–9). Even after both bills received royal assent, Jones's interest continued.

He secured a copy of the Judicature Bill after a confidential friend of the chancellor, probably with Thurlow's consent, had asked Jones to draft a report on the history of the Bengal judicature, including observations and recommendations. Because Thurlow had promised to bring in a Bengal bill, Jones's report should be vital. The summer circuit interrupted his progress, and intricate law business and the complexity of the report further delayed it. But Jones felt India to be so important that every English statesman should be "perfectly acquainted" with it. In December he concluded the report, which was generally disregarded, though it may have assisted Fox and other Opposition leaders. He had again conveyed his view that the Indians should be protected by their own laws and religions, and involvement with the legislation kept his name in the forefront relative to the judgeship. The turmoil about India would prevent any appointment in the near future; yet without the delay in appointing new judges entailed by the Parliamentary Commission of Enquiry into the Courts of Justice, he would have had little hope of obtaining the post.

Besides his Indian work and law practice, numerous social engagements kept Jones busy that summer. He attended the Club on 19 June and 3 July, for which he specially invited Gibbon. As their dinners were barely averaging seven members, he attended when possible. The proroguing of Parliament led to a suspension of meetings for a time. On the way to the Oxford sessions in early July, he dined with Lytton and then honored a dinner invitation from the Spencers at Wimbledon.

Jones was now the senior fellow at University College. He enjoyed perfect calm, as Wetherel was on vacation, and the college government was in Jones's hands. The Oxford assizes so tired him that he skipped the next three, joining the circuit at Hereford; but by the time he reached Haverfordwest, he had spent many days in sultry courts and many nights in drawing pleadings. His profession seemed secure, but what his colleagues considered success was actually drudgery in some administration as attorney general or solicitor general. He would not compromise his principles to become an MP, who only wore a senator's mask: "For these, and a hundred good reasons, I will certainly go to India for five or six years, if they are manly enough to send me" (2:488).

Alexander Wedderburn was on the English circuit, giving Jones a chance to observe the chief justice of the Court of Common Pleas. Despite Jones's known political opinions, he could not reject the attentions of this chief of his profession. Appreciating his integrity, Wedderburn defended the idea of a governmental appointment for a person of principles; otherwise, it might go to an unprincipled person, and it might provide the opportunity to make others happy. Jones promised to spend a few days at Wedderburn's estate.

After finishing at Cardigan, he stopped at Bristol to see Arthur Pritchard, a bachelor of his own age who occasionally copied for him. Their similar opinions and Pritchard's conscientiousness led Jones to offer an assistantship. But Pritchard preferred to have the same salary as a clerk and amanuensis in the country, minus the expense of urgent copying that had to be done in London.

Jones had an invitation to visit the Shipleys at Twyford, but there was not time. Certain points in the notes for his *Mu'allaqát* had to be checked at the Bodleian. He was modeling his translation on Lowth's *Isaiah,* with a dedication, preliminary discourse, and notes. Because he also worked on the Indian report, he could not submit the whole text to Nichols before returning to London, but he asked Nichols to typeset his translation of the first three Arabic poems.

In London his bankruptcy cases and other work monopolized two weeks. Jones caught up on his correspondence, informing Franklin that Paradise had been unable to go to Virginia. As the two years' grace would soon expire, he asked whether Paradise should travel by a French frigate or, if the Americans would permit, by an English ship to New York, then use a flag and proper certificates to reach Virginia. Disturbed by Lee's accusation that Franklin had engaged in fraudulent commercial transactions, Jones asked to be counted among Franklin's most faithful friends. Virtue was dead in England: "We have the *shadow* merely of a free constitution, but live in truth under the substance of despotism" (2:493–4).

Jones visited John Wilmot for a few days. His schedule was somewhat unpredictable, often being at the whim of the parties and attorneys. Thus he had not expected to attend the quarter sessions, but the bankruptcy list was suddenly shut. He remained at University College until 10 October, accepting invitations to dine at other colleges. Many Oxonians considered him a republican, "very unjustly, if they mean one, who wishes to see a republick in *England;* but very justly, if they mean one, who thinks a republick in the *abstract* the only rational, manly, intelligible form of government" (2:499). They sought his company, and he served the Whig cause by persuading some Tories that the Whig view was not so poisonous. Perhaps by degrees they would shift to true reason and social virtue.

Jones was not a republican in a literal sense; his politics derived from the constitution. He interpreted the current national troubles as stemming principally from the war and the enlargement of the king's powers. Indeed, his having jocularly characterized himself in younger days as a democrat in the Roman manner contributed to one view that he was the English Cato.[23] He did not hide his advanced Whiggism or his associations with Price, the Cartwrights, and Wilkes, besides his membership in the Honest Whigs and the Society for Constitutional Information. People knew of his political poems like *Ad Libertatem* and *An Ode in Imitation of Alcæus* and of his talks with rebel emissaries in Paris.

Naturally Jones was one of the many people suspected of having written the celebrated Junius letters. Later in *Gentleman's Magazine* he was said to have uniquely possessed the needed combined qualifications of lawyer, writer, patriot, and scholar.[24] But he was only twenty-one in 1767, too inexperienced to compose the series except for his observation of Spencer's political circles. Philip Francis was likely Junius.

Intricate business kept Jones in the Temple until late October, when Wedderburn made him drop everything to make the promised visit to Mitcham. He finished the enjoyable stay on 4 November, encountering Lady Spencer at Wimbledon. In fact, their walk was so pleasant that he was late for Bathurst's dinner.

Jones's intense reading had weakened his eyes, which were never strong after his childhood injury. Working at night by candlelight was imprudent, and so he had to write and read immoderately during the day. Because Pritchard was in the country, Jones could not dictate. Then he developed an inflammatory disorder. When Thomas Maurice requested help in securing any vacant curacy in London, Jones had to answer briefly. He would see the few London clergymen whom he knew, but feared that he could help little. Despite his illness, he attended the Club on 11 and 18 December, when Edward Eliot, Reynolds's associate, was elected.

One friend to whom Jones wrote lengthily despite his weak eyes was Parr. He had remained close to his old Harrow colleague. In 1780 his Greek "Character of Dr. Parr" had probably been written for Parr; this classical showpiece utilizes variant or obscure forms and coinings. It passes rapidly from subject to subject, perhaps representing Parr's typical train of thought, and suggests his idiosyncrasies, as in the opening third:

He is one whose character is not easy to define; for, being unlike all others, he does and says things most unlike himself; this is clear to see. He is one who is temperate and moderate, but nevertheless remarkable for his enjoyment of every kind of luxury and delicacy, drinking the wines which are most costly, eating the meats which are most tender, sleeping deeply, and preferring a scarlet-dyed couch to one not dyed at all, and one rather than two. And he is by nature quick to jest, to be quarrelsome, and to argue, but to call the quarrels camaraderie.[25]

Another passage anticipates Jones's later letter to Parr: "Once every five years, the head of state (or Prime Minister) ought to be put to the axe, not because he is a villain, but because he is head of state." Jones had considered Parr a staunch American supporter, but his *Discourse on the Late Fast* (London, 1781) suddenly defended the king. Jones's skimming discovered a masterly style and just religious sentiments; however, he smiled at Parr's exhortation to forgive the Americans:

They will *forgive you,* and *if possible, your* Country. I have been fighting your battles in many companies, and bearing ample testimony to your *integrity*. I find more difficulty in supporting your *reasons,* especially your sheet-anchor – "that we should unite in upholding Government, because our enemies are so numerous and virulent." What! must we, because we have many misfortunes already, add to them the last and worst of human misfortunes, a despotism in substance. (2:506)

Jones further suggested that wise men should diminish their calamities. Though not exulting at General Cornwallis's surrender at Yorktown, which effectively ended the war, Jones nevertheless felt "exceeding great joy."

He was particularly discouraged to find friends like Parr embracing the losing side, which seemed to have forgotten freedoms guaranteed by the settlements of the Glorious Revolution. A second turncoat was Pollard. Made penniless on Barbados by the recent great hurricane, along with other unpleasantness, Pollard became an opponent of America. In view of his previous politics, his letters further discouraged Jones.

Some friends had not changed. Assisted to a seat from Appleby, Pitt had joined Shelburne's Whigs, deriding the speech from the throne on 28 November 1781. He visited Jones to report Althorp's speech unsuccessfully advocating the withholding of supplies. Jones was delighted by this artistic orator's approbation of Althorp, whose understanding and judgment should make him an excellent future debater. Unfortunately, Jones felt, the pair were not destined to speak to better men in a better age.

Catching up with his correspondence on 13 December, he expected to shake off his cold and sore throat, then cease work for a month so as to devote himself to poetry and music. A local musician had nicely set one of his old songs to music, and having heard it sweetly sung, Jones intended to have the music copied for Mrs. Poyntz. Attending the Royal Society that night, he, Paradise, Daniel Solander, and others signed the certificate for Daniel Braithwaite, of the General Post Office.

Almost immediately Jones was in bed with fever, but by Christmas Day was well enough to travel. While resting at Oxford he philosophically integrated the arts into his view of life, refining the philosophy in his "Plan of an Essay on Education": "Man was born for *labour;* his configuration, his passions, his restlessness, all prove it; but labour would wear him out, and the purpose of it be defeated, if he had not intervals of *pleasure;* and, unless that pleasure be *innocent,* both he and society must suffer" (2:513–14). Jones dogmatically shared with Althorp his conclusion that the arts provide such pleasure, for family wealth afforded Althorp the means to a life of pleasure: "Mere pleasure, to which the idle are not justly entitled, soon satiates, and leaves a vacuity in the mind more unpleasant than actual pain." Only a just mixture of work and pleasure appears conducive to happiness. Jones's own relaxation gave way to preparations for the quarterly sessions. He had fully recovered when he finally reached London in mid-January.

Jones was soon in association with Burke – three times at the Club, but mainly in regard to Indian judicature. Indeed, his next book derived principally from Burke's having involved him in the legislation. The association had also disappointed him, for he had concluded that Burke would not lead England to genuine constitutional government. The Opposition was badly divided, and aspects of Burke's politics were counter to Jones's would-be ideal Whiggism. The two were good friends, but Burke was just too aristocratic. Then there had been the attempts to abolish the Welsh judicature and blight the great business of the petitions. Burke did not seem to think the executive influence too great; his system of national liberty seemed hopelessly sublime and obscure.

Their friendship had deepened through association partly built on Jones's scholarship. His judicial aspiration was gratified by their agreeing on a system of Indian justice based on Indian laws and religions. The subject of Warren Hastings had not yet come up between them; if it had, Jones would probably have jointly condemned the ruffians' actions in Benares. Now Burke requested additional help, in a more formal arrangement than the unpaid assistance the previous year. Too busy to call in person, Jones answered:

Nothing could be more flattering, nothing more honourable to me, than the design which you kindly intimated of employing my humble pen, in drawing part of the bill for the further improvement of the English judicature in India; for, although I am very sensible how little such assistance will be wanted, yet a call of that nature from a committee so enlightened as that, of which you are a member, must be considered by me as the highest honour I ever received. (2:520)

Nevertheless, Jones first had to learn the chancellor's attitude toward the bill, as well as the outcome of the attempt to recall Chief Justice Elijah Impey for questioning about Maharaja Nanda Kumar's execution for forgery. Thurlow's attitude was crucial. Either Jones must forget the Indian judgeship – as he was inclined to do after four years of waiting – or else accommodate himself as a principled individual to the inclinations of the man who seemed to have the appointive power.

Because Burke was Rockingham's friend and might be able to assist, Jones described his situation fully. Predilection for Oriental matters had induced him to apply, but the consequent suspense had ruinously prevented his attendance at Westminster Hall, excluding him from numerous cases that would otherwise have been his. He was still at the head in the Welsh assizes, and he was slowly gaining in the Oxford circuit. Nor would he despair of progress at Westminster if he could obtain a decision, however adverse. This dreadful blank in his life was undeserved, for his Oriental studies and temperament should make him useful in Bengal and perhaps result in important discoveries. The salary was not his principal object. He would spend much on payment to translators and interpreters, and on Oriental books and manuscripts, which Oxford would ultimately receive. But to no other politician would he mention these literary projects, as Burke knew Thurlow to be "a professed contemner of every thing graceful or ornamental in writing" (2:522).

Jones had earlier hinted to Burke that he preferred a seat on the Sadar Diwānī Adālat, the highest provincial court of appeal in civil suits, to the vacant puisne judgeship. He was not motivated by the higher salary of the latter post, but if it were continued and he could secure it, that £6,000 salary would be fine. In the Sadar Adālat he could use his Arabic and Persian in explaining Moslem law, while sitting alone with sole responsibility, whereas in the Supreme Court he would have to contend with three colleagues or else yield to their impetuosity. He shared Burke's opinion that the president of the Sadar Adālat should sit like a corporation recorder, without a sole deciding voice on appeals from the provinces: "No profit on earth could induce me to bear so vast a load on my reason and conscience, or to trust myself with so enormous a power." Actually, Jones's statement was expedient. Impey's acceptance of the lucrative presidency had provoked charges that the Sadar Adālat was no longer useful for settling disputes between individuals, as Impey now held appointments in both courts.

Jones gave Burke a copy of his new book, *The Mahomedan Law of Succession to the Property of Intestates,* which had the central purpose of helping British lawyers implement the East India Judicature Act. This had empowered the Bengal Supreme Court to hear cases involving Moslems; matters of contract and individual dealing were to be decided by Moslem law and usage. But judges could not justly rule without knowing Moslem law, for dependence on Indian lawyers was precarious. Even if these lawyers were unbiased or uninformed, judges must still base their judgment on others' reports unless they had a knowledge of Moslem jurisprudence and Arabic. Accordingly, Jones translated Ibn-al-Mulaqqin's *Bughyat al-bahith,* an authoritative poetic treatise on the Shafiite law of inheritance, "word for word, with a fidelity almost religiously scrupulous," in order to preserve legal exactness.

Nichols printed the book for Dilly in 1782. It has a preface, engravings of the eleven-part manuscript, a Roman verse-transliteration, and Jones's unrhymed verse- translation. He had not had time to compose extensive notes or a commentary on Moslem inheritance law, and because the translation had been done hastily, it was not good work. Nonetheless, although he later acknowledged mistranslations of technical terms not listed in the inadequate dictionaries, he caught the spirit of the poem, and there is little to correct in his general ideas.[26]

Refining the method introduced in his Persian *Grammar,* Jones hoped to "habituate the student of eastern languages to the reading of old *Arabian* manuscripts." His transliteration distinguished "every consonant and *long* vowel (the *short* ones are too vague and indeterminate) by a character invariably appropriated to it; so as *to give every full sound its own specifick symbol;* an advantage, which hardly any alphabet has, but which all ought to have." Thus he innovationally moved toward phonemic transcription, though he was representing written letters rather than sounds.

His contemporaries liked the book. In the *Monthly Review,* Gilbert Stuart praised Jones's deservedly eminent reputation: "On the present occasion, he has exerted his great knowledge in this department, with the view of promoting the exercise of justice in India" (June 1782, p. 442). This goal was paramount, but Jones must have anticipated enhancing his judicial qualifications by displaying such knowledge.

Franklin received a copy. Just before departing on the spring circuit, Jones expanded his associations with American leaders, implementing the thought that he had only implied to Burke. Jones had not been politically active until he was swept away by the fervor of his connections into extreme opposition. For two hours on 1 March he talked with Henry Laurens. The former president of Congress, recently released from the Tower in exchange for Cornwallis, described settlements flourishing seven hundred miles inland. Jones concluded that "every man among them is a soldier, a *patriot* – Subdue such a people! The king may as easily conquer the moon" (2:517).

Evidently Jones gave Laurens a letter from James Searle, because when he wrote that congressman on 5 March, he explained that Searle's "highly respectable friend" (presumably Laurens, who had not yet been acquitted) was restricted from writing. Jones's previous letter to Searle, written soon after their 1780 journey to Brussels, had apparently been lost. Searle had asked his opinion about some papers, but he had not had time to copy his notes. He hoped to meet Searle again, perhaps in America, for he would not grow old in England under the present governmental system. Jones's letter reports the Opposition's nineteen-vote majority on 28 February for ceasing hostilities, when the king had essentially answered: "I do not want your advice, and will do as I please." The Commons voted ironic thanks for the royal compliance, passing a warning that anyone who advised the king to continue the war was "highly criminal and an enemy to his country" (2:519). Jones did not yet realize that British military failures had doomed North.

He wrote Franklin a nearly identical letter, spending little time in answering Franklin's recent one. Although Jones conveyed no secret information, he had had someone posted in the Commons to bring him the results of the votes, which he now reported. Paradise was going to Virginia: "Should I accompany him, I shall again have the happiness of enjoying your conversation at Passy. I have no wish to grow old in England, for, believe me, I would rather be a peasant with freedom than a prince in an enslaved country" (2:517).

Jones had intended to follow the entire circuit, but he was barely in time for the Oxford assizes. Although the judgeship seemed remote, perhaps Shelburne suggested that Jones remain at Oxford, in view of the crescendo building in Parliament. After passing up the Shropshire assizes, he wrote

Burke an agonized letter, ending with a hasty footnote: "We have strong rumours here of an intended change of administration, in which the chancellor is said to be deeply concerned" (2:523). Indeed, Thurlow had made overtures to Rockingham. But as Hereford was one of Jones's best English assizes, he left Oxford without knowing of the planned Whig resolution to dissolve the ministry. At Gloucester he finished the circuit, having missed several assizes for the third consecutive time, mainly because of his scrambling for income and a judgeship that would not require a compromise of principles.

Jones's immediately returning to London suggests that someone wanted him available if there were a political upheaval. He had told Burke that he hoped to visit Burke at Easter, and Shelburne had once canvassed a borough for him. Before reaching town, he knew that Rockingham had formed a ministry, in which Shelburne became secretary of state for Home Affairs on 27 March. In London he worked on Indian matters for Burke, perhaps waiting for a summons. When he sent Burke congratulations upon the Whig ministry, just before leaving for the final Welsh assizes in Cardigan, he did not even know of Burke's appointment to two minor places. He may have wanted to see Laurens, to learn of any development in his American connections. If Thurlow did not pronounce a yes or no about the judgeship, "I will put myself out of it, and will accept a noble offer that has been made me by the noblest of men, among whom I may not only *plead causes,* but *make laws,* and write them on the bank of my own river under my own oak" (2:528). This invitation to migrate, probably from Laurens, might have led to Jones's being chosen to help frame the American Constitution, especially its balance of powers.

He had been disquieted for a month. He had earned a lot of money; yet clients' importunities and the general hurry added to his uneasiness. If wealth were the means to honor, he would be unhappy even with £40,000 a year, because he would have to sacrifice health and comfort, seldom seeing those whom he liked and spending his leisure with many whom he disliked. Few circuiteers had principles, selling their talents in the best market. On this circuit Jones had not really exulted at the Opposition's last-ditch victory. Congratulated at the judges' table on Althorp's becoming one of the three junior lords of the Treasury, he replied that England should be congratulated. But an unprincipled Scottish lawyer observed that it was always the Opposition's lot to complain. Now the Tories would start complaining, for Rockingham would not change things. Despising this idea too much to retort, Jones better employed himself by eating his turkey.

Despite his long yearning for a Whig ministry, he was troubled. The Tories were anticipating the coalition's dissolution in less than a year, as the fragile ministry depended on cordial Whig union and cooperation amid the deep divisions. Also, Jones was discovering an inclination to thank the king for removing the former ministers, but then to resume petitioning, as Middlesex, his own county, was doing. A petition from the associated counties had just been brought up in the Commons. Jones did not want the ministry to be bothered at this important moment: "Assist them to settle America, India, the islands, the navy, the army, the finances; when their great objects in those branches of government shall be attained, they are bound, by every tie, to bring back the constitution to its first principles" (2:526). No one must obstruct the coalition from keeping its pledge to end the war least disadvantageously. Once there was peace, Jones would still prefer civil war to monarchical or aristocratic power: "I wish to God, that every elector of Britain had as bright a bayonet as mine, with as much resolution."

After finishing a heavy caseload at Cardigan, Jones visited Charles Powell's castle near Brecon. A good Whig, Powell was spending a large fortune on "the duties of an upright magistrate, the improvement of agriculture, and the benefit of the indigent" (2:529). Even though such principles might be considered democratic, Jones would not part with them unless he was convinced that they were erroneous, even if they continued to delay his judgeship. Although the post would let him serve England by assisting two million Indians who were British subjects, he would not give up a single principle in order to gain it. These thoughts he penned to Burke.

Jones was returning home slowly, for the new ministry had not seemed to advance his interests. Sheridan had become Rockingham's undersecretary for foreign affairs; Fox, foreign secretary of state; and Dunning, chancellor of the Duchy of Lancaster. They could not really help, for Thurlow, who retained the law appointments in his continuing chancellorship, believed in sole patronage. If Jones approached someone in the ministry, Thurlow would object and again suspend him for years between the bench and the bar. He could not even mention the judgeship to Rockingham, who had politely entertained him. So he turned to Burke again, as he had previously done to Gibbon. Sounding as though Burke's posts of privy councillor and paymaster general of the forces were major ones, Jones congratulated Burke and England on "the glorious victory which consummate wisdom, unshaken virtues and splendid talents, so long exerted in vain, have at length obtained over mad pertinacity, crooked politicks, and criminal supineness" (2:531).

Jones recited his naive sequence to Burke. Chamier had directed him to apply to North. Then Chamier talked to Thurlow, who replied that North was the judge maker and that Jones had chosen to apply to North:

"I have no idea of *concurrent* patronage: I wish your friend well, and, as far as I know him, approve of him, but I shall hear nothing of the business, till the great seal is set to the patent." Thus Jones gave Burke information at least two years old, without having tried to learn the present opinion of the usually inflexible Thurlow. Now Jones was entreating his friends to inform him if anyone else were appointed: "The only thing I dread is a state of suspence for four years longer, which has often put me in mind of Homer's man in a dream, pursuing without advancing."

After a leisurely visit with Pritchard, Jones reached Oxford on 15 April. Letters were waiting, but he dined before opening them. Probably Burke's letter was in the pile:

Do not think a syllable in your Letter has escaped me. The world knows your Merits. . . . A New Set of men has succeeded. They mean well, and will act well. If they do not, in some way or other, distinguish you I think it will a little tarnish the Lustre of their Virtues. I shall probably have no great weight. But as far as my poor Voice goes, (and it is at present a little Hoarse with a cold) it shall not be wanting to call upon those in power, to add this to the rest of their good acts – that they rescue the Country from the disgrace of neglecting the most learned man it has.[27]

Shelburne's letter of 9 April galvanized Jones; Shelburne wanted to see him instantly. He put four horses to his chaise and traveled all night. Early the next morning he was presented to all the ministers, but the introduction was academic. For more than a fortnight Shelburne's undersecretaryship of state had been held open. Finally, not even knowing where Jones was, they had given it to another Whig. Had Parliament been dissolved, he would have had an immediate seat. His judicial ambition received strong encouragement, but when it became evident that his appointment was not imminent, Baron Ashburton (Dunning) paid him a long, flattering visit on 22 April. Jones penned eloquent thanks to Shelburne for the extraordinary kindness, asserting that no disappointment could diminish his attachment.

Thurlow was still the problem. Lloyd Kenyon, now attorney general, was Thurlow's close friend. As Jones knew that Kenyon had spoken kindly of him to the chancellor, perhaps Kenyon could help, particularly because Jones had never applied to Thurlow, for fear of offending. Not finding Kenyon at home, Jones initiated a correspondence. First he observed that his happiness did not depend on the judgeship, which he had been hoping to gain through the chancellor's favor; rather, it depended on the ending of the ruinous suspense. He was not conscious of having offended the chancellor, nor had he ever thought the post obtainable except by Thurlow's sole patronage. Yet he had been severely punished in his profession and domestic plans for years, at the most important time of his life. Robert

Chambers, whose prospects may have been poorer than Jones's, had deliberated for months before accepting an Indian judgeship, whereas Jones's four years of soliciting had not even elicited a rejection. Excepting the appointment, the best news would be speedy refusal. Would Kenyon immediately relay the news, when known, that either the post would not be filled in 1782, or ever, or that Jones would not be appointed?

His hopes waned. During the last three weeks, he had almost been an undersecretary, an MP, and a judge. Mentioned in the cabinet, Jones had the highest interest. But on 3 May a successful motion to recall Impey jeopardized the existence of the Sadar Adālat, if not of the Supreme Court. In view of the Court of Appeal, the vacancy was clearly not going to be filled in 1782. Jones could partly blame himself. Thinking that the new ministry had not helped him, he had dawdled on the way back from Wales, and he had not given key friends his circuit addresses. Nor had he been at Oxford to respond instantly to Shelburne's summons. Thurlow was hostile, and the parliamentary scramble over Bengal was further confusing the situation.

Jones decided to accompany Paradise to Virginia. During the next six weeks, while trying to plan the complicated trip, he resumed his role as poet and pamphleteer. *An Ode in Imitation of Callistratus,* his last political ode, complemented his *Ode of Alcæus.* He was a bit sensitive about this twelve-quatrain celebration of the change in ministries; for, when asked for a copy, he added annotations, because many friends had found the ode obscure. Drawing on Greek history, it is "a lawyer's poetry, and a deserter's too, who was not entitled to any favour from his muse" (2:581).

Jones's adaptation of Callistratus' famous scholium broadly compares the Whigs' peaceful accession to two patriots' slaying of the tyrant Hipparchus, which supposedly brought peace to Athens. Instead of driving a tyrant to death, the modern patriots Rockingham, Lennox, and Shelburne have brought blissful tidings:

> Rise, BRITANNIA, dauntless rise!
> Cheer'd with triple Harmony,
> > *Monarch* good, and *Nobles* wise,
> *People* valiant, firm, and FREE!

This patriotic verse, drawing on Jones's concept of a mixed republic, recalls Collins's verve in "Ode Written in the Beginning of the Year 1746." Other lines refer to thirsty blades and armed citizens, placing Jones squarely among the radicals, even if he did not have the remotest desire to use a sword.

He had Nichols print several copies privately, which he sent to various friends. Reprinted in *Gentleman's Magazine* (May 1782, p. 252), it and the better *Ode of Alcæus* were long celebrated in British democratic circles.[28] Apparently the eulogized trio of statesmen never learned of the Greek tyrannicides' doom or of the greater despotism that resulted because only one of the tyrants was killed, facts that made Jones's hasty analogy quite inept.

On 14 May he composed his third political prose work. It anonymously answers Shelburne's plan from Whitehall, which had just been circulated to the chief magistrates of towns and cities, to augment the nation's domestic force by raising temporary companies to provide for their own defense. The companies could not be moved unless there was invasion or rebellion, and the government would furnish their arms and ammunition. The plan alarmed some MPs, who charged that it was too democratic and dangerous. Jones liked the general idea, earlier proposed in his *Inquiry,* that local militias could suppress riots and resist invasion. However, Shelburne permitted the king too much power, admitting that the king had requested circulation of the plan.

Jones's "Plan of National Defence" contains a cover letter modeled on Shelburne's letter, the text of Shelburne's plan, and a point-by-point revision of the plan. Jones's letter, signed by "A Volunteer" as a kind of public communication, notes that the government plan was "conceived by some great mind, and intended for the noblest purposes." But its details are "*innovating,* harsh, unconstitutional, and big with alarming consequences; too *expensive* for the treasury, who have no treasures to lavish, and too *distrustful* of a generous and spirited people, who would *vigorously support* a government that *sincerely confided* in them."

Jones's plan, approved by a "Company of Loyal Englishmen," will help preserve the constitution; it is not too expensive for patriots or at all dangerous to a wise ministry. It fleshes out Jones's long-held ideas like "our constitution has a good defence in a well-regulated militia officered by men who love their country; and a militia so regulated may in due time be the means of *thinning* the formidable army, if not of *extinguishing* it" (1:275). His purpose was to preserve internal and external order, while preventing royal usurpation. Envisaging a force like Charlemont's volunteers in Ireland, he would have approved of its use for political freedom.[29]

Jones democratizes nineteen of Shelburne's twenty points. For example, an officer's rank would be determined by his contribution to the local defense fund rather than by the size of his property. The adjutant would be elected by the officers, not appointed by the king. Jones would have the officers enroll themselves; they would be commissioned by the high sheriff and chief magistrate. Arms would be purchased with local funds or officers' contributions rather than supplied by the government. Instead of having everyone receive pay, Jones would pay only the men needing it. This money would come from local funds, even during an invasion. Finally, instead of serving an unspecified time, a company would be discharged as soon as the invaders were repelled or the particular service was completed.

Jones's plan was never formally published. He may have wanted the Society for Constitutional Information to publish it, as on 17 May he wrote Thomas Yeates (the secretary) a long letter, which vanished after its sale by the Sotheby auction house in 1901.

Jones was now a member of this radical group. John Cartwright, Edmund's elder brother and a major in the Nottinghamshire Militia, was a founder in 1780. As the "Father of Reform" was advocating annual parliaments, universal suffrage, and the ballot, his Society for Constitutional Information attracted men of advanced views and published political works that regular publishers dared not touch.[30] Probably one of the Cartwrights or Thomas Day nominated Jones, who wrote Yeates: "I should indeed long ago have testified my regard for so useful an Institution, by an offer of my humble service in promoting it, if I had not really despaired, in my present situation, of being able to attend your meetings as often as I should ardently wish" (2:533). He noted that he was devoted to supporting the constitution, which the Society was designed to elucidate. No prospects or dangers could block this devotion. However, the just reducing of royal power might dangerously elevate the aristocracy, whereas the people should have all the substantial power: "On the people depend the welfare, the security, and the permanence of every legal government." Thus his mixed republic – composed of a good Crown, wise aristocracy, and a powerful people – tilted toward democracy. He had now overcome trepidation about anarchic citizens, as personally witnessed during the Gordon Riots.

A dedicated member, Jones wrote the Society a long letter when Henry Fielding's *Enquiry into the Causes of the Late Increase of Robbers* (London, 1751) alarmed him. In attacking social ills like gin drinking, Fielding argues that the constitution is "as variable as its weather." Considering this idea to be quite dangerous, particularly in view of Fielding's stature, Jones contends that the constitution is uniform and permanent:

This constitutional or public law is partly unwritten, and grounded upon immemorial usage, and partly written or enacted by the legislative power; but the unwritten, or common law, contains the true spirit of our Constitution; the written has often most unjustifiably altered the form of it; the common law is the collected wisdom of many centuries, having been used and approved by successive generations; but the statutes frequently contain the whims of a few leading men, and sometimes of the mere individuals employed to draw them: lastly, the unwritten law is eminently favourable, and the written generally hostile, to the absolute rights of persons. (2:553)

Legislation opposing the spirit of the constitution could be corrected by "the people or nation at large, who form, as it were, the high court of appeal in cases of constitutional equity; and their sense must be collected from the petitions which they present." Thereby Jones fitted petitions into his ideal government, in a political use of scholarship. He eschewed dilettantish scholarship done principally for itself, pursuing instead a more mature variety that could also serve humankind. He concluded that if the Society for Constitutional Information "will steer clear of party, [they] will do more good to Britain than all the philosophers and antiquaries of Somerset house with all their *royalties*" (2:577).

Although Jones had only recently met Major Cartwright, their similar politics ensured a closer friendship. Indeed, Cartwright's *Give Us Our Rights; or, a Letter to the Present Electors of Middlesex and the Metropolis Shewing What Those Rights Are,* which the society had just published, "ought to be written on the heart of every Englishman" (2:546), evidently in letters of gold, according to Jones's lost page of comments on the book. He also told Cartwright: "The people of England will never be a people, in the majestic sense of the word, unless two hundred thousand of the *civil* state be ready, before the first of next November, to take the field, without rashness or disorder, at twenty-four hours' notice." He had earlier urged Parr to organize a militia; now he was suggesting the total size and a deadline to a radical.

Jones notified Wilkes, his representative, that he intended to make a motion on militias at the next Middlesex meeting. He had hoped to hand-deliver the text of his motion, but had to enclose it in a letter praising the Commons' recent expunging of "the shameful resolution" that his friend Wilkes was incapable of sitting in Parliament (2:540). Now the crucial issue was "how the *civil state* is to be armed, not how the *military state* is to be reinforced." Because a lawyer could speak more gracefully on this issue than a soldier could, Jones would move:

That the committee now sitting be instructed, or a new committee appointed, to inquire into the most practicable and constitutional mode of enabling the sheriff and magistrates of this county to defend it by a legal force, and to assist government in defending the kingdom, in case of dangerous insurrection or invasion, and that the committee be desired to report their resolutions and plan of defence to the next general meeting of the county.

Thus he hoped to implement the details of his "Plan of National Defence."

The meeting called to order in the London Tavern on 28 May was of the "Quintuple Alliance," as the *Morning Chronicle* termed the electors from Middlesex and four other political divisions. Two resolutions were introduced in regard to improving parliamentary representation. These made Jones forget his motion and deliver an extemporaneous speech supporting petitions. He began with Blackstone's premise that the spirit of the constitution requires "a nearly equal and nearly universal representation." Emulating Pitt, he cited statutes to explode the doctrine of "virtual representation." Perhaps other counties would emulate the Quintuple Alliance and pass resolutions like the Middlesex ones.

By now Jones's speech was heavily political. He shifted to a favorite topic, the spirit of the constitution, thereby tripling the length of his speech. His epidemic ailment had not kept him at home, just as, when Roman liberty was endangered, Ligarius had risen from his sickbed and told his consoling friend, "If you have any business worthy of yourselves, I am well." The allusion was too dramatic, for this ailment was causing many deaths. Jones needed to discuss the constitution, he said, because "a very particular and urgent occasion . . . calls me for some months from *England*," a cryptic phrase that was to have repercussions. He urged purification of the constitution every few years by deleting the feudal echoes that creep into legislation when the form of the constitution is periodically changed to accord, supposedly, with its spirit. Because the audience was tiring of his legislative catalogue, he added rhetorically: "I hear a murmur among you, and perceive other marks of impatience. Indulge me a moment, and I will descend; but let me not be misapprehended." The royal influence must be reduced. He concluded: "If united, and dependent on Yourselves alone, you must succeed; if disunited, or too confident in others, you must fail." The English people would be happiest when freest, but would be freest only when England became the most virtuous and enlightened nation. This impromptu speech by Jones was soon to be published.

A general meeting of Middlesex gentlemen, clergy, and freeholders was held the next day at the Mermaid, called at several freeholders' request to consider addressing the king on the change of ministries and on needed parliamentary reform. Though Jones's friend Alderman James Townsend chaired the meeting, things did not go as Jones wished. First a bland motion to thank the king for the change was seconded. Next, as the *Public Advertiser* reported on 31 May:

Mr. Jones suggested an Amendment, to assure his Majesty of the good Intentions, and the zealous Determination of the County to form, and maintain a Plan of internal Defence, in compliance with the Proposition made by the Earl of Shelburn in his Circular Letter. He recommended this as a necessary Declaration of the Sense of the County, in a moment so urgent as the Present, when Time ought not to be lost in preparing a necessary Defence against Tumult or Invasion.

Thus Jones strengthened his planned motion. The radical John Horne Tooke seconded the amendment, but Townsend said that it might be improper. This was not the business for which they had assembled; indeed, it was so important that a new meeting should be advertised. When George Byng agreed, Jones withdrew his amendment, and the bland motion passed. After Tooke spoke at length on the need to petition the Commons about unequal representation, there was a unanimous vote to present the petition.

Before the meeting ended, Jones stubbornly moved: "That it be a Recommendation to the Committee to consider, and prepare a proper plan of Defence against Tumult or Invasion, to be reported at the next General Meeting for their Opinion and Adoption." Despite the unanimous approval, apparently the plan was never prepared. North's defeat and the reduced tempo of the war had weakened people's desire for such meetings, not to mention Jones's anticipated professional trip to America.

On 14 June, Dilly published Jones's *Speech to the Assembled Inhabitants of the Counties of Middlesex and Surrey, the Cities of London and Westminster, and the Borough of Southwark.* This fourth political pamphlet carried a bold advertisement:

Having been informed, that parts of my Speech on the 28th of May at the London Tavern were thought obscure, yet important, I have endeavoured to recollect what I then took the liberty to say, and have consented to let the argument go abroad in its rude and unpolished state. What offence this publication may give, either in parts or in the whole, is the last and least of my cares: my first and greatest is, to speak on all occasions what I conceive to be just and true.

This speech was hardly radical, drawing acclaim from lawyers and laypeople alike. The *Monthly Review,* quoting from the "judicious and spirited oration," praised the discerning orator for skillfully and successfully deriding the doctrine of virtual representation. The editors would not restate their own attack on the doctrine, they said, as they had already shown it to be ridiculous (August 1782, pp. 148–9).

Jones turned to what should be his greatest adventure, his projected voyage. The attractive American offer, coupled with the unhappy political situation at home, might persuade him to remain in America.

James River Property (1782–1783)

Realizing that Thurlow and the Court of Appeal would delay his judicial appointment at least until early 1783, Jones had agreed to accompany Paradise. Needing Franklin's help with the Virginia estate, the pair would sail from France. Paradise, who had been afraid to go alone, was delighted. Jones would serve as an advocate and witness, hoping to prevent a lawsuit. Friendship rather than the liberal payment was a major inducement, and he hoped to return before Christmas.

For the first time Jones would miss an entire circuit, a major source of income. Why not? Although the judgeship might have been filled without new legislation, Thurlow had thwarted his aspiration since becoming chancellor and would undoubtedly continue to do so. And as the Whigs had erred in letting the king retain a man whose views were so royalist, Jones despaired of the appointment and even the Whig prospects for now. Because he espoused the principle that citizens could migrate when their country suppressed liberty, perhaps his real future lay in Charleston or Pennsylvania. Laurens and Franklin might help him assist a government of separated powers based on near-universal suffrage and liberty, and Paradise would pay his fees in the form of choice property along the James River.

American friends had led him to wonder whether England was rejecting his qualifications. A lawyer of his capacities would have manifold opportunities in the new country, which, he firmly believed, had to be granted independence before there could be a peace treaty. Having first suggested a naive commercial pact in "A Fragment of Polybius," Jones had fully embraced the American cause after the Yorktown defeat. In view of the major French assistance, America would never desert France; only peace could preserve England.

Jones confided to Burke that permanent American residence was possible though improbable. Burke could assist him with the Sadar Diwānī Adālat, except that his experience with the Supreme Court vacancy had diminished his energies for a new solicitation. Because the voyage might be dangerous, Jones needed help: "If I could, without impropriety, ask Lord Keppel, through some common friend, for a pass to be used only in case of capture, directing all commanders of English vessels to give no molestation to my friend, myself, and my servant, but to let us proceed in our course, I should be glad to have such a security from delay" (2:538). But if there were any indiscretion in approaching the new first lord of the Admiralty, Jones would risk capture. Apparently Laurens had explained the travel situation, for Jones would not take an English ship to New York because of the difficulty then entailed in his getting to Virginia. Instead, he would take a foreign frigate: "A man who acts merely in his professional line, without taking any part in the civil war, has nothing to apprehend from law; and since I am not a man to leave my country, as if I fled from it, I shall make no secret of my intention, but shall apprise Lord Shelburne of it."

Expecting Burke to secure the pass, Jones asked Pritchard to accompany him as a friend and secretary, with lucrative pay. There would be no danger, and Jones would carry £1,000 for Pritchard in case of Jones's death. Pritchard would have a gentleman's status; his secretarial value would be immense. Even if he declined, he would remain second to Anna Shipley in Jones's will. Jones was undisturbed when the pass did not quickly materialize. He evidently talked with Shelburne, who suggested that he might become a peace commissioner and again encouraged him in regard to the judgeship, though it could not be filled before January.

While awaiting news about the pass, Jones attended to his practice. One case on 31 May kept him at Guildhall until 8:00 P.M. A package on his desk naggingly reminded him that Pritchard had still not copied the notes for his *Mu'allaqát* translation, so that it might be published. Then Pritchard unexpectedly visited London, accepting Jones's offer.

When Burke sent a note indicating that he could not help with the pass, Jones sought out John Lee, the new solicitor general, who felt that Shelburne rather than the Admiralty had jurisdiction. To be safe, however, Lee applied to Keppel. Because Shelburne professed to be Jones's patron, Jones decided to apply there. It was now 4 June, only two weeks before departure. His seven letters to Shelburne show the importance of patronage and the efforts that an honorable person had to make to obtain a responsible post without compromising principles.

Although Shelburne had said that Jones might call at any time, he chose to write so as not to inconvenience the secretary of state. He delicately pointed out that he could return from America before an Indian appointee could sail in a favorable season. If his frigate were captured, he could rejoice patriotically, though the delay would injure him as a lawyer on private business. A government pass to protect him against such possible delay therefore would be helpful. He and his client had nothing to do with the war; their purpose was to save endangered property. Jones became defensive: His client's children would remain behind in school as a pledge of their father's good conduct. But if there were any impropriety in the matter, Shelburne should forget it. Then Jones would risk capture, as he was not timid in just, professional acts (2:549).

He thanked Burke for the attempted help. Burke's flattering letter was ample compensation for Jones's four years of waiting for the judgeship as an unknowing slave to one man's caprice. He would not endure this situation for another year for all of India's wealth. At least Thurlow had been sufficiently tamed as to remain silent on recent Whig bills. No longer fearing Thurlow, Jones intended to call on Rockingham.

Presumably he did so. A two-day visit put his Oxford affairs in order, but on his return no communication from Shelburne was waiting. He was to leave within days, and recently the British navy had been intercepting French vessels. Ashburton observed that the form of the pass might be new and perhaps supplied the text that Jones copied out for Shelburne: "Whereas John Paradise and William Jones Esquires are going on their private business to North America, with two servants and baggage, I therefore require all officers and subjects of His Majesty not to impede or suffer them to be impeded in their voyage, but on the contrary to give them all the aid and furtherance in their power" (2:555).

Because Shelburne was not home when Jones tried to deliver the proposed pass, he sent a delicate cover letter. Upon his return before Christmas, he would show his devotion on any occasion. If there were an Indian opening, which was particularly in Shelburne's department, he would eagerly obey commands. Not mentioning that Shelburne had not answered his letter, he noted that he would be delayed if his French frigate were captured by a warship bound for England. For that contingency, as Ashburton had intimated, Jones was humbly enclosing the text of a pass that could serve every purpose but would be used only if absolutely necessary. However, if Shelburne preferred not to endorse it because of reasons that would certainly be wise, he should forget Jones's request and excuse the indiscretion. A P.S. reiterated the need for expedition.

The situation was quite sensitive, as Rockingham was fatally ill. Giving a pass to someone going on private business on an enemy warship to the American rebels perhaps required more authority than Shelburne had. What he did was to order an undersecretary's search for a precedent and to tell Jones the results, perhaps expecting that no such document covering an English colony in revolt would turn up. Pledged to end the war, Shelburne may have thought that Jones could better serve England by staying at home, ready to be a peace commissioner. Or, in view of his later actions, he may have been wondering whether Jones, whose American sympathy was well known, might not be migrating.

In a pleasant meeting Shelburne gave Jones new assurances about the judgeship. Concerned that Shelburne might have been upset, Jones sent his thanks from Dover, stating that he was as grateful as if a precedent had been found; departure from settled precedents always produced inconvenience. If Shelburne would pardon the rash request, Jones hoped to report upon his return that he had saved an indolent client's estate worth £50,000.

While waiting to sail, he wrote Parr cryptically: "On our return, we will explain to you the nature and object of our voyage" (2:559). As for the help that Parr was requesting, "You greatly overrate my power, and particularly my influence with Administration." If Parr knew Shelburne as well as Jones both knew and liked the minister, Parr would not believe the anonymous public attacks. Jones also knew Rockingham and that powerful circle, but dared not solicit preferment for friends yet. Just last week he had sounded out Kenyon, who had been trying vainly for two years to procure a benefice for someone through Thurlow. Perhaps upon his return Jones could help. Once Althorp, the wisest young man he knew, gained more influence, Althorp should be helpful.

Jones's party arrived in Paris at an unpropitious moment, when George III seemed determined not to grant independence. He had even drawn up his abdication, complete except for his signature. His aim in the unofficial negotiations was peace with union, though most of the Whig ministry and public opinion now wanted peace on any terms. General Guy Carleton, the commander in chief in America, had gone to New York to implement a policy of clemency that would do much for conciliation. He was to confer with Congress and General Washington, over the heads of the three American peace commissioners (who were instructed to demand independence) and unknown to France and Spain. Loyalists might be reestablished in power in an eventual pro-British government. Disguised agents, who would have to sympathize with the Americans but oppose independence, were said to be going to America to assist.[1]

Jones might not have been affected by the delicate situation if John Jay had not come to Paris. When Jay visited Franklin on 27 June, Jones was there. Franklin introduced Jones as a learned, active constitutionalist, who told Jay that he "despaired of seeing constitutional liberty reestablished in England; that he had determined to visit America, and in that happy and glorious country to seek and enjoy that freedom which was not to be found in Britain. He spoke in raptures of our patriotism, wisdom, &c."[2] Apparently thus contradicting his assurances to friends that he would return by Christmas, Jones mentioned Paradise's estate a few days later as a reason for his trip.

Jay liked Jones, exchanging several visits. Jones said that he was a rising character, had refused a lucrative Indian appointment, and had impressed prominent men. Discussing English politics one day, he mentioned his role and presented copies of his recent *Speech* at the London Tavern and another pamphlet. Surprised that someone of such rising expectations would be so smitten with American liberty as "to leave all, and follow her," Jay studied the pamphlets, which argued for a tripartite government based on the recorded, pure British constitution and near-universal suffrage. Two passages disturbed Jay. One was Jones's cryptic reference to his leaving for some months on a particular, urgent occasion. Jay suspected that his statements about Paradise and liberty were pretenses to cover a more important purpose; his vanity had revealed the evidence. As Jay had recently warned Robert R. Livingston against permitting British agents within the American lines, now Jay showed the two passages to Franklin, who was rather unimpressed because Franklin already knew the *Speech*. Also voicing apprehensions to General Lafayette, Jay refused to write recommendations for Jones.

Such speculation was becoming open, as in the London *Public Advertiser* of 26 June:

The destination of Mr. Jones is not Asia, as from his skill in Asiatic Languages might have been inferred, but *America;* and not having any private Concerns in any Part of America, it is supposed that the Object of his Departure is Business of a Public Kind.

When we call to Mind some other Circumstances connected with the above mentioned Mr. Jones, such as his very confidential Intimacy with all the Spencer Family, his peculiar Enthusiasm for Liberty of every Kind and in every Place, and above all, his Fame not only for Literature, but the Business of Politics, it seems to the highest Degree probable that Mr. Jones is now appointed, and surely with the best possible Reason appointed, to assist in the Pacific Negociation with America.

Franklin did warn Livingston about the "private agents sent into America to dispose minds there in favor of it, and to bring about a separate treaty there with General Carleton. I have not the least apprehension, that Congress will give in to this scheme, it being inconsistent with our treaties, as well as with our interest."[3] Still, he advised surveillance, with arrest or banishment if the agents tried to incite the people.

Actually, Shelburne had not provided the requested safe-conduct, which an agent would surely have had. None of Jones's letters to Shelburne hints of such a role, and those that he wrote shortly thereafter seem to exclude the possibility. Ashburton, who would have been chancellor except for the king's devotion to Thurlow, worked for Shelburne. There was no other powerful governmental friend whom Jones might have been secretly serving.

Not knowing of his letters seeking the pass, some American scholars have argued that he was an agent. For example, because Shelburne hoped to regain sovereignty over America on terms like those granted to Ireland, Jones was the emissary; Franklin supposedly advised Congress of his suspicion of Jones.[4] However, Jones now favored independence and would not have conspired against that one condition necessary to end the war. He had talked with Shelburne about being a peace commissioner and expected to enhance his qualifications on the trip, but his friendship with Shipley and Franklin made dissembling impossible. Teignmouth, who later knew Jones personally, concluded that such insinuations were exploded by the correspondence he used in constructing Jones's *Memoirs;* and he never saw the revealing letters to Shelburne. Surely Jones would have written Althorp about any undercover mission; no such letters have been found.

Just before leaving for Nantes, Paradise and Jones wrote Franklin to remind him of the promised recommendations. They wished him perfect health and hoped to pay their respects on their return. If Franklin had any lingering doubts, this reminder made him resolve them. In the recommendation to Jefferson he called Jones "a particular Friend of Mine, and a zealous one of our Cause and Country. I am sure you will be pleas'd with his Conversation, and therefore I make no Apology for recommending him to your Civilities." To James Bowdoin he recommended the pair as particular friends, men of learning and ingenuity, and staunch friends of America.[5]

In view of the speculation about the trip, Jones had a rather unpolitical stay in Paris, excepting his conversations with Franklin. A three-way discussion with the comte de Vergennes was to have repercussions. Jones saw the new architectural creations, a play at the new theater, and abbés whom he wanted to meet. Having studied L'Epée's universal sign language, he attended the abbé's course of lectures on the subject and became acquainted with the educator who was doing pioneering work with deaf-mutes. The duc de Nivernois was out when he called; then he was away when the duc returned the call. In general Jones rose at 6:00 A.M. and then read and exercised with a French sergeant, whose drills he practiced. After breakfast he spent the day in ceremonial or business visits.

Then Jones learned about Rockingham's death. He could only guess as to the successor, but he would not remain in England if the recent abominable system were even partly restored. Perhaps the new minister would be best for the country. When he heard of Shelburne's succession, but did not yet know that the Rockinghamites had refused to serve, he sent Shelburne formal congratulations: The king and people of England had wisely advanced Shelburne to the helm of government (2:561). Shelburne would harmonize royalty and liberty in the mixed constitution, ending Jones's suspicion of royal and aristocratic power: "The people will, I trust, have the happiness of seeing a patriot king and a patriot minister." Jones hoped to be home by December. Should his ship be captured, he would be consoled by knowing that he could express his regard for Shelburne more quickly. His letter shows no pique that he may have felt at not being given a post, and only indirect pique at not having a pass.

Just before leaving Paris on 15 July, Jones asked Franklin to forward a letter to Aleppo, perhaps in regard to his translation of the *Muʿallaqát.* He had no reason to hurry, as wartime exigencies made sailings unpredictable. At Nantes he received great civilities from Jonathan Williams, Franklin's nephew who was employed to inspect the arms being shipped to America. On the crowded, dirty docks, Paradise showed curious reservation if not fear, but had a ship been ready, they would have sailed. As none was, they prolonged their stay in what Paradise called the "Nantes hell-hole."

Over the next fortnight Jones inspected all ships that would soon leave for America. The best one was the *Annette,* scheduled for Philadelphia or Virginia. It would sail with other ships in late August. Returning from the docks one day, he found letters waiting that seemed to require his presence in London. Shelburne wrote that he had nothing more at heart than to procure a desirable Indian station for Jones, whose chances were now greatly improved. Another letter evidently raised Jones's hopes for marrying Anna.

He might remain in Nantes until late autumn; however, the frigates were full. No merchant ships with tolerable accommodations would sail for Virginia right away, and ships taking the southern route risked capture and conveyance to the West Indies. If Jones's ship were captured, he could not be home before the spring, too late for an Indian appointment. But if he made a quick trip to London, he could ascertain the situation, which would affect his likely marriage, and be back in Nantes before the *Annette* sailed.

A passport was needed for him and his servant to embark from Ostend. He outlined the situation to Franklin, explaining that family or professional affairs might prevent his voyage. If so, Paradise should go without him, as he had been fruitlessly entreating his friend to agree to do. Laurens had just arrived and would be happy to accompany Paradise. However, if Jones were to migrate, he needed information about practicing law in Pennsylvania and possibly helping frame American laws.

Adamant, Paradise would travel only with Jones, on whom their legal plans were based. When Jones promised to return in a few weeks so that they could sail as planned, Paradise concluded that Jones was abandoning him in favor of better opportunities. Depression seized him. Physically ill, he said that another week in Nantes would cost his sanity or his life, and Jones's prodding only increased his stubbornness. Jones cajoled him, partly in the interest of the estate, until Paradise, pushed too far, called Jones a false friend whom he never wanted to see again. As Franklin had now sent the needed passport, along with likely encouragement about migration, Jones angrily left.[6] The quarrel, Jones felt, had ended all obligations to Paradise.

When Paradise returned to Paris, he reported that the pair had parted and Jones had gone home. Jay told Livingston: "How this happened I never could learn. It was a subject on which Mr. Paradise was very reserved. Perhaps the sentiments of America, on General Carleton's overtures, had rendered Mr. Jones' voyage unnecessary."[7] When Paradise reached London, he was disillusioned and humiliated. Teignmouth, who presumably heard Jones's own explanation, concluded that Paradise's irresolution and indisposition prevented execution of the plan.[8] Jones's returning home would seem to end all possibility that he was an agent, though he evidently enjoyed the air of adventure and mystery about his three trips to Paris, which added to Jay's bafflement, culminating in the conclusion that he was indeed an agent. Rather than a selfless modern Ulysses rescuing his country in spite of itself, a country led by people who would not trust him to be a peace commissioner, Jones was a well-intentioned but self-appointed meddler, a romantic scholar rather than a political savior. These trips were ultimately politically useless. His one attempt at private diplomacy, "A Fragment of Polybius," failed.

Jones leisurely traveled through Normandy in mid-August. As the Oxford sessions were several weeks away, he took an excursion. After a day of sailing among the isles of Zeeland, he went from Rotterdam to Antwerp and back to Bruges, before paying the long-promised visit to Schultens at Leiden. Amid the warm hospitality there was helpful discussion of his *Mu'allaqát*. As Jones's notes were not yet printed, he needed to consult the manuscripts that Reiske had used in *Tharaphæ Moallakah* (Leiden, 1742). He met scholars like David Ruhnkenius, President des Brosses and a Greek critic; and Everardus Scheidius, whose Arabic study he encouraged.

There were exciting conversations and extreme civility in Leiden: "The character, indeed, of a man of letters, though very disadvantageous in life, has this advantage to a traveller in war time, that it operates as a kind of passport or flag of truce, and admits him, who bears it, into the company and confidence of his country's most vehement enemies" (2:568). This statement to Lady Spencer was Jones's most mature characterization of scholars as citizens of the world. Nationalistic loyalty can blur injustices by one's own country, whereas scholars can be more objective than politicians can and so should use their knowledge to achieve a just peace or other solution to international problems. Moreover, scholars should continue their research even during wartime, as research can transcend useless, military interludes in history.

Arriving at Margate on 9 September, Jones wrote Shelburne his most direct solicitation. He did not know whether the minister had received his congratulations from Paris, but cancellation of his voyage to America now made him immediately available for the judgeship. The difficulty in finding a suitable, safe ship was one of the main reasons for his return. Also, "it was impossible for me, consistently with my gratitude to your Lordship, for your noble and generous conduct towards me, to be absent so long from my country, which I might be called upon to serve in India, in some station for which you might be indulgent enough to think me qualified" (2:566). Having perfect confidence in the minister, he could say what he could not have said to any other:

If your kind intentions of opening a situation for me in Bengal should have their full effect, I will conform myself with the greatest fidelity to your instructions, and wishes; or, if you should think that I might be more useful at home, I will make a point, whether in or out of parliament, of supporting to the utmost of my humble abilities, your measures for the publick prosperity, and I shall be proud and happy to be guided through life by so great a statesman.

Because Shelburne was Jones's sole patron, he would place himself under the minister's protection and await commands at Oxford for the next two weeks. Actually, this letter did not compromise his principles, which Shelburne seemed to share. He had reconciled his idealism with the flawed real world of politics: "A man of high principle and transparent sincerity, Jones had the usual Celtic independence of spirit and pride, and would not compromise with his convictions even for India and the supreme opportunity this would afford for his genius as an Orientalist."[9]

Informing Althorp and Lady Spencer of the canceled voyage, Jones expressed dismay at the reports about the Rockinghamites' desertion of Shelburne: Men who loved England should sacrifice private animosity for public prosperity. His own role would depend on conversations with one or two friends, but he would like to pay his respects at Wimbledon first. So he became a house guest. During the restful stay he indulged in his old practice of writing letters while the ladies made morning visits.

Jones wrote Shipley that he would honor the long-standing invitation to visit Chilbolton if the family were going to be home after the circuit. He sent his respects to Mrs. Shipley and her five daughters, for whom he had hoped to bring back Virginia nightingales. Dissension had exploded his wish that the Whigs might harmonize in the political concert some time longer. He gently corrected Shipley's prediction that business and public responsibility would make *An Essay on Bailments* his last work. Many legal tracts had already been prepared, just as Sir Francis Bacon, Coke, and other figures had written voluminously without impairing lucrative careers. Because Jones wanted to become as great a lawyer as Sulpicius was, he would probably write as many volumes as Sulpicius supposedly wrote. The delay in the judgeship had injured him, but assiduity would recover the lost ground. Thus he reassured his prospective father-in-law about his profession and income. An invitation was immediately sent.

Jones delicately wrote Althorp, one of the three Treasury officers who had quit rather than serve under the man to whom Jones had committed himself. Althorp should condemn the bitter accusations, such as Fox's charge that Shelburne was protecting the destroyers of England's eastern possessions. Burke, John Lee, Frederick Ponsonby, and Sheridan had also resigned; at least Pitt's addition to the Treasury was a bright spot. England should regret Althorp's resignation, which could not have been motivated by anger or hate, Jones noted.

He visited Lytton on the way to Oxford. Shelburne's anticipated communication was not waiting, nor did it arrive as the days crawled by. As the sessions would begin in early October, he wrote his circuit friend James Eyre, who was urging him to visit the Eyre family seat: "[Shelburne] writes me word, that he has nothing more at heart than *to open some* situation for me in India. What this means I know not, but it looks like some new plan, which may probably hang undecided from session to session" (2:575).

Again, Jones turned to Kenyon, who had remained the attorney general. As the two had dined together just before his departure, he elaborately explained his return. The late sailing would have prevented his being home by Christmas and thus would have required sacrificing his reasonable aspirations, all for a weak client who refused to sail alone to save valuable property. This restrained interpretation was necessary to explain Jones's surprising return.[10] As Kenyon had always been indulgent and kind, Jones said: "My knowledge of your firm integrity and virtues, publick and private, makes me more desirous of cultivating your friendship than that of most men living" (2:573). Though his visit to Shipley would prevent his seeing Kenyon in Wales, Jones was inexpressibly anxious to be delivered from five years of ruinous suspense. Because Kenyon's last words to him had been so kind, he anticipated a successful intercession with Thurlow. He feared that he had unintentionally offended Thurlow, although in talking with friends earlier, he had always considered the man to have sole patronage.

Jones wrote to two other friends. Althorp received a defense of Shelburne, whose sincerity was being publicly questioned: "If he be *proved* a double-tongued and double-hearted monster, let him be sent to the tower with other royal savages: if there be no clear *evidence* against him, I think he must be raised, not depressed, by the accusation" (2:576). As Shelburne professed a system of mixed government, Jones would support him as long as he observed such principles. North had been too monarchical; Rockingham, too aristocratic. Jones accepted Althorp's laborious explanation for having reluctantly resigned the Treasury post.

Jones's sensitive letter to Burke explained that his return from Nantes had hinged on hopes for an Indian post, which he desired more than ever because of the division between his benefactors and friends. He would always appreciate Burke's friendship and glory, and he "lamented with real anguish the loss of the virtuous, amiable and excellent" Rockingham (2:580). He genteelly explained his support of Shelburne by quoting Shakespeare. Shelburne had been faithful and just to Jones; however, he would grievously answer for any ambitiousness. If the principles that he had professed proved to be delusive, no prospects anywhere could induce Jones's support.

Jones's three and a half weeks at University College were leisurely. For a while he was governor and almost sole occupant. When the quarter sessions ended and he still had not received a letter from Shelburne, he went to Chilbolton for what was to be his happiest month.

When the weather permitted, he joined Shipley for exercise in the field; and he gave language instruction to Georgiana, who was eight years younger than Anna. Anna was as charming as ever. There was pleasurable letter-writing. To the duchess of Devonshire he described his early life as a poet gathering roses without thorns, and his later life as a lawyer gathering thorns without roses. As she had assisted his efforts to raise the Whig standard at Oxford, she would be his patroness if he ever enjoyed Petrarch's *vita serena* and could finally compose "Britain Discovered," for she had reproved him for deserting Parnassus. Amid wild flights of imagination, the epic would convey his ideas on perfect government, to which the English constitution nearly approached. Thus he pleasantly contemplated his twelve-year-old plan.

Though Anna said nothing to permit him to utter what was in the back of his mind, he was again part of a delightful family, as he had been with the Spencers. Jones always seems to have wanted to be accepted into a large family, especially one with social prominence if not wealth. But soon he realized, dismayed, that he must leave to start the new term. Saying a long farewell to pleasure, he must face "the drudgery of drawing bills in equity, the toil of answering law-cases, the squabbles of the bar, and the most vexatious dissensions and conflicts in the political world" (2:582).

Jones had barely missed Shelburne's undersecretaryship, which might have changed his life; now time worked for him. Shipley's confidence in him had rekindled his determination to prosper as a barrister and enable him to support a wife. Jones had always rejected the notion of marrying for wealth, despite several opportunities; yet he did intend to marry. Indeed, his "Caissa" was partly autobiographical: "I was an early lover, as the poem was written at sixteen. In truth I have never ceased being in love from that age to more than the double of it, but some of my flames are married, others (more lamented) dead, and others surrounded with invincible obstacles." Anna had "good sense, and good temper, agreeable manners, a feeling heart, domestick affections, knowledge of the world and contempt of what is wrong in it – these were the qualities which I ever sought" (2:477, 586). She was highly virtuous, or Franklin and Lady Spencer would not have warmly praised her to Jones. All these reasons had persuaded him to propose, until he heard John Butler, then the bishop of Oxford, say that she was positively engaged. He desponded until he learned, probably from a letter received at Nantes, that Butler might be misinformed.

With his departure looming, Jones could conceal his feelings no longer, and on 25 October he confessed his love. When Anna explained, with captivating frankness, the source of Butler's mistake, "that heart, which I had the joy to find disengaged, I have had the happiness (and have I not reason to be vain?) of winning in exchange for my own" (2:587). Shipley consented to the marriage with a benevolence tempered by wisdom that made Jones love the virtuous bishop as a father. So did Mrs. Shipley and Anna's siblings, with flattering approbation.

After gaining all the Shipleys' consent, Jones informed Lady Spencer in an intellectual letter rich with French poetry. He anxiously wished that when they were united in marriage, she would continue the friendship with which she had honored them singly. His more intellectual letter to Althorp described the background leading up to his confession of love. He dispatched a servant to Midgham, hoping that William Poyntz could come to join in the happiness with his new family. Letters to the duchess of Devonshire and others also elicited congratulations. Jones thanked the highly complimentary Devonshires: "The felicity, which awaits me, is indeed a blessing of heaven, which I shall incessantly labour to render myself worthy of" (2:592).

Anna replied to her good friend Georgiana: "How can I describe to you half the Joy & happiness my heart feels in the Idea of the affection & friendship you express for my Mr. J – but how should it be otherwise you who have known his merits so long & who have a heart that is form'd to love everything that is good & wise. He absolutely Idolizes [you]" (2:592). Anna was willing to go to India; she would not discourage him from the post that he had long wanted and for which he had studied so hard.

Jones presumably informed Mrs. Montagu, who commented on the coming marriage of "the learned and ingenious Mr. Jones."[11] He wrote Franklin:

My profile will, I hope, have the honour of being hung up in your apartment with those of a family, whom you love and revere, and by whom you are loved and revered with the greatest cordiality. My connexion with the excellent bishop of St. Asaph, by my marriage with his eldest daughter (of whom I have heard you speak with approbation) is now settled, and will take place as soon as we can be united with a prudent attention to our worldly interests, and to the highest of all interests, our independence. . . . I am received with open arms into a family, which you and I have always known to contain a rare assemblage of publick and private virtues. We were always talking of you in Hampshire, and longing to enjoy again your sweet society. (2:593)

Jones sent regards to Franklin from the physician William Hodgson and other Honest Whigs. He said that Paradise, with excessive weakness, had told friends that Franklin and Jay had advised him it was unnecessary to go to Virginia to save the estate. Jones hoped that Paradise had not misunderstood.

Jones did not mention his own possible immigration, which he had contemplated only after he thought Anna was unavailable and England unsavable. If he had had no attachments, he might have accepted "an offer from some American leaders in several states to practise their old law among them and to hold the pen in framing their new laws" (2:590). When his hopes revived, the possibility weakened; Anna's acceptance and his anticipated Indian judgeship ended it.

From afar Jones had come to like India, although the lucrative pay was a greater attraction. He had given the Chilbolton address to key friends, so that the judgeship was never far from his mind. Burke, Kenyon, and

Lee wrote him; and Pitt sent a long, friendly message. Ashburton, who was to become Jones's most effective patron, was especially encouraging: "You will give me credit for not being indifferent about the important stake still left in India, or your particular interest in it, in which I consider that of the public so materially involved."[12]

Jones probably received a new promise from Shelburne. In any case, the new term required his return to London, and he needed to know whether the government meant to appoint him. Anna told Georgiana: "Shd this Scheme not take place he is determined to stick close to the Law which there is no doubt but he must succeed very well in, if his health should allow of the necessary confinement & attention but I have a thousand fears about it and shall therefore consider the India Plan in a very desirable light."[13]

Jones explained his dilemma to Lady Spencer, who in some ways had taken the place of his mother. Should he remain in judicial suspense until something was decided, or should he devote himself to his profession? The two goals could not be effectively pursued simultaneously. He had described his situation to Shipley, who so esteemed him that he needed an objective opinion. For five years Jones's income had averaged £600, but travel and other expenses took £200. His fellowship now paid more than £100, and his Oxford apartments and servants added the equivalent of another £200. All this and his small inheritance would provide a bachelor a perfect independence at Oxford and let him read Persian for the rest of his days. As a provincial counsel there, he could expand his library and keep horses.

Because life in London was much more expensive due to dress and the great distances, and because Jones's commissionership of bankruptcy paid less than £100, he could not properly support a wife and family there. The fact was, though he hardly realized it, he was not yet a successful barrister. So much time had been expended in pursuing the judgeship that, except for the Welsh circuit, his income was too limited for him to give up his college fellowship and take a wife, even after nine years of practicing law. Everything turned on India, but nothing was decided. Cornwallis expected to sail in February as the new Governor-General, if Hastings were recalled. North's friends had declared an armed neutrality in this matter, while Shelburne was overdoing encouragement and promises to Jones. The confusion made him wonder whether he should not delay marriage until he had the judgeship or else advanced himself in the Court of Exchequer with Pitt's help. Though he would be miserable until then, he would not expose Anna to the least danger, he told Lady Spencer: "I would covenant with trustees to leave all my present and future property at her sole disposal, in case of my death; and I have already appointed her my sole heiress, in case of accident before marriage" (2:600).

Lady Spencer replied that Jones was too modest. He was engaged to the woman he loved and was accepted in the Shipley and Spencer families. Shipley's politics coincided with his, as in their recent discussion about *The Principles of Government, in a Dialogue between a Scholar and a Peasant.* This pamphlet had been inspired by Jones's conversation with Franklin and Vergennes in Paris. Trusting in logic, he asserted that basic governmental principles could be made intelligible to uneducated readers. Vergennes denied the claim, and Franklin doubted it. To make his task harder, Jones composed a Socratic dialogue in French. When the trio met, Vergennes yielded, and Franklin ruled in Jones's favor.[14] Jones then translated the dialogue in London, and the Society for Constitutional Information published it anonymously as a free pamphlet.

In seven pages a scholar's questions guide a peasant into articulating political principles. These begin with the realization that the village club, which would be defended against a single member or members who attempted to seize unrepresentative control, is a weak, small free state. When asked the consequences "if the King alone were to insist on making laws, or on altering them at his will and pleasure," the peasant retorts that the king should be expelled. If the king tried to use his army to enforce his will, the nation should resist, "or the state would cease to be a state." Thereupon the scholar supplies a musket and advises the peasant to spend "an hour every morning in the next fortnight in learning to prime and load expeditiously, and to fire and charge with bayonet."

Locke provided much of Jones's general outlook on the nature and extent of human reason, especially Locke's *Two Treatises of Government,* which is much stronger than the dialogue. Jones stressed three democratic points: a body of volunteers, universal equality, and manhood suffrage.[15]

Dean William Shipley enthusiastically submitted the pamphlet to the local branch of the Society for Constitutional Information, which asked Jones to translate it into Welsh. But when Jones observed that it might do mischief, he was asked to hold off. Then Thomas Fitzmaurice, Shelburne's brother and now sheriff of Flint County, viciously attacked Shipley for having intended to publish a known libel. When Shipley defiantly reprinted and circulated a few English copies, Fitzmaurice transmitted a copy to the government, who ruled against a state prosecution. The king laughed at the thought, but Fitzmaurice persuaded the county grand jury to indict Shipley for publishing a seditious libel.

The action stung Jones as much as it did his future brother-in-law. Remembering the attempted coercion of his Oxford *Oration,* he had the society reprint the pamphlet in early 1783. The title page identified him as the author and a member, and he added Bishop Shipley's unsigned two-paragraph advertisement as a reply to Fitzmaurice's misrepresentations. Although Jones privately defended the constitutionality of his dialogue, the society hired the famous Thomas Erskine for the first trial. It ended in August 1784, when the jury ruled Dean Shipley guilty only of publishing the dialogue, as the judge had assumed the power of ruling it a libel. Erskine eventually won; Pitt and Burke helped in defending the freedom of the press against the judge's ruling. Fox's Libel Act of 1792 finally passed. Thus Jones's pamphlet led to the legal guarantee of a basic democratic principle: The jury has the right to decide whether the work is a libel.[16]

The dialogue was immediately famous as a denunciation of tyranny, although the public press was sometimes reserved. *Gentleman's Magazine* observed that it is "supposed to be by no mean hand"; the reader must judge whether it is seditious, treasonable, and diabolical. The advertisement was discreetly quoted to the effect that Locke would have to be judged a traitor if the dialogue were libelous (April 1783, p. 332). The *Monthly Review* praised Jones for carrying the great principles of liberty, on which constitutional government depends, to "their highest pitch of perfection" (October 1784, p. 349). Josiah Tucker's *Sequel to Sir William Jones's Pamphlet on the Principles of Government* (Cadell, 1784), negatively reviewed in the press, prompted Day's defense, *A Dialogue Between a Justice of the Peace and a Farmer* (London, 1785). Jones's dialogue remained famous for fifty years, with seven more editions or printings by 1831, replete with notes and historical commentary. It remains to this day a clear, dramatic exposition of basic rights.

Jones's pamphleteering ended with the anonymous *Letter to a Patriot Senator.* Printed by Nichols for Dilly, it proposes annual parliaments and wider representation. These advanced ideas were the logical culmination of principles that he had long been developing and that Major Cartwright was proclaiming. An MP has supposedly requested the author's ideas on representation, not as derived from metaphysical abstractions or Plato's *Republic,* but from "inquiry into the original frame and texture of our English government and the first elements of our civil polity." So the forty-page answer used "the rules and maxims transmitted to us by our forefathers, recorded in our venerable archives, and unfolded by writers of approved authority," which compose English constitutional law. There is predictable praise of Blackstone. The groundless distinction between personal and real property and between England's landed and trading interests has let the nobility and rich commoners control seats and become MPs, whereas the constitution permits suffrage to all subjects who are not extremely indolent or mentally incapable. The remedy is to restore the recorded constitution, with annual sessions so as to eliminate corruption.

The appended bill would widen parliamentary representation. Voters would sign a strict anticorruption oath, have an annual income of £25 to £50 from property or labor, and be at least twenty-one. Election officials would take an oath to make "a true return of the candidates elected." Elected MPs, with an income of £300 to £600, would take a comparable oath. The pamphlet ends with a defense of the bill: "The whole system, it will be said, is *democratical,* big with danger to publick peace, and evidently tending to a revolution, by giving to the people a greater share of power than is consistent with general tranquillity. Idle terrors! vain surmises!" Possible objections are rebutted: (1) Annual parliaments would not be too frequent; (2) the Scots would not have too large a share in Parliament; (3) there are not already too many oaths and felonies; (4) the plan is not too vast and impracticable, because Cicero demonstrated that industry and virtue can accomplish anything; and (5) the people are not grossly ignorant and abandoned. If the multitude are ignorant, they should be educated; if incorrigible, punished. Although the author does not expect such a bill to be enacted, it is a worthy experiment. As he does not fear personal inconvenience or seek approbation, the MP who requested the plan has the option of identifying or suppressing the author's name.

The pamphlet ends in the way that Jones sometimes ended his letters to Althorp, who may have been the unidentified MP and who may even have requested Jones's ideas on representation. Published on 3 May 1783, it is Jones's most mysterious writing. He never mentions it in his known correspondence; only recently has his authorship been verified. Perhaps the legal objectivity required by his judicial appointment led him to omit his name as author. The reviews were cautious. The *Critical Review* (May 1783, p. 404) and *Gentleman's Magazine* (October 1784, p. 768) simply reported the ideas. The latter was "credibly informed" that Jones was the author. After the storm from *The Principles of Government,* his final pamphlet moved smoothly into the stream of treatises leading toward the Reform Acts.

Overall, Jones's nine political works express the views guiding his personal and courtroom conduct. Drawing on the constitution at a time when England was threatened by external and internal disorder, he urges citizens to recognize and obey their ancient duty to protect their country. His *Letter* even suggests that the object of government is happiness for the greatest numbers, indicating acceptance of Jeremy Bentham's *Fragment of Gov-*

ernment (1776). These six essays and three poems are decidedly Whiggish. Jones's zeal for liberty came from a benevolent heart and an admiration of classical republics, and his political motives were pure.[17]

His political ideas were more theoretical than practical, as he admits in his *Letter.* The only idea that he tried to implement was local militias. He was a scholar, without the time to be a reformer. His findings could be useful, but he was usually more interested in pursuing the scholarship than in applying the conclusions. In March 1783 he indirectly declined the reformer's role by rejecting Edmund Cartwright's offer – probably inspired by Edmund's brother the major – to anthologize his political tracts. In 1782 Dilly published the second edition of Jones's *Inquiry,* which was hardly altered, in a seventy-five-page pamphlet containing his Oxford *Oration,* Middlesex *Speech* of 1780, and his letter accepting membership in the Society for Constitutional Information. Major Cartwright made political capital of this pamphlet, giving a copy to Fox (who promised to read it)[18] and then reprinting Jones's *Inquiry* and the 1782 *Speech* in 1819.

The *Moallakát* was Jones's major literary publication in 1782. Printed by Nichols for Elmsly on 1 December, it contradicted his statement in *Poems* that he would not translate the seven pre-Moslem poems; however, his praise of them had not enticed some other scholar to do so. Most of the work was done in 1781, but unable to finish revising the notes, he let the unbound sheets be sold with an advertisement requesting the purchaser not to bind them until Jones could prepare the preliminary discourse and notes. Scholars should submit their criticism and annotations.

The unbound edition has a dedication to Paradise, but the formal edition in 1783 omits this because of the quarrel. A cancel title omits the words "Notes, Critical, Philological, Explanatory" and "Preliminary Discourse," material that, in part, appeared in an essay in 1787. Both editions contain Jones's prose translations and Arguments, which summarize each plot and describe the metrics. His curious Roman-character transliteration of the original couplets is designed to encourage others to study Arabic if not translate the work. The book uses a sadly imperfect system and contains some real mistakes. For example, every consonant is transcribed as such, regardless of its function in the original. The translation itself has several errors.[19]

According to fanciful legend, the seven poems were adjudged best in a competition at the 'Ukaz fair, and then were transcribed in golden letters on Egyptian linen and hung on the Kaaba.[20] Imru'u 'l-Qays opens with the sorrowful poet's dramatic recollection of an adventure at a desert site where his mistress's tribe had encamped. He sat on her clothes while she was swimming until she had to come forth naked. 'Amr ibn Kulthúm also passionately describes his mistress's body. All the poems are hedonistic, as sensually conveyed in Ṭarafa's pleasures:

First, to rise before the censurers wake, and to drink tawny wine, which sparkles and froths when the clear stream is poured into it.

Next, when a warrior, encircled by foes, implores my aid, to bend towards him my prancing charger, fierce as a wolf among the GADHA-trees, whom the sound of human steps has awakened, and who runs to quench his thirst at the brook.

Thirdly, to shorten a cloudy day, a day astonishingly dark, by toying with a lovely delicate girl under a tent supported by pillars.

Jones nicely translates the anatomical descriptions of racing camels and the poets' self-praise. 'Antara brags: "Many a consort of a fair one, whose beauty required no ornaments, have I left prostrate on the ground; and the life-blood has run sounding from his veins, opened by my javelin like the mouth of a camel with a divided lip." The elderly Zuhair recalls his long-lost beloved before philosophically pronouncing maxims on war and peace, which Jones compares with Solomon's proverbs.

Jones's scholarly reputation had remained high since his *Commentariorum,* if a bit dimmed in Orientalism and now tilted toward law. This new book was a landmark in acquainting the West with the motif of kismet and would cause many echoes in English poetry.[21] Both his contemporaries and modern scholars have criticized his use of prose to keep as close as possible to the original meaning: "His talents for poetry need no commendation, as they are sufficiently known, and universally allowed, and surely they might have been displayed to great advantage in the present instance." Nonetheless, his prose shows "his extensive and critical knowledge" of Arabic.[22] The *Monthly Review* observed that it would be deemed temerity to criticize Jones's Oriental labors, as his translation "will add a fresh branch of laurel to his wreath" (October 1783, pp. 296–7). His book enjoyed long popularity, until superseded by Wilfrid Scawen Blunt's poetic *Seven Golden Odes of Pagan Arabia* (1903), but it merits a modern reprinting.

Jones had promised Gibbon a copy: "My *Seven Arabian Poets* will see the light before next winter, and be proud to wait upon you in their English dress. Their wild productions will, I flatter myself, be thought interesting, and not venerable merely on account of their antiquity" (2:480). Gibbon was more interested in Jones's Arabic scholarship: "His honourable mission to India has deprived us of his own notes, far more interesting than the obscure and obsolete text."[23]

In late December the third edition of Jones's *Grammar* appeared. Expecting the proroguing of Parliament to prevent action on the judgeship, he spent the holidays with the Shipleys. After the Oxford sessions in mid-

January 1783, he returned home to find the situation unchanged. Nor, despite the frequent promises, were Shelburne's political actions wholly pleasing: "Gratitude does not extend, I think, to the approbation of measures, which on a cool examination, appear injurious to the publick" (2:598). Jones did thank Shelburne for making provisional peace with America: "Were the nation as grateful as they ought to be, they would erect a statue to your Lordship, inscribed *Pacificator*" (2:601–2). If his own professional labors could secure honorable tranquillity for his declining years, Jones added wryly, he would finally compose his history of the war.

He scarcely concealed his disappointment to Shelburne, for the promise to open a place had principally motivated his abandoning the American voyage. As the preliminary articles had now been signed at Versailles, the encouragement for a peace commissionership had also been meaningless. He did not even mention India in his letter to Shelburne, who was actually much weaker than Jones thought. Somewhat at the king's mercy, Shelburne was caught in the conflict between the Court of Proprietors and the dissension-ridden Whigs.

The ending of the war had removed Jones's American sympathy as one of Thurlow's objections. So Jones turned back to Thurlow, through Kenyon. Having sprained an ankle, he could not call on the attorney general. He wrote that Ashburton had projected a new judicial management of British India, and because his own speedy marriage and happiness depended on the judgeship, Kenyon should place him in a favorable light with Thurlow. His defensive pronouncement, though not compromising his principles, must have galled him: "As to my politicks, which he has heard much misrepresented, his Lordship may be assured, that I am no more a *republican* than a *Mahomedan* or *Gentoo,* and that I have ever formed my opinions from what appeared to me, on the calmest inquiry, the true spirit of our constitution" (2:601). Jones thereby partly committed his fortunes to Kenyon.

The duchess of Devonshire made a direct appeal, which Thurlow answered tactfully:

Madam, – I think it very improbable, that I shall be consulted on the appointment of a Judge in India; without which it would be improper, in my situation, to interpose at all.

If I were called upon to recommend a fit person, I can assure your Grace, with much truth, and simplicity, that I know no opinion, upon which I shall rely more implicitly, for a just account of William Jones's character. The pretensions, which relate more immediately and peculiarly to the office, I should not expect to find much the subject of your Graces observations. But of other parts of Character, which are also important qualifications, no Person is more capable to discern.[24]

Such efforts were almost successful, until a Fox–North censure over the Versailles Articles led to Shelburne's resignation. As Jones despairingly wrote Burke, the waves of political change had driven his little skiff far from Bengal: "I certainly did not love lord Shelburne; nor had I any reason to love him for my own sake, or for that of the publick; but I must have been grateful to him, if he had kept his solemn promises, often repeated verbally and in writing, of placing me on the bench at Calcutta" (2:602). Moreover, Thurlow's continued presence in the ministry would let him obstruct the Rockinghamites until they could be overthrown. Jones might accept an invitation to become a lawyer in Pennsylvania, except for his love of England and many dear friends; or he could retire to Oxford on his small independence. Friends like Burke should decide: Should he resume his profession and forget India, or should he still hope for the judgeship? As Jones could not do both, Burke would be his oracle.

What he probably wanted most was encouragement. Retirement and marriage were financially incompatible, and he could hardly forget the judgeship, on which he had staked so much. But Shelburne did keep his promise in a last act as prime minister. George III approved Jones for the post for which he was ideally suited, writing Thurlow on 1 March:

I find from Mr. Townshend that Ld. Shelburne will think himself unkindly treated if Mr. Jones is not sent to the East Indies on the vacancy of Judge which has subsisted some years; I shall take it as a personal compliment to Me if You will consent to it. Ld. Ashburton answers for his being competent as a Lawyer, and his knowledge of the Eastern Languages is a very additional qualification. (2:604)

And Jones's service as a judge was to gratify the king, who had finally been led to think on a higher level about India.

Not yet knowing of Shelburne's help, Jones told friends that the appointment was due to Ashburton, who did assure the king that Jones was not only fit for the office but also the only one who was fit.[25] Ashburton's congratulations strengthened that view: "When I consider this appointment as securing to you at once, two of the first objects of human pursuit, those of ambition and love, I feel it a subject of very serious and cordial congratulation, which I desire you to accept" (2:604).

The Whitehall announcement of 4 March appeared in the *London Gazette:* "The King has been pleased to grant to William Jones, Esq. the Office and Place of one of the Judges of his Majesty's Supreme Court of Judicature at Fort William, in Bengal, in the Room of Stephen Cæsar Le Maistre, Esq. deceased." Jones thanked those who had helped, beginning with Ashburton. To Kenyon he expressed "warmest thanks for the kind part which you have taken in procuring my advancement, and with it every prospect of worldly happiness" (2:604). As Jones inquired about the warrant, which had been transmitted to the attorney general, he probably knew that Kenyon's efforts had helped little.

Perhaps his most elegant letter was to Shelburne: "Accept my warmest thanks for your signal kindness to me on all occasions and for your unremitted and zealous attention to my interest in recommending me to his Majesty as a proper person to supply the vacant place" (2:605). He had first admired the earl as a statesman. Now his attachment added gratitude to shared principles, and all his friendships would have been superseded had Shelburne been able to secure him a seat in Parliament. England "will owe all its future prosperity, if not its political existence, to the Peace, which your lordship so wisely made." But later, when Shelburne accepted the title of marquis of Lansdowne, Jones privately observed that Shelburne had changed the skin of his titles like a snake, "only to show in how many forms he can deceive" (2:853).

Jones's request for knighthood was communicated on 17 March. That same day the king gave Thomas Townshend permission to inform the new judge that he would be thus honored at the levee on 20 March. Thereupon he became Sir William.

Jones resigned his commissionership of bankruptcy. While preparing his effects for sailing, he continued to receive congratulations. Thanking Francis Hargrave, Jones expressed delight at being able to unite his profession with his predilection for Oriental studies. Edmund Cartwright wrote him twice.

The most pleasing congratulations came from Franklin, whom Hodgson had informed of Jones's "place of very great Emolument."[26] Franklin was also greatly pleased by the coming marriage, which was certain to be happy because the couple possessed so many amiable qualities. He hoped that Jones would return from corruptive India with much honestly acquired money and undiminished virtue. He enclosed a proof of his medal commemorating Saratoga and Yorktown, having altered the design and accepted the motto from Horace as Jones had suggested.[27] Their association was over. In the most furious days of the war a compassionate Englishman like Jones, who sought justice for America while remaining loyal to his country, had been friends with an enlightened American who yearned for a government of free people in England while inexorably pressing for American independence. Together they yearned for a government based on the pure English constitution, which was to underpin the American experiment in the balance of powers.

During his hectic final weeks in England, Jones attended the Club on 25 February and 11 March. On 25 March he said good-bye to Boswell,

Colman, Fordyce, Gibbon, Richard Marlay, Reynolds, and Steevens. Boswell's journal records little about the meeting: "We were well enough. But I find nothing in our conversation to pickle or preserve."[28] Presumably there were farewells to other members. Johnson wrote Chambers that Jones would report "the present state of the club, which is now very miscellaneous, and very heterogeneous," a condition that he had feared. The critic Edmond Malone told Percy about Jones's "emigration."[29]

Jones went to Oxford to arrange for transporting his books and resigned his fellowship as of 12 April. This followed Scott's resignation by one year and marked the end of the golden age of University College.[30]

Jones was married by special license on 8 April. Hannah More, expecting to meet the Shipleys at Mrs. Vesey's, was told that they had sent an excuse: "Anna Maria and Sir William were at that moment in the act of marrying. They will be now completely banished, but as they will be banished together, they do not think it a hardship. May God bless them, and may his stupendous learning be sanctified!"[31]

London Magazine perhaps expressed the public view:

He is now on his passage for India, and from the ideas which we have formed of his character, and from the opportunities which we have had of contemplating with admiration his exquisite taste, his extensive and diversified erudition, we may venture, without incurring the censure of rashness, to presage that his conduct, in the character of a judge, will render him even a great ornament to his country. (July 1783, p. 55)

Maurice later said that England never did a wiser deed than sending Jones to superintend Indian jurisprudence.[32] Certainly his judicial career was notable, but he probably would not have been appointed if Thurlow had had control of the matter. The parliamentary inquiry into the Bengal Supreme Court had occasioned much of the delay, though Jones's plain speaking and honest convictions contributed to it. The delay "may have cost posterity dear – for who can say what more he might not have accomplished, had he gone to India in 1778 and served there those lost years with Warren Hastings?"[33]

Jones had initially viewed the judgeship as a prestigious way to gain financial independence. Then he could begin his real public career at the peak of his powers, and he could redirect his country into constitutional practices. This attitude was somewhat ambiguous: He sought the post from a government that he attacked as a wicked despotism but that was perhaps the most liberal of the day. However, there had been rebuffs like Oxford's parliamentary rejection and Shelburne's not naming him as a peace commissioner. The Whig leaders on whom England's future seemed to depend were attacking one another instead of uniting to promote tranquillity. Jones slowly soured on public life and began to view India as a refuge where he could combine law and Oriental studies, insulated from the seemingly insoluble problems in England. More importantly, his industry and knowledge could help the Indians, in a startling motivation for eighteenth-century colonial administrators.

Jones was not yet aware of the dimensions of British oppression in India. Nor had he ever really considered that the people whom he would be judging had had no voice in his appointment, made while he was clamoring for liberty for both the British and the American people. Though in his letters he always spoke of the judgeship as the means to the independence that would later let him be a completely objective MP, he was nonetheless seeking wealth, which would inevitably come at the expense of the Indians whom he would be governing, regardless of the help that he could provide them. Basically altruistic and idealistic, he was nonetheless a commoner requiring social and political position before he could really serve people.

His pamphleteering ended when he sailed. Ironically, just as Jones was leaving, the grand jury was given the charge that Dean Shipley had published a libelous, seditious pamphlet tending to influence the king's subjects. So not even Jones's closing days were serene. After several attempts to see Kenyon, he sent a defense of his dialogue: "If the right of resistance be not law, we have no constitution; and, if we may not be *prepared* with arms, there never could be any effectual resistance: and the doctrine would be a mockery: if we give up these rights, we give up everything" (2:609). From the dockside he sent Kenyon a final statement, lamenting that he could not defend the doctrines before Kenyon and the jury, as advocate for Dean Shipley and the Whig interest. But Jones would live to see the successful outcome of the trial. The role of his pamphlet in the movement toward modern freedom of the press was one of his major, still little-known contributions to posterity.

8   A Vision in the Indian Ocean (1783–1785)

The judgeship gave Jones what he wanted most. The salary permitted an extremely happy marriage and ensured the independence he had long sought. It also offered large professional responsibilities, for he would not have accepted a post primarily for the salary. He would finally serve humanity, a goal requiring his return to Orientalism, which was to produce his major accomplishments and greatest fame as he deepened his knowledge of India.[1]

Jones was not exchanging an unsatisfactory political situation for an idyllic one, because the Regulating Act of 1773 had not created a smooth arrangement. Of North's appointees to the new Supreme Council, only Hastings was really knowledgeable about India; and Philip Francis influenced two other councilmen to form a majority in unending quarrels with him. As the Governor-General, Hastings was already having differences with the English ministry, and a near-feud soon developed. He was ably prosecuting the war to assist the wazir of Oudh, but Francis began to thwart his efforts and even usurp his authority. After he charged the fiery Francis with breach of trust, Francis was wounded in their duel in 1780 and returned home vowing revenge. Francis passed information to Burke, who decided that Hastings was the worst delinquent ever in India. This information figured prominently in the debates culminating in the decisions to recall Hastings and Chief Justice Impey. Then the Court of Proprietors rescinded the Court of Directors' order, leaving Hastings in the strange situation of having been ordered home to face prosecution while still officially serving as Governor-General.

A breach soon developed between the Supreme Council and the Supreme Court, as the Regulating Act had not defined or limited the divisions made in the governing authority of Bengal.[2] At times there was virtual war between them. The narrow-minded and arrogant Lemaistre had outbursts against Impey, which usually won John Hyde's support and thus split the court, further estranging the council. Impey implied that Hyde was out of his mind: "I must fear the return of his old disorder, but it is too delicate

195

a matter to touch upon. . . . He is an honest man, but a great coxcomb, his tongue cannot be kept still, and he has more pride and pomp than I have seen in the East."[3] Robert Chambers, who supported Impey in the quarrels, was the only one of the nine members of the court and the council whom Jones knew. Jones was little aware of the dissension into which he was moving.

The newlyweds hurried to Portsmouth, as the frigate *Crocodile* was scheduled to sail on 10 April. But when they stopped by Captain John Williamson's lodgings, he told them that the ship could not sail until the next day, presuming that he could complete his crew with men just paid from another voyage. Writing farewells, Anna was unhappy about going to India:

'Till I find myself travelling towards instead of from England, I can never feel so happy as I have been. . . . it will be my earnest & consistent endeavor to act as my duty now demands. I try to see things in as cheerful a light as possible, but my heart will act at the Idea of the distress I have felt, & occasion'd to those I ought to have made happy. (2:611)

She was, in truth, the favorite of her father, who lamented to Franklin: "She had more of that domestick kindness & attention which you know how to value; & which an old Man wants & delights in" (2:611). Though Shipley appreciated Jones's excellence, he was as deeply affected as if she had died, as there was little possibility of his ever seeing her again.

Jones wrote the directors of the East India Company to request that his judicial salary be commenced. A brief letter acknowledged Kenyon's affectionate wishes, but he chiefly defended *The Principles of Government.* A letter to Schultens promised to report Jones's Oriental discoveries, and one to Pritchard reported that his recommendations to Laurence Sulivan (chairman of the Court of Directors) and Orme might secure a Bengal post for his former clerk. He also wrote Pritchard's new bride.[4]

A letter went to Lady Spencer, who had just sent a pleasing servant. Anna was writing the Shipleys, Jones noted: "What confidence they place in me. . . . The moment shall never come in which I shall prove unworthy of that confidence" (2:611). He penned a letter to Althorp, in the spirit of the *Odyssey,* promising regular packets from exotic ports: "Can I be unhappy, when I possess so inestimable a treasure as my Anna? Can I be happy when I leave lord Althorp?" (2:613).

Novelty made the first two weeks at sea delightful. The almost-new *Crocodile,* while small, was an excellent boat. Williamson, who was later disgraced in a sea battle with the Dutch, was intelligent and obliging; and the officers had agreeable manners and fine sense. Jones established a schedule of Persian, law, and anything related to India, all of which he planned to study daily for six years. His recreation was chess; his exercise, walking for an hour. His greatest delight was the sweet society and conversation of Anna, whose spirits were wonderful in the new if not unappealing situation. After reaching the Madeiras in fifteen days, they were becalmed for another three. Jones amused himself by making sketches and answering two letters brought on board. As Pritchard wanted an Indian post, Jones advised consultation with Orme and Sulivan. Though the Regulating Act permitted the judges to appoint some officers on reasonable salaries approved by the Governor-General and Council, Jones did not suggest his own clerkship to Pritchard. He disapproved of sinecures. In his second letter he promised Ashburton that he would deliver the sealed letter to Impey as instructed. Ashburton's help with the judicial appointment had given Jones true happiness. Although he might eventually have attained his limited goals by means of incessant labor, only as a judge could he simultaneously gratify his curiosity about Asians, pursue his profession, and enjoy domestic comforts. He closed by defending *The Principles of Government:* He knew of no indictment for a theoretical essay on government, but he would not preach such views to the Indians anyway.

At Funchal the Joneses were entertained by the consul, remaining several days while supplies were loaded. On 14 May they went ashore on Cape Verde to have their clothes washed and to greet the Portuguese vice-governor, who provided eggs, fruit, water, and the like. The next morning Jones and Williamson rode to São Tiago. Anna remained on ship: "I should be quite afraid for Sir William but he is such a Salamander he is never hurt by heat. I own I long to be of their party & I believe shd. have been assez folle to have attempted it had he not exerted his *Authority*."[5]

In those days long voyages were unpleasant because of becalming, violent storms, shipwrecks, and even piracy. Water and food were inadequate, and the monotony of the days contributed to fatigue. Yet for the first time Jones had free hours. His studies overcame the unchanging vista, and his days were beneficial, even enjoyable. On 12 July he composed an unsequenced andrometer titled "Objects of Enquiry during My Residence in Asia,"[6] which first lists gigantic tasks related to his judgeship and Orientalism:

> Hindu and Moslem laws
> history of the ancient world
> Scriptural proofs and illustrations
> traditions about the Flood etc.
> Indian geography and politics
> best mode of governing Bengal

Asian mathematics and "mixed Sciences"
Indian medicine, chemistry, and anatomy
Indian products
Asiatic music, poetry, rhetoric, and morality
Shih Ching
accounts of Tibet and Kashmir
Indian trade, manufacturing, and agriculture
Mogul Constitution in *Fatáwá ʿÁlamgíríyat* and *Ain-i-Akbari*
Maratha Constitution

Of Jones's early Oriental studies, only the *Shih Ching* appears. He slights literature, which, he thought, held no practical value for the Indians.

The second part lists the publishing of the Gospel of Luke in Arabic, the Psalms in Persian verse, and law tracts in Persian or Arabic. The last part proposes "To compose, if God grant me Life" six long-projected works, all with Greek models. Heading these is "Elements of the laws of England," the large study that Jones had started even before his specialized book on bailments, which, along with Aristotle, would be his models. Next comes "The History of the *American* War. *Model* – Thucydides and Polybius." Thus Jones's associations with Gibbon, British leaders like Burke and Shelburne, and Americans like Franklin who had provided firsthand information, still inspired him, in his last reference to what might have been one of his greatest books. Third is his epic on the English constitution, "Britain Discovered," with Hindu gods as the machinery. Still excited by his recent consideration of his old plan, Jones now selected Homer as the model from among his other projections of Tasso and Virgil, but work on the poem would be delayed until he better understood Hinduism. The other three works are speeches, dialogues, and letters, modeled on Demosthenes and Plato.

Of the six works, Jones composed only letters, intended as geographical–cultural essays for his Atticus (Althorp). The first letter lengthily described his stop at Anjouan, Comoro Islands, on 27 July. It pictured the lush scenery and the uneducated, hospitable people on the island used as a coal depot. The ship was first surrounded by canoes; then the deck was crowded with the governor, lesser figures, and half-naked slaves. When the visitors repaid the call, Jones surprised the crowd by reading an Arabic inscription on a mosque. After the governor served dates and coconut milk in a sultry room so perfumed that the Joneses could hardly breathe, Jones examined the man's Arabic manuscripts. Expecting a present, the king's son exhibited his harem of miserable women in chador. The favorite's ankles were ringed with silver ornaments, which Jones silently perceived as fetters, as a rational being would have preferred to be an endangered wild beast instead of the prince's woman.

Jones's indignation was directly aroused when the prince described the islanders' profitable slave trade conducted in their own vessels. Jones demanded to know the law that permitted ownership of people. The prince replied that necessity was the justification, as pagans' captives were often starving: "If we buy them, they will live: if they become valuable servants, they will live comfortably; but if they are not sold, they must die miserably."[7] Jones retorted that the taking of slaves was the cause and effect of war, and it led to laziness among the owners. His religious argument was more effective to the Moslem prince: Child slaves might become Moslems if time were used for their religious instruction rather than in working them more. But obviously Jones was powerless, and there was the further question that he would soon be facing of whether a Western administrator can or should try to change another people's cultural habits except under extreme circumstances.

At exorbitant cost Jones hired guides for a hike into the jungle, where he rhapsodized over the flora. To the king he condemned the Europeans' harsh treatment of the natives and vainly hoped that no country would gain sovereignty over Anjouan, which provided supplies for European ships. Eventually he recast this letter into a form suitable for publication.

On 1 August the frigate sailed into the Indian Ocean. One evening when India lay ahead, Iran was to the left, and an Arabian breeze was blowing from the stern, Jones had a magnificent vision. The novel situation vividly recalled his youthful contemplation of Asian studies, in an almost mystical experience. He was alone on deck in an amphitheater almost encircled by the vastness of Asia, which was the nurse of sciences and the inventress of delightful arts. Asia was fertile in human genius, abounding in natural wonders, and infinitely diverse. Yet it was unexplored by scholars and contained solid, unused advantages. The vision led him to realize the necessity of creating an Asiatic Society.

Baron George Macartney, the governor at Madras, entertained the Joneses. He thought Jones well qualified for the judgeship. Anna had often seen him at Lady Spencer's and relayed news about Ireland.[8] When the ship reached Balasore, Jones notified Impey of his arrival and ordered a pipe of claret, which Impey paid for, because Jones had not yet received any salary.

The ship arrived at Chandpal Ghat, at the foot of Esplanade Row, on 25 September. The ceremonial landing of a Supreme Court judge was always impressive, but Jones's reception was much more so. Because of his reputation, he had been anxiously expected. Professional men were delighted to have a good jurist on the troubled court; Europeans and Indians alike rejoiced at having a magistrate known for probity, independence, and ability. Scholars welcomed a man whose erudition in Oriental languages was famous and whose books had assisted them.[9]

Chambers was at Benares, but he had offered his house until the Joneses could find their own. Impey was equally generous. Jones's sea dress was so unsuitable for Calcutta that he was measured for lighter clothes, and he purchased other clothes at Impey's expense until he could receive his salary. Ashburton's confidential letter and one from Shelburne were delivered to Impey.

Impey invited Hyde and others connected with the Supreme Court to breakfast; then they all went to Chambers's house to meet Jones before he was sworn in. Although Jones knew none of the advocates, officers, and attorneys, he mistook William Hickey for Hickey's older brother, whom he had known at Harrow.[10]

Hyde was well intentioned and mild mannered, but unenergetic. Impey was dependable, an attribute that appealed to Jones. Over the next two months the pair became friends. Impey supplied the court rules and orders, which Jones studied, as he would soon assume his duties. In further preparation, he worked with Arabic and Persian scholars in the mornings, and with Hindus and writers in the afternoons.

The friendship indirectly involved Jones in Burke's attacks on Hastings. Impey was being recalled on the charge that his trying and executing Nanda Kumar constituted legal murder. As Jones wrote Spencer (Althorp), who had succeeded to the title upon the earl's death, he would not attempt to influence someone who would be Impey's judge. However, Impey was "an agreeable good natured man, with respectable abilities" (2:624). Never changing this opinion, Jones presumably was pleased when Burke pronounced the official end of the charge in 1784 because of the improbability of proving it. In 1781 Jones had already condemned the loose talk in the Commons, in which Burke seemed to judge Impey without evidence.

It was Jones's warm friendship with Hastings that ended Jones's association with Burke. Jones's arrival was "a landmark in Indian history. It was also a day of rejoicing for the Governor-General and his small band of enthusiastic orientalists. Few official acts could have given Hastings greater satisfaction and pleasure than to welcome" Jones.[11] Jones was similarly, naturally drawn to this cultivated man, who innovationally wanted East India Company servants to be competent in Indian languages and to appreciate local traditions.[12] The consequent Indianization on intellectual and social levels harmonized with Jones's attitude toward Oriental studies and peoples. Anna also was struck by Hastings's charm, and the two couples became close.

In their first weeks in Calcutta the Joneses experienced "pleasures and pains, hours of amusement and hours of dullness, some few of sickness, and some minutes even of alarm" (2:622). Chambers's house was beautifully situated on the Hooghly, opposite other elegant gardens and soaring trees. Ships were anchored below: "The town is large and well-peopled, yet airy and commodious; the houses are in general well-built and some of them equal to palaces."

For a town house Jones rented the second story of a "commodious Upper Roomed House, situated in Old Court House Street, the corner of Wheeler's Lane."[13] He bought Anna a spirited horse; another necessary expense was £125 for a strong riding horse and £200 for four bay coach-horses. Like other couples of means, they sought a "garden house" away from the heat and noise. Theirs was at 8 Garden Reach, by the Hooghly. Early in the morning Jones would walk the five miles to town along the road from the Old Court House to the Esplanade.[14]

One of his first rulings was in the long-pending disposition of the twenty-three lakhs of rupees that the English had seized from Chait Singh, the former tributary raja of Benares whose maltreatment formed the serious charge against Hastings. Chambers ruled that the East India Company should have the prize money, but Hyde disagreed. The decision was left to Jones, "who, in a very able and impartial speech, entered into the whole of the case, and shewed clearly from the earliest annals of History, that plunder taken on the capitulation of besieged towns, belongs to those, who possess the power of making war and peace." So from the outset, Jones used his learning and rich historical perspective. Though the Supreme Court did not order the return of the plunder to the English army, ironically, Jones's ruling for the company was hailed by *Gentleman's Magazine* as possibly ending British rapacity in India.[15]

Hyde went to the country. Because Chambers was away and Impey was preparing to sail, Jones was a bit awed by his sobering introduction to the vast power wielded by European administrators: "All the *police* and *judicial* power, therefore, of this settlement, where at least half a million of natives reside, are in my hands: I tremble at the power, which I possess; but should tremble more, if I did not know myself" (2:623–4). Thus from the outset, he recognized himself as a helper rather than an exploiter. This attitude was extremely rare in colonial administrators, lay at the heart of his accomplishments in India, and was to bode well for the Indians whom he was to help govern.

Jones opened the sessions on 4 December, using the time traditionally given the judge, to deliver the first of his six biennial charges to the Calcutta grand jury. It begins with a statement: He has no personal zeal for any set of English ministers, and in any case his judgeship prohibits attachments. Totally breaking with his pamphleteering, he stresses the necessity of objectivity and ruling according to the law, however dubious it may be. The Supreme Court must ensure that "the *British* subjects resident in *India* be protected, yet governed, by *British* laws; and that the natives of these important provinces be indulged in their own prejudices, civil and religious, and suffered to enjoy their own customs unmolested." Perhaps naive, he knows no reason why this purpose may not be achieved, "consistently with the regular collection of the revenues and the supremacy of the executive government." The executive and the judicial branches must cooperatively promote the public good, without danger of colliding or diminishing the others' dignity; they must not impede governmental operations or the administration of justice. The result will be "the revival and extension of commerce in all the dependencies of *Britain,* the improvement of agriculture and manufactures, the encouragement of industry and civil virtues, by which her revenues will be restored, and her navy strengthened, her subjects enriched and herself exalted." This desired "result" shows that Jones, amid the colonial climate of his education and experience, had not yet considered that the Indians might deserve the constitutional rights of English subjects and certainly of Americans, whom he had strongly defended when that protection was threatened. Yet he was already laying the foundation for conditions fostering a system of Indian justice that would eventually allow constitutional liberties.[16]

The community's high expectation of the charge was gratified. In concise, appropriate language, it was adjudged as an elegant, "very sensible, pertinent charge" designed to harmonize the Supreme Court's relations with the Supreme Council and to inspire general satisfaction.[17] The law material was lucidly phrased to inform the jury of their responsibility. Jones also wanted to persuade the council that an independent judicature must help in providing justice by delivering legal judgments, and never personal opinions. He was providing a model for Indian jurisprudence while initiating instruction that would help make him one of the major European jurists to serve abroad. When he sent copies of this charge to England, the tradition began of periodicals reprinting his short essays. *Gentleman's Magazine* began the practice (August 1784, pp. 627–8), which was to ensure a wide audience for his writings.

Jones wasted little time in meeting the scholars in Calcutta. Hastings was more of a patron than a doer, but not so Charles Wilkins, a senior merchant in the East India Company who had started studying Sanskrit in 1778. Poor health in December 1783 led him to request transfer to Benares, a seat of Sanskrit learning, where he could improve his competence while on salary. Hastings approved this innovation, and Wilkins became the first European to master Sanskrit. He also knew Persian, giving Jones a ghazal by Háfiz. In turn, Jones shared the speculation that Etruscan lent many words to Latin and the false surmise that Etruscan writing was distantly related to Persian and Indian writing. Intrigued by Kama, he drafted a poetic hymn to this Hindu god of love, which he asked Wilkins to criticize.

A second new friend was Richard Johnson, a supernumerary on the Board of Revenue who knew Persian and was studying Indian music. Jones corresponded with these two men and invited Johnson to dinner on Mondays and Thursdays, when they would discuss Hinduism in the context of classical deities, for he had immediately realized that a knowledge of Hinduism was necessary for him to be an able jurist.

He talked with both men about an Asiatic Society, as they and a few other Englishmen were pursuing individual studies, without coordination or even interrelationship. Chambers's return from Benares reunited Jones with an old Oxford colleague and another friend who loved books, especially the Sanskrit manuscripts that he was collecting. Partly because of his rank as acting chief justice, Chambers sent out the invitations to the scholars in the Calcutta area, to meet in the Grand Jury Room on 15 January 1784 to form a literary assembly. That evening twenty-nine men received a copy of the Háfiz ode that Wilkins had selected and printed. Then Jones read "A Discourse on the Institution of a Society, for Inquiring into the History, Civil and Natural, the Antiquities, Arts, Sciences, and Literature, of Asia," which begins with a recounting of his dramatic vision in the Indian Ocean.

This programmatic essay projects the describing of Indian history, people, and culture in an interdisciplinary design. Instead of draining India, the British can make contributions, in a pursuit of scholarly ideals and goals. The only way to explore the vast area and utilize its many advantages is to form an Asiatic Society for unified investigation, which will provide entertainment and convey knowledge to humankind. Jones intuitively widened the scope from India to Asia, and will permit it to overlap into Africa and Europe when the stream of learning flows outside. The objectives are "MAN and NATURE: whatever is performed by the one, or produced by the other." As research areas, Jones lists all the disciplines then known. Original papers previously submitted to the secretary of the Society can be read at weekly meetings. Questions will be decided by a two-thirds vote, with a quorum of nine. Silently recognizing that successful research would require cultural interchange and mutual enrichment, Jones presents a carefully worded recommendation: "Whether you will enrol as members any number of learned natives, you will hereafter decide." He suggests three qualifications for membership: a voluntary desire, love of knowledge, and a zeal to promote it.

Thus the Society would differ from the Royal Society, which was plagued by wealthy aristocrats whom Banks sometimes nominated. Jones wanted to enroll active men of letters or science and to set high standards, and his dual objectives embraced Thomas Sprat's wish to record all works of nature or art that could come within the members' reach. He was not proliferating societies; he was creating a permanent research group and facility through an enlightened essay designing an international organization like the academy sketched in Bacon's *New Atlantis*. Scholars would cooperatively investigate major problems, inasmuch as no individual could search the whole realm of knowledge. This Society was original, for members would make comparative studies of all facets of a continent. By learning more about India than any other person, Jones would be a better judge. Naively anticipating no financial needs, he did not mention dues.[18]

The essay predicts the Society's slow, certain advance. It might emulate the Royal Society, which began as "a meeting of a few literary friends at *Oxford,* rose gradually to that splendid zenith, at which a *Halley* was their secretary, and a *Newton* their president." Once there were enough valuable papers, excluding lesser ones and mere translations, the periodical *Asiatick Researches* would be initiated. Though the Batavian Society of Arts and Sciences was started in 1778, Jones's Society rightly received the credit for inspiring the Oriental societies that followed, such as the Asiatic Society of Bombay (1804), Société Asiatique (1822), Royal Asiatic Society of Great Britain and Ireland (1823), and the American Oriental Society (1842).

When Jones finished delivering this First Anniversary Discourse, the audience passed a resolution thanking him for the essay, starting a tradition. They then constituted themselves as the Asiatic Society in accord with his purposes and agreed to meet every Thursday evening at 7:00.

The best-known charter members might be listed. Although Chambers and Hyde never composed any papers, Chambers attended about four times a year for a decade, whereas only Jones surpassed Hyde in attendance. Three other members were Johnson, Wilkins, and William Davy, Hastings's Persian secretary. Besides ten more who attended the important next meeting, there were Dr. Francis Balfour, Anna's physician and a student of Arabic borrowings in Persian; Reuben Burrow, a mathematician and astronomer; Charles Croftes, Bengal accountant general; John Shore, of the Secret Political Department and later the Governor-General; and the polyglot Henry Vansittart, the son of Bengal's former governor.

Because some of the men might have attended the founding meeting due to Jones's reputation or Chambers's influence, the next meeting was crucial; and so Jones was gratified when twelve men joined him on 22 January. Emulating the Royal Society, which had the king as its Patron, he wanted executive support to ensure cooperation. Thus he moved that the Supreme Council be asked to become Patrons as a token of the Society's respect. He, Hyde, Wilkins, and ten others signed the invitation. The ten were David Anderson, who negotiated the treaty with Mahadaji Sindhia; General John Carnac, commander of the British forces in India; William Chambers, Robert's brother and the Supreme Court's interpreter, who was to rival Hyde's loyalty to the Society; Charles Chapman, former Bengal commander in chief and Hastings's private secretary; Jonathan Duncan, later governor of Bombay; Francis Gladwin, Indian historian and super-intendent of the East India Company Press, who founded the *Calcutta Gazette;* Charles Hamilton, an Orientalist in India since 1776; Thomas Law, later on the Board of Trade and an American immigrant who would help establish the American national currency; George Barlow, Law's as-sistant and later acting Governor-General of Madras; and David Paterson, a senior member of the East India Company since 1776. Hastings and the Supreme Council elegantly accepted on 20 February: "We very much ap-prove and applaud your endeavours to promote the extension of knowledge by the means which your local advantages offer you in a degree, perhaps, exceeding those of any part of the *globe;* and we derive great hopes of your attainment of so important an end" (2:628).[19]

At the meeting of 22 January there were three nominations, with votes to be taken the next week, a procedure that never resulted in a rejection during Jones's tenure. Two of the nominees became his friends – Henry Richardson, president of the Chinsura Court of Justice; and Anthony Po-lier, a Swiss engineer with the British army. After Jones received permis-sion to offer Hastings the presidency, Anderson moved that Jones be vice-president.

Jones had three major, unannounced motives in inviting the Governor-General and Council to be Patrons. First was the important matter of Hastings's patronage of and possible personal contribution to scholarship; that is, he might be able to provide governmental funds for the group. Second, the group's research was dependent on the members' leisure in the enervating climate and thus needed official backing, possibly in securing released time from work. Third, the hostility between the Council and the Court might abate if the Council were involved in the Society, as all three Supreme Court judges were members. But Hastings modestly declined, stating that he lacked the time and intellectual stature of men like Jones.

Though hoping to be an active member, he yielded to "the Gentleman, whose genius planned the institution, and is most capable of conducting it to the attainment of the great and splendid purposes of its formation" (2:629). So Jones's effort to use the Society as a possible means to political improvement was not immediately successful, as he had feared, because of Hastings's responsibilities. When the declination was read on 5 February, Jones was unanimously asked to "reaccept" the presidency.

Only Law's description of two pillars near Patna had been presented since Jones's First Discourse. Another paper was read on 12 February, then Jones's tentative system for transliterating Persian into Roman orthography the next week, and a paper by Vansittart after a gap of one week. When the Supreme Council's acceptance as Patrons was read to the ten members present, two members of the council were guests, and John Stables's admission tied the council more closely to the Society. During these first seven meetings, eleven new members were elected, including the artist Samuel Davis, who was using Jai Singh II's observatory at Benares to identify Sanskrit astronomical allusions; John Herbert Harington, who was preparing an Arabic–Persian edition of Saʻdí; and the artist John Zoffany, R.A. All three became Jones's friends.

Hastings's declination elicited an urbane answer from Jones: "I trust, you will consider our act as proceeding solely from our anxiety to give you that distinction, which justice obliged us to give. As to myself, I could never have been satisfied, if, in traversing the sea of knowledge, I had fallen in with a ship of your rate and station, without striking my flag" (2:628–9). Promising to drop in that evening, Jones lamented that Hastings's departure would deprive Bengal of one of its greatest advantages. This letter partly compensated for his official one: As his salary had not been included in Hastings's order for paying the judges, he requested that an order be issued for his pay since embarkation.

The slow transportation to Europe meant that Jones's essays arrived months after he read them to the Society. In January 1785 *Gentleman's Magazine,* reviewing his First Discourse, observed that he was as much at home in the East as Addison had been in Italy: "A rich mine of Oriental literature, arts, and antiquities may reasonably be expected. Truly animated and interesting is the whole" (p. 50). Later the *Analytical Review* reprinted the essay (October 1789, pp. 202–6).

Jones's central purpose in founding the Society was scholarly. Because Europe contained few primary sources on India, his Indian scholarship began only after he gained access to the Sanskrit manuscripts mainly preserved by the Brahmans. Language was central to the Society and his research. In the First Discourse he noted that "the diversity and difficulty" of Asian tongues bar the advance of knowledge. Though he considered languages as the mere instrument of real learning, they must be mastered. This conclusion partly derived from his own experience. Famed for knowing Oriental languages, he knew no Indian ones. In Bengal he could speak Arabic with Moslem scholars only because of his work with a Syrian long before. Never having studied with a Persian informant, he had an unfortunate experience soon after arrival. A British friend who was fluent in Persian was sitting with him when some learned Indians came to pay their respects. Jones addressed them in his Persian, which he had learned from books. One of the Indians whispered to the friend that Jones should not use English, as they did not understand it. Because he was learned in Persian, he should use it. The friend chose not to mortify Jones,[20] who soon corrected his deficiency.

Besides his political and scholarly purposes in founding the Society, there was a human, moral purpose, which in some ways was the most important of all. As his coordinating the small nucleus of scholars in Bengal into a comprehensive program would enhance their individual findings and achieve a greater whole, potential scholars might perceive a worthy alternative to the usual immorality. Managing the Bengal trade gave Europeans a strategic position for amassing wealth by corruption, presents, and inflated contracts, despite governmental restrictions. The British succession to the Moguls presented opportunities for lavish drinking, gambling clubs, and the keeping of domestic slaves and concubines even by church officers, practices repugnant to Jones. If Europeans would devote their leisure to the Society, this immorality would be reduced. However, their work left them little leisure in an unhealthful climate, expensive setting, and usually without their wives. Officers seldom participated in the local culture, knowing little about it and, in any case, considering themselves superior to the Indians.

In short, the British were aliens among people who feared them.[21] Such conditions made it easy to succumb to temptation, Jones noted: "If our countrymen here will learn that wealth is not the only pursuit fit for rational beings, my object in proposing and supporting the Society will be attained" (2:868). Perhaps he saw himself as an indirect moral tutor of colonial Europeans, whose actions in Asia may never be wholly forgiven by Asians.

Jones was integrating his various purposes into a grand philosophical design. Achievement of one goal usually gave other benefits. Thus the reduction of European immorality would effect moral uplifting that would cause better treatment of Indians otherwise patronized or bullied, and the Indians would rise in dignity if not in their own esteem. The Society should unearth information immediately applicable to improving the British administration and thus the Indians' lot. Such thoughts inspired the research that was to flow from Bengal, as observed in the *Calcutta Gazette* of 3 June 1784:

The President possesses claims upon the gratitude of this settlement, which no compliments can ever repay, as he formerly promoted Asiatick knowledge by his elegant writings, and now prosecutes the same laudable design with more zeal and effect in person, and unites in himself the merit of instituting the Asiatick Society, and of advancing it towards perfection by the labours of his assistance, and the splendour of his example.

Amid the Society's early successes, Jones heard bad news about three friends. In "The Character of John Lord Ashburton" he movingly recalls his final meeting with Ashburton, whom he left with tears in his eyes because he did not expect to see the "memorable and illustrious man" again. Ashburton was democratic even in conversation, speaking no more than his just share and always listening attentively; but Jones's essay exaggerates his wit, "in which no mortal ever surpassed him, and which all found irresistible." In formal tradition Jones wishes "an honourable truth" to be inscribed on his own tombstone:

> With none to flatter, none to recommend,
> DUNNING approv'd and mark'd him as a friend.

The word *recommend* recalls Ashburton's help with the judgeship.

Zeal for Ashburton's fame prompted Jones to give his essay to the *India Gazette,* which printed it on 20 March. He asked Spencer to show it to friends, particularly the Club. *European Magazine* reprinted it in July 1800 (pp. 16–17). Jones's zeal was perhaps permanently recorded when a compliment from his essay was quoted in the Ashburton biography in the *Dictionary of National Biography.*

By contrast, he never considered eulogizing Samuel Johnson. A report about the old man's stroke in 1783 evoked only "Poor Johnson" (2:637). However, Johnson's influence is reflected in five allusions in Jones's later writings. He quoted the remark that as spiders would make silk if they could agree, "so men of letters would be useful to the public, if they were not perpetually at variance" (2:675). His strongest praise was in the Second Anniversary Discourse: "One of the most sagacious men in this age, who continues, I hope, to improve and adorn it, SAMUEL JOHNSON, remarked in my hearing, that, 'if NEWTON had flourished in ancient *Greece,* he would have been worshipped as a divinity.' " There was a singularly modern criticism in the Fourth Discourse: "SAMUEL JOHNSON's reasoning, on the extreme imperfection of unwritten languages, was too general, since a language, that is only spoken, may nevertheless be highly polished." Jones was much stronger in condemning the criticism of "Lycidas." Finally, he used the obscure word *redintegrate* from Johnson's *Dictionary* (2:820).

The two admired each other's learning. Johnson remarked that Jones praised the language sections of *A Journey to the Western Islands of Scotland* (1775); Jones often said that Johnson knew "a great deal of Greek." The duchess of Devonshire mentions a conversation shortly before the death of Johnson, who was "very entertaining about Sir William Jones's learning." Her "On the Death of Sir William Jones" quotes Johnson's famous praise:

> Unbounded learning, thoughts by genius fram'd
> To guide the bounteous labours of his pen,
> Distinguish'd him, whom kindred sages nam'd,
> "The most enlighten'd of the sons of men."

Finally, Johnson thought Jones "as splendid a literary character as any to be named."[22]

The third friend about whom Jones heard disturbing news was Burke, in a development that immediately stopped possibly highly salutary improvements in the British administration of India. While collaborating on legislation the two had agreed that "a perfect knowledge of India ... is now become an object of infinite importance to every British statesman" (1:352). This knowledge, which could help give India a just government, would come from scholarship and translations. As Jones later told Cornwallis: "I had communicated my sentiments to some friends in parliament and on the bench in Westminster Hall, of whose discernment I had the highest opinion" (2:795).

Jones was expecting to send Burke information and recommendations for legislative use, in a natural extension of his keen interest in comparative law. In February 1784 he wrote Burke that he would send, literally, a volume about the judicature, which was extremely imperfect and somewhat exceptionable. Regardless of the mode of reform adopted, Burke should "procure relief for a multitude of miserable insolvent debtors, from whose ship-wrecked fortunes not a splinter remains to satisfy their resentful creditors," through a statute like the one that periodically released English debtors (2:631). Otherwise, Indian debtors must endure a wretched existence in prison, which Jones had visited in disguise upon hearing of their plight. It was deplorable in the hot months. The Supreme Court hoped to submit a formal representation, but Chambers's absence and Hyde's inactivity left the matter up to Jones. Perhaps Burke would relieve the situation. Enclosing his First Discourse, Jones noted that Shipley would provide his first charge to the grand jury.

Because Burke had supported the 1782 resolution calling for all legal steps to remove Hastings for "having in sundry instances acted in a manner repugnant to the honour and policy of this nation, and thereby brought great calamities in India, and enormous expenses on the East India Company," Jones had reached a delicate point in his letter to Burke. He and Anna had made a special trip to town to see Hastings depart for Lucknow, but he knew little about this final attempt by Hastings to resolve matters with the wazir of Oudh: "The precise object of his journey I know not, as I disclaim all political connexions whatever in *India*, thinking them wholly inconsistent with the judicial character; and I promise you, that you shall never hear of any change in my conduct."

Burke had made what was perhaps just a casual remark to Shipley, but it struck at Jones's integrity. As Jones wrote Spencer, Burke had said: "If I *hear*, that *Jones sides* with *Hastings*, I will do all in my power to have him recalled" (2:636). Ever lamenting Burke's violence, Jones intended to expostulate sternly, as Burke should know that a judge could side with no one. No power could give Jones a political side: "If I am ignorant, let me be disgraced, if corrupt, let me be hanged: but let me not be menaced by every fiery fool, who may happen to measure my principles and conduct by his own." Hastings's rank did not influence Jones's friendship. They had similar amusements and fondness for Asiatic literature, and Hastings knew that the richest gem could not purchase one opinion by Jones. When Jones returned to England, Spencer should secure him a corner in the Commons if only for a session, so that he could rebut every audacious charge. There would never be a well-founded charge, Jones concluded to Burke.

In April 1784 Jones wrote Burke again, first promising to transmit nonpolitical observations on the Indian judicature and practicable means of improving it. His present purpose was friendly but serious expostulation about Burke's remark to Shipley, which he quoted. Instead of accepting hearsay, Burke should have disdained it as improbable and defamatory. Burke had often reproved Jones for ardor, while praising his integrity. The charter of justice had given Jones a multilateral side; no allurement could give him a political side. Hastings was a pleasant man of taste, a friend of letters; "but, whether his publick conduct be wise or foolish, I shall not, in my present station, examine" (2:645). If Jones ever testified in the Commons, he would speak the truth, attacking if Hastings were reprehensible but praising if merited: "You see, my dear Burke, that I am not deprecating your resentment, or entreating you to moderate your thunder against me; for, with the shield of justice and truth, I should not fear the most impetuous attack even of an *enemy*." As he could not fear a friend,

Burke should pour out the strongest eloquence if Jones were unjustly assailed. There would be no just provocation, he promised.

Soon Jones dispatched "The Best Practicable System of Judicature." This list of twenty-three enlightened recommendations, based on personally collected data, derived from the fundamental law of Bengal and the eastern provinces. The law was Islamic; however, pundits would resolve disputes among Hindus according to Hindu law, except in matters like crime and constitutional and fiscal administration. Three language-based recommendations explain Jones's early decision to learn Sanskrit, which would strengthen his knowledge of comparative law:

> *Digests* of *Hindū* and *Mahomedan* laws should be compiled by chosen *Conongōs, Mulavis,* and *Pundits,* and copies of them reposited in the treasuries of the several *Diwāneī Adālets.*
>
> The *laws* of the natives must be preserved inviolate; but the learning and vigilance of the *English* judge must be a check upon the native interpreters.
>
> The decrees in the *Sedr Adālet* must be conformable to *Hindū* or *Mahomedan* law, as the parties or defendants, shall be *Hindūs* or *Mahomedans.*

Jones further recommends that an effective tribunal protect the Indians against the British and permit Indian suitors to obtain justice cheaply and quickly, in an innovationally suggestive move toward Indian constitutional rights. Circuits should not be established because of the ruinous expense. He concludes: "A system like this, consisting of reciprocal checks and balances of power, would give satisfaction and security to the natives, the government, and the English subjects in India" (2:643–4).

Burke preserved but never legislatively used the enlightened document, which remained unpublished for almost two centuries. As it took five months for a letter to reach London, it was a year before Jones realized that Burke was not going to answer. His onslaught in the long impeachment trial slowly changed Jones's disappointment over the aborted cooperation into rancor, although his motives were honest. It was tragic that Burke and Hastings were antagonists, for both wished "to understand the religions and the languages of the East. Their common friendship for Sir William Jones, the eminent Orientalist, was no accident: it was a fundamental part of the nature of each."[23]

There was irony in Jones's attitude toward Hastings. Their friendship did not influence his feelings about injustice: Hastings's attackers simply had no real evidence. Thus Jones hoped for legal vindication, even as he privately condemned the man's political principles. Disavowing any thought of biasing Bishop Shipley, one of Hastings's judges, Jones told the bishop that he would speak out once the sentence was passed. Until then he would only say, because his opinion was unrelated to the trial, that Hastings's principles were "the quintessence of Eastern Despotism."[24] He was anticipating the modern view by approving of Hastings's general plans, while objecting to the sometimes unprincipled measures used to achieve the desired goals.

Certainly Burke wanted to further improve Indian judicature, but the rift with Jones ended all other collaboration. Jones never forgot Burke's possibly attempted coercion and the injustice, adopting an unscholarly attitude by refusing to read *Reflections on the Revolution in France* (1790): "I know it would vex me; but very grave unprejudiced men here assure me, that it has the honor of being the wickedest, the silliest, and the worst written book in our language: if you love that man, you will never find me your rival" (2:898). He annotated Bacon's parable "Make no friendship with an angry man, nor walke thou with a Furious Man," by adding the words "Edmund Burke to wit and Lloyd Kenyon." Burke apparently reciprocated the feeling: "Burke spoke on Abyss*inian* Bruce (*who, he said, made* Sir W. Jones a Dupe)."[25]

Their fourteen-year acquaintance had an important positive side: Their collaboration on judicature helped focus attention on the miserable conditions in India, and out of this concern came parliamentary improvement. Jones helped provide some of Burke's massive knowledge about India, even as Burke first stimulated Jones's Indian scholarship, especially his translation of Asiatic legal treatises. Finally, there was mutual literary, political enrichment.

In his early years in India, Jones was good friends with Chambers, who was collecting seven hundred to eight hundred primarily Sanskrit manuscripts at a total cost of £22,000. Chambers's criteria were completeness and condition rather than utility and scholarly value. There were grammars, dictionaries, almanacs, and treatises. Commendably, in the work he employed a *munshi,* a pundit, and Indian copying clerks, which assisted them professionally. Jones inscribed a copy of his *Moallakát:* "Given to Sir Robert Chambers by his respected friend Sir W. Jones the translator, 6 Nov. 1785."[26] However, Chambers was not fulfilling Dr. Johnson's expectation that he would inquire into Asiatic literature. Holding a lucrative post as fiscal of Chinsura, he desired money too much to pursue scholarship. He considered himself to be a close friend of Jones, who, he said, studied sixteen hours a day.[27]

Jones disliked Chambers's professional habits. After that senior judge became acting chief justice, there was "a tiresome and disgusting frivolousness of manners and conduct."[28] Whereas Impey had always taken his seat at exactly 9:00, Chambers seldom arrived before 11:00 and sometimes not until 1:30, while everyone waited. Jones's anticipated leisure time for study was thereby reduced; sometimes he wrote letters while waiting.

The sessions of June 1784 opened with a crowded calender. The grand and petit juries assembled soon after 8:00, but because Chambers did not come until 1:00, he did not finish swearing in the juries and delivering his charge until 3:00. By then it was too late to start a trial. The next morning Jones and Hyde took their seats at 9:00 and swore in the jury to try a prisoner whom they had arraigned. Etiquette required that they wait for Chambers. At 11:00 Hyde wrote an angry note asserting that he, Jones, and both juries had been waiting for two hours. Did Chambers intend to come? Just then Chambers arrived.

Jones was equally disturbed about some of the decisions of the Supreme Court, which lacked one judge. Convention required that the junior member be rather reserved. He wrote Pitt: "[I] should never think of proposing any alteration without the consent of my colleagues, one of whom I have not yet consulted" (2:663). Once when a Brahman servant complained to the police that his master had beaten him, the superintendents also beat him. Jones ruled that the superintendents-defendants should not have refused bail, for the case was bailable. No stripes should have been inflicted without a jury verdict, and the court should award full damages of five thousand rupees. Though condemning the superintendents' conduct, Hyde ruled that two thousand was enough. Chambers agreed, for a Brahman who had consented to be a servant should not make his fortune by a beating.[29] So the lesser sum was awarded.

During the first half of 1784 Jones attempted to schedule his letter writing, with a special letter book for Spencer every Sunday describing the week's activities. Countess Spencer and Shipley were other regular correspondents. Jones sent the Shipleys a detailed report of his finances; but it was to Spencer, the trustee of his marriage articles, that he planned to remit £5,000 to £6,000 in East India Company bills in early 1785. William Sloper, MP for St. Albans and Emilia Shipley's husband, was his other business agent. As Jones's instructions to Elmsly were general, his friends were invited to order any book for him that they liked.

Kenyon's active role against Dean Shipley continued to distress Jones. The hot-headed Master of the Rolls seemed perfectly mad. If, improbably, Kenyon could procure Jones's supersession because of *The Principles of Government,* suitable employment in Calcutta or at the English bar was assured. Jones hoped to answer Kenyon properly in the Commons, but it was as inconceivable that he would use the dialogue to raise sedition as it was for him to raise a church. Although convinced that the constitution required a scheme of equality, he knew that this was currently impracticable at home and inapplicable in India: "Millions of men are so wedded to inveterate prejudices and habits, that if liberty could be forced upon them by Britain, it would make them as miserable as the cruelest despotism" (2:642). This was not a statement of absolutism for British India, but a pragmatic recognition of unfortunate conditions that still prevail in many countries today.

Jones's correspondence included friends in India. He envied Wilkins's life with the venerable scholars of Benares, where daily advances could be made on untrodden Sanskrit paths. Unfortunately, life was too short and his responsibilities too long to learn Sanskrit, as Wilkins could acquaint him with the poetry, philosophy, and arts, which were poorly rendered into Persian. Jones was studying Indian music, aided by valuable manuscripts that Chambers had brought from Benares. As the *Yogavāsiṣṭha* apparently included much Platonic metaphysics and morality, Jones speculated that Plato had borrowed many ideas from Hindu sages.

Urging Johnson to compose a Hindu pantheon, Jones admitted his enthrallment to Sanskrit literature: "I am in love with the *Gopia,* charmed with *Crishen,* an enthusiastick admirer of *Rām,* and a devout adorer of *Brimha-bishen-mehais:* not to mention, that *Jūdishteīr, 'Arjen, Corno,* and the other warriours of the *M'hab'harat* appear greater in my eyes than Agamemnon, Ajax, and Achilles appeared, when I first read the Iliad" (2:652).[30] This exuberance recalls Jones's early remarks about the *Shāhnáma.* As he had three free months in the summer, he intended to rent a pinnace to go up the Ganges to Bhagalpur, where Charles Chapman was magistrate and collector and had invited the Joneses to stay, and then to inspect Sanskrit manuscripts at Benares.

Another correspondent was Patrick Russell, an acquaintance from the Royal Society. Jones invited the physician, who was encouraging Banks to study Indian botany, to send the Asiatic Society any curiosities found in travel and reading. He himself found something new daily.

Hyde was a local friend whom Jones often wrote. He offered to substitute as the rotating justice of the peace in the evenings if Hyde ever wished relief. He was trying to interest Hyde in a Persian translation of the *Śrīmad Bhagwatam,* one of the eighteen *Purāṇas.* Its novelty and wildness made it the most entertaining book that Jones had ever read: "[It] comprizes almost the whole of the *Hindu* religion, and contains the life and achievements of *Crishen*" (2:649).

His eyes were too weak for him to work by candlelight, and his morning leisure permitted little reading. He was stressing Arabic and Persian, as he wanted to talk with Indian scholars on his vacation. His Persian informant was the son of Nadir Shah's physician; his Arabic one, a native of Medina with a fine pronunciation. Jones normally rose before dawn and bathed after a ride. His health was reasonably good except for bad digestion, which he remedied by eating sparingly. His stomach was not strong, an indisposition that sometimes affected his whole frame. Good hours, gentle exercise, temperance, and cold bathing could not completely overcome the strain from his active mind: "I must be satisfied with a valetudinarian state of health" (2:633).

Anna also was not strong. In May she had a severe fever and rheumatism that persisted for days. The couple passed the spring with some sickness; the heat was still intense at noon, with incessant wind. They led a pastoral life in their garden house. Two sheep brought from Portsmouth, which had narrowly escaped the knife on ship, were pets, following Jones for bread. At night he was lulled to sleep by Persian nightingales, helping him understand the bulbul's prominence in Oriental poetry.

An incident in April illustrates his local associations. After Hastings donated land for a new Church of St. John, the senior chaplain solicited funds. Jones would not contribute as a private citizen, as a large place of worship was not necessary or a magnificent one proper anywhere. If a church were needed, the East India Company should build it. He attended only at Christmas. However, as the chaplain said that Chambers would subscribe as a judge, Jones agreed to follow his colleagues' lead. Shortly a committee approached him, and he restated his position. But when Hyde declined, Jones also refused, inasmuch as the bench had not discussed the matter. Next, Edward Hay, Hastings's undersecretary and secretary of the Secret Department, solicited Jones. He recapitulated the story, noting that Impey had refused to contribute before sailing. However, he pledged at least five hundred sicca rupees "to one of the principal purposes for which the Church itself is intended, and will so far, though not a contributor to its walls, promote the end of the erection" (2:640). That is, his contribution should be used for direct human assistance.

Jones wished to retain Hay's goodwill, as the reports submitted to the executive government – often kept secret because of their strategic value to the French or the Moslem prince Tipu Sultan – could be a rich source for his Asiatic Society. He was often successful when the author was a member. Thus Chapman provided his report on Cochin China. George Bogle had kept a journal while in Tibet, but although Hastings sent Dr. Johnson a copy, Hay did not give Jones the manuscript.[31] Hay did supply

Samuel Turner's report of a trip to Tibet.[32] Jones was unsuccessful with Isaac Titsingh, the Dutch chief at Chinsura, who sent his essays to the Batavian Society.

Jones was seizing every opportunity for knowledge. When an Abyssinian who had supposedly traveled with James Bruce arrived in town, Jones sought out the man. After hearing an Arabic description of Gondar and a "Syrian physician" who was undoubtedly Bruce, he composed "A Conversation with Abram, an Abyssinian, Concerning the City of Gwender and the Sources of the Nile," which he supplemented with "On the Course of the Nile," developed from further reading. Jones read the two brief papers to the Society, urging the publication of Bruce's travel account. The experience deepened his respect for Bruce, who had actually followed the Blue Nile.

Besides the first seven meetings, Jones also attended the next fourteen. Attendance ranged from seven to fifteen members, averaging ten. On 18 March he read his treatise on Persian music, later expanded into "On the Musical Modes of the Hindus." On 25 March he seconded the nomination of Hay and accepted Henry Richardson's gift of Persian books. On 8 April he nominated Turner, who read his own Tibetan report to two members of the Supreme Council (John Macpherson and Stables), Hyde, Jones, and eleven others. On 10 June, Jones read a paper by Ali Ibrahim Khan, chief magistrate of Benares, which Hastings had transmitted; and Law presented a collection of medical materials from a king. Thus, after only five months, Indian scholars were already starting to support the Society. On 17 June was William Chambers's account of the Mahabalipuram sculptures.

A principal purpose of Jones's summer trip up the Ganges was to open new sources, as he wanted the members living along the river to collect materials for the archives and write on new subjects. But in late June a severe fever compelled his early departure up the Hooghly. Confined to his couch for weeks, he reached the site of Clive's victory. When Anna took a walk and exposed herself to danger, he composed "Plassey-Plain, a Ballad, Addressed to Lady Jones," in fourteen mock-heroic quatrains that show her frolicking near the battlefield before she trips into the palms. Knowing that cobras must be near, she is undaunted: "Who fears offence that ne'er offends?" Parakeets and elephants cannot warn her that awed tigers pant "for so fair a food," as she does not know their Eastern languages. But if ONE (Jones) had known of her peril, "He ne'er had found a resting place."

Jones had also recently composed "Lines from the Arabic" for Anna. As three quatrains of this minor ode are in the Hastings papers, he may have presented them to Hastings.[33] A lover agonizes over his beloved, like a mother lark caught in meshes that hauntingly prevent her return to her nestlings.

Three days after Jones wrote "Plassey-Plain," he had a serious relapse. At a friend's house Shore found him "languid, exhausted, and emaciated, in a state of very doubtful convalescence; but his mind had suffered no depression, and exhibited all its habitual fervour. In his conversation he spoke with rapture of the country, of the novel and interesting sources opened to his researches, and seemed to lament his sufferings, only as impediments."[34] On 14 August he was able to write one paragraph to Richard Johnson: "A violent fever, from which I am not yet recovered, interrupted my letter, and still prevents my finishing it. I must continue here till my emaciated body can bear the heat on the water, when the sun has power. I shall then proceed by Boglypore and Patna: I fear not to Benares" (2:653).

After a daylong trip to Jangipur, his fever almost abated, although he was extremely weak. The couple went on to Bhagalpur and stayed with the Chapmans, where Jones had another major relapse. Fever then flux so emaciated him that he could not sit up; he could not dress himself and "could almost as easily fly as walk" (2:654). His own mortality was impressed on him during these months, as in a sensitive prayer that he composed:

O thou Bestower of all Good! if it please thee to continue my easy tasks in this life, grant me strength to perform them as a faithful servant; but if thy wisdom hath willed to end them by this thy visitation, admit me, not weighing my unworthiness, but through thy mercy declared in Christ, into thy heavenly mansions, that I may continually advance in happiness, by advancing in true knowledge and awful love of thee. Thy will be done![35]

Jones regained his strength slowly. It would have been madness to return to steaming Calcutta, although the new term demanded his presence on 22 October. He generally observed Dr. John Fleming's instructions to avoid intense application while convalescing, but the physician-zoologist let him examine flowers and lent the works of Linnaeus, whose taxonomy delighted him and held implications for his language research. His fascination with botany was so strong that only during the worst paroxysms did he cease comparing Linnaeus's descriptions with the plants brought to his bed. Describing a blossom was especially exciting when it was not in Linnaeus, and he could employ the taxonomy for himself; Anna drew and colored the exotic plants.[36] Thus Jones laid a foundation for his later botanical work.

Letters arrived for him. The Pritchards had landed. Answering from his bed with an effort, he granted them use of his Calcutta study and dressing room until his return. Pritchard could have his clerkship, which currently required little work, and a lesser post. Besides living prudently, Pritchard should gain the goodwill of Hyde, "one of the best men living" (2:655). Jones would not make Pritchard an attorney, which would provide a moderate fortune, until he qualified himself by attending an honest attorney and constantly observing court sessions.

From London the geographer James Rennell had sent the Society a paper on Bhutan and Tibet. Rennell's description of the Himalayas intrigued Jones. Having brought Samuel Davis's computations and some eyewitness observations with him, just after sunset one day he saw the 23,997-foot Chomo Lhari. Jones's calculations showed it to be at least 244 miles away, which he explained in a note to the paper.[37]

While convalescing he drafted a comparative essay about Hindu gods and "The Enchanted Fruit; or, the Hindu Wife." This elegant mock-heroic in 287 couplets is purely literary, based on the *Mahābhārata* story of the princess Draupadī. Because an enchanted fruit had been shot off a tree by one of the five Pāṇḍava brothers and could not be rejoined to the bough, they and their wife-in-common must confess their worst faults. Their admissions of revenge, rage, intemperance, avarice, and pride cause the fruit to rise to within ten cubits of the bough; Draupadī's confession of vanity raises it eight more. Only when she blushingly admits that she once let her Brahman teacher kiss her is the fruit rejoined.

Jones has a Hindu woman boisterously speak about harems:

> Prepost'rous! that one biped vain
> Should drag ten house-wives in his train,
> And stuff them in a gaudy cage,
> Slaves to weak lust or potent rage!
> Not such the *Dwāper Yug!* oh then
> ONE BUXOM DAME MIGHT WED FIVE MEN.

Yet the poem lacks verve and drama, partly because of Jones's scholarship. Trying to convey local color across the vast cultural and linguistic gap, he extensively transliterates Sanskrit words for foods, geography, and aspects of Hinduism. In addition, obtrusive footnote explanations help the poem fail as an Anglo-Indian romance based lightly on an Indian plot, though he enjoyed composing it and believed in its orthodoxy. Reviewers like the Orientalist John Parsons were polite: As it was too long to analyze and too elegant to illustrate, "let those who have a taste for delicacy, as well as sprightliness and vivacity, gather the fruit for themselves" (*Monthly Review*, June 1787, p. 482). But this verse tale set a kind of model that attracted Romantics like Byron and Southey to the form.

When word arrived in Bhagalpur that Hastings was coming, Jones joined the welcoming crowd on 24 October at 10:30 P.M. He was virtually a skeleton in his wrists and ankles in his last conversations with the man who whetted his appetite for Sanskrit. Having just seen Wilkins's translation of the *Bhagavad-Gita,* Hastings had written an introduction on the spot and later helped get the book published by the East India Company. Jones remained enthusiastic: "I long to see the Geita, of which you gave me a taste in this room. The ascent of Crishen from earth was not more afflicting to Erjun than your departure will be to [me]" (2:660). As Hastings sailed soon thereafter, their collaboration never materialized, prevented by the long delay in Jones's appointment. But the two couples were close, as Anna indicated: "Now farewell my ever respected friend may every blessing you have so justly earned attend you & may my Sir William and I live to return & see you in the possession of them, & renew those happy days we have passed already with our valuable & much valued friend."[38]

Jones refused to abandon his only chance to visit Benares. The partial regaining of his strength permitted the couple to proceed to Patna, where he became severely sick but insisted on making the arduous trek to see the Gaya inscriptions. They followed the Ganges to Benares, where his visit to Davis's observatory led to his only systematic cooperation with a fellow member, which he had envisioned as the Society's procedure. He deepened his association with Wilkins and met Kāśīnāth Śarman, Wilkins's pundit.

Too weak to search for manuscripts for the archives, Jones visited the ancient university and conversed with pundits through an interpreter. One mentioned the *Mānava-Dharmaśāstra,* an intriguing law-book that was to shape the rest of his life. Despite his slower pace, "Maulavys, Pendits, and Rajas pressed me so close, that my mornings were wholly lost, except one" spent with Ali Ibrahim Khan (2:658), the first Indian to have contributed a paper to the Society. Ali's pundits would not make a Persian translation because of the book's sanctity, but Ali promised to have one made as a guide for the Supreme Court's judgments involving Hindus. As Jones's sense of duty would not let him remain long, he left Benares on 24 December. At Patna he had started a letter to Hastings when the Sanskrit *Mānava-Dharmaśāstra* arrived from Ali. After excitedly inspecting it, he asked Law to arrange for a Persian translation at Gaya, then sailed to Bhagalpur, where the air was so dry and fresh that he regretted having to leave.

Jones wanted to see Charles Grant, a Society member who was the commercial resident at Malda, and to visit Gaur before reaching Calcutta in February, so as to avoid traversing the Sundarbans in the heat. He reached Malda in a convalescent state on 17 January 1785. Grant wrote in his journal: "I went with Sir W. and Lady Jones to Gour, taking the great tank in our way. Sir W. was curious at Gour only about the remains of art. The Mosque of the Adunah was the best thing we saw in our excursion – a curiosity worth a visit."[39] Jones was fascinated by the gigantic Adina Masjid, but was so weak that he could not stay long in the nearby magnificent ruins, which were dangerous because of wild animals. He left with regret.

Sleeping in the pinnace, he came ashore early Sunday to join the highly religious Grants at family prayer and church. As he often read religious works on Sunday, he had brought Thomas Secker's *Sermons on Several Subjects* (London, 1770–1), from which he read a sermon aloud. The two couples spent the rest of the day in restrained, useful talk. The Joneses remained for two weeks, taking the rides thereabouts and enjoying the setting. Their observance of the Grants' strict customs impressed Grant: "Sir W. is astonishing in variety and depth of learning, facility and variety of genius, and is polite and entertaining in a high degree." This observation provides further insight into Jones's character and success in polite society. He had long ago learned to be highly considerate of others' feelings. This sensitivity, together with fine conversational abilities, complemented an impressive knowledge that was communicated as permitted by decorum and always with a becoming modesty. He did not display his learning; there was no intellectual arrogance in his conversations with Grant. The two were to be closer when Grant was appointed to the Board of Trade in Calcutta, later becoming a Clapham leader.

The Joneses followed the Padma River into the Sundarbans, a wide delta area at that time sixty to eighty miles long. The dense jungle harbored pirates, prompting them to avoid the narrow passes. Once they sailed within two yards of a tiger, which gazed at them indifferently. As they penetrated the delta more deeply, it became hotter, even at night, than Jones had ever been in a vapor bath. Until then he had not realized the power of the Indian sun, which much affected Anna.

In the intense heat Jones wrote Pitt as a friend, not as a subject to his minister. Penning the long letter was difficult, but even in his weakness he could not forget his duty to the Indians. Perhaps in the back of his mind during his Ganges odyssey was the need to cooperate with an MP in helping them. No letter from Burke had been waiting at Malda, and Jones's former classmates Sheridan and Fox were equally assailing Hastings.

Pitt was a likely helper. His India Act weakened the East India Company by establishing a Board of Control and a Privy Council, with the Bengal Governor-General gaining more power over the Bombay and Madras Presidencies. The act, the details of which Jones had not yet seen, did not correct the prevailing bad conditions and injustice. So, four steamy days from Calcutta, Jones described the debtors' prison to Pitt. Though the judges' official letter on the subject might be awaiting his signature, he asked Pitt to procure "the insertion of a special clause in the next bill for the relief of insolvent debtors, or rather by a separate bill for those in India" (2:662). A noxious pond, together with the close confinement, made the prison worse than the worst Western dungeon. Unnecessary violation of the concept of impurity made Hindus further miserable. As imprisonment was the only known way to promote justice, all that could be done for now was to mitigate this necessary evil. Some Indians had been imprisoned for years; their counsel thought that they could be relieved only by an expensive equity suit: "The higher order of natives both speak and write indignantly on the subject of our *English* prison," a fact that repelled Jones.

Better oaths were also needed; Indians must risk punishment if they fraudulently concealed property when taking the oath. Jones recommended that a Supreme Court judge be able to sit as a justice of the peace and make civil judgments, instead of having to defer decision to the Court. The Calcutta police needed improvement, perhaps by adding twenty gentlemen to the commission for the peace. Jones would report other important problems once he analyzed them, despairing of nothing under Pitt's guidance. He had ordered Persian versions of the oldest law-book in Sanskrit, which he was almost tempted to learn so as to verify the court pundits' opinions. He had translated *Al Sirájiyyah,* on Moslem law, which he planned to print. Overall, "a *good system* of *laws,* a just *administration* of them, and a *long peace,* will render this country a source of infinite advantage to Great Britain." Although this conclusion did not mention advantages to Indians, Jones's entire letter was about their well-being.

As Pitt apparently did not answer the letter, Jones's last hope of a parliamentary implementer of his recommendations was stillborn. Just as Burke did not use "Best Practicable System," Pitt never followed up the recommendations. This further opportunity to ameliorate aspects of Western colonialism, which might have somewhat countered the developing Indian hostility toward European rulers, was lost. But as Jones's pinnace sailed out of the Sundarbans toward Calcutta, he was buoyed up by his hopes.

9   A Sacred Oriental Language (1785)

Jones reached Calcutta after an absence of seven months. For a time "reduced to a skeleton by fevers of every denomination, with an obstinate bilious flux at their heels," now he felt reasonably recovered (2:666).

The political situation had changed; he personally felt the loss of Hastings. Macpherson, the senior member of the Supreme Council, was acting as Governor-General. He required officers to list their notices in the *Calcutta Gazette,* provoking an editorial on 3 March on freedom of the press.

During his year and a half in Bengal, Jones had fostered some cooperation between the council and the Supreme Court. Now overtures were made to Macpherson:

I always thought before I left England, that a regard for the public good required the most cordial union between the executive and judicial powers in this country; and I lamented the mischief occasioned by former divisions. Since I have no view of happiness on this side of the grave, but in a faithful discharge of my duty, I shall spare no pains to preserve that cordiality which subsists, I trust, and will subsist, between the government and the judges. (2:668)

Citing Bacon on the need for statesmen to relieve their minds from the fatigue of business, Jones enclosed "The Enchanted Fruit," which, he hoped, might amuse Macpherson. The composing had not been solely recreational, for a knowledge of Hindu manners was useful to a judge. Nor was Jones's allusion to statesmen accidental. Since his tutorship, he had sought to educate others, using correspondence to suggest proper ideals to Althorp. In a sense, his "Best Practicable System" had been instructional. In various letters he advised successive Governors-General: Hastings, Macpherson, Cornwallis, and Shore.

As the intimacy of Calcutta permitted greater directness than in his early suggestion of principles for Gabriel, Jones told a grateful Macpherson: "Your kind and pleasing letter ... shews that your mind can grasp the whole field of literature and criticism, as well as that of politics, and that in the manner of ancient rulers in Asia, particularly Cicero, the governor of Cicilia, you unite the character of the statesman and the scholar" (2:672).

He was ready to assist whenever needed. When Macpherson remarked that he felt safe only in fixed unanimous opinions of statute law, he was supplied maxims for interpreting legal writings. Jones lent Raleigh's *Cabinet-Council* (London, 1658), which contains "wise aphorisms and pertinent examples; it is rather the common-place book of some statesman, than a well digested treatise, but it has amused me on a second reading" (2:680). Macpherson reciprocally supplied the writings of the Scottish philosopher Adam Ferguson. Considering that Macpherson had been dismissed from the East India Company and was being charged with bribery when added to the Supreme Council, it is revealing that Jones devoted so much time to him. But such was Jones's desire for public good.

Their association partly prompted Macpherson's judicial reliance on the Supreme Court, from which he quickly requested rulings. First, the Court held that a person accused of delinquency by a foreign power (France) should not be handed over to that power, because one's local allegiance gave one the protection of English law guaranteeing liberty until there was due process. Here Jones's views on the constitution surely prevailed. Next was a complex ruling on jurisdiction in cases not involving treason and felony in Indian territories governed by Britain. Third, the Court ruled that only a special commission of oyer and terminer in England could try a certain accused man.[1]

Their association benefited the Calcutta Madrasah, which Hastings had founded at his own expense to advance the knowledge of Moslem law and to train Indian lawyers and judges. Joining the Asiatic Society, Macpherson proposed that a knowledgeable member visit the college monthly under his direction to investigate the troubles there. Students had testified that Mujd-ud-din, the head, was taking their allowances and leaving them without subsistence, a charge outside Jones's cognizance as a justice of the peace.

Because the head was also a *maulvi* of the Supreme Court, Jones welcomed the proposal. After the Society selected William Chambers to make the visits as a service to the government, Macpherson consulted with Jones about a new regulation that improved the situation.

The Society had languished during Jones's Ganges trip. Four meetings were adjourned, with no papers read. On 17 February 1785, Stables, Hyde, Wilkins, and four others joined Jones. He nominated George Perry, an assistant to the surveyor general, and read Henry Richardson's letter offering to perform services in England, like Shore's recent offer. No paper was read.

The meeting of 24 February attracted twenty-seven members, the largest number since the founding. The other two judges, Macpherson, and Stables came. Jones seconded the nomination of Joseph Champion, who was completing a translation of Firdausi's poetry. Then Jones read his Second Anniversary Discourse, which, in his weakened condition, had been difficult to compose. Utilizing information from his trip, it asks the Society to advance the general good by "many useful and interesting tracts, which, being too short for separate publication, might lie many years concealed, or, perhaps, irrecoverably perish." The goal is "truth unadorned by rhetorick."

National welfare and individual benefit will flow from research into Indian topics. Because the ancient Indians prized medical skill, their medical books should be located "without loss of time; lest the venerable but abstruse language, in which they are composed, should cease to be perfectly intelligible, even to the best educated natives, through a want of powerful invitation to study it." The Society should seek works on agriculture, chemistry, and music and should translate Sanskrit literature. Jones proudly announced Wilkins's plans to translate the *Śrīmad Bhagwatam* or even all of the *Mahābhārata:* "If we may form a just opinion of the *Sanscrit* poetry from the specimens already exhibited, (though we can only judge perfectly by consulting the originals), we cannot but thirst for the whole work of VYASA." The Society should translate mathematical books; and "if some standard *law-tracts* were accurately translated from the *Sanscrit* and *Arabick,* we might hope in time to see so complete a Digest of *Indian* Laws, that all disputes among the natives might be decided without *uncertainty,* which is in truth a disgrace, though satirically called a *glory,* to the forensick science."

Besides this Sanskrit labor, members should make sketches of architectural remains and draw up detailed geographical descriptions. The Indian plant and mineral systems needed to be fitted into the Linnaean classification. Nothing was purely theoretical, for there were applications, particularly in Europe. Thus research on botany could help diet and medicine, research on chemistry could lead to new manufactured products, and research on architecture could result in beauty and sublimity. If each member were to describe

such manuscripts as he had perused or inspected, with their dates and the names of their owners, and to propose for solution such *questions* as had occurred to him concerning *Asiatick* Art, Science, and History, natural or civil, we should possess without labour, and almost by imperceptible degrees, a fuller catalogue of Oriental books, than has hitherto been exhibited, and our correspondents would be apprised of those points, to which we chiefly direct our investigations.

Such work was almost inexhaustible.

The year before, Jones had recognized that his colleagues might have rejected the concept of an Asiatic Society if he had tried to force Indian members on them. Now a year had passed, and his suggestion that there be a vote on the matter had been quietly ignored. This time he approached the delicate subject from a different angle: "Much may, I am confident, be expected from the communications of *learned natives,* whether lawyers, physicians, or private scholars, who would eagerly, on the first invitation" submit studies in a cooperative investigation. Persian and Hindi notices might be circulated to explain the Society's purposes, and an annual medal "with inscriptions in *Persian* on one side, and on the reverse in *Sanscrit*" might be awarded for the best essay. This suggestion of an award like the Royal Society's Copley Gold Medal was successful, and accordingly, Indians besides Ali Ibrahim Khan contributed. Wherever Jones went, he sought Indian scholars, collecting information about their education, specialization, and age. His notebook[2] lists eight "Learned Men at Calcutta," with similar lists for places as far removed as Benares. His reason for this endeavor was bold and simple: Research would inevitably point to some needed changes, which were impossible without the Indians' full cooperation. The Indian intelligentsia must trust their European fellow researchers if the Society were to advance knowledge collectively through cultural encounters. Jones was increasingly appreciative of and sympathetic to ancient Indian culture, and it was this demonstrated view that chiefly secured the Indians' active support and helped ensure his own advances. He was trying hard to get the Society to recognize this vital point.

Yet his Second Discourse has an ethnocentric strain despite his scholarly objectivity. For example, he states that some Indians want to advance knowledge but that most desire, not unreasonably, to gain favor. While recognizing the superiority of European talents, members must not condemn Asians, whose research may supply many valuable hints "for our own improvement and advantage." Although this strain soon faded as Jones discovered the richness of Indian philosophy, his bias surfaced intermittently, particularly because he lived and worked among prejudiced Europeans.

A summary of his Society activities until his autumn vacation is as follows: He attended all twenty meetings, whose attendance ranged from seven to fifteen. On 3 March he read Francis Light's description of a Balinese religious document on tree bark.[3] On 24 March he presented his "On the Gods of Greece, Italy, and India," which was to be much revised. The following week he read his never-published translation of an Italian version of part of a *Purāṇa.* On 7 April he seconded the nomination of Thomas Deane Pearse, commandant of the artillery; and enumerating the titles of papers delivered to date, he proposed their publication.

Sometimes Jones had to use all his leisure to conclude research. Thus on 14 April he told Wilkins that he did not expect to finish his essay for that evening's meeting. Could Wilkins read a supposedly completed translation of a Sanskrit inscription? When the answer was negative, Jones worked intensively to finish translating an Indian physician's Persian essay on elephantiasis, which details a crystalline arsenic treatment and several case histories. Jones added an introduction describing his humane aim, recommending that Europeans test this and other putative cures. Once a cure was verified, elephantiasis, which was rare in Europe, could be eradicated. Such a magnificent goal and procedure for cooperation between East and West to help the Asians, as bridged by the Society, intellectually anticipated the transformation of mercantilism into the modern Commonwealth and exemplifies the larger human benefits that he almost invariably visualized in his research, beyond the general purpose of advancing knowledge. Jones titled this remarkable essay "On the Cure of the Elephantiasis, and Other Disorders of the Blood."

On 5 May he read "On the Second Classical Book of the Chinese," a springboard essay for his more comprehensive Seventh Discourse. Describing the *Shih Ching* and Confucius' remarks on it, the essay solicits research from all of Asia. Seeking to learn about Chinese literature, Jones had urged Whang Atong to translate the *Shih Ching*, a suggestion gently declined on the grounds that no one could be found to devote the requisite years to that large collection. He invited Atong to bring Chinese artists to Bengal if the government would subsidize the project. But despite the public and artistic advantages, he was too realistic to request the funds: "We must wait for a time of greater national wealth and prosperity, before such a measure can be formally recommended by us to our patrons at the helm of government." Thus Jones projected a government-financed exchange arranged by a learned society, like modern Fulbright programs. In his essay he included his early versions from the *Shih Ching*, "The Verbal Translation" and "The Paraphrase," which later were often anthologized. The former, in six eighteenth-century quatrains, is not at all Chinese.[4]

On 19 May he presented his never-published essay on possible affinities between Hebrew and Devanagari writing; on 2 June, his note on Rennell's account of Bhutan and Tibet; and on 7 July, Wilkins's translation of a Sanskrit royal grant. A member's description of the famed Sanskrit university at Nabadwip (Nadia), presented on 28 July, persuaded Jones to spend his vacation there. With no new essay available on 11 August, seven members heard Charles Hamilton's paper on the madhuca tree again and then adjourned because of Jones's coming vacation.

Meanwhile, he was heavily engaged in hearing cases, one of which, on

11 March, involved a raja. Jones made a note to himself: "When a principle of *law* is certain, we have nothing to do with its consequences. I presumed yt. in this case there had been no *agreement* to be subject to our jurisdiction. Had there been one, the motion I think shd. have been granted."[5] He wrote Wilkins that in Hindu matters, only correct Hindu law should guide the judges, who were entirely dependent on Indian lawyers, "through our ignorance of Shanscrit" (2:666).[6]

Because one of the two pundits employed by the Supreme Court had died, Jones again wrote Wilkins when Kāśīnāth recommended Govardhana Kaul, who should be examined by learned pundits like Kāśīnāth. Would Wilkins consult Kāśīnāth, so that Jones might act on the recommendation? If the university at Tirhut were still conferring degrees in Hindu law, the judges might request applicants from there and Benares. The appointee should be universally approved, as Hindus must be convinced that the Supreme Court made decisions based on the best information. This was a striking change in administrative policy, designed to build Indians' confidence in British judicial decisions.

Jones frequently consulted with Wilkins. When a book arrived from Ali Ibrahim Khan on 1 March, he immediately reported his puzzlement. Its Persian title differed from the Sanskrit one, which he deciphered as "Dherm Shāstr Menu Smrety." When the promised Persian version arrived, he hoped to read the original if a pundit would assist him. Wilkins often helped Jones. He had certain slokas copied from the *Śrīmad Bhagwatam,* because Jones had heard that they contain pure theology and sound philosophy and wished to engrave them. He made suggestions for Jones's poetic hymns to Hindu divinities, as will be seen. For Jones's second charge to the grand jury, Wilkins answered the query of "whether the crime of perjury be expiable by any religious acts or atonements, and what kind of oath, if any, is held so solemn, that no expiation or absolution will atone for a wilful violation of it" (2:677). Having found some complicated rules on oaths in the *Mānava-Dharmaśāstra,* Jones further utilized Wilkins's scholarship in judicial rulings.

Jones's charge on 10 June discusses forgery, imprisoned debtors, masters who beat their servants fatally, and the willful violation of oaths, since the docket contained such cases. His discussion is woven into a theme of the jury's proper attitude toward the Indians. Because a single charge was too short to convey Jones's enlightened system of Indian justice, he was presenting it in segments. He recommends indictment for forgery as only a misdemeanor, for the British penalty of death cannot be legally extended to India. The brutal death of a European's slave girl provokes his indignation: "I make no scruple to declare my own opinion, that *absolute un-*

conditional slavery, by which one human creature becomes the *property* of another, like a horse or an ox, is happily unknown to the laws of *England,* and that no human law could give it a just sanction." In his own household, children rescued from misery are treated like other servants and will be so informed when they are old enough to differentiate servantship from slavery. (Unfortunately, his policy had no effect, as slavery was not abolished in Delhi until 1812.) Jones warns that juries must be constantly on guard against perjury, by Europeans or Asians. Jurors should view crimes severely but criminals compassionately: "Avoid by all means the slightest imputation of injustice among those, whom it is the lot of *Britain* to rule; and, by giving them personal security, with every reasonable indulgence to their harmless prejudices, to conciliate their affection, while we promote their industry, so as to render our dominion over them a national benefit." Here, despite Jones's stress on gaining the Indians' confidence, some ethnocentrism is evident.

He had now realized his earlier naïveté in asserting that he knew no reason why Hindus could not be governed by their own laws. As none of the judges knew Hindu law, they had to rely on pundits who might be incompetent or corrupt. Only in Sanskrit could dependable law be found; so Jones again found that knowledge was often language based and especially valuable when applied to a predetermined end of improving peoples' lives. For almost two years he had hoped that Wilkins might supply certain needed legal information. Wilkins did help in preparing an oath to ensure Hindus' truthful testimonies, but would not serve as an encyclopedia ready to seek and transmit requested data. Wilkins was just not interested in law.

Nor were problems resolved as smoothly as they might have been in England. Thus Jones prepared reliable Moslem oaths, but the Armenian who was to engrave them lost his father and stopped working for a time. Then, trying to determine the proper Hindu form from Sanskrit books with pundits' advice, Jones relied too much on *maulvis,* who made errors on the plate. Wilkins had another copy of the Moslem oath printed, also checking the Persian and Hindi oaths. Jones supplied the oath to Chapman, suggesting that it might be useful. Law was asked to query his pundit: (1) How should Hindus be examined in court? (2) Can Brahmans give absolution for perjury? and (3) Should Hindus swear by the Ganges or any other holy thing or word?

The Supreme Court pundits' opinions constituted Jones's largest problem. His aspiration to know more about India than anyone else did could not be fulfilled through a secondary source like Wilkins, who would soon return to England. Wilkins would probably work only on grammars and dictionaries, but this focus in no way diminished his accomplishments in providing "more advantages in *Indian* literature than *Europe,* or *India,* can ever sufficiently acknowledge." The departure of this "very ingenious member, who first opened the inestimable mine of *Sanscrit* literature," would deprive the Society of accurate, solid information.[7]

The term lasted two months and fatigued Jones. The constant sitting in court every morning, together with the irksome duties of justice of the peace every afternoon, made him fear for his health. So in late August the Joneses fled as fast as their pinnace could transport them from Calcutta's heat and humidity and the friends who continually dropped in. Though enjoying their conversation, he could not indulge himself without neglecting his studies; healthful isolation would permit uninterrupted scholarship.[8] Instead of a traditional hill station, he selected Krishnagar, Nadia's head station, sixty miles north of Calcutta. He rented a cottage near the ancient university.

Jones had now decided "to learn the rudiments of that venerable and interesting language which was once vernacular in all India" (2:680). Learning about Sanskrit literature exhilarated him, but his chief purpose was to be able to verify the pundits' legal opinions. Later he often said that his primary goal was to gain justice for the Indians; by then his enthusiasm for Sanskrit and especially the literary treasures had become a virtual drive.

Nehru gives a dramatic account of Jones's experience at the university. He expressed a desire to study Sanskrit, but no Brahman would teach the sacred language to a foreigner, even for handsome payment. After much difficulty, a *vaidya,* or medical practitioner, agreed under "peculiar and stringent conditions."[9] No evidence for this account has been found, but some chronology may be instructive. In the Preface to *A Code of Gentoo Laws,* Halhed complained that pundits would not teach him Sanskrit, despite Hastings's official requests, so that he had to translate a Persian version. In 1778 Wilkins began studying Sanskrit with "a pundit of liberal mind." By the time of H. T. Colebrooke's study in 1791–3, Brahmans were allowing access to their sciences and the Vedas.

Jones sought a tutor at Nadia in 1785, at a time when the Brahmanic faculty were on vacation. The choice was a pleasant *vaidya,* who was not attending the seasonal Durgā ceremonies because he was not a Brahman: "[Rāmalocana] has taught grammar and ethics to the most learned Brahmins, and has no priestly pride, with which his pupils in general abound" (2:687).[10] He was employed continuously, and Jones's successful study contributed to the Brahmans' change of attitude by Colebrooke's time. Jones's notebook shows his appreciation of Rāmalocana: "Most of ye. learned *Brāhmans* were his pupils in *Grammar.* . . . [He] teaches *Grammar* at *Nadīyā* and has 20 or 25 scholars! betw. 65 & 66 yrs. old." It ranks eighteen pundits by reputation. Nadia had about five hundred students in October, with one thousand for the whole year, but it was "much on the decline."

The pundit began teaching Jones all that he knew about Sanskrit, in accordance with native grammarians' analysis, which has survived in India and the West.[11] Though Pāṇini was "an inspired Saint, on the *pronunciation* of vocal sounds," Jones considered his work to be "so abstruse, as to require the lucubrations of many years, before it can be perfectly understood. . . . there can be little occasion to travel over so rough and gloomy a path."[12]

A European's learning Sanskrit at that time was an extraordinary achievement. The grammars and dictionaries were in Sanskrit manuscripts, and the rote repetition and memorization of texts were foreign to Jones's habits. Dependence on the pundit further slowed his study. Although Latin was vaguely similar in structure, he had never encountered anything like the strings of morphemes fused by sandhi that constituted the texts. A distant comparison might be for a non-English speaker in A.D. 5000 to learn today's English from transcriptions like *waja,* representing *what,* the past-tense form of *do,* and *you.*[13] Jones's knowledge of Persian was helpful, inasmuch as Old Persian and Sanskrit developed from Indo-Iranian: He frequently encountered cognates that he remembered from early Persian.

Because this would be his last language, he wanted to learn it "more grammatically and accurately than the indolence of childhood and the impatience of youth" had let him learn any other (2:718). His basic vocabulary was the *Amarakośa,* containing about 12,608 words, which he translated.[14] His chief grammar was Durgādāsa's *Mugdhabodhaṭīkā,* which he considered "an excellent Grammar, comprehensive, methodical, and concise." The two hundred pages contained all that a learner needed to know, but Jones also used the *Sārasvatīprakriyā* and *Siddhāntakaumudī.* He arranged to take "the father of the university" back to Calcutta, hoping to read the *Hitopadeśa:* "My great object is the Dherme Sastra, to which I shall arrive by degrees" (2:682). Learning Sanskrit was to "facilitate his investigations in history and the study of man" in the context of translating this law book.[15]

Jones's decision to learn Sanskrit can be partly traced back to Hastings. Smoothing the way by means of his appreciation of Indian civilization, Hastings recognized that British fortunes could best be advanced by solicitous attention to local religions, customs, and laws.[16] To assist the Supreme Court, he asked a commission of Brahmans to collect authoritative legal passages. Because no European knew Sanskrit, their collection *Vivādār-*

ṇavasetu was rendered into Persian, which Halhed was assigned to translate. In terms of contemporary European knowledge of sources, the book was rather carefully planned, and the pundits faithfully transcribed the Sanskrit passages. Although the Brahman compiliers inspected Halhed's resulting *Code of Gentoo Laws,* his translation never enjoyed authority. It was slightly executed, lacked references, and abounded in errors. The Persian version that he used was done "by a Muselman writer from the Bengal dialect, in which one of the Brāhmans (the same who has corrected my Sanscrit copy) explained it to him. A translation, in the third degree from the original, must be, as you will easily imagine, very erroneous," as Jones later evaluated the translation to a friend (2:821).[17]

As Halhed's *Code* was not useful to the Court, Jones wanted a dependable digest. Law had persuaded a wealthy Hindu to arrange a Persian translation of the *Mānava-Dharmaśāstra,* which fascinated Jones. This Brahmanic code, which specifies domestic rules, seemed to be basic to the Hindu portion of a digest. Studying the Persian version, Jones gradually realized that he must translate the original. The Court could not use the Persian version: "[It], like all others from the *Sanscrit* into that language, is a rude intermixture of the text, loosely rendered, with some old or new comment, and often with the crude notions of the translator; and, though it expresses the general sense of the original, yet it swarms with errours, imputable partly to haste, and partly to ignorance."[18]

Sanskrit was only part of Jones's daily studies at Krishnagar:

> *Morning* – One letter.
> Ten Chapters of the Bible.
> Sanscrit Grammar.
> Hindu Law, &c.
> *Afternoon* – Indian Geography.
> *Evening* – Roman History.
> Chess. Ariosto.[19]

His daily letters were mainly answers to scholarly friends in India. He gave jocular encouragement to Patrick Russell: "I shall be impatient to see the fruit of your learned labours. Our society goes on slowly; and hot-bed fruits are not so good to my taste as those which ripen naturally" (2:680–1). As Russell was collecting specimens and drawings, rather than assisting in Banks's idea of botanical transplantation within the British Empire, the "hot-bed" allusion was serious. Russell had become the East India Company's naturalist in the Carnatic upon John Koenig's death, and Jones wanted to secure Linnaeus's works when Koenig's library was sold.

Jones proudly informed Wilkins of his Sanskrit study: "Your time is too precious, and you spend it too nobly in your own studies, for me to think of engaging much of it, except on extraordinary occasions" (2:682). He thanked Law for the Persian version of the *Mānava-Dharmaśāstra*, "the most curious work, that has yet emerged from the gloom of Sanscrit. I am proceeding slowly, but surely, in the study" (2:685). Sanskrit was as difficult for Jones to learn as Greek had been.

He had originally planned to stay in India for six years, until he could save enough money to serve independently in Parliament or elsewhere in his prime. But his responsibilities were too demanding to permit a time-table. Even the establishing of a reliable Hindu oath was difficult. The heat, life in a city surrounded by salt marshes without drainage or sani-tation, the understaffed Supreme Court, and his slow progress on Sanskrit suggested a longish tenure. Anna wrote her sister that she was reconciled to staying several more years, news that was relayed to Franklin.[20]

Jones was willing to extend his residence partly because of a growing affection for the tantalizing culture: "If temperance and composure of mind will avail, I shall be well; but I would rather be a valetudinarian, all my life, than leave unexplored the Sanscrit mine which I have just opened" (2:687). In England he had known little or nothing about Indian literature. No Sanskrit manuscripts had been published, partly because no one had emulated Edward Pococke's model of bringing the texts to Europe; the first Sanskrit grammar was not published until 1790. Colonial Europeans had seen the vast, ruined temples but believed the nonliterate "black men" to have produced little literature. After Hastings and Shore returned to England, Jones's major fellow admirer of the ancient civilization was Wil-kins, whose health was not good, but he would usually help when asked.

The delicate, cosmic conceptions of Hindu divinities had so intrigued Jones that soon after his arrival he composed the first of nine hymns. Written within five years for his literary pleasure, they use descriptions he collected from various sources. Each is introduced by a brief Argument comparing the divinity with a Greek and/or Roman one, though his com-prehensive interrelating was reserved for the essay "On the Gods of Greece, Italy, and India," which he was continuing to revise. In choosing deities to poeticize, he had no overall plan to honor a certain number or develop a common theme. A hymn was written when he had the time and inclination.

Jones asked Wilkins to criticize his draft of "A Hymn to Camdeo," which was inspired by a passage in the *Bhaviṣya-purāṇa*, and incorporated some of the corrections. His Argument opens on a pioneering comparative note: "[Kama], to whom the following poem is addressed, appears evi-dently the same with the *Grecian* EROS and the *Roman* CUPIDO; but the *Indian* description of his person and arms, his family, attendants, and attributes, has new and peculiar beauties." Jones wove most of Kama's at least twenty-three epithets into eight ten-line stanzas modeled on Milton. Kama's bow of sugarcane or flowers, with its string of bees and its arrows tipped with blossoms, can provoke amorous feeling; but when Kama daringly tests an arrow on Siva, Siva's flame reduces him to a mental essence. The hymn maintains high quality from the outset:

> What potent God from *Agra's* orient bow'rs
> Floats thro' the lucid air, whilst living flow'rs
> With sunny twine the vocal arbours wreathe,
> And gales enamour'd heav'nly fragrance breathe?
>   Hail pow'r unknown! for at thy beck
>   Vales and groves their bosoms deck
>   And ev'ry laughing blossom dresses
>   With gems of dew his musky tresses.
> I feel, I feel thy genial flame divine,
> And hallow thee and kiss thy shrine.

When Jones read the hymn to the Society, they applauded and called it the only correct specimen of Hindu mythology yet to appear. Considering it new and quite original, he sent it to friends in England, where it could become known and perhaps advance his early wish to rejuvenate British poetry. When it appeared with his First Discourse and first charge to the grand jury in the pamphlet *A Discourse on the Institution of a Society* (1784), the usual laudatory reviews followed. The *Monthly Review* called the hymn a charming performance that "will equally delight the admirers of genuine and elegant poetry, and the lovers of Eastern allegory" (November 1784, p. 357). *Gentleman's Magazine* also liked it, quoting three stanzas (January 1785, pp. 50–51). It was reprinted in the *Annual Register* of 1784–5 (pp. 137–8) and Dr. Johnson's *Works of the English Poets* (1:668). And John Courtenay alluded to it in his "Moral and Literary Character of Dr. Johnson," giving only Johnson more space than Jones:

> Here early parts accomplish'd JONES sublimes,
> And science blends with Asia's lofty rhymes:
> Harmonious JONES! who in his splendid strains
> Sings Camdeo's sports, on Agra's flowery plains;
> In Hindu fictions while we fondly trace
> Love and the Muses, deck'd with Attick grace.[21]

In April 1785 Jones sent Wilkins a draft of "A Hymn to Nārāyena," requesting additional epithets for a new stanza: "The subject is the sublimest that the human mind can conceive; but my feeble Muse cannot do justice to it. How I lament my inability to read the two Purāns of the *Egg* and the *Lotos!* The doctrine is that of Parmenides and Plato" (2:669). The epithets from Wilkins were shaped into what became the fifth of seven eighteen-line stanzas. Jones's Argument suggests the complexity of his most poetical, profound explanation of Hinduism: "A complete introduction to the following Ode would be no less than a full comment on the VAYDS and PURĀNS of the HINDUS, the remains of *Egyptian* and *Persian* Theology, and the tenets of the *Ionick* and *Italick* Schools." There also are biblical allusions and Miltonic echoes in this delicate story of the Spirit of God. Stimulated by the *Mānava-Dharmaśāstra,* Jones imaginatively presents Brahma the Creator in a grand view:

> First an all-potent all-pervading sound
>   Bade flow the waters – and the waters flow'd,
>   Exulting in their measureless abode,
>   Diffusive, multitudinous, profound,
>   Above, beneath, around;
> Then o'er the vast expanse primordial wing
>   Breath'd gently, till a lucid bubble rose,
>   Which grew in perfect shape an Egg refin'd:
>   Created substance no such lustre shows,
>   Earth no such beauty knows.
> Above the warring waves it danc'd elate,
>   Till from its bursting shell with lovely state
>   A form cerulean flutter'd o'er the deep,
>   Brightest of beings, greatest of the great:
>   Who, not as mortals steep,
>   Their eyes in dewy sleep,
>   But heav'nly-pensive on the Lotos lay,
> That blossom'd at his touch and shed a golden ray.

Praise of the hymn began with a eulogistic poem in the *Calcutta Gazette* of 26 May 1785. After a Calcutta periodical published it, it gained a temporary place as one of Jones's best-known poems. In the *Monthly Review,* John Parsons praised it as "very poetically conceived, and vigorously, as well as elegantly, expressed" (May 1787, pp. 417–18); and *Gentleman's Magazine* reprinted it (February 1787, pp. 109–10). Its fame reached America, where Emerson printed the "fine pagan strains" of a stanza as one of his favorites.[22]

Jones's other seven hymns, which also contain many names that jar Western readers, are poorer, though he had the praiseworthy intention of adding to English the Sanskrit borrowings needed to communicate Hindu cultural and religious concepts, like the inkhorn terms of the Renaissance, and to provide new and exotic images for Western poetry. In May 1785 Jones sent Wilkins a stanza to Indra and requested Indra's most poetic names, parentage, and attributes. He expanded this into the first three stanzas of twenty-one stanzas of four to eleven lines. The poet sees a vision at Benares, in which the King of Immortals and the "empyreal train" bestride the Sun's bright beam.

The hymn to Sarasvati was completed about September. The thirteen stanzas of thirteen lines dramatize the Hindu Minerva Musica's invention of the sciences and the Necklace of Musical Modes, and show Jones's deepening knowledge of Indian music.

His hymn to Ganga was composed in late 1785. The thirteen stanzas of thirteen lines, in a form borrowed from Thomas Gray, celebrate the goddess's birth, wanderings, and nuptials. The persona, a Brahman centuries earlier, prophesies British toleration and equity. Though Jones sent a copy to Hastings, he was not satisfied with the ode, reacting to Davis's allusion to a scenic waterfall by offering to insert a description if Davis would paint it. Jones never did, although composing poetry rested his mind after his intensive deliberations on the bench.

His sixth hymn, written in September 1786, uses most of Surya's nearly fifty names or attributes in twelve seventeen-line stanzas: "Every image, that seemed capable of poetical ornament, has been selected from books of the highest authority." His principal source was an episode from the *Mahābhārata* and Wilkins's translation of the *Bhagavad-Gita*. In the Argument he transliterates a description of a demon, which he compares with Milton's demons. An autobiographical comment answers the divinities' question "What mortal pours the strain":

> Say: "From the bosom of yon silver isle,
> Where skies more softly smile,
> He came; and, lisping our celestial tongue,
> Though not from *Brahmā* sprung,
> Draws orient knowledge from its fountains pure,
> Through caves obstructed long, and paths too long obscure."

When Francis Gladwin initiated *Asiatick Miscellany; Consisting of Original Productions, Translations, Fugitive Pieces, Imitations, and Extracts from Curious Publications* in 1785, that Society member probably expected to include Jones's hymns to attract readers. The periodical would publish literary works unsuitable for the scholarly *Asiatick Researches*, thereby helping disseminate Oriental literature. Other local Europeans contributed, but Jones was by far the most extensively represented in the first two volumes, with the six hymns, "The Enchanted Fruit," four minor translations of Sanskrit and Arabic verses, and two other works.

His "Tales and Fables by Nizami," a prose version of twenty exempla in the *Makhzanu'l-Asrár*, is an exercise for learning Persian. Only after many years had Jones translated these from the shortest poem in the *Khamsa*. He sacrificed elegance and idiom for scrupulous fidelity, partly as practice in making Persian versions of Sanskrit works. Above each English sentence he provides the Persian.

"On Parent Knees," another translation from the Persian, became a standard English poem. It is brilliant in compactness and universal theme:

> On parent knees, a naked, new-born child,
> Weeping thou sat'st, while all around thee smil'd:
> So live, that, sinking in thy last long sleep,
> Calm thou may'st smile, when all around thee weep.

Jones probably sent a copy to Mrs. Thrale, who transcribed the "very pretty" quatrain; another went to Mrs. Montagu.

In the *Monthly Review,* Parsons calls Jones's works the "highest ornaments" in *Asiatick Miscellany.* In the spring of life, Jones attained the triple character of linguist, poet, and critic. Now in the bloom of manhood, possessing unimpeachable integrity and attractive manners, he is poet, philosopher, and critic (May 1787, pp. 514–15). The two volumes of *Asiatick Miscellany* were reprinted in Calcutta and London in 1787. When *European Magazine* (January 1787, p. 34) concluded that this was the Asiatic Society's journal, Jones reacted: "[We] mean to print no scraps, nor any *mere* translations." As the notion became more prevalent, he vigorously denied it: "We had nothing to do with the Miscellany of Mr. Gladwin & his successors, which has been erroneously imputed to us" (2:770, 814–15).

A third volume, titled *The New Asiatic Miscellany* (1789), contains Jones's seventh hymn, which was composed in ten to twelve intensive hours in September 1788. The fourteen eighteen-line stanzas to Lakshmi were principally inspired by the *Bhagavad-Gita.* Foreshadowing Shelley, the hymn allegorizes Lakshmi's qualities as the world's great mother and preserving power of nature. Jones's Argument urges Europeans to study Hinduism, complementing his earlier urging them to study Persian and Arabic literature:

We may be inclined perhaps to think, that the wild fables of idolaters are not worth knowing, and that we may be satisfied with misspending our time in learning the Pagan Theology of old *Greece* and *Rome;* but we must consider, that the allegories contained in the Hymn to LACSHMĪ constitute at this moment the prevailing religion of a most extensive and celebrated Empire, and are devoutly believed by many millions.

This recommendation that Europeans study Hinduism exemplifies Jones's capacity to be completely dispassionate in viewing Oriental religions and his placing them in other contexts.

His other two Indian hymns, introduced by one Argument, were composed by 1788. The hymn to Durgā, inspired by Kālidāsa's *Kumārasam-*

bhava, is the longest of the nine. It tells the story of the dread Kālī, who does not pay a tribute to love but it reconciled with Siva in a mystic wood. The hymn to Bhavani describes in ten octets the power of fecundity of the Indian Isis, who causes river dragons' iron breasts to melt with passion. Both employ the syllabic measures of Pindar's First Nemean Ode. To practice his classical Greek and provide a comparison with the Hindu pair, Jones made a word-for-word poetic translation of Pindar's ode. All three were published posthumously.

Contemporaries applauded Jones's hymns. Their versatility, originality, and transmission of a profound, novel world to the West can still be commended. His borrowings from the Bible, Milton, Gray, and Pindar are harmonized into a rich reflection of Sanskrit literature. The hymns are Jones's most original and creative poems, with attractive, even resplendent imagery. They are true odes, each with an intricate structure and a majestic evolution of thought, probably the most successful English examples of their kind between Gray and Wordsworth.[23] The subjects provide the chief originality and help make Jones the first Anglo-Indian poet, who merits a small place in that restricted circle boasting Rudyard Kipling. Jones was the first European to poetically celebrate key divinities of the Hindu pantheon, treating the vast subject with profound knowledge, experience, and enthusiasm.[24] His humanistic evocation of the Hindu spirit and grandeur communicates the myths, attitudes, and beauty. His treatment of nature, the Hindu Creation, and the general romantic aura sometimes elevates stanzas to a level suggesting that he might have been a good poet had he pursued a literary career. His sincerity everywhere shows through.

Jones partly evokes the sensuous, delicate Indian atmosphere by transliterating place-names and other proper nouns. Though usually phonetically accurate, these strange words constitute stumbling blocks that are one reason why even his hymns to Narayana and Kama are not fine English poetry. This is the familiar problem of his learning. Having experimented with intrusive footnotes in "The Enchanted Fruit," he scrupulously avoids them in the hymns and burdens his Arguments with a bewildering array of information. Some contemporary periodicals omitted these little scholarly essays, leaving the reader without an explanation of the names. Sometimes Jones had added a stanza simply to present more epithets, thereby making his subject culturally remote for most Western readers. But if the hymns are not poetry of the highest order, they are nonetheless aflame with enthusiasm and knowledge.[25]

Except for a few minor works that will be mentioned later, Jones had completed his poetic activities. He did more to introduce Europeans to the Eastern Muses, particularly through essays and translations, than perhaps any other writer had. The earlier *Arabian Nights Entertainments* emphasized the grotesque and incredible, neglecting the human elements, whereas Jones altered the Western concept of the East by showing that there was poetry in Shiraz.[26]

Contemporaries ranked him among the greatest living poets. But a decade after his death, critics like Francis Jeffrey began to question the occasional pedantry and the fine polish suggesting classical affectation: "The greater part of his poetry is so learned and elaborate, that the perusal of it is rather a labor than a relaxation."[27] Yet Jones held a place as a standard poet for half a century after Alexander Chalmers included him in *The Works of the English Poets* (1810):

[His poems] indicate a taste so greatly refined, that there can be no scruple in admitting him to a very high rank among modern poets. He has presented to the English reader a new set of images, and opened new sources of the sublime and the pathetic by familiarizing the scenery and manners of the eastern regions. The judgment with which those are selected leads us to regret, that his original productions are few, since it is universally acknowledged that, independent of the languages and versification, both polished to a high degree of excellence, they are distinguished for true poetical fancy, ardour, and sensibility. (18:440)

For decades Jones's poems appeared in collections, until the reassessment following the rejection of advocates of dead languages like Sanskrit, together with the emergence of Tennyson and Browning, challenged his literary rank. Thus "To the name of poet, as it implies the possession of an inventive faculty, SIR WILLIAM JONES has but little pretension. He borrows much; and what he takes he seldom makes better. Yet some portion of sweetness and elegance must be allowed him"; and "He cannot, however, be called a poet of an original genius; any peculiarity of inspiration that may seem to distinguish some of his compositions is for the most part only the Orientalism of the subject, and of the figures and images. He is a brilliant translator and imitator rather than a poet in any higher sense."[28] Yet *An Ode in Imitation of Alcæus* and "On Parent Knees" have remained standard English poems, and the inclusion of "A Persian Song of Hafiz" in *The Oxford Book of Eighteenth Century English Verse* (1926) may have restored its place.

In view of his many translations, imitations, and paraphrases, Jones was one of the least spontaneous and original poets. Rather, his temperament required the study and use of others' great thoughts. He realized in poetry what he gathered as a scholar, by assimilating an amazing knowledge into his poetry.[29] As a contemporary pointed out, Calcutta had few literary men.[30] Lacking the stimulation of a Reynolds or a Dr. Johnson, Jones had all the more reason to devote his leisure to scholarship. His real literary achievement was an indirect role in comparative literature, by giving the West a new vista of themes, styles, images, and metrics. His contributing to the partial Orientalization of some Romantics and a few later poets accomplished his original goal of helping rejuvenate the literary current, of quickening the imagination of writers from Gibbon to Tennyson, and of American transcendentalists like Emerson and Thoreau. One way to measure his influence is to count the footnotes of acknowledgment by Byron, Southey, Tennyson, and the like.

We can complete this account of Jones's activities in 1785 by summarizing his Society's five meetings after he returned from Krishnagar. On 10 November he read a letter from William Marsden, whom he nominated for membership, though the young linguist was in England. He read the bishop of Llandaff's gratifying letter of 19 July, in which Llandaff said that the Society "was very much desired by all men of an enlarged turn of mind," and he praised the broad plan "by so skillful an Architect" (2:681). He made theological queries such as possible Indian accounts of the fall of man, Judaic elements in the caste system, and hints in ancient religion that the Indians possibly came from Noachic stock.

There had been a similar letter in December 1784 from Sir George Yonge, the secretary for war, who enclosed "Heads of Enquiry, which myself and Others in this part of the world, think of Importance to be made in India as well as in Europe, in order to obtain, and diffuse, if possible a more extensive knowledge of Antiquity the most remote, and thereby to reconcile the various opinions of Mankind, or at least to discover the truth" (2: 681). Yonge's fourteen language-based questions reflect Jones's success in establishing the importance of such research. For example, the first asks about ancient Indian religion and history; the second, about inscriptions pertaining to the origin of man. The twelfth concerns the early languages of India, including a possible original source; the thirteenth, the ancient words of key "Objects in Religion and Nature," including pronouns and names for God, time, and heaven. Yonge's letter initiated a correspondence with Jones.

Only seven of Jones's colleagues attended the Society meeting of 17 November, when no paper was read. On 8 December, General John Carnac nominated Titsingh; Jones seconded the mandarin's name. On 15 December there was Wilkins's translation of an inscription at Gaya. On 29 December, Macpherson, Chambers, Hyde, and seven others gathered to hear Wilkins read another translation. Overall, in 1785 there were two adjournments and twenty-seven meetings, the largest number during Jones's tenure. The Society's newness was still stimulating, and varied papers were being composed. The group's future thus seemed secure; some of his projections were bearing fruit.

Other circumstances were just as satisfying. Anna was well again. Jones had sent £5,000 home and expected to transmit another £5,000 soon. His assistance to Governor-General Macpherson, whom he could not help but like, had contributed, to date, to the greatest cooperation between the Supreme Council and the Supreme Court. For the first time in his life, Jones was using his research to develop ideas that he could transmit directly and even successfully to a receptive executive.

10   A Genetic Explanation: Indo-European
        (1786–1787)

The Society's first meeting of 1786 was held on 19 January. Jones, Hyde, and four others heard a translation of a brief Persian history. Jones seconded the nomination of John Gilchrist, an assistant surgeon who was questioning the East India Company's policy of having its servants gain some command of Persian, the language of the courts and government but not of the people. Stimulating the study of Hindustani, Gilchrist was preparing a dictionary to facilitate communication with Indians. Jones, however, never assisted, loving languages but preferring the classical to the vernacular. Sanskrit so fascinated him that there was little time for Hindi. Had he lent his talents and influence to Gilchrist's mission, conceivably Macaulay's Minute of 1835 might have been forestalled, and perhaps even a decision might have been made to use an Indian language rather than English in Indian schools.[1]

The meeting of 2 February attracted Macpherson, Stables, Chambers, Hyde, and thirty-one others. Because members knew that Jones was devoting his Third Discourse to India, this attendance was the largest during his tenure. According to the schedule in his andrometer, he would not distill all his knowledge into multivolume works until his early fifties. He was still collecting data, directly in the Society and through European exchanges that he was fostering. Jones's system is implicit in his Anniversary Discourses, which show a preliminary integration of Oriental knowledge, although scholars stress the famous philological passage in the Third Discourse.

Beyond its role in the history of linguistics, this passage has an overall context in a sequence of eight Anniversary Discourses within a general plan and a uniform approach. The First Discourse traces the purposes, guidelines, and procedures of the Society. The Second projects a detailed research program as the objective. These general essays are balanced by the Third, which is specific and introduces a titanic sequence:

The *five* principal nations, who have in different ages divided among themselves, as a kind of inheritance, the vast continent of *Asia,* with the many islands depending

241

on it, are the *Indians,* the *Chinese,* the *Tartars,* the *Arabs,* and the *Persians: who* they severally were, *whence* and *when* they came, *where* they now are settled, and *what advantage* a more perfect knowledge of them all may bring to our *European* world, will be shown, I trust, in five distinct essays; the last of which will demonstrate the connexion or diversity between them, and solve the great problem, whether they had *any* common origin, and whether that origin was *the same,* which we generally ascribe to them.

Five separate Discourses then treat the five peoples; the Eighth Discourse, the islanders. Each discusses the languages and letters, philosophy and religion, sculptural and architectural remains, and written memorials of arts and sciences. The Ninth Discourse attempts to solve the "great problem" that Jones first posed, and the Tenth sketches the benefits of such knowledge.

His philological passage is buried in the "languages" section of the Third Discourse. His method led him to reject etymological speculation in favor of empirical evidence in reaching hypotheses, and to add language to the three classical sources of knowledge, which he uses after providing a linguistic underpinning. Rejecting Jacob Bryant's speculative approach, Jones reaches conclusions that let him fit linguistic data into interdisciplinary study. Etymological postulates proceed empirically from provable facts; etymology thus studied may divulge valuable data suggesting the affinity of some languages. The experimental hypothesis of probable affinity is then tested and refined by grammatical data.

At this time scholars were still trying to locate the Garden of Eden and verify Newton's dating of Jason's search for the Golden Fleece. Although the new geology was shaking some prescientific tenets, humankind was still believed to have originated in the Middle East. Though Jones hoped to trace the inhabitants of the area back to a single source, his desire for commonality did not lead him to posit linguistic affinity before weighing the evidence. Rejecting the myth that the Tower of Babel episode caused the original language to diverge into other tongues, he empirically reached his innovational formulation of common source. He later stated:

I should ill deserve your indulgent attention, if I were to abuse it by repeating a dry list of detached words, and presenting you with a vocabulary instead of a dissertation; but, since I have no system to maintain, and have not suffered imagination to delude my judgment; since I have habituated myself to form opinions of men and things from *evidence* . . . I will assert nothing positively, which I am not able satisfactorily to demonstrate.[2]

Jones's philological passage was a tested conclusion; his reasoning can be partly reconstructed. Scholars like Dr. Johnson had chronologized the Germanic descendant languages into Anglo-Saxon (i.e., Low German), Francic (High German), and Cimbric (North Germanic). Other recognized, obvious language groups in Europe were Romance (French, Italian, and Spanish) and Slavic (Russian, Polish, Bohemian, and Serbian). Greek belonged to none of these and had a larger relationship. Latin had affected some of these because of its preponderant cultural influence.[3] Jones was probably aware of the suggestions of Filippo Sassetti (c. 1585) and Father Coeurdoux (1767) that Sanskrit had an affinity with Greek and Latin, and of the incisive observations on the similarities between Greek and Latin, made about the time of the birth of Christ. But as no one had deduced common source as the explanation, the suggestions were absorbed into the unscientific thinking of the day. They might even have strengthened the false conclusion that Latin came from Greek, or even Greek from Sanskrit. In 1779 Jones had spoken of an "almost primæval," single ancestor of Persian, Greek, Latin, and the Celtic languages, as exemplified by certain Persian–Greek cognates.

A classical scholar, he also knew German and Persian. When he encountered a precise formulation of Sanskrit grammar or sandhi, his excellent memory often supplied a similar feature from one or more of the other four languages. The school reworking of Pāṇini that Jones evidently used contained the most thorough analysis of phonology and morphology that he had ever seen. Within months he perceived "relationships between Pāṇini's explicitly stated basic morphemes and the similar, implicitly intuited basic morphemes which he already knew."[4] Besides the numerous cognates, there were grammatical resemblances to strengthen his revolutionary hypothesis.

Jones had worked himself into a position in which a comparison of certain languages with Sanskrit was almost necessary. Pāṇini rigorously described the inflections, derivations, and combinations, as well as syntactic usages, of his own speech.[5] An analysis of Greek and Latin by this model would have been vastly taxing if not impossible, for linguists had not yet devised a method for reconstructing primitive forms. Jones's time could be better spent on sweeping questions like tribal migrations and the origin of peoples; he considered language study to be really valuable only when the findings could help humankind, in an early envisioning of applied linguistics that today has developed much of the focus that he was seeking in the 1780s. His current interest was comparative anthropology in terms of the Indians' possible common origin with certain other Asians, where cultural history could be anthropologically enlightened and enriched.

Avoiding folk etymology, Jones effectively employed experimental procedure. Apparently weighing similarities on the basis of probabilities, he found common origin to be a sounder hypothesis than borrowing or coincidence, which, instead of one explanation, would require a fresh hypothesis for every similar pair. The only tenable explanation was a genetic relationship, and his breakthrough was in realizing that such a relationship was possible and that the source language was a previously unknown one that might no longer be spoken because it had changed into languages that had become Sanskrit, Old Persian, and others. He could hardly have reached this conclusion without using phonetic similarity, morpheme by morpheme, and perceiving the systematic nature of the resemblances. His few examples illustrate some of the sound shifts that Jacob Grimm, no doubt building on Rasmus Rask, would later identify and group under a governing principle. Jones would have considered such pre-Grimm methodology as rather trivial points within his integrated historical goals.

The problem that he faced was to find an analytical method that would separate actual cognates from similarities caused by chance or borrowing. Later he specified some of his criteria: (1) The analyst must be "perfectly acquainted" with the relevant languages; (2) the meaning of possible cognates must be identical or nearly identical; (3) vowels cannot be disregarded; (4) there can be no metathesis or consonantal insertions; and (5) phonetic correspondence cannot be postulated solely on articulatory position.[6] Coupled with these criteria were his stress on evidence, partly motivated by his barrister's training and courtroom experience, and by the extensive data and method he had observed in the great Linnaean binomial nomenclature. So he meticulously avoided poor transliterations (which could make an Asiatic word seem phonologically closer to a European word than it actually was), and he relied on basic vocabulary rather than on exotic items (which might be borrowed).

Apparently no one helped Jones construct his hypothesis. Halhed's *Grammar of the Bengal Language* (Hooghly, 1778) provocatively describes some forms in terms of Sanskrit kinship, in a kind of overview of North Indic languages derived from Sanskrit. Several comparisons of Sanskrit–Greek and Sanskrit–Latin hint at Sanskrit as the parent tongue. Jones annotated his copy of the book; but there is no reference to Halhed in the Third Discourse, nor any evidence that they discussed the subject in the few weeks in 1784 when they could have talked in Calcutta.

Nor did Wilkins have a direct impact on Jones's thinking. Jones corresponded with Lord Monboddo, an early anthropologist, whom he had often met at Shipley's. Monboddo's *Of the Origin and Progress of Language* mentions the possible affinity of Greek and Sanskrit.[7] Monboddo's comparative bent, together with the comparative questions sent by Yonge and Llandaff, may have enhanced Jones's zeal in independently reaching his lucid conclusion in the Third Discourse:

The *Sanscrit* language, whatever be its antiquity, is of a wonderful structure; more perfect than the *Greek;* more copious than the *Latin,* and more exquisitely refined than either, yet bearing to both of them a stronger affinity, both in the roots of verbs and in the forms of grammar, than could possibly have been produced by accident; so strong indeed, that no philologer could examine them all three, without believing them to have sprung from some common source, which, perhaps, no longer exists; there is a similar reason, though not quite so forcible, for supposing that both the *Gothick* and the *Celtick,* though blended with a very different idiom, had the same origin with the *Sanscrit,* and the old *Persian* might be added to the same family.

Jones's use of the word *family,* though not implying a family tree, was taxonomically vital, greatly surpassing Dr. Johnson's simple and partly erroneous genealogical conception for a restricted portion of Germanic. In his letters of 1786–7 Jones often characterized Sanskrit as the sister of Greek and Latin. His formulation may have been the first to use the word *family* to describe groups of languages derived from some earlier source in common. Some Linnaean botanists' use of the tree diagram in the mid-eighteenth century does not diminish his achievement in applying this botanical concept to explain language similarities, a cross-disciplinary insight that was absent from contemporary language theorists. Because plants and animals were known to be mutable, why should not languages also be mutable? This and later generalizations by Jones ultimately became the final, definitive rejection of the idea that God gave Hebrew to the first human being as a direct gift and that all languages came from Hebrew, an idea that Herder had earlier attacked in part.

Yet Jones's philological passage is not free of error when viewed from modern perspective. The value judgments about Sanskrit reflect contemporary thought, and the assertion that "Gothick" was blended with a different idiom mistakenly implies that speech mixture can explain the differences between the structure of Germanic sounds and morphemes and that of non-Germanic Indo-European ones. Jones cautiously leaves open the possibility that the source (Indo-European) might still survive.[8] He shows no insight into the necessary reconstruction of earlier languages that lack written records. The concept of a family tree with successive branches, much less the wave theory, is hardly to be found in the passage. His reference to similar grammatical forms is vague, though he correctly differentiates paradigms of cognate verbs in Greek–Hindi and German–Greek. Finally, he does not suggest the concept of sounds shifting from their original forms, though he must have had a pioneering insight into the shifts, which are vital to his explanation.

These errors, unrecognized by his contemporaries, made Jones's hypothesis all the more revolutionary; for, among his previously conventional linguistic formulations, this was brilliant and far reaching in the history of ideas. In a prescientific matrix he discarded the trivial and erroneous, specifying common source as a definition of relationship that still holds. As no one had previously explained similarities in this way, he can be called the first modern linguist. This was "the first known printed statement of the fundamental postulate of Indo-European comparative grammar; more than that, of comparative linguistics as a whole."[9] That is, languages could be grouped into families; members of a single family derived from a common archetype. Thereby Jones linked linguistics with the sciences in a universalist view, applying historical and comparative methods to language study. By relating Sanskrit to some European tongues, he added a cultural link to the ties between East and West.[10]

His hypothesis excited nineteenth-century scholars, who filled in the details of his suggestion of comparative linguistics. The common Western languages had been described, and now one of the world's most famous linguists had related them to a language once spoken by a supposedly savage people of a greatly different religion and culture. This identification massively shook the ethnocentric Western view of the colonial world that Europeans had conquered, particularly their view of India. After Jones introduced Sanskrit and the view that languages could be productively compared, Rask, Franz Bopp, Grimm, and Karl Verner showed that sounds shift systematically, like the Germanic consonant shifts explained by Grimm's and Verner's laws. Friedrich von Schlegel, making the error that Jones had avoided, proposed Sanskrit as the ancestor of Greek, German, and Latin. Because Sanskrit's chronological and geographical world was too distant to explain languages like Latin by means of borrowings and "corruption," Schlegel identified Sanskrit as the primitive source.[11] Jones deserves a high place in the history of linguistics, contrasting with the contemporary speculative theorizing of Bryant, Monboddo, and John Horne Tooke and anticipating modern linguists' reliance on facts.[12] Later discovering more evidence, he concluded that "the ancient language of Ireland had certainly an affinity" with Sanskrit (2:770–1), an affinity proved by Bopp in 1839.

Except for the philological passage, Jones's Third Discourse is disappointing. Some of his thinking set out in adjacent paragraphs may be contradictory and is unsystematic. His treatment of India is superficial, and his sources are often secondary ones like Dionysius and Orme. Jones is provocative if facile: "Nor is it possible to read the *Vedānta*, or the many fine compositions in illustration of it, without believing that PYTHAGORAS and PLATO derived their sublime theories from the same fountain with the sages of *India.*" He thought that such statements seemed to confirm Pythagoras' dependence on India, whose main ideas can be found there in the sixth century B.C.[13] The more that Jones learned about Indian philosophy, the more certain he was that Pythagoras had traveled extensively in the East. In August 1787 he said: "Need I say what exquisite pleasure I receive from conversing easily with that class of men, who conversed with Pythagoras, Theles and Solon, but with this advantage over the Grecian travellers, that I have no need of an interpreter" (2:756).

In composing the long Third Discourse after six to seven hours in court and then duty as a justice of the peace in the afternoon, Jones had exhausted himself. As Anna's health was also in question, as soon as the Discourse was read to the Society, the couple boarded a sloop for Chittagong, the eastern limit of British India. He had long wanted to observe the countryside and customs there.

Jones's final act before sailing was to sign the judges' joint protest about Macpherson's new method of salary payment, which was the outgrowth of the financial distress in the three Indian presidencies. The back pay due the armies had raised fears of mutiny, and people with money were reserving it for immediate use or buying up the East India Company's enormously depreciated paper. As not a rupee could be raised by the usual company drafts, Macpherson used the cash in the treasury to pay the troops. Explaining his severe economy to the judges, he said that he wished to help: Bonds issued in lieu of salary would carry lucrative interest. However, these paid only 8 percent redeemable in England; and the judges were pinched and made "contemptible in the eyes of the natives, and of their own servants," as Jones wrote Macpherson (2:690). The new method was so intolerable that he and Hyde would have to resign the following season. The only reason why he had not complained in person, besides signing the joint letter to Macpherson that he had composed and his colleagues had much softened, was to spare the Governor-General "the pain of defending indefensible steps." Unable to pay his physician or *munshis,* Jones had had to sell East India Company bonds at a 30 percent discount and to borrow rupees for food. The judges were willing to receive half their salary, with the remainder to be paid on fair terms later. Fortunately, they had misunderstood the method, so that their generous offer was never considered. Macpherson's explanation satisfied them, whereupon the Board of Control delightedly thanked him for his boasted reduction of £1,250,000 expenditures.

Jones had a personal reason for spending the hot season in Chittagong. Charles Croftes, now the chief collector there, had been Jones's local financial agent until his stroke. Jones and others had taken his and Richard

Johnson's joint bond for £5,000. The Joneses accepted Croftes's invitation and stayed a fortnight with them, though they had planned to spend only a few weeks in "this Indian Montpelier, where the hillocks are covered with pepper vines, and sparkle with blossoms of the coffee tree" (2:692).[14] Jones did not have to be in court until mid-June, and the setting was so relaxing that he rented a house in nearby Jafrabad. It stood on a hill overlooking the sea, with a mountain behind, and it had a fine study.[15]

One of his most pleasurable activities was scholarship, which again embraced Orientalism. It had three major facets in Chittagong. Jones had hired a Parsee refugee as his Persian informant, and the two continued their daily schedule. Three lists of primarily literary titles in his notebook suggest an emphasis that could only indirectly improve his judicial capacities. His "Order of Persian Reading" is revealing – 'Aṭṭár's *Pand-nama,* Háfiz, Nizámí's *Makhzanu'l-Asrár,* Firdausi's *Yúsuf va Zulaykha,* Sa'dí's *Bústán* and *Gulistán,* Rúmí's *Mathnawí, Sháhnáma, Ta'rikh-i-Nadiri,* Naṣíru'd-Din's *Akhláq-i-Náṣirí, Anwár-i-Suhaylí,* and *Zafar-nama.* Besides the duplications in the other two lists, there are four more sources – *Chahár Darvísh,* Hátifí's *Laylà va Majnún, Khamsa,* and Zoroaster.

The *Sháhnáma* appears on all three lists. Jones read this old love twice: "If I can bring the Persian epic poem to Europe in an English dress, I shall be as far below Lycurgus as Firdusi is below Homer, but shall think the analogy just, and my country will be obliged to me" (2:607). He was planning a tragedy based on Firdausi's story of Sohrab and Rustum, which he frequently revised. Employing a chorus of Persian magi, he intended to portray the customs exactly, but he never seriously started translating the whole story. The only survival is an eighteen-line epode.[16]

As the *Makhzanu'l-Asrár* also appears on all three lists, Jones may have translated "Tales and Fables by Nizami" if not "On Parent Knees" in Chittagong. When "On Parent Knees" appeared in *Asiatick Miscellany,* this literary by-product of his Persian studies was on its way to posterity. He may have done two other translations at this time. First, "An Ode of Jami," in Persian form and measure, preserves the double character of the fourteen lines. Weaving Jámí's name into the last couplet, he successfully imitates the ghazal.[17] Second, Jones's "Song" celebrates the coming of spring in four sestets, beginning "Wake, ye nightingales, oh, wake!" Reprinting it, the Philadelphia *Port Folio* rhapsodizes: "We have always derived uncommon pleasure and instruction from the writings of SIR WILLIAM JONES. More Learning and More Fancy can scarcely be found, in any modern books, than we are regaled with in the various pages of this all accomplished writer" (4 May 1805, p. 134).

His linguistic scholarship resolved a serious problem confronting Oriental studies. A European who needed to write Arabic, Persian, or Indic words employed a "notation peculiar to himself; but none has yet appeared in the form of a complete system; so that each original sound may be rendered invariably by one appropriated symbol, conformably to the natural order of articulation, and with a due regard to the primitive power of the *Roman* alphabet."[18] Such inconsistency caused confusion in the identification of Asian persons and places, to the point that one person or place might be construed as two persons or places, or vice versa. Because Jones wanted his Society to provide "more correct information" on Asian history and geography than Greek scholars had given, he first drafted a system "more universally expressive of Asiatick letters." It transliterated only Persian; then he expanded it to accommodate Sanskrit and Arabic, while refining it "by careful observation and long experience." In Calcutta he had had plates engraved for his "Dissertation on the Orthography of Asiatick Words in Roman Letters," which he completed in Chittagong.

Most of the long essay is devoted to the transliteration of Devanagari writing, for Jones required consistency in *Asiatick Researches*. The two existing systems were inadequate. As William Davy's was chiefly built on the pronunciation of the words being represented, it posed problems when a sound or distribution did not occur in English. For example, a Persian would not be able to comprehend most of Davy's transliterations. Halhed and Wilkins advocated a scrupulous rendering, letter for letter, "without any particular care to preserve the pronunciation" of Sanskrit. But Jones wanted something more universal. A key problem was the "disgracefully and almost ridiculously imperfect" English spelling, particularly vowels. So as not to create more difficulty for the already troublesome Calcutta printing, he decided against inventing symbols, gaining the needed extra ones by adding French diacritics to existing letters: "Each original sound may be rendered invariably by one appropriated symbol, conformably to the natural order of articulation. . . . a perfect system of letters ought to contain one specifick symbol for every sound used in pronouncing the language to which they belonged." His primitive phonemic transcription is a pioneering attempt to approximate the original sounds. This was the first formal essay on transliteration and held the germ of ideas eventually culminating in the International Phonetic Alphabet. As he does not really attempt to represent the reductions made in rapid speech, much less intonation, his Jonesian System represents words in isolation, not sequences. He sometimes attempts to normalize dialectical variations. That he did not always know how to determine a standard form is shown by variants in his correspondence like *pandit, pendit,* and *pundit.* Accommodating only three languages, his system deliberately excludes tonal languages like Chinese.

The Society voted to make Jones's essay the lead essay in *Asiatick Researches* 1, as it would be the key to other essays. The Society and some later groups adopted the system presented in this first scientific paper on Indic–Persian. Though Gilchrist modified Halhed's system by devising a vowel transliteration to convey a consistent, fairly accurate pronunciation in English symbols, Jones's system was slowly refined by scholars: "As a result of a kind of natural selection or survival of the fittest, the practice of all Oriental scholars – *so far as Āryan languages* are concerned – is settling down into an acceptance of Sir William Jones's principles."[19] The practicality of his principles allowed "greater exactitude than he was able to do himself, a sufficient tribute to their validity."[20] His effort to standardize Oriental spelling, based on the principle of accurately representing the original sounds within a perspective of general phonetics, started scholars on the road toward the International Phonetic Alphabet. The emphasis on Sanskrit that he helped foster can be followed to Grimm and Verner: "The first long but slow steps away from the awkward fumblings of early European scholarship were taken only when Hindu phonetics had come to be thoroughly known to Sanskrit scholars and had been introduced by them into the stream of European scholarship."[21]

Jones's essay concludes with "a very curious passage from the *Zend*" supplied by his informant. Other passages show that, since his *Lettre*, he had worked with Avestan and with Pahlavi inscriptions on coins. Anquetil praised Jones for founding the Asiatic Society; but his *Oupnek'hat* (1801–2), a Latin collection of the Upanishads, accused Jones of "most wanton and (apparently) premeditated misrepresentation," charging that the "Zend" passage is actually Persian in Zend characters, as Jones could not distinguish Modern Persian from Avestan. This charge revived the old issue, prompting a nationalistic letter in the *Monthly Magazine*. After attempting a rebuttal, it asserts that Anquetil has few justifiable pretensions to "first rate talents, elegant accomplishments, various, extensive, and recondite literature," and that his charges insult Englishmen (December 1805, pp. 418–21).

In addition to Persian and linguistics, Jones's second major study in Chittagong was the digest of Indian law. Because he might have to request help for such a vast project, he wrote Macpherson:

I have begun a translation of Menu into English. . . . What I can possibly perform alone, I will by God's blessing perform; and I would write on the subject to the Minister, Chancellor, the Board of Controul, and the Directors, if I were not apprehensive that they who know the world, but do not fully know me, would think that I expected some advantage either of fame or patronage, by purposing to be made the Justinian of India; whereas I am conscious of desiring no advantage, but the pleasure of doing general good. I shall consequently proceed in the work by my own strength, and will print my digest by degrees at my own expense, giving copies of it where I know they will be useful. One point I have already attained; I made the pundit of our court read and correct a copy of Halhed's book in the original Sanscrit, and I then obliged him to attest it as good law, so that he never now can give corrupt opinions, without certain detection. (2:699)

Jones's last major study in Chittagong was botany. Since his introduction to botany at Bhagalpur, he had been describing all the blossoms that he could procure. Drawing was Anna's chief amusement, and she sketched each flower after he examined it. This procedure was linked to his Sanskrit reading, which was turning up many names. He enjoyed the challenge of finding and describing the plants if they still grew in India, and then of checking Sanskrit medical books to learn the benefits from the plants.

Jones also indulged in other reading and correspondence. Having brought a small library from Calcutta, he reread Adam Ferguson's *Essay on the History of Civil Society* (Edinburgh, 1767), and one morning at breakfast he read George Forster's *Sketches of the Mythology and Customs of the Hindoos* (London, 1785). The biggest book he studied was Orazio della Penna's eight-hundred-page *Alphabetum Tibetanum* (Rome, 1762). He had brought a letter case "full of scraps, narrative, descriptive, geographical, political, botanical, historical" for use in letters (2:691), but his three major studies prevented his initiating a regular scholarly correspondence. Nor did he finish expanding his notes into an essay on Anjouan.

In long letters Jones reported his Chittagong activities to Macpherson, Davis, and Hyde, who was looking after Jones's affairs in Calcutta. He wrote brief letters to Thomas Caldecott, George Hardinge, and Spencer. As the salary situation had not yet been resolved, he advised friends not to come to India: "Our salaries are unpaid, and we are forced to borrow money for our daily rice" (2:693).

There was one dramatic event during the three months. King Bodawpayā, having annexed Arakan by force, led an army up to Cox's Bazar with the evident intention of extending Burma's frontiers. An East India Company regiment was encamped there with fieldpieces that would stop the Burmese. Jones knew the major in command, for whom he puzzled out the Burmese general's insolent letter. Excitedly but vainly he thought that he might record the anticipated battle as a historian.

Having promised to be in Calcutta by mid-June, Jones was planning a route that would permit visits with his friends along the way. As Anna had regained her strength, the Joneses anticipated an odyssey. They wished to see the burning well near Chatigan, and then Dacca. But they were slaves to the season. When they left Dacca, they expected to be home in eight days. Recalling their vapor bath the previous year, they were still in Kumarkhali on 15 June, awaiting word that the Jalangi had enough water for passage, as the heat was too great for them to attempt the Sundarbans.

When Jones finally reached Calcutta, there was an even heavier schedule than usual. Soon the Supreme Court was entangled in a case involving Macpherson's unsavory friend Sir Robert Sloper, the Bengal commander in chief, whose recall had been ordered. The Supreme Council requested a ruling on Sloper's precedence at council meetings when the Governor-General was absent. The court's unanimous ruling that Sloper would preside proved to be academic, for an amendment to Pitt's India Act had deprived him of the council's second seat and an annual £10,000. Apparently Macpherson did not try to influence Jones, nor did Sloper's kinsman William attempt to do so after opposing the amendment in the Commons. Jones would have rebuffed any attempt to influence his ruling; however, there would be repercussions.

Jones did seek patronage for a deserving friend. Joseph Emin, whom Burke had helped, had gone to Armenia to arouse his countrymen against their oppressors. Eventually he abandoned his idealistic plans and came to Calcutta, where Jones became his generous patron and forwarded his letter to Mrs. Montagu.[22] Jones thanked Macpherson for the kind attentions to Emin: "Many in England will be equally thankful. He is a fine fellow; and if active service should be required, he would seek nothing so much, as to be placed in the most perilous edge of the battle" (2:700). Emin's colorful life and belief in liberty led Jones to encourage his autobiography, and Jones may have subsidized the *Calcutta Gazette*'s publishing *The Life and Adventures of Joseph Emin, an Armenian; Written in English by Himself* (1792).

Proud of his supposed skill in English, Emin wrote Mrs. Montagu: "My gardian Angel Sir William Jones has been so good as to correct the wrong spelling and faulse English of it. Lady Jones and several Gentlemen have seen it and approved of it." He also told her: "By virtue of indifatigable study of Sr. Wm. Jones & the Arts & Sciences may florish, which have already began to shew a head, & to shine out. He is an honour to his Country! yes he is the glory of it."[23] The poor English demanded Jones's extreme patience and many hours, but his final editorial report to Emin tactfully avoided mentioning his labors on the long manuscript:

I send back the last number of your Narrative with my very hearty thanks for the pleasure which the whole work has given me; it has been highly interesting to me; but, as there is no reasoning on tastes I cannot be sure that it will be thought equally interesting by others; the style remains wholly your own; for I have corrected only those errors in language and orthography, which were unavoidable in an English work written by a native of Hamadan. (2:806–7)

Jones recommended deleting the self-approbation and "the Asiatick style of panegyrick," which Emin loved but which offended English taste. He did not correct the dedication, but Pearse "would not be pleased with it, and I cannot be accessary to any thing that appears even in a questionable shape." He was sorry but not surprised at Emin's failure to transplant an English-style constitution to Armenia. A democracy, though the only natural form of government, could not last: "The lazy, (who are the majority of every estate) must continue poor and weak, while the few who are diligent grow wealthy and powerful, and the chief use of a king is to keep down the pride and imperiousness of the few." A mixed republic, by contrast, was likely to be permanent.

Only Jones and Mrs. Montagu subscribed for as many as five copies of the book. Conceivably Jones's connection with it may have been the reason for Burke's not subscribing, for Burke wrote: "Since that time none of those who governed India, either abroad or at home, have been my particular friends. Some, perhaps, have been ill-disposed towards me."[24]

Jones also encouraged Richard Johnson. Urging publication of Johnson's fine manuscript of Háfiz as "a valuable acquisition to the publick," he was delighted when Johnson began preparing it for the press: "I hope some years hence to offer up a copy of it on the tomb of the divine poet" (2:702). Sometimes Jones copied an impressive Persian couplet and sent it by way of a servant. Johnson, in turn, loyally supported the Asiatic Society, presenting Arabic plates to illustrate Jones's "Dissertation on Orthography." Borrowing Johnson's large copy of Rúmí, Jones rapturously inscribed his own manuscript of the great mystic:

So extraordinary a book as the Mesnavi was never, perhaps, composed by man. It abounds with beauties, and blemishes, equally great; with gross obscenity, and pure ethicks; with exquisite strains of poetry, and flat puerilities; with wit, and pleasantry, mixed with dull jests; with ridicule on all established religions, and a vein of sublime piety: it is like a wild country in a fine climate overspread with rich flowers, and with the odour of beasts. I know of no writer, to whom the Maulavi can justly be compared, except *Chaucer* or *Shakespeare*. (2:735)[25]

Before the Supreme Court recessed and Jones made his annual autumn retreat to Krishnagar, he was instrumental in awarding damages against an attorney, in a relentlessly evenhanded implementation of the law, whether the offender was European or Indian. The *Calcutta Gazette* reported on 20 July: "The judgement gave general satisfaction, and must evince the impartiality of the court in thus discountenancing one of its own officers for having offended, even in so slight a degree, against the laws they are bound to declare."

Yet there was one outrageous decision in an important case. Frederick Deatker, a Danish constable in Calcutta, had broken into George Tyler's house with a search warrant for another man. Not finding the man there, Deatker secured a writ from Hyde charging Tyler and a captain with rescuing his prisoner and assaulting him, although the wanted man had never been at Tyler's. Sepoys marched the falsely charged pair to a jail housing drunken seamen. After William Hickey persuaded Hyde to hear Tyler's servants, who had witnessed everything, Hyde released the pair. Determined to make an example of Deatker, the pair brought separate suits for trespass, assault, and false imprisonment. Deatker's plea of justification argued that he was fulfilling his duty. His brother and three other men swore direct contradictions of Tyler's eyewitnesses, but the lie was so blatant that Chambers threw out their testimony. After the counsel presented their arguments, Chambers asked Jones to speak first.

Jones spoke for two hours in pointed, elegant language. He lamented that custom required the junior judge to deliver his sentiments first, without the opportunity to refine them from Chambers's argument. This was the most outrageous oppression that he had heard of in the British dominions; no one would be safe if such a wretch could range uncontrolled in the guise of a public peace officer. Jones's blood boiled at hearing the facts proved and then at hearing Deatker and four others commit perjury and subornation. Deatker should be made an "example of the consequences of attempting to violate the mild and benign laws of that country he was living under." Jones ruled for the full damages asked by Tyler.

Hyde believed the perjurers, who established a plea of justification; and Chambers ruled similarly in "a long and incoherent rhapsody." When treble costs were awarded to the defendant in both cases, Jones asserted that he could not be silent. In a minority opinion of increased severity, he attacked Deatker's misconduct throughout the affair. All magistrates acting as justices of the peace were liable to a civil action if they acted wrongly; otherwise, Jones would be very uneasy and would not act. He vainly reasserted that both plaintiffs should be awarded the full amount requested in their suits. Later the captain had the sepoys court-martialed; but they were freed on the grounds that they had acted under a superior's order, which, however, must never again cause degrading, improper service. Hickey and his friends were feted and drank Jones's health "three times three." But as the captain soon left India and as Tyler never appealed to a higher court, Deatker's tyranny triumphed.[26]

After the Supreme Court recessed, Jones and Anna discussed the future as their pinnace moved up the Hooghly. The harsh climate determined them to stay in Bengal no longer than 1790. In a letter he cautioned his sister-in-law to keep their decision secret, or applicants would press for his judgeship and possibly shove him out early. If Anna's health compelled her earlier departure, he would "remain like a man with a dead palsy on one of his sides; but it were better to lose one side for a time than both for ever" (2:703). When she recently had had an enfeebling bloody flux, the worst Indian disorder, he had feared for her life. Reflection told him that he might not have survived the terrible loss. Her dysentery had stopped, but her debility was slowing her recovery despite the medicines and special diet. Jones had often mentioned the advisability of her return, although the separation would inexpressibly anguish him. Anna would have £15,000 immediately, and he would join her when the sum was doubled. Her affectionate resolution not to leave gave him keener pain, as it was clear that she would never be well in Bengal.

Jones's systematic nature was disturbed by the hundred unanswered letters that had accumulated since last autumn. The duties of his judgeship and the study of Sanskrit laws permitted him to correspond only once a year. So, while Anna wrote volumes beside him, he started this autumn task. Though consuming many hours, correspondence was part of the eighteenth-century dissemination of ideas. In his "Objects of Enquiry" he had projected writing letters like those of Demosthenes and Plato.

Of Jones's hundreds of known Indian letters, the small number found suggests that he wrote many more that autumn than the ten that have been found. He probably answered most of the hundred. His correspondents are important in their own right; his topics, of intellectual interest. He did not compose a model letter and then copy sections as partial answers; rather, he responded to each individual. To Patrick Russell and William Shipley (the bishop's brother), he reported giving the compositor the first essays for *Asiatick Researches* 1, which would be printed on the East India Company Press when it was not in official use. As accuracy was imperative and as Society members were "men of business, in commerce, revenue, or judicature," the periodical could not proceed rapidly (2:715).

A frequent topic in Jones's letters to those who knew Anna was her health. To those interested in Sanskrit, like Hastings, he reported completing his first long translation. In his Third Discourse he had praised "the most beautiful, if not the most ancient, collection of apologues in the world: they were first translated from the *Sanscrit,* in the *sixth* century . . . and are extant under various names in more than twenty languages; but their original title is *Hitōpadēsa,* or *Amicable Instruction."* His familiarity with Bidpai's French version was one reason he selected these tales for practice in translating.

This first of his four Indian prose versions was a translation of two recensions.[27] Rāmalocana read the originally oral stories aloud to Jones, who imitated the pronunciation and made a literal translation. He was struck by their resemblance to Jesus' teachings in the first forty-three chapters of Ecclesiasticus; the prose-poetry of these four major tales of the *Pañcatantra* was wonderfully useful in his learning Sanskrit. His version was finished in October 1786.

The tales are tied together by an "envelope story": A king asks a philosopher to teach morality to his erring sons. The method is traditional, through fables told by a crow, tiger, or other animal. The moral is often in epigrammatic verse from sacred writing, which Jones conveys in prose. When he must stipulate the form of the maxim and uses phrases like "According to the couplet" or "He heard a person read these couplets," his prose form is jarring.

The fables are dramatic. In "On War," peacocks defeat the geese who confide in crows friendly with the peacocks. The moral is "May you, when you reign, fight not always with elephants, with horsemen, and with infantry! but may your enemies, overthrown by the winds of wise counsels, be driven for protection to the mountains!" After hearing the last fable, the princes understand the perfect system of royal duties, which coincided with Jones's view of such duties.

Continuing his transliterative advances, he usually defines the Sanskrit item in his text:

a raven named *Laghupatanaca* or *light-wing*
. . . .
a prince of pigeons named *Chitragriva,* or *painted-neck*
. . . .
with some *Cusa,* or *holy grass*

Such glosses slow the narrative flow, even as his italics impair the visual effect. Yet the method is superior to his earlier explanations in footnotes or introductions, and he is clearly trying to add Sanskrit words that he considered valuable for the English language.

His literal version is in the rather formal style of the day, with long sentences containing parenthetical matter that convey a biblical, proverbial quality. He maintains verbal fidelity, employing some imaginative phraseology to communicate the vivacity. His diction is choice and vigorous, though his command of Sanskrit was not yet good.[28] Not expecting to publish the version, Jones did not polish it much. Wilkins, who credited himself with first translating the work into English, sent Jones a copy of his 1787 translation, perhaps not knowing about his friend's unpublished version. Jones was sensitive about the matter, later remarking that he had done his translation three years before Wilkins had any thought of doing one. After its posthumous publication in Jones's *Works* (1799), the Orientalist Alexander Hamilton observed that it clears up several of Wilkins's confused passages; yet a literal version cannot convey the humor, vivacity, beauty, and sublime morality of the original. Today an occasional critic ranks Jones's version among the best,[29] but Sir Edwin Arnold's is recognized as better literature.

The rest of Jones's important Krishnagar correspondence of 1786 may be summarized. To Davis, now assistant to the collector and registrar at Bhagalpur, Jones agreed that a tree entirely charred in a rock fissure was curious: "I should rather impute it to some phosphorick or pyrophorick substance, (such as nitrous acid and phlogiston, or perhaps vitriolick acid mixed with a mineral) which took fire as soon as the air was admitted by the perforation of the rock, and formed a real charcoal of the oil and earth of the vegetable" (2:705). This explanation exemplifies a premise in his andrometer: Education can never be complete because it is cumulative. One must master new disciplines that are developed. Jones felt that he had now mastered the only two subjects in encyclopedias that he had not previously understood. Although botany was better suited to the Indian climate than chemistry, it was not more alluring: "Both are the language of God to his creatures in the stupendous volume of nature; and the creator may be named, without impiety, the Almighty Chemist" (2:752). He was reading Macquer's *Elements of the Theory and Practice of Chymistry* (London, 1764) and *Dictionnaire de chymie* (Paris, 1778). In doing Macquer's experiments with acids he burned his fingers, but this new knowledge explained the charring of the tree; scientific principles should operate everywhere.

To Russell, Jones wrote about botany (2:707–8). He longed to see Russell's collections, although he personally preferred to describe fresh plants rather than to study a herbal. He had not begun to collect specimens but just described as well as he could, using Latin for brevity. He had examined many *Pentapetes,* which, according to Koenig, had more filaments than Linnaeus assigned: "I find the description of Linnæus to be correct; but there is no accounting for the variety of a protean plant." Besides truth, a practical value was involved; when immersed in water overnight, one of the local fleshy blossoms formed cooling mucilage and might substitute for Arabian gum.

Because scholarship should be disseminated, Jones urged Russell to publish two recent essays. Thus *To the Honorable Major General Sir A. Campbell* appeared in Madras in 1787. Though he offered to read the proofs if the Bengal government would print the essays, he must have been disappointed when Russell's "Account of the Tabasheer" appeared in *Philosophical Transactions* of 1791, rather than having been submitted to *Asiatick Researches*.

Possibly at Macpherson's suggestion, Jones wrote Charles Boughton-Rouse, secretary of the Board of Control, to whom he had recently sent a calligraphic letter in Persian like his *jeu d'esprit* to Prince Czartoryski (2:727–9). Jones needed the secretary's advice about an objective closely connected with his duties if not the prosperity of British India – "the Administration of Justice among the natives according to their respective systems" (2:720). Because Pitt must be extremely busy (and had not answered Jones's letter about the debtors' prison), he had not written Pitt again. He did not know Henry Dundas, the board's acting director; nor could he write Dundas on a subject that should also be addressed by Chambers and Hyde. Hence he was writing as a friend who had heard Boughton-Rouse eloquently speak in the Commons on the wisdom of the law that gave the Indians the protection of their laws.

As the Indian pundits or *maulvis* generally lacked integrity or could be bribed, Jones always made them produce the book containing the particular Sanskrit law. His improved Arabic and a year's study of Sanskrit now let him check their translations: "Another year will place me on firm ground; but as it cannot be expected that future Judges will take the trouble to learn two difficult languages, I wish much to see compiled and printed a complete Digest of Hindu and Musliman Laws, on the great subjects of *Contracts* and *Inheritances*." Soon he hoped to print his translation of *Al Sirájiyyah*.

During his vacations, unaided, he could do no more than continue translating the *Mānava-Dharmaśāstra*. Assistance might be granted from London: "I could neither ask, nor accept it here. To compile a Digest like that of Tribonian consisting solely of original texts arranged in a scientific method, I must have two Pandits, two Maulavis, and two Writers, one for Sanscrit and one for Arabic." As these should be the most learned men, their monthly cost would total 1,000 sicca rupees. A three-year arrangement would cost 36,000 rupees, excluding printing expenses. Jones would purchase the needed manuscripts that he did not already own, and he would deposit them with the Supreme Court. If the East India Company could assist, he would write Pitt, Dundas, and the directors; except that ancient customs no longer prevailed, he would emulate Bacon and address the king. Jones must not raise any suspicion of patronage for six Indians.

Here he was implementing his idea of involving great Indian pundits and *maulvis* in paid governmental service, as only the Indians could really understood their laws.

Jones praised Ghulám Husain Khan's history *Siyar-ul-Mutakherin*, which he would provide if Boughton-Rouse did not have a copy. Ghulám's *jaghire* let him make his own arrangements for collecting revenue within his jurisdiction during his lifetime, but he deserved a reward for this scholarship. His sons would be left in want unless the property was made an *altamgha-enam*, the equivalent of the rent-free grant that successive Mogul rulers had renewed to the original grantee's descendants.

Jones also informed Boughton-Rouse "that the Judges gave no opinion concerning the legality of General Sloper's Appointment, that they never obtrude their opinions, nor have interfered since I have been here in a single measure of the executive Government; that we were never consulted on that Commission or any other." Jones had not known that its legality had been questioned until he saw an old London newspaper report of Dundas's telling the Commons that the Supreme Court had ruled that two laws cast doubt on Sloper's actions as commander in chief because Sloper's commission had not had the king's sign manual to it. Burke had then criticized the judges' supposedly ruling on the constitution and the appointment; he said that it was highly improper for them to be consulted, for they had nothing to do with politics (echoing Jones's words to Burke) and should not interfere. Jones was upset that such folly should be imputed to him: "The hasty fire which my friend Burke was pleased to scatter against us, as *giving advice* (which we never gave) and perplexing *Government with Cavils* which in truth we never made, I at least disclaim it wholly."

Jones now felt ill will toward Burke, having just prematurely congratulated Hastings for "full triumph over the rancour of your enviers; for such they really are rather than your enemies" (2:717). Hastings's fame should spring up again with luxuriance proportioned to humility. Jones told Hastings that Wilkins's return to England had forced Jones to turn to Sanskrit for a knowledge of Indian jurisprudence at its fountainhead. His study had already helped in an important case, in which the pundits' divergent opinions led him to translate the original tracts and choose the best. He had memorized a pleasing episode in Wilkins's version of the *Bhagavad-Gita* after comparing the entire text with the Sanskrit. The version seemed perfect: "But, as a learner, I could have wished that it had been still more literal, and that the verses had been numbered, and every thing put in the Sanscrit printed in Italicks, like our excellent translation of the Bible."[30]

Jones's letter to William Shipley apologized for his long delay in accepting a corresponding membership in Shipley's Kentish Society for Promoting Useful Knowledge, which was improving the Maidstone jail. This was the first scholarly exchange between Jones's Society and a European one. The Maidstone suggestions about preventing infection might be helpful, although the Indians' habit of sleeping in any available draft reduced the danger of infection. Perhaps Jones's Society could make a discovery that might be useful in England. Shipley had sent a tract describing a method for rescuing drowning persons, which might be useful in India. Thus Jones received accounts of possibly useful scholarship, requesting research on agriculture and mechanical arts, which the Indians neglected.

Jones agreed with Orme that every line of Greek literature was "a gem of exquisite beauty," but that Roman poetry was bright from borrowed rays (2:716). By contrast, Sanskrit and Arabic literature was original, sublime, and beautiful. Even Virgil would appear indifferent in a verbal translation. To appreciate Virgil, one must read the original.

Jones answered Arthur Lee's letter on 1 October, just after receiving it. Peter Elmsly was their intermediary, enclosing Lee's letters in the frequent parcels of books mailed to Jones. John Paradise was not a proper person to forward mail, as Jones explained:

When in 1782, at his earnest solicitation and simply through pity and affection for a helpless creature, I would have accompanied him to America, giving up two circuits and exposing myself to the hazard of losing my judgeship, he took fright at Nantes, and by his mad conduct exposed both himself and me to publick derision. We there separated; and, on his return to London, he told the basest and most contemptible lies, which he had the meanness afterwards to disavow. (2:713)

Uneasy about the American civil disorder preceding the Constitutional Convention, Jones expressed the hope to Lee that the States would become *United* in substance. American commerce and agriculture should so augment its wealth that its difficulties should vanish. He hoped for American trade with India, "but that not being my department, I can take no measures for that purpose." His principles were unchanged; he still wished for universal liberty for all peoples, of which the Indians were currently incapable: "Few of them have an idea of it; and those, who have, do not wish it. They must (I deplore the evil, but know the necessity of it) they must be ruled by an absolute power." This was not a lingering Western bias, but simply a practical realization of the state of contemporary Indian political capacities.

Jones's scholarly correspondence left little time for writing to Spencer in the old instructional vein. He did pen two letters about his finances, sending the original and two copies of a bill on the East India Company for £590 by separate ships, as only one out of three letters ever reached

England. In the unlikely event that the directors would not accept the bill, his lawyer William Hamilton should charge the Bengal Presidency with the expenses of protest and reexchange. Spencer should deduct his own expenses and spend £100 on silver for University College, paying Jones's debts to the Royal Society and the Society of Antiquaries if any money remained. Jones enclosed a copy of Charles Croftes's bond for £5,000, which Richard Johnson was guaranteeing since Croftes's death.

Jones had earlier sent Spencer his "Ethick Epistle." Now he added three couplets:

> Before thy mystick altars, heav'nly Truth,
> He kneels in manhood, as he knelt in youth:
> Thus let him kneel, till this dull form decays,
> And life's last shade be brightened by thy blaze.
> Then shall his soul, now lost in clouds below,
> Soar unconfin'd, and unconsuming flow.

Inspired by Isaac Barrow's eighth sermon, he copied the couplets, titled "The Concluding Sentence of Berkeley's *Siris,* Imitated,"[31] in his copy of *Siris,* as his thoughts upon ending his fortieth year.

About the time that Jones had reached Krishnagar, Cornwallis had arrived in Calcutta. Jones quickly sent a note congratulating the new Governor-General and India on the appointment. Anna's recent illness kept him from paying his respects in person, but he promised to hasten to Calcutta in October to do so. Cornwallis wrote on the note: "Recd. Sept. 23. Ansd. Sept. 23." Jones was to provide more help to this executive than to any other.

Meanwhile, Macpherson was unhappy at being replaced, though he had made no effort to eliminate the corruption among East India Company servants. He secured legal opinions to the effect that only the king could remove him. He even appealed on the basis that Cornwallis's appointment had injured him, but his final effort was rejected. Jones gracefully complimented Macpherson's governmental thrift: "Magnum vectigal est parsimonia, is an aphorism which I learned early from Cicero. The public, if they are grateful, must wish that you had attended as vigilantly to your own vectigal, as you have wisely and successfully to theirs" (2:727).

Jones thanked Macpherson for releasing and transmitting Samuel Turner's governmental report on a lama's inauguration, which he read to the Society on 2 November. This was only the third meeting of 1786. Five weeks later, twelve members heard a missionary's paper on borax, after which there was another month's gap. Because of Jones's long absences, Wilkins's departure, and the other members' general lack of interest, only four meetings were held in 1786.[32]

By rising at dawn, Jones was able to continue his Sanskrit scholarship. Then he could spend an hour on Sanskrit daily; this sister of Latin and Greek charmed him. During the term his principal writing was the examination of witnesses or notes of arguments, when he and a colleague were on the bench for at least five hours, with another two hours in chambers. He knew that if he did not protect his health after such strain, he would soon die, like so many Europeans in Calcutta before him.

In November the Supreme Court spent a day in hearing an East India Company officer's complaint about ill treatment during his confinement for debt. Jones agreed with his colleagues that the officer deserved to be put in irons because he was trying to start a mutiny, and they reprimanded him.[33]

An important case was the King *v.* Collipersaud Ghose, who was tried under 2 George II. c. 25, s. 2 for stealing a treasury order. This statute placed such theft on the same footing as that of chattels of like value. In a trial lasting until 1:00 A.M. on Christmas Eve, Chambers ruled that the statute did not extend to Calcutta. Hyde disagreed and Jones doubted. Ghose's conviction paralleled Nanda Kumar's, which had caused Impey's recall; however, Ghose was only "burnt in the hand" and imprisoned for two years.[34]

A continual strain on Jones was the health of Anna, who kept him informed even when he was in court, as in a note: "I am up & feel easy & comfortable much is the effect of the Laudenum I know; but let us enjoy the blessing while it lasts" (2:726). The next day she needed an opiate; and he summoned Francis Balfour, John Fleming, and Nicholas Fontana – the three most learned, experienced doctors in the country. The next night they returned. Balfour gave her artificial Spa-water, which soon took effect. They kept "her body constantly open. She is naturally of a contrary habit, and this creates a difficulty; but, while they keep up a continual discharge of whatever is collected in the bowels, they are sure of keeping off a fever, which alone I dread. I rely on God; and pray to him incessantly" (2:726). She regained her appetite, and they thought that she would soon be completely well; still, they advised a colder climate. She forbade their mentioning that subject again.

In the moments free from worry, Jones discussed chemistry with the three doctors. He had lent a tract to Fontana, the author of *Observations on the Diseases to Which Europeans Are Subject in Warm Climates* (Leghorn, 1781). They suggested that he procure Fourcroy's *Elémens d'histoire naturelle et de chimie* (Paris, 1786), Llandaff's five-volume *Chemical Essays* (Cambridge, 1781–7), and Bergman's *Physical and Chemical Essays* (London, 1784) from Elmsly. Thus these four Society members inspired one another in their study of chemistry.

Only eighteen members heard Jones's Fourth Discourse on 15 February 1787, the smallest attendance at any of his anniversary papers. Jones's association with Cornwallis was bearing fruit; he attended, as did Shore, who had returned to sit on the Supreme Council and preside over the Board of Revenue.

Jones's admittedly cursory observations in the Third Discourse erroneously hypothesize the Hindus' immemorial affinity with the old Persians, Ethiopians, Egyptians, Phoenicians, Greeks, Tuscans, Scythians, Celts, Chinese, and Japanese. In the Fourth Discourse he treats pre-Islamic Arabia, using data gathered for his never-finished *Mu'allaqát* essay. His languages section partly derives from his comparison of Sanskrit, Greek, Persian, and German, which, he says, delight in compounds and bilateral verb roots. The four differ lexically and grammatically from Arabic, which had a common origin with Hebrew and Chaldean. This fundamental postulate for the Semitic family expands Jones's innovational "family" concept to fit non-Indo-European languages. He argues simplistically: The Arab intelligentsia prior to the Islamic revolution were theists, and the lower classes were stupid idolaters. The only pre-Islamic philosophy that he has discovered is ethics, which was depraved for a century before Muhammad. The arts were poetry and rhetoric until the Arabs burst over the whole area with military genius. Jones ends by reporting the printing of the first sheets of *Asiatick Researches* 1: "If the learned in *Europe* have not raised their expectations too high, they will not, I believe, be disappointed: my own imperfect essays I always except."

He held six more Society meetings before his annual Krishnagar sojourn; the attendance averaged twelve. At the first two there were papers on alkali and distilling. Carnac had sent six ancient plates inscribed with Sanskrit, which Jones translated for the 29 March meeting. This was "An Indian Grant of Land in Y.C. 1018," the first of his three epigraphic translations. Edmund Morris, who became a superintendent of the Company Press, was nominated on 12 April, with Jones seconding the nomination.

On 4 May he read "On the Literature of the Hindus," his translation of a Sanskrit paper communicated by Govardhana, to which he had added a long commentary. Jones shows fine appreciation of the variety and richness of Sanskrit writings, but does not mention his difficulty in securing the complete Vedas, which he needed for preparing the commentary. Anthony Polier, now at Lucknow, had needed a raja's permission to get the four books, traditionally said to have been composed by Vyāṣa. A cursory inspection told Jones that "even a learner of *Sanscrit* may read a considerable part of the At'harvavēda without a dictionary; but that the style of the other *three* is so obsolete, as to seem almost a different dialect."

Govardhana's paper discusses true knowledge in Hindu sacred literature, Hindu law, Buddha's writings, and six atheistic philosophies. Jones describes the Vedas, transliterates a passage into the Jonesian System, and praises the *Ramayana* and the *Mahābhārata*. Though not naming any secular literature, he mentions "the *Nātaca*, which answers to the *Gāndharvavēda*, consisting of regular *Dramatick* pieces in *Sanscrit* and *Prācrit*." Tantalizingly he compares Indian and Greek philosophers – Gautama with Aristotle, Jaimini with Socrates, and Vyāṣa with Plato – noting that a comprehensive comparison would require a volume. After outlining Hindu law and language scholarship, Jones nationalistically urges the British to provide an accurate knowledge of Sanskrit and its valuable works. Here is the first good example of the kind of cultural encounter that he was seeking for the Society: An Indian scholar provided basic Indian knowledge, and a European related it to European knowledge, with mutual enrichment.

Two months later Reuben Burrow read two essays on mechanics. The *Calcutta Gazette* of 12 July praises their many useful and original propositions. Jones informed the Society of the proposal by Morris and John Herbert Harington (the secretary) to publish *Asiatick Researches* at the Company Press at their risk, with any profits to accrue to them. The members asked him to conclude the agreement.

Some of his most scholarly local correspondents were Society members. Polier has been mentioned; Johnson and Shore were now Jones's chief fellow appreciators of Oriental culture, a quality that he wished to extend. Shore lent two copies of the *Dabistan,* an Indian treatise on twelve religions that Jones read twice and that misled him about Persian history and languages: "It contains more recondite learning, more entertaining history, more beautiful specimens of poetry, more ingenuity and wit, more indecency and blasphemy, than I ever saw collected in a single volume. . . . On the whole, it is the most amusing and instructive book I ever read in Persian" (2:739).

Shore provided access to an intriguing work by Rādhākānta Sarman, a revered Brahman about eighty-four years old who was his pundit. This explanation of the *Purāṇas* contained lists of Indian kings from the earliest times, but the proper names were "so murdered, or so strangely disguised in Persian letters" that Jones was tantalizingly mystified (2:735). He had his writer make a copy, leaving every other line blank, so that he might interpolate a literal English translation. He enjoyed speaking Sanskrit with Rādhākānta but was less effective than with Rāmalocana, with whom he used it continually. Jones was now so fluent that Indian lawyers could never impose an erroneous opinion on him.

Although he did not make the official translation of Bodawpayā's conciliatory letter to the English, he read it minutely for Shore. The Burmese king, who seemed to be an ambitious dog but would act like a lion if permitted, was proposing a commercial treaty, with self-praise and justification of his own ruthlessness. Jones advised Shore: "We may be gainers by his gold and ivory; but I have no inclination to taste his sweet and delicious petroleum, which he praises so highly" (2:736).[35]

Shore was one of the few local friends with whom Jones talked politics. He had kept his word of ruling by the law. The news about politics in England made him rejoice that he was in Asia; those with whom he had spent some of his happiest hours and hoped to spend many more on his return home seemed to be trying to tear one another to pieces. He could only wish that right and justice would prevail, while he discharged his duties and then relaxed with Sanskrit literature. The pair also shared personal feelings. Jones cheered up Shore when he desponded about having left his new bride in Europe, in order to return to a deplorable revenue system and an antagonistic Macpherson. When Shore was ill, Jones recommended a musical prescription of Italian composers.

Pearse, another of Jones's correspondents, sent Burrow's observations on Hindu astronomy. Jones gracefully suggested that Burrow string his loose pearls into an essay. As he claimed an astronomical idea that had been earlier published by Le Gentil, the essay needed a footnote reference. *Asiatick Researches* required scholarly quality and documentation:

I wish we could prevail on him to omit his Theology: that Moses wrote any of the psalms, may be true; but ought not to be roundly asserted without proof; and that Jesus was ever in India would be still harder to prove. Besides, many pious Christians deny, that the doctrine of the Trinity is to be found in the Gospel. Let that be as it may, the question seems unconnected with Astronomy. (2:738)

Jones did not want to discourage Pearse. That loyal attendee had read a paper to the Society, besides contributing a meteorological journal and astronomical observations to the forthcoming first volume.

Another scholarly correspondent was John Henry Cox, whose ship traded directly between Canton and America. He had lent Jones a curious Chinese text and was trying to arrange for a translation of the *Shih Ching*. Because the Chinese, unlike the Brahmans, did not keep their ancient literature a mystery, Jones suggested that a mandarin might dictate a literal version to an interpreter, who could transcribe it in a European language.

Jones would grudge no expense. Whang Atong had sent the original text, a translation of which was still Jones's great, never-fulfilled objective.

In March 1787 the Supreme Court issued a writ of habeas corpus to an English magistrate to produce an Indian and explain the imprisonment. The magistrate scribbled "not in custody" on the writ. Chambers and Hyde wanted to give him until noon the next day to comply, but Jones opposed delay: "*Habeas Corpus* was the most *remedial* procedure known in our law, and ought not to be defeated or even evaded in the smallest degree."[36] After a writ of attachment was issued, the magistrate delayed the permitted twenty-four hours before appearing with the Indian, who was instantly discharged. Thus the law operated, but more slowly than Jones wished.

His third charge to the grand jury was an "eloquent speech, replete with humanity and sound sense," conveying "elegance, perspicuity, and legal knowledge."[37] The necessary brevity permitted him to elaborate only on the "grievous offences" on the court calendar. Thus murder is the most atrocious crime by a rational member of civil society: As a peasant woman had seen three soldiers stab her husband, the jury must uphold English honor. Jones recommends the serious treatment of even petty complaints, just as the crushing of baby serpents protects against their later venom. The jury must prevent "offences against good morals and good order, which spring from the dissolute manners of the populace, and branch out into all the disorders and evils" that can affect humankind. Until there is an ordinance against "stupefying drugs, which are easily procured from the fields" and afford cheap gratification, the jury is the Indians' protection. Dives and brothels are indictable as public nuisances. Lacking a good police system, Calcutta is afflicted with robbery. Also, some educated Indians commit perjury, which greatly complicates the discharge of public duty. Until Jones can discover a more binding Hindu oath, there must be exemplary punishment of perjury and subornation.

Interweaving suggestions for reform, Jones laments that the jury meets only twice a year. The guilty and the innocent thus suffer up to six months' imprisonment, a condition inconsistent with benign law. The jails must maintain justice, without exactions and cruelty. England must "never be justly reproached for inhumanity; nor the severest of misfortunes, loss of liberty, be heightened under our government." Here again was an injunction that colonial European jurors were not accustomed to hearing.

The importance of the oath was soon manifested in a case of a European who had murdered an Indian. Requesting a more solemn form of oath to prevent perjury, the prisoner's advocate recommended Jones's mode from the recent charge – the use of sacred fire or the presence of the idol. Jones responded that he had not proposed these with certainty, but only suggested that they would be more binding: "It was impossible to go further, as there was no *certainty* respecting it."[38] Chambers agreed, for different sects would require different oaths because of the varied idols worshiped.

After the case Jones went home to Garden Reach, where he always slept and where the couple kept herds and flocks. His schedule was rigorous. Rising before 4:00 A.M. during the term, he walked the five miles to Fort William before taking a palanquin to the courthouse. Bathing and breakfast took an hour, and at seven he read Sanskrit with Rāmalocana. Then an hour was spent in reading with an Arab one day and with a Persian the next, except on Saturday, when he corresponded with Moslem scholars. After the attorneys arrived at 9:00, he sat on the bench for five hours. At 3:00 he dined with friends and conversed until nearly sunset, when he and Anna returned home. After tea they read; he usually read Italian aloud until they retired at ten. For four months a year, his duty as justice of the peace took three evenings a week.

During vacation, at Garden Reach in the summer or at Krishnagar in the autumn, Jones slept later. After his bath and coffee, he read Sanskrit. At about 11:00 he read English or Italian to Anna for an hour, with theology on Sunday. Then he pursued the day's tasks until dinner. At sunset he walked two or three miles, accompanied by Anna in a sedan chair. Their evening was spent in reading.

The conservative couple seldom gave parties. One of Parr's friends described dinner with them. Jones wore white Indian dress. Cheerful and agreeable, in a fine voice he called, "Othello," whereupon a large turtle crawled to his chair and was fed. He said that he would free it except that it was safer with him than in the Ganges.[39] Nor did the couple participate in the gala activities in Calcutta. For example, a large crowd attended the Governor-General's New Year's party in 1788. After a midnight dinner, dancing continued until 4:00 A.M., while the devotees of the god of wine paid their allegiance. The Joneses' names are conspicuously absent from the list of prominent people there.

Jones always attended the Society meetings, which were nonsocial. As dinner was not served, he may have emulated Banks by starting a select dining club on Thursday, the meeting night. His notebook lists fourteen names entitled "Club." The order of the familiar ones is interesting – Henry Vansittart, Johnson, Wilkins, Gladwin, Burrow, Shore, William Chambers, Chapman, Croftes, Harington, and Law. Jones did not include his fellow judges. The *Calcutta Gazette* of 18 August 1785 might have been referring to this club in announcing the establishment of an India Club in London under the Asiatic Society's denomination, designed to promote fellowship and tend to the East India Company's interests: "a similar Club is to be formed in Calcutta, with a view to the cultivation of a mutual intercourse."

When a large assemblage consecrated the Church of St. John on 28 June 1787, Jones did not even attend that Sunday. Hyde, who also had not contributed to the construction, and Chambers were there, as well as Cornwallis. Unconcerned about such appearances and public religion, Jones went to church only on Christmas Day, though he was privately pious. Implicit in his andrometer is a religious superstructure superseding everything; "preparation for eternity" was the culmination, the most severely predetermined goal of his life. As he told Davis just before his death, his Christian belief was a reasoned decision based on "the fulfilment of the prophecies."[40] It had a philosophical, humanistic element. In Jones's Eighth Discourse he criticizes religions produced by ignorance and supported by fraud. By contrast, the Bible contains, "independently of a divine origin, more true sublimity, more exquisite beauty, purer morality, more important history, and finer strains both of poetry and eloquence, than could be collected within the same compass from all other books, that were ever composed." He copied these lines in his Bible, prefaced by the comment that he regularly and attentively read the Scriptures. He stresses their antiquity: "The unstrained application of them to events long subsequent to their publication is a solid ground of belief, that they were genuine predictions, and consequently inspired." Yet his Eighth Discourse rejects proselytizing: Because religious belief is each person's absolute property, Jones would never obtrude his belief on free minds. The note in his Bible was often reprinted in articles praising the Christianity of learned people.[41]

Jones's surviving prayers are intensely pious, as in one that he composed upon awakening at sea in July 1783: "Graciously accept our thanks, thou Giver of all Good, for having preserved us another night, and bestowed on us another day. O, grant that on this day, we may meditate on thy law with joyful veneration, and keep it in all our actions, with firm obedience." A later one is more intellectual: "Father and God of Mercy give me Wisdom, the assistant of thy seats: send her from thy holy heavens, from the seat of thy greatness; that she may be present with me, and labour with me, and teach me what is acceptable to Thee!"[42]

Jones's scholarship strengthened the intellectual underpinnings of his religion. Thus his botanical study discovered a more exquisite lecture in every flower and berry than any theologian could write: "The sublime doctrine of final causes is no where so beautifully proved and illustrated as in the plants of the lakes and forests, when their different parts and the uses of them are minutely and attentively observed" (2:902). Jones was not cynical about theologians, for sermons and other religious works formed a valuable part of his library. Barrow, who impressed Jones as perhaps the most impressive theologian partly because of his profound learning, might have been "the sublimest mathematician, if his religious turn of mind had not made him the deepest theologian of his age."[43]

Some of Jones's minor poems show a spiritual element. One was inspired by Barrow:

> As meadows parched, brown groves, and withering flowers,
> Imbibe the sparkling dew and genial showers;
> As chill dark air inhales the morning beam;
> As thirsty harts enjoy the gelid stream;
> Thus to man's grateful soul from heaven descend,
> The mercies of his Father, Lord, and Friend!

Another derived from Coke's translation from the Latin, which Jones redid:

> Six hours to law, to soothing slumber seven,
> Ten to the world allot, and *all* to Heaven.[44]

His letters often mention his prayers for Anna, for he felt constant anxiety about her precarious health. If she were well, he would be the happiest man alive: "I am united by mutual affection to the most angelic of women."[45] If she remained generally well and did not have to precede him to Europe, his life would be complete. They were ideally happy, as she shared his interests and enthusiasms.[46] After a severe seasoning, his own health was restored.

Their savings were gratifying. He had remitted East India Company bills for £5,911, and in July 1787 he sent bills for five months' salary of £2,950. As Johnson had paid the £5,000 on the bond, Jones expected to send another £4,000 soon, remitting all his government bills on the directors. Company bills were now the only safe means, and he had to hold £5,400 in company bonds. William Hamilton's latest statement showed savings of £16,000 to date, after paying Jones's debts. In four years Jones hoped to double that sum, after which he would consider resigning. If he did not have £30,000 by then, he might remain in his Indian exile, for he would not live in England without perfect independence.

As he left for Krishnagar to begin reading the *Śakuntalā*, the most important book of his career, he was pleased. A fine tribute was then being serialized by *European Magazine* in the July, September, and October 1787 issues. Jones is praised beyond almost any contemporary:

The man of whom all this and much more might be said, is now only in the bloom of manhood; possessed of integrity unimpeached, and of manners the most attracting; in his judicial capacity, the glory of the British name in India; and as a scholar, still indefatigable in those pursuits, which render him at once the patron and example of the poet, the philosopher, and the critic. (p. 5)

The public was certifying Jones's successful amalgamation of Oriental scholarship and juridical duties, though his modesty made him relatively oblivious of his great reputation.

The couple reached Krishnagar about 4 August. Intending to remain two months, Jones enjoyed his stay so much that he extended it. One joy was their cottage, which he purchased, together with acres of meadow and gardens:

How preferable is this pastoral mansion, (though built entirely of *vegetable* substances; without glass, mortar, metal, or any mineral but iron nails from its roof to its foundation) to the marble palaces, which you have seen in *Italy!* It is a thatched cottage with an upper story, and a covered *verone,* or *veranda,* as they call it here, all round it, well-boarded and ten or twelve feet broad; it stands on a dry plain, where *many a garden flower grows wild.* (2:743)[1]

He began his annual correspondence. His duties consumed the other nine months, when, though rising before sunrise, he had no time for writing letters, not even on Sunday, which Anna used for that purpose. Pritchard had once assisted, but he was wasting away from consumption. At Krishnagar, Jones decided to write Spencer one page a morning, a goal that he pursued into September. Anna's generally good health sometimes permitted her to copy his page, increasing the chance that one of the two pages would reach England, but he had no time to make copies of his fifty necessary letters.

Two were to Samuel Parr and John Wilmot. Parr had recommended a senior merchant and two barristers, whom Jones had treated courteously but could not advance because the Supreme Court had nothing to give that a barrister in good business could accept. Wilmot had recommended a well-qualified Calcutta attorney, who later received Jones's clerkship upon Pritchard's death. Jones avoided discussing politics with Wilmot, who disagreed with his view of "the great principles of government and legislation, the majesty of the whole nation collectively, and the consistency of popular rights with legal prerogative" (2:781–2).

Having received a long letter from Hastings, Jones was restrained on that subject to Spencer, considering it a crime to bias a judge. Anyway, he did not know the legal evidence for the charges. When Caldecott sent

271

Sheridan's long speech conveying the fourth charge for maltreating Oudh, Jones did not read it, because for sixteen years he had required evidence for all assertions: "I have no leisure to examine proofs in a business so foreign to my pursuits. . . . If Hastings and Impey are guilty, in God's name let them be punished; but let them not be condemned without legal evidence" (2:778).

Jones urged Spencer to practice street fighting to defend liberty; thus he reexpressed trust in militias. Properly, politics was the "exercise of talents, which, if no accident destroy their effect, will render a nation, if corrupt, virtuous; if poor, wealthy; if weak, powerful; if despised, formidable; if ignorant, wise" (2:748). Instead of remaining aloof from the bitter Whig strife, Jones would not have chosen Spencer's calm course if in Parliament, despite the hostility to political knight-errantry. In his opinion Bengal had a just government under Cornwallis and Shore, who were popular and had the best intentions. Shore had "every talent that a man in his station ought to possess, together with accurate knowledge of the revenues" (2:746). Jones was always independent, not requesting patronage even for those who deserved it, because the public might think that he would repay it with a biased ruling.

Spencer was chiefly aiding Jones by receiving his East India Company bills and investing in a fund or other good security. Jones was barred from honorable trading in diamonds and silk and prohibited from exporting gold. He was transmitting every other monthly bill. Thus he was excited when he heard that the director's decision about the method of salary payment had arrived in Calcutta, for, if the company bills were not to be honored in London, he would encounter much delay in remitting his savings. The new arrangement extended the term for compensating bondholders and decreed 5 percent interest to be paid in installments beginning in ten years. Because he had purchased his bonds at a discount and thought the company's credit was as good as that of the public funds, he accepted the poor terms. He transmitted his July and August bills, planning to send £5,000 soon. With luck he could have £30,000 in four more years.

Though Jones's desire for independence was a major reason for his decision to remain in India for ten more years, he did not esteem money, having modest tastes and interests. Mere money would not compensate for a situation that he disliked; actually, he loved India, enjoying fluent conversation with sages' descendants in their ancient language. They were astonished by his progress, not knowing how much the affinity with Greek and Latin helped him. Their children copied his Sanskrit verses. One signified that "as the thirsty antelope runs to a pool of sweet water, so I *thirsted* for all kinds of knowledge, which was sweet as nectar." The raja copied it, his son memorized it, and his Brahmans entered it in the poetic records. Then a Brahman challenged Jones's use of *triṣṇā,* arguing that it meant "thirsty for water," not for learning. Replying that Jones was a poet and consequently inspired, Rāmalocana produced an authority proving that the word could mean "any ardent desire." The raja and the Brahmans thereupon called Jones a *kshatriya,* and he was welcomed at the university, where he conversed familiarly with the Brahmans.

Determined to know Sanskrit perfectly, he studied it the most elaborately of the numerous languages that he had mastered. Of the several Sanskrit dictionaries that he had collected, the best was more than eighteen centuries old and arranged somewhat like Comenius: "I have employed a Brahman and a Bengal boy, who understands English, to translate the Sanscrit vocabulary; and they have already brought me ten thousand *words;* but *things* are my great object; since it is my ambition to know *India* better than any other European ever knew it" (2:751). Jones had always preferred classical languages rather than their vernacular form, and the study of Sanskrit law continued his long love of comparative law.

The Brahmans' recognition and appreciation of his fluency do not explain his devotion to Sanskrit, for he did not pursue scholarship to gain approval. His study had discovered "half a million of Stanzas on sacred history & literature, Epick and Lyrick poems innumerable, and (what is wonderful) Tragedies and Comedies not to be counted, above 2000 years old, besides works on Law (my great object), and Medicine, on Theology, on Arithmetick, on Ethicks, and so on to infinity" (2:747). The non-Brahman Indians did not know this treasure from an Indian court that was formerly one of the most brilliant in the world and that was their heritage:

Suppose Greek literature to be known in modern Greece only, and there to be in the hands of priests and philosophers; and suppose them to be still worshippers of Jupiter and Apollo: suppose Greece to have been conquered successively by Goths, Huns, Vandals, Tartars, and lastly by the English; then suppose a court of judicature to be established by the British parliament, at Athens, and an inquisitive Englishman to be one of the judges; suppose him to learn Greek there, which none of his countrymen knew, and to read Homer, Pindar, Plato, which no other European had even heard of. Such am I in this country. (2:755–6)

The preface to Jones's *Sacontalā* (the title of his translation of the *Śakuntalā*) summarizes his major discovery. In England he had found a reference in the missionaries' *Lettres édifiantes et curieuses* (Paris, 1717–76) to "many books, called Nātac, which, as the Brāhmens assert, contain a large portion of ancient history without any mixture of fable." In Bengal he sought these books. The Brahmans corrected some of his misinformation but provided no real insight. Abounding in fables, *natakas* were supposedly "extremely popular works, and consisted of conversations in prose and verse, held before ancient Rajas in their publick assemblies, on an infinite variety of subjects, and in various dialects." Apparently they were moral or literary dialogues; Europeans believed that they were discourses on dancing, music, or poetry. At length Rādhākānta surprisingly observed that *natakas* were publicly staged in Calcutta during the cold season, similar to what the English called *plays*. When Jones inquired as to the most universally esteemed, Rādhākānta "answered without hesitation, Sacontalā, supporting his opinion, as usual among the Pandits, by a couplet."

Jones took a supposedly correct copy to Krishnagar in 1787. Assisted by Rāmalocana, he started translating it into Latin, "which bears so great a resemblance to Sanscrit, that it is more convenient than any modern language for a scrupulous interlineary version." He communicated his excitement to Spencer at reading a patently major work of world literature by Kālidāsa,

the Indian Shakespeare, or Metastasio, who was the chief poet at the court of Vicramāditya near two thousand years ago. The dramatick piece, which is neither Tragedy nor Comedy, but like many of Shakespeare's fairy-pieces, is called *Sacontalā,* and the story is this.

A pious man, whose name was Viswamitra, or Universal Friend, had by his devotion attained such power over all nature, that Indra, the God of the Firmament, began to fear, lest his own dominion might be in danger, and to check the ambition of the Saint, commanded an *Apsara,* or Celestial Nymph, to descend from heaven and seduce the hermit from his vows of Chastity. She – What she did, you shall hear to-morrow morning, *si je ne dors pas. Adieu!*

5 Sept. She – (for the Saint had the weakness of other mortals) overpowered his austerity, and was delivered of a lovely daughter who was named Sacontalā. The child, being born on earth, was necessarily to go through life before she could be admitted into Swerga, or the heaven of Indra; to which her mother ascended, having intrusted her to the care of another holy man, whose name was *Canna.* After she had received a divine education, she was seen in a forest by Raja *Dushmanta,* when he was hunting, and her beauty inflamed him with such passion, that he married her. Soon after the nuptials a Brāhman, named *Durbāsa,* visited the king, who being in a very thoughtful mood on account of some publick business, took no notice of him; which disrespect so provoked the *Brāhman,* that he pronounced this imprecation against *Dushmanta:* "May she whom thou lovest best forget thee, and not recollect thee till she has seen the ring on thy finger." *Dushmanta,* not attending to him, or disregarding the curse, went, as it was his custom every morning, to bathe in a sacred pool called *Sasitirt'ha* or the *Moon's Pilgrimage,* and, sprinkling his head with the water – but, as it is noon, you shall know what he did to-morrow, "if the Sultan allow me to live another day." Farewell!

6 Sept. He dropped his ring, which had his name on the gem, and which he had shown to Sacontalā, when he first saw her, to convince her that he was the Raja; but he did not perceive his loss, and, on his return to the palace, he went to the apartment of the Queen, who expressed great displeasure at the intrusion of a

perfect stranger. He was astonished at her reception of him, and more so, whe she denied, that she had ever seen him before. He was going to ask her, if she haa forgotten the ring, which he showed her in the forest, but found with amazement, that it was not on his finger. This made him suspect that she was a Sorceress, and a harlot; but he only ordered her to be confined in the interior part of the palace, with a few maids to attend her. The order was no sooner obeyed, than her mother, the nymph, prevailed upon Indra to raise a violent storm of thunder, in which Sacontalā vanished from the palace; and the king hearing of her supernatural escape, was confirmed in his opinion that she was an enchantress. But – Farewell!

7 Sept. A fisher in the pool of *Sasitirt'ha* caught a large Ro'hitamatsya (which, by the way, is one of four most delicate fish in this country) and, on opening it, found a ring; which, being very poor, he carried for sale to a publick market. He first offered it to a servant of the king's household; who, seeing the name of Dushmanta on a fine gem, carried it, with the fisher, to the first Minister. The *Vazir,* or *Amātya* (which is the Sanscrit name for Prime Minister) perceived that the ring had a fishy smell, and, having heard the testimony of persons who saw the fish opened, dismissed the man with a reward, and informed the Raja of it; who put the ring on his finger again, and so sincerely repented of his behavior to *Sacontalā,* that he retired to a forest, & led the life of a hermit; leaving his Amātya to manage the affairs of Government. One day, as Dushmanta was wandering near the extremity of the forest, he saw a beautiful little boy playing with a young lion, and – Who he was You will know, if you are patient. Farewell. . . .

9 Sept. *Dushmanta* was surprized at the sight, and put some questions to the child, who gave him ingenuous & pertinent answers; but, when the Raja said, that he was a stranger in that forest, the boy, who had been instructed in the laws of hospitality, invited him to take refreshment in his mother's house. The king accompanied him, and – but I must break off. (2:766–8)

Jones never concluded this summary of the plot, even though he was near the end. He may have finished his Latin version of the play that autumn.

His initial dedication to Sanskrit is explained by its connection with the needed digest of inheritances and contracts. Fluency in Sanskrit and Arabic would enable him to perform better juridical service. The Hindus considered their laws to be sacred. Justice and policy required the use of their laws in governing, and the improvement of justice made Hindus happier. Jones's personal rule was to acquire some new knowledge of human beings or nature daily: "Instead of carrying my knowledge to market, I will publish all my new works here for the effectual relief of the Insolvent Debtors in our prison" (2:756). Like Trajan, he did not want a single day to pass unless he relieved someone's distress. For that reason, he had analyzed Bacon's knowledge supposedly attainable by humans, in order to determine the parts he had attained, those he wished to attain, and those not worth attaining.

Jones's deepening knowledge of Sanskrit was increasingly drawing on works lacking legal applications. Part of his fascination with Hinduism came from such religious information, a by-product of which was his nine hymns.

One study flowed into another. Thus Kālidāsa's allusion to *svarga* led Jones to a new investigation: "They believe, all souls advance from birth to birth, rising and falling, till they are free from any taint of evil, and then ascend above Swerga to the heaven of heavens, where they are absorbed in the divine nature, from which, as from a fountain, they had originally flowed" (2:765–6). This concept seemed "incomparably more rational, more pious, and more likely to deter men from vice" than the Christians' endless punishment. If Jones were a missionary in India, he would not teach Christianity as the religion of the Messiah, which the Koran disputed, though Hindus would have less difficulty in accepting the Thirty-nine Articles. Rather, he would prove Isaiah's antiquity, then show "the conformity of his prophecy with the life and death of Jesus, and of no other man recorded by History" (2:758).

In September 1787 Jones's appreciation of Hinduism led him to incorporate the Hindu pantheon into his dusty plan for "Britain Discovered." This projection of an Anglo-Indian *Aeneid* revived his fascination with the epic tradition. Discarding most of the action once planned for classical deities, he has Siva convene the divinities to oppose Britan's founding of Albion, "a wonderful nation, who will possess themselves of her [India's] banks, profane her waters, mock the temples of the *Indian* divinities, appropriate the wealth of their adorers, introduce new laws, a new religion, a new government, insult the *Brāhmens,* and disregard the sacred ordinances of *Brihmā.*" Britan (royalty) founds Albion in accord with legend, marrying Albina (liberty) as united in the English constitution, but Jones has the attending druid recommend "the government of the *Indians* by their own laws."

This was Jones's last work on the epic. It was not related to the law digest, and he drafted only four stanzas and the prose Arguments of the twelve books. It was "perhaps the last attempt to embody that dream of the men of the Renaissance, the new Iliad or Aeneid reborn in a modern vernacular tongue, the 'national epic' which was to teach both patriotism and morality."[2] In a sense, the druid's recommending a government according to Indian laws was Jones's anticipatory answer to the later imperialism of Macaulay and others. Had he not died early, he might have devoted his retirement to a fine epic, as he had the requisite knowledge and probably the literary talent. As the *Southern Literary Messenger* observed, "We cannot see why the adventures of the Tyrian Prince might not have been as well wrought up as those of Ulysses, Æneas, Godfrey, or Vasco da Gama."[3] Hindu acceptance is problematic, for Jones was planning "a curious medley of classical, medieval, and Hindu mythological characters and situations" in a classical mold.[4] He solicited suggestions for his plan, stating that he would finish the epic if he lived. His only inflexible decision was to use blank verse, rejecting heroic couplets in keeping with the movement away from neoclassicism.[5]

Music, which Hindus considered an art practiced in heaven before being revealed to humankind, was the second of Jones's Sanskrit studies unrelated to the digest. It had flourished in Vikramāditya's reign, but had so declined since the Moguls that it was now almost lost in Bengal. Jones wrote an essay on Hindu music, which he later combined with his study on Persian music. Polier had procured Somanātha's *Ragavibodha* and let Jones's writer copy it. Jones was collating this book of beautiful verse, which seemed concise and obscure but might suggest improvements for European music. He hoped to summarize it as soon as *Asiatick Researches* 1 was printed.

Except for his correspondence, the digest, and the *Śakuntalā,* his major work that autumn was botany. Having collected the Sanskrit names of a thousand plants, he was dissecting and describing all that he could find. He urged Spencer to read Linnaeus' *Philosophia botanica:* "You will then use his other works only as a dictionary, in which you will find every flower, when you know its genus and species" (2:752). Jones's search was now more thorough, partly because of requests from men like Yonge.

A Botanic Garden had been established on St. Vincent, with intensive cultivation of sixteen acres. Yonge wanted to transplant there valuable plants from the East Indies and South America. Thus Admiral Rodney had brought cinnamon in 1782; later, Captain William Bligh brought breadfruit. Jones relayed Yonge's new request to Russell: As the king wished "to improve the commerce of the West-India islands, and to provide the British troops on service there with medicinal plants" (2:775), Russell should send a box or two of seeds. This garden gratifyingly exemplified Jones's view of the necessary utility of scholarship; he would contribute whatever assistance he could, relaying any unfinished commissions to individuals able to complete them. He also applied to Cornwallis, who had already obeyed the king and spoken to Robert Kyd. Kyd, the superintendent of the East India Company's new Botanical Gardens in Calcutta, promised to transmit all the curious seeds that he could collect.

Having failed in preserving seeds on a long voyage, Jones asked Yonge for suggestions. The seeds of sago palms from the East Indies and of West Indian sandalwood had been covered with wax but had not germinated in his garden. He promised Yonge many valuable medicinal plants perhaps "applicable to the Military Service" (2:771). Spices were less promising, though cinnamon flourished in gardens near Calcutta, and pepper was plentiful in Chittagong. "Due Culture" might make Indian coffee as fine as mocha. As for commercial plants, Jones awaited Yonge's instructions. During the hot season he drank pomelo juice as a daily, "admirable Preservative against Feverish Heat." Addition of wormwood salt produced a syllabub that could cure a slight fever: "If you think it likely that our sort may be finer than the West Indian, I will send you a Box of Seeds."

Jones had long been exchanging information with Russell, who had inquired about pedalium, which Jones had not been able to find. Russell doubted the scientific value of searching in medical books for the virtues of the three hundred medical plants mentioned in the Sanskrit dictionaries. Jones, while agreeing that the books were not always accurate, considered them valuable because they suggested useful experiments. James Anderson, the physician general at Madras, had sent him some cocci, which he put in a solution of tin in aqua regia to make fine red ink. But Anderson had sent Banks his essay on an insect that London chemists had proved was not a cochineal. Jones was finding that Linnaeus' *Genera plantarum* (1737) and *Species plantarum* (1753), which constituted his dictionary, were barbarously written: "I grieve to see botany imperfect in its two most important articles, the *natural orders* and the *virtues* of plants, between which I suspect a strong affinity" (2:776).

Jones enlisted Russell in what was becoming his major search for spikenard. Relating literature to science by identifying plants mentioned in Sanskrit books, now he sought their classical and biblical names, if any. Like John Ray and others, he wanted to expel myth and mystery by making taxonomic identification: "What is the natural order, class, genus &c. of the plant? What was the spikenard in the alabaster-box of the Gospel? What was nardi parvus onyx? What did Ptolemy mean by the excellent nard of Rhangamutty in Bengal?" (2:777).

Sanskrit provided other rich information, some of which Jones transmitted to Europe. Charles Vallancey, who founded the school of writers theorizing about the Irish past without studying the manuscripts or languages, misunderstood Jones: "On communication of these names of our Druidical mythology, Sir W. Jones encouraged my pursuit, and was convinced, as I am, that the first Eastern Colonists that settled in Ireland, were the Indian Scythæ, whom Berosus says settled on the Indus and Ganges, in the fortieth year of Belus, the Nimrod of the Scriptures."[6] In his Third Discourse, Jones had posed a linguistic affinity between Celtic and Scythian; but he privately mocked Vallancey's deriving Irish from Persian and Sanskrit: "According to him, when silly people gave me the surname of *Persian,* they in fact called me *Irishman.* Do you wish to laugh? Skim the book over" (2:769). Yet apparently Jones was undisturbed by Vallancey's use of his name in *A Vindication,* supposedly "Proved from the Sanscrit Books" (Dublin, 1786). He asked the antiquarian Joseph Cooper Walker to convey his best regards to Vallancey, whose work he had read twice with great pleasure: "We shall soon I hope see faithful translations of Irish histories and poems. I shall be happy in comparing them with the Sanscrit" (2:770). He encouraged Walker's studies.

Jones was always modest about his own accomplishments. Lauding Wilkins's translation of the *Bhagavad-Gita,* he urged Wilkins to render the rest of the *Mahābhārata:* "You are the first European who ever understood Sanscrit, and will, possibly, be the last. I go on pleasantly, have read an excellent grammar, and translate all I meet with" (2:782). Jones could not predict whether his humble labors might contribute to posterity; "but if GOD continue my existence in this perishable state, I will persist in putting forth *branches, leaves,* and *flowers,* and in *adorning that Sparta* (to use the Lacedæmonian phrase) which He has allotted me" (2:746).

Jones refused to exploit his success with Sanskrit. When private letters predicted that he would be named chief justice upon Impey's resignation, he told Spencer that this was morally impossible: "I am content, my dear lord, with my present station. I often repeat this verse of a Persian poet: 'Mine is the kingdom of Liberty and the treasury of Content, which a Monarch could not easily gain by the sword" (2:755).

Jones had not forgotten his Society. Publication of *Asiatick Researches* 1 was slow, with only eight sheets printed when he left for Krishnagar, though there were enough materials for two volumes. The East India Company kept the Press busy with Orders and Regulations most of the time. Unlike the members of the Royal Society, all of Jones's colleagues had a full-time profession and had to devote some of their leisure to caring for their health. The world should be surprised at how much the Asiatic Society had accomplished.

To Law, Jones gently suggested the quality required for chemical essays. Law's loose notes were pleasurable, but European scholars expected something more extensive than notes extracted from letters. Law should compose a memoir on porcelain modeled on Llandaff's essays on alabaster, for *Asiatick Researches* needed formal essays of the sort published in *Philosophical Transactions.* An essay conveying general propositions must contain details of experiments, without a chink in the argument, which Jones illustrated by amending some of Law's formulations. He asked detailed questions about resources and possible useful manufactures in Bihar.

Although Jones knew Llandaff's five volumes well, he read Anna one of the essays every morning, so as to involve her in his activities. Llandaff's resolution to abandon chemistry in deference to the usual notions about a prelate's proper functions was surprising: "If I were a bishop, and must black my hands, I would rather black them with charcoal than with poli-ticks" (2:753). Jones was doing experiments from Macquer's *Elements:* "I exhibited a fine silver tree to my black philosophical friends, and have shown them so many wonders by making sulphur, nitre, and other mixed substances, that they look upon me as another *Abúsina."* Thus he mastered the remaining discipline in encyclopedias, for which he had previously not had time.

Ever the teacher, Jones urged five-year-old John Charles, Viscount Al-thorp, to study Comenius. He sent his poetic translation of a passage in the *Bústán* expressing his own views: (1) kindness to all creatures, which was an article of God's religion delivered to man; and (2) the necessity of work, which gives virtue and happiness. Later he revised the first couplet for his Tenth Discourse:

> Ah! spare yon emmet, rich in hoarded grain:
> He lives with pleasure, and he dies with pain. (2:753)[7]

Both versions were widely reprinted.

Because Spencer had not understood the last line of his "Ethick Epistle," Jones added three couplets explaining that he desired no fruit from their friendship except as the crown for the poem:

> To me, no sweeter fruit his friendship brings;
> I ask no boon of nobles or of kings:
> Should they, and all their train desert my cause,
> Their country slighted and their country's laws,
> Yet many a friend, attentive to my call,
> Would give me strength, and GOD above them all. (2:754)

Even Countess Spencer received discreet instruction: "I trust your Lady-ship can by this time read Isaiah; it is much easier to learn Hebrew without points than chess; and all genuine Theology is built on Hebrew learning" (2:784).

Shore had lent Jones a copy of Háfiz, which he read twice. Then having composed a mediocre five-quatrain imitation of Ovid, Shore sent it anon-ymously. Ironically, Jones liked its pathos so much that he dispatched it to Shore with a little lecture: "Excessive grief is neither full of tears, nor full of words; yet if a dramatic poet were to represent such grief naturally, I doubt whether his conduct would be approved" (2:784–5).[8] He also sent Kháqání's *Habsiyya,* "the wildest and strangest poem that was ever writ-ten" (2:763). He provided the meter so that Shore could correct any errors. Jones noted that Rādhākānta had refused a Supreme Court punditship, presumably because of religious scruples, and had no way to avoid bor-rowing more money. As Jones was already paying his Indian scholars more than he could well afford and was employing more Brahmans than he had time to hear, perhaps he and Shore might jointly help. They did so.

He finished "Remarks on the Island of Hinzuan or Johanna" at Krishnagar, continuing the habit of working on at least one translation or essay there. The catalyst was recent Arabic letters from Anjouan: "The behaviour of our sea-officers is very brutal; and, not to mention the dishonesty of many, they treat the islanders like dogs. Surely this is abominable" (2:760). This long geographical essay was designed to show the progress of civilization in an Arabian colony, and, after it appeared in *Asiatick Researches* 2, was often serialized.[9]

Jones's reading aloud to Anna that autumn drew the couple even closer. Thus on 6 August they read and then discussed chemistry. When she turned to her own voluminous correspondence, he resumed his morning schedule, which she did not hesitate to interrupt. Once she asked him to tutor her in algebra. Soon after they finished the lesson, she excitedly brought in an equation that she had solved, laying it upon the scholarly page that he was composing.

He read her so much Petrarch that he memorized whole sonnets, for they were planning to visit Italy on their way home. They read all of Ariosto, Tasso, and Metastasio's ten-volume *Opere drammatiche* (Paris, 1775–9), reserving Dante for the winter. He read Birago Avogaro's 445-page *Historia Africana* (Venice, 1650) to her in two weeks. Jones feared talented men who rise to power, like the African emperor who murdered men so as to make a hell-broth of their brains.

Their theological reading was on Sunday. Richard Price's *Sermons on the Christian Doctrine* (London, 1787) reconfirmed Jones's beliefs. Price speculated that future punishment would be temporary, with the time proportioned to the offense, but doubted that he could document this view from the Bible. However, Jones knew of many biblical proofs and viewed eternal punishment as blasphemous to divine justice: "I would give up Scripture rather than embrace it. *Eternity* of pain, if *eternity* means for *endless duration* must be disproportioned for any offence" (2:765). He liked *Sermons* so much that he congratulated Price. Though despairing of liberty in England, he hoped to finish his life there "in studying those parts of knowledge which are connected with the duty of good citizens, and in conversing with you and a few others who love their country" (2:819).

The chalybeate water that Anna continually drank kept her stomach in fairly good order, although once she was extremely ill for a fortnight from eating a bad onion. Otherwise, she frolicked with the flocks of sheep that ate from their hands, as in a scene from the golden age. They were given a tiger cub, which, being of the royal breed, would become huge; it gamboled with its foster-mother goat and Anna. Jones's own health was fairly good, although his constitution could not withstand the steady weakening from illnesses every few months.

The term began on 22 October with the usual heavy schedule. There were three important cases. First, the Supreme Court heard rival claims for the estate of an Englishman who had died intestate. The judges unanimously gave the administration to the principal creditor, but Jones noted that the court lacked option or discretion and could only specify the principal creditor: "He reprobated the idea of a *discretionary power* being vested in a Court of Law – it would be dangerous and mischievous to the Public."

Second, the court resolved the long-pending case of F. B. Thomas, who had been discharged from his surgeonship because of John Bristow, a prominent local citizen. The complex questions of fact and law made Jones rule on the basis of what he considered the general feelings of humankind. He had to read the voluminous evidence thrice, before ruling that Thomas's suit should be dismissed because no malice had been proved. Thomas's insulting bill had left Bristow three alternatives. Bristow could not submit, nor should he have challenged Thomas to a duel, and so he had requested a court-martial. Jones's colleagues ruled otherwise, with Hyde admitting that he had had less time for the case than Jones because of "avocations." They awarded Thomas five thousand rupees.

In the third case a cook was tried for assaulting another European. He said that he had mistaken his victim for someone else and asked the man's pardon. However, Jones told the jury that they had to determine only whether there had been an assault; the court would consider any extenuating circumstances in pronouncing sentence. Because the law forbade even the smallest assault, if the cook had touched someone in anger, "it was to all intents and purposes an assault." He was sentenced to imprisonment until he could pay the fine.[10]

Jones held three more Society meetings in 1787, for a total of ten that year. On 1 November he read his "Remarks on Hinzuan"; on 22 November, a Devanagari translation. Polier's essay on the Sikhs attracted only eight members on 20 December. In 1788 there were perhaps only five meetings.[11] The group was losing much of the spirit that Jones had originally imparted, as scholars like Wilkins left. On 7 February only five joined Jones. Hyde nominated Henry St. George Tucker, a young East India Company clerk. Jones seconded the name of this future company director and nominated Thomas Daniell, who had recently arrived to paint Indian scenery. Charles Grant, now Jones's neighbor, did the seconding.

Then Jones read his "On the Chronology of the Hindus," prepared from extensive Sanskrit sources and discussions with pundits. His ultimate purpose was to identify a sequence of Indian events and their dates that accorded with attested Western ones, so as to clarify "a subject in itself so obscure, and so much clouded by the fictions of the *Brāhmans*," who had "designedly raised their antiquity beyond the truth. . . . we must be satisfied with probable conjecture and just reasoning from the best attainable data." Actually, his task was herculean: "Until the vast store of knowledge enshrined in Sanskrit literature and inscriptions could be translated, the story of India, prior to the Muhammadan invasions of the eleventh century A.D., as recorded by the people themselves, remained an absolute blank."[12] The Brahman keepers of the sacred books, convinced that Hindus had an almost infinite past, hardly helped him. Even today, *The Cambridge History of India* notes that many dates accepted by its editors are either approximate or conjectural (1:640).

Jones rejects Brahmanic opinion after opinion as a monster "repugnant to the course of nature and to human reason." This first systematic Western attempt to date Hindu events tentatively rejects the "received" view, because the three Hindu ages were mainly mythological and the fourth traceable no earlier than 2000 B.C. He concludes that his explanation, while still obscured by poets' imagination and astronomers' riddles, is not particularly inconsistent with Western chronology: "The hypothesis, that *government* was first established, *laws* enacted, and *agriculture* encouraged in *India* by RAMA about *three thousand eight hundred* years ago, agrees with the received account of NOAH's death, and the previous settlement of his immediate descendents." Jones's appended "Chronological Table" begins with Adam and Manu I in 4006 B.C., proceeds past Noah and Manu II in 2949 B.C., and ends with Nadir Shah. However, unless Sanskrit astronomical books date the colures precisely, there will admittedly be loose traditions in his sequence, such as the centaur Chiron, whom Newton placed in the Golden Age but who may never have existed. Thus Jones leaves the door open for his discovery crowning this pioneering effort to start putting the labyrinth of Indian mythology and culture into a dependable sequence that Western historians would later use.

The meeting of 21 February attracted Cornwallis, his fellow judges, and nineteen others to hear his Fifth Discourse. The second longest of his eleven Anniversary Discourses, it is the least eventful, partly because he admittedly had little knowledge of the Tatar languages: "The gross errours of *European* writers on *Asiatick* literature have long convinced me, that no satisfactory account can be given of any nation, with whose language we are not perfectly acquainted." Jones postulates a single earlier language, different from the two that sired Sanskrit and Arabic, respectively, as the source of Turkish and other tongues. He has found a void in Tatar language and letters; the only real poetry was war songs, because, anthropologically, the Tatars were ferocious and nonliterate. Here Jones was somewhat influenced by William Robertson's pioneering typological description of society as evolving from savagery to barbarism to European-style civilization. He has found no more traces of philosophy in Tatary than in ancient Arabia, nor many impressive monuments and inscriptions. After defending his opinion that Tamerlane did not write *Institutes,* Jones concludes that he has proved most of Asia to have been immemorially possessed by Hindus, Arabs, and Tatars, who are so different that "if they sprang originally from a common root, they must have been separated for ages." His future Discourses will consider whether the Persians and Chinese are equally different or have derived from an intermixture: "To what conclusions these inquiries will lead, I cannot yet clearly discern; but, if they lead to truth, we shall not regret our journey through this dark region." Mirages offer attractive but false conclusions.

At the meeting of 27 March he presented two short essays and read a paper by Polier, who had just left India. "On the Pangolin of Bahar," a physiological complement to Jones's botanical investigations, was the first of three such essays. This sound description was his first serious work with physiology, in which he minutely compared the pangolin and even the contents of its stomach with Buffon's description.

This study whetted his appetite: "We cannot venture to say more of this extraordinary creature, which seems to constitute the first step from the quadruped to the reptile, until we have examined it alive, and observed its different instincts." This evolutionary formulation may have been stimulated by Buffon or by John Hunter's lectures challenging the doctrine of immutability. When Jones was sent a pangolin from the mountains, he returned it because it was uncomfortable in the heat. In his Tenth Discourse he insists on humanitarianism:

Could the figure, instincts, and qualities of birds, beasts, insects, reptiles, and fish be ascertained, either on the plan of BUFFON, or on that of LINNÆUS, without giving pain to the objects of our examination, few studies would afford us more solid instruction or more exquisite delight; but I never could learn by what right, nor conceive with what feelings, a naturalist can occasion the misery of an innocent bird and leave its young, perhaps, to perish in a cold nest, because it has gay plumage and has never been accurately delineated, or deprive even a butterfly of its natural enjoyments.

A creature should be studied when in a state of natural freedom, or at least should be made as happy as possible if it must be confined. If other species exist for humans' good and instruction, they must not be treated cruelly. The Hindus' and Buddhists' respect for all life had strengthened Jones's feelings; he opposed killing an animal except for a vital need like food, a view that helped discourage zoological research in the Society. He himself never considered becoming a vegetarian.

His second paper was "Inscriptions on the Staff of Fírúz Shah," a mature epigraphic effort. Realizing that inscriptions in Indian temples contain valuable information, he innovationally requests members to sketch monuments and copy inscriptions that they encountered in their work. Polier had copied those on the lat of Firoz Shah III, at Delhi. Jones was unable to translate the Pali characters, the ancestor of modern Devanagari, which proclaim Aśoka's edicts; but the usual mode of decipherment, he says, might lead to discovery of the language. His paper translates the Sanskrit on the lat.

William Steuart, assistant resident at Hyderabad, also copied these inscriptions, as well as the Gupta Sanskrit poetry on the Iron Pillar, near Delhi, which Jones hoped to translate but never did. Steuart's letters reveal the scholarly exactness with which Jones had infused him. Poor copies were first made "by fixing Deer skin (Gold baiters leaf) on the stone, and with a Pencil or Pen drawing the Characters in the most minute manner." Then Steuart had his workers rub charcoal on the letters, securing an almost perfect copy. He scoured the nearby countryside for ancient inscriptions. Jones copied others in his memoranda, including one from Aśoka's pillar at Allahabad and another in a French translation.[13]

After a long lapse, nine members assembled on 3 July, when Jones nominated an East India Company writer and seconded another nomination. Thirteen next met on 6 November, to hear a paper on Europeans' preserving their health in India.

Even though the Society might be languishing, Jones was elated by two triumphs in 1788 – governmental support of his digest and finally the publication of *Asiatick Researches* 1. The Supreme Court's need to have reliable Hindu law had led him to study the requisite laws in the original Sanskrit, as the Persian translations were inadequate. He assembled a Hindu staff after Rāmalocana became his pundit, recognizing that a joint effort of Indian pundits and Europeans was required in the search and interpretation. By then his zeal for scholarship would have made him continue studying Sanskrit even if he did not often observe the danger in relying on Indian lawyers.

Jones had wanted to translate the *Mānava-Dharmaśāstra* almost from his first sight of the book. It was so relevant to his judicial work that economy demanded its complete translation, which the English judges could use in conjunction with the digest. Brahmans told him it was the acknowledged basis of Hindu law and institutions; he seemed to regard its relation to the digest as the Roman Institutes stood in regard to Justinian's digest.[14] He was making progress on the version when he wrote to Boughton-Rouse.

Evidently his friend replied that he could ask the Bengal Presidency for help without implications of patronage or ambition. He discussed the digest with Cornwallis, who had the public good at heart and strongly approved. When Henry Dundas enthusiastically approved the project, Jones promised to make an outline, which pundits and *maulvis* could fill in accurately: "The Brahmans are so highly gratified with the attention shown to their laws and literature, that they have entirely shaken off the habits of reserve, which the Moguls had caused by their sternness and intolerance; and the Muselmans, who also believe their laws to be divine, are not less pleased" (2:791). This was a major advance, for the Brahmans were willingly helping an unbeliever to work with their sacred laws.

Encouraged, he wrote the Governor in Council a formal letter on 19 March 1788 (2:794–800). The Indians were now gratifyingly protected by their own laws, but the necessary British dependence on Indian lawyers continued to create problems for the judges. In England, Jones had mentioned the obvious remedy to friends in Parliament and on the bench – a "complete Digest of Hindu and Mohammedan laws, after the model of Justinian's inestimable Pandects, compiled by the most learned of the native lawyers, with an accurate verbal translation," which could be deposited in the Sadar Diwānī Adālat and the Supreme Court as a standard of justice. The Indians needed permanent security in matters of contracts and inheritances, to which the Supreme Court was restricted in disputes between Indians. The scope of the digest would be reduced by Raghu-Nandana Bhaṭṭācharya's twenty-seven volume *Dayatattwa* on Hindu law and by the five-volume *Fatáwá ʿAlamgíríyat*. Though Halhed had faithfully performed his part in producing the *Code*, "the Persian interpreter had supplied him only with a loose injudicious epitome of the original Sanscrit, in which abstract many essential passages are omitted."

For the new compilation Jones proposed to hire a pundit from each of Bihar and Bengal, and a *maulvi* from each of the two Moslem branches. Their monthly salary would total 800 sicca rupees, with 200 more for two writers of Devanagari and Arabic. To ensure diligence, the project would be limited to three years, at a cost of 36,000 rupees. Jones would have cheerfully borne this expense, except that he already paid his private staff of Indians more than 500 rupees a month. The Bengal government should pay the additional 1,000.

The director-translator must know Arabic and Sanskrit and have enough knowledge of juridical principles and legislation to plan the digest, supervise its compilation, and make a perspicuous English translation that could command some authority. Jones noted, immodestly, that he was one of the few people with such composite qualifications even in his low degree. He would have preferred someone else but would volunteer rather than never see the digest done: "I offer the nation my humble labour, as far as I can dispose of my time consistently with the faithful discharge of my duty." If this offer were accepted, Cornwallis should nominate the pundits and *maulvis.* Then, every morning before beginning his judicial schedule, Jones would translate their compilations of the preceding day. He described basic sources like the *Mānava-Dharmaśāstra* and *Al Sirájiyyah,* not mentioning his unpublished translation of the latter.

The Governor-General accepted the offer the same day. Because Jones wanted "to promote a due Administration of Justice, it becomes interesting to humanity; And it is deserving of our peculiar Attention as being intended to increase and secure the happiness of the numerous Inhabitants of the Company's Provinces" (2:801). The digest would reflect the greatest honor upon the Bengal Presidency, which was fortunate to have an eminently qualified person motivated by general benevolence. The paymaster would make monthly disbursements at the orders of Jones, who should select the Indian scholars.

For the Bengal pundit, Jones chose Rādhākānta, a distinguished Brahman. His other five nominations were also excellent. On 1 May the Governor in Council expressed "perfect Confidence in the Propriety of the Selection" (2:803), which made an important contribution to India. Jones's persuasion of the Bengali scholar Jagannātha Tarkapanchanan to be the compiler further demonstrated the Indians' growing enthusiasm about working in the miniature research complex that he had created in his own staff. Indian scholars now recognized that he was not a Westerner who was seeking to force their culture into a Western mold, but, rather, that he was an objective scholar who foresaw the need for creative evolutionary collaboration between East and West. From the early moments of his Society he had believed that real advances would come only when Indians participated in the research; now Jagannātha's work with the digest enlisted his talents on behalf of Bengalis. The Governor in Council approved a salary of three hundred rupees monthly and another one hundred for assistants, in a Minute of 22 August: "His Opinion, Learning and Abilities are held in the highest Veneration, and Respect by all Rank of People and the Work will Derive infinite Credit and Authority both, from the Annexation of his Name as a Compiler & from his Assistance" (2:803).

Cornwallis reported to the Court of Directors on 3 November:

Few circumstances have therefore given me a more sincere gratification than the voluntary public spirited proposition of Sir William Jones to engage in the arduous undertaking. . . .

The thorough knowledge which Sir William has acquired of the Eastern languages joined to the extent of his literature and the strength of his natural abilities constitute qualifications for executing the Work that he has undertaken, which perhaps cannot in any other man be paralleled; And considering it singularly fortunate for this Government to be able to obtain the assistance of such a person, I could make no hesitation in granting from the public purse the moderate Monthly Sum that he required. . . . if it can be accomplished according to the original Plan, it will justly render the name of its Author dear to the Natives of the Country. (2:803)

Approval was granted in London on 28 April 1790: "Our Opinion of the utility of the Work is greatly strengthened from the consideration that it is to be executed under Sir William's immediate inspection; and we are as sensible as you can be of the degree of public spirit, and general benevolence which he has manifested" (2:803).

Jones minutely planned the digest, listing the sources more systematically than Hastings and Halhed had done for the *Code.* The Brahmans, working under a European's direction in constructing a digest of their laws, admired and helped refine his arrangement.[15] He spoke Sanskrit so fluently that they considered him a pundit. If he kept his health and finished the digest, it would be "the standard of justice to eight millions of innocent and useful men" (2:813), his frequently voiced goal that inspired his Brahman colleagues.

Jones's drive for knowledge was bringing additional responsibilities. Besides editing *Asiatick Researches,* he had two manuscripts ready to publish. His botanical investigations were greatly widening because of Yonge's commissions, his search for spikenard, and his cooperation with Banks. Accustomed to receiving queries about all disciplines, often accompanied by specimens, Banks maintained a vast international correspondence. His implicit high standards were paralleled by the scientific level of Jones's eight letters to him between 1788 and 1792. He had an informal network of collectors in India like Russell and William Roxburgh (the pioneer exponent of Indian flora), to whom Jones had gravitated. Science was Banks's passion; "public service through the applications of science was his constant aim."[16] This master coordinator used people in diverse fields and locations to make the Royal Society a leading scientific center, and Jones was a fascinated participant.

Banks wanted help with his personal herbarium; but preferring to work with living plants, Jones provided assistance to the St. Vincent Garden and the Royal Botanic Gardens at Kew. Banks had designed the Kew imperial center for interchange to study the problems of transplantation and acclimatization, while advancing botanical exploration and experiment.[17] Of the almost seven thousand exotic plants brought into English cultivation, most were obtained by Banks's collectors. Jones's involvement required him to be comprehensive in his botanizing. Although the pair had not preplanned this cooperation, his zeal and far-ranging Society made him particularly valuable.

Desiring more connection between his and Banks's groups, Jones asked Polier to deliver some curiosities to Banks: "I wish I knew what plants or animals of this climate would be *agreeable* (I know that none would be *new*) to you. I had destined for Lord Mulgrave a beautiful royal Tiger, as gentle as a Spaniel, who was nursed by a She-Goat in my house; but the cold of this season killed it" (2:786). Jones also dispatched some Madeira to Dr. Johnson's Club.

Upon receiving three commissions from Banks, he broke his rule and answered at once, promising a later report from Krishnagar. First, Banks wanted Jones's reaction to Sir William Herschel's speculative "Account of Three Volcanos in the Moon" (*Philosophical Transactions* for 1787), in an attempt to involve Jones in astronomy. Jones related the supposed discovery to some highly delighted Brahmans, though one pundit suspected an error in Herschel's observation. Second, Banks requested Dacca cotton. When John Bebb, the commercial agent at Dacca, reported that it could not be procured immediately, Jones worked on the matter for three years, first transmitting a pincushion of the finest cotton and Bebb's letter describing the specimens provided. As Bebb collected them in varying degrees of ripeness, Jones arranged several transmissions. Some were sent to Yonge; others were carried by friends going to Europe. But the pods would not vegetate, and Banks complained. Jones's agent, who had been at Dacca and in the West Indies, felt that either Jones had sent a poor specimen, or else Banks was mistaken about the comparative quality: "[The] agent insists that the texture of the Dacca Cotton is much finer than that of the American Islands" (2:894).

The third commission involved books that Banks had lent to the recently deceased George Perry. These had been sold at auction when Jones was away, and he could not even recover Banks's copy of Penna's *Alphabetum Tibetanum*. He would seek out a passenger to deliver a box containing the roots of an Arakan plant esteemed an excellent bitter, while he sought the seeds and flowers: "from the experiments that I have tried with it on myself, I should prefer it to Columbo root, & I wish it could be tried in London" (2:790).

Jones maintained a local correspondence throughout 1788, rather than writing letters only in Krishnagar. A letter to Shore in February shows his integrity even to that close friend. The establishment of the Supreme Court had superseded the local jurisdiction at Fort William, without adequately providing for the Calcutta police, which badly needed reforming. Cornwallis met with the court to consider his applying to Parliament for the power to establish an efficient police system. He proposed that a superintendent be able to convict offenders, so as to reduce the corruption in criminal courts and restrict Indian control. Misunderstanding the results of the meeting, Jones wrote Shore a partly legal letter opposing summary conviction and punishment: Supposed necessity should not prompt abandonment of the spirit and form of judicature in criminal cases, as the system had been approved by the wisdom of a thousand years. It was not necessary to handle offenders without a jury, as Parliament could empower the Governor in Council to appoint six to twelve justices of the peace, who could appoint subordinate peace officers. Also, a superintendency suggested a foreign system and constitution. Jones recommended quarterly sessions and the compiling of a list of three hundred persons qualified to serve in rotation on petty juries. As he felt that Britishers and Indians would prefer trial by jury, Parliament should be asked only for the power to appoint justices by annual commission. If Cornwallis chose to mention the judges' concurrence in his application, Shore should remind him that Jones was opposed. However, the matter had a salutary end.

It did not affect Jones's association with Shore, who sent him lovely passages from Waḥshí's elegies. He often wrote an immediate answer while the bearer waited. That summer Shore composed some stanzas that Jones praised as worthy of Catullus: "I rejoice that you have it in your power to relieve your mind by poetical imagery; it is the true use of the fine arts" (2:809). They talked about the *Śakuntalā,* of which Jones finished a word-for-word English translation of his own interlinear Latin.

Although his eyes were strained from intensive reading, he answered Law's letters about chemistry. To the question of whether Chinese kaolin was argillaceous, Jones suggested an experiment to resolve the matter if it seemed important. Because Law had decided against writing regular essays, his detached paragraphs must remain private hints for inquiry rather than appear in *Asiatick Researches* 1, which needed a drawing of the madhuca tree. Fearing that he had been unclear, Jones wrote Law a second letter and then a third in May: "I meaned 'The *Flower* and the Leaf' on a little stalk drawn with a pen, to be etched at Calcutta on copper on a page as large as that, on which I now write. I annex a sketch of Anna Maria's to show what I mean" (2:805).

Law partly shared Jones's zeal for botany. An undated letter illustrates how Jones used his Society to collect for the Gardens at St. Vincent and Calcutta:

Dear Sir Wm.
I have the pleasure to enclose the leaf of a Palm tree at the Cape which Mr. [Thomas] Lyon calls the gauze tree & which he says he does not know has ever been particularised

Yrs ever with esteem &c
T Law–

On 7 August the *Calcutta Gazette* published one of Jones's two finished works. Printed by Manuel Cantopher, this Persian book by Hátifí was sold for "the Insolvent Debtors in the Prison of Calcutta. Price, one gold Mohr, ready money only." Jones observes in his English preface that even if all the copies are sold, giving the trustees twelve thousand sicca rupees, few debtors will be freed. Perhaps public charity will help, but multitudes "will perish, and all must wish to perish" before Parliament could relieve the rest. This precedent-setting effort paralleled Jones's practice in England of donating legal help to the poor. His *Sacontalā*, fifth charge to the grand jury, and *Al Sirájiyyah* were to appear in the same way.

Besides its unbiased humanitarianism, Jones's new book had a literary purpose. His rare manuscript by Hátifí was so aesthetically valuable that he wanted Indian and other readers to know it. Of the dozen poetical versions of *Laylà va Majnún*, this one by Jámí's nephew was esteemed the simplest and most moving. Too busy to edit his manuscript, besides lacking sources for notes, Jones had it printed at his own expense. Ali Ibrahim Khan helped by adding a Persian notice about Hátifí. A last-minute addition to the preface notes that the text is "unhappily far from being correct." At least Jones was able to proofread Cantopher's printing five times, carefully comparing it with two other manuscripts that he finally procured. His name does not appear on the title page; only a "W. Jones" at the end of the preface indicates his association. Upon receiving a copy, Reviczky praised the Persian printing as the most elegant that he had ever seen.

Jones's summer term of 1788 required labor beyond that of any English bar: "We have been sitting seven hours a day, sometimes whole nights, for three months together, and that without any assistance from juries except in criminal cases" (2:820). Once he had to read cases from 9:00 A.M. to 2:00 P.M. the next day during the hot season. He was now happier with his colleagues, enjoying a relationship permitting him to offer critical suggestions before they made their judicial ruling. Thus in beginning some equity cases he wrote Chambers a note: "When it is necessary to assert a fact we must give the adverse party an oppy. of answering it." The gratifying reply was "Yes, whenever it can possibly be answered."[18]

Cornwallis requested rulings, especially on delicate cases from Bombay. As the Supreme Court's only leisure was on Sundays, they had to delay considering an indictment against a Charles Johnstone, who may have composed *Chrysal, or the Adventures of a Guinea* (London, 1760–5). They refused to give an extrajudicial opinion, which was rendered only in emergencies when requested by the Governor in Council on general questions about the government's rights or powers because the long delay in securing judgment from England would create public danger or great inconvenience. Moreover, a superior court should not advise the oyer and terminer, over which it had no jurisdiction. The Bombay judges should have quashed the indictment if they thought it bad: "This we beg leave to offer to their consideration as a general rule of conduct and not as an intimation of our Sentiments" (2:810–11).

The problem of the Madrasah reemerged. While praising the regulation by "which some of the most learned Mahomedans in this Country have been consulted," the Board of Revenue charged that Mujd-ud-din was guilty of negligence and misconduct and had brought many improper persons into the school. Therefore, when the students burglarized a leading citizen's house, the board ordered his removal.[19] Though Hastings had esteemed Mujd-ud-din, Jones's conversations had shown him to be a man of shallow learning.

The Supreme Court was adjourned to 17 October. Before departing for Krishnagar, Jones showed his usual generosity. The drought had caused famine, and he donated one thousand sicca rupees to the Calcutta relief (his colleagues gave five hundred), promising one thousand more if the rice harvest did not end the shortage. The Governor-General traditionally subscribed the largest sum; Jones invariably gave the second largest. For example, Jones gave two hundred rupees to a Madras orphanage for Protestant girls, five hundred to soldiers and seamen of the Bengal Squadron, five hundred to a hospital for Indian relief, and one thousand to the Fund of the Free School Society. He and Anna were on the Committee for the Relief of Debtors, and each contributed four gold mohurs annually.

During his month at Krishnagar, Jones's study of Arabic and Sanskrit and the Indian jurisprudence written in those languages superseded everything except necessary correspondence. He devoted his mornings to friends like George Hardinge, writing concisely and promising longer letters next year. To Lady Eleanor Butler, a Llangollen recluse for fifty years, he sent his annual report of his reading, in answer to her report. He asked a favor of Caldecott:

Pray assure all who care for me, or whom I am likely to care for, that I never, directly or indirectly, asked for the succession to Sir E. Impey, and that, if any indiscreet friend of mine has asked for it in my name, the request was not made by my desire, and never would have been made with my assent. . . . I have enough, but if I had not, I think an ambitious judge a very dishonourable and mischievous character. Besides, I never would have opposed Sir R. Chambers, who has been my friend twenty-five years, and wants money, which I do not. (2:816–17)

Jones probably did not know that Bishop Shipley had solicited William Wilberforce, Pitt's close friend:

Mr. Pitt might be reminded that Sir William has all the talents, abilities, and virtues the wisest minister could wish for in the man whom he destined to fill so important an office. Lord Ashburton, when Sir William was first appointed, took leave, as he told me, to assure his majesty that he was not only fit for the office, but that he was the only one that was fit. . . . Sir William has an enlarged, active, and liberal mind; and your great friend will seldom have the opportunity, by promoting a single man, of doing so signal a service to his country and to mankind. (2:816)

As events proved, the prime minister did not want Jones to be the chief justice.

One of Jones's longest letters that autumn was to Arthur Lee, whom he intended to visit in America. Young Englishmen should "finish their education by visiting the United States instead of fluttering about Italy, and strive rather to learn political wisdom from republicans than to pick up a few superficial notions of the fine arts from the poor thralls of bigotry and despotism" (2:821). Hoping to see Franklin before the old man died, Jones lamented the continued disunion between Franklin and Lee.

Jones's economy in correspondence was not always understood. Although the two had once been close, he did not write to Thomas Day, who complained privately: "I never expected, in the multiplicity of his affairs, that he would find room for idle correspondence. And it is a lesson . . . that all the real, disinterested friendship in the world may be compressed into a surprizingly small compass."[20] Jones even lacked the time to compose a daily page to Spencer, whom he did write the longest letter of his stay. He reported that he had saved £20,000, but as his goal was £30,000 before he would contemplate resignation, it was too early for him to purchase land in England.

Jones hardly economized on scholarly correspondence. He thanked William Shipley for the Royal Society of Arts' *Transactions,* which had delighted a learned friend in Calcutta. Jones hoped that *Asiatick Researches* I could soon be sent to Europe, he proudly told Banks, implying an exchange of publications with the Royal Society. Banks collected such proceedings.

In answer to Lord Monboddo's query about the relation of India to the origin of language and humankind, Jones sent his Third Discourse, which was to tantalize the anthropological theorist. As for the Brahmans' philosophy, Jones responded that he had seen enough to be convinced that Vedantic doctrines are Platonic.

As this promising collaboration began, another ended when Russell sailed. Jones had been too busy to criticize Russell's materials on the plague, which had also been sent to Adam Smith. Nor did he have time to examine flowers. His own search for fresh spikenard had gone nowhere; the physicians on his Sanskrit staff knew it only in a dry state. Jones bid his chief botanical collaborator a sad farewell.

He read aloud to Anna daily. After a week's introduction to Spanish, she was able to read Cervantes' minor novels with facility, and he read her another. They read Boccaccio for recreation in the evenings. Jones finished reading *The Wealth of Nations,* which was so pleasurable that they decided to return to it again and again. His informal instruction was bearing fruit: Anna knew more about "law, physick, and divinity" than most graduates (2:813).

She continued to be "not ill." Though she was apparently never to be well in Bengal, his hopeful "Etrenne" to her had not really been contradicted thus far:

> May health & joy my Love await,
> Throughout the year of eighty-eight.
> No murmurs then I'll make at Fate;
> Nor curse Bengal, nor Blackie hate.
> But thankful will I ever date,
> This new-born year of eighty-eight. (2:783)

Jones's delicate efforts to persuade the Shipleys to urge her return to England had prompted no real attempts to alter her resolution not to leave early. Because of her great love for him, he seldom mentioned the matter to her. His own health was reasonably good when they returned to Calcutta.

Jones's most important writing in 1788 was his fourth charge to the grand jury, which mainly discusses the crimes on the docket. It maintains a continuity with his previous three charges by stressing the kinds of crimes that he had not yet described, so as to assist the jury in finding or rejecting the bills of indictment. Perjury or subornation so damages a judicial system, he points out, that culprits should be sentenced under a Renaissance statute calling for imprisonment and nailing them to the pillory by their ears (or else paying a heavy fine). In criticizing Europeans who abase the Indians' morals, Jones recommends an investigation of the dangers in Calcutta at night, with attention to streets where European castaways have taverns.

Though Parliament has not legislated reform, the jury can still improve social conditions by meting out severe punishment.

The best punishment for cheating is imprisonment, which affluent Indians fear more than a fine or public censure. Jones defines the conditions constituting murder, providing details in a case involving three *chokidars,* who were to be acquitted through the jury's observance of his general instructions. The Supreme Court is divided on the issue of forgery. As he and Chambers think it is not a capital crime in British India, but Hyde disagrees, a Renaissance statute should be the guide until the highest authority decides. Again, Jones urges attention to the conditions in the jail, the prisoners' condition, and the jailers' conduct. Finally, jurors should be willing to have more frequent sessions, in order to preserve the constitutional mode of trial and thus to prevent possible summary jurisdictions.

Local newspapers reported that "many ladies of distinction attended – the Court was very full – and every auditor paid the strictest attention. . . . his nervous manner of delivering it, fixed an impression on every susceptible mind that cannot easily be effaced." Jones displayed "Learning and Knowledge, communicated in elegant, tho' unaffected language, equally characteristic of the Lawyer and the Citizen," transmitted with that "manly eloquence and constitutional exposition of the Law, which ever distinguish the speeches of the learned Judge."[21] The jury's judgments followed his guidelines in case after case. The charge was published on 8 December on the front page of the *India Gazette,* which, a week later, urged implementation of his recommendation of quarter sessions.

Despite his compassion, Jones approved swift punishment, as evidenced in several revealing cases. A sepoy, convicted of murdering a slave, was executed two days later. Sentenced for murdering his corporal, a European private was executed within forty-seven hours. And an Indian adjutant, charged with killing another Indian, had his sentence of execution in four days delayed for four days when the Court approved his request.[22]

Jones's major triumph of 1788 was the publication of *Asiatick Researches* 1. He had projected an annual volume once enough good essays were available, but there had been delays. Meanwhile, he established the library and archives that became the basis of the Society's superb manuscript collection and its large collection of coins, copper plates, busts, and drawings. The delays permitted him to construct a high-quality first volume. He did the proofreading, adding notes when an author was unavailable to answer his queries, as in the case of Wilkins. Jones asked for Davis's sketch of the Mahabalipuram ruins to illustrate William Chambers's paper on those ruins. If Daniell would then make an etching, the sketch could be printed; however, Daniell was upcountry. Jones had to postpone the matter until the next volume, which, he told Davis, should contain one of Davis's essays on Sanskrit astronomy. As the binders finished the book in late December, the volume carried a date of 1788, though it did not appear until 19 January 1789. The printer was Cantopher; the price, fifty sicca rupees.

Sixteen of the twenty-seven essays in *Asiatick Researches* 1 are by scholars like Burrow and Wilkins. Ten of Jones's contributions have already been described – his "Dissertation on Orthography," his first three Anniversary Discourses, "An Indian Grant of Land in Y.C. 1018," "Inscriptions on the Staff of Fírúz Shah," "On the Literature of the Hindus," "On the Pangolin," "Conversation with Abram," and "On the Course of the Nile." After the latter two were reprinted in *Scots Magazine* (App. 1789, pp. 646–8) and *European Magazine* (December 1789, pp. 406–8), their popularity helped dispel the doubt that James Bruce had really made the expedition.[23]

Jones's eleventh contribution was "On the Gods of Greece, Italy, and India." Composed in 1784 and expanded into his second longest Indian essay, this once-celebrated comparison begins by condemning undocumented arguments. Only facts can prove that an "idolatrous people must have borrowed their deities, rites, and tenets from another; since Gods of all shapes and dimensions may be framed by the boundless powers of imagination, or by the frauds and follies of men, in countries never connected." Jones generalizes tantalizingly, in a comparative vein reminiscent of his famous philological passage:

When features of resemblance, too strong to have been accidental, are observable in different systems of polytheism, without fancy or prejudice to colour them and improve the likeness, we can scarce help believing, that some connection has immemorially subsisted between the several nations, who have adopted them: it is my design in this essay, to point out such a resemblance between the popular worship of the old *Greeks* and *Italians* and that of the *Hindus;* nor can there be room to doubt of a great similarity between their strange religions and that of *Egypt, China, Persia, Phrygia, Phœnice, Syria.*

Jones promises to be circumspect. Thus he will sketch only the striking similarities between the chief classical and Hindu gods, which must be superficial because of his brief Indian residence, busy schedule, and lack of classical sources. Actually, the slow uncovering of Sanskrit sacred literature may have been stimulating his natural human desire to be the first to reveal the treasures. His yearning to find universal connections among cultures and religions pushed him toward dubious conclusions partly drawn from the accidental phonetic similarity of divinities' names. He makes important but hasty generalizations from imperfect data, many of which had been collected for his hymns.[24]

This essay on Hindu divinities, drawing on sources like the *Purāṇas* and Jayadeva, pioneered a method of comparative mythology. Jones was the first to print drawings of several of the gods. Unfortunately, he generally identifies Janus with Ganesha, Saturn with Noah and Manu, Jupiter with Indra, and Apollo with Krishna. While outlining major similarities between Jupiter and the Hindu triad, he does not specify the original system, and he wrongly speculates that Egyptian priests traveled to the Ganges. His digression on missionaries predicts that certain features in Islam and Hinduism will prevent conversion. And so missionaries should translate into Persian and Sanskrit the most persuasive Christian elements: Isaiah, other prophets, evidence of the predictions, and Jesus' life. Quiet distribution of these translations might convert educated Indians. Characteristically, Jones does not seem to have communicated his suggestion to the missionaries in the Bengal schools, as he felt that Indians had a right to their own religion.

His essay had a quick, powerful impact in Europe, with *Gentleman's Magazine* calling it a learned, ingenious proof of affinity (May 1801, p. 441). His startling conclusions tied a remote Oriental religion to familiar classical ones and started Western scholars on a path that eventually exposed the errors in his pioneering essay, though occasionally today there are echoes of his superficiality and dubious etymology. The essay has only historical significance today,[25] but without it the conceptions and methods of comparative mythology might have been delayed.

The *Calcutta Gazette* of 22 January 1789 praised the variety of information and entertainment in *Asiatick Researches* 1, which should entitle it to much commendation. Ships took seven hundred copies to Europe, and a specially bound copy was sent to Dundas, with a suggestion that the king would honor the Society by accepting it. *Asiatick Miscellany* had whetted the public appetite for exotic material; now Jones's Society had initiated a study of Indian culture. His essays were singled out in glowing reviews of the volume.[26] When the king accepted his copy, expressing satisfaction at the scientific progress in India and praising the digest, Jones's achievements received their highest commendation to date.

12   An Indian Renaissance (1789)

In artistic implications for posterity, 1789 was Jones's most important year. It began with Yonge's acceptance of his offer to help to transfer Asia's spicy forests to St. Vincent. Indirectly apologizing for having to ask Shore to relay Yonge's letter to Kyd, Jones could assist only as much as the digest would permit. He asked Claud Martin, who was to be Cornwallis's aide, to send Yonge all the seeds that could be collected.

Jones's association with Shore remained literary. When Jones's *maulvi* composed a Persian poem on the subject of Thomas Parnell's "The Hermit," Shore made a copy. Jones asked Shore to explain a Homeric episode to the Indian, who might imitate it. Shore sent an amatory ode by Waḥsí, which almost equaled Metastasio's on the subject and surpassed other Persian odes that Jones knew. Jones's chief fellow appreciator of Persian was now Richard Johnson, whom he and Anna sometimes visited on weekends. Johnson lent him a copy of the *Sháhnáma,* which he pleasurably read aloud.

One reason for Jones's emphasis on Persian was his Sixth Discourse for the Society on 19 February. It is his most unreliable discourse, despite his assertion that his long, attentive study can supply more positive information on Persia than on any other nation. He reaches four dubious conclusions. First, there was a powerful Hindu monarchy in Persia long before the Assyrian empire. Second, the language of the first Persian empire was the mother of Sanskrit, Greek, Latin, and Gothic. Third, Persia was the center of population, knowledge, and arts before the other Oriental nations developed. Finally, the founders of Arabia, India, and Tatary originally migrated from Persia. These conclusions raise questions for a later Discourse: Has Asia produced groups distinct from the Hindus, Arabs, and Tatars; and has intermixture of the three in different proportions led to diversity? Thus Jones moves toward a hypothesis of common origin and anthropological diffusion.

Much of his evidence is linguistic, which permits generalizations about Persian history and languages but causes errors. For example, Jones identifies the legendary Kay-Khusraw as Cyrus, and the legendary Píshdádí kings as Assyrians. He derives *Cambyses* from the Modern Persian *Kambakhsh,* and *Xerxes* from *Shíru'í.* A larger error leads him to doubt the genuineness of the Zend books. Studying the *Sháhnáma* while projecting his tragedy about Rustum, he discovered hundreds of nouns that seemed to be pure Sanskrit. Many Persian imperatives were Sanskrit verb roots: "The moods and tenses of the *Persian* verb substantive, which is the model of all the rest, are deducible from the *Sanscrit* by an easy and clear analogy." Hundreds of cognates, too numerous to be borrowings gained by political and commercial intercourse, named "parts of the body, natural objects and relations, affections of the mind, and other ideas common to the whole race of man." As linguists did not yet know that the Indo-Iranians had migrated together over many years, so that their perhaps already diverging dialects shared some lexicon and inflections, Jones tentatively concluded that Persian and the Indic languages came from the ancient Brahmans' language. But he was "inexpressibly surprized to find, that six or seven words in ten were pure *Sanscrit"* in the *Zend-Avesta.* Because Anquetil and the Persian compiler did not know Sanskrit, "the language of the *Zend* was at least a dialect of the *Sanscrit,* approaching perhaps as nearly to it as the *Prácrit,* or other popular idioms, which we know to have been spoken in *India* two thousand years ago." Therefore, "the oldest discoverable languages of *Persia* were *Chaldaick* and *Sanscrit,"* from which Pahlavi and Avestan descended, respectively.

Part of this error is terminological, for Jones was pioneering in plotting the complicated Iranian subfamily. If we can interpret *Chaldaick* as Old Persian, he rightly names it as the source of Pahlavi. He had earlier realized that Latin and Greek were not descended from Sanskrit. Now, misled by the close genealogy of Sanskrit and Avestan, he named Sanskrit as the source of Avestan, thereby perhaps blocking him from later discoveries. Ironically, he used Anquetil's data for his major linguistic error. He did epigraphic study, vainly seeking Devanagari letters in inscriptions copied from Persepolis. One misleading source was the *Dabistan,* which opens with "a wonderfully curious chapter" and contains evidence that he considered unexceptionable. This commendation caused a vogue that was not dispelled for a century, but it eventually helped scholars see the truth.

The Discourse concludes with a problem – "By what means we can preserve our Society from dying gradually away, as it has advanced gradually to its present (shall I say flourishing or languishing?) state." Although it has subsisted for five years without any expense to its members, now each member should purchase a copy of *Asiatick Researches* 1, which costs only the equivalent of a fellow's annual contribution to the Royal Society.

They also should try to sell the volume in London. The Asiatic Society will meet in vain unless original papers are presented; papers will be collected in vain unless they can be published without exposing Morris and Harington to considerable loss. Only united efforts can rival the French contribution to universal knowledge and transmit the Society's discoveries to Europe.

The impression of this first volume had to be sold, for Morris and Harington would not risk a second loss. Jones probably wrote Elmsly, who agreed to sell it and thus ensured the Society's solvency. Only to close friends did Jones reveal his pessimism: The organization would die without his dynamism and scholarship. When he was away, the meetings were adjourned. But he intensified his efforts, composing more papers and urging members to write essays or help editorially so that the journal might appear regularly.

Another group to which Jones remained loyal was Johnson's Club. When Banks wrote that politics had found its way into the Club, "whose members meet reciprocally to impart & to receive new ideas," Jones was saddened. He would never intrude his principles upon men of science: "If, on my return to Europe, ten or twelve years hence, I should not find more Science than Politics in the Club, my seat in it will be at the service of any Politician." Indeed, "the rancour of contending parties fills with thorns those particular societies, in which I hoped to gather nothing but roses" (2:843, 849). He also continued to pay his dues to the Royal Society and the Society of Antiquaries.

His statement about science reflects his view of politics as "the narrow selfish squabbles of interested factions" (2:828). Though he congratulated Wilkins for abstaining from such activity, the British domestic squabbling upset him. A divisive issue was the French Revolution, which Price and Fox championed but which Burke attacked. Jones was privately hostile to this attack, while maintaining public detachment from political matters. As Shore remarked, probably thinking of Jones: "Although we have some sturdy democrats amongst us, political questions, upon the whole, are discussed here with tolerable moderation." The barrister William Burroughs also knew Jones well: "The flame of liberty burns very ardently in his mind, and has, I fear, consumed everything monarchical and aristocratical."[1]

Jones always had difficulty in reconciling his idealism with realities. Struggling to adjust his drive for knowledge and his love of England and the constitution to his realization of the ubiquitous corruption, he exemplified "intellectual and moral vigor, and the willingness to endure the anguish it can produce."[2] His judicial vow kept him independent of everyone in the government. The Indians had been so cheated by European lawyers that they mostly settled their differences by arbitration. They publicly condemned Chambers and Hyde and wished for the pair's speedy departure; indeed, Jones was the only judge in Calcutta whose integrity was not questioned. Indefatigable, he deserved his reputation.[3] He had always scheduled his studies so as to learn something useful, but until now he had never had to devote virtually every free minute to study, for his duties consumed most of his time.[4] He was scrupulously impartial in procedures and rulings, manifesting the concentration and incisiveness that characterized his scholarship. No investigation was too bothersome if justice could be served.

There was an intriguing case in January 1789, when Martirus Shabin was accused of publishing a bond. The penalty under 5 Elizabeth c. 14 was a fine, imprisonment, the pillory, and the cutting off of one ear. Because Chambers had suggested it be applied to Nanda Kumar (who was executed), either Chambers was culpably timid then or else had changed his mind by 1789.[5] Shabin was convicted under this milder statute.

In February the Supreme Court considered the long-standing case of whether John Bebb was entitled to the considerable profits from providing the government with carriage cattle. Quoting Latin, Jones methodically eliminated all alternatives but his judgment:

In cases of trust, it is the express province of equity to discover the motives, to search the hearts of parties; here the motive has been discover'd, and that motive was lucre in *Morgan,* the desire of enriching himself with that which belonged to another. A man who does a wrong Act, may lose by it, but he cannot gain by it. According to these principles, there must be, in my opinion, a decree in favour of *Bebb* for the profits admitted by the answer of *Morgan.*

The Court awarded Bebb 2,603 Bombay rupees and costs.

Jones's ruling in July also prevailed: No insurance could be paid on a ship lost at sea without proof that the loss occurred within the time covered by the policy. He "laid it down as a settled principle, that the proof on the side of the party who affirms, must be stronger than of him who denies, and that in the former case, such evidence must be given, as would induce a jury to believe the affirmative to be true, which the circumstances here would not amount to."[6]

Another action is revealing. An Indian sought admission as a suitor, *in forma pauperis,* without taking an oath. He presented a Sanskrit book on oaths, asserting that Siva had composed it to prohibit swearing by the water of the Ganges. He said that it had been copied from a manuscript twelve years before, but Jones's Sanskrit competence discovered impudent fraud not twelve days old. He ordered the man to bring him the original in ancient Sanskrit, or he would know that deception was intended.

Anna's health was a continuing concern to Jones in the first half of 1789. They were an ideal couple. Before marriage he had sometimes mentioned to close friends the idea of having children, but later he ceased such references. The explanation may be implied in Anna's remark to the duchess of Devonshire: "You will have just one dozen & a half [babies] to make amends for setting about it so late.– I shall never set about it at all."[7]

Her health was fair until the hot season, when some newspapers arrived that reported her elderly father's death. Because the report might have been untrue, Jones could not prepare her for the news, which would exacerbate her already enervated condition. Although he would not be able to conceal the news very long, he destroyed the newspapers and had Shore seal all her letters in a packet to him. He withheld these until one came from her wisest friend, Countess Spencer, whose handwriting he recognized and who would tenderly present the dreadful message. But Anna still suffered tremendously: "The shock my spirits received by the fatal news my English letters brought me, last year, can never be recover'd. You, Mr. Hastings, knew & will have lamented that best of Men as a friend! & will therefore easily imagine what we who mourn a Parent in him must suffer: but this is a subject my mind is yet unable to bear –." She herself was concerned about Jones, who left Garden Reach before sunrise on weekdays. Despite demanding duties and an "application to his studies that would kill half the men in Europe," he maintained fair health by "early rising & regular hours & no suppers & above all avoiding the Sun."[8] Even in a temperate climate his schedule would have been strenuous: "Think what it is in this!"[9]

In 1789 Jones began an intensive correspondence with Samuel Davis, a close friend to whom he wrote at least thirty-eight letters about astronomy. When Davis visited Calcutta, their mutual curiosity branched out into chemistry and natural phenomena. Jones had realized that he could not investigate ancient Indian chronology without delving into Sanskrit astronomy, as some primeval events were recorded in astronomical mythology. As he was too busy to attempt dating the colures from Sanskrit references, Davis's investigations filled a gap in his research design for the Society and assisted his plotting of Indian chronology. Thereby he implemented his cooperative design for one of the few times during his Bengal residence.

His encouragement finally elicited Davis's bulky "On the Astronomical Computations of the Hindus." Though Jones agreed to correct the proofs, his eyes were too weak and his duties too demanding to correct the tables, in which a minute error might be important. He asked Davis's pundit to list all the proper names and scientific terms in Devanagari, transliterated "according to the component *letters; for,* as there are many provincial modes of *pronouncing* them (four of which I have been obliged to learn) we have no sure guide, but the *letters* themselves" (2:829). Through examples Jones made discreet corrections in the essay.

Because Davis wanted Robert Chambers to read it, Jones followed instructions, suggesting that Chambers owned Bhaṭṭotpala's commentary on the *Bṛhat-Saṃhitā,* which was said to be an incomparable work and might be useful. Harington copied Davis's essay, so that it might be revised before it was typeset. But the pundit had omitted several names from the requested list, which Jones intended to append as a glossary.[10] Jones spent more time on this essay than on any other colleague's, for it was the Society's first major work on astronomy. He presented it at the meeting of 16 April, meanwhile urging Davis to stop Daniell on the way back through Bhagalpur long enough for Daniell to etch the Sanskrit figures. Jones had compiled a list of Sanskrit astronomical books but had mislaid it and was able to supply Davis with only forty-six titles. After trying to date Bhāskarāchārya, the pair turned to his poetic masterpiece *Siddhānta-śiromaṇi.* Its two highly original mathematical parts, which Davis summarized from his pundit, excited Jones, who hoped that one part might be on universal arithmetic. If the ancient Hindus had used algebra, "we shall possibly find rules and methods, which may be substantially useful" (2:833).

Davis asked Robert Saunders, a Tibetan traveler who was now a surgeon at Bhagalpur, whether he had seen any fresh spikenard. As Ptolemy had written that it abounded in the north and northeast, Jones requested information about the Linnaean order and genus from Saunders, who supplied some facts. Jones then queried him as to "whether the curled locks of it, which the druggists sell dry, are the roots of the Baccharis, or only bundles of fibres shooting from the bottom of the stem" (2:831). Linnaeus considered spikenard to be an Andropogon.

Such data were intended for *Asiatick Researches.* The chronology of the second volume shows Jones's devotion to the Society, in addition to his heavy judicial labors and work on three Sanskrit translations and the law digest. By late February 1789 all the materials, which he personally selected, were ready for typesetting. He reminded Davis about the Mahabalipuram drawing, which was needed as a frontispiece to be etched by Daniell. By 17 April the volume was being printed, but Davis's revised paper still had not arrived. On 4 May, at William Chambers's urging, Jones wrote Davis that Daniell might arrive in time to etch the now-located drawing. On 12 July, with two hundred pages printed, he again requested

Davis's paper. Harington agreed to handle matters if it arrived while Jones was at Krishnagar. Meanwhile, Daniell was sketching somewhere up-country.

The strenuous proofreading had so weakened Jones's eyes that Dr. John Fleming forbade his reading aloud to Anna; nonetheless, he finished his second major prose translation from the Sanskrit. He had begun rendering Jayadeva's *Gīta Govinda* as a translation exercise, but his admiration of the twelfth-century lyric drama made him go further and polish his version. To convey the precise meaning, he sacrificed the poetry of this episode from Vishnu's incarnation as Krishna. Not adding one image or idea, he italicized his prose version of the several songs in order to mark their location. The plot intrigued him. Krishna abandons Rādhā to wanton with the gopis, until, repentant, he invites her to his bower. Initially despairing, she finally comes. Thereby he frees himself from mere physical allurements and finds peace with her, an action that Jones considered an allegory depicting "the reciprocal attraction between the divine goodness and the human soul."

The highly moral Jones feared that he might offend Europeans, to whom he wished to introduce the drama. His solution was simple: He translated nothing that he judged too bold for Western taste. Because the drama sometimes revels in physical passion, he set a model for later translators by scissoring out Sarga 12. Thus Krishna's suggestive speech in the marriage bower ends with the invitation "O! let affliction cease: and let ecstasy drown the remembrance of sorrow." Without indicating an omission, Jones discreetly continues: "In the morning she rose disarrayed, and her eyes betrayed a night without slumber." Yet he conveys overall sensuality, as in the gopis' reaction to Krishna:

One of them presses him with her swelling breast, while she warbles with exquisite melody. Another, affected by a glance from his eye, stands meditating on the lotos of his face. A third, on pretence of whispering a secret in his ear, approaches his temples, and kisses them with ardour. One seizes his mantle and draws him towards her, pointing to the bower.

The local color nicely comes through in this linguistically competent version, showing a gopi dancing around Krishna in a "sportive circle, whilst her bracelets ring, as she beats time with her palms."

Jones sent Shore a copy in June, even though one aspect disappointed him: When he had first read the songs in the drama and considered the mode in which each song was anciently sung, he had hoped to find the music. Unsuccessful, he concluded that this Indian art had "faded for want of due culture" over the centuries. The songs are still mainly a mystery, for music was taught orally rather than handed down in written records that he wanted to print as a scholarly complementation.[11]

Gītagōvinda: or, the Songs of Jayadēva, published posthumously in Jones's *Works* in 1799, roused much less interest than did his other Sanskrit translations, partly because its beauty particularly depends on the lyricism. But he wanted to give Europe the substance of one of India's greatest lyric works, which he could best do with literal prose. He was not concerned that he was the first to translate it. The *Monthly Review* observes that he did not spiritualize it: His "extremely sweet and delicate" style conveys the Indian imagery (App. 1794, p. 574).

Jones may have sent this new translation to Wilkins, whom he congratulated for informing people about Indian literature: "You have the honour of being the first European . . . who possessed a knowledge of Sanscrit" (2:828). Although the *Mānava-Dharmaśāstra* should be left to Jones, Wilkins could translate the other Sanskrit works.

Anna and Jones left for Krishnagar on 22 August. His annual epistolary duty required him to answer fifty long letters from Europe and fifty short ones in eight weeks. Two letters to Walter Pollard agreed that aristocracy was dangerous and an enfeebled democracy unacceptable. Although the wise few should conduct basic government, the people should nonetheless retain the judicature and the ultimate power to repress tyranny. So the Americans should not reject popular government, lest they become "like the deluded, besotted, Indians, among whom I live, who would receive Liberty as a curse instead of a blessing, if it were possible to give it them" (2:847). Jones questioned Pollard's praise of Pitt, who had all the craft of the oldest minister: "What is a minister but a servant of a single frail and fallible man, who wears a crown?" (2:840). Thus Jones used an Indian extreme to rebut Pollard's criticism of America, just before Pollard's return to England to embrace the British system.

Walker was again Jones's intermediary for Irish scholars. *Historical Memoirs* (London, 1786) had pleased Jones, and he would be much interested in Vallancey's *Comparaison de la langue punique et de la langue irlandoise* (Paris, 1781): "I heartily rejoice that such men as Col. Vallancey and yourself are labourers, for the sake of the publick, in so abundant a mine" (2:842).

Jones answered Czartoryski's new letter. The prince grieved at not having the proper means to cultivate Persian: "The acquisition of a language will always appear to me much more valuable than that of a desert."[12]

There were local letters to answer, as well. Declining William Steuart's invitation to send epigraphic commissions, Jones suggested another mission: "If you should meet with an Astronomical Brahman, who can write down the Sanscrit names of the constellations (except those in the Zodiack, which I have) and can point them out to you on a fine starry night, you will do me great service" (2:839). Jones knew only the names of the "12 Signs, the 27 Lunar Mansions, the Great Bear, the Pole-star, and Canopus." As the Hindus had named many zodiacal stars, "if we can ascertain their places in the great epochs of their history, we shall fix their chronology by our certain knowledge that the equinox goes back one degree in about 72 years." Thus he pursued a question for "A Supplement to the Essay on Indian Chronology," which he was preparing.

Besides reporting to Shore on his reading, Jones wrote Hyde. One letter answered Hyde's request to alleviate the misery of Captain Peter Horrebow, who had been convicted of assaulting and forcibly carrying Indians to Ceylon to sell as slaves. Of the 150 children on board under British colors, 20 had died and the rest had been sold. In July, Jones had joined in the Supreme Court's first such verdict, sentencing the European to three months' imprisonment, fines, and a huge security. Though Hyde and Chambers now wanted to approve the prisoner's petition for release, Jones knew of no legal precedent: "I have no compassion for him; my compassion is for the enslaved children and their parents" (2:845). Any losses suffered were no more than Horrebow deserved, nor would his wife's health be restored by his release. He himself was not ill. Still, Jones would approve the release if Hyde could find a precedent; he probably knew that there was none. A second letter reveals his compassion when justice was not compromised. Recollecting a recently sentenced man, he agreed to the immediate discharge suggested by Hyde.

Besides his autumn letter writing, Jones finished some other work, so that he could concentrate on law for the next eleven months. His eyes were improved enough to read Anna all twenty volumes of Francesco Guicciardini's *La Historia di Italia* (Florence, 1561). He also composed four essays and prepared materials for his Seventh Discourse for his puny, rickety Society.

"On the Antiquity of the Indian Zodiac," based on inadequate sources and influenced by Brahmans, rejects Jean-Étienne Montucla's view that the Indian zodiac was borrowed from the Greeks or Arabs. Jones argues for an earlier source, out of which both the Greek and the Indian zodiacs developed, perhaps before the Hindu progenitors' dispersal: (1) The Brahmans were too proud to borrow their sciences; (2) the Indian signs differ too much from the Greek ones to be copies; (3) the names and forms of the Indian lunar constellations differ from the Arabic ones; (4) literary or scientific intercourse between the Brahmans and the Arabs is unproved; and (5) the Indian zodiac has great antiquity. Finally, "the practice of observing the stars began, with the rudiments of civil society, in the country of those whom we call *Chaldeans;* from which it was propagated into *Egypt, India, Greece, Italy,* and *Scandinavia.*"

Thus Jones was the first to defend the originality of Indian astronomy, although that part of it "with any claim to scientific precision is more or less Greek."[13] His essay was read to the Society on 5 November. When a scholar of his renown challenged the standard view, defenders of his revolutionary premise quickly arose. Carried too far by the extent of his discoveries to perceive the Greek resemblances and simply amend the standard view, he unintentionally stirred up a heated controversy. Most scholars eventually agreed that at least the twelvefold division had derived from Greek influence, but the matter is so shrouded in antiquity that some modern scholars still share his view.

Jones's second essay was "On the Musical Modes of the Hindus." This product of Sanskrit research initiated Western study of Indian music, by comparing Hindu and Western music. His humanistic desire for the exchange of knowledge with Europe underlay this much-revised paper drafted in 1784. The Society was in a unique position to study Indian music, having access to instruments and Sanskrit sources on composition. Besides learning about a delightful subject, members could extend the general knowledge about music. Because the climate made it difficult to keep instruments in tune, in his essay Jones concentrated on theory rather than on Indian musical instruments. He was adding the subject of comparative music to his cultural knowledge, though music is "subordinate in its functions to pathetick poetry, and inferior in its power to genuine eloquence."

Jones describes Hindu musical effects in terms of the association of ideas and the mutilation of the regular scales. Certain strains suggest certain ideas, as each Indian season is represented by a separate primary mode. Why these modes have distinct properties and may convey particular emotions may be unanswerable until scholars determine why each color in a rainbow has an analogous particular effect on the eyes. Yet that aesthetic fact should be considered by performers, so as not to reduce all the modes to dull uniformity. Jones's sources are the *Rāgānarva* (Sea of passions), *Sabhavinod* (Delight of assemblies), *Sangīta-darpana* (Mirror of music), and *Sangīta-ratnākara* (Jewel mine of music). Not specially praising the last two, which today are the most esteemed, he recommends Somanātha's *Ragavibodha* (Doctrine of musical modes), which he had closely studied. He transliterates Somanātha's scale, providing a detailed description of the vina and a drawing of its fingerboard, in the first known written use of *vina* in English. Borrowing little from his earlier essay on Persian music, Jones ends on a bittersweet note. Political changes have kept this admirable system of music from becoming standard in India; other studies now dictate his own farewell to music.

"On the Spikenard of the Ancients," the first of two botanical essays, recounts the unsuccessful search by Jones and many botanists and physicians. Thomas Law finally obtained fresh plants from Nepalese travelers, but these were mistakenly planted at Gaya and flourished for a time. Arabs had first told Jones about the extensive distribution of *Valeriana jatamansi,* which he erroneously concluded to be the biblical nard (it is *Valeriana wallichii*). Initially accepting Linnaeus's view that spikenard is gramineous and an Andropogon, Jones had Dr. James Anderson send him some *Andropogon nardus,* which he studied and then expressed "dissent, with some confidence as a philologer, though with humble diffidence as a student in botany." From a reliable drawing he posited the distinguishing features of the Gaya transplant but could make no conclusions about its virtues. Because botanical philosophy seeks to discover the uses of the vegetable system, he would not apologize for lacking a plan to apply this new knowledge to a useful end; experiment underpins knowledge.

Jones's fourth essay that autumn, "The Design of a Treatise on the Plants of India," related to his new botanical letter to Banks. Mentioning Sir Gilbert Blane's efforts to identify the Indian nard, Banks had apparently asked Jones for help. Blane had received a dried specimen of Andropogon from his brother William at Lucknow, which he concluded to be the true nard. Jones had also received some, which had not yet flowered. Requesting fresh plants for transmission to Banks, Jones decided that this was not Ptolemy's nard. So he tentatively rejected Blane's mistaken formulation before it appeared in "Account of the Nardus Indica, or Spikenard" (*Philosophical Transactions* of 1790).

Jones's search for spikenard anticipated his efforts to identify the water flowers, vines, and creepers mentioned in the Sanskrit drama that he would shortly introduce to a startled Europe and an India generally unaware of its literary heritage. By utilizing various collectors, he contributed to a "botanizing" over a goodly part of India. Their findings were fed into his research design, with emphasis on cataloguing nonmicroscopic flora and discovering any uses. Because most of the plants were inadequately or not at all described, this step was tedious but necessary. Banks wanted detailed studies, but Jones's schedule and weak eyes prevented his examining minute blossoms, especially the grasses that most interested Banks. As a compound microscope was not available, he could not magnify plant tissue: "I am no Lynx like Linnæus" (2:844).

But Jones was cooperating, though one of Banks's queries had been unsuccessfully pursued: "I am not partial to the *Priyangu,* which I now find is its true name; but Mr. Shore found benefit from it, & procured the fresh plants from Aracan, which died unluckily." Jones thought it was quite bitter and less pleasant than calumba. Still, it needed more tests before its tonic benefits, if any, could be determined. Again he suggested testing it in London, a premise that must have pleased Banks, as they agreed that knowledge should be made useful. Thus reciprocating commissions, Jones concluded: "Since the death of Koenig, we are in great want of a professed Botanist." Perhaps he was vainly hinting that Banks might subsidize such a post, like the exploration and collecting that Banks was financing elsewhere.

Jones's botanical study was now his most scientific, even if posterity has rightly stressed his linguistics. Linnaeus's grouping the species of each order into genera, introducing modern binomial nomenclature, was one reason. Jones strongly felt the temptation to describe all the flowers that he saw daily, similar to what had taken Linnaeus to the subarctic tundra. The new system made classification "one of the easiest, instead of one of the most difficult, biological exercises."[14] Jones was correcting errors, even as he supplied the taxonomy for previously unknown plants. The goal was a single comprehensive flora that would permit everyone to agree on the identity and description of any specimen, which was a major problem into the nineteenth century.

If this veered from medieval naturalists' goals, Jones's utilitarianism still embraced theirs: "Infinite advantage may be derived by *Europeans* from the various *Medical* books in *Sanscrit,* which contain the names and descriptions of *Indian* plants and minerals, with their uses, discovered by experience, in curing disorders."[15] Having collected the names of three hundred supposedly medicinal plants, as well as of seven hundred others, he intended to test their virtues as claimed in the medical books. This study became his programmatic "Design of a Treatise on the Plants of India," his last essay of 1789.

The first step in Jones's intended comprehensive treatise was to write the plants' correct names in Roman orthography and "in *Sanscrit* preferable to any vulgar dialect," as vernaculars will change and the treatise must be intelligible to posterity. Once the plants were classified and described, their possible uses in medicine, diet, and manufacturing would be determined by experiment. Though generally following the Linnaean system, Jones rejects the names assigned to the twenty-four classes: "The allegory of *sexes* and *nuptials,* even if it were complete, ought, I think to be discarded, as unbecoming the gravity" of scientists. His five sample descriptions include the madhuca tree, or *Bassia latifolia,* with the observation that it yields "by distillation, an inebriating spirit, which, if the sale of it were duly restrained by law, might be applied to good purposes."

Jones was also projecting an autobiography in three parts: student, advocate and barrister, and finally judge.[16] He did not mention this to Parr and Bennet, whom he had once asked to compose his biography if he did not return from a trip. Both later refused to surrender his letters for the biography that Teignmouth was to write. Parr may have wanted to compose it; Bennet expressed another reason: "I do not think myself justified in sending letters; and I have some of a late date, containing bold opinions about men and manners."[17]

Although Jones had completed his poetic career, he outlined two sets of unwritten poems.[18] One was "Odes in Four Books: Celtic, Saxon, Norman, Teutonick. Object: to praise great *Warriours, Patriots,* and *Statesmen,* who have flourished in Britain, and to recommend them as objects of imitation by *Englishmen.*" The other was "Hymns in Four Books. European Asiatick African American. Object: to recommend universal toleration by showing that all nations, even the most idolatrous, agree in the *essentials* of religion, a belief in one GOD, Creator and Preserver, and in the future state of reward and punishment."

By far the most important event for Jones in 1789 occurred on 8 October, when his *Sacontalā, or the Fatal Ring: An Indian Drama by Cālidās: Translated from the Original Sanscrit and Pracrit* was published by Joseph Cooper in Calcutta. Although it did not carry Jones's name, the 183-page book was his greatest translation. His use of interlinear Latin to bridge between the exoticness of antique India and eighteenth-century Europe is of linguistic interest. Latin's greater closeness to Sanskrit in age and richness of inflections (compared with Modern English) could assist initial accuracy in a language that he knew well, because, from the first, he was envisioning an artistic English version that would faithfully transmit the drama. His decision anticipated the one in modern theory of translation: A literal version precedes the literary.[19] As the last step required an artist, he naturalized the foreign idioms and polished his English syntax into a "pleasing and authentick picture of old Hindū manners, and one of the greatest curiosities that the literature of Asia has yet brought to light" (preface).

This procedure required great linguistic competence, for there was a paucity of Sanskrit loanwords in English. Even the massive Indic borrowing during the Renaissance had added few words denoting Indian flora, fauna, mythological place-names, Hinduism, and foods, which could transmit the exotic biota and culture. Latin afforded no semantic help. Yet Kālidāsa's love of nature required communication of the wild Himalayas and primeval forests, palace gardens with their mango blossoms, and lovely fish. Jones's transliteration of key lexical units entailed the unraveling of Sanskrit sandhi, which was further complicated by the unrepresentative English spelling. "The Enchanted Fruit" had failed partly because of his intrusive explanatory footnotes, and his *Hitōpadēsa* had only pointed the way toward internal definition of his transliteration.

Now Jones's Romanized Sanskrit item helps capture the local color by naming plants and animals. Eschewing footnotes by adding inconspicuous explanations as needed, he employs 118 different transliterations, usually in unitalicized self-defining contexts like "the hard wood Samī; this Mādhava creeper; ruddy as the Bīmba fruit." Such unfamiliar nouns edge his English toward Sanskrit without reducing his narrative quality, while innovationally representing non-European things better than many later translations do. If an existing loanword incorrectly represents the Sanskrit, the Jonesian System provides his spelling: "How I wish thou hadst been seized by a tiger or an old bear, who was prowling for a skakāl." This variant of *jackal* is not recorded among those listed in the *Oxford English Dictionary* since its first record in 1603. Few of his transliterations are listed there, though later usages are sometimes given, whereas he may have been the first to write *avatar, Brahman, champac, lat, nargileh, sloka, vedanta,* and *vina*. Few of Jones's transliterations were naturalized, but his device, if not his system, guided Romantic poets like Byron and Southey.[20]

There was a major textual problem: The *Śakuntalā* has survived in two principal recensions. The Devanagari one, shorter and more concise, is probably older and better than the more diffuse Bengali one. Jones's Bengali manuscript was not even a good version, as it contained interpolation and repetition. Though he had no reason to suspect the existence of a more concise version, his keen aesthetic sense is reflected in his preface, in which he comments perceptively on the verbosity: "The piece might easily be reduced to five acts of a moderate length, by throwing the third act into the second, and the sixth into the fifth; for it must be confessed that the whole of Dushmanta's conversation with his buffoon, and great part of his courtship in the hermitage, might be omitted without any injury to the drama."

Two decisions handicap Jones's version. First, he does not attempt dialectal variation. His preface explains that men of rank speak pure Sanskrit in classical drama. To elevate their dialogue, the Sanskrit dramatist uses verse, as is done for much of Dushyanta's dialogue. But not knowing the various social dialects, Jones employs only prose. He observes that women speak Prakrit; "the low persons" speak the dialects of their provinces. But he makes no serious effort to convey the social level. His dialogue is rather dignified and formal for all characters, whether fisherman, police chief, sage, or king, thereby losing Kālidāsa's marvelous quality of social differentiation.

Second, Jones again exercises moral restraint. In Arthur W. Ryder's "standard" version, the stage direction in the love scene instructs that Dushyanta "lays his hand upon her,"[21] whereas Jones provides "He gently draws her back." In this lovely scene Ryder translates:

D: Why should I not have my way? (He approaches and seizes her dress.)
S: O sir! Be a gentleman. There are hermits wandering about.

Jones writes:

D: How! must I then fail of attaining felicity? (Following her, and catching the skirt of her mantle.)
S: (Turning back.) Son of Puru, preserve thy reason; oh! preserve it.– The hermits are busy on all sides of the grove.

Because Jones tones down descriptions of her swelling breasts, his Western readers are unaware of Kālidāsa's simultaneous earthiness. His philosophy of translation permits such moderating if the version is supposedly improved for culturally different readers who will never read the original and might be offended by the Guptas' sexual directness. If he violated contemporary Western literary morality, Europeans might reject the play and thereby void his efforts.

Overall, Jones's achievement is high. He faithfully communicates the somewhat frail plot from the *Mahābhārata*. The rich creation of both an individual and a universal woman, the sensitive relationships between a man and a woman in love, the evocation of emotion, and the appreciation of nature produce a work of literature, Jones's intuitive goal. Despite stating that he will not evaluate the characters and actions, his preface reveals his attitude in the epithet "our illustrious poet, the Shakespeare of India," which was permanently associated with Kālidāsa.[22]

Jones's *Sacontalā* altered European public opinion: A land valued for material wealth also had a great literature. He opened a mine as rich in legend and mythical lore as was Greek and Elizabethan drama; the mine was to divulge work after startling work. This landmark in comparative literature excited more European interest than had perhaps any similar Oriental translation except the *Arabian Nights Entertainments* and Bidpai.[23] Perceiving that the work deserved a place in world literature, Jones introduced it to the West and started its rise to world esteem. Its beauties were recognized by his numerous reviewers, more than had previously reviewed one of his books.

The *Analytical Review* began the commendation (August 1790, pp. 361–

73). *Gentleman's Magazine* concluded: "It is generally believed that we are indebted for this specimen of the genius of the Indian Shakespeare to Sir William Jones, the great reviver of Indian literature . . . which, nobody can deny, contains fine passages" (November 1790, pp. 1013–15). The *New Annual Register* of 1790 considered the drama to be a present to every reader of taste interested in the rich exuberance of Kālidāsa's genius (p. 241). Thomas Ogle termed it a pleasure for all readers with taste and particularly for those curious about ancient Oriental literature (*Monthly Review,* February 1791, p. 137). The *Annual Register* of 1791 described it as "a delicious treat" possessing dignified moral sentiment, warm expression, delicate characters, simple conception, and glow of coloring (pp. 193–4).

A literary contemporary's reaction is perhaps typical:

You will be much pleased with it. There is much fancy and much sentiment in it, – much poetry too, and mythology: but these, though full of beauties, are often uncouth and harsh to the European ear. The language of nature and the passions is of all countries. The hero of the piece is as delicate and tender a lover as any that can be met with in the pages of a modern romance.[24]

The *Sacontalā* created a sensation on the Continent. Georg Forster made a quickly famous translation into German in 1791, and Goethe celebrated it in a beautiful lyric:

> Willst du die Blüthe des frühen, die Früchte des späteren Jahres,
> Willst du was reizt und entzückt, willst du was sättigt und nährt,
> Willst du den Himmel, die Erde, mit einem Namen begreifen;
> Nenn' ich, Sakontalā, Dich, und so ist Alles gesagt!

> If you want the bloom of the early, the fruits of the later year,
> If you want that which attracts and delights, if you want what satisfies
>   (one's appetite) and nourishes,
> If you want to grasp heaven and earth in one name,
> I'll name you, Sakuntalā, and all has been said with it.

In the prelude to *Faust,* Goethe emulated the Indian dramatic convention by having the theater-owner converse with his colleagues. Herder also was excited and became an important intermediary for the acceptance of Jones's works in Germany and their influence on German Romanticism. Jones's version was translated into French in 1803, and then the French one into Italian in 1815; Emerson's father reprinted it in Boston.[25] There were versions in Dutch (1792), Danish (1793), Swedish (1821), Polish (1861), Thai (1920?), and an incomplete Russian one in 1792, among others.

This first translation of the *Śakuntalā* was Jones's finest literary contribution to India. Of course, he did not discover it; the Brahmans had preserved the corpus of India's greatest dramatist. Nor did his version directly affect the people, who did not know English. It was for a primarily European audience. Not until Governor-General Wellesley's College of Fort William, after 1800, was there real movement toward the translation of Sanskrit literature into Indian vernaculars, with wide printing and distribution, ending the Brahmans' intellectual monopoly.[26] Jones's work on the *Śakuntalā* and other classics contributed to the development of the Indians' new self-esteem:

We had nothing but some shreds of our past memories, some dim recollections of what we were and what we did . . . a race advancing fast towards complete degeneracy and intellectual bankruptcy, through an ignorant denial to itself of its own heritage. Jones . . . acted as the golden wand that slowly made us shake off the sleep of ages. . . . he perhaps unconsciously, supplied one of the strongest forces for a revival, a renaissance, of our national culture in India.[27]

Later, Indians could take pride in their heritage and face colonial administrators who boasted of a Shakespeare and a powerful army. As Nehru concluded: "To Jones and to many other European scholars India owes a deep debt of gratitude for the rediscovery of her past literature."[28] The excellent Indology of later Indians in Calcutta was the eventual consequence. Jones emphasized basic human values and the needed cultural–material exchange between East and West. The result was larger than even his tolerance and universalism envisioned, transcending his goal of replacing the distorted European view that India was an ancient land of savages without a fine culture, with the truth that India had richly contributed literature and other arts and sciences to world culture.

There is a paradox, however, in Jones's introducing Sanskrit drama to the West and helping stimulate a national revival in India. His determination that England should properly govern by Indian laws impelled him to learn Sanskrit, and his *Sacontalā* was partly a by-product of these studies. So his means to the end had more important consequences than did the law digest itself, though he believed that literary study should have practical as well as artistic goals. Like the Italian humanists, he elevated an area in world culture by discovering the Hindu golden age for the West. He also implemented his old idea that such translations might rejuvenate English poetry, for his *Sacontalā* and other works contributed to the Oriental strain in Romanticism.

Jones's preface ends with a plea for the study of Sanskrit: "It is my anxious wish that others may take the pains to learn Sanscrit, and may be persuaded to translate the works of Cālidās: I shall hardly again employ my leisure in a task so foreign to my professional (which are, in truth, my favourite) studies" except to translate the *Mānava-Dharmaśāstra* and the digest. He praises Kālidāsa's epics *Kumārasambhava* and *Raghuvaṃśa*, as well as *Vikramorvaśī, Meghadūta,* and *R̥itusaṃhāra,* and the works of other authors. But he finally obeyed this old promise to stop his translating.

The book does not carry Jones's name as translator, but most reviewers found internal evidence in the preface to identify him. There was an identical, reset issue in London in 1790; and Cooper's London printing followed in 1792, with many editions since then. Because Jones's name appears in none of these, Banks wrote him about a disturbing review in the *Critical Review,* which reported:

An Indian drama without the name of the translator, or any testimonies of its authenticity, will undoubtedly at first excite suspicion; and, in an age fertile in literary forgeries, may at once be overlooked or despised. But the suspicion and contempt cannot be lasting: every page will convince even the most incredulous reader. . . . much of the beauty depends on the peculiarities of the plants so often mentioned. . . . In our extracts we have given sufficient proofs of its merit, and we can only add our thanks to the translator for bringing it within the sphere of our attention. Our suspicions, however, are scarcely quieted, for oriental manners and oriental imagery may be easily imitated. (January 1791, pp. 18, 20, 27)

Upset to find the drama's authenticity questioned, Jones elaborately demonstrated to Banks that the biota mentioned were actually in India, giving wry intensity to his efforts to identify the plants in Linnaean terms. But he never dignified this one hint of possible forgery by making a public reply.

When Jones left Krishnagar that autumn, he was pleased. He had composed four essays for his Society, and his greatest literary work had been published. The drama would introduce the West to a culture stretching backward fifteen centuries to the brilliant Gupta period, at a time when blue-painted tribesmen were ravaging the Joneses' native Anglesey. He had finally struck it rich after two decades of scholarly exploration.

13   A Burning Tropical Sun (1790–1791)

Besides concentrating on his two Oriental law translations in his leisure, Jones spent much time in 1790 on matters related to his Society. Richard Johnson was leaving India because of poor health. Jones hosted a farewell party at the first of the year, at which he recommended Johnson to Banks as "one of the most distinguished of the Company's servants in India for ability as a public man, & for knowledge of various kinds & agreeable manners" (2:854).

Shore's departure interrupted another friendship. After completing the decennial revenue settlements (in which Jones assisted), he also left because of poor health. As he later said of Jones: "At the Gardens, he was my neighbour. . . . I have often regretted, as I flatter myself he also did, that our different avocations prevented our meeting as constantly as we both wished."[1]

Jonathan Duncan, another charter member of the Society and now superintendent at Benares, was helping resolve the revenue problem. He sent Jones a manuscript of the rare *Nāradasmriti,* a part of the "divine law" in the Smritis usually considered a supplement to the *Mānava-Dharmaśāstra.* As Cornwallis had told Jones of Duncan's treaty with the Infanticides, Jones hoped that it would be "the means of preserving the lives of thousands." He equally condemned thuggee, "the sordid priestcraft of Durgā's ministers" (2:855, 856). These were cultural conditions that, in his view, could conceivably be cooperatively eliminated without trampling on Indian customs.

Davis finally sent the revised "On the Astronomical Computations of the Hindus," which Jones proofread for *Asiatick Researches* 2. Morris and Tucker helped with the calculations, and the sixty-two pages were printed. As Daniell had not yet returned to etch the copper plates, the inexperienced portrait painter John Alefounder etched the Sanskrit. Jones directed such labors all year until the volume appeared.

Inspiring Davis to use European scholarship, Jones recommended Jean-Sylvain Bailly's *Histoire de l'astronomie moderne* (Paris, 1779–82), despite

316

the weak fifth volume of 1787: "I anticipate your triumph over M. Bailly, whose late work, I presume, you have read. His materials are full of errors" (2:857). As Bailly presumed that no European could decipher the *Sūrya-siddhānta*, which initiated scientific Indian astronomy, Jones nudged Davis toward Sanskrit. By translating it from the original with Brahmans' assistance, Davis would have a great advantage over Le Gentil and other Continental scholars. This version would deserve separate printing.

As Jones's research on Indian chronology required data that he lacked the time (and observatory) to collect, he sent Davis a list of the twenty-seven yuga stars in the order of the lunar mansions. Davis supplied the table of longitudes, latitudes, and right ascensions, as well as an elegant drawing of the Indian ecliptic.[2] Learning about Varāha-mihira's *Brhat-Saṃhitā* from his pundit, he sent a Sanskrit passage, which Jones considered of great importance in determining the antiquity of Indian literature:

I am so young in Astronomy (having only read the first book of Newton's Principia, and gone through the ordinary course of the Elements, Conick Sections, & Fluxions) that you must not be surprized at my errors; but I cannot, with Harris's chart before me, understand how the *tenth* degree of *Bharani* could only be 3° 40′ eastward of the equinoctial colure in the time of the Argonauts, which colure (*Newt. Chron* p. 89) did in the end of 1689 cut the Ecliptick in ♉ 6° 29′ 15″ (2:858)

In dating Vyāsa, legendarily contemporary with Krishna, Jones identified Vyāsa as Parāśara's son. He was using Harris's *Stellarum fixarum hæmisphærium australe* (London, 1690), which claims that "all the stars in the Brittanick Catalogue are carefully laid down" for 1690. Because Davis's Sanskrit passage was full of errors, Jones studied it with Rāmal-ocana, who decided that it was inexplicable. Persevering, Jones read it aloud and discovered a meter that enabled him to reconstruct the passage, which was later verified by the correct copy that a pundit brought. He corrected key passages in his manuscript of Bhaṭṭotpala's commentary, thereupon dating Parāśara.

"A Supplement to the Essay on Indian Chronology" recounts the process. Some of the passage is reproduced in three ways – in Devanagari, transliterated in the Jonesian System, and translated. Here Jones pursued his own suggestion of using data regarding the colures to date ancient events more precisely, in a blend of the prescientific and the scientific. Elsewhere he accepted the new geological discoveries, but in this essay he relies on "Genesis" for his cosmic scheme. His elaborate study of Jason's voyage dates it forty-five years earlier than Newton did, although he does not take a stand on Jason's reality: "The whole *Argonautick* story (which neither was, according to HERODOTUS, nor, indeed, could have been, originally *Grecian*), appears, even when stripped of its poetical and fabulous ornaments, extremely disputable." Jones illustrates the Indians' "fabling and allegorizing spirit" by translating from the *Bhagavad-Gita,* in an exuberant, sometimes fallacious quest to correlate the events in "Genesis" and Hinduism:

> Whatever be the comparative *Hindu* scriptures, we may safely conclude, that the *Mosaick* and *Indian* chronologies are perfectly consistent; that MENU, son of BRAHMĀ, was the *Ādima,* or *first,* created mortal, and consequently our ADAM; that MENU, child of the Sun, was preserved with *seven* others, in a *bahitra* or capacious ark, from an universal deluge, and must, therefore, be our NOAH . . . and that the dawn of true *Indian* history appears only three or four centuries before the *Christian* era, the preceding ages being clouded by allegory or fable.

Yet, in view of the Brahmans' misinformation and Western ignorance of the Vedas, Jones was fortunate to discover what he did, and later would cap in a revelation that more than compensated for his errors in comparative mythology.

"A Supplement to Chronology" was not finished in time for the Society's meeting on 4 February, when after a disturbing gap of three months, Jones read an essay by William Roxburgh to eleven members. Three weeks later he, Cornwallis, Chambers, Hyde, and twenty-four others met. One of the two nominees whom he seconded was Burroughs. The occasion was Jones's Seventh Discourse.

In this he advances the question already sequentially developed, though his evidence is admittedly sparse: "Whence came the singular people, who long had governed *China,* before they were conquered by the *Tartars?*" Of the four usual answers, he easily rejects the view that the Chinese have dwelt for ages if not from eternity in China. The missionaries' view that they sprang from the same stock as the Arabs and Jews is harder to disprove. Their dissimilarity in manners and arts indicates that they were not anciently Tatars. Long inquiries lead Jones to accept the Brahmans' view that the Chinese were originally *kshatriyas* who abandoned the privileges of their caste and wandered into their eventual homeland. Mixing with the few Tatar inhabitants and unifying the area, they eventually developed a different appearance and language.

Jones's meager knowledge of Chinese linguistic and ethnic chronology ranges from inadequacy to error. For example, he erroneously equates Buddha with the legendary Fohi, pronounces Chinese philosophy to be "in so rude a state, as hardly to deserve the appellation," and offers flimsy parallels between Chinese and Hindu ceremonies and superstitions. Yet for ethnology he had to rely on the controversial Bailly and Le Gentil and on secondary literary sources like Couplet.[3] His best sources were the *Lun Yü* and the *Shih Ching,* which he still hoped to translate in a grand plan to enrich the West culturally through language. He promises to consider in a later Anniversary Discourse whether the three peoples anciently in Asia "had one common root, and, if they had, by what means that root was preserved amid the violent shocks, which our whole globe appears evidently to have sustained."

No particular harm was done by Jones's Seventh Discourse, even when the *Annual Register* of 1799 praised "the most perfect accuracy" of his associating Buddha with Fohi (p. 503). China belonged in his ambitious series, but it was simply outside his competence. He was as incautious as he had been about Anquetil; yet his endeavors began English sinology. A worthy precursor of the nineteenth-century British sinologists, Jones attempted calligraphy and printed Chinese characters in *Asiatick Researches*.[4] Burrow gave him a 488-page "Chinese Alphabetic Dictionary with an Index of the Characters Arranged under the 214 Keys,"[5] in which he wrote: "The letters A & B must be procured from *China*. If the letters A & B can be supplied, the book will be inestimable." Jones defined each word in Latin and supplied Roman transliterations of the logograms in the index.

On 1 April, the Society's third meeting of 1790, he read his "Design of a Treatise on the Plants of India," and in June he presented "A Supplement to Chronology" and "On the Spikenard." His Krishnagar sojourn delayed the fifth meeting until November, when his special efforts attracted nineteen members. Jones nominated two people – Le Gentil as an honorary member and then a friend who had promised to dissect a pangolin. He seconded the nomination of Arthur William Devis, who was to paint his full-view portrait, and delivered his "On the Musical Modes." The December meeting attracted only seven members for a geographical paper. Although the Society met only six times in 1790, Jones was still envisioning vast responsibilities: "*Give us time, we may say, for our investigations, and we will transfer to* Europe *all the sciences, arts, and literature of* Asia." A major goal was to procure accurate descriptions of animals and hundreds of medicinal plants "from actual examination, with accounts of their several *uses* in medicine, diet, or manufactures."[6] Even today, such scope and comprehensiveness sound more like a WHO program than one scholar's idealism.

Though Jones hoped to disseminate knowledge more widely than the Royal Society usually did, there were large obstacles. He had to rely on Bengal's unsophisticated facilities and typesetters; sometimes he needed an unusual font. Also, when his eyes were weak, colleagues had to help with the proofreading. He sought to enlist men of special talents. Daniell's wanderings had delayed Jones's plan for first-rate etchings, and the local silversmith was dilatory. Jones did secure the services of Alefounder, holder of the Royal Academy's silver medal. His encouraging Devis's membership had a similar motivation.

Jones had won Indian scholars' full cooperation in the law digest, but few were contributing to the Society. Their role was still much more limited than was needed if India were to be fully investigated and if real cultural advances were eventually to be made. Usually he inspired the Indians' essays for the Society, which were then read to the members by a European. His colleagues' unwillingness to accept Indian members had not been ameliorated by his personal model of having an enthusiastic staff of pundits. He had not initiated the idea, but now each of the scholarly members kept a full-time pundit. In this way, Jones was setting the stage for a climate in which English Orientalists could build an enduring relationship with the Bengali intelligentsia, supplying Western knowledge to the Indians who were working to effect change. Following in his footsteps, H. T. Colebrooke, William Carey, and others contributed to this collaboration and the discoveries.[7] But not until 1829 could Indians participate directly in the Society's role in the Bengal renaissance.

Jones's view of these culturally different people at first was not democratic. A member of a ruling nation that considered itself superior in knowledge, discipline, and organization, he was a product of that educational system. Although he generally kept a latent bias enchained, sometimes it shockingly emerged: "I was forced to borrow of a black man, and it was like touching a snake" (2:694). The "deluded, besotted" Indian peasants presently lacked the capacity to participate in his ideal democracy (2:847). But increasingly, when he needed to know more about the Indians in order to help them, the foreign administrator was obscured under the sympathetic friend and disinterested seeker of knowledge. "[He] regarded the natives with the reverential interest of the newcomer, and [George Nesbitt] Thompson mentions a conversation in which he 'mounted his Hindoo Pegasus' and expressed his belief that the Hindus were the Gymnosophists of the ancients, and needed only mild laws, not harsh measures, to restrain their naturally philosophical instincts."[8] Jones made a strenuous effort to understand the Indians on their own terms: "His achievement was greater than 'tolerance'; it often appears genuine acceptance of values very different from European ones."[9] His research was never done in a spirit of Ripley's "Believe it or not"; rather, he was a detached investigator who accepted all beings as creatures of God, whether European or Asian, or human or nonhuman.

Seeking to expand his understanding of Hinduism, Jones seldom let his Christian beliefs block his appreciation. Great ideas appealed to him, but occasional tenets might be questioned:

Each sect must be justified by its own faith and good intentions: this only I mean to inculcate, that the tenet of our church cannot without profaneness be compared with that of the *Hindus,* which has only an apparent resemblance to it, but a very different meaning. One singular fact, however, must not be suffered to pass unnoticed. That the name of CRISHNA, and the general outline of his story, were long anterior to the birth of our Saviour, and probably to the time of HOMER, we know very certainly.[10]

He frequently praised the Hindu concept of the hereafter, as compared with the Christian eternal punishment.

Jones's humanism was humanitarian. He considered infanticide and sacrifices to Kālī to be unrepresentative of sound Hinduism, comparable to the claims that the Virgin Mary had appeared in Italy in 1294, which did not invalidate Christianity. If he privately disparaged the caste system, he was publicly silent on untouchability, because it was a basic Indian custom. What he did do was to try to improve health and sanitation in the jail, where this concept particularly affected prisoners.

In the spring of 1790 Jones's schedule averaged seven hours daily as a judge, with another two hours for the digest and reading to Anna. On 10 June he made his fifth charge to the grand jury. As he had previously instructed the jurors on all kinds of cases, this time his short discourse discussed "the general form of the Oath, which you have taken, and every material word, which occurs in it." The oath, never before treated in a charge, was admittedly complicated. Grand juries sometimes found it ambiguous, and friends often asked him about it. In clear legal terms he analyzed the four parts and the intent of the law – "the pole-star, by which you are to direct your course." He concluded: "Like perfect historians, you will not fear to say any thing that is true, nor dare to say any thing that is false; but will so act in every part of your duty, that the innocent may approach the tribunal without apprehension of danger, and the guilty leave it without complaining of injustice." Thus, in hearing cases, he continued to instruct jurors about objectivity, truth, and procedures.

A juror thought this charge was so important that he gave it to the *Calcutta Gazette,* which printed it on the front page on 1 July "as a most valuable and instructive lesson to all future Grand Jurors." The Company Press published it for two rupees, with the proceeds to go to insolvent debtors, as Jones requested.

He was planning to delay his return to Europe until he saved £30,000. Then Countess Spencer disturbingly remarked that the interest on that sum would provide a very moderate income "for the Joneses." He intended to retire in comfort and had estimated an annual need of £1,200 to ensure such comfort: "It would certainly be lunacy in me to leave at my age a fine income, half of which is fully adequate to all purposes of human happiness" (2:864). A total of £25,339 had been sent home, £1,500 would be paid when his note on Bishop Shipley's estate matured, and another £1,000 could soon be transmitted. If he were insulated and solitary, he would never leave India: "But my affections have a magnetick power, and attract the iron of my republican spirit."

The long sittings and heavy duties of business left Jones little time for vacation; not even Sunday was a day of rest. When the couple went to Krishnagar, his hope of writing many long letters had been reduced to the necessity of answering only his correspondents' specific points. His chief occupation again was the digest, which was vast and difficult. Yet he was proceeding confidently, speaking Sanskrit daily with Brahmans and hoping to understand it as well as he did Latin. One hour nightly was reserved for reading to Anna.

Jones wrote few personal letters that autumn. Anna's sister Emily Sloper had sent him a speech by Thomas Erskine, provoking his criticism of the wealthy, former liberal: "I never mind what advocates *say,* but what they prove; and I can only examine *proofs* in causes brought before me" (2:872). To John Wilmot he sent a hearty wish to the French people for a successful revolution and "an end of all the tyrannies, which the laziness and vices of nations have suffered to be established" (2:870). As for their mutual friend Chambers, who wanted a larger salary, Jones had done everything in his power to end Chambers's cruel suspense about the long-promised promotion to the chief justiceship.

He was less direct to Macpherson, who had mentioned Jones's possible major advancement, probably to the chief justiceship. Though honored, he would decline because he needed no addition to his fortune. An ambitious judge was a threat to public justice; indeed, Jones would favor a law requiring judges and bishops to remain for life in their original appointments. Actually, Lord Grenville, the secretary of state for the Home Department, had written Dundas:

Pitt has received a letter from you respecting a Mr. [William] Dunkin whom you seem to think a proper person to be appointed a judge at Calcutta. But this presupposes that one of the present judges is to be made Chief Justice. I confess there appear to me strong objections to placing either Chambers or Jones in that situation, and Pitt seems to feel them at least as strongly as I do. We wish however to receive your ideas on that subject; and if you agree with us, it would perhaps be better to take a new Chief Justice from the English Bar.[11]

Dundas may have been hoping to advance Jones by recommending Dunkin, a former officer of the Sadar Dīwānī Adālat. Dundas was showing keen interest in the Indians' welfare, partly kindled by Jones and the digest project.[12] Shortly Dundas agreed that Dunkin's appointment hinged on the promotion of Jones or Chambers, of whom he knew nothing except from his correspondence with Jones and from secondhand praise of Chambers. If Pitt and Grenville objected strongly, they were probably right.

Perhaps the pair feared Jones's latent politics. His earlier pamphleteering was not forgotten, despite his political silence publicly and his judicial–scholarly achievements in India. He still held advanced principles, as Pitt might have heard from mutual acquaintances. Chambers was under threat of parliamentary censure for supposed offense against the Regulating Act and Charter, but was not questioned on the charge. His official promotion to chief justice in January 1791 proved his virtual acquittal.[13] Dunkin's simultaneous appointment finally restored the Supreme Court to full strength.

Jones's probably last letter to Arthur Lee did not mention a possible visit to America or Franklin's death, but he told Price: "I had flattered myself with a hope of making a visit to our venerable friend at Philadelphia before the retreat which I meditate to my humble cottage in Middlesex – but God's will be done" (2:867). Anna's poor health had principally caused him to abandon that hope, but perhaps they would live to see free government in Europe.

Edward Jerningham's gift of *Poems on Various Subjects* (London, 1786) had delighted Jones, who could not reciprocate, as the digest prevented him from composing verse. The diplomat Harford Jones had sent Waḥshí's *Farhád u Shírín,* which some admiring *maulvis* had copied. Despite its beauty, Jones still preferred Nizámí. Pleased that his Persian writings had helped the diplomat, he was sorry that he lacked the time to do more. He reported on William Francklin, who, after joining the Asiatic Society, was to dedicate to Jones the translation *The Loves of Camarúpa and Cámalatá, an Ancient Indian Tale* (London, 1793).

Jones also wrote a friend who had assisted Colonel Polier at Oxford. This association ensured that Polier's manuscript of the Vedas would be given to the Bodleian Library rather than to the British Museum, as Polier had earlier promised Banks, with the condition that Jones and Wilkins have access to it. Jones next thanked William Shipley for promoting judicious projects and ingenious inventions and promised to disseminate the Kentish Society's work.

Jones was still helping old friends like Thomas Maurice, who decided to write a needed history of India. Though Maurice knew the classical sources, only Sanskrit could provide primary data. His general plan was encouraged: "Jones afforded the clue which has directed my path through this dark and intricate labyrinth. I have cautiously adhered to the outline which his pencil drew, and have in no instance deviated from my honoured guide." Maurice was urged to learn Persian so as to consult other key sources. He published Jones's letter, deleting only the candid remarks about "friends" who were less than zealous in advancing Maurice's projected history. This probably included Jacob Bryant, whom Jones had criticized when devising a proper methodology for using etymological scholarship. Jones had much to do with starting Maurice on a notable career in Orientalism.[14]

His most scholarly letter that autumn answered Monboddo's elaborate query about the source of the languages and arts of the peoples named in Jones's Third Discourse. Monboddo hypothesized that humans had originated in Asia, spreading over the earth in migrations chiefly traceable by language. Ingenious, inaccurate data led him to conclude Sanskrit to be the ancient language of Egypt: "The question is, whether the Egyptians learned the language from the Indians, or the Indians from the Egyptians, or both from some other nation." If the Egyptians learned Sanskrit in India, were the Indians self-taught, or did they learn it from another nation?

The universalism in this wild speculation appealed to Jones, which pleased Monboddo: "You say you incline to believe that not only the Egyptians, but the Indians came from Chaldaea. If you can make out this, it will be a great discovery at least to me, who have not so much as a conjecture about the origin of either of these two nations." When Jones suggested caution, Monboddo argued that the Egyptians took their arts and sciences into India and perhaps went to Japan: "In both these countries there are Idols to be seen, of black men with woolly hair, flat noses and thick lips." Did Jones know of such idols? Mistakenly believing certain words to be common to all languages, Monboddo concluded that "there was one primitive Language from which all other Languages are descended; and that this Language was the Language of Egypt, the parent country in my opinion of all Arts and Sciences." This suggestion of comparative anthropology anticipated the modern view that humankind evolved from one ancestral stock, and the theory of Elliot Smith and others that most elements in world culture evolved in Egypt. Jones was interested in the matter and obtained a small statue of Buddha, which Anna later sent to Monboddo.[15]

Upon his return to Calcutta, Jones answered a letter from Richard Morris, Jr., who wanted to publish his uncle Lewis Morris's place-name dictionary and requested Jones's opinion of the long manuscript. Even though it was fascinating to a Welsh linguist, the project received only Jones's usual promise to promote it but not to influence subscriptions. He barely had time to maintain membership in the Cymmrodorion Society of Morris's father.

Jones's association with Cornwallis was prospering. After the vestiges of the struggle between the Supreme Council and the Supreme Court disappeared, the ensuing cooperation was improving the government of Bengal. Cornwallis's desire to advance the public good had been demonstrated by his support of the law digest, and his procedure in reformation was gratifying. He met with the Court several times to harmonize on principles for legislation that would improve the Calcutta police. An appointed superintendent would maintain order and arrest suspects but would have no magisterial and judicial functions, so that Jones's constitutional emphasis evidently prevailed. The reorganization became part of the Cornwallis Code in May 1793. Three judges at each of the four circuit courts would act in civil and criminal cases.[16]

Cornwallis needed help from an experienced jurist. Having worked with law for two decades and possessing keen scholarly powers, Jones advised energetically. Probably he saw himself as a tutor to a good administrator, and India benefited when he assisted in the judicial reformation. For an entire morning he studied Cornwallis's draft and supplements of a "Minute on the administration of criminal justice in the provinces," which cautiously moved toward English law, with English agencies to replace the Indian ones, without really violating Indian law. His intention was to write all his objections unreservedly: "I found nothing to which I could object, and did not meet with a single paragraph to which, if I were a member of the Council I would not heartily express my assent" (2:877).[17] Cornwallis delightedly transmitted Jones's approving report to London.

Both men benefited from the association. This Minute led to the establishment of circuit courts, which Jones's "Best Practicable System" had opposed; yet it implemented his wish that *maulvis* help the English judges. Cornwallis was not a lawyer; he knew nothing of Islam or the Indian temperament and depended on Jones's research, which pointed toward a case law and the ending of the more barbaric Moslem punishments. Having an exaggerated regard for the English legal system, Cornwallis convinced Jones of the need for a police superintendency, once he accepted the constitutional bars on the position. So in the effort to codify existing law and procedure into regulations, Jones played a leading role.[18]

Just as Jones helped Shore make the perpetual revenue settlements covering the zamindars, he suggested principles and details for the innovational Cornwallis Code that founded the Indian Civil Service and became the legal basis for new territories. His views are reflected in provisions such as (1) magistrates with reasonable judicial power, aided by local police heads, will hear and decide civil suits; (2) Moslem law will be followed in criminal cases, but will be superseded by English law in punishments like mutilation; (3) in civil suits between Hindus, a pundit will assist the judge on matters of inheritance and caste; and (4) unjust decisions can be overturned through a system of appeal. The code was consonant with Indian law, in harmony with Jones's feelings since his work on Indian judicature in 1781, but English agencies administered justice.

Jones's pleasant relationship with Cornwallis was never as close as that with Hastings, for Cornwallis was not a scholar or literary man. Nor did Jones have time to be convivial, in view of his research and nightly reading to Anna. Still, he could supply immense learning and keen interest in reform. Cornwallis later summarized his own attitude at a dinner with Pitt and others: "Afraid of Sir William Jones; and always found him much to do, and took him into his council; where otherwise he might have thwarted."[19] But Jones's influence led to Cornwallis's informal assistance to scholarship. Duncan's appointment to Benares led to the founding of the Sanskrit College of Sarasvati Bhawan, where Kāśīnāth, who had compiled a Sanskrit dictionary for Jones, became the head professor, in another notable advance for Indians' scholarship. The Governor-General also supported the Asiatic Society, which Jones had ensured by soliciting Cornwallis's acceptance as its First Patron.

The last of *Asiatick Researches* 2 was finally printed. The publication date was 1790, but numerous corrections delayed it until 19 January 1791, when Cantopher advertised it for fifty sicca rupees. Jones gave the manuscripts for the third volume to the press. Remembering the king's praise of the first volume, he informed Dundas that Elmsly would bind special copies for Dundas and the king.

Half of the twenty-eight more formal papers were by Jones's colleagues, including a Sanskrit translation by Wilkins, and Roxburgh's essay on an insect, which expanded a Linnaean class. Although Roxburgh's revision "Chermes Lacca" appeared in *Philosophical Transactions* of 1791, the fact that this F.R.S. permitted the Asiatic Society to publish the original draft indicates Jones's success in competing with Banks. Burrow contributed notes for the appendix.

All but two of Jones's contributions have been discussed: the Fourth through the Seventh Anniversary Discourses, "The Design of a Treatise," "On the Antiquity of the Indian Zodiac," "On the Chronology of the Hindus," "On the Cure of the Elephantiasis, and Other Disorders of the Blood," "On the Second Classical Book," "On the Spikenard," "Remarks on Hinzuan," and "A Supplement to Chronology." These included all his new essays except his charges to the grand jury.

"On the Baya, or Indian Gross-Beak" is Jones's translation of a *maulvi*'s brief paper from Delhi. He interpolates philological and utilitarian observations such as that the grosbeak's "flesh is warm and drying, of easy digestion, and recommended, in medical books, as a solvent of stone in the bladder or kidneys; but of that virtue there is no sufficient proof." His source makes this the poorest of his three physiological papers.

Excepting the zodiacal paper, the most important essay in the second volume was Jones's "On the Indian Game of Chess." Without using Sanskrit sources, Thomas Hyde's *De ludis orientalibus* (1694) had credited the Hindus with originating chess. Jones was fascinated by the description of a four-handed dice game in the *Bhaviṣya-purāṇa,* which he partly translated in extending Hyde's opinion. This game was more complex yet more modern than the Persian one. Elaborately etymologizing the word *chess,* Jones speculated: "It was invented by one effort of some great genius; not completed by gradual improvements, but formed, to use the phrase of *Italian* criticks, *by the first intention."* Sanskrit sources seemed to prove that chess was developed in India; one rule even governed pawn advancement. Mentioning the ancient view that chess had existed for four thousand to five thousand years, Jones stated only that it was introduced into Persia in the sixth century A.D. Many modern authorities agree that it was played in India before it is known to have been played elsewhere.[20]

European praise of the second volume delighted the Asiatic Society. The *Monthly Review* reviewed it seriatim, concluding: "When we consider the importance and excellence of the aggregate, we look with dread toward any accident that may impede the progress of the Society's researches. We read with great sorrow the close of the President's Sixth Discourse, and we heartily wish to unite our exertions with his 'to promote the sale of the work in London.' "[21]

Jones's Advertisement in the volume articulated his international view of advancing and disseminating knowledge. It transcended direct cooperation with the Royal Society, for it might simply have appeared in *Philosophical Transactions:*

It may greatly conduce to the advancement of useful knowledge, if the learned Societies established in *Europe* will transmit to the Secretary of the Society in *Bengal* a Collection of short and precise Queries on every Branch of *Asiatic* History, Natural and Civil, on the Philosophy, Mathematics, Antiquities, and Polite Literature of *Asia,* and on Eastern Arts, both Liberal and Mechanic; since it is hoped that accurate Answers may in due time be procured to any Questions that can be proposed on those subjects; which must in all events be curious and interesting, and may prove in the highest degree beneficial to mankind.

The response was excellent. Yonge and Llandaff had not waited for an invitation to submit wide-ranging questions. Banks's commissions, though intended for his botanical projects, tied in the Royal Society; and William

Shipley had started an exchange with his Kentish Society. The mathematician John Playfair, whose "Remarks on the Astronomy of the Brahmins" had just appeared in *Transactions of the Royal Society of Edinburgh,* submitted "Questions and Remarks on the Astronomy of the Hindus": "They will, perhaps, be forgiven to one who feels himself deeply interested in the subject to which they relate, and who would not lose even the feeblest ray of a light, which, without the exertions of the *Asiatic* Society, must perish for ever." Jones answered three of the questions in his Eleventh Discourse and publicly thanked Playfair when he printed Playfair's "Questions and Remarks" in *Asiatick Researches* 4. The Edinburgh *Transactions* shortly announced the election of Jones, Roxburgh, and Dr. James Anderson to membership (3:23–25).

The Advertisement also stimulated American societies. Perhaps Franklin's death prevented an association with the American Philosophical Society, and Jones's own death prevented his seeing three important responses. Ezra Stiles, the president of Yale University, submitted a voluminous inquiry. Eliphalet Pearson sent an involved biblical question from the American Academy of Arts and Sciences, and requested Oriental manuscripts for Harvard University, which had none: "It may ultimately be most for the benefit of mankind, that these ancient records of truth should be deposited in each quarter of the globe." This tied universities to the Asiatic Society. James Sullivan reported Jones's election to membership in the Massachusetts Historical Society and enclosed books intended to initiate "an intercourse of true philanthropy . . . to support that harmony in the great family of mankind, on which the happiness of the world so much depends." He requested facts about natural history.[22]

In 1791 Jones held eight meetings of the Asiatic Society. On 19 January he read "A Royal Grant of Land in Carnāta," his annotated prose translation of a fifty-four-stanza Devanagari inscription on the great pagoda of Conjeeveram, which he calls "conformable to the rules" of Sanskrit verse. On 24 February his two fellow judges, all the Supreme Council except Cornwallis (who was leading the army against Tipu Sultan), and twenty-nine others heard his Eighth Discourse. This long essay on Asian "borderers, mountaineers, and islanders" richly expands his concept of language families, and provides further proof that a close study of his linguistics requires consideration of all of his Indian essays. He had done more work on Arabic, annotating his copy of John Parkhurst's *An Hebrew and English Lexicon, Without Points* (London, 1762).[23] Completing the conceptions that had been advanced by Scandinavian philologists earlier, Jones places Ethiopic in the Semitic family, "not only from the great multitude of identical words, but (which is a far stronger proof) from the similar grammatical arrangement." He innovationally classifies the Gypsies' Romany as an Indic language, but was understandably troubled by its differences from the Indic languages spoken in Bengal. Unfortunately, William Marsden's dubious data misled him into concluding that Sanskrit had given rise to languages from Madagascar to the Philippines. The Hellenic group includes Aeolic, Doric, and Attic, with Phrygian perhaps related. Jones similarly subdivides Germanic into the equivalent of High and Low German, and North and East Germanic. Naturally he never mentions Tocharian and Hittite, which were discovered later. He specifies a Finno-Ugric family containing at least Finnish, Hungarian, and Lappish. He even projects how a language can diverge into a mutually unintelligible tongue in four to five centuries: "Ferocious and hardy tribes, who retire for the sake of liberty to mountainous regions, and form by degrees a separate nation, must also form in the end a separate language by agreeing on new words to express new ideas; provided that the language, which they carried with them, was not fixed by writing and sufficiently copious." Overall, this important linguistic essay relates various peoples to the ancient Hindus in terms of cultural diffusion, primarily through migration.

This essay is also Jones's best use of the inscriptions that his colleagues were copying from pillars and caves for him, in a grand design intended ultimately to collect reliable copies of all inscriptions in the subcontinent. Just as he had studied Sanskrit astronomy to help date events, now he used a new kind of evidence to help reconstruct India's past. He introduced a subject matter and method of comprehending Indian archaeology "in a devout spirit of inquiry, affecting the interests of humanity and the truths of holy writ."[24] This epigraphic pioneering again enlarged European intellectual horizons, ultimately suggesting a kind of sociology of knowledge in which disciplines are intertwined and may be best studied as a field such as Orientalism.

At the meeting of 17 March there was a personal triumph: Jones nominated Dr. Anderson. Dr. Nicolas Fontana presented a paper about a voyage. On 21 April the attendance rose to seventeen, but on 16 June only eight heard two papers sent by Roxburgh and then agreed to adjourn until after Jones's vacation at Krishnagar. By then 150 pages of *Asiatick Researches* 3 had been printed.

Once the term began on 7 January, Jones had hardly an hour's leisure during the day, even on Sundays, for four months. One trial in January consumed two weeks of nine-hour days. Speaking Sanskrit fluently by now, he was polishing his translation of the first nine chapters of the *Mānava-Dharmaśāstra*. Between breakfast and the sitting of the Supreme Court he worked on it, charming the Indians: "Making their slavery lighter by giving them their own laws, is more flattering to me than the thanks of the company and the approbation of the king, which have been transmitted to me" (2:885). This characterization of British rule as Indian slavery was his strongest private statement to date and shows the value of his help to Indians within the overall administration.

Jones still read to Anna nightly; in seven years they had crossed so much literary ground that even he was surprised to recollect the many volumes. Among them, Pietro della Valle's *Viaggi* (2nd ed., 1658–63) was delightfully instructive because of their familiarity with Asia. Jones's favorite was Francesco Guicciardini, a lawyer who had refused to mix in the world when Florentine laws were no longer respected: "I wish to imitate him by abandoning the Metropolis for ever and retiring to an *Arcetri,* as he did at the age of fifty . . . in a studious and tranquil retirement" (2:902).

Early in 1791 Anna was ill again but recovered. Apparently Europeans could not be inured to the harsh climate; those who stayed the longest seemed to be the most susceptible. Temperance and moderate exercise had kept Jones healthy since his near-fatal fever, despite his heavy schedule. Yet he now felt more fatigued after seven continuous hours on the bench, and he anticipated a calm weekend at Garden Reach more.

In February he sent home £3,000 in China bills, projecting two more such transmissions over the next two years. Then he might begin saving for the expenses of the return voyage, presuming that the interest would permit as comfortable a life as he now enjoyed in Bengal. He would not necessarily retire, for he had not abandoned all hope that the people's part of the English constitution might be invigorated. If so and if he were in Parliament, he would attempt some such proposition in the form of a resolution; but because his principles had not changed, the Commons seemed unappealing unless there was real hope of doing good in a time of public danger. So he would seek tranquillity on a Sabine farm, far from the bustle of London. Except for Anna and beloved friends like Spencer, that retreat might otherwise be in the United States. The couple wanted a country house, with a pasture for horses and a garden for studying botany. The interest on their savings or a well-secured annuity should easily support their modest wishes, and they had no needy relatives.

In the first half of 1791 Jones spent considerable time in encouraging Society members. Duncan had begun work on Indian history. Francis Wilford was engaged in an investigation complementing Jones's findings, grandly promising to be the new Rennell of Indian geography. Taking Jones's applause to heart, he zestily urged his pundit to find Sanskrit references to Noah and Noah's three sons. When he reported startling treasures in the *Skanda-purāṇa* and sent a chart supposedly of the Nile and adjacent countries, Jones added the silent hope that it *was* a treasure. Prodding his obliging pundit, Wilford went to Benares and soon reported that he had located a Sanskrit account of Africa, Europe, and even of Britain by name. When Jones requested proof, the pundit forged and discolored a sheet that was placed in the *Padma-purāṇa*. After Wilford read a paper to the Society that included the pundit's "minutely exact" translation of the supposed Sanskrit, there were to be repercussions. Jones, who would have detected the forgery, never saw the sheet.

He subtly conveyed Le Gentil's "challenges" to Davis, who was working with Brahmans in translating the *Sūrya-siddhānta*. Also inspired to compose "On the Indian Cycle of Sixty Years," Davis was now ready to learn Sanskrit. Because this had been Jones's hope all along, he tried a stronger challenge: Only Davis could divulge the treasures in Varāha-mihira, as accurate information would not come from Bailly or Playfair. Half an hour's daily study of the *Sārasvatīprakriyā* for two or three months would permit Davis to read Sanskrit with ease. Jones lent the short book at Davis's request: "Do not mind the Brahmens, who affect to despise this grammar, because it is *easy:* it is so, but it is perspicuous and elegant, & will fully answer your purpose. I would not advise you to get the rules by heart, but merely to read the book with your Pandit" (2:880–1). Here Jones rejected the traditional memorization, which he had done, to suit the situation.

In early September the Joneses left for Krishnagar. Their pinnace was barely out of town before he began paying his annual tribute of letters. Burroughs had lent a laudatory communication from the earl of Charlemont, and because he had added his own praise, one of Jones's most graceful letters was required. Receiving praise, though unmerited, from someone who deserved the highest praise pleased even rough classical moralists. Presumably Charlemont liked Jones because of his belief in freedom. Friendship so based had a strong attraction for Jones: "Were I to hear of a man at the extremity of the globe, who maintained those principles and carried them into action, I should instantly find my heart struggling to unite itself with his" (2:887). Conversely, Jones would never willingly associate with men who professed the opposite principles.

Long letters went to Spencer and Spencer's mother. Jones commended George Hardinge, now the senior justice of Brecon, for the unimpressive sonnets later published in *The Miscellaneous Works in Prose and Verse of George Hardinge* (London, 1818). But he criticized their political themes, "which add very little to the graces of poetry" (2:891), conveniently forgetting his own political poetry.

Perhaps Jones's last letter to Hastings was composed in October. Their correspondence was mainly advanced by Hastings, who also wrote Anna.

As she wrote him: "You are very kind in your good wishes & solicitude about my Sir William & me."[25] The growing public opposition to the parliamentary attacks again evoked Jones's premature congratulations: "You will, I doubt not, have obtained a complete triumph over your persecutors; and your character will have risen, not brighter indeed, but more conspicuously bright, from the furnace of their persecution" (2:899). Even here he avoided legal ramifications, not even naming Burke. Although Burke, who made highly polished speeches against the supposed heart of the Bengal corruption, dropped most of the charges, Hastings's ordeal was to drag on until 1795. Jones's rancor was intense.

He wrote scholarly letters to the physician Jean-Baptiste Le Roy, Sir John Sinclair, and Banks. Sinclair, the president of the Board of Agriculture, was collaborating with Banks in trying to crossbreed merino sheep in order to produce finer wool. He requested information about Asiatic wool, or soft hair, and enclosed various tracts and wool specimens, which Jones circulated. Jones was too busy to help much himself, but Bebb and Robert Kyd promised to seek the information. Although Bengal wool was coarse, Jones explained that fine Kerman wool might be procured from sheep in Bombay: "The shawl goats would live, I imagine, and breed in England; but it is no less difficult to procure the females from Cashmir, than to procure mares from Arabia" (2:890). Even though he approved of the breeding scheme, he contributed nothing to the project that would establish the modern British wool industry. Such correspondence helped inform him that improvement depends on the careful selection of males and females to breed stock with progressively fewer defects and greater perfections. He was also instructed in Banks's related methodology for vegetables, in which warm-climate plants were grown on the spot so as to adapt them to the new climate. Thus the concept of directed evolution became clearer to Jones, whose Christian beliefs were not affected by it.

Banks was concentrating on botany, and as the East India Company was consulting Banks about economic plants, Jones became more involved with Kyd. Seeking to transplant the Malacca sago palm and Persian date palm to Bengal as resources against famine, Banks secured Cornwallis's cooperation.[26] Besides wishing to have all the Indian plants represented in Kyd's Calcutta Gardens, Jones hoped to introduce Arabian, Persian, and Chinese plants. He participated in investigations with Kyd, who submitted "Remarks on the Soil and Vegetation of the Western Side of the River Hooghly" for *Asiatick Researches*.[27]

Jones's botanical searches were no longer random. Early fascinated by natural history, he was pleased to contribute to making Kew the botanical Mecca. No doubt he appreciated its potential for the tropical empire as grandly conceived by Banks, that dominating figure in science.[28] The knowledge would be used to help people around the world. Since Banks's initial commissions, their association had deepened until Jones was being asked to do regular collecting and even transporting. This work was important, but he would not neglect his law digest for something that had considerably lower priority for him. When Banks requested more help than he had been giving Yonge, who had the official responsibility for St. Vincent, Jones made his excuses:

I talked on the subject to Lord Cornwallis, who told me the King himself had mentioned it to him; & I took for granted, that it would be made a public official measure. As a private man, I can do little in that way; for I know few Captains; & those whom I do know I seldom see. It was with great difficulty that I got a passage for a Cratæva Marmelos; and heaven knows what became of it. In short, if you wish to transfer our Indian plants to the Western Isles, the Company must direct Kyd and Roxburgh to send them & their own Captains to receive them & attend to them. (2:891)

Perhaps thinking of Banks's funding of explorations, in contrast with his own need to earn his livelihood and use his leisure for research at his own expense, Jones reiterated his Society's need for a traveling botanist of John Koenig's quality. Unconcerned about the East India Company's commercial obligations, he would prefer a full-time scholar; yet he was not so naive as to think that even Banks's influence could help. The company, like the Royal Society, did not fund research, which was done without support of salary, equipment, or travel. As scholarship was pursued because of one's devotion to finding the truth, Jones had to operate his Society in the way that Banks ran the Royal Society. However much he would have liked the government to subsidize botanical study, there was no pension or privilege.

Koenig had bequeathed his manuscripts and drawings to Banks. When Roxburgh forwarded them to Banks, Jones was not pleased:

God knows whether any use honorable to his memory will be made of his manuscripts. . . . I wish poor Kœnig had left his papers to you; Banks has too much of his own to employ him, and Macpherson, who loved the sage, would I dare say have persuaded Lord Cornwallis to raise the best monument to his memory, a good edition of his works. (2:706–7)

Expeditious publication was the appropriate way to present one's findings. Jones was too busy to edit the papers, but his Society needed access to the data. Thinking that nothing had been done with the papers, he asked Banks either to print them or send a copy: "We will send you in return, not only the correct Sanscrit names, but the Plants themselves; or at least the Seeds, *if you can prevail on any Captain to take care of them.*" The following year Jones made a public reminder: "We may be sure, that the publick spirit of that illustrious naturalist [Banks] will not suffer the labours of his learned friend [Koenig] to be sunk in oblivion."[29]

Jones sent Banks a miniature state of the art in Indian botany. Roxburgh would do much on the coast if he could get relief from his terrible headaches. In Bengal there was no assistance, as the East India Company would not subsidize botanical travel. Jones had neither strong eyes nor time, but he and Anna had examined 170 Linnaean genera:

She brought home a morning or two ago, the most lovely Epidendrum, that ever was seen; but the description of it would take up too much room in a letter: it grew on a lofty Amra; but it is an air-plant, & puts forth its fragrant enameled blossoms in a pot without earth or water. None of the many species in Linnæus correspond exactly. (2:892)

In a letter in February 1790 Banks had asked about several matters, on which Jones reported. His knowledge of James Bruce was from *Travels,* all five volumes of which he had read to Anna, except for certain frank descriptions. They were so entertaining that he forgave Bruce's botanical and Arabic mistakes, but he clearly was unaware that Bruce had traced the source of the Blue Nile. Second, he reported that the madhuca tree was a bassia. Banks had compared Charles Hamilton's essay on the tree with Koenig's statement that it had sixteen filaments; however, Jones found not one blossom in fifty to have sixteen filaments. Koenig had undoubtedly seen such a character, "but he should not have set it down as constant. I frequently saw 26 & 28 filaments, sometimes 12; & the average was about 20 or 22." Finally, Pearse's claim that Saturn had seven arms was disproved by the mythological drawings of the planets that Pearse had secured. Nor had Jones seen a Sanskrit epithet like *seven-armed.* He regretted the death of Pearse, who "had an ardour in his character, which might have brought some light out of smoke.– He showed his paper about the prediction of Comets and even of Earthquakes by the Brahmens & was so offended by our credulity, that we were obliged to print his dull papers merely to keep him in tolerable humour."

When Banks again inquired about spikenard in March 1791, Jones was uncertain: "We have Nards in abundance, Acorus, Schœnus, Andropogon, Cyperus, &c. &c"; but he had no evidence that the Greeks meant only a fragrant grass. He thought Ptolemy's nard was a valerian. Banks's questions about the flora mentioned in the *Sacontalā,* which had entertained Banks, elicited a list of botanical names, in a fusion of literature and science at once expanding Jones's botanical goals. Initially, Jones's search had been literary, but the Linnaean classifications were valuable in their own right. Wishing to be Banks's neighbor upon retirement, he asked Banks to watch for "a pleasant Country house to be disposed of in your part of Middlesex with pasture-Ground for my Cattle and Garden-ground enough for my amusement" (2:895).

When a Hindu friend brought Jones a flower celebrated in the Vedas, he could not find it listed in Linnaeus or Reede's *Horti Malabarici pars prima* (Amsterdam, 1673–1703). So he sent it to Banks to learn the Linnaean name. Banks also met with no success in Reede; Jones had found few names correctly written in Sanskrit or Arabic in the twelve volumes.

After offering to send his two hundred Sanskrit, Persian, and Arabic manuscripts to Banks, in January 1792 Jones dispatched them with a bill of lading: "Should I live to have the pleasure of seeing you again, you will have the goodness to let me take the manuscripts, with the care of which I now trouble you: should I die, you will deposit them in the library of the Royal Society, so that they may be lent out without difficulty to any studious men" (2:906). He was not forsaking his own Society; he expected to use them in England, after completing the digest, where they would be available for European scholars. Later, after Jones's death, Banks wrote a careful letter giving Anna no opportunity to retrieve the manuscripts, which would be received "with infinite respect to the memory of the donor & the conditions stated in his letter minutely attended to."[30]

Overall, Jones helped give more unity and design to Banks's Indian collecting. Their association embraced more disciplines than was the case when Banks asked a British doctor to collect plants. Ironically, Jones's endeavors may have reduced the Asiatic content in *Philosophical Transactions,* because his colleagues published in *Asiatick Researches.* He sent copies of individual essays, which Banks, anticipating the exchange of offprints, catalogued into a splendid personal library. In turn, Jones's own essays were more scientific as a result of Banks's influence, and his botanical taxonomic work ramified and deepened his vastly important concept of common source as an explanation of language similarities. That is, his scientific predecessors had shown that at least some flora and fauna were not immutable, and he conceived the vital corollary that a language can comparably die or change into another language. For a scholar, linguistic changes through time might be as revealing as biota were for Buffon and Linnaeus. Perhaps linguistics required a model from the sciences in order to become modern.

In personal exploration and collecting, Banks operated on a much more international scale, if less comprehensive than Jones's research design for a smaller area. India was just one source for Banks, and Jones's Society was a remote Asian intellectual center. By contrast, Banks's London house and library constituted a leading scientific meeting place; his informal gatherings anticipated international congresses. Unfortunately, Jones was the only scholar who was strategically placed in a research complex like the one that he had constructed. Had there been others, the advent of international cooperative projects might have been hastened.

Their correspondence, exemplifying the contemporary utilization of letters to advance research, increased Jones's love of botany. It was his favorite amusement at Krishnagar: "A more delightful study could not have been found; nor could we have had a finer field for it than India" (2:884). Anna also preferred botany. Although she enjoyed the reading that he selected usually for instruction, she had greater delight in illustrating his description of a plant after they had examined it. Their curiosity was neverending: "Anna has brought me a new flower, and we are going to hunt for it in Linnæus" (2:899).

Her health seemed so good that Jones did something very untypical: So as to avoid the Calcutta heat, they remained in their delightful Krishnagar cottage for an extra week, despite his duties on the bench. During that intimate autumn, of her own accord she promised to sail in January 1793 to preserve her health, when they should have £33,000. She would live with her mother until he returned to England. Then they would settle in a retreat perhaps selected by Banks, "with comfort and absolute independence, perfectly at our ease, yet with a wise frugality that may enable us to be properly liberal" (2:901).

For six months beginning on 1 November 1791, Jones daily spent seven hours on the bench and two more in his chambers. Dunkin's arrival did not appreciably lighten the Supreme Court's burden; it only permitted earlier hearings. Dunkin was quite direct. For example, Robert Morris, a former violent supporter of John Wilkes, wrote the judges individually that he wished to practice as an advocate. Though Dunkin urged the court to tell Morris that he was unworthy of a place, the other judges saw no reason to hurt Morris's feelings when he might have seen the error of his ways. They therefore informed him that there were already enough advocates. But he came to court in a wig and gown, accusing the judges of partiality and injustice. He was put down. Speaking third, Jones also upheld the original decision.[1]

Dunkin did not participate in the Society, although Jones presumably provided an invitation to the last three meetings of 1791. On 1 September, Jones seconded the nomination of the artist James Hoare, who was to collect Arakan plants for him. There was a paper by Roxburgh.

On 17 November, Jones presented "The Lunar Year of the Hindus," consisting of his introduction and calenderlike outline of Raghu-Nandana Bhaṭṭācharya's report on Hindu rites and ceremonies. Jones used two Sanskrit almanacs and other sources to verify the tables in this curious report,[2] making some omissions and carefully italicized additions. Inserting his prose translation of a passage from the *Bhaviṣya-purāṇa*, he makes intriguing classical comparisons. His conclusion is programmatic: "If the festivals of the old *Greeks, Romans, Persians, Egyptians,* and *Goths,* could be arranged with exactness in the same form with these *Indian* tables, there would be found, I am persuaded, a striking resemblance among them; and an attentive comparison of them all might throw great light on the religion, and, perhaps, on the history, of the primitive world." But it failed to stimulate other scholars.

Hyde and seven others heard Jones's "On the Mystical Poetry of the Persians and Hindus" on 8 December. This unusual poetry "consists almost wholly of a mystical religious allegory, though it seems on a transient view to contain only the sentiments of a wild and voluptuous libertinism." It is "a figurative mode of expressing the fervour of devotion, or the ardent love of created spirits towards their beneficent Creator," which has long prevailed in Asia. Jones cites Isaac Barrow and Jacques Necker to suggest the epitome of Vedānta and Sufism,[3] providing prose versions of Háfiz to illustrate Sufic mysticism. He also translates twenty-six couplets of Rúmí's *Mathnawí,* in the first European translation from that great work. Later titled "Verses, Translated from the Persian," it contains fine lines:

> Oh, more than GALEN learn'd, than PLATO wise!
> My guide, my law, my joy supreme arise!
> Love warms this frigid clay with mystick fire,
> And dancing mountains leap with young desire,
> Blest is the soul, that swims in seas of love,
> And long the life sustain'd by food above.
> With forms imperfect can perfection dwell?
> Here pause, my song; and thou, vain world, farewel.

Using Sufic sources, Jones was the first European to discuss the complex subject authoritatively.[4] He appended his translation of *Gīta Govinda* as a Hindu example.

In 1792 the Society met only five times. Seven members heard Davis's "On the Indian Cycle" on 9 February. Jones later thanked him for correcting the French errors: "You will have the honour of being the first European who drew a knowledge of Indian Astronomy from the fountainhead" (2:907).

On 23 February the Supreme Council, Isaac Titsingh, and twenty-seven others heard Jones's Ninth Discourse, "On the Origin and Families of Nations." Jones's belief in the unity among peoples extends Monboddo's anthropological speculation by relating language change to his concept of language families:

If the human race then be, as we may confidently assume, of one natural species, they must all have proceeded from one pair. . . . They must people in time the region where they first were established, and their numerous descendants must necessarily seek new countries, as inclination might prompt, or accident lead, them; they would of course migrate in separate families and clans, which, forgetting by degrees the language of their common progenitor, would form new dialects to convey new ideas.

Jones's desire for universalism prompts his speculation that "the inhabitants of *Asia,* and consequently, as it might be proved, of the whole earth, sprang from three branches of one stem." Rejecting Monboddo's view that some words are used in common by descendants of the three peoples, Jones declares Noah's language to be irretrievably lost. Then he wildly speculates that the only human family after the Flood established themselves in northern Persia, and that they eventually multiplied into the Arabs, Hindus, and Tatars – again overlooking the Negroid and Dravidian peoples of India.

Jones criticizes Bryant, who used ingenuity and erudition in his etymological conjecturing and was skilled in classical languages, but knew no Asian tongue except possibly Hebrew: "It will hardly be imagined, that I mean by this irony to insult an author, whom I respect and esteem; but no consideration should induce me to assist by my silence in the diffusion of error." Etymological license would derive almost any word from any other. When Bryant learned of this criticism, "he became so exasperated, that not all the high encomiums so liberally paid by his friend, in the same dissertation, to his talents and virtues, could, for a long time, appease" him. He wrote Maurice:

As to Sir W. Jones, he is by many thought to shew great duplicity, and to be very unfair in his allegations. I have written my opinion of his behaviour for my own private amusement: for I shall hardly send it into the world: especially while he is abroad. When he returns, I may probably let him see it. A writer more inconsistent and so often in opposition to himself, I never encountered.[5]

On 5 April the *Calcutta Gazette* published the first of Jones's two books of 1792. Fearing that the long-preserved Sanskrit manuscripts could still be lost, he wanted to make a literary work inexpensively available both to Western scholars and Indians in Bengali characters. His belief that the Indians should know and appreciate their own heritage underpinned his major contributions to India, but this time his effort was impractical. Indian literacy was so restricted that there could be little serious education even by mass printing of the literature, though he was anticipating the College of Fort William and its major translations. He had no time to publish other Sanskrit texts, but his annotations show how carefully he studied them.

Jones chose the short, juvenile *Ṛitusaṃhāra*. It is quite inferior to the *Śakuntalā*, and its eroticism must have shocked him. Although his puritanical delicacy would not have let him translate it into English, perhaps his integrity required a text with graphic physical descriptions and actions, a Sanskrit literary characteristic. But he would not use Western taste to censor Indian literature presented to the Indians. Only when introducing it to the West did he feel justified in employing omission and restraint. Only his Advertisement is in English:

This book is the first ever printed in *Sanscrit:* and it is by the press alone, that the ancient literature of *India* can long be preserved: a learner of that most interesting language who had carefully perused one of the popular grammars, could hardly begin his course of study with an easier or more elegant work, than the *Ritusanhāra,* or *Assemblage of Seasons.* Every line composed by *CĀLIDĀS* is exquisitely polished; and every couplet in the poem exhibits an *Indian* landscape, always beautiful, sometimes highly coloured, but never beyond nature: four copies of it have been diligently collated; and where they differed, the clearest and most natural reading has constantly had the preference.

The collating was a formidable task. Jones sent Wilkins a copy of the 144-quatrain book, "which Morris has printed, and which you are the only man in Europe who can read and understand" (2:914).[6]

Jones finished polishing his translation of the *Mānava-Dharmaśāstra* and began copying it, but had to stop to compose a charge to the grand jury on 9 June, his last and most important charge. As no penal case is too insignificant for a grand inquest, his purpose is to defend trial by jury, as the view that summary jurisdiction might handle slight offenses could lead toward arbitrary power. He reiterates ideas from his political pamphlets: Citizens can keep arms to protect themselves, possessions, and country; and English counties should be able to defend themselves against riots, insurrections, or invasions, so that a standing army is not needed. If counties are ever unable to defend themselves, trial by jury is the only way to preserve the constitution. Arbitrary power is "commonly slow at first, and imperceptible to all but the vigilant, like the creeping of a tiger at night." The convenience of summary jurisdiction could lead to the loss of other rights, which always entail troublesome duties. Jury trial must be preserved for the Indians, or they might better never have been governed by the British. Thus even in Calcutta, Jones remained in the political vanguard by stressing this right, at a time when Fox was legislating a related freedom in the Libel Act.

Jones's six charges set a theme for future Indian jurisprudence and reflect a vision based on a veneration of English laws. Delivered with captivating oratory, they exhibit philanthropy, humanity, lucid legal exposition, and elegant phraseology.[7] In the *Monthly Review,* Alexander Hamilton evaluated the charges: "These impressive addresses, besides affording an admirable model of dignified composition, throw considerable light on the state of society among the lower orders" in Bengal (June 1800, p. 129).

Wilford's expanding revelations also required Jones's time. Regarding him as a pillar of the Asiatic Society, Jones proofread the 168-page "On Egypt and Other Countries Adjacent to the Cálí River, or Nile of Ethiopia," which was serially delivered on 5 July, 16 August, and 5 November. Among the mistakes in the Sanskrit passages copied for Jones, one singular error indicated that the verses were modern. So he added a cautious footnote to Wilford's essay: Though Jones believed that the ancient Hindus knew about the Nile, "we must ever attend to the distinction between *evidence* and *conjecture;* and I am not yet fully satisfied with many parts of Mr. WILFORD's Essay, which are founded on so uncertain a basis as *conjectural* Etymology." By early 1794 Jones suspected that Joseph Harris's chart "had been shown by missionaries or other Europeans to very modern Pandits" who were Wilford's sources (2:926).

However, there was serious later damage. Convinced that the ancient Brahmanic literature contained references to Greek mythology and Genesis, Wilford had created a demand with his insistence and liberal rewards. For years he produced translated passages supposedly naming Greek divinities, Noah, and others. There was joy in Europe until the coincidences proved so startling that inspection of the Sanskrit manuscripts revealed the deceptions. Wilford's acknowledgment of his gullibility helped confirm the later charge that the crafty Hindus had duped their rulers, while supplying ethnocentrists like Macaulay with ammunition against the early Orientalists. Even today, Wilford's expansive statements are sometimes cited by writers on ancient religion.[8]

Because Jones died before the forgeries were exposed, the apparent extension of his comparative vein and Wilford's geographical advances pleased him. By the time of his 1792 Krishnagar sojourn, *Asiatick Researches* 3 was nearly printed. The short vacation permitted little time for letter writing, as he was concentrating on the law digest. In view of Anna's plans to sail in February, he now planned to remain in India only long enough to complete it. His departure must not jeopardize the stability of the Society, for Davis was making discoveries in astronomy, Wilford in geography, and others in natural history. Jones would contribute from his rural retirement in England.

Soon after he returned to Calcutta in late October, his second book of 1792 was finally published. This was only part of his intensive work with Arabic. "The Order of Arabick Reading" in his notebook was the *Arabian Nights Entertainments,* al-Búṣírí's *Burda* (The Mantle), the Koran, ʿAli ibn Abi Ṭálib's works, Al-Harírí's works, *Muʿallaqat,* and the *Hamása.* He listed the best books of Moslem law as *Fatáwá ʿÁlamgíríyat,* Al-Kuduri's *Institutes of Mohammedan Law,* and Al-Nasafí's *Kanz al-daqáʾiq,* together with their commentaries.

Jones's new law book was Siráj al-Dín's *Al Sirájiyyah: or the Mohammedan Law of Inheritance.* Hastings had asked Muhammad Kasim, later a *maulvi* on Jones's digest, to make a Persian translation of *Al-Sajáwandí* and the commentary *Sharifiah.* Though a good translation, Kasim's six-hundred-page version blended the text, commentary, and his own notes. As an English translation of this standard Moslem inheritance law would supplement the Arabic part of the digest, Jones read the original Arabic three times and condensed his version into fifty pages. Printed at his own expense, the book appeared on 19 November. It was priced at sixteen sicca rupees and was sold for the benefit of insolvent debtors.

It is a summary, so that readers would not have to search through criticism, unusual literature, and anecdotes to find the needed principle or law. Utility is Jones's object, although he includes the Arabic for those who wish to consult it. His brief preface claims that the work can answer any question on the Moslem law of succession. Today it remains the basis on which judicial interpretation of this branch of Indian law has been built. His excellent version has more or less preempted efforts in this branch; his lucid exposition is the work of a finished scholar. Perhaps he should have translated more excerpts from the original, which Muhammad had praised, except that he never intended such an ambitious undertaking.[9] Jones gave a copy of his version to Cornwallis; another went to Dundas.

Dundas was also sent a copy of *Asiatick Researches* 3 for the king. Appearing at the end of 1792, this five-hundred-page volume met Jones's revised, biennial goal, although it was actually published on 17 February 1793. He had modeled the periodical on *Philosophical Transactions,* but its Asiatic content continued to differentiate it. Each of his first two volumes had had a fuller meteorological journal than that kept at the Royal Society "by order of the President and Council." Now, wishing to include all of Wilford's long essay and deciding that the journal was not useful enough to justify such extensive space, Jones dispensed with it (Banks received Pearse's 1773–89 meteorological records). He was securing some East India Company servants' reports to the government, while organizing an investigation primarily of India, in a wide search. Major Charpentier de Cossigny, who became the Society's second honorary member, sent Chinese plants.

Most of the essays in *Asiatick Researches* are descriptive and polished. Rejecting personal letters or detached notes even from friends, Jones screened previously delivered papers before accepting them. Because the topics were original, he did not face Banks's problem of having to reject ingenious papers describing personal discoveries already known to scholars. Yet that very originality required circumspection, even the writing of editorial notes for others' papers. When a friend's essay recommended that members make Asiatic commonplace books, Jones supplied the mainly botanical examples, which reveal the orderly way in which he organized data for later use.

Besides his editorial additions, *Asiatick Researches* 3 contains his Eighth and Ninth Discourses, "A Royal Grant of Land," "On the Musical Modes," "The Lunar Year," "On the Mystical Poetry," and his translation of *Gīta Govinda.* "On the Fruit of the Mellori," his note to Fontana's essay on the Nicobar Islands, merges science and humanitarianism. Tentatively identifying the *Pandanus Leram* as the ketaka mentioned in Sanskrit literature, Jones suggests that the Bengalese variety of the tree might be improved by planting "the male and female trees in the same place, instead of leaving the female, as at present, to bear an imperfect and unproductive fruit, and the distant male to spread itself only by the help of its radicating branches." This idea moves toward the modern one of producing fertile stable hybrids by crossing members of the same genus. Here Jones again questions the immutability of species, a doctrine generally accepted up to Darwin's day: Each modern species could not have been descended from an original entity or pair, unchanged since the Creation.[10] Four transplanted Nicobar trees were flourishing in Kyd's Botanical Gardens: "A fruit weighing twenty or thirty pounds, and containing a farinaceous substance, both palatable and nutritive in a high degree, would perhaps, if it were common in these provinces, for ever secure the natives of them from the horrors of famine." Thus Jones borrowed Banks's idea of transplanting food sources within the empire, to recommend a way to combat the famines that were so common in that part of the world. This was another startling departure from the usual colonial administrators' concerns. The Calcutta Gardens were to furnish vast numbers of useful and ornamental plants around the world.

Asiatick Researches 3 upheld the great expectations in Europe. There were glowing reviews and increased reprints of Jones's essays. Volumes 1 through 3 supplied the materials for the four-volume *Dissertations and Miscellaneous Pieces Relating to the History and Antiquities, the Arts, Sciences and Literature of Asia* (London, 1792–8). Half of the first volume is by Jones, as the preface observes:

To the exertions of one Gentleman, whose various excellencies panegyric might display in the warmest terms, without being charged with extravagance, the ENGLISH settlements in the EAST INDIES are indebted for an institution which has already exhibited specimens of profound research, of bold investigation, and of happy illustration, in various subjects of literature; – subjects which, until the present times, had not exercised the faculties of EUROPEANS; but which, being produced to publick notice, will enlarge the bounds of knowledge, increase the stock of information, and furnish materials for future Philosophers, Biographers, and Historians.

Gentleman's Magazine included his entry in "A List of Living English Poets":

Sir William Jones, the Orientalist, now a Judge in India, is son of a celebrated Mathematician, was educated at University College, Oxford, and afterwards called to the Bar, at which he practised till he left England. His very early acquirements in elegant literature, as his Latin Commentary on the Asiatic poetry evinces, his uncommon facility of learning languages, the richness of his fancy, and the copiousness of his diction, render him one of the most extraordinary characters which England has furnished. (June 1792, p. 505)

He was now one of the most famous scholars and poets of the day.

Paradoxically, as the Asiatic Society's fame expanded, Jones's devotion to the two legal translations intended to be his greatest books reduced his time available for the Society. The four meetings held in 1793 tied the number held in 1786. After a lapse of almost four months, Cornwallis and the Supreme Council, Chambers, Hyde, and twenty-three others assembled on 28 February to hear Jones's Tenth Discourse.

His original objectives had stressed benefits for England, with only incidental advantages for Asians. His enriched intellectual–cultural goals had provided the vision concluding his Ninth Discourse:

[Particular advantages] may result from our sedulous and united inquiries into the history, science, and arts, of these *Asiatick* regions, especially of the *British* dominions in *India,* which we may consider as the centre (not of the human race, but) of our common exertions to promote its true interests; and we shall concur, I trust, in opinion, that the race of man, to advance whose manly happiness is our duty and will of course be our endeavour, cannot long be happy without virtue, nor actively virtuous without freedom, nor securely free without rational knowledge.

The Tenth Discourse defines the "particular advantages" as the conveniences and comforts of social life, its innocent pleasures, and the gratification of curiosity. Besides the intellectual benefits, historical research might discover practical suggestions for the Indians' prosperity. In astronomy "an accurate knowledge of *Sanscrit* and a confidential intercourse with learned *Brāhmens,* are the only means of separating truth from fable." Then Jones describes an allusion in an old Sanskrit book that led him to identify the Sandrocottus of Greek sources as the Maurya Emperor Chandragupta. He sketches his reasoning tantalizingly, without exploring the implications of the identification. He had been as baffled as others were by the Greek versions of Sanskrit names, and now this find would permit later historians to work back and forth around it in correlating Indian dates and events with known classical ones. Jones's dramatic presentation, which appeared in *Asiatick Researches* 4, was a major uncovering of ancient India. British scholars, generally unaware of an identification of the same names in 1772, used Jones to begin a verifiable history: "Gradually Indra and Agni, Brahme and Brahma were ranged in chronological order; whilst Vishnu and Siva were forced to give up their claims to remote antiquity."[11] Indian history was thus placed within the context of world history, and the world could more easily use the richness of Sanskrit learning and overall culture to advance world culture. Indian coins and especially the epigraphy that Jones was using supplied him with information to identify most of the needed names and events. His programmatic suggestions in the Tenth Discourse, while overshadowed by the Chandragupta formulation, include a collaborative description of Asian birds, animals, insects, reptiles, and fish. Besides analyzing minerals, "we cannot employ our leisure more delightfully, than in describing all new *Asiatick* plants in the *Linnæan* style and method, or in correcting the descriptions of those already known, but of which dry specimens only, or drawings, can have been seen by most *European* botanists."

On 21 March only five members joined Jones to hear Playfair's "Questions and Remarks" and Jones's congratulatory memorandum on Shore's appointment as Governor-General. On 11 July he and nine others heard two papers. Then there were no meetings for five months.

The first term of 1793 was strenuous. A long breach-of-promise suit against a prominent judge ended with the jilted woman's receiving twenty thousand rupees. In another case the General Bank sued to recover certificates worth nine thousand rupees. Dunkin did not think that an argument was necessary for his judgment, because legal diligence had not been exercised in securing the bank's endorsement. Having delayed speaking in order to study cases that might be relevant to India, Jones concluded that "as a juror he had no doubt that in this case there were grounds to excite suspicion and enquiry," and that the General Bank should recover the nine thousand rupees and interest. The other judges supported Jones.

In March the Bengal Presidency gave a dinner to celebrate Tipu Sultan's surrender at Seringapatam. Untypically, Jones attended, perhaps because the Supreme Council, Supreme Court, and senior military officers were urged to participate.[12] He evidently did not stay for the dancing, because Anna does not seem to have accompanied him. He was uneasy about her during the early months of 1793, though she was not really ill and was beginning to question her decision to return to England. During the cool season she felt good and so fretted about leaving him that she resolved to remain another year.

On 9 July he gave his manuscript translation of the *Mānava-Dharma-śāstra* to the Governor in Council. If the government would order it to be printed, he would correct the proofs and then complete the digest and its introductory discourse within two more vacations. Edward Hay replied: "[Cornwallis] is highly sensible how much the public and the Country at large are indebted to you for the great trouble you have taken in preparing this great and most useful Work" (2:917). It would be printed at the Company Press; the superintendents were awaiting Jones's orders.

A second cause for joy was the return of Shore, whose commission

permitted succession to the Governor-Generalship when Cornwallis relin-
quished it. Shore found his

friend, although somewhat debilitated by the climate, in a state of health which
promised a longer duration of life than it pleased Providence to assign to him. The
ardour of his mind had suffered no abatement, and his application was unremitted.
The completion of the work which he had undertaken, occupied the principal
portion of his leisure, and the remainder of his time which could be spared, was
as usual devoted to literary and scientific pursuits.[13]

The two neighbors resumed their literary discussions.

During the third term Jones had free time only at night and on weekends.
Anna was so sick that he did not risk going to Krishnagar, far from her
doctors. But in September they rented a picturesque house at Bandel,
overlooking the Ganges. They visited eighty-nine-year-old Jagannātha, "a
prodigy of learning, virtue, memory, and health" (2:923). He and his family
were comfortable on the monthly pension of three hundred rupees that
Jones had recommended; thus an Indian was treated in retirement like
British governmental employees, in another move toward Indian rights.

For the second consecutive autumn Jones neglected his correspondence.
He asked Davis to write a paper on the Hindu astrolabe to embellish the
materials now ready for *Asiatick Researches* 4, and suggested that a model
of Jai Singh II's observatory at Benares would be a fine ornament for the
Society meeting room in Calcutta. Jones's main request was for flowers
and leaves of the famous tamāl tree, the *Xanthochymus pictorius*.

He reviewed his recent years to Spencer. His ten years in India would
have been his happiest except for Anna's incessant ill health. But she had
finally decided to end her suffering by sailing in November, and he would
follow in two years, the moment the digest was done. Here his love for
Anna partly overcame his zeal for Sanskrit knowledge, which he would
give up, as well as a life without political or financial worries, and the
opportunity to help people who considered him their judge and legislator.

In his concern for Anna's health, Jones forgot his own. When the cool
season blew in, he neglected to dress warmly after a strenuous botanical
excursion: "The consequence of neglecting her advice was, that I had an
acute rheumatism, when I went to bed. The fever lasted only two days,
but the rheumatick pains in my shoulder remained" (2:923–4). Though the
pains caused him to be late for the new term, he arrived on 26 October,
as the *Calcutta Gazette* reported, "we are happy to say in perfect health."
But he was weaker than was thought.

Anna's heavy baggage went to the *Princess Amelia,* which put out to
sea "with a fair wind" on 7 December. In a sense Jones had chosen between
the digest (and the Indians) and life with Anna, for he could have accom-

panied her. Both had anticipated his choice when the unhappy moment came; she too considered the digest more important than their supposedly temporary separation. He would never see her again.

With the ship went part of Jones's strength, for Anna's departure left a vacuum in his life. No more could she encourage him to rest or read to her when he had overtaxed himself, as he habitually did because of his drive for knowledge. No more could they enjoy botanical ramblings and read Italian. The marriage had been so perfect that he found himself alone for the first time in eleven years. Though he mixed more in society, his heart was on the *Princess Amelia*. Nor did his assiduity on the digest let him forget his loss, which was necessary to preserve her life.

The entire income from their savings was placed at her disposal. Because she took along £7,000 and his Indian property was worth £12,000, by 1795 the savings should total £50,000. His will of 30 December 1793 left his estate real and personal to her. She was to be executrix for his English property, and the executor for the Indian property was to pay all debts and give her the proceeds.[14] Still concerned about their financial independence, Jones visited Shore one evening to discuss the matter. Knowing his moderation and economy, Shore assured him that he had ample funds,[15] and he resolved to leave in 1794. He was not penurious. His contributions to charity and particularly the salary of his personal Indian staff show a liberality overshadowing the modest circumstances in which the couple chose to live.

Attendance at the Society rose to fourteen on 19 December, when Jones seconded the nomination of Roxburgh. He read his "On the Loris, or Slowpaced Lemur" on 2 January 1794, at which time he seconded the nomination of Kyd. Thereby he directly involved another key botanist and made a more formal connection with the Calcutta Gardens. This physiological paper was one of three that he delivered during his last months. His pet loris "had died without pain, and lived with as much pleasure as he could have enjoyed in a state of captivity." Jones's data on the form, habits, name, and distribution are succinct. He confirms Linnaeus' description except for a few details, but considers Buffon's short account to be unsatisfactory. He includes a drawing, one of Anna's last, partly because Buffon's was so unrepresentative.

Governor-General Shore and the Supreme Council, Chambers, Hyde, and twenty-nine others heard Jones's Eleventh Discourse on 20 February. The number tied the largest attendance to date, as people knew of his plans to leave and anticipated that this Discourse would be his last. The meeting was more convivial than usual, with toasts of liquid rubies from Shiraz.

"The Philosophy of the Asiaticks," Jones's last Discourse, presents a fivefold definition of the term *science*. He expects few benefits from medical books, despite his astonishing discovery of an Upanishad devoted to human internal organs. Metaphysics and logic constitute an almost new field for study. According to the *Dabistan,* Brahmans communicated to Callisthenes "a technical system of logick" that was to underpin Aristotelian method: "If this be true, it is one of the most interesting facts, that I have met with in *Asia.*" Jones has often found perfect syllogisms in Brahmanic philosophy; indeed, the ideas in Newton's theology and part of his philosophy also appear in the Vedas. Jones praises Asiatic ethics and jurisprudence. After outlining natural philosophy, he praises the *Sūrya-siddhānta* as the great desideratum on Indian astronomy. Finally, he asserts that the supremacy of God is more piously and sublimely expressed in Sanskrit, Persian, and Arabic (in the Koran) than in any other language except Hebrew.

Jones's eleven Anniversary Discourses tingle with enthusiasm, that of a scholar discussing topics heretofore unknown in the West. They are an introduction to Asia, in an effort to instruct and tantalize others to follow paths that he was illuminating but had no time to explore. And he was successful, though some of his work was rendered obsolete and occasionally invalidated by scholarship that his pioneering generalizations stimulated. His ingenious, perceptive mind sometimes drew dubious conclusions from data that, at the time, he could not know were inadequate. The *Asiatic Annual Register* of 1799 deemed the Discourses his most valuable writings, containing new materials in a flowing, perspicuous, and highly classical style.[16] Modern scholars partly agree, pointing to his philological passage, the Sandrocottus identification, and lesser discoveries. That these materials came principally from his Sanskrit studies is poetic proof that he had mastered it better than any other foreign language.

Jones now spoke the "language of the gods" fluently and could intensively study "India's national legislation, an intimate knowledge of which was indispensable to a rational and humane administration."[17] Because almost every page of the emerging digest contained extracts from the *Mānava-Dharmaśāstra,* he had translated it first. Disdaining the poor Persian translation, he worked from the original Sanskrit, making an interlinear Latin version of the difficult parts. He read the Sanskrit three times, while studying the commentaries. *Institutes of Hindu Law: or, the Ordinances of Menu, According to the Gloss of Cullūca, Comprising the Indian System of Duties, Religious and Civil* was printed on 1 March 1794. After its posthumous publication on 3 July, all the copies went to the Governor in Council for distributing.

This last major translation by Jones was especially difficult to do. Theological matter is always complex because of mysteries that can only be transcribed, which "would be sacrilegious and radically inaccurate to transpose or paraphrase."[18] This complexity was compounded by the remote time, culture, and language. There were no contemporary informants to verify a meaning that he puzzled out or the answers that Brahmans gave to his constant questions. Yet this first translation of the Brahmanic code was a monumental achievement requiring the simultaneous abilities of lawyer, literary critic and writer, and Sanskritist. Bearing few traces of irresponsible emendation, the twelve-part code is "a complete social manual and portraiture, a poetic creed of deity and pneumatology, an account of the origin of man and of the world."[19] Beginning with the creation of the world, it ends with the means of escape from the consequences of deeds committed in transmigration. It defines the creation of the castes and their individual status.

Jones's preface is distinguished by polish, humanity, and comparative insights. The code, he states,

contains abundance of curious matter extremely interesting both to speculative lawyers and antiquaries, with many beauties, which need not be pointed out, and with many blemishes, which cannot be justified or palliated. . . . In a country happily enlightened by sound philosophy and the only true revelation, it must be remembered, that those laws are actually revered, as the word of the Most High, by nations of great importance to the political and commercial interests of *Europe,* and particularly by many millions of *Hindu* subjects, whose well directed industry would add largely to the wealth of *Britain,* and who ask no more in return than protection for their persons and places of abode, justice in their temporal concerns, indulgence to the prejudices of their own religion, and the benefit of those laws, which they have been taught to believe sacred, and which alone they can possibly comprehend.

Jones overvenerates these ordinances that Brahma mythologically gave to Manu, whom Hindus revere as the first man and holiest legislator. Hastings had made them the mainstay of his government. Not knowing that they were probably a Brahmanic compilation, Jones considers Manu a real person who spoke a language resembling "that of the *Vedā,* particularly in a departure from the more modern grammatical forms." The Hindu lawyers' reverence for the ordinances led him to decide mistakenly that current Hindu law rested mainly on them, a conclusion that Colebrooke and later scholars were to correct.[20] Jones elaborately dates the code as about 1280 B.C., thereby creating a controversy that is still not wholly resolved except for agreement that he accords the code an undeserved antiquity.

Jones's translation is so masterly that modern lawyers prefer it to more scholarly ones like that of Georg Bühler, who observed: "I am indebted to Sir William Jones' great work, which, in spite of the progress made by Sanscrit philology during the last hundred years still possesses a very high value."[21] It went through numerous editions and reprintings until 1911 and is still worthwhile reading, with a "fine, lofty, vigorous, and slightly archaizing style, reminding one not infrequently of the King James Bible."[22] Besides ensuring the preservation of a valuable text, it served as the basis of later Anglo-Indian case law confirming the primacy of custom over written law, primarily through Jones's translation of book 1, verse 108: "Immemorial custom is transcendent law, approved in the sacred scripture, and in the codes of divine legislators."[23]

The voluminous contemporary reaction to Jones's book uniformly praised the public zeal motivating his years of labor in his free time at his own expense. His preface was said to be masterly, eloquent, and elegant, with an excellent style seldom seen in literal translations. Conveying learning and judiciousness, the book is a great acquisition for the Christian and historian and stimulates important reflections. It contains more new, curious material than any other work of the age and illuminates Hinduism more than have all previous publications combined.[24] The *Asiatic Annual Register* of 1799 might have been speaking for all of Europe in acknowledging Jones's great accomplishment: He had finally changed British public opinion toward India – "it proves, beyond all dispute, that the people of India had made great advances in civilization, at a period when the nations of Europe were in the rudest stage of social life" (p. 11).

Like all of Jones's Sanskrit work, this book had a special impact in Germany, where his version was translated in 1797 and was to influence scholars who became fine Sanskritists. His phrase about the tribes who speak the language of Aryas had an indirect effect. Pliny and his English translator had used the Latin form of the word, but Jones introduced the translated phrase to Europe. This combined with his description of a golden age when early Hindus "were splendid in arts and arms, happy in government, wise in legislation, and eminent in various knowledge,"[25] to set the stage for the change of his language use of the word *Aryan* to a racial one, as in the theories of Max Müller and Nazism. His version was translated into French in 1833.

Jones did little more on his law digest. He had made a major accomplishment by introducing into government service scholarly Brahmans, pundits, and *maulvis,* whose affection he had earned. By demonstrating that a European could cooperatively gain and use Hindu legal knowledge to help the Indians, he set a model that inspired scholars like Jagannātha, Rādhākānta, and Ali Ibrahim Khan to greater accomplishments, in contrast with the colonial government's usual practice of offering Indian scholars no intellectual stimulus. After the Hindu portion of the digest was completed to Jones's satisfaction, two pundits continued to help him collate the six folio volumes. In March 1794 he divided these into nine volumes; only the infirm Rādhākānta was assisting now.

Jones's death left the digest to Colebrooke, whose labors on it won him fame as a Sanskritist. When he started, he anticipated finishing in six months, but the translating took two years. Publication of *A Digest of Hindu Law on Contracts and Successions, with a Commentary* (Calcutta, 1797–8) marked an epoch in Indian administration. Judges were no longer dependent on pundits,[26] and some ancient texts may have been saved. There was a fourth, revised edition in 1874. John Flaxman's sculpture at University College appropriately depicts Jones forming the digest from the sacred books that pundits are reading to him amid Indian foliage.

Jones also supervised the compilation of four volumes of Shia law, which Shore nominated John Baillie to translate. The Company Press published only Jones's first volume, *A Digest of Mohummudan Law, According to the Tenets of the Twelve Imams, Compiled, Under the Superintendence of the Late Sir William Jones* (1805). By then Baillie, who had mastered Arabic and Persian in Jones's model, was a professor at the College of Fort William.

On 1 March 1794 Jones sent Dundas copies of his *Institutes of Hindu Law* for the king, Dundas, and the East India Company directors:

I, therefore, entreat you, Sir, to lay before His Majesty my humble supplication for His gracious permission to resign my judgeship in the year 1795, or (if the Digest should not then be completed) in 1796; it being my anxious wish to pass the remainder of my life in studious retirement, though devoted, as I ever have been, to the service of my King and my Country, and of that recorded Constitution, which is the basis of our national glory and felicity. (2:928)

While leaving the door open for further service, Jones implied his political independence in this last official letter.

Dundas might have assisted Jones toward such service. He had John Bruce, the company's historiographer, send Bruce's *Historical View of Plans for the Government of British India, and Regulation of Trade to the East Indies* (London, 1793). Bruce also requested information on the political and commercial aspects of Indian history, topics that would have excited Jones a few years earlier. But Jones was secretly too worn out and in pain to encourage a new correspondent.

His interest in botany and astronomy was undiminished, as was his encouragement of his colleagues in Bengal. Colebrooke's submission of "On the Duties of a Faithful Hindu Widow" received a flattering acknowledgment. Indicating that he might accept it for *Asiatick Researches,* Jones had it read on 3 April, his last meeting. Francis Balfour, Davis, Devis, Harington, Edmund Morris, Tucker, and six others attended. Jones seconded a nomination and, despite his pain from a tumor that he had recently discovered, read part of his long "Botanical Observations on Select Indian Plants."

This was his crowning work in botany, for which Roxburgh named the famous Saraca tree the *Jonesia asoca,* "Consecrated to the remembrance of our late President, the most justly celebrated SIR WILLIAM JONES, whose great knowledge of this science, independent of his other incomparable qualifications, justly entitles his memory to this mark of regard."[27] Jones's essay describes seventy-eight plants "selected for their novelty, beauty, poetical fame, reputed use in medicine, or supposed holiness." Having examined them with "ardent zeal for the most lovely and fascinating branch of natural knowledge," he provides the classical names, synonyms or epithets, and Indian-language names, in an Indian Kew miniature of classification and description.

Jones intended to expand the essay, which derived from his "Catalogue of Indian Plants." This index, transliterated in the Jonesian System, lists 419 plants, about half of which he identifies in Linnaeus. Another 10 percent are tentatively identified. Elsewhere, he names 53 plants in his pioneering list of plants growing between Kidderpore and Arifnagar, in Calcutta.[28]

Jones also composed "Additional Remarks on the Spikenard of the Ancients." He had enjoyed rereading Gilbert Blane's essay, but felt it necessary to state his objections "with all the freedom of a searcher for truth, but without any diminution of that respect, to which his knowledge and candour justly entitle him." Jones recapitulates his arguments, adding classical evidence: "The true nard is a species of *Valerian,* produced in the *most remote* and hilly parts of India, such as *Nēpāl, Morang,* and *Butan,* near which PTOLEMY fixes its native soil." A prince had attempted to send him ten living plants from Bhutan, but all died en route to Calcutta. Impressively enough, Roxburgh now concurred in Jones's mistake about *Valeriana jatamansi.*

Apparently Jones's last letters were to Davis, the last on 24 March. He was helping reconstruct the career of Jai Singh II. Davis had sent drawings for an intended book on Indian constellations, and Jones promised to translate the Sanskrit. As his survey had discovered only one tamāl tree in the province, he renewed his invitation for Davis to visit him, "like Crishna, decked with holy Tamāla blossoms" (2:931). The fruit and buds sent were not sufficiently developed, and he chided Davis. Ironically, Davis's last transmittal was of the wrong plants, which Jones identified as a previously unknown hypericum.

Asiatick Researches 4 was published soon after Jones's death. Besides his editorial notes, it contains his Tenth and Eleventh Discourses, "Additional Remarks on the Spikenard," "Botanical Observations," "A Catalogue," and "On the Loris," his smallest representation in the four volumes. Perhaps this journal best proves the success and long-term value of his decade-old Society.

One measure of that success was his persuasion of colleagues who were fellows of the Royal Society to give their essays to him rather than to Banks. Wilkins contributed five essays, primarily translations of inscriptions; Roxburgh, five on botany. Marsden supplied a paper on Indic languages. However, Patrick Russell and Robert Saunders sent their materials to Banks.

The Asiatic Society was now fairly secure. Although it lacked a place of its own, the public room in which it met would be adequate for years. Once Elmsly agreed to sell *Asiatick Researches* in London, the worry about publishing costs ended. The fourth volume was greeted with much applause, as the Society's fame spread, and up to 1839 there were numerous reprintings and pirated editions in London. The praise was echoed in America. The first four volumes were translated into German in 1795–7, enhancing Jones's towering reputation in Germany, where he had always had the most scholarly influence on the Continent and from where great philologists would come. Two volumes appeared in French in 1805, raising his French stature. The quality was to continue. On 1 May 1794 thirty-one members approved Chambers's motion to invite Shore to be their new president. When that charter member accepted, Jones's ideal was achieved: Their president was the Governor-General and a scholar, thus ensuring official support.

Jones's "Desiderata"[29] shows that he was not planning to cease his Oriental studies when he returned to England. For Arabia he projected a pre-Islamic history and translations of the *Hamása* and Al-Harírí's divan. For Persia there would be a history, an edition of the *Farhang-i-Jahángírí* (for which he had prepared the notes), and a translation of Nizámí's *Khamsa*. A Tatar history and a translation of the *Shih Ching* were also projected. Most of the vast tasks were Indian:

1. Purāṇic geography
2. Description of Indian plants
3. A Sanskrit grammar, from Pāṇini and others

4. A Sanskrit dictionary
5. Ancient music and theater
6. Medicines and methodology
7. Translations of the Vedas, *Purāṇas, Mahābhārata,* and *Ramayana*
8. Ancient philosophy, mathematics, and astronomy
9. Purāṇic constellations and their mythology
10. Pre-Moslem history

Having studied the *Siddhāntakaumudī* in 1792, Jones intended to edit this fairly modern recension of the Pāṇinian grammar. As for the projected dictionary, he was editing the two alphabetical volumes that Kāśīnāth had compiled for him and for which he had prepared a Latin version. "Botanical Observations" was the beginning of his botanical book.

It seems inconceivable that Jones expected to translate the Sanskrit sacred literature and the two epics. Yet his accomplishments were so great that even today they are impressive, and these works fitted into his plan to enrich cultures through language. He translated a story from the *Ramayana* and some Vedic fragments.[30] These include materials from the *Yajur-Veda* and the sacred Gāyatrī prayer from the *Rig-Veda,* intended for a projected "On the Primitive Religion of the Hindus" designed "to remove the veil from the supposed mysteries of the primeval Indian Religion." Although he was not the first non-Hindu to discover the prayer, in about 1791 Jones had difficulty obtaining "access to a shrine so studiously concealed by the *Hindu* priests." First he tried to talk with his assembled pundits about Hinduism, but they were so reticent that he resorted to conversation with individual Brahmans. Each one privately answered Jones's questions except about the Gāyatrī, until he translated for them Newton's concluding General Scholium of the *Principia* into Sanskrit. It was then that he acquired and translated the prayer. He also rendered Śankara Āchārya's sixteen-stanza *Mohamudgara* (Mallet of the ignorant).[31]

Jones's expertise in Sanskrit allowed him to direct what was becoming a meticulous uncovering of Indian civilization, without any relief from his heavy judicial duties. He devoted his leisure to a remarkable search for truth, not expecting to be relieved from work so as to study Sanskrit, as Wilkins had been. Though not ceasing to work in the mine of Indian literature, he never neglected his public duties, which, he felt, should supersede everything else. He believed that his scholarship could best help the Indians through his legal works. Championing India's cultural tradition, he "sought to learn from it, not efface it with an imported English veneer, or write it off as backwater barbarism."[32] He was driven to scholarship by immense energy and industry. Like Posidonius "the Athlete," whom he sometimes quoted, he could subordinate illness to intellect. He had begun to study botany during his severe fever in 1784, when the plants had to be brought to his sickbed. In his final months his tumor was so painful that only his dedication, culminating in his *Institutes of Hindu Law,* permitted him to pursue scholarship.

Jones's early experience had demonstrated that Orientalism could provide only a meager living, so that much of his early life was devoted to a struggle for a lucrative position. Yet he observed how wealth encouraged vice and how power in government could endanger the constitution. Although he originally went to India mainly to secure the wealth and position necessary to later political and financial independence, his drive for knowledge soon submerged his materialism. Through research and his Asiatic Society's exchanges he sought enlightenment for humankind. The intense study of faded manuscripts affected Jones's health; it did not improve his position.

His intense labors had gravely weakened him. About 20 April 1794 he stayed out late on his nightly walk, talking in an unhealthful situation. Calling on Shore, he complained of ague but said he would take some medicine, for "an ague in the spring is medicine for a king." When he did not feel better after a few days, his doctor was summoned. He explained that the tumor on his right side, as big as his fist, had appeared four or five months earlier. As it had come of itself, he had supposed that it would go away by itself, and precious time would have been spent in seeing a doctor. He had continued to walk the ten miles to and from town daily, in such severe pain that he said he would not endure such months again for all the world's riches and honors.

Jones's trouble was inflammation of the liver, which was common in Bengal. Although the inflammation was too advanced for medicines to help, they were administered. Aware of his condition, he nonetheless told Shore, who offered to sit with him, that he was better and that his mind was easy. Indeed, on the night of 26 April the doctors thought him better and recommended that he leave on the next ship, proposing to salivate him and prepare him for the voyage. But the next morning a servant ran to Shore's and reported that his master was delirious. When Shore reached Jones's Gardens, another servant said that Jones had requested tea, drunk it, and died. He was "lying on his bed in a posture of meditation; and the only symptom of remaining life was a small degree of motion in the heart, which after a few seconds ceased, and he expired without a pang or groan. His bodily suffering, from the complacency of his features and the ease of his attitude, could not have been severe."[33] Thus died at forty-seven a great scholar, Orientalist, and human being.

15   Jones Today

Jones's death was a catastrophe that "spread a gloom over the public mind in India, Native as well as European; and was deplored by none of his friends more deeply, both on public and private accounts, than by the Governor-General." As Shore wrote his wife, "At my durbar yesterday I had proofs of the affection entertained by the natives for Sir William Jones. The Professors of the Hindu Law, who were in the habit of attendance upon him, burst into unrestrained tears when they spoke to me, and grief clouded many countenances. His death is really a national loss."[1]

Many such testimonies could be mustered to demonstrate the high regard in which Jones was held by the Indian intelligentsia and even the common people of Calcutta. When this regard is compared with the attitude of other conquered peoples (e.g., the Aztecs' view of Cortes), it is clear that Jones used his office quite differently from the way other Europeans did, and that the governed people loved him for his efforts on their behalf. Simultaneously, he earned the equally high regard of the West for his achievements in India, and at his death was renowned in the West not for his colonial administrative actions but for the intellectual distinctions earned primarily in his spare time from his judicial duties. This dual exaltation makes him almost unique among the many notable individuals who have served in such administrative capacities. At his death Jones was one of the most celebrated men in the world. Few other people throughout history have achieved such wide and high distinction during their lifetime.

This assessment derives primarily from his literary and linguistic achievements. We have indicated that although Jones's reputation as a major poet in his own right began to wane after 1810, it was not until the advent of Victorian poets like Tennyson and Browning that he was relegated to the role of a minor eighteenth-century poet, known principally for three short poems. By the twentieth century, general anthologies seldom included even those poems. But in the interval, scholars had realized that his literary impact was chiefly that of influencing the European Romantics and a few American writers, and Jones became known as a Romantic precursor who

ASIATIC SOCIETY
BICENTENARY

1784-1984

SIR·WILLIAM·JONES

MDCCXLVI-MDCCXCIV

The Asiatic Society Logo.

may have done more to introduce Oriental elements into Western literature than perhaps has any other poet. The 1984 bicentenary celebrations heightened this appraisal and advanced him into the perspective of comparative literature. His introduction of new images, styles, and themes to the West, in systematic efforts to reinvigorate European poetry, ultimately raised his stature in general literary history. What he did was to gather, integrate, and transmit a synthesized body of data from a part of the Orient that had been known by the various trading companies since about 1600, but known only in a distorted and intensely ethnocentric way. Correcting the image and revealing the spirit of kinship and unity in space and time, by such poetry and other writings Jones in his way helped stimulate a new renaissance in the Western mind. Cultural pluralism was at hand, and clearly this impact went far beyond literature.[2]

Linguistically, as we have previously said, throughout Jones's life, this first modern linguist demonstrated the values of learning languages. His famous memorandum listing the twenty-eight that he had studied,[3] in view of his enormous reputation based on language, offered a model for commoners who, deep into the nineteenth century, were continually exposed to essays extolling how this commoner had achieved great distinction through study. Invariably his scholarly achievements, presented chiefly in terms of his philological pronouncement about the common source of some languages, were emphasized. Jones dramatically and convincingly showed the world that the written treasures contained in languages could entertain, instruct, and morally uplift people. He learned Sanskrit under difficult conditions in leisure moments when he might have been resting after a strenuous term. He was not the first European Sanskritist; Wilkins was.

But it was Jones's philological passage and *Sacontalā* that dramatically introduced the West to Sanskrit. Out of his pioneering eventually came modern linguistics; and his discoveries speeded up the future development of learned societies devoted to the editing and interpreting of Sanskrit texts, and the dynamism of modern Sanskrit universities scattered throughout India (in comparison with the sad state of Sanskrit universities in India in the early 1790s).

In a prescientific matrix Jones analyzed data in a surprisingly modern way, sometimes using sets of triple cognates selected for their similar forms and synonymy, as he recognized that many data from many languages were needed to demonstrate his "family" concept. This concept had little provable direct influence, however, on the major nineteenth-century comparativists, all of whom used his work. These Germanic scholars assembled whatever ideas they could find, which they published under their own name, often without notes to indicate others' work that they used, although Friedrich von Schlegel and others paid tribute to Jones's work, and Jacob Grimm partly rewrote the second edition of his *Deutsche Grammatik* so as to take Ramsus Rask's work into account.

The bicentenary celebrations apprehended Jones's overall literary, language, linguistic, and ultimately integrated Oriental contributions. They perhaps raised his stature as an outstanding translator and even theorist of translation. More importantly, they showed that he provided the clue to the scientific study of languages, as based on historical change. He gave the philologists who followed him much of what they needed – the concepts of genetic change and language families, reliance on basic rather than esoteric vocabulary, much of the methodology, and even cautionary warnings (e.g., the dangers of etymological speculation and similarities based on contact and borrowings). On the other hand, he remained undecided, and perhaps unaware of his indecision, between the typological and the genetic classification criteria in historical linguistics, as did some other eighteenth-century scholars. If Jones's 1786 paper is considered as a whole, we find him suggesting that Hindi could not be descended from Sanskrit because its grammatical structure was so different, even as he was noting Hindi's vast inheritance of Sanskrit vocabulary that linked the two languages genetically.

Overall, Jones drew many disparate threads together into one theoretical formulation, while discarding numerous false premises of the day, in a kind of integrative method that characterized most of his work. His projections of various Indo-European branches and several non-Indo-European families triggered dynamic activity in the following decades, together with the consequent development of language-change theories and genetic classificatory methodology.[4] He was a featured topic at the 1986 Rice University Symposium on the Genetic Classification of Languages, when projections for linguistic advances for the next two hundred years were made.

Linguists have rightly stressed Jones's philological passage since it first appeared in 1786, and it still may be his outstanding specific intellectual contribution to the world. It is one of the most quoted formulations among all scholarly formulations in all disciplines. In the history of ideas it stands as one of the great conceptions that attempt to explain human beings and their intellectual–cultural advances. In some ways it ultimately separated language from religion as clearly as Darwin later separated science from religion. It moved language study away from mythology, speculation, and intuition, and toward the sciences. In its ramifications, this passage may even be comparable to discoveries like Copernicus's and Galileo's breakthrough into scientific astronomy, and to Darwin's integrated explanation of organic changes. It belongs in this elite set of conceptions of world knowledge.

Jones's language research widened European intellectual horizons by introducing various Oriental cultures and subject matter, particularly Sanskrit literature and thought. He sought East–West cooperation and mutual advancement in a spirit of universal tolerance that respected ancient non-European cultures, despite his years in the courts of colonial England. When he uncovered a treasure unknown to the West, he wished to make it known in world literature, while enriching European readers. As he wanted the Indians to know their glorious past, he initiated that movement by printing the *Ṛtusaṃhāra*. Perhaps his greatest contribution to them was helping them rediscover their past culture and gain the national pride essential to their renaissance in a colonial situation. Jones's ultimate achievements were in Orientalism, in which his drive for encyclopedic learning was unceasing. In India his studies gradually stressed the advancement of people. He loved his fellow-beings, irrespective of religion, race, or culture, as he viewed all cultures as being generally equal and deserving of moral, intellectual, and aesthetic enrichment.

As no single person could accomplish the vast interdisciplinary goals that Jones envisioned, he created a unique learned society to collect, organize, and disseminate the overall cultural values of Asia to the world. This society should cooperate with other societies on other continents to bring maximum utility and intellectual and artistic enlightenment to the world. When one considers some scholars' attitude toward learned societies today, it is obvious that some societies might learn much from Jones. He planned a research design for a continent, disseminating the multidisciplinary findings while offering a kind of intellectual answering service for Asia. He anticipated the application of knowledge across national boundaries and oceans. His Asiatic Society, rich in the heritage with which he endowed it, continues to advance and disseminate knowledge, as exemplified in the 1984 celebrations. It is a major research institute in Asia that concentrates on Asia, one of several far-flung Asiatic Societies around the world and the one that he founded. A further measure of his success is reflected in the fact that several of these are in Asia – for example, in Bombay, Madras, and Bangkok.[5]

In sacrificing his life to such goals, Jones showed the world that it was possible for one to use a colonial position to accomplish goals that would be colossal even today. He proved and popularized the rich advantages of studying other peoples' languages and especially their culture, gaining information that would then be integrated into the advancing of world culture. He showed the world that learning can serve people and that scholars can make interesting, important contributions to society. This was a way toward world humanism and universal tolerance. His transmittal of cultural and linguistic Sanskrit knowledge to the West is comparable in its way to Marco Polo's opening the magical world of Cathay to a startled Europe, even as the resulting cooperation with Indians helped lead to an Indian renaissance. Jones never made a scientific discovery like the circulation of blood or devised a taxonomy like the classification of the animal kingdom, but his discovery of classical India for Europe is somewhat comparable (as is the reverse – his salutary influences on future Indians). Sir William Jones remains one of the greatest intellectual explorers of all time, and his views and the model of his life again beckon to a troubled world.

Appendix: Five New Letters by Jones

The following four previously unpublished letters to William Adams have an important bearing on the 1780 Oxford election, important people who were involved, and British politics during the American Revolution. (The Gloucestershire County Council kindly permitted them to be published here. The letter of 3 May 1780 is torn.)

3 May [1780] – Midnight.

Dear Sir,

Is it possible for me to repent of the part, which my friends take, when it has already yielded me such fruit as your two letters, although unhappily I have lost your wishes on this occasion? No; I cannot repent of it; and it has already yielded me much fruit of a similar nature. From this moment I apply to no man living for his *vote;* and to you, indeed, I only applied for *advice:* But I must follow the example of Dr. Scott in soliciting the exertions of my intimate friends: to more than one of my bosom friends, hardly known to him, he has personally applied at a time when he had requested me to keep silence on his intentions, as not yet ripe, which prohibition he forgot to remove; and by this forgetfulness has wholly engaged Burke, half engaged Dunning, and invaded my most heartfelt friendships. I should grieve, if this matter should end in a breach between Scott and me: but I am a plain Briton, as my father was, and must speak out. I am far from thinking myself too late: my friends assure me that all the *literary* and *Whig* interest in the nation will be exerted for me. What a soul-ennobling idea, to be a member, and a Whig member, for so illustrious a body of constituents! At the Roman bar the process called *divinatio* was a kind of previous question – "Who shall prosecute *Verres*"? Shall it be Tully or Hortensius? This case is similar: What gremial member shall oppose Sir W. Dolben? Shall it be one, whose principles have always been declared, or one whose profession is *moderation,* but whose sentiments are not avowed? More than this I dare not say consistently with propriety, as you are engaged for my competitor. I lament that the purity of our Academical elections should be sullied. If you recollect my defense of Oxford against a Frenchman who attacked us in three volumes of invective and misrepresentation, you will see that I have ever vindicated the chastity of our proceedings on this occasion.– Lettre à Monsr. A. p. 27. 28.

I am, with unfeigned and truly respectful regard, dear Sir,

Your grateful and faithful servt.
W. Jones.

If the parliament should not speedily [be] dissolved, I shall regret my exi[t] in twelve month from Oxford, w[] the purity of the election will for[] appearance. Be this my excuse f[or] waiting upon you, if I pass through the []

Temple 12 May 1780.

Dear Sir,

The paper, which I took the liberty to enclose to you, and which was written printed and circulated by my worthy and zealous friend Mr. Paradise of St. Mary Hall, having been uncandidly ascribed to me, I entreat you to contradict so disingenuous a report, if it should happen to be made in your hearing. Mr. Paradise, having read all my letters, has copied many of my words and phrases, and the facts and arguments were collected by him from my conversation; but I had no hand in the composition. Another report, that I did not mean to stand a poll, is equally groundless. I daily and hourly meet with so many promises and so much encouragement, that I shall stand a poll, if parliament be dissolved ever so soon. I meet every day with many friends who revere you highly, and grieve that we are adverse on this occasion. Dr. Scott takes an extraordinary line here, his friends representing him every where as a Whig, whereas to my knowledge and to the knowledge of hundreds, his principles are highly monarchical and hostile to popular government; nor is this a secret, but what I never knew him conceal. I am, dear Sir, with high respect,

Your much obliged and faithful Servt.
W. Jones

Temple 15 May 1780.

My dear Sir,

Be assured, that it was not without the most exact enquiry that I determined to stand a poll. Had I no prospect of succeeding myself, I would certainly decline; but my enquiries end in the liveliest hopes, and my prospect grows brighter and brighter every hour. No man that lives has a higher respect than I have for the excellent men, the ornaments of literature, the teachers as well as examples of virtue, who are generally resident in our University, but as I find that they do not form one *fourth* part of the whole elective body, which is dispersed in different parts of the kingdom and which is never collected but upon pressing occasions, in which the state is interested, I resolved to indulge my friends in their eager desire to make a general canvass of all the literary and Whig interest of the nation: the answers and promises, which they daily receive are such as give me the greatest encouragement; and, if the parliament be not very speedily dissolved, I have strong hopes of success against both Sir William and Dr. Scott, who ought to stand upon *the same political interest,* for reasons which I will presently explain. Having thus made a sufficient trial of my strength, I hastened to apprize my friends of my resolution to stand a poll; especially as an uncandid report, no less groundless than unhandsome, of *my having declined,* had been circulated by some friends of my competitors. I assure you, dear Sir, that I am incapable of magnifying my own interest beyond the truth to which I will steadily adhere on this occasion as on all others: my supporters and well-wishers are many of the greatest personages in this kingdom both for rank and property, who have a strong interest in our University as the place, where their children and posterity will possibly receive their education.

Every day I receive actual promises of votes from persons resolved to attend at any warning: and, in fact, I am determined to know by the clearest proof how I stand in the affection of our great Academical body, of whom I certainly have not deserved ill. This is not the case of a professorial chair or an University-place, which, however important and valuable, are bestowed by the resident masters, at least in most cases: no; the question now is, who shall protect the Academical body, the laws, and the constitution, at a time of all others the most alarming; and I have not a doubt but that more masters will come from distant counties, than have been known to attend for a considerable number of years. Dr. Scott was always a man, whom I have been zealous to serve, whom I every where praised, especially to the heads of his profession, and whom I sincerely respected for his deep erudition and cultivated mind; but there never was, nor could be, any great cordiality between us on account of the wide difference between our political sentiments; he, every where, at least in my company, professing high notions of prerogative and power and combating every proposition favourable to popular government; whilst I, from my early youth, have considered our constitution as analogous to a game at chess, where the king is respected and preserved from all danger, but where the principal strength consists in the pawns, or people, although the pieces, or nobles, have also no small share in the mixed system. In a word, I always knew and know Dr. Scott to be what is called a Tory, with this favourable difference, that Sir W. Dolben is one from family prejudice, Dr. Scott from deep thought and principle. Knowing this as I do, I could not but be surprized to find that Dr. Scott should *now* be proclaimed the opposition-candidate, and should stand upon the Whig interest. His real strength is his literary merit, which is confessedly great; but, as for politicks, his true line, to the knowledge of hundreds, is that on which Sir William stands. I consider myself, and am considered, as the only *Whig* candidate; and, when a flag of truce was brought me the other day with a singular prospect of *an union of interest,* I declined it for two important reasons, 1. because Mr. Page's seat is, and ought to be, firm, by the unvaried custom of the University, 2. because I could not form any *political* union with a man, whose principles were the reverse of my own; and for this I appealed to the knowledge of the very person, who brought the proposal; for I am not speaking from private conferences with the doctor, but from his open conversation in many companies: from both I am confident, that Dr. Scott is not a Whig any more than I am a Tory; and you will judge whether I will be made the instrument of deluding the Whigs by representing him as one of their number. Certainly I will not; but will say, with Aristotle, that *I love Truth* (and I will add, *my country*) *better than I love Plato.* I shall be grieved, if this competition should extinguish the intimacy of Dr. Scott and me; but I shall comfort myself; for I am persuaded, that the only indissoluble bond of friendship is *idem sentire de republicâ.* As to Sir William, I have known him almost as long as I have been well acquainted with Scott, and (literary merit apart) I do not see why one candidate will not serve his country as well as the other. Your exhortation to overlook any little eagerness of my competitor in first applying to my most intimate friends, has the greatest weight; but what am I to think of the following facts, which I wrote down instantly, that I might be perfectly correct? On Friday night 28 April, the doctor called on me to ask my advice and solicit my interest: this I promised, on condition that my friends did not declare me a candidate: had I not determined not to declare myself, I should have started at the same time with him. I had two Oxford friends in the next room: said the doctor "This must be kept *secret* for the present"! "It shall be secret, said I, from all the world, till you permit me to disclose it." I understood from him, that the matter was not ripe. I saw numbers of friends that evening, to whom I was mute as to Oxford. The next morning I breakfasted with Wenman, to whom I said nothing, not having received Scott's permission. I had not left Wenman ten minutes before Scott was with him, and almost obtained an engagement from him. No permission for me to disclose the secret. On the same morning Scott's hand bills were printed and dispersed at Oxford, his express having set out from London soon after he had been with me. On the same morning (while he kept my lips fast locked) he applied to Dr. Hunter, who promised to write to Dr. Smith. Hunter and Wenman are both my intimate friends. This I heard by accident, and then thought myself at liberty to consult you, dear Sir, for whom I have and ever shall have the most undissembled veneration on account both of your extensive learning and amiable manners.– I found next day, that on the same 29th of April (my lips being still sealed by Scott's desire) he had been with my excellent friend Sir Josh. Reynolds requesting him to solicit Mr. Dunning's influence for him, whilst he knew that Mr. Dunning is my great professional friend – Then I wrote my second letter, six or seven friends having previously called on me with offers of service, four of the number being voters. At the same time my friend Edm. Burke was applied to for the doctor and engaged, whilst the doctor himself had imposed silence on me, suggesting that the affair was not ripe, and *forgot* to remove the seal – When I told this very true story to Dr. Johnson, he said – "I hope it *was forgetfulness.*" So do I too, my dear sir, very heartily: be it as it may, it was that very *forgetfulness,* which gained him the start at Oxford, and prevented my friends from applying in time to you. Having written thus seriously, I will relieve you, my dear sir, with an incident almost ludicrous. Our very good friend the dean of Gloucester has, very innocently, been the cause of my losing some favour at Oxford. You may remember the copy of his book against Locke, which he lent me when I had the honour of meeting him at your house. In the margin of that copy, I scribbled, by his desire, such remarks as occurred to me: they were, I am sure, inoffensive; and our worthy friend himself thanked me for them. That copy with my notes I lent Mr. Coulson, who was requested by Mr. Mortimer of Lincoln to lend it him. I never knew till now that others had seen it; and I sent it as soon as it was returned, to the Dean. Now, my Zealous, my too Zealous, friend Mr. Paradise writes me word, that Mr. Williamson told him, that a certain pamphlet "concerning the interest of Church or State had been handed about the University with marginal notes said to be in my hand, which had given infinite offence." It is really very comfortable to me to find, that the retired and studious life, which I have always led, has so far prevented me from doing any bad action, that nothing worse can be found than writing a few private observations in an unpublished book for the inspection, and by the desire, of the author, and of an author, so respectable as the dean of Gloucester.

It is time, I think, to desist from troubling you.– I anxiously hope, that your amiable family are well, and that you will long enjoy that health and happiness, which you so highly deserve. At the quarter-sessions I will have the pleasure of seeing you, and we will talk of literature and philosophy, leaving political and election interests for others to discuss, who have nothing else to discourse on. Prosperity attend you! and believe me to be, my dear Sir,

Most faithfully yours
W. Jones.

Lambs' Buildings Temple.
4 Sept. 1780.

Dear Sir,

Permit me to renew a correspondence (too long unhappily intermitted) by informing you, that, as the parliament is dissolved, I decline giving the University any farther trouble and am heartily sorry for that, which has been already given them. I do not use words of form, when I say, that it is not *possible* for any man to love and respect the learned body more zealously and sincerely than I do; and that your self in particular have not a more respectful admirer or a friend more sensible of all your excellent qualities than, dear Sir,

Your very obedient and faithful Servt.
W. Jones.

If Dr. Scott stands a poll, I shall be ready to perform my promise of giving him my vote, as I am no longer his competitor; but if Dr. Wetherell ever supposes that I shall either obey his mandate, or be solicitous about his good or bad word and opinion, he will find himself exceedingly mistaken. I would not say to him (for very obvious reasons) what I say to you, my dear Sir, that

λίσσομαι εἵνεκ' ἐμεῖο μένειν· πάρ' ἔμοιγε καὶ ἄλλοι
οἵ κέ με τιμήσουσι, μάλιστα δὲ μητίετα Ζεύς

[Others will honor me, and Zeus who views the whole world most of all (*Iliad* 1. 11. 174–5).]

No – while the respectable person, to whom I write, shall think my intentions just and my heart good, I shall hear without pain that Dr. Wetherell charges me with wishing to *overturn that constitution,* to *preserve* which I would sacrifice my peace of mind or even my life, but which he certainly does not understand or does not regard.– My best respects to your very worthy family.

The following letter to Richard Johnson shows how Sanskrit appreciators like Jones were enriched by Sanskrit culture, in this case transforming an otherwise pedestrian note by elevating a Hindu image into a striking figure of speech. (Published with permission of the Princeton University Library.)

27 Nov. 1787.

My dear Sir,

Durgà waits upon you: When we proposed also to attend you at Russa next Sunday, it did not occur to us, that we should have no moon on our return: we must therefore postpone that pleasure till the God, who bears a black antelope in his bosom, shall again enlighten us. I am, dear Sir,

Yours ever faithfully,
W. Jones.

Notes

Introduction

1. Translation of Raymond Schwab, *The Oriental Renaissance* (New York: Columbia University Press, 1984), p. 122.
2. David Kopf, *British Orientalism and the Bengal Renaissance* (Berkeley and Los Angeles: University of California Press, 1969), pp. 241, 272, 263–4.
3. See Schwab, *The Oriental Renaissance,* p. xxiii.
4. Kopf, *British Orientalism,* p. vii.
5. Quoted in Kopf, *British Orientalism,* p. 274.

1. A Barbaric Oriental Conqueror (to 1770)

1. See Morris's letter to William of 1 January 1748, Teignmouth's *Memoirs of the Life, Writings and Correspondence of Sir William Jones* (London, 1807), 1:2–4. Teignmouth's *Memoirs* constitutes the first two volumes of the thirteen-volume *The Works of Sir William Jones.* Hereafter cited as Teignmouth and *Works,* respectively. See the *Dictionary of National Biography* (hereafter cited as *D.N.B.*) entry for William and *The Dictionary of Welsh Biography down to 1940* (London, 1959), pp. 522–3. *The Mathematical Papers of Isaac Newton,* ed. D. T. Whiteside and M. A. Hoskins (Cambridge, 1967–), contains many references to him. Llewelyn G. Chambers has kindly supplied new materials from his forthcoming work on Welsh mathematicians.
2. Hugh Owens, "Additional Letters of the Morrises of Anglesey," *Y Cymmrodor* 49 (1947–9):253. Teignmouth (1:5) dates his birth as 1680.
3. Society records show that he was never vice-president, contrary to the *D.N.B.*
4. In Stephen Peter Rigaud's *Correspondence of Scientific Men of the Seventeenth Century* (Oxford, 1841).
5. Charles Hutton, *Mathematical Tables* (London, 1785), p. 117.
6. Sir Henry Lyons, *The Royal Society 1660–1940* (Cambridge, 1944), p. 173.
7. Teignmouth, 1:14–18.
8. Ibid., 1:21–22. Italics in all quotations are in the original.
9. *A Philosophical Survey of Nature* (London, 1763), p. 69.
10. Of November 1762, *The Letters of Sir William Jones,* ed. Garland Cannon (Oxford, 1970), 1:3. References to *Letters* will be given in the text by volume and page nunber(s) when possible, and some quotations will be in translation.
11. Teignmouth, 1:29.
12. Ibid., 1:28.
13. Warren Derry, *Dr. Parr: A Portrait of the Whig Dr. Johnson* (Oxford, 1966), p. 7.
14. *The Works of Samuel Parr, LL.D.,* ed. John Johnstone (London, 1828), 1:18–21.
15. Seventeen lines are in Teignmouth, 1:31. "Saul and David," written at thirteen to satirize

the inordinate love of novelty, is in *Thraliana,* ed. Katharine Balderston (Oxford, 1942), 1:237–40. A mature Latin declamation, written for the school upon Jones's leaving Harrow, is in *Gentleman's Magazine* 68 (May 1798):373–4.

16. Rosamond Bayne-Powell, *The English Child in the Eighteenth Century* (London, 1939), p. 101.
17. Parr, *Works,* 1:15.
18. In *Analyse du jeu des échecs* (London, 1749).
19. Sir Thomas Ireland, *An Exact Abridgment in English of the Eleven Books of Reports of . . . Sir Edward Coke* (London, 1650).
20. Bennet to William Davies Shipley of November 1795, and Parnell to Lady Jones after 1794, in Teignmouth, 1:34 and 49, respectively.
21. In Teignmouth, 1:53. From Odes, II. xiv ("Eheu fugaces, postume"). The lost holographic collection contained other translations, imitations, and "Saul and David."
22. Teignmouth, 1:54.
23. Ibid., 1:198. See Richard Crakanthorpe's *Introductio in metaphysicam* (Oxford, 1619) and *Logicæ libri quinque* (London, 1622), the standard textbooks then, and Franco Burgersdijck's *Idea philosphiæ moralis* (Leipzig, 1623).
24. Mary was fatally burned in 1801. See Lætitia-Matilda Hawkins's *Memoirs, Anecdotes, Facts, and Opinions* (London, 1824), 1:247–53.
25. He used Golius' *Lexicon Arabico-Latinum* (London, 1653) and Erpenius' *Arabicæ linguæ tyrocinium* (London, 1656).
26. A. S. Tritton, "The Student of Arabic," University of London *Bulletin of the School of Oriental and African Studies* 11 (1946):695. Hereafter cited as *BSOAS.*
27. Teignmouth, 1:57–58.
28. Simon Digby's review of *Letters,* in *BSOAS* 34 (1971):170.
29. A. L. Rowse, "Welsh Orientalist: Sir William Jones," *History Today* 21 (1971):64.
30. Preface to his English abridgment, *The History of the Life of Nader Shah,* in *Works,* 12:317. His explanation to Reviczky of 29 January 1770 (1:44) slightly varies from this public one: Christian VII had heard of Jones and summoned him to London, where the Danish king personally showed him the manuscript and requested the translation. See Hertha Kirketerp-Moller's "Nader Shah, Christian VII og William Jones," Det Kongelige Bibliotek *Fund og Forskning* 9 (1962):114–27.
31. Thomas Maurice, *Memoirs of the Author of "Indian Antiquities,"* 2nd ed. (London, 1821), pt. 1, p. 76.
32. Laurence Lockhart, *Nadir Shah* (London, 1938), p. 296. See G. S. P. Freeman-Grenville's *The Muslim and Christian Calendars* (London, 1963). A bibliographical evaluative description of Jones's books and of reviews of them can be found in Cannon's *Sir William Jones: A Bibliography* (Amsterdam, 1979).
33. *Monthly Review* 42 (App. 1770):508–9.
34. *Works,* 12:340.
35. In Asiatic Society Library, Calcutta. James Northcote's portrait of Jones as a young man is in the National Museum of Wales.
36. On its founding on 2 January 1769. See Charles Robert Leslie and Tom Taylor's *Life and Times of Sir Joshua Reynolds* (London, 1865), 1:319.
37. Memoranda Book, British Library (hereafter cited as *BL*), Add. MS 32336.
38. The back covers of the Buttery Accounts record the number of guests at the six annual holiday dinners at University College Hall, when a special charge was made for wines. By checking those dates when Johnson is known to have been at Oxford, and when Scott or Chambers was present and there was a guest, one can guess whether Johnson attended. The daily accounts do not tabulate the number of guests.
39. Victoria County Histories, *A History of Oxfordshire* (Oxford, 1954), 3:69.

40. Maurice, *Memoirs*, pt. 2, p. 148.
41. Teignmouth, 1:111.
42. His propositions are in Teignmouth, 1:115–17.
43. Teignmouth located only Jones's "Plan" (1:154–8).
44. Locating only Jones's discourse, Teignmouth summarized it (1:158–60).
45. A partial copy of Voltaire's first-person answer of 16 May is in the Bodleian, M.A. Eng. Lett. C229, f. 140.
46. See a nationalistic condemnation in *Monthly Review* 45 (December 1804):339.
47. Having introduced himself to Chinese only the previous summer, he did not know Percy's English version of the ode in *Hau Kiou Choaan* (London, 1761), 4:233–4, made from an English form and a Portuguese translation.
48. It is labeled absurd in a letter in *Gentleman's Magazine* 72 (February 1802):104.
49. In Teignmouth, 2:429–43.
50. Of 21 October 1766, *Memoirs of the Life of the Right Honourable Sir John Eardley Wilmot, Knt.*, ed. John Eardley-Wilmot (London, 1802), p. 117.

2. Delicate Arab Maidens and Liquid Ruby (1770–1772)

1. Frederick W. Hilles, "Self-Portrait of the Great Orientalist," *Yale Review* 60 (1971): 266–7.
2. Rosane Rocher's review of *Letters*, in *Journal of the American Oriental Society* 92 (1972):515. Hereafter cited as *JAOS*.
3. *Works*, 5:243.
4. A. J. Arberry, *Asiatic Jones: The Life and Influence of Sir William Jones* (London, 1946), p. 33.
5. Arberry, "Orient Pearls at Random Strung," *BSOAS* 11 (1946):701–2.
6. Ibid., p. 703.
7. V. de Sola Pinto, "Sir William Jones and English Literature," *BSOAS* 11 (1946):687.
8. Of 30 March 1774, *The Letters of Samuel Johnson*, ed. R. W. Chapman (Oxford, 1952), 1:403–4.
9. *Eclectic Review* 1 (January 1805):35.
10. R. M. Hewitt, "Harmonious Jones," *Essays and Studies by Members of the English Association* 28 (1942):48.
11. "Jones's *Persian Grammar*," *Classical Journal* 35 (March 1827):122.
12. Charles Wilkins published *A Dictionary, Persian, Arabic, and English* (London, 1829). Ultimately the East India Company subsidized Francis Johnson's 1,420-page revision of Meninski (London, 1852).
13. Indignantly responding in *An Apology to John Richardson* (n.p., 1778?), Bryant denied that most of his evidence rested on etymological deduction. In an expanded *Dissertation on the Languages, Literature, and Manners of Eastern Nations* (Oxford, 1778), Richardson then charged that Bryant's system was unsound and utilized etymological "allegations."
14. Marzieh Gail, *Persia and the Victorians* (London, 1951), p. 28. See Arthur D. Waley, "Anquetil-Duperron and Sir William Jones," *History Today* 2 (1952):23–33.
15. Edward G. Browne, *A Literary History of Persia* (reprint) (Cambridge, 1951), 1:49. See also Holger Pedersen, *Linguistic Science in the Nineteenth Century* (Cambridge, Mass., 1931), p. 25.
16. Translation in Gail, *Persia and the Victorians*, pp. 28–29.
17. Waley, "Anquetil-Duperron and Sir William Jones," p. 31.
18. December 1771, p. 498; and Suppl. 1771, p. 605, respectively.
19. Of 28 November 1771, Teignmouth, 1:192–3.
20. Browne, *Literary History*, 1:49–50, 57.

21. Preface to *Poems,* in *Works,* 10:199; Introduction to the abridgment *History,* ibid., 5:415; and "To the University of Oxford" (in 1:367), respectively.
22. R. E. R.'s letter of 30 October 1804, *Monthly Magazine* 19 (February 1805):32.
23. Browne, *Literary History,* 1:57.
24. Pedersen, *Linguistic Science,* p. 26. See Max Müller's *Chips from a German Workshop* (New York, 1887–90), 1:80.
25. Alexander Chalmers, "The Life of Sir William Jones," *The Works of the English Poets* (London, 1810), 18:434; and *Journals of Ralph Waldo Emerson* (Boston, 1909–14), 10:139, respectively.
26. The prefatory discourse of the lost "Essay" is in Teignmouth, 2:455–93.
27. Of 27 March 1771, ibid., 1:167–8.
28. *Works,* 10:359–60.
29. Pinto, "Sir William Jones," p. 687.
30. See Frédéric Alliey's translation, *Poèmes sur le jeu des échecs* (Paris, 1851).
31. Harold Mantz, "Non-Dramatic Pastoral in Europe in the Eighteenth Century," *Publications of the Modern Language Association* 31 (1916):439.
32. Pinto, "Sir William Jones," pp. 689–90.
33. M. H. Abrams, *The Mirror and the Lamp* (New York, 1953), p. 87. See David Newton-De Molina's "Sir William Jones' 'Essay on the Arts Commonly Called Imitative,' " *Anglia* 90 (1972):147–54.
34. To William Mason of 25 May 1772, the Yale edition (hereafter cited as Yale ed.) of Horace Walpole's correspondence, ed. W. S. Lewis, 28:35–36.
35. Pinto, "Sir William Jones," p. 688.
36. "The Debt to Asiatic Jones," 28 September 1946, p. 464.

3. Persian Jones and Constitutional Law (1772–1777)

1. Lucy Sutherland's review of *Letters,* in *South Asian Review* 4 (1971):262.
2. Walter Pollard's observation, in Maurice, *Memoirs,* pt. 1, p. 87.
3. The epitaph is in Teignmouth, 1:204–5.
4. Maurice, *Memoirs,* pt. 1, p. 87.
5. Ibid., pt. 2, pp. 156–62. The couplets are in *An Essay on Epic Poetry,* 4:235–48, in *Poems by William Hayley* (Dublin, 1782), 2:70–71.
6. Sent to Hawkins on 7 April 1772 (1:111–12). This version is much like that in *Annual Register* of 1778, p. 205. Garrick's "Upon the Earl of Chatham's Verses to Mr. Garrick" (1772) declined the counterinvitation to visit Pitt's "small roof."
7. John Blackman, *A Memoir of the Life and Writings of Thomas Day* (London, 1862), p. 29; and Sir S. H. Scott, *The Exemplary Mr. Day 1748–1789* (London, 1935), p. 39.
8. "Sir William Jones and Mr. Day," *Mirror* 12 (26 July 1828):64.
9. Ralph M. Wardle, *Oliver Goldsmith* (Lawrence, Kans., 1957), p. 251. A record of the evenings is in Percy's Memoranda Book, BL Add. MS 32336, ff. 160, 170, 177.
10. Archibald Shepperson, *John Paradise and Lucy Ludwell* (Richmond, Va., 1942), pp. 89, 121.
11. Of 3 November 1772, BL India Office Library, Orme Correspondence, 41:87.
12. Boswell, *Life of Johnson,* ed. L. F. Powell (Oxford, 1934–50), 1:477. Also see L. F. Powell's "Sir William Jones and the Club," *BSOAS* 11 (1946):818–22; and Cannon's "Sir William Jones and Dr. Johnson's Literary Club," *Modern Philology* 63 (1965):20–37.
13. Memoranda Book, BL Add. MS 322336, f. 176.
14. Boswell, *Johnson,* 2:235–40; and *Private Papers of James Boswell,* ed. Geoffrey Scott and Frederick A. Pottle (1929–34), 6:130.

15. Boswell, *Johnson*, 4:115, 433; and *Johnsonian Miscellanies*, ed. G. B. Hill (Oxford, 1897), 1:287, respectively.
16. Entry of 25 August 1773, Boswell's *Journal of a Tour to the Hebrides with Samuel Johnson*, ed. Frederick A. Pottle and Charles H. Bennett (New York, 1936), pp. 78–79.
17. See "Genuine Character of Omiah" in "Characters," *Annual Register* of 1774, pp. 61–63.
18. Garrick lent Parr the costumes for several classical plays.
19. William Reginald Ward, *Georgian Oxford; University Politics in the Eighteenth Century* (Oxford, 1958), p. 259.
20. Jackson's *Oxford Journal* of 26 June 1773. See the 10 July issue and *Gentleman's Magazine* of July 1773 (pp. 350–2).
21. Of 1769, Teignmouth, 1:200–1.
22. Tritton, "The Student of Arabic," pp. 696–7.
23. Arberry, "Persian Jones," *Asiatic Review* 40 (1944):193.
24. Of 20 November 1773, Francis Hardy's *Memoirs of the Political and Private Life of James Caulfeild, Earl of Charlemont*, 2nd ed. (London, 1812), 1:346.
25. Of 2 March 1774, Teignmouth, 1:209.
26. J. A. Stewart, "Sir W. Jones' Revision of the Text of Two Poems of Anacreon," *BSOAS* 11 (1946):669–71.
27. *History*, ed. J. B. Bury, 4th ed. (London, 1911), 6:33, n. 82.
28. Of 9 February 1778, "Five New Letters by Sir William Jones," *Philological Quarterly* 51 (1972):952.
29. Reported by Henry Hawkins in Lætitia-Matilda Hawkins's *Memoirs*, 1:244–5.
30. Ibid., 1:246.
31. Acts 34 and 35, Hen. VIII, c. 26. See W. Llewelyn Williams, "The King's Court of Great Sessions in Wales," *Y Cymmrodor* 26 (1916):1–87.
32. Woide told Michaelis: "Mr. Jones is very young, likeable, and has a lot of different interests and is good in all of them." See letter of 13 October 1774, *Literarischer Briefwechsel von Johann David Michaelis* (Leipzig, 1796), pp. 103–4.
33. The MS is no. 154 in "A Catalogue of Sanskrit, and Other Oriental Manuscripts," *Works*, 13:424.
34. Derry, *Dr. Parr*, p. 332. His grandson, Bulwer-Lytton, depicted him as the elder Caxton in *The Caxtons*.
35. Maurice, *Memoirs*, pt. 1, p. 74. His translation of "Ad Lunam" is on p. 74. See pt. 2, p. 139.
36. See Cannon, "The Andrometer and Performance-based Teacher Evaluation," *Educational Forum* 38 (1974):305–13.
37. The rental books show that he took his chambers, which included "One pair of Stairs," in his name in midsummer of 1775 at £35 per annum. There is no mention of Day, who has been said to have shared these chambers.
38. See "History of Europe," *Annual Register* of 1775, pp. 63–77.
39. Epistle dedicatory to *Speeches of Isæus*, in *Works*, 9:4.
40. Maurice, *Memoirs*, pt. 1, pp. 84 and 86, respectively.
41. Her society's work is detailed in John Burrows's many letters to her between 1774 and 1785, at Althorp.
42. Orme's undated fragment may have been an introduction for the trip to Rome: "Dear Sir, Mr. William Jones, a Gentleman of the bar, and known to the world for his great Learning is coming from Paris. He is a friend for whom I have the highest regard & Esteem. I desired him to be had an—" (Orme Collection, 147.2:18).
43. Of 10 January 1775, MS at Althorp.
44. *Bibliotheca Parriana. A Catalogue of the Library of the Late Reverend and Learned Samuel Parr, LL.D.* (London, 1827), pp. 522, 203, and 506, respectively.

45. See Lowth's letter to Benjamin Wheeler of 1777, Parr's *Works*, 1:99.
46. Quoted by Pollard around June 1778 to Maurice, in Maurice, *Memoirs*, pt. 2, p. 152.
47. "To G. Hardynge, Esq." is in Teignmouth, 2:78. Hardinge's letter to Althorp of 13 July 1777, at Althorp, lavishly praises Jones.
48. Of 18 October 1777, Richard Henry Lee, *Life of Arthur Lee, LL.D.* (Boston, 1829), 1:119–20.
49. BL Add. MS 30866, f. 70. Jones's address is recorded in Wilkes's third address book, Add. MS 30892, f. 57.

4. The Athenian and Eleutherion (1778–1780)

1. Jones was referring to 12 Geo. III, c. 73, s. 13.
2. *The Letters of Warren Hastings to His Wife*, ed. Sydney C. Grier (London, 1905), p. 249.
3. Robert Gore-Browne, *Chancellor Thurlow* (London, 1953), p. 125.
4. Of 5 July 1778, "Memoirs of the Life of Sir William Jones, M.A.," *Annual Biography and Obituary* (London, 1817), 1:458–9.
5. Preserved in vol. 5 of Reiske's *Oratorum Græcorum* (Leipzig, 1770–5).
6. Miniatus Bononiensis, *Oratorum Græciæ praestantissimorum* (Hannover, 1619), pp. 360–590.
7. S. G. Vesey-FitzGerald, "Sir William Jones, the Jurist," *BSOAS* 11 (1946):812–13.
8. Chalmers, *Works of the English Poets*, 18:435.
9. Of 5 January 1780, "Five New Letters by Jones," p. 953.
10. Athanase Auger, *Œuvres complettes de Dêmosthene et d'Eschine* (Paris, 1777); and Hieronymus Wolfius, *Demosthenis et Æchinis principum Græciæ oratorum opera* (Basel, 1572), 6 vols.
11. Derry, *Dr. Parr*, p. 32.
12. James Madison Stifler, *"My Dear Girl"* (New York, 1927), pp. vii–viii, 218, 225–6.
13. Shepperson, *John Paradise and Lucy Ludwell*, pp. 133–7.
14. Hector Charles Cameron, *Sir Joseph Banks* (London, 1966), p. 125.
15. Of 1 January 1778, Teignmouth, 1:282.
16. Of 31 December 1778, ibid., 1:291–2.
17. Of 3 October 1778, ibid., 1:284.
18. Of 26 November 1778, ibid., 1:292.
19. Boswell, *Johnson*, 4:183.
20. Ibid., 3:371.
21. Boswell, *Private Papers*, 13:233.
22. Powell, "Jones and the Club," pp. 821–2.
23. Maurice, *Memoirs*, pt. 2, p. 139.
24. To Mrs. Thrale of 5 June 1782, in A. M. Broadley's *Doctor Johnson and Mrs. Thrale* (London, 1910), p. 142.
25. To William Mason of 5 February 1781, Yale ed., 29:104.
26. Carl B. Cone, *Torchbearer of Freedom* (Lexington, Ky., 1952), pp. 54–55.
27. John Carswell, *From Revolution to Revolution: England 1688–1776* (New York, 1973), p. 142.
28. See "A Fragment of Polybius from His Treatise 'On the Athenian Government' " (1:290–6); and Cannon's "Sir William Jones and Anglo-American Relations during the American Revolution," *Modern Philology* 76 (1978):29–45.
29. James Parton, *Life and Times of Benjamin Franklin* (Boston, 1884), 2:333; and William C. Bruce, *Benjamin Franklin Self-Revealed* (New York, 1917), 2:313.
30. By Jared Sparks, ed., *The Works of Benjamin Franklin* (Boston, 1840), 8:366–7.
31. Shepperson, *John Paradise and Lucy Ludwell*, p. 149.

32. Of 14 October 1779, Franklin's *Works,* 8:395.
33. The 1780 memorandum is in Teignmouth, 1:343–4; the two-circle one and that on classical books is in BL Add. MS 8889.
34. Charles Richard Weld, *History of the Royal Society* (London, 1848), 2:138–9.
35. The letter is in *The Correspondence of James Boswell with Certain Members of the Club,* ed. Charles F. Fifer (New York, 1976), 3:77.

5. An Ass Laden with Gold (1780)

1. Ward, *Georgian Oxford,* p. 276.
2. Charles Parker's letter of 1780, Warwickshire P.R.O.
3. Of 23 May 1780, Teignmouth, 1:314.
4. To William Mason of 19 May 1780, Yale ed., 29:36.
5. Of 9 May and 6 June 1780, Johnson's *Letters,* 2:356, 365–6, respectively.
6. A copy is in Bodleian, Gough Oxf. 90, 96 (66). In *Letters* (1:366–7), it is probably his Oxford printed address from which the *D.N.B.* concludes that Jones was an unsuccessful candidate for the lord almoner's professorship of Arabic in May 1780. The post was vacant, but there is no evidence that he applied for it.
7. Parker's letter to Newdigate, in Newdigate Collection, B. 2141, on loan in Shire Hall of Warwickshire County Council from F. H. M. Fitzroy Newdigate.
8. *Annals of the Club 1764–1914* (London, 1914), plate 3. See Langton to Boswell of 18 May 1780, Boswell's *Correspondence,* 3:106–7.
9. This handwritten ledger is at Worcester College.
10. Ward, *Georgian Oxford,* p. 278.
11. Letter, Reginald Blunt, *Mrs. Montagu "Queen of the Blues"* (Boston, 1923), 2:84.
12. Cartwright's letter is in Teignmouth, 1:310.
13. Of 30 May 1780, Mary Cartwright Strickland's *A Memoir of the Life, Writings, and Mechanical Inventions, of Edmund Cartwright* (London, 1843), p. 44. When Parr asked for another copy of *Ad Libertatem,* Jones noted that the supply was exhausted: "Paradise has engaged to re-print it, with notes, historical and explanatory" (2:505).
14. Of 30 May 1780, Hartley MSS, Berkshire P.R.O. D/EHY F88.
15. Review of Teignmouth, *Critical Review,* 3rd series, 4 (January 1805):16.
16. Translation of Schultens of 2 June 1780, Teignmouth, 1:317–18.
17. See *London Evening-Post* and *St. James's Chronicle* of 8 June for accounts of the Temple during the riots.
18. Ward, *Georgian Oxford,* p. 278.
19. Peter Douglas Brown, *The Chathamites* (London, 1967), p. 364.
20. To John English Dolben of 26 October 1780, Christ Church MS 353/5.
21. Arberry, "New Light on Sir William Jones," *BSOAS* 11 (1946):673.
22. Brown, *The Chathamites,* p. 363.
23. September 1780, p. 436. "To William Jones, Esq." is also in *European Magazine* 6 (September 1784):234.
24. See L. G. Mitchell, "Univ., Sir William Jones and the 1780 Election," *Oxford University College Record* 4 (1973):257–62.
25. Shepperson, *John Paradise and Lucy Ludwell,* p. 149. Also see Arberry's *Asiatic Jones,* pp. 14–15.
26. Of 9 October 1780, Franklin's *Works,* 8:505.

6. Politics: Writings and Activism (1780–1782)

1. The late James Osborn supplied these dates from "The Club: the First Half-Century," which he was constructing from the meeting records and other documents.

2. Of 27 November 1780, Teignmouth, 1:347.

3. Undated proposal to John Price (*Letters*, 1:446–9).

4. To the earl of Strafford of 31 August 1781 and to the countess of Upper Ossory of 4 September 1781, Yale ed., 35:362; 33:387–8, respectively.

5. Sir N. William Wraxall, *Historical Memoirs of My Own Time*, ed. Richard Askham (London, 1904), p. 386. See Hayley to Samuel Rose of 26 June 1795, in *Memoirs of the Life and Writings of William Hayley, Esq.*, ed. John Johnson (London, 1823), 1:470.

6. Of 28 May 1781, Teignmouth, 1:359.

7. "Sir William Jones," *Penny Magazine* 8 (Suppl. to April 1839):122.

8. Pinto, "Sir William Jones," p. 692.

9. In *The Autobiography and Correspondence of Mary Granville, Mrs. Delany,* ed. Lady Llanover, 2nd series (London, 1862), 2:539–41.

10. Ibid. The poem is in 2:500–1.

11. Ibid. The poem appeared as "To the Nymph of the Spring" in *Monthly Magazine* 17 (May 1804):348; and in *Port Folio* 5 (4 May 1805):135.

12. The lyric is in Teignmouth, 2:505–7; the poorly printed doggerel is in Schultens's papers.

13. The poem is in Teignmouth, 2:506–7.

14. Of 6 May 1781, *The Papers of Thomas Jefferson,* ed. Julian P. Boyd (Princeton, N.J., 1950–4), 5:610.

15. For example, when "two gentlemen" landed from the *Vengeance* on 26 July, they were charged with carrying on a treasonable correspondence (*Gentleman's Magazine*, August 1781, p. 388).

16. Sir William Holdsworth, *A History of English Law* (London, 1938), 12:393.

17. Joseph Story, *Commentaries on the Law of Bailments,* rev. 3rd ed. (Boston, 1843), p. x.

18. Vesey-FitzGerald, "Sir William Jones, the Jurist," p. 813.

19. Holdsworth, *History of English Law,* 11:220.

20. "Hoffman's Course of Legal Study," *North American Review* 6 (November 1817):46.

21. Jones's copy of Littleton, annotated and interleaved for his translation, is in BL 708.g.22. His "law" memorandum is Add. MS 8889.

22. See notes in Bury's ed., 3:80; 4:487, 496; 5:325; and 6:33, 245.

23. Arberry, "New Light," p. 679.

24. August, October, Suppl. 1817 (pp. 133–4, 295–6, 582–3, respectively); and May 1818 (pp. 402–3). In *A Statistical Method for Determining Authorship* (Gothenburg, 1962), p. 85, Alvar Ellegard tested *Poems* in rejecting Jones as a viable candidate. See the list in *Junius: Including Letters by the Same Writer Under Other Signatures,* ed. John Wade, new ed. (London, 1855), 1:xxiv.

25. Translation by Roy Hyde of the Bodleian's printed copy, MS 1004, f. 244.

26. Tritton, "The Student of Arabic," p. 698.

27. Undated; see Cannon, "Sir William Jones and Edmund Burke," *Modern Philology* 54 (1957):177.

28. Pinto, "Sir William Jones," p. 690. It is in W. J. Courthope's *A History of English Poetry* (London, 1910), 6:24.

29. Vesey-FitzGerald, "Sir William Jones, the Jurist," p. 810.

30. C. B. Roylance Kent, *The English Radicals* (London, 1899), p. 86.

7. James River Property (1782–1783)

1. Shepperson, *John Paradise and Lucy Ludwell,* pp. 158–61.

2. Jay to Livingston of 17 November 1782, in Francis Wharton, ed., *The Revolutionary Diplomatic Correspondence of the United States* (Washington, D.C., 1889), 6:12.

3. Of 28 June 1782, Franklin's *Works,* 9:348.

4. William V. Wells, *The Life and Public Services of Samuel Adams* (Boston, 1865), 2:166–7. Franklin did not mention Jones in his precautionary letter to Livingston (*Works*, 9:348).

5. Both of 15 July 1782, Jefferson's *Papers*, 6:194; and Edward E. Hale and Edward E. Hale, Jr., *Franklin in France* (Boston, 1887–8), 2:214, respectively.

6. Shepperson, *John Paradise and Lucy Ludwell*, pp. 167–80.

7. Of 17 November 1782, Wharton, ed., *The Revolutionary Diplomatic Correspondence*, 6:14.

8. Teignmouth, 1:355. By contrast, Shepperson asserts that Jones's actually straightforward letter had poisoned Franklin's mind (pp. 176–80). Parton (*Life and Times of Franklin*, 2:481) explains Jones's departure primarily on the basis of Paradise's absolute terror of the sea, which made Paradise take to his bed.

9. Rowse, "Welsh Orientalist," p. 61.

10. Shepperson asserts that Jones's eloquent defense made him consider himself the injured party; his spreading this interpretation helped weaken Paradise's self-confidence pathetically (*John Paradise and Lucy Ludwell*, pp. 177–80).

11. Of 4 December 1782, John Doran, *A Lady of the Last Century (Mrs. E. Montagu)* (London, 1873), p. 307.

12. Of October 1782, Teignmouth, 1:403–4.

13. Of 13 November 1782, Devonshire Collections, Chatsworth, Derbyshire.

14. Jones's summary, Parr's *Bibliotheca*, p. 441.

15. Vesey-FitzGerald, "Sir William Jones, the Jurist," p. 811.

16. See Cannon, "Freedom of the Press and Sir William Jones," *Journalism Quarterly* 33 (1956):179–88; and *Erskine's Select Speeches*, ed. Nathaniel Chapman (Philadelphia, 1807–8), 2:2–119.

17. See Vesey-FitzGerald, "Sir William Jones, the Jurist," pp. 810–11; Francis Jeffrey's review of Teignmouth, *Edinburgh Review* 5 (January 1805):340; and Cannon's "Jones and Anglo-American Relations."

18. Letter of 29 July 1798, *The Life and Correspondence of Major Cartwright*, ed. F. D. Cartwright (London, 1826), 1:248.

19. Tritton, "The Student of Arabic," p. 695.

20. See Reynold A. Nicholson, *A Literary History of the Arabs*, 2nd ed. (Cambridge, 1930), pp. 101–21.

21. Satyendra Nath Ray, "Sir William Jones's Poetry," in Suniti Kumar Chatterji, ed., *Sir William Jones: Bicentenary of His Birth Commemoration Volume, 1746–1946* (Calcutta, 1948), p. 154.

22. Review, *London Magazine* 52 (July 1783):59, 55. Zuhair's poem is reprinted in *Calcutta Gazette* of 13 and 20 May 1784.

23. Gibbon's footnote is in *History*, 5:325.

24. Undated, "Selections from the Letters of Georgiana Duchess of Devonshire," *Anglo-Saxon Review* 2 (1899):68–69.

25. Shipley's quoting of Ashburton of 12 November 1787, *The Correspondence of William Wilberforce*, ed. Robert and Samuel Wilberforce (London, 1840), 1:47.

26. Of 6 March 1783, American Philosophical Society Library.

27. Letter of 17 March 1783, Franklin's *Works*, 9:500–1. Jones's help became widely known; thus Adams quoted the motto in 1817, *Statesman and Friend: Correspondence of John Adams with Benjamin Waterhouse, 1784–1822*, ed. Worthington Chauncey Ford (Boston, 1927), p. 132.

28. *Private Papers*, 15:184.

29. Of 19 April 1783, Johnson's *Letters*, 3:18; and *The Percy Letters*, ed. David Nichol Smith and Cleanth Brooks (Baton Rouge, La., 1944), 1:12, respectively.

30. William Carr, *University College* (London, 1902), p. 193.

31. Letter of 29 March 1783, *Johnsonian Miscellanies,* 2:200.
32. *Indian Antiquities* (London, 1800–1), 1:13.
33. Arberry, *Asiatic Jones,* p. 39.

8. A Vision in the Indian Ocean (1783–1785)

1. Sutherland, review of *Letters,* p. 263.
2. *Memoirs of Sir Elijah Impey, Knt.,* ed. Elijah B. Impey (London, 1850), pp. 53–59.
3. To Thurlow of 28 November 1776, Sir James Fitzjames Stephen, *The Story of Nuncomar, and the Impeachment of Sir Elijah Impey* (London, 1885), 1:36–37.
4. Of April 1783, untraced since its sale. See Sotheby's *Catalogue of a Valuable Collection of Autograph Letters, Forming the Hayley Correspondence* (London, 1878).
5. Of 15 May 1783, Devonshire Collections.
6. In Teignmouth, 2:3–4.
7. "Remarks on the Island of Hinzuan or Johanna," *Works,* 4:290.
8. Reported in Macartney's letter of 12 October 1783, *The Private Correspondence of Lord Macartney,* Camden 3rd series, ed. C. Collin Davies (London, 1950), 77:223.
9. Teignmouth, 2:11.
10. *Memoirs of William Hickey,* ed. Alfred Spencer (New York, 1923), 8:155.
11. A. Mervyn Davies, *Strange Destiny: A Biography of Warren Hastings* (New York, 1935), p. 423.
12. Kopf, *British Orientalism,* p. 17. Though a bit dated by the time of the Asiatic Society Bicentenary, this is still the main book on the British Orientalists' achievements and their conceptual contributions to Western knowledge.
13. "To let" notice in *Calcutta Gazette* of 29 May 1794.
14. Joseph Emin, *Life and Adventures of Emin Joseph Emin,* 2nd ed. (Calcutta, 1918), p. xx.
15. September 1784, p. 708. See *India Gazette* of 29 November. The three Calcutta newspapers fully reported the Supreme Court's major cases during Jones's tenure.
16. Richard W. Bailey's review of *Letters,* in *Michigan Quarterly Review* 11 (1972):213.
17. *India Gazette* of 6 December 1783; it appears in the 10 January 1784 issue. See Teignmouth, 2:13.
18. See Cannon, "Sir William Jones, Sir Joseph Banks, and the Royal Society," *Notes and Records of the Royal Society of London* 29 (1975):105–30; and Cannon, "Jones's Founding and Directing of the Asiatic Society," BL *India Office Library and Records Report for 1984–85,* pp. 11–28.
19. Details of the meeting are in MS Proceedings, Asiatic Society Library.
20. William Dick to Scott of 23 August 1819, *Familiar Letters of Sir Walter Scott* (Boston, 1894), 2:55.
21. Suresh Chandra Ghosh, *The Social Condition of the British Community in Bengal 1757–1800* (Leiden, 1970), pp. 1–4; and H. T. Colebrooke, *Miscellaneous Essays* (London, 1873), 1:19, 28–29.
22. The remark of 15 September 1777 is in Boswell's *Johnson,* 3:137; Jones's praise, in *Johnsonian Miscellanies,* 2:363; the duchess's letter to Lady Spencer of 7–10 September 1784, in "Selections from the Letters of Georgiana Duchess of Devonshire," *Anglo-Saxon Review* 2 (1899):78; the poem, in Teignmouth, 2:513; and William Bowles's report, in Boswell's *Johnson,* 4:524.
23. Robert H. Murray, *Edmund Burke. A Biography* (London, 1931), p. 346.
24. Of 8 August 1781, "Five New Letters by Jones," p. 954.
25. The annotation is in *Of the Advancement and Proficiency of Learning* (Oxford, 1640), p. 391, published in *Catalogue of the Library of the Late Sir William Jones* (London,

1831), p. 8; and Boswell's entry of 23 January 1790, in *Private Papers*, 18:24. See Cannon's "Jones and Burke."

26. T. Hannas and L. Hannas, Catalogue no. 13, *English Verse* (1962), no. 412.
27. Dick to Scott of 23 August 1819, *Familiar Letters of Scott*, 2:55.
28. Hickey, *Memoirs*, 3:198, 218.
29. *Calcutta Gazette* of 8 December 1785.
30. Peter Marshall kindly corrected the tentative identification of the addressee. It was Johnson, not Wilkins.
31. BL Add. MS 19283.
32. On 13 April 1784, National Archives of India, "Descriptive List of Secret Department Records," vol. 5, no. 28.
33. BL Add. MS 39898, f. 30.
34. Teignmouth, 2:38–39.
35. Ibid., 2:41–42.
36. Some of his and Anna's sketches are in the Royal Asiatic Society in London. See Raymond Head, "Divine Flower Power Recorded," *Country Life* 176 (1984):703–5.
37. Teignmouth, 2:46–48.
38. Of 3 March 1786, BL Add. MS 29169, f. 485.
39. Henry Morris, *Life of Charles Grant* (London, 1904), p. 82.

9. A Sacred Oriental Language (1785)

1. Of 14 and 16 April and 29 July 1785, Bodleian MSS Eng. Hist. c. 80, ff. 19, 20–1, 41, respectively.
2. In Osborn Collection, Yale University.
3. See H. P. Clodd's *Malaya's First British Pioneer; the Life of Francis Light* (London, 1948).
4. T. C. Fan, "William Jones' Chinese Studies," *Review of English Studies* 22 (1946):310.
5. "Notes of Legal Cases Argued in Bengal," BL Add. MS 8885.
6. The MSS of thirteen of his published letters to Wilkins are in the India Office Library.
7. "A Dissertation on the Orthography of Asiatick Words in Roman Letters" and Third Anniversary Discourse, *Works*, 3:261, 46, respectively.
8. Teignmouth, 2:65.
9. Jawaharlal Nehru, *The Discovery of India* (New York, 1946), p. 317.
10. See Murray Emeneau's review of *Letters*, in *Language* 47 (1971):962–3.
11. Ibid., 960–1.
12. "On the Literature of the Hindus," *Works*, 4:94, 107.
13. See Colebrooke, *Miscellaneous Essays*, 1:53–54. Parcel 698 contains some of Jones's translation exercises, including addresses to Ganesha and Sarasvati possibly by Śankara Āchārya. His phonetic list and annotations show his sandhi formulations.
14. After finishing his version on 27 July 1788, Jones states: "Of *eighteen*, or more, *Sanscrit* Dictionaries this is universally esteemed the principal: it was composed in easy blank verse by Amarasinha, a great scholar. . . . The words are here disengaged from the metre, and only the *roots* of them, or *crude nouns*, are exhibited. This book has a *tícà*, or *Comment*, in which all the words are *etymologically* analysed." The Texas A&M University Library has Jones's manuscript volume; Colebrooke published an English interpretation in 1808.
15. Translation from Borrow to Mr. Usóz of 28 July 1839, William I. Knapp's *Life, Writings, and Correspondence of George Borrow* (London, 1899), 2:282.
16. Kenneth Stunkel, "English Orientalism and India, 1784–1830," *Ohio University Review* 11 (1969):49.

17. See Colebrooke, *Miscellaneous Essays,* 2:73–74.
18. Preface to Jones's translation, *Works,* 7:87.
19. Teignmouth, 2:29–30.
20. Catherine to Franklin of 30 September 1785, Stifler, *"My Dear Girl,"* p. 260.
21. Boswell, *Johnson,* 1:223.
22. *Parnassus* (Boston, 1875), p. 180.
23. Pinto, "Sir William Jones," p. 692.
24. Edward F. Oaten, *A Sketch of Anglo-Indian Literature* (London, 1908), p. 32.
25. *C.H.E.L.,* 14:370.
26. Hewitt, "Harmonious Jones," p. 43. See T. Walker's "A Lecture on the Character and Writings of Sir William Jones," *Illinois Monthly Magazine* 2 (September 1832):559.
27. *Edinburgh Review* 5 (January 1805):331–2.
28. Henry Francis Cary, "Sir William Jones," *Lives of English Poets* (London, 1846), p. 384; and George L. Craik, *A Compendious History of English Literature and of the English Language* (New York, 1877), 2:414, respectively.
29. Hewitt, "Harmonious Jones," p. 49; and R. K. Das Gupta, "Sir William Jones as a Poet," in *Sir William Jones: Bicentenary of His Birth Commemoration Volume, 1746–1946* (Calcutta, 1948), pp. 162–3, respectively. See S. Viswanathan's "Hymns of Sir William Jones," *Aryan Path* 40 (1969):487–93, 543–50.
30. William Burroughs of 8 December 1789, *The Manuscripts and Correspondence of James, First Earl of Charlemont* (London, 1894), Hist. MSS Com., 13th Rep., App., pt. 8, 2:112.

10. A Genetic Explanation: Indo-European (1786–1787)

1. John Clive defends the Minute in *Macaulay: The Shaping of the Historian* (New York, 1973), pp. 364–76; cf. Cannon, "Evangelical Christianity in British Bengal Schools," *History of Education Quarterly* 13 (1973):445.
2. Sixth Discourse, *Works,* 3:111–12. See Hans Aarsleff, *The Study of Language in England, 1780–1860* (Princeton, N.J., 1967), pp. 127–31.
3. See Johnson's genealogical chart of Germanic languages in the preface to his *Dictionary of the English Language* (London, 1755); and Pedersen, *Linguistic Science,* p. 21.
4. Murray Emeneau, "India and Linguistics," *JAOS* 75 (1955):149.
5. Leonard Bloomfield, *Language* (reprint) (New York, 1956), p. 11.
6. Ninth Discourse, *Works,* 3:198–200. See Cannon, "Jones's 'sprung from some common source': 1786–1986," in Sydney Lamb, ed., *Sprung from Some Common Source* (Stanford, Calif., 1990).
7. (Edinburgh, 1774), 2:530–1.
8. Pedersen, *Linguistic Science,* p. 18.
9. Franklin Edgerton, "Sir William Jones: 1746–1794," *JAOS* 66 (1946):232. Charles F. Hockett calls it "the birth of modern linguistics . . . the first breakthrough," in "Sound Change," *Language* 41 (1965):185.
10. Suniti Kumar Chatterji, "Sir William Jones: 1746–1794," *Sir William Jones: Bicentenary of His Birth Commemoration Volume, 1746–1946* (Calcutta, 1948), p. 92; and Kalidas Nag, "Foreword," ibid., respectively.
11. Pedersen, *Linguistic Science,* p. 21.
12. Bailey, review of *Letters,* p. 211.
13. Herbert H. Gowen, *A History of Indian Literature* (New York, 1931), p. 138.
14. Also see Anna to Hastings of 3 March 1786, BL Add. MS 29169, f. 485; and Thomas Henry Davies to Jones of 26 September 1786, MS at Althorp.
15. Josiah Bateman, *The Life of the Right Rev. Daniel Wilson, D.D.* (London, 1860), 2:167.
16. In Teignmouth, 2:512–13.

17. John D. Yohannan, "The Persian Poetry Fad in England, 1770–1825," *Comparative Literature* 4 (1952):149. The ode is in Teignmouth, 2:501; and *Gentleman's Magazine* 74 (September 1804):856.

18. "A Dissertation on the Orthography of Asiatick Words in Roman Letters," *Works*, 3:253.

19. Sir Monier Monier-Williams, "The Duty of English-speaking Orientalists in Regard to United Action in Adhering Generally to Sir William Jones's Principles of Transliteration, Especially in the Case of Indian Languages," *Journal of the Royal Asiatic Society of Great Britain and Ireland* for 1890, p. 615. The quarrel had been heated. See H. T. Prinsep's "On the Adaptation of the Roman Alphabet to the Orthography of Oriental Languages" and Sir Charles Trevelyan's "Defence of Sir William Jones's System of Oriental Orthography," *Journal of the Asiatic Society of Bengal* 3 (June, August 1834):281–8 and 413–17, respectively.

20. Alfred Master, "The Influence of Sir William Jones upon Sanskrit Studies," *BSOAS* 11 (1946):806. Relating local speech sounds to English metropolitan orthographic practices, Jones represented the vowels as in Italian and the consonants as in English, a principle adopted by the Royal Geographic Society in 1836, preceding development of the IPA. See A. N. Tucker, "Orthographic Systems and Conventions in Sub-Saharan Africa," *Current Trends in Linguistics* 7 (1971):618.

21. Emeneau, "India and Linguistics," pp. 149–50.

22. It was enclosed in Jones's packet to her containing *Asiatick Miscellany*.

23. Of 15 January 1789 and 15 August 1791, Emin, *Life and Adventures*, 2:491, 494–5, respectively.

24. Of 29 March 1789, *The Correspondence of Edmund Burke*, ed. Thomas W. Copeland (Chicago, 1965), 5:456.

25. See Nicholson's ed. (London, 1925–40), 8 vols.

26. Hickey, *Memoirs*, 3:247–58; and *Calcutta Gazette* of 17 August and *India Gazette* of 14 August 1786.

27. No. 22 in Wilkins's Catalogue, *Works*, 13:410; and no. 449 in Jones's *Catalogue*, p. 19.

28. Edgerton, "Sir William Jones," p. 237.

29. For example, Carl Holliday, *The Dawn of Literature* (New York, 1931), p. 101. See Hamilton, *Monthly Review*, 2nd series, 32 (June 1800):133–4.

30. When Hastings reported this qualified criticism, Wilkins said with some acrimony: "I was not translating *for the use of schools*" (Hastings, *Letters*, p. 349).

31. In Chalmers, *Works of the English Poets*, 18:462.

32. See Sibadas Chaudhuri, ed., *Proceedings of the Asiatic Society* (Calcutta, 1980) for a partial publication of the Manuscript Proceedings for 1784 to 1800.

33. *India Gazette* of 13 November 1786.

34. Stephen, *Story of Nuncomar*, 2:33; *India Gazette* of 1 January 1787.

35. A translation of Bodawpayā's letter is in Teignmouth, 2:111–14.

36. *India Gazette* of 2 April 1787.

37. *Calcutta Gazette* of 14 June and *India Gazette* of 11 June 1787, respectively.

38. *India Gazette* of 18 June 1787.

39. William H. G. Twining, ed., *Travels in India a Hundred Years Ago* (London, 1893), p. 456.

40. Davis's MS note is in Teignmouth, 2nd ed. (London, 1806), p. 370, in the W. S. Lewis collection, Farmington, Conn.

41. As in *Gentleman's Magazine* of February 1799, p. 162; and Suppl. 1815, p. 585.

42. The shipboard prayer and the undated one are in Teignmouth, 2:42 and 513, respectively.

43. "On the Mystical Poetry of the Persians and Hindus," *Works*, 4:212.

44. In Teignmouth, 2:258; and "Sir Wm. Jones," *Notes and Queries* 12 (1861):396, respectively.

45. To her father of 8 August 1787, "Five New Letters by Jones," p. 954.
46. Arberry, *Asiatic Jones,* p. 22.

11. Sanskrit Literary Treasures (1787–1788)

1. The ruins were still visible in the college grounds in the 1850s. See W. S. Seton-Karr's *The Marquess Cornwallis* (Oxford, 1898), p. 109.
2. Pinto, "Sir William Jones," p. 689. The Arguments and the stanzas are in Teignmouth, 2:444–54.
3. "The Poems of Sir William Jones," *Southern Literary Messenger* 15 (December 1849):726.
4. Chatterji, "Sir William Jones," p. 94.
5. In the context of the writing of a national epic, Hayley laments the abandonment of Jones's plan, in *An Essay on Epic Poetry* (London, 1782), 4:373–82.
6. "On the Oriental Emigration of the Ancient Inhabitants of Britain and Ireland," in William Ouseley, ed., *The Oriental Collections* (London, 1797–9), 3:31.
7. A variant holograph is in BL India Office Library, MSS Eur. D. 491.
8. "Philemon" is in Teignmouth, 2:131–2.
9. In the weekly *Calcutta Gazette* of February 1791; *European Magazine* of September–December 1791, pp. 177–80, 281–4, 343–6, 449–50; and *Scots Magazine* of October–December 1791, pp. 469–72, 527–32, 581–6.
10. Reported in *India Gazette* of 5 November 1787; and *Calcutta Gazette* of 15 November and 27 December 1787, respectively.
11. The Manuscript Proceedings are missing between November 1788 and 4 November 1789.
12. Sir George Dunbar, *A History of India from the Earliest Times to the Present Day* (London, 1936), p. 4.
13. Steuart's letters of 10 November 1788 and 3 February and 24 March 1789, together with numerous inscriptions and Jones's draft of the Phoenician writing system, were acquired by BL India Office Library in Parcel 699. See Jones's "MS Memoranda," BL Add. MS 8889; and Cannon's "Early Indian Epigraphy and Sir William Jones," *Journal of the Asiatic Society* 19 (1977):1–13.
14. Sir Henry Maine, *Dissertations on Early Law and Custom* (London, 1883), pp. 2, 4.
15. Teignmouth, 2:154–5. See Kopf, *British Orientalism,* pp. 275–91.
16. Edward Smith, *The Life of Sir Joseph Banks* (London, 1911), p. vii. See also Cannon's "Jones, Banks, and the Royal Society."
17. Cameron, *Sir Joseph Banks,* pp. xii, 63.
18. Of 28 October 1788, Jones's "Notes of Legal Cases Argued in Bengal," BL Add. MS 8885.
19. Ibid. His name is in a list of twenty-three *maulvis* in Jones's notebook.
20. George Gignilliat, *The Author of Sandford and Merton* (New York, 1932), p. 240.
21. *Calcutta Chronicle* of 11 December, *India Gazette* of 15 December, and *Calcutta Gazette* of 11 December 1788, respectively.
22. *India Gazette* of 22 December 1788; and *Calcutta Gazette* of 5 January 1792 and 11 July 1793, respectively.
23. See letter in *Gentleman's Magazine* 67 (August 1797):642–3.
24. Müller, *Chips from a German Workshop,* 4:99–105; and Colebrooke, *Miscellaneous Essays,* 1:235–6.
25. Edgerton, "Sir William Jones," p. 233.
26. See Thomas Ogle's serial essay in *Monthly Review,* App. 1789, pp. 648–53; and March–April, App. 1790, pp. 317–29, 431–45, 559–68, respectively. Chambers sent Percy a copy. See Percy to Boswell of 24 April 1790, Boswell's *Correspondence,* 3:294.

12. An Indian Renaissance (1789)

1. To Charles Grant of 21 October 1793, Charles John Shore's *Memoir of the Life and Correspondence of John, Lord Teignmouth* (London, 1843), 1:262; and to Charlemont of 22 November 1791, Hist. MSS Com., 13th Rep., 2:178, respectively.
2. Patricia Meyer Spacks's review of *Letters,* in *Journal of English and Germanic Philology* 70 (1971):324.
3. Burroughs to Charlemont of 8 December 1789 and 22 November 1791, Hist. MSS Com., 13th Rep., 2:111–12, 177.
4. "Sir William Jones," *Penny Magazine* 8 (Suppl. to April 1839):123.
5. Stephen, *Story of Nuncomar,* 2:33–34.
6. *Calcutta Gazette* of 26 February and 6 August 1789, respectively.
7. Of 9 December 1785, Devonshire Collections.
8. Anna to Hastings of 1 February 1790, BL Add. MS 29172, f. 26.
9. Anna to the duchess of Devonshire of 9 December 1785, Devonshire Collections.
10. Parcel 698 contains the list, with many items translated in Jones's handwriting.
11. Gowen, *History of Indian Literature,* p. 417.
12. Of 20 September 1788, Teignmouth, 2:179.
13. Gauranga Nath Banerjee, *Hellenism in Ancient India,* 2nd ed. (Calcutta, 1920), p. 165.
14. A. Rupert Hall, *The Scientific Revolution 1500–1800,* 2nd ed. (Boston, 1962), pp. 292, 283–4.
15. "On the Literature of the Hindus," *Works,* 4:106.
16. Outline in "Explanations of Sanskrit Characters," BL Dept. of Oriental Printed Books, Art. 4.
17. Of 11 February 1795, Parr's *Works,* 1:473. Bennet was reacting to a form letter:

> Bolton Street
> Feb. 23, 1795

Sir

You will I am sure agree with me in thinking that, from the very deservedly high estimation in which Sir William Jones was held in the Literary World, it becomes a duty incumbent on his friends to collect & preserve such of his productions as are to be met with.

Under this impression I am desired by my sister Lady Jones to request that you will favor her with any Letters from her late Husband (not of a private nature) which may happen to be in your possession. She proposes making a similar application to all Sir Williams Correspondents having good reason to believe that such a step would have been by no means disapproved by Sir William Jones himself.– Permit me to request the Honor of an answer to this House.

I am Sir

> your very obedt. Humble Servt.
> *W D Shipley*

Anna's first choice of biographer was Hayley, whom Spencer rejected. See her letter of 13 April 1796, at Althorp.
18. "Plans of Knowledge," in Parcel 698.
19. Ronald A. Knox, *On English Translation* (Oxford, 1957), p. 4.
20. Edna Osborne, "Oriental Diction and Theme in English Verse, 1740–1840," *Humanistic Studies of the University of Kansas* (Lawrence, Kans., 1916), 2:23. See Cannon, "Sir William Jones's Introducing the *Śakuntalā* to the West," *Style* 9 (1975):82–91.
21. *Kalidasa: Translations of Shakuntala and Other Works,* Everyman's Library (London, 1920), p. 34. See Cannon, "Sir William Jones Revisited: On His Translation of the *Śakuntalā,*" *JAOS* 96 (1976):528–35.

22. A few ethnocentric reviewers later objected. It is "not perhaps a very philosophical opinion, for neither the human mind nor human life did ever so exist in India, as to create such kind of faculties as those of Shakespeare," *Blackwood's Edinburgh Magazine* 6 (January 1820):418.

23. Zenaïde A. Ragozin, *The Story of Vedic India* (New York, 1895), p. 86; and *Edinburgh Review* 108 (July 1858):257.

24. Mrs. Barbauld to Mrs. Beecroft of September 1790, *The Works of Anna Lætitia Barbauld* (London, 1825), 2:83.

25. In *Monthly Anthology* 2 (June, August, September, October, November, December 1805):360–6, 409–13, 466–72, 520–6, 573–83, 639–56, respectively. See Klaus Karttunen and Krister Karttunen's review of Cannon's *Sir William Jones: A Bibliography,* in *Acta Orientalia* 44 (1983):275–87.

26. Kopf, *British Orientalism,* p. 114.

27. Chatterji, "Sir William Jones," pp. 82–87.

28. *The Discovery of India* (New York, 1946), p. 317.

13. A Burning Tropical Sun (1790–1791)

1. To Lady Shore of 27 April 1794, Shore's *Memoir,* 1:286.

2. Parcel 698 contains Jones's yuga list and the drawing, on which he wrote: "This margin is about an inch (or a little more) too high for the volume of our Transactions." John Gilchrist reprinted the drawing in his *Grammar, of the Hindoostanee Language* (Calcutta, 1796), p. 316.

3. Fan, "William Jones' Chinese Studies," p. 312. See Ho Ping-ti, *The Cradle of the East* (Hong Kong, 1975); and K. C. Chang's review in *JAOS* 98 (1978):85–91.

4. See Arthur D. Waley, "Sir William Jones as Sinologue," *BSOAS* 11 (1946):842; and Fan, "William Jones' Chinese Studies," pp. 304, 314.

5. In BL India Office Library, MSS Eur. C. 119 (no. 68 in Wilkins's Catalogue, *Works,* 13:416).

6. "The Design of a Treatise" and "On the Pangolin," *Works,* 5:1; 4:359, respectively.

7. Kopf, *British Orientalism,* p. 5.

8. Hastings, *Letters,* p. 249. See Chatterji, "Sir William Jones," p. 87.

9. Spacks's review of *Letters,* p. 323.

10. "On the Gods," *Works,* 3:393–4.

11. Of 14 September 1789, *The Manuscripts of J. B. Fortescue, Esq., Preserved at Dropmore,* Hist. MSS Com., 13th Rep., App., pt. 3 (London, 1892), 1:510. See 1:519.

12. Holden Furber, *Henry Dundas, First Viscount Melville, 1742–1811* (London, 1931), p. 296.

13. Impey, *Memoirs,* p. 352. See his letter to Charles Jenkinson of 31 December 1785, BL Add. MS 38409, f. 36.

14. See Maurice's Prefaces, *The History of Hindostan* (London, 1795–9), 2:v; and 3:v. Jones's letter of 10 October 1790, which is not in *Letters,* is in 3:vi. See Maurice's tribute *An Elegiac Poem* and Hayley's *Elegy on the Death of the Honorable Sir William Jones* (both in London, 1795).

15. On 11 July 1794; abstract in *Fourth Report of the Royal Commission on Historical Manuscripts* (London, 1874), 4:520. Monboddo's letters of 20 June 1789 and 20 June 1791 are in Cannon's "The Correspondence between Lord Monboddo and Sir William Jones," *American Anthropologist* 70 (1968):559–61. See Smith's *The Diffusion of Culture* (London, 1933).

16. *The Cambridge History of India* (New York, 1922–37), 5:451–3.

17. Minute of 3 December 1790, State Archives of West Bengal Government, Revenue Dept. Proceedings, Education Dept., Calcutta. See *Cambridge History,* 5:436.
18. See Arthur B. Keith, *A Constitutional History of India 1600–1935,* 2nd ed. (London, 1937), p. 109; and Edward J. Thompson and G. T. Garratt, *Rise and Fulfilment of British Rule in India* (London, 1934), p. 196.
19. Wilberforce's diary entry of 29 May 1802, in Robert Wilberforce and Samuel Wilberforce, *The Life of William Wilberforce* (London, 1838), 3:49.
20. Duncan Forbes, *The History of Chess* (London, 1860), pp. 1–2; Jones's essay is annotated on pp. 286–94.
21. In 7 (App. 1792):559–77; 8 (App. 1792):495–507; 10 (App. 1793):502–11; and 11 (App. 1793):544–55.
22. Stiles's letter of 18 January 1794 and Pearson's of 2 February 1795 are in Yale University Library; Sullivan's of 7 February 1795 is in Teignmouth, 2:314–16.
23. In BL no. 12904, f. 23.
24. Translation of Friedrich von Schlegel, *Lectures on the History of Literature* (London, 1885), p. 329.
25. Of 1 February 1790, BL Add. MS 29172, f. 26.
26. Cameron, *Sir Joseph Banks,* p. 83.
27. Kyd's four letters to Jones of 1791–2 and "Remarks" are in BL India Office Library, MSS Eur. F. 95.
28. Cameron, *Sir Joseph Banks,* p. xii. See Brown, *The Chathamites,* p. 408.
29. "On the Fruit of the Mellori," *Works,* 5:53–54. See Anders Jahan Retzii, ed., *Observationes botanicæ sex fasciculis comprehensæ; accedunt J. G. Koenig descriptiones monandrarum et epidendrorum in India orientali factæ* (Leipzig, 1791).
30. Of 7 February 1795, in Cannon's "Jones, Banks, and the Royal Society," p. 226. Wilkins's Catalogue of the MSS is in *Works,* 13:401–26. They are described in Charles H. Tawney and Frederick W. Thomas, *Catalogue of Two Collections of Sanskrit Manuscripts* (London, 1903), pp. 1–40; and E. Denison Ross and Edward G. Browne, *Catalogue of Two Collections of Persian and Arabic Manuscripts* (London, 1902), pp. 1–76. The MSS are in BL India Office Library.

14. Scholar-Martyr (1791–1794)

1. Hickey, *Memoirs,* 4:59–64.
2. Parcel 698 contains the two – "Varānas Almanack" and Jones's annotated Nabadwip almanac for 1789.
3. Parcel 698 contains the draft of his translation of Necker's long passage.
4. Arberry, "Persian Jones," p. 194. *European Magazine* displayed his Rúmí version as "never before printed in any European Publication," in 25 (February 1794):141. It is also in *Gentleman's Magazine* 64 (January 1794):66–67; and *Annual Register* 34 (1794):424–5.
5. Maurice, *Memoirs,* pt. 2, p. 34; Bryant's letter of 8 July 1794 is on p. 36.
6. See Herman Kreyenborg's facsimile ed. (Hannover, 1924).
7. Shore's Discourse, *Works,* 3:xv; and Teignmouth, 2:293.
8. See Müller, *Chips from a German Workshop,* 4:105–15; Colebrooke, *Miscellaneous Essays,* 1:239–40; and Wilford's explanation in Teignmouth, 1:xv–xvii.
9. See Vesey-FitzGerald, "Sir William Jones, the Jurist," p. 814; and Tritton, "The Student of Arabic," p. 698. William Amer reprinted it (London, 1869), and there was a second edition (Calcutta, 1890).
10. Hall, *Scientific Revolution,* p. 298.
11. Charlotte Speir, *Life in Ancient India* (London, 1856), p. 222. See Joseph de Guignes,

"Réflexions sur un livre indien intitulé Bagavadam," *Histoire de l'Académie Royale des Inscriptions et Belles-Lettres* 38 (1772):322.

12. The two cases and the dinner are described in *Calcutta Gazette* of 24 January, 7 February, and 28 March 1793, respectively.

13. Teignmouth, 2:221–2.

14. BL India Office Records, Bengal Wills 1793–4, L/AG/34/29/8. William Fairlie was granted probate on 3 May 1794.

15. To Lady Shore of 27 April 1794, Shore's *Memoir*, 1:288. See *Gentleman's Magazine* 64 (Suppl. 1794):1205; 65 (February 1795):111–12; and 67 (April 1797):322.

16. "Books," p. 215. There is similar phraseology in *Annual Register* of 1799, p. 504. See *Gentleman's Magazine* 71 (April, May 1801):346–7, 439–41.

17. Ragozin, *Story of Vedic India*, p. 84.

18. George Steiner, *After Babel* (London, 1975), p. 249.

19. Schlegel, *Lectures*, p. 114.

20. See Gowen, *History of Indian Literature*, pp. 165–6; Vesey-FitzGerald, "Sir William Jones, the jurist," p. 814; and Maine, *Dissertations*, pp. 4–7, 12.

21. *The Laws of Manu*, in *The Sacred Books of the East* (Oxford, 1886), 25:cxxxiii.

22. Edgerton, "Sir William Jones," p. 233.

23. *Works*, 7:108. See Robert Lingat, *The Classical Law of India*, trans. from the French (Berkeley, Calif., 1973), pp. 197–8.

24. Summarized from *European Magazine* 30 (October and November 1796):252–6, 335–9; *Scots Magazine* 58 (December 1796):838–9; *Monthly Review* 21 (App. 1796):542–51; *British Critic* 8 (November 1796):544–5, and 9 (January 1797):55–58; and *Annual Register* of 1799, p. 507.

25. The phrase is in *Works*, 8:65; the "golden age" passage, in 3:32.

26. Colebrooke, *Miscellaneous Essays*, 1:71–75.

27. "A Description of the Jonesia," *Asiatick Researches* 4:355. Parcel 698 contains some translations that Jones made for his essay "Botanical Observations."

28. In Parcel 698.

29. In *Works*, 3:xi–xii.

30. Ibid., 13:343–61, 367–81, respectively. Parcel 698 contains these fragments.

31. Ibid., 13:382–4. Parcel 698 contains the manuscript, with Jones's interlinear Latin version, the only known complete text showing his methodology. His corrected English prose translation is preceded by a note: "The following version of the poem is disengaged from the stiffness of a verbal translation; but all the images in the original, which would bear an *English* dress without deformity, are carefully preserved; and, though much is omitted, nothing is added." Parcel 698 also contains annotated, untranslated manuscripts – the first three chapters of Śrīharsha's *Naiṣadhācarita*, Sivadāsa's version of *Vetālapañcaviṅśati*, and Rāmadeva's *Vivdvanmodataraṅgiṇi*, besides slokas and a pundit's unpublished Sanskrit letter to Jones. Parcel 699 (India Office Library) contains an extract from Varāhamihira's *Pañca-Siddhāntikā*. See Cannon, "Sir William Jones and the Association between East and West," *Proceedings of the American Philosophical Society* 121 (1977):183–7.

32. Kenneth Stunkel, "English Orientalism and India, 1784–1830," Ohio University *Review* 11 (1969):63.

33. Teignmouth, 2:261. See the diary quoted in Kathleen Blechynden's *Calcutta Past and Present* (London, 1905), pp. 157–8. Anna, who lived until 1829, reproached herself severely for having left Jones, though he had been well then and she would have sacrificed her own life by remaining. See Elizabeth Shipley to Sarah Ponsonby of 26 January 1795, in *The Hamwood Papers of the Ladies of Llangollen and Caroline Hamilton*, ed. Mrs. G. H. Bell (London, 1930), p. 274.

15. Jones Today

1. Shore, *Memoir,* 1:285; and letter of 1 May 1794 (1:289).
2. Cannon, "The Construction of the European Image of the Orient," *Comparative Criticism* 8 (1986):186.
3. In Teignmouth, 2:264–5.
4. See Cannon, "Jones's 'sprung from some common source.' " Among several fine linguistic reappraisals, at least three should be mentioned here: Winfred P. Lehmann, "Philology to Linguistics: Constructive to Literary Study," SCMLA *South Central Journal* 1 (1984):132–9; Jean-Claude Muller, "Early Stages of Language Comparison from Sassetti to Sir William Jones," *Kratylos* 31 (1986):1–31; and R. H. Robins, "The Life and Work of Sir William Jones," *Transactions of the Philological Society* for 1987, 1–23.
5. There is a quite different argument, concentrating on the Arab peoples, in Said, *Orientalism,* p. 324.

Selected Bibliography

Manuscript Sources

Asiatic Society, Calcutta. Manuscript Proceedings.
British Library (BL), Department of Manuscripts. Papers of Warren Hastings, Sir William Jones, Earl of Liverpool, Thomas Percy.
  India Office Library and Records. Parcel 699 of Jones's Papers, Orme Correspondence.
Cannon, Garland. Parcel 698 of Jones's Papers.
Devonshire Collections, Chatsworth, Bakewell, Derbyshire. Family Papers.
Oxford, University of:
  Bodleian Library, Department of Western Manuscripts.
  University College. Buttery Accounts.
Royal Society of London. Journal Books.
Yale University, Beinecke Library. James Osborn Collection.

Printed Sources

Periodicals

Analytical Review, or History of Literature, Domestic and Foreign 5 (1788) to 28 (1798).
Annual Register, or a View of the History, Politics, and Literature 1 (1758) to 79 (1837).
Asiatic Journal and Monthly Register for British India 1 (1816) to 40 (1843).
Asiatic Society of Bengal. *Asiatick Researches; or, Transactions of the Society Instituted in Bengal* 1 (1788) to 20 (1839).
British Critic, a New Review 1 (1793) to new series, 18 (1822).
Calcutta Gazette; or, Oriental Advertiser 1 (1784) to 33 (1800).
Edinburgh Review 1 (1802) to 136 (1872).
European Magazine and London Review 1 (1782) to 86 (1824).
Gentleman's Magazine 1 (1731) to 223 (1867).
India Gazette; or, Calcutta Public Advertiser, 1783–94.
Jackson's *Oxford Journal,* 1772–83.
Journal of the Asiatic Society of Bengal 1 (1832)–.
London Chronicle or Universal Evening Post, 1772–83.
London Evening-Post, 1772–83.
Monthly Magazine, or British Register 1 (1706) to 96 (1842).
Monthly Review 1 (1749) to 4th series, 3 (1838).
New Annual Register, or General Repository of History, Politics, and Literature, 1780–1806.
North American Review 1 (1815) to 247 (1939).
Public Advertiser, 1772–83.
Quarterly Review 1 (1809)–.

St. James's Chronicle; or, the British Evening Post, 1772–83.
Scots Magazine 24 (1762) to 79 (1817).
Universal Magazine of Knowledge and Pleasure 43 (1768) to new series, 12 (1809).
Westminster Review 1 (1824) to 23 (1835).

Books and Articles

Aarsleff, Hans. *The Study of Language in England, 1780–1860.* Princeton, N.J.: Princeton
    University Press, 1967.
Arberry, Arthur John, *Asiatic Jones. The Life and Influence of Sir William Jones.* London:
    Longmans Green, 1946.
    "New Light on Sir William Jones." *Bulletin of the School of Oriental and African Studies*
    11 (1946):673–85.
    "Orient Pearls at Random Strung." *Bulletin of the School of Oriental and African Studies*
    11 (1946):699–712.
    "Persian Jones." *Asiatic Review* 40 (1944):186–96.
Asiatic Society, Calcutta. *Proceedings of the Asiatic Society: 1784–1800.* Vol. 1. Ed. Sibadas
    Chaudhuri. Calcutta: Asiatic Society, 1980.
Bailey, Richard W. Review of Jones's *Letters. Michigan Quarterly Review* 11 (1972):210–13.
Boswell, James. *The Correspondence of James Boswell with Certain Members of the Club.*
    Vol. 3. Ed. Charles N. Fifer. New York: McGraw-Hill, 1976.
    Life of Johnson. Ed. G. B. Hill, revised and enlarged by L. F. Powell. 6 vols. Oxford:
    Clarendon Press, 1934–50.
    Private Papers of James Boswell from Malahide Castle. Ed. Geoffrey Scott and Frederick
    A. Pottle. 18 vols. Privately printed, 1929–34.
Brown, Peter. "Sir William Jones." In Peter Brown, *The Chathamites,* pp. 339–420. London:
    Macmillan, 1967.
Browne, Edward G. *A Literary History of Persia.* 4 vols. (1929). Cambridge: Cambridge
    University Press, 1951.
Cameron, Hector Charles. *Sir Joseph Banks* (1952). London: Angus and Robertson, 1966.
Cannon, Garland. "The Construction of the European Image of the Orient: A Bicentenary
    Reappraisal of Sir William Jones as Poet and Translator." *Comparative Criticism* 8
    (1986):167–88.
    "The Correspondence between Lord Monboddo and Sir William Jones." *American An-
    thropologist* 70 (1968):559–61.
    "Freedom of the Press and Sir William Jones." *Journalism Quarterly* 33 (1956):179–88.
    "Jones's Founding and Directing of the Asiatic Society." British Library *India Office
    Library and Records Report for 1984–85,* pp. 11–28.
    "Jones's 'sprung from some common source': 1786–1986." In Sydney Lamb, ed., *Sprung
    from Some Common Source.* Stanford, Calif.: Stanford University Press, 1990.
    "The Literary Place of Sir William Jones." *Journal of the Asiatic Society* 2 (1960):47–61.
    Oriental Jones: A Biography. London: Asia Publishing House for the Indian Council for
    Cultural Relations, 1964.
    Sir William Jones: A Bibliography of Primary and Secondary Sources. Vol. 7. Library and
    Information Sources in Linguistics. Amsterdam: John Benjamins, 1979.
    "Sir William Jones and Anglo-American Relations during the American Revolution."
    Modern Philology 76 (1978):29–45.
    "Sir William Jones and Dr. Johnson's Literary Club." *Modern Philology* 63 (1965):20–37.
    "Sir William Jones and Edmund Burke." *Modern Philology* 54 (1957):165–85.
    "Sir William Jones, Language, and the Asiatic Society." *Indian Horizons* 22 (1973):5–21,
    27–45.

Sir William Jones, Orientalist: A Bibliography. Honolulu: University of Hawaii Press, 1952.

"Sir William Jones's Indian Studies." *Journal of the American Oriental Society* 91 (1971):418–25.

"Sir William Jones's Introducing the *Śakuntalā* to the West." *Style* 9 (1975):82–91.

"Sir William Jones, Sir Joseph Banks, and the Royal Society." *Notes and Records of the Royal Society of London* 29 (1975):205–30.

"Sir William Jones's Persian Linguistics." *Journal of the American Oriental Society* 78 (1958):262–73.

Chalmers, Alexander. "Sir William Jones." In Chalmers, ed., *The Works of the English Poets,* 18:427–511. London: J. Johnson, 1810.

Chatterji, Suniti Kumar. "Sir William Jones: 1746–1794." In Suniti Kumar Chatterji, ed., *Sir William Jones Bicentenary of His Birth Commemoration Volume 1746–1946,* pp. 81–96. Calcutta: Royal Asiatic Society of Bengal, 1948.

Colebrooke, Henry Thomas. *Miscellaneous Essays.* Ed. Sir T. E. Colebrooke (1837). 3 vols. London: Trübner, 1873.

Derry, Warren. *Dr. Parr: A Portrait of the Whig Dr. Johnson.* Oxford: Clarendon Press, 1966.

Dictionary of National Biography (D.N.B.).

Digby, Simon. Review of Jones's *Letters. Bulletin of the School of Oriental and African Studies* 34 (1971):169–72.

Dodwell, Edward, and J. S. Miles. *Alphabetical List of the Honourable East India Company's Bengal Servants from the Year 1780 to the Year 1838.* London: Longman, 1839.

Edgerton, Franklin. "Sir William Jones: 1746–1794." *Journal of the American Oriental Society* 66 (1946):230–9.

Emeneau, Murray. "India and Linguistics." *Journal of the American Oriental Society* 75 (1955):145–53.

Emin, Joseph. *Life and Adventures of Emin Joseph Emin 1726–1809.* 2nd ed. Calcutta: Baptist Mission Press, 1918.

Fan, T. C. "William Jones' Chinese Studies." *Review of English Studies* 22 (1946):304–14.

Foster, Joseph. *Alumni Oxonienses: The Members of the University of Oxford, 1715–1886.* 4 vols. Oxford: Parker, 1887–8.

Franklin, Benjamin. *The Works of Benjamin Franklin.* Ed. Jared Sparks. Vols. 8 and 9. Boston: Hilliard, Gray, 1836–40.

Gibbon, Edward. *The History of the Decline and Fall of the Roman Empire.* Ed. J. B. Bury. 7 vols. 4th ed. London: Methuen, 1906–20.

Gowen, Herbert H. *A History of Indian Literature from Vedic Times to the Present Day.* New York: D. Appleton, 1931.

Hall, A. Rupert. *The Scientific Revolution 1500–1800.* 2nd ed. Boston: Beacon, 1962.

Hastings, Warren. *The Letters of Warren Hastings to His Wife.* Ed. Sydney C. Grier. London: William Blackwood and Sons, 1905.

Hawkins, Lætitia-Matilda. *Memoirs, Anecdotes, Facts, and Opinions.* 2 vols. London: Longman, 1824.

Head, Raymond. "Divine Flower Power Recorded: Sir William Jones (1746–94)." *Country Life* 176 (13 September 1984):703–5.

Hewitt, R. M. "Harmonious Jones." *Essays and Studies by Members of the English Association* 38 (1942):42–59.

Hickey, William. *Memoirs of William Hickey.* Ed. Alfred Spencer. 4 vols. New York: Knopf, 1923.

Hilles, Frederick W. Review of Jones's *Letters. Yale Review* 60 (1971):259–67.

Historical Manuscripts Commission. *The Manuscripts and Correspondence of James, First Earl of Charlemont.* Vol. 2, 13th Report, App., pt. 8. London, 1894.

Hodson, Major V. C. P. *List of the Officers of the Bengal Army.* 4 vols. London: Constable, 1927–8; Phillimore, 1946–7.

Hunter, W. W. *The Imperial Gazetteer of India.* 14 vols. 2nd ed. London: Trübner, 1885–7.

Impey, Sir Elijah. *Memoirs of Sir Elijah Impey, Knt.* Ed. Elijah B. Impey. London: Simpkin, Marshall, 1850.

Jefferson, Thomas. *The Papers of Thomas Jefferson.* Vols. 5 and 6. Ed. Julian P. Boyd. Princeton, N.J.: Princeton University Press, 1950–4.

Johnson, Samuel. "History of the English Language." In Johnson's *Dictionary of the English Language.* London, 1755.

Johnsonian Miscellanies. 2 vols. Ed. G. B. Hill. Oxford: Clarendon Press, 1897.

The Letters of Samuel Johnson. 3 vols. Ed. R. W. Chapman. Oxford: Clarendon Press, 1952.

Jones, Sir William. *Catalogue of the Library of the Late Sir William Jones.* London: W. Nichol, 1831.

"Five New Letters by Sir William Jones." Ed. Garland Cannon. *Philological Quarterly* 51 (1972):951–5.

The Letters of Sir William Jones. 2 vols. Ed. Garland Cannon. Oxford: Clarendon Press, 1970.

The Works of Sir William Jones. 13 vols. London: John Stockdale, 1807. (Teignmouth's *Memoirs of the Life, Writings and Correspondence of Sir William Jones* constitutes Vols. 1 and 2.)

Kopf, David. *British Orientalism and the Bengal Renaissance.* Berkeley and Los Angeles: University of California Press, 1969.

Lehmann, Winfred P. "Philology to Linguistics: Constructive to Literary Study." SCMLA *South Central Journal* 1 (Spring–Summer 1984):132–9.

Maine, Sir Henry. *Dissertations on Early Law and Custom.* London: John Murray, 1883.

Master, Alfred. "The Influence of Sir William Jones upon Sanskrit Studies." *Bulletin of the School of Oriental and African Studies.* 11 (1946):798–806.

Maurice, Thomas. *Memoirs of the Author of "Indian Antiquities."* 2nd ed. London: W. Bulmer and W. Nicol, 1820–2.

Mitchell, L. G. "Univ., Sir William Jones, and the 1780 Election." *Oxford University College Record* 6 (1973):257–62.

Müller, Friedrich Max. *Chips from a German Workshop.* 5 vols. New York: Scribner, 1887–90.

Muller, Jean-Claude. "Early Stages of Language Comparison from Sassetti to Sir William Jones." *Kratylos* 31 (1986):1–31.

Nicholson, Reynold A. *A Literary History of the Arabs.* 2nd ed. Cambridge: Cambridge University Press, 1930.

Oxford English Dictionary (OED). Ed. J. A. Simpson and E. S. C. Weiner. 20 vols. 2nd ed. Oxford: Clarendon Press, 1989.

Parr, Samuel. *Bibliotheca Parriana. A Catalogue of the Library of the Late Reverend and Learned Samuel Parr, LL.D.* London: John Bohn and Joseph Mawman, 1827.

The Works of Samuel Parr, LL.D. 8 vols. Ed. John Johnstone. London: Longman, 1828.

Parton, James. *Life and Times of Benjamin Franklin.* Vol. 2. Boston: Houghton, Mifflin, 1884.

Pedersen, Holger. *Linguistic Science in the Nineteenth Century.* Trans. John Spargo. Cambridge, Mass.: Harvard University Press, 1931.

Pinto, V. de Sola. "Sir William Jones and English Literature." *Bulletin of the School of Oriental and African Studies* 11 (1946):686–94.

Powell, L. F. "Sir William Jones and the Club." *Bulletin of the School of Oriental and African Studies* 11 (1946):818–22.

Ragozin, Zenaïde A. *The Story of Vedic India.* New York: Putnam, 1895.

Robins, R. H. "The Life and Work of Sir William Jones." *Transactions of the Philological Society* for 1987, pp. 1–23.

Rowse, A. L. "Welsh Orientalist: Sir William Jones." *History Today* 21 (1971):57–64.

Said, Edward W. *Orientalism.* New York: Viking, 1979.

Schlegel, Carl Wilhelm Friedrich von. *Lectures on the History of Literature.* (Translated from the German.) London: George Bell and Sons, 1885.

Schwab, Raymond. *The Oriental Renaissance.* Trans. G. Patterson-Black and V. Reinking. New York: Columbia University Press, 1984.

Shepperson, Archibald Bolling. *John Paradise and Lucy Ludwell.* Richmond, Va.: Dietz Press, 1942.

Shore, Charles John, ed. *Memoir of the Life and Correspondence of John, Lord Teignmouth.* 2 vols. London: Hatchard and Son, 1843.

Spacks, Patricia Meyer. Review of Jones's *Letters. Journal of English and Germanic Philology* 70 (1971):321–4.

Stephen, Sir James Fitzjames. *The Story of Nuncomar, and the Impeachment of Sir Elijah Impey.* 2 vols. London: Macmillan, 1885.

Stifler, James Madison. *"My Dear Girl."* New York: George H. Doran, 1927.

Sutherland, Lucy. Review of Jones's *Letters. South Asian Review* 4 (1971):261–4.

Teignmouth, Lord. See Jones, *Works.*

Tritton, A. S. "The Student of Arabic." *Bulletin of the School of Oriental and African Studies* 11 (1946):695–8.

Vesey-FitzGerald, S. G. "Sir William Jones, the Jurist." *Bulletin of the School of Oriental and African Studies* 11 (1946):807–17.

Waley, Arthur D. "Anquetil-Duperron and Sir William Jones." *History Today* 2 (1952):23–33.

Walpole, Horace. *The Yale Edition of Horace Walpole's Correspondence.* Ed. W. S. Lewis. New Haven, Conn.: Yale University Press, 1937–.

Ward, William Reginald. *Georgian Oxford; University Politics in the Eighteenth Century.* Oxford: Clarendon Press, 1958.

Index

Some subjects also appear under *Bengal, Calcutta, England, Hindu, India, languages, Oxford,* or *Sanskrit.* Birth and death dates sometimes differ from scholar to scholar; the ones given here are the usually accepted ones. Standard abbreviations are used such as *b.* "born," *Bt.* "baronet," *d.* "died," and *fl.* "flourished."

Aarsleff, Hans, ix, xii
Abingdon, earl of (Willoughby Bertie, 1740–99), 122
Abu 'l-ʿAlá al-Maʿarrí (973–1057), 17
Abu 'l-Fidá (d. 1331), 35
Actinia, 106
Adair, Serjeant James (c. 1743–98), 72
Adam, 283
Adams, John (1735–1826), 138, 150, 375
Adams, William (1706–89), 114–19 *passim,* 134, 362–6
Addison, Joseph (1672–1719), 6, 48, 50, 143, 206
agriculture, 224, 260, 283
Alcaeus (c. 600 B.C.), 146
Alefounder, John (d. 1795), 316, 319
ʿAli ibn Abi Ṭálib (c. 600–61), 341
Ali Ibrahim Khan (d. 1793?), 216, 219, 225, 227, 291, 350
Alleyne, John (d. 1777), 69
Althorp, Lord, *see* Spencer, George John
Amarakośa, 230
Amarasiṃha (fl. 4th century), 377
America, 152, 328
  Jones's possible migration to, 97, 162, 171–4, 183, 205, 330
  Jones's view of and sympathy with, 145, 157, 161, 192, 202, 293, 305
  trade with, 86, 260, 265
American Academy of Arts and Sciences, 328
American Oriental Society, 204
American Philosophical Society, ix, 328
American Revolution, 81, 174–6, 190
  Jones's and other Britishers' view of, 75,

82, 88, 91, 97, 114, 125, 136
  and Jones's trips to Paris, 99–102, 137–8, 174–8
  military events of, 77, 84, 102–11 *passim,* 156
  and Parliament, 71, 103
Anacreon (572?–?488 B.C.), 64, 65
Anderson, David (1750–1825), 205
Anderson, Dr. James (1737–1809), 278, 308, 328, 329
andrometer, 71, 197, 241, 257, 268
Anjouan, Comoro Islands, 198–9, 251, 281
Annual Register, 49, 147, 233, 313, 319
Anquetil-Duperron, Abraham-Hyacinthe (1731–1805), xv, 42–44, 54, 70, 119, 250, 362
ʿAntara (6th century), 36, 189
anthropology, 243, 284, 298, 324, 329
Anwár-i-Suhaylí, 248
Apollo, 297
Apollonius (3rd–2nd century B.C.), 64
Arabian Nights Entertainments, The, 7, 20, 49, 238, 312, 341
Arabic literature, 17, 51, 63–65, 142–3, 260
Arabs, xv, xvi, 242, 263, 284, 298, 306, 318, 339, 385
Arakan, 251, 289, 309, 337
architecture, 224, 242
Arden, William (1731–68), 11, 30
Ariosto (1474–1533), 231, 281
Aristotle (384–322 B.C.), 10, 24, 51, 198, 264, 348, 364
Armenia, 252, 253

391